AN EYEWITNESS HISTORY

CHILDHOOD IN AMERICA

Catherine Reef

☑® Facts On File, Inc.

In memory of Linda Reef

Childhood in America

Copyright © 2002 by Catherine Reef

All rights reserved. No part of this book may be reproduced or utilized in any form or by any means, electronic or mechanical, including photocopying, recording, or by any information storage or retrieval systems, without permission in writing from the publisher. For information contact:

Facts On File, Inc.
132 West 31st Street
New York NY 10001

Library of Congress Cataloging-in-Publication Data
Reef, Catherine.
   Childhood in America / Catherine Reef.
     p. cm.—(Eyewitness history)
   Includes bibliographical references and index.
   ISBN 0-8160-4438-4 (hardcover)
   1. Childhood—United States—History. 2. Adolescence—United States—History. 3. Children—United States—Social conditions. 4. Youth—United States—Social conditions. I. Title. II. Series.
   HQ792.U5 R345 2002
   305.23'0973—dc21   2001040319

Facts On File books are available at special discounts when purchased in bulk quantities for businesses, associations, institutions or sales promotions. Please call our Special Sales Department in New York at (212) 967-8800 or (800) 322-8755.

You can find Facts On File on the World Wide Web at
http://www.factsonfile.com

Text design by Joan M. Toro

Cover design by Cathy Rincon

Printed and bound in the United States of America

VB FOF 10 9 8 7 6 5 4 3 2

. . . what is childhood
But after all a sort of golden daylight,
A beautiful and blessed wealth of sunshine . . .

—Henry Timrod, "Dramatic Fragment"

CONTENTS

ACKNOWLEDGMENTS

I wish to acknowledge the many librarians and collection curators who made possible much of my research, especially those at the Library of Congress and the University of Maryland libraries. My son, John S. Reef, helped with some of the many tasks involved in putting together a book of this scope, and I thank him. I also thank the editor of *Childhood in America,* Nicole Bowen, for her willingness to take on challenging projects and her competence in carrying them out.

INTRODUCTION

In June 1920, a writer named Annie Winsor Allen remarked in the *Atlantic Monthly* that the ages from 12 through 18 had become "the most wasted years of life." Only recently had psychologists defined these years as adolescence, a distinct stage in human development. Allen complained that during this time that had been "taken from adult life and added to childhood," boys and girls ran "in a kind of entertaining squirrel-cage, many of them with a notable impatience and a smarting sense of futility."

The teenage restiveness that Allen described is familiar to anyone who came of age in 20th-century America, because adolescent angst has come to be viewed as a universal experience. Yet in 1920, as Allen indicated, awareness of this emotional state was new. She—and many of her readers—remembered when people age 12 to 18 commonly shouldered adult responsibilities.

Boating on Belmont Lake, Long Island, in the 1920s *(Brown Brothers)*

Remarks such as Allen's demonstrate that society's concept of childhood has evolved, although historians debate how much it has changed and when. Some students of history have even speculated that childhood itself is a relatively recent invention in the Western world. Most prominent among these is the French historian Philippe Ariès. In 1960, Ariès observed that artists in the Middle Ages painted young people smaller than adults but rendered the two groups alike in every other way. He noted that children portrayed in paintings of the 12th and 13th centuries had the body proportions and musculature of adults and wore clothing identical to that of grown men and women. Ariès rejected the notion that such portraits resulted from artists' ignorance of children's anatomy and insisted that children look like adults in the art of the Middle Ages because their society made no distinction between the two groups. Children joined adults in work, worship, and recreation as soon as they were physically able to do so. There was, Ariès said, "no place for childhood in the medieval world."

Other historians have reached similar conclusions about children living as recently as the 18th century. They, too, found evidence in children's clothing, asserting that a person's style of dress denotes his or her place in society, and that if children and adults dress identically, their social position must be the same. Some have conjectured that the system of apprenticeship widely used in Europe and America, wherein boys were signed over to artisans for a specified number of years in order to learn a trade, demonstrated that parents thought of their children as property. It has also been suggested that because many children died in the first months and years of life, parents felt little affection for them.

Among those presenting evidence for the opposing view—that some concept of childhood existed in earlier centuries—is the American historian Linda Pollock, who studied hundreds of diaries and journals written between 1500 and 1900. As she read accounts of 16th-century parents spending the night at the bedside of a sick child or worrying about a son's education, she concluded that at least as early as the 1500s, Europeans acknowledged that children differed from adults and that children passed through several stages of development before reaching maturity.

Whether human beings developed an awareness of childhood as distinct from adult life at a particular time in history is an issue that may never be adequately resolved, because little is known about the day-to-day existence of children living more than two centuries ago. What is certain, though, is that most historians did not discover childhood until the late 20th century. Just as scholars began in the 1960s to study intensively the historical experience of African Americans, and in the 1970s the experience of women, at the start of the 21st century they were looking at the experience of children. According to Jay Mechling, professor of American Studies at the University of California at Davis, "children remain the last underclass to have their history written from their point of view."

"THE PHOTOGRAPHY OF TIME"

Presenting history from children's points of view poses a problem, however. With the exception of a small number of letters and diaries, the children of past eras have left very little written evidence of their lives. Historians are forced to rely almost exclusively on the observations and remembrances of adults. Thus, it is easier to learn what adults thought of children and remembered of childhood than about children themselves. There has been concern, too, that adults are less reliable witnesses. Memories can become distorted with time, and even the most conscientious of memoirists might exaggerate, downplay, or omit key details.

Adults' desires to conform to the values of the present day can cause them to alter accounts of the past in ways that children, with their natural candor and limited experience of the world, do not. "Adults are finished products," historian James Marten of Marquette University has remarked. "Children are much more interesting." Nevertheless, age does afford advantages. Adult witnesses have acquired greater insight and a broader understanding of the context in which events occurred.

Some of the adults whose memoirs are cited in this book have themselves commented on the difficulty of accurately recalling their childhoods. "Whether everything was as I have written about it I do not know—only that this is how the photography of time pictures it. The colors may be too dark or too bright," stated Anne Gertrude Sneller, who was born in 1883 and grew up in Onandoga County, New York. George Gallarno of Iowa, an orphan of the Civil War, made a similar confession: "Visions come to me, but whether they are real visions of actual experiences, especially in the earliest years, retained somewhere in my memory, or whether they are recollections of facts related to me, I am unable to clearly determine." In contrast is the certainty of L. MacRae Bell, who survived the 47-day Union siege of Vicksburg, Mississippi, in the spring and summer of 1863. She wrote, "I do not think a child could have passed through what I did and have forgotten it."

There are ways to verify the accuracy of many childhood memories recalled in adult life. Especially when the experience remembered is a major historical event, such as a Civil War battle, the facts related can be compared with other, accepted, sources. Also, memoirists often write about the past in similar ways, so that even recollections of day-to-day life gain credibility through repetition. So many writers have detailed the cruelty of 19th-century schoolmasters and the discomforts of the classroom, for example, that readers can safely conclude that the typical school of the 1800s was an unpleasant place.

SHARING THE WORK

Americans who wrote about growing up in the late 18th and early 19th centuries often described in loving detail the work that they did as children. Daniel Drake, who had been a child in 19th-century Mayslick, Kentucky, told the readers of his memoir, "I must reconduct you to the corn-field, the scene of my earliest labors and most cherished recollections." People like Drake were born into a society that valued hard work and, because most Americans farmed, probably into farming families that needed the labor of every able member. By the age of seven or eight, boys had joined their fathers in the field to plow, sow seed, pull weeds, hoe, and harvest ripened crops. Girls helped their mothers with the myriad tasks that kept the household running, from preparing and preserving food to weaving cloth and laundering clothes. Older girls looked after their numerous siblings. Having eight to 10 offspring, on average, in a time of high infant and child mortality ensured parents that some of their sons and daughters would make it to maturity and also provided an agricultural workforce.

There was at least a 20-percent chance that a child born in the early national period (roughly from 1780 until 1830) would die before reaching maturity. More children died from illness than from any other cause. Contagious diseases such as smallpox, influenza, and whooping cough claimed many lives. Yellow fever and malaria often proved fatal as well, especially in the South, while typhoid fever spread in the water supplying towns and cities, where 20 percent of Americans lived in 1800.

Urban children also worked. At age 14 or so, a boy might be apprenticed to an artisan, such as a blacksmith or carpenter, to learn a trade by which he would one day earn his livelihood. It took several years for an apprentice to reach the level of journeyman and be paid for his work, but many parents could not wait that long if they had an immediate need for any wages their sons or daughters could earn. The children of these adults often worked as servants or in the factories that were proliferating in eastern cities. By the start of the 19th century, manufacturers desperate for labor were putting children to work. With the manufacturing process broken down into a series of steps, a factory child performed the same task over and over again, six days a week, sometimes for 12 hours a day or more. For all of this drudgery, he or she earned about 50 cents. After 1840, as the immigrant population in northeastern cities rose, whole families worked together in tenement sweatshops making goods for more affluent members of society.

Although some forward-looking individuals objected to child labor because it prevented children from being educated, society as a whole viewed the workplace as a school that taught such worthwhile attributes as industry and ingenuity. In addition, it was widely accepted that working was preferable to idleness, which promoted vicious habits. Secretary of the Treasury Alexander Hamilton spoke for many Americans when he said in 1791 that "women and children are rendered more useful, and the latter more early useful, by manufacturing establishments, than they would otherwise be."

Indeed, children in the young United States devoted much of their energy to being useful, but they still had time left over for play. The few toys that they owned were handmade—things like kites, carved wooden boats, and cloth dolls. Children joined with adults in community recreational activities such as dances and church socials. They also observed and participated in life's somber rituals, such as the events surrounding death. Parents saw no reason to shield children from the dying and the dead, and in fact sometimes made sure that they witnessed the final moments of a dying sibling or other loved one.

Many children also attended school during the early national period, at least for a little while. Public schooling developed at the local level in the United States, as communities established schools according to specifications outlined by state legislatures beginning about 1800. These early schools varied in quality, but they consistently brought students of all ages together in one room under the tutelage of a single teacher. A school was likely to be a wood-frame building that was poorly constructed, furnished, and ventilated.

Throughout the 19th century, American schools were renowned for their odor. Instructors tended to be poorly educated themselves; often they took low-paying teaching jobs because nothing better was available. One of their principal duties (and for some, one of their principal pleasures) was applying corporal punishment to maintain order.

The opinion prevailed that education was less important than work, so communities were reluctant to raise taxes for schools. In addition, farmers thought nothing of keeping their children home from school during the growing season to help with the crops.

Private schools also were opened in the early 19th century, especially in cities. Until about 1830, infant schools enjoyed popularity in Boston and elsewhere. Accepting children between the ages of 18 months and 6 years, these schools essentially were day-care centers for the children of factory workers that offered some instruction in reading and deportment. At the same time, churches operated Sunday schools, which doled out academics heavily laced with religion; and charity schools, which welcomed the children of the poor.

Private education appealed to the aristocratic planters of the South, who engaged tutors or sent their sons and daughters to elite boarding schools. Missionaries operated schools for some of the free black children living in the South, but most of the region's children had no formal education.

A British pedagogue, Joseph Lancaster, had a strong but brief influence on the nascent U.S. and Canadian school systems. Lancaster devised a system of mass education in which one instructor taught as many as 1,000 pupils by relying on student monitors for assistance and imposing strict regimentation of behavior. Of more lasting impact was the work of an American academician, Horace Mann. Mann, who was secretary of the Massachusetts Board of Education in the 1840s, worked to elevate the teaching profession by promoting teacher training and enlightened pedagogical methods.

THE PUSH WEST

The children who labored on farms or in factories in the first half of the 19th century or who endured schooldays that were uninspiring at best were an optimistic group living in an exuberant time. The writer Lucy Larcom, who went to work in a New England textile mill in the 1830s at the approximate age of 10, vividly described the predominant mood of that era:

> Vistas opened in every direction. New horizons were lifting themselves. The untrodden peaks, the unpenetrated forests, the prairies untraversed, were all around, just far enough off to give scope to the most inclosed landscape. There was boundless breathing-room for everybody. There were the hopes and possibilities which are more to the imaginative seeker than attainment. The simple phrase, "the far West," was like a talisman, rich with suggestions and beckonings.

Fertile soil, the mild climate of California and the Pacific Northwest, and the chance to escape the corrupting influence of eastern civilization lured tens of thousands of young families to the West beginning in the 1840s. For children crossing the Great Plains by wagon train, there was never a dull moment.

A child helps to brand cattle on the Cal Snyder ranch, Custer County, Nebraska, in 1888. *(Nebraska State Historical Society)*

By day they saw herds of bison that appeared limitless, and by night they covered their heads with bedding as colossal thunderstorms moved across the level ground. Having been raised on stories of Indian attacks, they often feared the approach of Native Americans. Yet in time they discovered that the Indians were less of a danger than diseases such as cholera and scurvy, which consigned pioneers of all ages to shallow trailside graves.

The majority of children survived the trip west and settled into a life that was an unusual combination of hard work and unbounded freedom. Frontier children had to share in the labor if their families were to survive. Boys and girls gathered food and helped to prepare it, tended livestock, carried water, hunted, and plowed and planted fields. Settler children on the western range learned to ride horses as skillfully as children in the 20th century learned to ride bicycles. On horseback, they moved confidently over miles of open country. Many girls made a difficult adjustment, though, as they approached adulthood and society pressured them into adopting a traditionally feminine lifestyle.

There were varied experiences of childhood in every period of U.S. history. While settlers were moving onto western lands and bringing up their young in what was to them new country, the region's Native American children were being raised in a traditional manner. By the 1840s, most of the surviving Indian population lived west of the Mississippi River and was composed of ethnic groups that either were indigenous to the area or had been forced out of the East.

Climate and geography strongly influenced Native American life. Thus, the Navajo (Dineh) raised sheep on the fertile grazing land of the Southwest, while the peoples of the Pacific Northwest fished. The Cheyenne, who relied on buffalo meat for food and buffalo hides for clothing and shelter, stayed on the move, following the great herds across the plains.

Despite this diversity, some aspects of life were common to all Indian children. They all began to help with the work that sustained the family and community at an early age. Boys might build boats, tend sheep, plant crops, fashion weapons, or learn to hunt. Girls prepared food, cared for younger children, made clothing, and practiced traditional crafts. "We followed our fathers to the fields and helped plant and weed," said a Hopi man recalling his childhood in the Southwest. "We joined the women in gathering rabbitweed for baskets and went with them to dig clay for pots. We watched the fields to drive out the birds and rodents, picked peaches to dry in the sun."

Schooling took the form of instruction from elders in the culture's myths and time-honored practices—its rituals and songs—and in the ways of the natural world, where humans were the equals of other forms of life. Adolescents underwent rites of passage that involved spiritual quests and tests of courage.

SLAVERY AND THE WAR TO END IT

An altogether different experience of childhood in the United States was that of the African Americans who grew up in slavery prior to 1865. Theirs was American childhood at its harshest; they lived in drafty, sparsely furnished cabins and consumed a diet that was deficient in vitamins, calcium, protein, and calories. Their clothing was inadequate, they grew up unschooled, and they regularly saw adults being whipped or subjected to other tortures. The permanent separation of parent and child—the result of one or the other being sold—was a common occurrence that no doubt caused much psychological trauma.

And then there was the work. Slaveholders assigned farm chores and household duties to children as young as eight. These youngsters fed livestock, fetched and carried, washed dishes, and served in the white people's kitchens or at their tables. Older children, like most enslaved adults, labored in the fields raising cotton, tobacco, rice, and sugar, the principal plantation crops. The older children pulled weeds, removed insects pests from growing plants, and helped with the harvest. "It was hard back breaking work for a little fellow and the hours were sometimes awfully long," stated Robert Anderson, an ex-slave, in his memoir. Some boys avoided field work when they were apprenticed to learn a trade.

Incredibly, former slaves who wrote or spoke about childhood mentioned not only work, hardship, and cruelty, but also play. They described running and jumping; fishing and swimming; singing; and ballgames played with rolled-up yarn. As Josiah Henson, who had grown up in slavery, reminded the readers of his autobiography, "however hedged in by circumstances, the joyful exuberance of youth will bound at times over them all."

The enslaved people became free Americans in April 1865, with the Union victory in the Civil War. Children—Union and Confederate—participated in that war directly as soldiers or indirectly as citizens on the home front. Not only did boys younger than 18 (the minimum legal age for enlistment) sign on with state regiments, but they also served as drummers, for whom the Union army had no age requirement until 1864. Boy soldiers saw combat throughout the South; thousands died from wounds they received or from diseases picked up in camp. Children were also among the inmates of military prisons.

The majority of children in the North, who did not go to battle, worked in their communities on behalf of the war effort. Permitted access to military encampments that would be unthinkable today, children provided direct aid in the form of food and supplies to soldiers moving through their towns. Children made items to be sold at fundraising fairs sponsored by the U.S.

Sanitary Commission, a charitable organization, or that they set up and ran by themselves at home.

Military engagements were the stuff of play for most northern children, while southern children had a more direct experience of war. For example, children were among the residents of Vicksburg, Mississippi, who spent the spring and early summer of 1863 living in hillside caves while Union forces bombarded their city. Children were also among the citizens of Confederate states who fled their homes in advance of the approaching Union army. People left the besieged countryside for cities such as Richmond and Atlanta. Families from Arkansas and Louisiana sought refuge in Texas, where children accustomed to being waited on by slaves learned to do chores and care for themselves.

Runaway slaves formed a second group of wartime refugees. With southern landowners involved in the war, enslaved people left the plantations in ever-increasing numbers and appealed to Union military leaders for protection. Men among the escapees often enlisted in African-American army regiments, and some boys found employment as officers' servants. But for most of the refugees from slavery—children, women, and old men—hunger and homelessness characterized life behind the Union lines.

In the aftermath of war, many of these children and their parents returned to the farms of the South and lived hard lives as sharecroppers. Thousands of these children received at least some education in schools operated by the U.S. Freedmen's Bureau, which was a federal agency, and various religious and charitable organizations. Thousands of others who were still in the care of plantation owners, their labor too valuable to lose, were bound as apprentices, often against the wishes of their parents.

In the North and in the South, children were reunited with fathers mustered out of the army in the months after the war ended. Fathers numbered among the 620,000 war dead, however, so a great many children had to cope

The Indiana Soldiers' and Sailors' Orphans' Home Band performs at a gathering of the Grand Army of the Republic, an organization of Civil War veterans, ca. 1900–15. *(Library of Congress)*

with the loss of a parent. Americans responded to the economic hardship these children faced by opening orphanages. Most of these operated on an ad hoc basis, closing their doors for good once the soldiers' orphans had reached maturity, but some were still caring for children in the 20th century.

A Faith in Institutions

Nineteenth-century Americans typically dealt with needy or delinquent children by placing them in orphanages or correctional institutions. At a time when epidemics could cost large numbers of children one or both parents and when there were no public-welfare programs to support the poor, society had to find something to do with impoverished and troublesome young people. Although New Orleans Quakers responded to a yellow-fever epidemic by opening an orphanage in 1817, prior to mid-century orphaned children frequently wound up in poorhouses or almshouses. These institutions were in actuality dumping grounds for the unwanted poor: the ill, the insane, and the aged. They offered an unsuitable environment for children, and by the 1850s, due to the efforts of hardworking social reformers, the number of orphan asylums in the United States was growing. There would be 613 by 1880.

For children who got in trouble with the law or—especially if they were girls—exhibited moral laxity, there were houses of refuge or reformatories. These institutions were intended to be schools as well as correctional facilities, but brutal punishments and forced labor usually took precedence over spelling and arithmetic. The authorities considered it a successful outcome to place a graduate as a farm laborer or indentured servant.

Not all reformers viewed institutions as the best environment for poor and orphaned children. "It would be as wise," said Charles Loring Brace, founder in 1853 of the Children's Aid Society, "to put a hundred patients, diseased of innumerable maladies, in some immense hospital, and apply a universal treatment by machinery . . . as to place a hundred abandoned, ignorant, vicious children, each with his separate moral malady, under the drill arrangement of some public institution." Brace was a firm believer in "placing out," or settling urban children in rural foster homes to permit them to reach maturity in a family setting. Between 1854 and 1884, the Children's Aid Society's "orphan trains" carried more than 60,000 children from New York City to homes in New England and the Midwest.

Juvenile courts, which began to appear at the turn of the 20th century, kept youthful offenders out of institutions by addressing the root causes of unlawful behavior, such as family and financial issues, and by assigning probation officers to children accused or convicted of crimes.

Reformers of the early 20th century lobbied for child-labor legislation at the state and national levels. The National Child Labor Committee, founded in 1904, had persuaded 35 states to regulate the labor of people age 16 and younger by 1914. The first federal child-labor law, the Keating-Owen Act of 1916, banned interstate trade of goods produced by children, but the Supreme Court declared it unconstitutional in 1918. A 1919 attempt by Congress to impose similar restrictions was also ahead of its time and met the same fate as the Keating-Owen Act.

Employees of the Alexandria Glass
Factory, Virginia, June 1911,
photographed by Lewis Hine
(Library of Congress)

HOLDING CHILDREN DEAR

The concern for the welfare of society's children that characterized the second half of the 19th century coincided with a shift in the way that many adults viewed the individual child. As society became more urban and middle class, family size diminished. The child's familial role as a worker declined, and adults now idealized his or her purity and innocence. Children's clothing—their sailor suits, soft dresses, bows, and curls—symbolized their privileged status. Affluent parents purchased an array of dolls and mechanical toys for their young, and mothers had time to read the latest child-rearing manuals, which counseled them to consider a child's level of physical and mental development when offering guidance or administering discipline.

Older values persisted among the working class and immigrants, groups in which large numbers of offspring continued to be the norm and children helped to support their families. In the late 19th and early 20th centuries, millions of people left southern and eastern Europe to make their homes in the United States. Immigration reached a peak in 1907, when 1.5 million newcomers passed through U.S. ports. The children of immigrants strained urban public schools, not only because they filled classrooms beyond capacity, but because most teachers had no idea how to cope with their inability to speak English and with their foreign customs and dress. Schools embarked on a course of Americanization, emphasizing U.S. history and culture and proficiency in English.

WHAT PEOPLE REMEMBERED

Whereas memoirists writing about childhood in the early national period frequently described the work that they performed, those who grew up in the decades after the Civil War more often wrote about play. Reminiscences abound from this period of favorite dolls, backyard ballgames, and the vandalism that had come to be expected of boys.

Recollections of childhood from the early 20th century compete for the reader's attention with the opinions of numerous experts who had applied science to the process of child development. Prominent among them was G. Stanley Hall, who affixed the name *adolescence* to the transitional period between childhood and adulthood, and who saw the entire history of the human race mirrored in the maturation process. Psychologist John Broadus Watson had many parents raising their children by the clock and believing that demonstrations of affection between parent and child were unnecessary and even harmful. Meanwhile, educator John Dewey was advocating learning by doing and persuading teachers to link lessons to children's interests and experience.

Once again in the early 20th century, war became a significant experience for American children. During the years of U.S. involvement in World War I, 1917 and 1918, children learned in school the patriotic attitudes that the government wanted them to adopt. Because the fighting took place overseas, children's wartime activities were limited to home-front efforts, such as resource conservation, bond purchases and sales, and gardening. Teenage boys in several states temporarily replaced farm laborers who were serving overseas.

Conditions were right in the prosperous decade that followed World War I for the emergence of a distinct youth culture. With spending money and access to automobiles, young people of the Roaring Twenties rejected society's standards of dress and decorum. Short skirts, smoking and drinking, frank discussions of sex—the older generation did not know what to think. Were parents to blame for this display of moral laxity? Or did the behavior of the young reflect a healthy break from the false goodness of the past? Such questions became irrelevant after October 29, 1929, when the U.S. economy collapsed and the party ended.

CHILDHOOD IN THE GREAT DEPRESSION

As unemployment climbed to 24.9 percent in 1933, adults worried about current or potential joblessness and dwindling financial reserves. Children, meanwhile, struggled to understand recent changes in their households that might have included despondent, discordant parents; frugal meals; mended, hand-me-down clothing; and loss of the family car. Children who were old enough contributed their earnings from part-time jobs, but even the strictest economizing was not enough to save a great many homes. Some families moved in with kinfolk, and others came apart. Parents separated; poverty forced some mothers and fathers to send children to financially stable relatives or orphanages; teenagers left home to wander the nation's highways and hitch rides on freight trains.

Privation was often worse in rural areas than in cities. Because country schools lost more funding proportionally than city schools did, they were more likely to discontinue programs, shorten terms, or fold. By April 1, 1934, some 20,000 rural schools had closed. Rural children also suffered higher rates of disease, much of which could have been prevented by adequate public-health measures.

Beginning in 1933, President Franklin Delano Roosevelt sent a flurry of legislation to Congress. These laws, known collectively as the New Deal, aimed to ease the economic crisis by shoring up banks, aiding business recovery, and creating jobs. Several New Deal programs were of great benefit to youth. The Civilian Conservation Corps (CCC), established on March 31, 1933, employed 2.5 million boys and young men from families receiving public assistance. The government housed the CCC workers in military-style camps and put them to work on forestry and conservation projects. "It is all voluntary, if there is anything voluntary in a drowning man clutching at a straw and a hungry man grabbing a job and forage," commented one journalist in 1933. The National Youth Administration (NYA), another New Deal program, gave work-study jobs to high school and college students and vocational training to people age 16 to 25 who were out of school.

Such programs did little to help the farmers of the American Southwest who watched their soil dry up and blow away as drought devastated the region in the 1930s. Children were prominent among the people fleeing the "dust bowl," as this section of the country came to be called. Most of those who left traveled to California in search of jobs in that state's famed agricultural industry. The majority of these refugees failed to find steady work, with the result that their children went without adequate food, shelter, and clothing. Small children died of starvation and disease; the raggedness and regional accents of the older children drew taunts from native-Californian classmates.

The New Deal did benefit young African Americans, whose families were hit especially hard by the depression. The CCC and NYA, for example, enrolled African Americans in proportion to their numbers in the population. Not only was unemployment higher among blacks than among whites, but private relief agencies often refused to assist them. Those religious and charitable organizations that did aid African Americans stretched their resources to the limit, but they provided many black children with meals, shelter, medical care, and recreation.

At that time, much of the African-American population was moving from rural southern communities to northern urban industrial centers. The reasons for this population shift, known as the Great Migration, included poor living conditions in the South and perceived opportunities in the North.

Between 1916 and 1940, the North offered about 1.5 million people an escape from fear and oppression. The North beckoned with jobs in factories for adults and educational opportunities for children, although it turned out not to be the Promised Land that migrants anticipated. The only jobs open to black adults paid meager wages, and blacks were restricted to renting homes in poor, rundown sections of cities. Also, the schools that African-American children attended were segregated by custom rather than by law. These children suffered disproportionately from hunger and disease, and they were more likely than white children to die in the first year of life.

PITCHING IN TO WIN A WAR

New Deal initiatives helped to ease the hardship, but it was not until the end of the depression decade, when U.S. factories began producing the weaponry of World War II, that the economy truly started to mend. The sudden entry of the

United States into that war, following the Japanese attack on Pearl Harbor on December 7, 1941, stunned Americans of all ages and races. The first months of war were a frightening time for American children, as blackouts and school air raid drills made many of them worry that bombs would fall on them.

Children adjusted to changes in family life brought on by the war. Fathers and older brothers were drafted or enlisted in the armed forces, and many mothers were among the millions of adults who went to work in defense plants. Children used to having their mothers at home were now cared for by relatives or neighbors, placed in day care, or left to manage on their own. The availability of high-paying defense jobs lured people from rural communities to midwestern and West Coast manufacturing centers. For the children of these workers, moving to such a city as Detroit or Seattle often meant adapting to electric lighting, school buses, and other common features of 20th-century life.

The government called on citizens to conserve food and manufactured goods and to contribute scrap materials to the war effort. Children were energetic gatherers of scrap metal, which was converted into weapons and vehicles of war. They collected old tires for their badly needed rubber, and they scavenged for other usable commodities. Once again, children spent their coins on war stamps and bonds, and they provided reading material, knitted garments, and baked goods for the men and women in uniform.

Wartime conditions bred prejudice against the people of enemy nations and mistrust of Americans of German, Italian, or especially Japanese descent. In March 1942, the U.S. government began a mandatory evacuation of Japanese Americans from their homes on the West Coast to camps in remote western regions. As adults gave up their livelihood, children were forced to part with friends, pets, and toys. For nearly three years, these children would live and attend school in cramped, drafty barracks. Japanese Americans would wait until 1988 for the federal government to apologize for this violation of their civil rights and offer monetary compensation for their losses.

In 1942 children in San Juan Bautista, California, parade on school grounds with scrap metal they have collected for the war effort. *(Library of Congress)*

Japan's surrender on August 14, 1945, ended World War II and heralded the return of fathers from active duty. These men and their children worked at getting to know one another again, while children whose fathers had died in battle made different kinds of adjustments.

THE BABY BOOM

Following World War II, millions of GIs came home with marriage on their minds. The number of marriages taking place in the United States reached a high in 1946 of 118.1 per 1,000 single females age 14 and older, and it was not long until the birth rate skyrocketed. More than 76 million babies were born in the United States between 1946 and 1964—the baby-boom years.

Such a large segment of the population passing through childhood and adolescence influenced the way that all Americans lived. The housing industry responded to the needs of young families by constructing suburban subdivisions in which residents were dependent on the automobile for transportation. Businesses producing toys, foodstuffs, and other products aimed at young consumers earned huge profits. As the children entered their teens and developed a taste for rock and roll, Americans young and old heard this raucous music pouring from juke boxes and radios.

Americans who were young during World War II had the radio for entertainment; the children of the baby boom were the first to have television. The TV set also became the means by which children experienced newsworthy events, such as the assassination of President John F. Kennedy in November 1963 and the first moon landing in July 1969.

The writer Joyce Maynard, herself a baby boomer, described the late 1950s and early 1960s as a time when "fantasy existed mostly in the form of Mr. Clean and Speedy Alka-Seltzer." Maynard wrote, "We were sensible, realistic, literal-minded, unromantic, socially conscious and politically minded. . . . It was not a time when we could separate our own lives from the outside world."

This generation's highly developed moral and political consciousness caused many of its members to reject the materialistic, goal-driven lifestyle prevalent in the United States and to pursue self-expression and self-knowledge. Millions of teens and young adults sought heightened awareness through hippie culture, with its colorful, unisex fashions, free love, and drug use. The hippie movement came into full flower in August 1969, when 400,000 people attended the Woodstock Music and Arts Fair in the Catskill Mountains of New York.

In the late 1960s and early 1970s, members of this politically aware generation demonstrated against U.S. involvement in the Vietnam War. Some of the protests escalated into confrontations between student protesters and police and National Guard units. On May 4, 1970, Americans were shocked to learn that one such encounter on the campus of Kent State University in Ohio had ended with four students dead of gunshot wounds.

These protests were partly inspired by the achievements of the civil rights movement, victories that young African Americans helped to win. In 1955 and 1956, for example, black children were among the citizens of Montgomery, Alabama, who boycotted that city's buses until they were guaranteed the same rights and courtesies that white passengers enjoyed. In September 1957, black teenagers faced a hostile white mob and armed National Guardsmen to integrate Central High School in Little Rock, Arkansas. These courageous young people placed themselves in danger to improve conditions for their race. They escaped harm, but some children lost their lives in the battle for equal rights. Most memorable were the four girls killed in the bombing of a Birmingham, Alabama, church on September 15, 1963.

CHILDHOOD'S END?

Forty years ago, Philippe Ariès suggested that childhood as a distinct stage in life did not exist in the Middle Ages. Today some researchers speculate that childhood is disappearing and that the young increasingly face adult situations. Certainly there is evidence to support this disturbing yet intriguing claim.

Like children living in the early 19th century, many of today's youngsters have little time for unstructured play. With large numbers of mothers in the workforce, toddlers spend the equivalent of a workweek in day care. At the same time, parents keen on promoting early intellectual achievement are enrolling small children in academically oriented preschools and kindergartens. For older children, playing ball now means joining an adult-supervised organization; going to summer camp means learning to use computers or speak a foreign language.

There is evidence that children are becoming sexually experienced at progressively younger ages. Sexual activity—even promiscuity—is no longer a rarity among middle-school students. A number of causes for this trend have been proposed, including frequent exposure to sexually explicit material in the media, the behavior of national leaders and celebrities, and the high divorce rate. In 1997, it was estimated that 50 percent of all couples marrying for the first time would divorce within 10 years and that 60 percent of second marriages would end in divorce.

Children at the start of the 21st century often dress like adults in designer clothing and, in the case of girls, provocative styles. But the similarity between adult and child fashions has taken on a new twist. Writing in the *Wall Street Journal* in October 2000, journalist Amy Finnerty noted that women are now

Schoolyard games, Morton County, North Dakota, 1940
(Library of Congress)

dressing like little girls in tiny T-shirts and clothing emblazoned with cartoon characters.

It may be that mothers and fathers encourage precocity. Today's children live in a nation where sixth and seventh graders bring guns to school and open fire on their classmates, where children need information about drugs and AIDS. The semblance of maturity may provide some protection in a dangerous world.

Notes to the Introduction

p. ix "... taken from adult life ..." Annie Winsor Allen, "Boys and Girls." *Atlantic Monthly,* June 1920, p. 796.

p. x "... no place for childhood ..." Philippe Ariès, *Centuries of Childhood: A Social History of Family Life* (New York: Alfred A. Knopf, 1962), p. 33.

p. x "... children remain the last underclass ..." Jay Mechling, "Oral Evidence and the History of American Children's Lives." *Journal of American History,* September 1987, p. 579.

p. xi "Adults are finished products." Quoted in Dale Russakoff, "On Campus, It's the Children's Hour." *Washington Post,* November 13, 1998, p. A1.

p. xi "Whether everything was as I have written ..." Anne Gertrude Sneller, *A Vanished World* (Syracuse, N.Y.: Syracuse University Press, 1964), p. vii.

p. xi "Visions come to me ..." George Gallarno, "How Iowa Cared for Orphans of Her Soldiers of the Civil War." *Annals of Iowa,* January 1926, p. 163.

p. xi "I do not think a child ..." L. McRae Bell, "A Girl's Experience in the Siege of Vicksburg." *Harper's Weekly,* June 8, 1912, p. 12.

p. xi "... I must reconduct you ..." Daniel Drake, *Pioneer Life in Kentucky* (Cincinnati: Robert Clarke and Co., 1870), p. 47.

p. xii "... women and children are rendered ..." Quoted in Grace Abbott, *The Child and the State.* Vol. 1, *Legal Status in the Family, Apprenticeship and Child Labor* (Chicago: University of Chicago Press, 1938), p. 277.

p. xiii "Vistas opened in every direction." Lucy Larcom, "Among the Lowell Mill-Girls: A Reminiscence." *Atlantic Monthly,* November 1881, p. 611.

p. xiv "We followed our fathers ..." Quoted in Richard Erdoes, *The Rain Dance People* (New York: Alfred A. Knopf, 1976), p. 187.

p. xv "It was hard back breaking work ..." Robert Anderson, *From Slavery to Affluence: Memoirs of Robert Anderson, Ex-Slave* (Hemingford, Neb.: The Hemingford Ledger, 1927), p. 11.

p. xv "... however hedged in by circumstances ..." Josiah Henson, *Father Henson's Story of His Own Life* (Boston: John P. Jewett, 1858), p. 19.

p. xvii "It would be as wise ..." Charles Loring Brace, *The Best Method of Disposing of Our Pauper and Vagrant Children,* p. 10.

p. xx "It is all voluntary ..." "Doughboys of 1933 Off to the Woods." *Literary Digest,* April 29, 1933, p. 22.

p. xxii "... fantasy existed mostly ..." Joyce Maynard, *Looking Back: A Chronicle of Growing Up Old in the Sixties* (London: Michael Joseph, 1973), p. 5.

1

The Youth of a New Nation
1790–1850

One way to approach the culture of a distant place or time is to explore the issues that occupied people's minds. A hot topic of debate among New Englanders in the late 18th and early 19th centuries was the fate of the souls of children who died in the first years of life. Did God welcome them into heaven or condemn them to hell?

This was a complex question to resolve. New England society in the early national period was strongly influenced by the Puritanism of its founders. The Puritans had accepted the doctrine of original sin, the teaching that every person inherited Adam's depravity. Sin tainted all human deeds; no one escaped corruption, not even a newborn babe. Each individual had to seek salvation through God's grace, but children who died before developing the faculties of language and reason never had the chance to commit themselves to God.

Scripture offered no answer, because divine wisdom was dispensed strictly on a need-to-know basis. The Creator revealed eternal truths to facilitate salvation and not merely to satisfy human curiosity. Even the most indulgent of ministers could offer grieving parents no guarantee that God would grant their lost child a place in heaven, so fathers and mothers coming to terms with God's will looked for reasons within themselves and blamed their own shortcomings for his wrath. Some wondered whether they had offended the Almighty by forming too strong a worldly attachment to their child.

Religion cast a fainter shadow on family life and childbearing outside of New England. For example, a secular culture had evolved in the Chesapeake region, which was settled by Catholics and Protestants. Dwelling too heavily on the tenets of Christianity would have created a moral dilemma for the residents of Maryland and Virginia, whose economy was based on the labor of enslaved Africans.

Americans in both the North and the South used the word *infancy* when referring to the first six years of life, when children were principally in the care of their mothers. The term *adolescence* did not yet exist. People perceived that childhood continued until age 18 or even beyond age 20. Puberty arrived later than it does today, occurring on average at age 15 in girls and at 16 in boys. Physical growth was a slower process as well. Many young men were 25 years old before they had reached their full height. In addition, record keeping was careless, especially in rural areas, and many parents quickly lost track of their children's ages. Size and ability to work counted more than chronological age.

LARGE, WORKING FAMILIES

Nearly every American who came of age between 1790 and 1830 grew up in a big family, with an average of seven to nine siblings. Families with more than 10 children were not uncommon. Such large numbers of offspring frequently resulted from more than one marriage; that is, a widowed man who remarried might have had several children with each of his wives. For parents, having lots of children made good economic sense: More children meant more workers. In a nation that was predominantly agricultural, the family formed the basic unit of production.

Boys as young as seven or eight worked beside their fathers in the fields. They stood behind plows, sowed seed, and pulled up weeds. They labored especially hard during the late-summer harvests. With their mothers, girls performed the many tasks that were relegated to women. They assisted in food preparation, in everything from cooking meals to churning butter, making cheese, and collecting eggs from the hen house. Women and girls also made the family's clothing, literally from scratch. They harvested flax and spun linen thread for weaving; they scoured and carded, or combed, wool and wound it into yarn. Older girls looked after their younger brothers and sisters, and most likely they had several, for as a rule women bore children for most of their reproductive lives, from soon after marrying in their late teens or early 20s through their late 40s.

Children joined the adults not only in work but in worship and social activities as well. Young people took part in dances and quilting bees. They belonged to temperance societies, debating clubs, and other groups dedicated to self-improvement. Children were dressed like miniature adults, with boys past infancy wearing men's-style shirts and breeches and girls wearing long dresses that might have had rigid stays sewn inside to foster upright posture.

Children were exposed to emotional issues that later generations would consider inappropriate for their age. In particular, many children of the early 19th century had a strong familiarity with death. Parents encouraged children's exposure to the dead and dying, because death was a natural process, part of life and even of childhood, something it was best to learn about early. At a time when adults and children commonly died at home, some parents made sure that children were present to witness the dying moments of a sister or brother.

The demands of work left little time to play, but most children had a few homemade toys. A girl might have developed her sewing skills by making the small number of dolls that she owned. Girls played with dollhouses, dolls' cradles, and paper dolls. Outdoors they rode on swings; indoors they recited poetry. Boys, who generally favored active games, built wigwams and pretended to be Indians or rode hobbyhorses and live ponies. Boys flew kites, sailed toy boats, and combed the natural world to collect rocks and birds' eggs. Children in wealthy families might own toys that had been purchased, such as miniature tea sets and lead soldiers, but such items were beyond the budgets of most American households.

Girls in Wethersfield, Connecticut, weed an onion patch in this 1780 print. *(Courtesy Wethersfield Historical Society)*

The number of objects crafted specifically for children was small. Mothers and older sisters made swaddling clothes and quilts for babies. There were standing stools to hold small children erect and cradles for babies to rest in beside the hearth during the day. Babies slept near their mothers at night, while two or more older children frequently shared one bed. In some homes, boys and girls slept in the same room; in others, they slept apart.

For the American colonists founding a nation in the wilderness, there had been no one to depend on but themselves. The citizens of the young United States valued self-reliance, and they allowed their children greater freedom than

A rare depiction of play from early 19th-century America: girls jumping rope *(The Saint Louis Art Museum)*

European parents did. European travelers in the United States, accustomed to formality at home, remarked on the familiar relations that existed between American parents and their children. Some criticized the impudence of American youth who voiced opinions in conversations as if they were the equals of adults, but others found it refreshing.

Despite the premium placed on autonomy, children old enough to move around had to be watched closely to see that they did not fall into the fire, brush against a candle and ignite their clothing, or swallow pins or other small objects. Outdoors, young children needed to be protected from falling into a stream and drowning, wandering into a livestock pen, or ingesting poisonous berries or leaves.

DISEASE POSED A RISK

Children from birth through age 16 made up half the U.S. population for most of the period between 1790 and 1830. Having a big family not only kept the homestead running, it also gave parents confidence that some of their offspring would reach maturity, barring a severe epidemic. Parents were thus reasonably assured that there would be adult children to look after them, should they reach old age.

Children throughout early America succumbed to contagious diseases such as smallpox, yellow fever, and influenza, as well as intestinal and respiratory infections. Epidemics of measles, whooping cough, and scarlet fever claimed many young lives, and tuberculosis was a common killer of children age 10 and older. The poor died disproportionately from typhoid fever, which spread through the water supply, and typhus, which was carried by fleas and lice.

In New England during the early national period, between 20 and 30 percent of live-born children died before reaching maturity. The death rate for children under five was highest in coastal regions of the South, where humidity and warm temperatures facilitated the spread of disease. In late summer and early fall, when malaria and yellow fever were at their peak, families with the means to do so vacated coastal and river cities, such as Charleston and Savannah, taking refuge in cabins in the piney woods. In all regions, however, the first year of life brought the greatest risk of death. The time of weaning, usually around age two, was especially hazardous as well, probably because it was then that children were first exposed to microorganisms in food.

Medical treatment made being sick even more perilous. Doctors treated intestinal worms—a common malady—with calomel, a strong purgative containing mercury. Some children died from this remedy, while others sustained permanent damage to the digestive tract. Purging was also a popular treatment for infectious disease, as was bleeding, which was accomplished either by applying leeches to the skin or by lancing a vein.

In the early 19th century, doctors in London and Paris were demonstrating the ineffectiveness of bleeding and purging and the potential for mercury to cause disease. Physicians and surgeons in the United States read the European findings in medical journals, but many continued to employ the old methods anyway. The influential Philadelphia physician Benjamin Rush, a member of the Continental Congress and a signer of the Declaration of Independence, called for the treatment of all diseases by a single method, "depletion," which entailed bloodletting and purging. The more acute the illness, Rush advised, the more aggressive the curative measures. Other American doctors justified their practices by claiming—erroneously—that diseases were more severe and spread more rapidly in the New World than in Europe.

New Englanders practiced a crude form of smallpox inoculation in which they inserted dried material from the pustules of an infected person under the skin of a healthy individual's arm or leg. This type of inoculation caused some fatal cases of smallpox, but it did provide a measure of protection. In 1792, when more than 9,000 Bostonians received inoculation, the death rate from vaccination was roughly 2 percent. About 12.5 percent of city residents who caught the disease naturally in the same year died from it. In 1799, Harvard physician Benjamin Waterhouse read of the British doctor Edward Jenner's success using the less virulent cowpox virus to immunize people against smallpox. Waterhouse experimented with cowpox vaccine in the United States, trying it first on his five-year-old son. As more people were inoculated with cowpox, vaccination became a safe procedure.

CHILDREN IN TOWNS AND CITIES

By 1800, one-fifth of Americans lived in cities and towns. Among them were failed farmers who had come to find work as well as their dependents. Lacking assets and marketable skills, many displaced farm families joined the ranks of the poor, a class that would grow in numbers and visibility throughout the 19th century. In towns as in rural settings, children's labor contributed to their families' well-being, but the kind of work that children did depended to a large extent on their parents' position in the community.

A poor child might gather kindling or herd someone else's livestock. A girl could be hired as a housemaid, while her seven-year-old brother might be employed as a "boy of all work"—a servant who performed a variety of tasks, such as running errands, drawing well water, and chopping wood. Children also became beggars. It was not uncommon for a city dweller to find a little girl at the kitchen door with a basket over her arm, asking for scraps of bread and meat.

Some poor and abandoned children were placed in indentured servitude, either by their parents or by local authorities. An indentured child was bound by contract to an employer for a specified period, typically seven years. Indentured girls were required to do domestic work, while boys served artisans or tradesmen. The hours were long and the labor hard. The practice of indentured servitude began in the colonial period, when men and women worked for a four- to seven-year term in exchange for their transportation to the New World. Some colonial indentured servants were deported prisoners whose labor had been sold for the price of their passage. Indentured servitude was more common before 1830 than after, but it continued until the end of the 19th century in northeastern cities. Public records indicate that in Philadelphia and other urban areas, most of the children bound as indentured servants were of Irish heritage.

If state or church authorities determined that a child was in need of being properly cared for, they might arrange for him or her to be "placed out." Such a child—and he or she was invariably poor—was assigned to be an unpaid laborer for a family who in turn agreed to provide food, shelter, clothing, and some schooling until the child came of age.

A common career path for a town or city boy from a more stable financial background began when he was apprenticed to a skilled craftsman, at the approximate age of 14. While an indentured servant was engaged only to work, an apprentice was taken on to both work and learn. Whether they studied carpentry, coopering, printing, or shoemaking, boys had similar experiences of appren-

Boy apprentices figured prominently on a silk banner carried by the Society of Pewterers as they marched in New York City to celebrate ratification of the Constitution, July 23, 1788. *(Collection of the New-York Historical Society, negative no. 1176)*

ticeship. They spent several years under the artisan's tutelage, practicing every step in the manufacturing process. An apprentice graduated to become a journeyman, or paid worker, in the master's shop, and hoped to be a master himself in time.

YOUNG WORKERS FOR THE FACTORIES

The population of the United States grew by more than 35 percent between 1790 and 1800, rising from 3,929,214 to 5,308,483. A similar increase occurred between 1800 and 1810, when the population reached 7,239,881. Immigration from northern Europe accounted for much of the growth. The population was spreading westward as well, and by 1810, more than 1 million people lived west of the Appalachian Mountains. As individual craftsman found it increasingly difficult to meet the public's needs and the traditional manufacturing system began to collapse, the Industrial Revolution reached America's shores. A new commercial institution, the factory, would satisfy the great demand for goods. Factory owners would owe much of their success and their profit to the cheap labor of children.

Production first moved out of the home and artisan's shop in Great Britain in the 18th century, when the manufacture of textiles became mechanized. The flying shuttle, invented by John Kay in 1733, speeded the process of weaving. In 1769, Richard Arkwright developed the spinning frame, a machine that simultaneously spun several threads for weaving. Fifteen years later, a Scottish-born instrument maker named James Watt perfected an efficient steam engine for powering factory machinery.

Hoping to eliminate foreign competition from the start, Parliament outlawed the export of textile equipment and barred textile workers from traveling overseas. The legislation failed to prevent Samuel Slater, who had been apprenticed to Arkwright, from sailing to New England with the plans for state-of-the-art British textile machinery committed to memory.

Working in partnership with the owners of an established textile firm, William Almy and Moses Brown, Slater constructed his first cotton mill at Pawtucket, Rhode Island, in 1790. By the early 19th century, many more mills had been built in the United States, and the factory system had spread to other industries—to the manufacture of firearms, clothing, timepieces, and shoes. There were too few men available to work, so factory owners hired women and children. The first workers hired by Almy, Brown, and Slater were nine boys from poor families living near the mill. By 1801, 100 children aged four through 10 worked for Slater and his partners.

Manufacturers profited from child labor because children commanded lower wages than adults did. A young woman could expect to earn $3.25 per week in a New England mill, while a child's wages could be as low as 33 cents per week. Children working for Samuel Slater earned 50 cents a week, enough for a pound of sugar, a pound of flour, and a bushel of potatoes at the company store. Manufacturers insisted that employment taught children the Puritan values of hard work and thrift. They pointed out that having jobs kept many children (and sometimes their widowed mothers) from depending on charity.

In truth, there was little learning on the job for children in factories. They performed tedious, repetitive work that required a low level of skill. Under the factory system, the manufacturing process was broken down into a series of steps, and a worker performed a single step in the process again and again. It was widely thought that children's little fingers were well suited to handling thread, so child workers repaired broken threads on looms and replaced empty bobbins. They performed these tasks quickly, while the machines operated, to avoid slowing the pace of production. Other children spread cleaned cotton on the carding machines, which combed it, or passed the carded fibers through the roving machines that rolled it into loose bundles that were ready for spinning. The smallest workers darted under machinery to clean up dust and loose threads that had fallen onto the floor.

The exact number of children working in early 19th-century American factories is unknown. In 1810, Albert Gallatin, secretary of the treasury under President Thomas Jefferson, surveyed 87 textile mills from New England through Baltimore and determined that 3,500 of the 4,000 workers in those mills were women and children. Some 20th-century historians have estimated that one-third to one-half of New England mill workers were age 16 or younger. These children put in the same long days as adult factory workers did, standing or walking for 12, 14, or even 16 hours a day, six days a week. In one Philadelphia factory in 1838, children walked up and down four flights of stairs, carrying boxes on their heads, from 5:00 A.M. until 7:00 P.M. each workday. It is no wonder that working children had swollen ankles and were often exhausted.

Like adults, children were expected to be punctual and awake and alert on the job. Those who were tardy had their wages docked, and the chronically late were dismissed. Some bosses resorted to corporal punishment when children worked slowly or inattentively. Although there were reports of child laborers suffering broken bones at the hands of their employers, such brutality was rare. It was in a mill owner's best interest not to injure his workers too severely. Disability or death resulting from a mechanical accident was a greater risk than physical punishment at a time when there were no laws setting standards of workplace safety.

Many children living in the cities of the Northeast toiled alongside their parents and siblings in home sweatshops. Families working in this manner performed one step in the manufacture of an article of clothing or other item and were paid according to the number of pieces completed. Home sweatshops became common after 1840, as the population of immigrants increased. The population of New York City, which was 96,373 in 1810, totaled 312,710 in 1840 and 515,547 in 1850, largely because of immigration. Other cities experienced similar growth. For example, Baltimore, a city of 46,555 in 1810, had a population of 169,054 in 1850. In 1790, there had been no American cities with 50,000 residents. By 1850, nearly half a million people lived in cities that large.

RAISING VIRTUOUS CHILDREN

After 1830, birth rates declined in the Northeast. For one thing, there was less arable land available, which meant that farmers' sons who came of age were increasingly forced to establish themselves far from home or to seek employment in towns and cities. Farmers in developing rural regions therefore began to limit the size of their families. For another, industrial development brought into being

An unidentified Maine family, ca. 1850. Because young boys and girls were dressed alike at this time, it is impossible to determine the sex of the children in dresses; however, the kinds of toys they hold indicate that the two middle children are probably boys. *(New York State Historical Association, Cooperstown, New York)*

a new middle class of manufacturers and merchants in New England and indirectly softened prevailing attitudes toward children—at least among business and professional people. Middle-class New Englanders expected less work from their children and stopped viewing them as an economic asset. Parents in this group lavished more attention on each son or daughter, and the bond between mother and child grew stronger.

The thinking of this new industrialist class was influenced less by their Puritan heritage and more by the Enlightenment, the trend in thought prevalent in 18th-century Europe prior to the French Revolution. The thinkers and writers of the Enlightenment expressed confidence in the ability of human reason to reveal the secrets of the universe. Inspired by Isaac Newton's discovery of universal gravitation in the 1680s, they placed no limit on humans' ability to discern God's laws and improve their nature. Another important precursor of the Enlightenment, one who influenced attitudes toward child development, was the 17th-century English philosopher John Locke. In his *Essay Concerning Human Understanding,* published in 1690, Locke had called the newborn child's mind a *tabula rasa;* it was a blank slate, morally neutral, he wrote, ready to be shaped by experience. According to Locke, human nature developed gradually as children interacted with the environment.

Infants who died were now deemed too pure for the evils of the world. It was children past infancy who risked damnation, who needed to repent and seek God's grace. Death rates remained high among the young, so it was imperative that they receive moral training. Mid-19th-century children learned to honor their mothers and fathers; to display good manners, which were an outward sign of their principles; to treat others with kindness, friends and strangers alike; and to work hard—in short, to adopt virtues that would cause God to look favorably upon them. Popular guides to raising children published after 1830 by Bronson Alcott, Lydia M. Child, and others advocated a gentle approach to nurturing these qualities. Previously, most written advice on child rearing argued for severe beatings as a disciplinary measure.

Adults expressed their newfound reverence for children at Christmas, a holiday that Americans only began to celebrate in the 1820s. By 1830 even strict Calvinist congregations were holding Christmas services. Immigrants from Germany brought evergreens into their homes and covered them with festive decorations, and native-born Americans adopted the practice. It was not long before parents were telling their children to expect gifts from Saint Nicholas, the patron saint of children, who was associated with holiday giving in Europe. The name Santa Claus is an American corruption of the Dutch dialect name *Sante Klaas.*

At Christmas, children waited for Santa Claus to fill their stockings with fruit, candy, nuts, coins, and small toys. Clement Clarke Moore, a teacher of Greek and Eastern literature at the General Theological Seminary, created the image of the robust, red-suited Santa Claus so familiar to Americans today in his 1822 poem, "An Account of a Visit from St. Nicholas." Moore modeled his Santa on a portly Dutch neighbor of his father, who lived in New York State.

COMING OF AGE

In the first half of the 19th century, the transition from childhood to independence was gradual and unique for every individual. There were no universal rites of passage and no usual age for finishing school, moving out of the home, or embarking on a career. There were 14-year-olds living away from home and supporting themselves and 18-year-olds still dependent on their parents and working on the family farm. Volunteer militias set a minimum age for membership, usually 18, but these ceremonial and social organizations frequently admitted younger members. Girls began keeping company with young men between the ages of 14 and 18.

Consistent with the culture of self-reliance, boys were encouraged to strike out on their own, to acquire land away from their family, possibly to the west. Girls faced a different prospect. Society expected them, upon reaching maturity, to stifle their independence, to marry and devote themselves to family and home.

CHRONICLE OF EVENTS

1690

John Locke publishes his *Essay Concerning Human Understanding.*

1733

John Kay's invention of the flying shuttle speeds the process of weaving.

1769

Richard Arkwright invents the spinning frame, a practical machine for spinning thread.

1784

James Watt perfects an efficient steam engine for powering factory machinery.

1790

The population of the United States is 3,929,214.

Samuel Slater constructs his first cotton mill at Pawtucket, Rhode Island.

1790–1830

The average American family has eight to 10 children.

Most children live on farms and participate in the work necessary to sustain the family.

Children age 16 and younger constitute half the U.S. population.

Twenty to 30 percent of children born alive will die before reaching maturity.

Poor and abandoned children are placed in indentured servitude in northeastern cities; this practice will continue until the end of the century, but it will lose popularity after 1830.

1792

In Boston, 9,000 people are inoculated against smallpox; 2 percent of them die as a result.

Of the Bostonians who contract smallpox naturally, 12.5 percent die.

1798

Vaccination with cowpox makes smallpox inoculation a safe procedure.

1800

One-fifth of Americans live in cities and towns.

The population of the United States is 5,308,483, showing an increase of 35 percent from 1790.

1810

The U.S. population is now 7,239,881.

The population of New York City is 96,373; Baltimore's population is 46,555.

More than 1 million people live west of the Appalachian Mountains.

Secretary of the Treasury Albert Gallatin concludes that 3,500 of 4,000 workers in 87 eastern textile mills are women and children.

One-third to one-half of New England textile-mill workers are age 16 or younger, according to 20th-century estimates.

1822

Clement Clarke Moore publishes "An Account of a Visit from St. Nicholas," the poem that establishes the popular American image of Santa Claus.

1830

Birth rates begin to decline among the middle class in New England; parents are influenced by the thinking of John Locke.

Parenting guidebooks published after this year advocate a kind, gentle approach to bringing up children.

1840

New York City's population is 312,270.

1850

Immigration brings the population of New York City to 515,547 and that of Baltimore to 169,054.

EYEWITNESS TESTIMONY

. . . [O]ld Brindle [the cow] was then a veritable member of the family, and took her slop at the cabin door, while the children feasted on her warm milk within. The calf grew up in their companionship, and disputed with them for its portion of the delicious beverage which she distilled from the cane and luxuriant herbage in which she waded through the day. It was my function when our rival was likely to get beyond its share, to take it by the ears, and hold it away till mother should get ahead; and many a tough struggle did I have.

Daniel Drake recalling the years 1788 through 1794, when he was a child in Mayslick, Kentucky, Pioneer Life in Kentucky, *p. 44.*

To prepare the new field for cultivation required only the axe and mattock, but the cultivation itself called for the plow and hoe; both of which I recollect were abundantly rude and simple in their construction. Deep plowing was not as necessary as in soils long cultivated, and if demanded would have been impracticable, for the ground was full of roots. After a first "breaking up" with the coultered plow, the shovel plow was in general use. In such rooty soils it was often difficult to hold the plow and drive the horse; it was the employment of small boys, therefore, to ride and guide the animal—a function which I performed in plowing time for many years; and it was, I can assure you, no sinecure. To sit bareback on a lean and lazy horse for several successive hours, under a broiling sun, and every now and then, when you were gazing at a pretty bird, or listening to its notes, or watching the frolic of a couple of squirrels on the neighboring trees, to have the plow suddenly brought to a dead halt by running under a root, and the top of the long hames to give you a hard and unlooked-for punch in the pit of the stomach, is no laughing matter, try it who may.

Daniel Drake recalling the years 1788 through 1794, when he was a child in Mayslick, Kentucky, Pioneer Life in Kentucky, *p. 45.*

Swinging by grape-vines was, in general, a joint amusement, as was hunting nuts, haws, pawpaws, and other fruits, when in season. The boys climbed trees after bird's nests and grapes, and for the enterprise. It was sometimes a matter of ambition to see who could climb the highest. Now and then several would ascend the same tree, and be clinging to its trunk at the same time; or two would start on the opposite sides of one tree and strive for the greater elevation. Occasionally a luckless squirrel would be driven up a detached tree when, if it were not too lofty, he was assailed with clubs and stones, by which (rarely) he would be killed; but more commonly led to jump from its top, when not very high, and run for a taller tree.

Daniel Drake recalling the years 1788 through 1794, when he was a child in Mayslick, Kentucky, Pioneer Life in Kentucky, *pp. 148–49.*

In the winter nearly all the boys went to school, and in the summer, those large enough to work, staid at home and worked on the farm; going barefoot till cold weather came again. This going barefoot in a new country, among small stumps and roots, is a bad business. The feet get sore, and then to go in the woods among the ground yew, was exceedingly annoying to sore feet. It was however the fashion of the country and could not be avoided; for shoes were not to be had, except for winter, when a "cat whipper" came to the family, with kit, and made them.

Levi Beardsley describing conditions in Otsego County, New York, ca. 1795, Reminiscences, *in Louis C. Jones, ed.,* Growing Up in the Cooper Country, *pp. 62–63.*

Although I was blessed with kind parents, who cared for all my wants, yet I soon learned that human life was not designed to be a scene of continuous enjoyment, but a school of discipline, where, by a series of trials, instructions and struggles, are brought into activity and developed the nobler faculties of a soul-life—where we are shown the beauty and effulgence of an unveiled eternity!

Richard Cecil Stone writing about his early childhood, ca. 1798–1805, Life Incidents of Home, School and Church, *p. 1.*

The first of my children that I inoculated, was a boy of five years old, named Daniel Oliver Waterhouse. I made a slight incision in the usual place for inoculation in the arm, inserted a small portion of the [thread infected with cowpox], and covered it with a sticking-plaster. It exhibited no other appearances than what would have arisen from any other extraneous substance, until the 6th day, when an encreased redness called forth my attention. On the 8th, he complained of pain under the inoculated arm, and on the 9th, the inoculated part exhibited evident signs of virulency. By the 10th, any one, much experienced in the inoculated small-pox, would have pronounced the arm infected. The pain and swelling under his arm went on, gradually encreasing, and by the 11th day from inoculation, his febrile symptoms were pretty strongly marked. . . .

The inoculated part in this boy, was surrounded by an efflorescence which extended from his shoulder to his elbow, which made it necessary to apply some remedies to lessen it; but the "symptoms," as they are called, scarcely drew him from his play more than an hour or two; and he went through the disease is so light a manner, as hardly ever to express any marks of peevishness.

Benjamin Waterhouse, 1800, A Prospect of Exterminating the Small-Pox, in Robert H. Bremner, ed., Children and Youth in America, Vol. 1: 1600–1865, pp. 302–03.

I was always in bondage through fear of death, until the grace of God delivered me from it, by the forgiveness of my sins. I was, perhaps, uncommonly exercised with gloomy thoughts on this subject, in the very early part of my life. I used to lament bitterly, that I must die, when but a small child. I used to meditate upon the subject and thought if I must die, I would beg to be buried near by the house of my parents, for I could not bear the thoughts of being deposited in the lonesome grave-yard.

Ray Potter writing about his thoughts in 1802, the year he turned seven, Memoirs of the Life and Religious Experiences of Ray Potter, p. 18.

I was an exceedingly delicate child, and my mother was often warned that she could "have me with her but a short time." I remember being much petted and indulged during my first years (probably on account of the fragility of my constitution), and also being several times prostrated for a week or more after a day's visit with my little cousins.

Emily C. Judson, who spent her first years in Eaton, New York, recalling her life ca. 1802, in A. C. Kendrick, The Life and Letters of Mrs. Emily C. Judson, p. 15.

IN Memory of
Thomas K. Park Junr
and thirteen infants,
Children of Mr.
Thomas K. Park and
Rebecca his wife

Inscription on a Grafton, Vermont, family gravestone, 1803, in Dickran Tashjian and Ann Tashjian, Memorials for Children of Change, p. 257.

About two years after my mother died, my brother, whose name was Milton, and who, being about two years older than myself, was my most intimate playmate in the family, followed her to the grave. This was a great loss to me; for he was a bold, generous, active boy, and my spirit chimed in with his more than with any other member of the family. I loved his reckless daring, and restless activity. He was seized with a nervous or brain fever, and, in a few days, was dead.

I have a vivid recollection of his death. It was midnight; I was in my bed, and, with the rest of the family, was called up to be present at the closing scene. I came down in haste; entered the room; my dying brother and playfellow was sitting in a chair. All the family were standing around. I stood near my brother. He spoke not a word—did not seem to see or know any of us. That room was silent, disturbed only by the short breathings of my dying brother, and the stifled sobs of the loving ones around him. How I longed to hear that brother's voice speaking to me! But he ceased to breathe, and was laid on the bed. Then came the funeral, of which I remember only the neighbors coming in, and the last look at my playmate and bedfellow brother, as he lay in his coffin. He looked so pale, and seemed so still and silent! I could not understand it.

Henry Clarke Wright remembering his brother's death, ca. 1805, Human Life, in Louis C. Jones, ed., Growing Up in the Cooper Country, pp. 98–99.

When about ten years old, I was put by my father to work for a farmer, about three miles from home, through the season. During the time I staid here, I was inexpressibly unhappy. Removed from the company of my parents, and among strangers, I was in a situation to have my mind overwhelmed with foreboding thoughts of death and eternity; and added to those reflections on these subjects which were *ordinary*, was the idea that the world would be destroyed that season. There was to be an extraordinary conjunction of the planets that season, and some one had declared that a conflagration of our earth would certainly take place at the same time. . . .

But the summer passed away—the world stood unshaken, and I returned in autumn to my father's house. . . . The ensuing spring I was engaged to Mr. K.

of Cranston, a kinsman of my father. He filled a number of important offices in the State and town. He kept a grocery store in which I attended; worked in the garden, &c. in the summer, and attended school in the winter. He was remarkably kind and indulgent, and never gave me an angry word that I recollect, during the two years which I lived with him.

Ray Potter of Providence, Rhode Island, writing about events occurring between 1805 and 1807, Memoirs of the Life and Religious Experiences of Ray Potter, *pp. 18–19.*

Among the very few times that [my father] ever attempted to correct me by whipping, one occurred as follows, when I was about ten or twelve years old. We were plowing, with two yoke of oxen. He was holding; I was driving. The leading oxen were young and not well trained, and almost every time we came round the field, as we crossed the path leading to the barn, these leaders would run off. This would wake up father, and call out the reproof: "Careless boy!" "Take better care of those steers!" I would determine to do better; yes I *would*. I would keep them right the next round! But I was a dreamy boy, as my father was a dreamy man. I would forget, and off they would go again! At length on one occasion I did remember—I kept the leaders straight. There was not a word said, and on we went, I rejoicing that I had kept my resolution. But the next round I forgot myself, and off they went again! My father was angered. "You careless boy! You don't try to mind your business! Those leaders have run off every time we have passed this place since we began." I said, "No, father, they did not run off the last time." He said, "They did; you tell that which is not true." I replied, "I say the truth; they did not run off the last time round." He replied, with greater anger, "Don't contradict me!" I replied again, "I kept them straight the last time round." He seized the whip, took it from my hand, and whipped me severely, saying, "Will you now contradict me again?" I looked him in the face and said, "Father, you may whip me to death, if you please, but I shall say with my last breath, I kept them straight forward the last time round." He again raised the whip, looked me with an indescribable expression in the eye for a moment, then threw the whip upon the ground, went to his plow, and bade me drive on.

Richard Cecil Stone, who was 10 years old in 1808, Life Incidents of Home, School and Church, *pp. 2–3.*

In 1809–10, my mother having no help, and my sister being nearly two years younger than myself, I used to help milk, set the table, make the coffee, bake buckwheat cakes, etc., etc., and this part of my education I have valued very much. . . . As mother rose very early, we would get the milking and other work done in time for school, which was never neglected, except on hog-killing day. The school was vacated in harvest time, when I would work in the field, gathering sheaves, raking after the wagon, handing sheaves on the barrack or mow. I often assisted the men in the mornings and evenings when I went to school, by which I learned to do many things that were afterwards of use.

Benjamin Hallowell, a native of Cheltenham Township, Pennsylvania, who was 10 years old in 1809, Autobiography of Benjamin Hallowell, *p. 12.*

One of my playmates had induced me to purchase of him, for three or four coppers I had saved, a whistle he had whittled out of a piece of willow wood. My incessant whistling led to inquiries by my father, who, having shown me how simple was the process of making a whistle, added: "Neal, I am afraid that thou wilt come out of the little end of the horn if thou spendest thy money so foolishly." I replied: "I'd rather come out of the little end than stick in the middle."

The prompt confiscation of the whistle fixed in my memory the parental admonition that children should always be respectful to their parents.

Neal Dow writing about his childhood in Portland, Maine, ca. 1810–15, The Reminiscences of Neal Dow, *p. 30.*

Idleness was regarded by my parents as a dangerous evil and a sin against one's self, and I was brought up to look upon useful employment as not only tributary to health and strength, but as a divinely appointed safeguard from many otherwise inevitable misfortunes. There were many ways in which a boy about a New England home of my time, in such a community as Portland then was, could make himself useful. My parents sought to guard me from the mischief, which, as I was made to believe, "Satan always finds for idle hands to do." If I ever had any natural disinclination to be usefully employed, parental training soon corrected it.

Neal Dow writing about his childhood in Portland, Maine, ca. 1810–15, The Reminiscences of Neal Dow, *pp. 30–31.*

INDUSTRY & SLOTH.

What a sight! The sluggard stretched out in his bed with the bright light shining upon him and his mother and sister at work as busy as bees. Let him lose his breakfast two or three times and he will learn better ways.

A pictorial lesson published in the 1850s by the American Sunday-School Union of Philadelphia teaches children to value industry over sloth. *(Courtesy The Winterthur Library: Printed Book and Periodical Collection)*

When I was a boy a murderer was hung on Munjoy Hill. He had been convicted of killing, in a town adjoining Portland, an officer who was attempting to serve some sort of legal document upon him. The inhabitants generally from all the surrounding country, as well as from Portland itself, flocked to the scene, as to a feast, and a gala day was made of it, the people picnicking on the hill near the gallows. Boy-like, I wished also to view the horrible sight, as some of the boys in my neighborhood were allowed to do, with their parents, but my father forbade it. My Uncle Jonathan, who was a sea-captain, was then visiting our home, and he was about to give me a glimpse of it through a spyglass from the scuttle [opening with a lid] of our roof when I was summarily summoned down-stairs by my father, to my great and unreasonable wrong, as I then thought. *Neal Dow writing about his childhood in Portland, Maine, ca. 1810–15,* The Reminiscences of Neal Dow, *p. 44.*

Yesterday my little son appeared very sick. I was awake with him most of the night, and was apprehensive of two disorders, one in consequence of a bad fall, the other the effect of having been exposed to an infectious disease. But, blessed be my gracious Lord, he has disappointed me. Instead of putting the cup of mourning into my hand, he has dissipated all my fears, and caused me to rejoice in his sparing mercy. My heart failed me. I thought I should sink under the affliction of a separation from my child; not because God had not a perfect right to do what he pleased with his own, but from the extreme natural sensibility of my disposition, which is my snare.

Susan Huntington, July 22, 1812, Memoirs of the Late Mrs. Susan Huntington, of Boston, Mass., *p. 50.*

There is scarcely any subject concerning which I feel more anxiety, than the proper education of my children. It is a difficult and delicate subject; and the more I reflect on my duty to them, the more I feel how much is to be learnt by myself. The person who undertakes to form the infant mind, to cut off the distorted shoots, and direct and fashion those which may, in due time, become fruitful and lovely branches, ought to possess a deep and accurate knowledge of human nature. It is no easy task to ascertain, not only the principles and habits of thinking, but also the causes which produce them. It is no easy task, not only to watch over actions, but also to become acquainted with the motives which prompted them. It is no easy task, not only to produce correct associations, but to remove improper ones, which may, through the medium of those nameless occurrences to which children are continually exposed, have found a place in the mind. But such is the task of every mother who superintends the education of her children.

Susan Huntington, February 7, 1813, Memoirs of the Late Mrs. Susan Huntington, of Boston, Mass., *p. 57.*

I do not like the punishment of whipping, unless when the child exhibits strong passion, or great obstinacy. It ought to be the last resort. Neither do I like those punishments which are chiefly directed to the selfish principles of our nature, as depriving a child of cake, sweetmeats, &c. I should rather aim to cherish feelings of conscious rectitude, and the pleasure of being beloved. I would have a child consider his parent's declaration that he is not good, his worst punishment. For instance, if your little boy has done very wrong, I would tell him he must not stay with mama, or must not take a walk, or see the company, or that he must eat his dinner alone; and all, because he is not good enough to be indulged these usual privileges. But there are some cases in which the use of the rod is indispensable.

Susan Huntington, March 8, 1814, Memoirs of the Late Mrs. Susan Huntington, of Boston, Mass., *p. 76.*

. . . [I]f children were demons, fit for hell, would God have given them that attractive sweetness, that mild beauty which renders them the most interesting objects on earth, and which compels us to shrink with horror from the thought of their everlasting ruin? Let those who support this sad doctrine contemplate the countenance of infancy, its unfurrowed brow, the smile with which it rewards the caresses of parental affection, and the tranquillity which sleep diffuses over its features. Who has not felt the turbulent passions of his nature calmed by the sight of childhood; and is this winning child, whom God has adorned with charms the most suited to engage the heart, abhorred by God, and fit only for the flames of hell?

William Ellery Channing, "Dissertation on the Sinfullness of Infants," August 1814, p. 248.

It appears to me that three simple rules, steadily observed from the very germ of active existence, would make children's tempers much more amiable than we generally see them. *First!* Never to give them any thing improper for them, because they strongly and passionately desire it; and even to withhold proper things, until they manifest a right spirit. *Second.* Always to gratify every reasonable desire, when a child is pleasant in its request; that your children may see that you love to make them happy. *Third.* Never to become impatient and fretful yourself, but proportion your displeasure exactly to the offence. If parents become angry, and speak loud and harsh, upon every slight failure of duty, they may bid a final adieu to domestic subordination, unless the grace of God interposes to snatch the little victims of severity from destruction. . . .

Dear children! I tremble for you, when I reflect how dangerous is the path in which you are to tread, and how difficult the task of directing you in safety.

Susan Huntington, March 27, 1815, Memoirs of the Late Mrs. Susan Huntington, of Boston, Mass., *pp. 100–01.*

I wanted very much to learn a trade, to use tools and be a builder, and many inquiries were unsuccessfully made for a situation of the kind in Philadelphia. At length, Nathan Lukens, of Horsham [Pennsylvania], my mother's first cousin, offered to take me as an apprentice. He was both a carpenter and joiner, and I was much pleased with the idea of living with him. . . .

I was pleased with the business. Nathan had a lot of about twenty acres, in which was corn, etc., and when it was needed we worked on that, where I could make a full hand now, and we would then work in the shop by candle-light.

The hardest part was when we would have to sit up till midnight or after, making and polishing a coffin for a funeral next day, I having to hold the light.

But the business of the trade suited me. The winter was employed in joiner-work in the shop, which was kept warm and comfortable. . . . Nathan made a fine large secretary of mahogany, with secret places for deeds, bonds, etc., very ingenious and very handsome. Any part that I could do, on that or his other works, he put me at.

Benjamin Hallowell, who began his apprenticeship in October 1815, when he was 14, Autobiography of Benjamin Hallowell, *pp. 27–29.*

When I was about twelve years old, I saw the first elephant exhibited in Maine. It was a great wonder, and the people thronged into Portland from many miles around, on foot, on horseback, and in every conceivable kind of conveyance, except what would now be regarded as convenient and comfortable for such use. The animal was exhibited in the stable-yard of a tavern. . . .

The elephant remained on exhibition for some time. If I mistake not, it was the first ever brought to the country, and was as much of a wonder to adult as to youthful spectators. On its way out of Maine the poor brute was shot in the town of Alfred by a farmer who was incensed because its owners had taken so much money from the farmers.

Neal Dow recalling events of 1816, The Reminiscences of Neal Dow, *pp. 46–47.*

Being the older son of a poor and hard-working farmer, struggling to pay off the debt he had incurred in buying his high-priced farm, and to support his increasing family, I was early made acquainted with labor. I well remember the cold summer (1816) when we rose on the eighth of June to find the earth covered with a good inch of newly fallen snow,—when there was frost every month, and corn did not fill till October. Plants grew very slowly that season, while burrowing insects fed and fattened on them. My task for a time was to precede my father as he hoed his corn, dig open the hills, and kill the wire-worms and grubs that were anticipating our dubious harvest. To "ride horse to plough" soon became my more usual vocation; the horse preceding and guiding the oxen, save when furrowing for or tilling the planted crops. Occasionally, the plough would strike a fast stone, and bring up the team all standing, pitching me over the horse's head, and landing me three to five feet in front. In the frosty autumn mornings, the working teams had to be "baited" on the rowen or aftermath of thick, sweet grass beside the luxuriant corn (maize); and I was called out at sunrise to watch and keep them out of the corn while the men ate their breakfast before yoking up and going afield. My bare feet imbibed a prejudice against that line of duty; but such premature rising induced sleepiness; so, if my feet had not ached, the oxen would have had a better chance for corn.

Horace Greeley describing the farm chores he performed in 1816, when he was five, Recollections of a Busy Life, *p. 38.*

As to the amusements of my boyhood, they were few and simple. My eldest brother wrote on one occasion that he had only half an hour during the day for play. Life was regarded as real and earnest and children were less indulged than they are now, and life was to them more sombre.

In summer we bathed in the bay when the tide was high; the game of ball was played, but not reduced to such a system as it now is, and foot ball was not practised. There was, too, the shooting of wild pigeons, which were very abundant in their season. . . .

In winter our amusements were ready to hand. After a heavy fall of snow, making drifts from ten to twenty feet in depth, we boys delighted to jump from the roof of house or shed, sinking almost out of sight in the soft, white yielding cloud, which had come from the skies and spread itself out beneath, apparently for our special fun. Burrowing in those grand drifts on the sides of ravines, we would cut out, like the inhabitants of Petra, from the solid rock, halls and corridors, which delighted us like the creations of Aladdin and his lamp. In these rooms we could have carpets of straw, and even build fires, with snow chimneys to conduct the smoke away, thus imitating the ice cabins of the Esquimaux. We built snow forts with supplies of snowball ammunition; some, as large as one's head, were bombshells to be hurled on our enemies. The fort would be attacked and defended with great valor, generally by imaginary British and American troops. They would last for weeks, almost as if made of clay. The sliding was perfect by day and by night; often we went down hills, perhaps a quarter of a mile long, with railroad speed, the cold air making every nerve tingle with pleasure.

Joseph Packard writing about childhood in Wiscasset, Maine, in the 1820s, Recollections of a Long Life, *pp. 24–25.*

Having loved and devoured newspapers—indeed, every form of periodical—from childhood, I early resolved to be a printer if I could. When but eleven years old, hearing that an apprentice was wanted in the newspaper office at Whitehall [New Hampshire], I accompanied my father to that office, and tried hard to find favor in the printer's eyes; but he promptly and properly rejected me as too young, and would not relent; so I went home downcast and sorrowful. No new opportunity was presented till the Spring of 1826, when an apprentice was advertised for by the publishers of The Northern Spectator, at East Poultney, Vt. . . . My father was about starting for the wide West in quest of a future home; so, not needing at the moment my services, he readily acceded to my wishes. I walked over to Poultney, saw the publishers, came to an understanding with them, and returned; and a few days afterward—April 18, 1826—my father took me down, and verbally agreed with them for my services. I was to remain till twenty years of age, be allowed my board only for six months, and thereafter $40 per annum in addition for my clothing. So I stopped, and went to work. . . .

Horace Greeley relating events occurring in 1822 and 1826, Recollections of a Busy Life, *pp. 61–62.*

About this time I had my first experience of death in our own family. I had been at funerals, and had some strange and vague thoughts about death, but nothing definite remained in my mind. But now the whole subject was to be brought before me in a new light. I was to see one very near and dear to me sicken and die. My sister . . . contracted a severe cold which settled on her lungs and brought on consumption. She failed

rapidly, and in the early summer went to her heavenly home. I was much with her. . . . The day she died she talked freely with all the family, and placing her hand on my head, with angelic sweetness gave me her dying charge.

Heman Dyer remembering his sister's death ca. 1825, Records of an Active Life, *pp. 14–15.*

From early life I had heard that somebody had, sometime and somewhere, said, that infants not a span long were in hell, and that hell was doubtless paved with their bones. And I must admit that for once, traditionary fiction retained a verbal accuracy of statement not surpassed by written documents. Until, however, I became acquainted with the state of things in Boston and its vicinity, I had supposed this rumor was a falsehood, which, upon the principle of moral affinities, had found its element, and had flowed down, in its own proper channel, among the irreligious and vicious, and was a part of the imagery which adorned the drunkard's song.

Lyman Beecher, January 1828, "Future Punishment of Infants Not a Doctrine of Calvinism," p. 43.

Removed with my parents to Pratt's Hollow [New York], a small village, where there was a woolen factory, and immediately commenced work at splicing rolls. We were at this time very poor, and did not know on one day what we should eat the next, otherwise I should not have been placed at such hard work. My parents, however, judiciously allowed me to spend half my wages (the whole was one dollar and twenty-five cents per week) as I thought proper; and in this way, with numerous incentives to economy, I first learned the use of money. My principal recollections during this summer are of noise and filth, bleeding hands and aching feet, and a very sad heart.

Emily C. Judson, who began work in April 1828, in A. C. Kendrick, The Life and Letters of Mrs. Emily C. Judson, *p. 16.*

Infant education commences with the very dawn of infant existence. At this early period, maternal care should be chiefly interested in securing the physical comfort and happiness of its sweet charge, by the invariable exercise of the kindest and tenderest offices of affection and love. The infant's helplessness and innocence appeal in the strongest and most persuasive language for safety and protection to the mother's heart. Her feelings will prompt her to attend to its numerous wants, and by the exercise of those charities, which the author of her nature, has wisely fitted her to confer, to anticipate, supply, and relieve them. It is by these repeated acts of affection, that her infant becomes conscious of the existence of the benevolent being, from whom its happiness is derived. The sweet fountain from which it draws nutrition, the soft bosom on which it reposes, from whose embrace it awakes to meet the eye of maternal fondness, and the caress of maternal love, awaken in its breast the feelings of conscious affection; and denote the commencement of its *moral* life. As an agent of the divine instructer, the mother will feel herself entrusted with a spirit, destined for immortality, on which she is urged, by every consideration, to shed that redeeming influence, which alone can preserve it from earthly pollution, and conduct it to the skies.

"Maternal Instruction," 1829, pp. 54–55.

I have a friend, whom all her acquaintance agree in calling 'a remarkably smart woman;' intelligent and

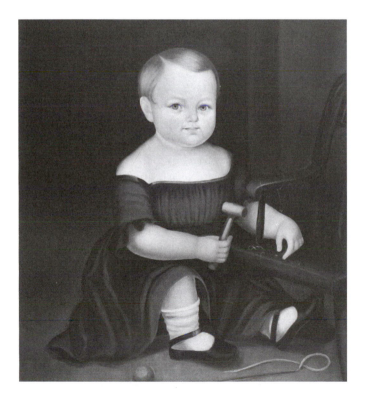

Posthumous portrait of Edward W. Gorham of Springfield, Massachusetts, 1844, by Joseph Whiting Stock. Contemplating this portrait helped young Edward's parents to grieve. *(New York State Historical Association, Cooperstown, New York)*

kind-hearted she certainly is; but . . . unfortunately she has no consistency of character, no habits of self-control.

She gives her children enough of good advice, and more than enough of good whipping; yet they are the most unpleasing, troublesome little varlets, I ever knew. The reason is plain; there is no uniformity in her government, and her children do not understand it. When she is at leisure, and feels happy, she will allow her little tribe to ask her a million questions, and will praise them for wishing to understand the reason of everything; but when she is hurried or petulant, their inquiries are repulsed with, 'How you tease me!' 'You must not ask so many questions!' 'If you do n't keep out of my way, I will whip you.' This system could produce but one result; the children watched their mother's moods, and governed themselves according to her temper, without any distinct idea of what was right and what was wrong. Her oldest boy is in the habit of saying to his brothers and sisters, 'You must not ask mother to-day, because she is cross. Wait till she has company, and then she won' n't mind what we do.' He had often heard his mother say, 'Company spoils children; I always let them do as they have a mind to when strangers are here, just to keep them quiet.' The use he made of the remark is but an ordinary proof of the shrewdness and observation of children. A more direct method to make children turbulent and troublesome before company could not have been devised; yet the woman who adopted this shortsighted policy was neither stupid nor ignorant. When I reasoned with her, her answer was, 'I have not domestics enough to take the care of my children off my hands, as rich people have; when I have company, I must keep them still in any way I can.' Had this injudicious mother scrutinized her own motives very severely, she would have found that indolence was the principal cause of her mismanagement.

"Hints with Regard to the Management of Very Young Children," January 1830, pp. 28–29.

It is important that children, even when babes, should never be spectators of anger, or any evil passion. They come to us from heaven, with their little souls full of innocence and peace; and, as far as possible, a mother's influence should not interfere with the influence of angels.

Lydia M. Child, 1831, The Mother's Book, *p. 3.*

Some distinguished writers on education have objected to dolls, as playthings which lead to a love of dress and finery. I do not consider them in this light. If a mother's influence does not foster a love of finery, I think there is very little danger of its being produced by dressing dolls. I like these toys for various reasons. They afford a quiet amusement; they exercise ingenuity in cutting garments, and neatness in sewing; they can be played with in a prodigious variety of ways; and so far as they exercise the affections, their influence is innocent and pleasant.

Lydia M. Child, 1831, The Mother's Book, *p. 57.*

Amusements and employments which lead to exercise in the open air have greatly the advantage of all others. In this respect, I would make no difference between the management of boys and girls. Gardening, sliding, skating, and snow-balling, are all as good for girls as for boys. Are not health and cheerful spirits as necessary for one as the other? . . .

When I say that skating and sliding are proper amusements for girls, I do not, of course, mean that they should mix in a public crowd. Such sports, when girls unite in them, should be confined to the inmates of the house, and away from all possibility of contact with the rude and vicious. Under these circumstances, a girl's manners cannot be injured by such wholesome recreations.

Lydia M. Child, 1831, The Mother's Book, *pp. 58–59.*

A knowledge of domestic duties is beyond all price to a woman. Every one ought to know how to sew, and knit, and mend, and cook, and superintend a household. In every situation in life, high or low, this sort of knowledge is a great advantage. There is no necessity that the gaining of such information should interfere with intellectual acquirement, or even with elegant accomplishments. A well regulated mind can find time to attend to all. When a girl is nine or ten years old, she should be accustomed to take some regular share in household duties, and to feel responsible for the manner in which it is done,—such as doing her own mending and making, washing the cups and putting them in place, cleaning the silver, dusting the parlor, &c. This should not be done occasionally, and neglected whenever she finds it convenient; she should consider it her department.

Lydia M. Child, 1831, The Mother's Book, *pp. 146–47.*

Our little daughter S. W. N. was born January 5th, 1832. . . . Before she was quite a year old, we began to correct her for crying. This has been a severe but wholesome discipline. It has taught her a command over her feelings, which we trust may be of great service to her in subsequent life. Now, when she is grieved or displeased, unless she is in bad humor from bodily suffering, she will suppress the disposition to cry, often with a very perceptible struggle and effort. But, even when she is unwell, and bursts into a loud cry, we generally correct her, until she suppresses it. . . . In this discipline, we sometimes used the rod; but more frequently shut her in a room alone, til she became quiet.

"Extract from a Mother's Journal," Mother's Magazine, *1834, in* History of Childhood Quarterly, *Winter 1976, p. 320.*

All that a parent can do for his child during the first few months of its life, is, to promote its health and consult its enjoyments within the limited circle to which its faculties are confined. With the immediate care of it, of course the father will have little to do; but it will be both proper and interesting for him to know the general rules for the treatment of an infant. Warm clothing should envelope it, from the soles of the feet to the neck, by night and day, graduated according to the surrounding atmosphere, but no bandage should strongly compress its tender form. Daily washing is necessary to keep the skin in a healthy state; its delicate organs should not be pained by strong light, loud or jarring sounds.

It should be fed and put to sleep when nature requires it, but as early as possible should be habituated to regular periods for both. It will be for the comfort both of parents and child if it be put to sleep from the first without rocking or carrying. Habit will reconcile children to many things of this kind. Some judicious persons believe that the use of a cradle is dangerous to the brain; and this may be easily believed, while we see how violently some nurses rock their children when they wish to force them into a slumber. It is certainly better to dispense with it where it can be done with ease. Violent jumping and throwing up of children is to be avoided.

Theodore Dwight, Jr., 1834, The Father's Book, *pp. 27–28.*

Till the United States cease to be republican, and their vast area is fully peopled, the children there will continue as free and easy and as important as they are. For my own part, I delight in the American children. There are instances, as there are everywhere, of spoiled, pert, and selfish children. Parents' hearts are pierced there, as elsewhere. But the independence and fearlessness of children were a perpetual charm in my eyes. To go no deeper, it is a constant amusement to see how the speculations of young minds issue, when they take their own way of thinking, and naturally say all they think. Some admirable specimens of active little minds were laid open to me at a juvenile ball at Baltimore. I could not have got at so much in a year in England. If I had at home gone in among eighty or a hundred little people, between the ages of eight and sixteen, I should have extracted little more than "Yes, ma'am," and "No, ma'am." At Baltimore, a dozen boys and girls at a time crowded round me, questioning, discussing, speculating, revealing in a way which enchanted me. In private houses, the comments slipped in at table by the children were often the most memorable, and generally the most amusing part of the conversation.

Harriet Martineau, an English traveler in the United States from 1834 through 1836, Society in America, *pp. 310–11.*

One [event] that occurred when I was three years old made a lasting impression. My parents took me to see the body of a young married woman who had been my mother's "help" and had evidently liked me well, for she had called me "Haddie's baby." On a board supported on two chairs her body was laid out covered with a white sheet, and two large copper pennies wrapped in paper lay upon her eyes. I don't remember that I was frightened, but there was mystery.

William Watts Folwell, who was born in Romulus, New York, and was three years old in 1836, The Autobiography and Letters of a Pioneer of Culture, *p. 3.*

We younger girls entered upon the usual routine of grammar-school study at Lowell [Massachusetts], and were nearly prepared for the high school, when it was found necessary that one or more of us should take up our share of the domestic burdens, which my mother had found too heavy to bear alone. I, being larger for my years, and apparently stronger than my sisters nearest me in age, was taken from school and began to work in the mill in my twelfth year. . . .

That children should be set to toil for their daily bread is always a pity; but in the case of my little workmates and myself there were imperative reasons, and we were not too young to understand them. And the

regret with which those who loved us best consented to such an arrangement only made us more anxious to show that we really were capable of doing something for them and for ourselves.

Lucy Larcom, who started to work in a textile mill in 1836, "Among the Lowell Mill-Girls," pp. 599–601.

I began to reflect upon life rather seriously for a girl of twelve or thirteen. What was I here for? What could I make of myself? Must I submit to be carried along with the current, and do just what everybody else did? . . .

In the older times it was seldom said to little girls, as it always has been said to boys, that they ought to have some definite plan, while they were children, what to be and do when they were grown up. There was usually but one path open before them, to become good wives and housekeepers. And the ambition of most girls was to follow their mothers' footsteps in this direction; a natural and laudable ambition. But girls, as well as boys, must often have been conscious of their own peculiar capabilities,—must have desired to cultivate and make use of their individual powers. When I was growing up, they had already begun to be encouraged to do so. We were often told that it was our duty to develop any talent we might possess, or at least to learn how to do some one thing which the world needed, or which would make it a pleasanter world.

Lucy Larcom recapturing her thoughts in 1837, A New England Girlhood, *pp. 156–57.*

For children, berrying was play, pure pastime; it brought no money to their pockets. For the first hour it was infinitely exciting; by the next, we wanted something else, and it was difficult to keep us in order. . . .

To hide and play games was one means of escape from the fatigue of the slow filling berry pails. Then such a quiet fell over the pasture that our elders knew some mischief was afoot. We were promptly discovered, scolded and warned that we must fill our pails before we could play.

As milking time approached we gathered up stray hats, aprons and handkerchiefs and prepared to go home. We painted each others' cheeks with the red blood of huckleberries and crowned our heads with leaves of the birch and oak, stalks of indigo weed or broad fern fronds that hung down over the face like green veils. Thus freaked and marked, walking in single file, our mothers and elder sisters behind us, shouting, leaping and laughing, we presented something as near a

Bacchic procession as could be found in a community enshrouded in the black cloak of John Calvin.

John Albee recalling berry picking in Bellingham, Massachusetts, ca. 1840, Confessions of Boyhood, *pp. 135–37.*

[My mother] always depended on me to catch the geese for picking, to run down fowls when needed for the kitchen, and to run to the neighbors for fire if ours had gone out. I commonly brought it on a big chip covered with a few smaller ones. . . . My services were much in request for errands, especially as I grew older. At times I was sent up to Squire Miller's for a dose of "pink 'n seeny [pinkroot and senna]," when a vermifuge [cure for intestinal worms] was in demand.

We were three miles from the post office, and I was the mail carrier. At least once a week I was mounted on a colt with a sheepskin strapped on his back and a single riding bridle. Trotting was a hard gait for me, and that colt was generally put to the gallop.

In the summer time I made frequent excursions, not on galloping colts but on the sturdy farm horses, to the blacksmith shop to have them shod or have a ploughshare sharpened.

William Watts Folwell remembering his childhood on a New York farm in the 1840s, The Autobiography and Letters of a Pioneer of Culture, *pp. 6–7.*

As my mother possessed no land nor any means to send me to academy and college, it was early decided to apprentice me to a trade with some good master. . . .

Accordingly in my eighth year I was turned over to an uncle, my father's only brother, who lived in the next town. He was a boot maker with four sons of his own. At once I found myself cut off from all the objects and persons I had ever known, thrown into a strange world, my own lost as completely as if I had gone to another. I found myself introduced to a small room up a flight of stairs at the end of the shed of my uncle's house. The room was full of windows, all of which looked in the direction of my lost home; it had a number of low shoemaker's benches ranged along three of its sides. Here my uncle and two of his sons made boots. I was directed to one of the benches and began by being taught how to use a waxed end and stitch the counters of bootlegs. Never in my life before had I been pinned to one spot for any length of time save on a school bench; never before set at any work that

was not or that could not be made half play. A deadly homesickness at once seized upon me, of which I could not be cured by all the kindness and encouragement of my uncle and aunt. . . . But no treatment harsh or kind could cure a homesick child, and one day my uncle said he was going to see my mother, and that I was to go with him. Oh, how my spirits recovered themselves! I never thought of the return; only to go, to be once more in my own home, with my own river, fields and companions, filled me with ecstasy. I went and did not return.

John Albee, who was eight in 1841, Confessions of Boyhood, *pp. 148–53.*

Although not the most useful lad on a farm, I liked certain kinds of farm work very well. Ploughing was my favorite employment. I drove the team with the lines passed over my back and under one arm, and at fifteen turned a furrow, my father said, as well as any man. In those lonely but pleasant hours in the field, with no companions but the kind, dumb, steady-going horses, I made a great many verses, which I retained in my memory and wrote down after the day's work was done.

John Townsend Trowbridge, who was 15 in 1842, My Own Story with Recollections of Noted Persons, *p. 54.*

Swimming, hunting, fishing, foraging at every season, with the skating which the waters of the rivers and canals afforded, were my joy; I took my part in the races and the games, in football and in baseball, then in its feline infancy of Three Corner Cat, and though there was a family rule against fighting, I fought like the rest of the boys and took my defeats as heroically as I knew how; they were mostly defeats.

William Dean Howells writing about his childhood in Ohio in the 1840s, Years of My Youth, *p. 19.*

My world was full of boys, but it was also much haunted by ghosts or the fear of them. Death came early into it, the visible image in a negro babe, with the large red copper cents on its eyelids, which older boys brought me to see, then in the funeral of the dearly loved mate whom we school-fellows followed to his grave.

William Dean Howells writing about his childhood in Ohio in the 1840s, Years of My Youth, *p. 19.*

The next effort to make a craftsman of me was in my tenth year. I was put under the hands of a millwright. . . .

The terms of my apprenticeship included a new suit of clothes each year, and that I should be sent to school in the summer. The clothes were never forthcoming and my mother had to furnish them. My master gave me my boots for winter and shoes for summer, but I went barefooted seven months of the year. This was no hardship. How I hated to wear shoes on the only day when it was compulsory, Sunday. It cost me tears to learn to tie a double bow knot with my shoestring, as my master insisted upon my doing, and this was the only thing during my apprenticeship that he took pains to teach me—to tie a shoestring. He was a silent, self-absorbed man with a stern manner, a square set jaw, wide mouth and ponderous ears. He was very fond of his two little girls, three and four years old; but he never had a kind word for me. However, he was not peculiar in this respect. Boys were not cosseted in those days, but made to feel the rod and keep their place.

John Albee, who was 10 years old in 1843, Confessions of Boyhood, *pp. 156–59.*

. . . I fished to my heart's content. There was an old mongrel dog at my heels wherever I went, and together we hunted woodchucks and squirrels without a gun. . . . In the autumn I set snares for partridges which I sold to the Boston stage drivers for ninepence apiece. Well do I remember the high hope with which I entered the silent wood in early morning to examine my snares, the exhilaration when I found a poor partridge in the noose, limp and dead, with a white film drawn over her eyes. . . . The sale of partridges furnished me with considerable spending money; for what I spent it, I know not.

John Albee describing how he hunted as a boy, ca. 1843, Confessions of Boyhood, *pp. 159–60.*

There was a small group of boys, seven or eight years old, who were inclined to follow my lead. We had absorbed Indian stories, and at first these gave the staging for our pastimes, but when we came into possession of "The Pirates Own Book" the Indian performances seemed tame, and we were launched on a downward career. We found caves where we met and consumed the booty, which at first consisted of the product of raids on the home pantries; we even learned to make the necessary keys. Before long our feasts included fruit and green corn from the fields of unrelated owners. Then we appropriated cider and wine. In time we bor-

rowed boats, and later actually took permanent possession of one which we succeeded in hiding. This not only widened our range of operations, but also gave them the final stamp of piracy. We had the conventional quarrels in division of spoils, and I still bear the scar of a stab in my leg.

Raphael Pumpelly recalling games in Owego, New York, ca. 1845, My Reminiscences, *p. 17.*

. . . [A]t ten years and onward till journalism became my university, the printing-office was mainly my school. Of course, like every sort of work with a boy, the work became irksome to me, and I would gladly have escaped from it to every sort of play, but it never ceased to have the charm it first had. Every part of the trade became familiar to me, and if I had not been so little I could at once have worked not only at case, but at press, as my brother did.

William Dean Howells, who was 10 years old in 1847, Years of My Youth, *p. 18.*

If there is any truth in the adage so often quoted in recent years that "We learn to do by doing," surely the farm is the place where the boy, more than anywhere else, learns to do many things—more different things than he can learn anywhere else. Beginning very early, when he is told to "mind the baby," as the years pass by he learns to leave his play and do numberless chores about the house and on the farm. He brings in wood from the wood-pile for the kitchen stove, he saws and splits it, prepares kindling, feeds the pigs, plants corn and potatoes, sows grain, weeds the garden, picks apples, makes cider, drives the cows to pasture in the morning and brings them up at night, leads the horse to water, harnesses the horse, drives to the gristmill and gets the corn and rye ground. . . . He milks the cows, drives oxen, mows grass, spreads hay, rakes hay, lays the load, and mows it away in the barn, drives the team to plow, or rides the horse to plow between the rows of corn, then learns to hold the plow. . . .

If he has a loving and lovable mother, he will sometimes help her in the kitchen by wiping the dishes. Occasionally he will be up early in the cold winter mornings and build the kitchen fire before either father or mother appears.

William A. Mowry describing a boy's duties on a family farm, ca. 1848, Recollections of a New England Educator, *pp. 12–13.*

2

Schooling the Children
1777–1867

As the 18th century drew to a close, U.S. leaders faced tremendous challenges. One was to mold a diverse population of former colonists, scattered over a large expanse, into men, women, and children who viewed themselves as Americans—a single people with a common heritage.

The early United States was a nation of Europeans, Africans, and Native Americans. European Americans—the dominant ethnic and cultural group and therefore the population that most interested U.S. leadership—were largely of English descent. Still, one-fourth of the people in Pennsylvania were of German heritage and spoke German as their primary language. French Huguenots and the Dutch had helped to settle New York; and Louisiana, with a large population of French-speaking Roman Catholics, would be granted statehood in 1812.

Many thinkers of the period advocated centralized schooling as a potentially unifying force, but in doing so they endorsed measures that flew in the face of traditional Puritan thinking. The Puritans had taught that education belonged in the home and that parents were a child's proper teachers. In the Puritan community, orphans or children whose parents were unable to teach them learned under the guidance of a minister or attended a private school operated by a neighborhood woman. Thus, any schools that existed were locally run. There were no minimum qualifications for teaching, nor was there a standard curriculum. No laws required children to be in attendance.

By the late 18th century, how and what children were to be taught became questions for debate. Thomas Jefferson contended that only the educated could enjoy the full rights of citizenship and protect themselves from tyranny. In 1779, 40 years before founding the University of Virginia, he presented a plan for a statewide school system to the Virginia Assembly. He proposed that all free children attend public school for three years at the state's expense, with optional continued study to be privately financed. The elementary-school curriculum would include reading and writing as well as the history of the ancient world, England, and the United States. The course of study in secondary schools would prepare students for college. It was to cover Latin, Greek, English grammar, geography, and higher mathematics. Because Jefferson favored total separation of church and state, his plan—which the Virginia Assembly rejected—omitted religious instruction.

Philadelphia doctor Benjamin Rush put forth a plan for a public-school system for Pennsylvania in 1786. Because of the state's large population of Germans eager to pass along their cultural heritage, Rush called in his plan for reading and writing to be taught in both English and German. In contrast to Jefferson, he argued for inclusion of religion in the curriculum and use of the Bible as a textbook. Rush's plan, like that of Jefferson, amounted to much rhetoric and no results.

Noah Webster wrote about education in the 1780s and was far more influential. Webster was a teacher in Goshen, New York, when he perceived that language could be a medium for uniting the American people. He set out to mold the English taught in schools into a unique "Federal English" shaped by the usage, grammar, and idioms of ordinary Americans. Webster had observed, for example, that Americans employed the word "smart" when the British would use "clever," and that Americans often said "I reckon" instead of "I think." He altered the spelling of some words to reflect American pronunciation. Thus, "lustre" became "luster," and "humour" became "humor." He hoped that standardizing the language might also help to eliminate regional dialects.

Between 1783 and 1785, Webster published *A Grammatical Institute of the English Language,* which comprised the *American Spelling Book,* known to generations of American schoolchildren as the "Blue-Backed Speller"; a grammar text; and a reader. At first Webster opposed using the Bible in school, but he gradually relaxed his position on religion in the classroom, and in 1798, he appended a moral catechism onto his reader. Webster's opus would remain in print for a century and sell millions of copies. Many of the Americanisms that he incorporated into his text became standardized, while others were discarded. For instance, Americans have never accepted the grammatical construction "you was," which Webster insisted was correct.

Although learned people from Virginia to New York perceived that addressing the need for public schools would benefit the nation, U.S. leaders declined to make schools a national concern. Nowhere does the Constitution discuss education; instead, the power to establish and regulate schools was implicitly handed over to the states when the Tenth Amendment was ratified on December 15, 1791, as part of the Bill of Rights.

In 1800, eight of the 16 states mentioned education in their constitutions. Pennsylvania, for example, required a school in every county; Vermont and Massachusetts called for one in every town. The Massachusetts legislature also enacted two important laws that gave the state school system the structure it would retain through the 1880s. The first law, passed in 1789, obligated each town of 50 households to support a school for six months of every year and to employ a schoolmaster to instruct the young in reading, writing, and arithmetic as well as "decent behavior." A town of 100 households was compelled to support its school for the entire year, while a town where 200 families lived had the added burden of hiring a grammar-school instructor proficient in English, Latin, and Greek. (Although the term *grammar school* has come to mean "elementary school," it originally referred to a higher-level institution where Latin and Greek were taught.) All teachers had to be U.S. citizens and had to provide written certification of their qualifications and morals from a member of the clergy or a selectman (a town official). In addition, grammar-school teachers had to be college-educated.

The second law, passed in 1827, divided communities into school districts, decreed that citizens would support their local schools through taxes, and eliminated religion from the curriculum and textbooks. Ministers were barred from supervising public schools, but they were permitted to encourage school attendance.

New York, like Massachusetts, was a leader in public education. When Governor George Clinton took office in 1777, churches, charities, and private citizens operated all of New York's schools. In 1786 Clinton prodded the New York Legislature into establishing a school system supported by $50,000 annually and requiring the counties to match the state's contribution. By 1822, children in every New York county—more than 350,000 of the state's 371,000 school-age children—were attending public school. New York was the first state to centralize control of its schools by creating the position of superintendent. This individual worked to improve the common, or public, schools; supervised the spending of school funds; and reported to the legislature on educational issues.

SCHOOLS VARIED IN QUALITY

School conditions and the quality of instruction differed from one community to another, even in forward-looking states such as New York and Massachusetts. At one extreme, Boston's schools were a model of efficiency. In 1789, the city established six coeducational schools for children age seven and older. Three were writing schools, offering instruction in writing and arithmetic, and three were reading schools, where the focus was on language arts: reading, spelling, English grammar, and composition. Boston also had a grammar school.

In other communities, all children within a given radius attended a single school, regardless of age. There was no grading; as many as 80 pupils studied together under one instructor, who sat behind a crudely built desk on a raised platform. Students wrote their exercises in ink, because pencils, a new invention, were too expensive for everyday use. Metal pen points became popular around 1830; before that time, young scholars wrote with quill pens. They lined sheets of paper for their lessons with a ruler and a piece of lead. Where paper was scarce, children wrote their lessons in chalk on slates that were wiped clean at the end of the day.

After 1836, McGuffey readers became an important presence in American schools. William McGuffey was on the faculty of Miami University in Oxford, Ohio, when he published the first two volumes in a series of six elementary-school readers. The McGuffey readers, which progressed in difficulty from the alphabet and simple texts to selections from Jefferson, Shakespeare, and the Bible, stressed morality and practical knowledge. They were employed in American classrooms through the 1920s and introduced millions of immigrant children to standard English. Many historians of education consider them to be the most influential schoolbooks in U.S. history.

Economy-minded school districts, hoping to keep taxes low, balked at the expense of providing roomy, well-constructed school buildings. One-room, wood-frame schoolhouses were the rule. In many districts, pupils who ranged from small children to young men sat on backless benches that kept the youngest ones' feet dangling in the air. Desks, if any were provided, were of a single size—too large for some students and too small for others. A stove in the center of the room heated the typical 19th-century schoolhouse in winter and did so unevenly at best. The children sitting closest to the stove grew drowsy from the warmth, while those near outer walls struggled against the cold as icy air blew in through cracks, crevices, and broken windows.

Despite the draftiness, the chief complaint against 19th-century schools was poor ventilation. Schools were renowned for foul odors and fetid air. In 1847, Michigan's school superintendent became ill simply from breathing while visiting a school. In 1858, the atmosphere in a Groveland, Massachusetts, school gave a school-committee member a severe headache. People wondered how schoolmasters and students tolerated the situation and decided that they had grown accustomed to the stench.

Public schools were also famously deficient in sanitary facilities. In 1857, 244 of the 276 public schools in Erie, Pennsylvania, lacked outhouses. In 1860, 4,600 schools in Illinois were similarly wanting. Sometimes, the front step or the side of the school building served as a makeshift privy. Connecticut's school superintendent speculated in 1848 that the lack of privacy for the performance of bodily functions was the reason many parents kept their daughters home from school.

It was not just girls who stayed away, though. Attendance by all students tended to be irregular. Farm families sent their children to school only when it was convenient. Rural mothers found it helpful to have their young children in school in summer in order to be relieved of caring for them throughout this busy time of year. Because sons were needed to work in the fields during the growing season, many boys attended school only in winter. Additionally, some farmers' sons age 12 to 14 sought winter employment and returned to school after an absence of several years, when they were nearly full-grown.

Apprentices frequently were entitled to a month or two of schooling each year according to their contracts. Work so exhausted factory children, however, that the majority had no time or energy left for school. Fears that generations of child laborers growing up illiterate would threaten U.S. democracy led to the first compulsory education laws. In 1813, Connecticut passed a law requiring manufacturers to provide children in their employ with instruction in reading, writing, and arithmetic. This law had little impact, though, because it was not enforced. An 1836 Massachusetts law prohibited the employment of any child under 15 who had not attended school for three months in the previous year. Other states enacted legislation requiring working children to attend school that was patterned on the Massachusetts law.

THE ROD AND FERULE

The presence of so many boys and young men made winter schools noisy, chaotic places. In the early 19th century, schoolmasters kept order with rods. The frequent and severe beatings that they administered would be called abusive today, but at the time teachers and school committees insisted that strict discipline was necessary to maintain order in the classroom. Parents supported the practice, too, because they expected the schools to turn out obedient, respectful children. When Bronson Alcott, father of Louisa May Alcott, taught school in Connecticut in 1823 and refused to beat his pupils, the community called for his dismissal.

A 19th-century schoolteacher takes disciplinary action. *(Courtesy The Winterthur Library: Printed Book and Periodical Collection)*

By the 1830s, reformers were working at the local and state levels to improve the quality of public schools. These individuals promoted education as a way to broaden young minds, develop potential, and build character. The most notable of the reformers was Horace Mann, secretary of the Massachusetts Board of Education between 1837 and 1848, whose work had an impact throughout the United States. Mann elevated the teaching profession by founding the *Common School Journal,* a publication for educators, and calling for teacher training. He spoke out against harsh pedagogical methods and religious influence in the classroom, and in his many lectures to the public, he called on every young American to achieve his or her own victory for humanity.

As the Puritans' view of human beings as corrupt yielded to the Enlightenment's belief in human potential, educators and parents thought anew about whether sparing the rod spoiled the child. School committees began to advise teachers to use moral arguments to encourage good behavior, even though they usually backed their teachers when parents complained about beatings in school. The states showed little interest, however, in regulating this issue. In 1867 New Jersey became the first state to outlaw corporal punishment in its schools, but it would remain the only state with such a law for more than a century, until Massachusetts passed a similar one in 1972.

The growing presence of women in the classroom also reduced the incidence of whippings. Women had traditionally taught in summer, when young children were in the majority in classrooms, and men had taken over for the rest of the year. Finding suitable male teachers willing to accept the salaries that most schools offered was a chronic problem, though. Despite laws like the one in Massachusetts that set standards for teachers, schoolmasters as a group were poorly educated. Some gave their employers reason to question their morals, and others were dependent on alcohol. By 1840, the number of women teachers was increasing as school committees learned that competent women were willing to teach for low salaries. Although women relied less on the rod and ferule to maintain order than men did, female teachers were occasionally known to dole out physical punishment.

THE GROWTH OF PRIVATE SCHOOLS

Privately supported schools sprang up in the Northeast at the same time that public school systems were being developed; reformers with social or religious concerns established most of them. In the early 19th century, infant schools served children of the poor between the ages of 18 months and 6 years. These schools stressed good manners, which were thought to be a manifestation of discipline and morals, and attempted to impose order on the lives of their pupils, many of whose parents worked in factories. The infant-school movement began in Scotland in 1816; the first in the United States opened in Hartford, Connecticut, in 1827. Infant schools were soon operating in cities and towns throughout the Northeast, and for a while they enjoyed public support. A belief in early instruction, especially in reading, was a legacy from the Puritans, who thought that young children needed to know how to read the Bible in order to seek salvation.

After 1830, as American society became more secularized, educational authorities argued against schooling children under five years of age. Doctors and other experts claimed that too much intellectual activity at a tender age might overstimulate the brain, leading to epilepsy, imbecility, or insanity. Benefactors withheld funding from infant schools, the public withdrew its acceptance, and the movement died out.

Protestant groups responded to the needs of older children by opening Sunday schools and charity schools in churches, public schools, or rented spaces. Volunteer teachers staffed the nondenominational Sunday schools and offered lessons in reading, writing, and arithmetic along with strong doses of religion, morals, and manners. In Boston the Society for the Poor opened its first Sunday school on May 11, 1817, and was operating five schools by the summer of 1818. Classes were held all day, with a break at noon, and instruction emphasized Bible readings, prayer, and hymns. Most church-run charity schools restricted enrollment to the poor, although some, such as those of the Quakers in Pennsylvania, welcomed all children.

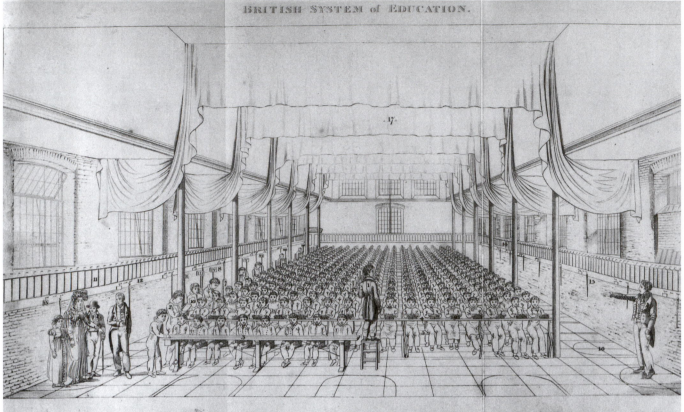

BRITISH SYSTEM of EDUCATION.

INTERIOR of the CENTRAL SCHOOL of the BRITISH & FOREIGN SCHOOL SOCIETY, BOROUGH ROAD.

The interior of a British monitorial school, 1837. The "General Monitor of Order" stands front and center, while subordinate monitors stand to the left of each row. All take direction from the master, right. *(Department of Special Collections, Syracuse University Library)*

Private schools that accepted public funds formed the foundation of New York City's school system. In 1806, the New York Free School Society opened its first institution for poor children. Thomas Eddy, a wealthy Quaker affiliated with this organization, perceived that educating the sons and daughters of all of the city's poor would require a great deal of money. Searching for a way to cut costs, he investigated a method of education that had been developed in England.

The Lancasterian system, named for its inventor, Joseph Lancaster, employed older students as monitors. The monitors took over much of the work of operating the school, allowing one teacher to manage as many as 1,000 pupils. While the teacher sat at his desk, monitors marched between the rows of students to give instructions and keep order. There were monitors to take attendance, monitors to supervise recess, and monitors to oversee the work of other monitors.

Lancasterian schools thrived on order. People who attended them as children recalled strict regimentation, with all students hanging up their coats in unison. Children were required to position their hands in a specific way while reading (the left hand cradling the spine of the book and the right index finger extended and ready to turn the page). They were also taught to fold their hands when listening, in order to demonstrate that they were paying attention. Interest in Lancasterian education spread beyond New York to other cities and towns. In 1818, Joseph Lancaster traveled to Philadelphia at the request of that city's board of governors to organize a model school there.

SEPARATE SCHOOLS FOR AFRICAN AMERICANS

The proliferation of public and private schools that occurred in the first half of the 19th century was largely confined to the North. School development lagged south of the Mason-Dixon Line and the Ohio River, because the dominant planter class did not want to educate African Americans. Slaves were denied education by law, but 100,000 free African Americans lived in the South in 1810, constituting 5 percent of the free population. It was true that white missionaries were operating schools for black children and that some free blacks had opened schools of their own. But there were too few of these institutions to educate all of the South's free African-American children. In the agrarian, predominantly rural setting of the South, most planters saw no need to educate poor white children either. Parents who could afford to do so hired tutors for their own children or sent them away to boarding schools.

In 1803, the city council of Washington, D.C., established a board of education to provide schooling to the children of poor white residents. The school system was to be funded by taxes on slaves, dogs, and a variety of licenses, including licenses to operate a carriage or a tavern; to sell wines and liquor; to offer theatrical performances; and to peddle items from door to door.

Northern cities and towns provided schools for African-American children, but they almost always educated them apart from white students. African-American religious leaders in Boston opened a Sunday school for black children in 1817. Boston's first primary school for African Americans opened on August 7, 1822. Its first pupils numbered 47, but enrollment expanded so quickly that the School Committee soon established two more schools for African Americans. Many of the students were from poor families, and it was not unusual for boys and girls as old as 12 to enter school illiterate.

By 1831, a militant antislavery movement had grown up in the North. As southern states began outlawing schooling for free African Americans, these activists—the abolitionists—pressured northern communities to integrate their schools. Theirs was a tough battle: Some New Englanders were as zealous as southern plantation farmers in their opposition to educating African Americans.

In 1832, Prudence Crandall, a Connecticut Quaker, was forced to close her girls' boarding school in the town of Canterbury because her neighbors so vehemently protested the admission of an African-American student. When Crandall next opened a school exclusively for African Americans, the people of Canterbury did everything possible to impede her efforts. Crandall was arrested for violating a hastily passed law against educating African Americans from outside the state and briefly incarcerated. She endured insults, the school was vandalized, and its windows were broken. In 1834, she admitted defeat and gave up the school. Crandall moved with her husband to Illinois.

By the mid-1840s, several Massachusetts towns had desegregated their public schools, but Boston's remained strictly segregated. In 1846, as Frederick Douglass and other African-American leaders defended the right of black children to attend neighborhood schools with whites, 86 African Americans petitioned the city's primary-school committee to end racial separation. They called the practice demeaning and said that it violated their children's rights. The committee rejected the petition, stating, in short, that because state law did not mandate integration, they were not required to make any changes.

A mob attacks Prudence Crandall's school for African-American girls in this illustration from the *Anti-Slavery Almanac* of 1839. *(Library of Congress)*

In 1849, an African American, Benjamin Roberts of Boston, took the school committee to court for denying his daughter Sarah permission to attend the school nearest her home. The case reached the Massachusetts Supreme Court, where Roberts was represented by a young attorney, Charles Sumner, who would later distinguish himself as an advocate of equal rights. Sumner argued that it was impossible for segregated schools to offer the same curriculum to all children, and that a school restricted to one social group—to one race, religion, or economic class—must differ significantly from a school that was open to all children regardless of social distinctions. Segregation, Sumner said, made a mockery of the concept of equal rights. More than 100 years later, Thurgood Marshall would make similar statements in the United States Supreme Court while arguing the case *Brown v. Board of Education.*

Chief Justice Lemuel Shaw ruled in Benjamin Roberts's case that the principle of equal rights guaranteed by the state constitution permitted the assignment of black and white children to separate schools, and Sarah Roberts continued to attend an all-black school. Just six years later, the Massachusetts legislature outlawed segregation by race, effectively reversing Shaw's decision. The other northern states would pursue a similar course of school desegregation after the Civil War.

U.S. SCHOOLS: A WORK IN PROGRESS

When the United States became a nation, there was general, if informal, agreement on the need for schools. Proceeding largely through trial and error, state legislatures, city councils, and religious and charitable organizations established public and private school systems, gradually setting standards for teachers and outlining curriculums. By 1860, the district school system was firmly in place in many northern communities. The states were beginning to protect the right of children to attend school by passing mandatory education laws, although the earliest such laws had little impact. African Americans and other concerned men and women had taken the first steps toward integrating America's schools and securing equal educational opportunity for all.

CHRONICLE OF EVENTS

1777

George Clinton becomes governor of New York; all schools in New York are privately run.

1779

Thomas Jefferson proposes a statewide school system to the Virginia Assembly; the assembly rejects Jefferson's plan.

1783–85

Noah Webster publishes *A Grammatical Institute of the English Language,* a series of textbooks attempting to standardize American spelling, grammar, and usage.

1786

Benjamin Rush unveils his plan for a public school system for Pennsylvania.

The New York legislature allots $50,000 per year for public schools.

1789

A Massachusetts law requires towns of 50 households to employ a teacher and support a school for six months per year; towns of 100 households are required to support a school for the entire year; towns of 200 households must also employ a grammar-school teacher.

Boston establishes six coeducational elementary schools and a grammar school.

1791

December 15: The Tenth Amendment to the Constitution, ratified on this date as part of the Bill of Rights, states that all powers not delegated to the United States belong to the states or to the people. These powers include the right to establish schools.

1798

Noah Webster adds a moral catechism to his reader.

1800

Eight of the 16 states mention education in their constitutions.

1803

The Washington, D.C., City Council creates a board of education to provide schools for poor white children.

1806

The New York Free School Society opens its first school for poor children in New York City.

1810

Up to 100,000 free African Americans are living in the South.

1813

Connecticut passes the nation's first compulsory education law, requiring manufacturers to provide child laborers in their employ with instruction in reading, writing, and arithmetic.

1817

May 11: The Society for the Poor opens its first Sunday school in Boston.

Inspired by the society's activities, Boston's African-American ministers open a Sunday school for black children.

1818

The Philadelphia Board of Governors invites Joseph Lancaster to establish a model school in that city.

The Society for the Poor is operating five Sunday schools in Boston.

1822

More than 350,000 of the 371,000 children of school age in New York are enrolled in school.

August 7: Boston's first primary school for African Americans opens.

1823

A Connecticut community calls for the dismissal of its schoolmaster, Bronson Alcott, who refuses to beat his pupils.

1827

The Massachusetts Legislature creates a system of school districts, requires citizens to support their local schools, and eliminates religion from the public-school curriculum.

The first infant school in the United States opens in Hartford, Connecticut.

1832

Community protests against admission of an African American force Prudence Crandall to close her girls' school in Canterbury, Connecticut.

1833
Prudence Crandall opens a school for African-American girls and is arrested and taunted.

1834
Prudence Crandall moves from Connecticut to Illinois.

1836
The first McGuffey readers are published.
A Massachusetts law prohibits the employment of any child who has not attended school for three months during the previous year.

1837–1848
Horace Mann serves as secretary of the Massachusetts Board of Education; he brings professionalism to teaching and encourages educational reform both within Massachusetts and nationally.

1840
The number of women teachers is increasing.

1840s
Some Massachusetts towns desegregate their schools.

1846
Eighty-six African Americans petition the primary-school committee to end school segregation in Boston.

1847
The malodorous air in a schoolroom sickens Michigan's school superintendent.

1848
The Connecticut school superintendent speculates that a lack of proper toilet facilities prevents many girls from attending school.

1849
African American Benjamin Roberts takes the Boston primary-school committee to court for denying his daughter permission to attend the school closest to her home; the Massachusetts Supreme Court rules that school segregation does not violate the principle of equal rights as guaranteed by the state constitution.

1855
The Massachusetts legislature outlaws segregation by race.

1857
Thirty-two of the 276 public schools in Erie, Pennsylvania, have outhouses.

1858
A Massachusetts school-committee member develops a headache from the atmosphere in a school.

1860
In Illinois 4,600 schools lack outhouses.

1867
New Jersey becomes the first state to outlaw corporal punishment in its schools.

EYEWITNESS TESTIMONY

My father had learned me my letters some time before we had a school, and I could spell ba, and soon after baker. I remember his first teaching me my letters. There was A, with two feet, i with a dot, round o, Q with a tail, crooked S, T with a hat, &c. &c. After six or seven families had settled within striking distance, it was decided that a school house must be built, and a summer school started for the children. The house must be near water, and must be built where it would best accommodate its patrons; accordingly a place was selected, the neighbours made a bee, came together, cut away the underbrush, and the trees, that were near enough to endanger the house. They cut logs, drew them to the place, and put up a log house, small but low, and the roof nearly flat for several years; and covered with bark. One side was so much elevated by an additional log, that the water would run off, and subsequently rafters were added, making an ordinary roof, but no floor overhead. The floor beneath was made of split logs, hewed to make them smooth; and some narrow benches made from split logs, supported by legs, were put in for the scholars. There were no writing tables or desks, but these were added afterwards when they wanted to educate larger boys, and were made by boring into the logs, and driving pins to support a sloping board for a writing table, so that those who wrote sat with their faces to the wall, and their backs to the teacher.

Levi Beardsley, who was born in 1785 in Otsego County, New York, Reminiscences, *in Louis C. Jones, ed.,* Growing Up in the Cooper Country, *pp. 59–60.*

Father and his neighbors were not indifferent to the education of their children; but they were all new settlers, all poor, and all illiterate, and hence had not the means or conception necessary to the establishment of a good school, even had it been possible to procure a competent teacher. In a year or two after our removal [to Kentucky, ca. 1788] a small log schoolhouse was erected by the joint labor of several neighbors, about half a mile north from his house, and just beyond the "line" of his "place." It was entirely in the woods, but one of the wagon roads leading into the Lick passed by its very door. In the winter, light was admitted through oiled paper by long openings between the logs; for at that time glass was not thought of. It was one story high, without any upper floor, and about sixteen by twenty feet in dimensions, with a great wooden chimney, a broad puncheon floor, and a door of the same material, with its latch and string. . . .

The first teacher who wielded the hickory mace in this academy was Jacob Beaden. . . . He was a recent immigrant from the eastern shore of Maryland, and an ample exponent of the state of society in that benighted region. His function was to teach spelling reading, writing, and cyphering as far as the rule of three; beyond which he could not go; and his attainments in that branch harmonized, as to quality and compass, with his erudition in the others. The fashion was for the whole school to learn and say their lessons aloud, and a noisier display of emulation has perhaps never since been made.

Daniel Drake recalling his first school in Mayslick, Kentucky, where he lived from 1788 through 1794, Pioneer Life in Kentucky, *pp. 143–45.*

There is one general practice in schools which I censure with diffidence, not because I doubt the propriety of the censure, but because it is opposed to deep-rooted prejudices: this practice is the use of the Bible as a schoolbook. There are two reasons why this practice has so generally prevailed: the first is that families in the country are not generally supplied with any other book; the second, an opinion that the reading of the scriptures will impress upon the minds of youth the important truths of religion and morality. The first may be easily removed, and the purpose of the last is counteracted by the practice itself.

If people design the doctrines of the Bible as a system of religion, ought they to appropriate the book to purposes foreign to this design? Will not a familiarity, contracted by a careless disrespectful reading of the sacred volume, weaken the influence of its precepts upon the heart?

Noah Webster, 1790, "On the Education of Youth in America," pp. 49–50.

. . . [T]he principal defect in our plan of education in America is the want of good teachers in the academies and common schools. By good teachers I mean men of unblemished reputation and possessed of abilities competent to their stations. That a man should be master of what he undertakes to teach is a point that will not be disputed, and yet it is certain that abilities are often dispensed with, either through inattention or fear of expense.

To those who employ ignorant men to instruct their children, permit me to suggest one important idea: that it is better for youth to have *no* education than to have a bad one, for it is more difficult to eradicate habits than to impress new ideas. The tender shrub is easily bent to any figure, but the tree which has acquired its full growth resists all impressions.

Noah Webster, 1790, "On the Education of Youth in America," p. 57.

Although at five I was familiar with story books, and could read without hesitation any plain reading, yet I was never taught at home as a regular exercise. I read my books oftentimes aloud, and, finding a hard word or unintelligible sentence, sought aid. Nor did I, in my early childhood days, ever attend school. Rhode Island had not in those days, nor for years afterwards, any public schools; but private schools, more or less convenient, and more or less properly taught, were in operation all over the State. My father sent me to one of them *two weeks,* when I was about five years old. The teacher kept me the whole two weeks in one lesson, and I knew it by rote before going to school. My father, learning this, took me out of school, saying "he would send me no longer to such a blockhead."

Richard Cecil Stone, who was five in 1803, Life Incidents of Home, School and Church, *pp. 5–6.*

The severest duty I was ever called to perform was sitting on that little front seat, at my first winter school. My lesson in the Abs [alphabet] conveyed no ideas, excited no interest, and, of course, occupied but very little of my time. There was nothing before me on which to lean my head, or lay my arms, but my own knees. . . . How my limbs ached for the freedom and activity of play! It sometimes seemed as if a drubbing from the master, or a kick across the schoolhouse, would have been a pleasant relief.

But these bonds upon my limbs were not all. I had trials by fire in addition. Every cold forenoon, the old fire-place, wide and deep, was kept a roaring furnace of flame, for the benefit of blue noses, chattering jaws, and aching toes, in the more distant regions. The end of my seat, just opposite the chimney, was oozy with melted pitch, and sometimes almost smoked with com-

bustion. Judge, then, of what living flesh had to bear. It was a toil to exist.

Warren Burton writing about his first winter term at the common school in Wilton, New Hampshire, in 1804, when he was three years old, The District School as It Was, *pp. 18–19.*

The whole school is arranged in classes; a monitor is appointed to each, who is responsible for the cleanliness, order, and improvement of every boy in it. He is assisted by boys, either from his own or another class, to perform part of his duties for him, when the number is more than he is equal to manage himself.

The proportion of boys who teach, either in reading, writing, or arithmetic, is as one to ten. In so large a school there are duties to be performed, which simply relate to order, and have no connexion with learning; for these duties different monitors are appointed. The word monitor, in this intitution [sic], means, any boy that has a charge either in some department of tuition or of order, and is not simply confined to those boys who teach.—The boy who takes care that the writing books are ruled, by machines made for that purpose, is the monitor of ruling. The boy who superintends the enquiries after the absentees, is called the monitor of absentees. The monitors who inspect the improvement of the classes in reading, writing, and arithmetic, are called inspecting monitors; and their offices indeed are essentially different from that of the *teaching monitors.* A boy whose business it is to give to the other monitors such books, &c. as may be wanted or appointed for the daily use of their classes, and to gather them up when done with; to see all the boys do read, and that none leave school without reading, is called the monitor-general. Another is called the monitor of slates, because he has a general charge of all the slates in the school.

Joseph Lancaster explaining the monitorial system of education, 1805, Improvements in Education, as It Respects the Industrious Classes of the Community, *pp. 37–38.*

The commands that a monitor usually gives to his class, are of a simple nature: as, to go in or out of their seats: 'In'—'Out.' The whole class do this at one motion—they learn to front, or go to the right or left, either single or double. They 'show slates,' at the word of command; take them up, or lay them gently down on the desk, in the same manner. . . .

Another command is, to 'sling hats,' which is always done on coming into school; and, 'unsling hats,' which is always done on leaving it. This alludes to a very convenient arrangement, which prevents all the loss of hats, mistakes, and confusion in finding them, which would naturally occur among so large a number of boys. It saves all shelves, nails, or places where they are usually put in schools. It prevents them all going to put hats on the nails or shelves, and all going to get them thence, before they leave school. These are great advantages—as, with eight hundred boys in school, they save sixteen hundred motions, unavoidable on the usual plan, both morning or afternoon—motions that, before this arrangement was made, produced much inconvenience in the school; and complaints were made, almost daily, of boys losing their hats, which have ceased since this arrangement. All these advantages are gained, and inconveniences are avoided, by every boy slinging his hat across his shoulders, as a soldier would sling his knapsack: by which means he carries it always about him, and cannot lose it without immediately missing it.

Joseph Lancaster, 1805, Improvements in Education, *as* It Respects the Industrious Classes of the Community, *pp. 109–11.*

I always had a thirst after reading. At a very tender age my parents were frequently under the necessity of using their authority in compelling me to leave my books at a late hour, and retire to my bed. History was my delight. It was a great mercy that I possessed this taste for books, for without it, I should not have attained a common school education, as my privileges for obtaining it were quite limited. My parents being poor, and having a large family, it became indispensibly necessary that I should be put to labour as soon as my age would possibly permit. I however generally made a shift, after having worked through the summer for wages, to obtain a place in the winter where I could be allowed my board and the privilege of going to school for what I could do independently of my school hours. I pursued my studies closely when I had the opportunity, rising at 4 o'clock in the winter season, and devoting the hours between this and sunrise, to English grammar, so that I might attend to other branches in school. In this way I acquired a tolerable English education, was considered qualified to teach a school myself, which I engaged in at different times, with general satisfaction, and was also employed for

about three years as clerk of a manufacturing establishment in my native town. My father however being a mechanic himself, and considering it an indispensible duty binding on himself to give all his sons a trade, I accordingly commenced working with him at the carpentering business, and acquired a knowledge of that art.

Ray Potter recalling his education and first employment near Cranston, Rhode Island, ca. 1805–10, Memoirs of the Life and Religious Experience of Ray Potter, *pp. 15–16.*

I conceive the education of our youth in this country to be peculiarly necessary in Pennsylvania, while our citizens are composed of the natives of so many different kingdoms in Europe. Our schools of learning, by producing one general, and uniform system of education, will render the mass of the people more homogeneous, and thereby fit them more easily for uniform and peaceable government.

Benjamin Rush, 1806, "Of the Mode of Education Proper in a Republic," in Essays, Literary, Moral and Philosophical, *pp. 7–8.*

. . . [T]he only foundation for a useful education in a republic is to be laid in Religion. Without this there can be no virtue, and without virtue there can be no liberty, and liberty is the object and life of all republican governments.

Such is my veneration for every religion that reveals the attributes of the Deity, or a future state of rewards and punishments, that I had rather see the opinions of Confucius or Mahomed inculcated upon our youth, than see them grow up wholly devoid of a system of religious principles. But the religion I mean to recommend in this place, is that of the New Testament.

It is foreign to my purpose to hint at the arguments which establish the truth of the Christian revelation. My only business is to declare, that all its doctrines and precepts are calculated to promote the happiness of society, and the safety and well being of civil government. A Christian cannot fail of being a republican.

Benjamin Rush, 1806, "Of the Mode of Education Proper in a Republic," in Essays, Literary, Moral and Philosophical, *p. 8.*

Persons too lazy to work, and unfit for other profitable employments, were usually engaged as pedagogues. School-books were scarce, but of divers kinds. . . . Highly favored were the children who owned Webster's spelling-book, then just coming into use. For reading, every pupil brought to the school such book or books as were found in his family—they might be the Columbian Orator, Scott's Lessons, the Arabian Nights, Robinson Crusoe, the Bible or fragments of it, or anything else in print, historical or fictitious, didactic or heroic, solemn or amusing. This diversity in school-books was not so inconvenient as a modern teacher might suppose. Schools were not divided into classes, but every pupil "said" or read his own lesson. A slate and pencil, with paper and ink for the advanced students, completed the outfit for an education in the "Old-Field Schools." In most of them neither a dictionary, a grammar, nor an arithmetic could be found.

Jeremiah Bell Jeter, who attended school in Bedford County, Virginia, ca. 1807–12, The Recollections of a Long Life, *p. 4.*

It is time to inquire after the attainments of the pupils in these plain, rural schools. Of course, they did not learn much. If most of the teachers had ever heard of accent or emphasis, they furnished to their scholars no proof of their knowledge. Of punctuation, they had some vague conception. He was deemed the greatest proficient in reading who could read the fastest. The teacher would often call out to the pupil, reading with breathless velocity: "Mind your stops!" and the teaching in punctuation was limited to this stern command. Spelling was the only branch of learning cultivated successfully in these schools. The pupils spelled in classes, the best spellers ascending to the head and the worst descending to the foot of the class. By this means an emulation was excited among them, which made them quite ready in spelling the words found in their meagre school vocabulary.

Jeremiah Bell Jeter, who attended school in Bedford County, Virginia, ca. 1807–12, The Recollections of a Long Life, *p. 5.*

The pupil might love his books, but far more he loved the hour for his amusements; he might eat his lunch with a sharp relish, but he had a much keener appetite for the sports of the play-hour. All the scholars looked forward with thrilling interest to the time when the shadow of the sun on the door-sill of the school-house indicated the arrival of meridian. All ears were then attentive to hear the words by which the commencement of the joyous "Play-time" was invariably announced by the schoolmaster: "Lay by your books."

That sentence instantly changed the school-room into a babel. Books, slates, pens and paper were cast aside, and the demon of uproar seemed to be unchained. The homely lunch was speedily disposed of, and all were ready for the desired amusements. The girls betook themselves to the shady bowers and all the mimic arts of housekeeping. The sports of the boys took a wider range. The favorite amusements of the time were marbles, cat, base-ball, prisoner's base, steal-goods, and the like. The popular athletic sports were running, wrestling, jumping, chasing the fox, and boxing, an exercise that sometimes caused more pain than pleasure. Some of the lads attained to great expertness in these plays. I remember one who was an incomparable dodger. The most skillful thrower might stand close by him, and casting a ball at him with the greatest care and force, would be more likely to miss than to hit him.

Jeremiah Bell Jeter, who attended school in Bedford County, Virginia, ca. 1807–12, The Recollections of a Long Life, *p. 9.*

I tried every expedient I could devise, to gain the privilege of staying at home [from school], for which it is but justice to myself to say, there was some excuse in the severity of the teacher, who went about the school-room carrying under his arm a large rod or switch, which would resound from a back here and another there, every little while, and sometimes on a whole bench-full successively, from which I did not escape. Being very sensitive and nervous, the sound of a stroke on another hurt me almost as badly, it seemed, as if it had been on myself. I dreaded going to school *exceedingly,* and thought any expedient, which was not criminal, would be justifiable, that would relieve me from a day of such agony.

Benjamin Hallowell, who attended school in Cheltenham Township, Pennsylvania, ca. 1808, when he was nine, Autobiography of Benjamin Hallowell, *pp. 6–7.*

Two months before I had attained the age of three years, I was taken home by my grandfather Woodburn to spend a few weeks with him, and sent to school from his house,—the school-house of his district being but fifty rods from his door. . . . Hence, I lived at my grandfather's, and went thence to school, most of each

Winter and some months in Summer during the next three years.

My first schoolmaster was David Woodburn Dickey, a nephew of my grandfather, a college graduate, and an able, worthy man, though rather a severe than a successful governor of youth. The district was large; there were ninety names on its roll of pupils,—many of them of full-grown men and women, not well broken to obedience and docility,—with an average attendance of perhaps sixty; all to be instructed in various studies, as well as ruled, by a single teacher, who did his very best, which included a liberal application of birch and ferule.

Horace Greeley, who was three years old in 1814,
Recollections of a Busy Life, *pp. 42–43.*

I was sent very early to school, a common district school. My first experience made a wonderful impression upon me. . . . When my mother had made me ready and I set out with an older brother to whose hand I clung very tightly, I thought it was a great affair, and my mind had some very big thoughts on the way. But when I entered the school-house my wonder and amazement knew no bounds. So many children I had never seen together before. I could not imagine where they all came from! And then there was the master, a man grown, sitting by a table, and on the table were some books, a ruler, and his heavy walking stick. The sight of all these things filled me with profound awe. Perhaps I was a little, perhaps a good deal, scared. At any rate I had a kind of awful feeling. The master did not look or act like other people. I could hardly keep my eyes off from him, but gazed at him as a kind of superior being. One little incident is fresh in my memory. A little boy, older than myself, was called up to the master to say his letters. I can now see him standing by the knee of the teacher and intently following the point of the penknife as it pointed out each letter, and I can hear him call out in his loudest voice the names of the letters, one after another, sometimes right, and sometimes wrong, until he was brought up all standing at the letter S. He looked steadily at it for some time, and scratching his head, without saying a word, he went round on the other side of the teacher and took another look at it, twisting and turning all the time, but keeping perfectly silent, and yet very much puzzled. At length the teacher said, "Well, what is it? what does it look like?" Straightening himself up and looking the teacher in the face he said, "It looks like dad's saddle-bags." This created quite a laugh in the school, but there was no laugh in me. The matter was too important, and I felt too deeply for that.

Heman Dyer, who first attended school in Shaftsbury,
Vermont, ca. 1815, Records of an Active Life,
pp. 9–10.

The capital start given me by my mother enabled me to make rapid progress in school,—a progress monstrously exaggerated by gossip and tradition. I was specially clever in spelling,—an art in which there were then few even tolerably proficient,—so that I soon rose to the head of the "first class," and usually retained that position. It was a custom of the school to "choose sides" for a "spelling-match" one afternoon of each week,—the head of the first class in spelling, and the pupil standing next, being the choosers. In my case, however, it was found necessary to change the rule, and confide the choice to those who stood second and third respectively; as I—a mere infant of four years—could spell, but not choose,—often preferring my playmates, who could not spell at all.

These spelling-matches usually took place in the evening, when I could not keep my eyes open, and should have been in bed. It was often necessary to rap me sharply when "the word" came around to me; but I never failed to respond; and it came to be said that I spelled as well asleep as awake. I apprehend that this was more likely to be true of some others of the class; who, if ever so sound asleep, could scarcely have spelled worse than they did.

Horace Greeley, who turned four in 1815,
Recollections of a Busy Life, *p. 44.*

On one side [of the schoolhouse] was a large open fireplace, which with its entrance door occupied the whole space. In this great heater, in the cold winter, not less than half a cord of green wood was consumed each day, roasting half the school and leaving the other half nearly frozen during the process. The seats and benches were made of half-planed hemlock or spruce boards, and were arranged on three sides of the house, in amphitheatre style. The back seats were designed for the older boys and girls, and the front seats for the little ones sent to school to relieve the mothers of their care at home. These seats were so wide that the child's back could not be supported, and so high that his feet could not touch the floor. A more complete rack of torture and machine for making cripples could hardly be invented. Yet these children were kept upon these hard benches all day long, relieved only by short recesses, with nothing to do but play, if they dared.

In one respect that old schoolhouse was a model of its kind, far superior to many of more modern construction; it was well *ventilated*. Its huge open fireplace, spacious chimney, loose windows, and half-nailed covering boards invited the passing breeze and gave free circulation to the pure mountain air. No pupil ever contracted consumption from breathing impure atmosphere in that temple of knowledge.

Hiram Orcutt describing the school he attended as a child in Acworth, New Hampshire, ca. 1820–23, Reminiscences of School Life, *pp. 14–15.*

Added to the rough and tumble of schoolboy sports, and battles of snowballing, some pupils lived two miles away, making four miles' walk each day over rough or snow-drifted roads. The dinner-basket was a necessity; and even the rats and mice which had gained residence in the old schoolhouse were dependent for their living upon the crumbs that fell from the benches, when they failed to gain access to the full basket. Still we were not much annoyed by them.

Hiram Orcutt recalling his schooldays in Acworth, New Hampshire, circa 1820–23, Reminiscences of School Life, *p. 16.*

. . . [T]he teaching of composition in any form was never attempted. Writing in copy-books was allowed, but not *taught*. In reading, the pupil acquired the habit of uttering improper sounds, mispronouncing words, and the incorrect expression of sentences. In arithmetic, he was required only to "do the sums," without understanding the principles or reasons. It was never suggested that a correct knowledge of this or any other branch of study would be of any practical benefit in the business of life. The study of geography consisted of committing to memory long lists of names and figures, to be forgotten before the next recitation. Grammar was, and continued to be, one of the seven wonders of the world. As a result, the best graduates from this school could not have estimated the measure and value of a pile of wood, could not have expressed correctly a simple sentence, or written a creditable letter to their mothers.

Hiram Orcutt recalling his schooldays in Acworth, New Hampshire, ca. 1820–23, Reminiscences of School Life, *pp. 21–22.*

The innovative educator Bronson Alcott, ca. 1852 *(Photograph courtesy of the Louisa May Alcott Memorial Association)*

The province of the instructor should be simple, awakening, invigorating, directing, rather than the forcing of the child's faculties upon prescribed and exclusive courses of thought. He should look to the child to see what is to be done, rather than to his book or his system. The Child is the Book. The operations of his mind are the true system. Let him study these carefully and his success is sure. Let him follow out the impulses, the thoughts, the volitions, of the child's mind and heart, in their own principles and rational order of expression, and his training will be what God designed it to be—an aid to prepare the child to aid himself.

Bronson Alcott, September 21, 1828, The Journals of Bronson Alcott, *Vol. 1, p. 12.*

After [the children] had finished eating, the teacher told them he would read them a story, if they would like to hear one. They all held up their hands in token of assent, and entreated him to read about Peter Parley. So he took up the book, and began, first telling them what the name, Parley, meant, and asking the meaning of the difficult words as he went on. He asked them, in one instance, what 'miserable' meant? One said, 'not comfortable,' another 'poor,' and another pointed to the fire, (which was quite out,) and said, 'That is a *miserable* fire.' The teacher asked what 'violently' meant? 'Hard,' 'quick,' 'strong,' were some of the answers. But one of the children got down off his seat, and stamping with his foot, shouted in a loud voice, '*That is violently!*' After a while, the teacher shut up the book, and they all exclaimed. 'Oh! *do* finish the story.' 'If you don't, you are a naughty man,' said one. 'Am I?' said the teacher, looking at him with a smile. 'Oh! no—But do read some more.' By this time they had all got into confusion; and the teacher put the book upon his knee, and said, 'Why don't I go on?' 'Because we are all making such a noise,' they replied. He did not bid them be still, but waited patiently until they had brought themselves to order, and then read on. When he had finished, he told them he was very glad they had *governed themselves.* When he sent them to their seats, he bid each one remember not to talk; then he gave them their slates, and wrote on the black board: 'Day' 'this' 'is' 'cloudy' 'a'—and told them he was going to make a sentence out of these words. One or two of them read it off directly; he told the rest; and they all wrote it upon their slates.

"Account of a Visit to an Elementary School," 1829, *pp. 74–75.*

An infant school may be best described, perhaps, as something which resembles, not so much a school, as a large nursery, and the object of which is to provide for its little inmates employment and amusement, not less than instruction. A number of young children, varying, in different instances, from fifty to one or even two hundred in amount, and embracing all diversities of age, from that of about six years down to that of eighteen months, are assembled to spend the day under the care of a teacher, furnished with the requisite aid of one or more female assistants. . . .

The *intellectual* instruction imparted at these schools, is restricted to a few simple but useful and interesting elements. It embraces the rudiments of arithmetic, a good degree of progress in reading and orthography, some information about animals, plants, and minerals, and the various substances composing

articles of daily use in household affairs or the arts of life. . . .

But the peculiar feature in the infant school system, is, the excellence of its *moral* instruction, by which the pupils, instead of being made passive recipients of injunctions and silent listeners to truth, are allowed a free and varied intercourse with each other and with their teacher, and are made active and spontaneous agents in their own improvement. The moral lessons of the infant schools, if they ever can be detached from the other departments of instruction and exercise, may be briefly said to resemble, as nearly as possible, the tender, affectionate, and judicious management of a well regulated nursery.

"Observations on Infant Schools," 1829, *pp. 8–9.*

. . . [I]nfant schools are needed on the score of *health,* not less than of mental improvement. To the children of the poor, home has generally few opportunities to afford for healthful recreation. The common air and light of heaven are often in a great measure denied to infancy in this condition; the unaided vigour of the constitution is left to struggle with hindrances, and not unfrequently sinks under the evils of neglect. Our primary schools seldom offer any salutary counteracting influence to early injuries of this nature: they are too generally situated so as rather to prolong or aggravate them. A change, it is gratifying to observe, is now making, by which, it is to be hoped, spacious and pleasant rooms will be furnished for these schools, and the health and comfort of the teachers and the children secured. But this change, desirable as it is, produces of course no change on the condition of infancy—nothing to counteract the disadvantages of damp, unwholesome, unventilated rooms, at that susceptible period; and it is one great purpose of infant schools to provide airy and comfortable rooms, in which the little pupils may spend most of the day. Were no other good whatever effected by these schools, who can estimate the benefit thus conferred by them on the community?

"Observations on Infant Schools," 1829, *p. 18.*

. . . [T]he interesting subject of Infant Schools is becoming more and more fashionable. . . . We have been told that it is now in contemplation, to open a school for the infants of others besides the poor. If such a course be not soon adopted, at the age for entering primary schools those *poor* children will assuredly be the richest scholars. And why should a plan which promises so many advantages, independent of merely relieving the mother from her charge, be confined to children of the indigent?

Ladies Magazine, *February 1829, in Carl F. Kaestle and Maris A. Vinovskis, "From Apron Strings to ABCs: Parents, Children, and Schooling in Nineteenth-Century Massachusetts," p. S52.*

Infants, taken from most unfavorable situations in which they are ever placed, from the abodes of poverty and vice, are capable of learning at least a hundred times as much, a hundred times as well, and of being a hundred times as happy, by the system adopted in infant schools, as by that which prevails in the common schools throughout the country. The conclusion most interesting to every friend of education is, that the infant school system can be extended through every department of the *popular education*. And that in any school district where there is interest and liberality enough to raise Ten Dollars to procure apparatus, a *beginning* can be made the present season.

Boston Recorder and Religious Transcript, *July 9, 1829, in Dean May and Maris A. Vinovskis, "A Ray of Millennial Light," p. 62.*

Such as were far enough advanced had foolscap writing paper sewed together, to make a writing book, and at the top of the sheet the Master wrote in his best hand, often very bad, a copy. "Be virtuous and you will be happy," and similar old moral saws. They also had slates, upon which they laboriously worked out sums in addition, subtraction, multiplication and division, while the very clever pupils ventured into fractions, and even into "single rule of three," which was the extreme limit to which the Master was expected to go. The teachers, as a rule, were Scotch-Irish, of American birth, with now and then an Englishman, or smart young native. There were generally from thirty to forty pupils. The master would begin with the smaller ones, calling them one by one, and going over the alphabet several times with each; then the next larger, who could spell words of two or three letters; then those who could master two syllables, who were ranged on a line, and spelled in turn, those missing standing down the rank, to give space to the correct speller; then followed those advanced to three or more syllables, who went through the same exercise; then those who could read in the "Introduction," which contained no hard words, who in turn read sentences; then the advanced ones, who

read from the "English Reader," made up of selections from standard English authors. This round of classes consumed the time until recess. After recess those who studied arithmetic carried their slates, one by one, to the teacher, who looked over the work they had done, or the examples he had set for each, correcting and assisting the pupil when at fault, after which he examined the copy books. The same program as before recess was afterwards gone through with the younger ones. The afternoon exercises were the same as those of the forenoon, with the addition of a general spelling class, consisting of all who had advanced to three syllables, and in that class there was great emulation as to who could get to the head of the class the oftener, the pupil once at the head being always put to the foot to work his way up again.

Seymour D. Carpenter, *who attended school in Lancaster, Ohio, between 1831 and 1836,* Genealogical Notes of the Carpenter Family, *pp. 77–78.*

Many physicians of great experience are of the opinion, that efforts to develope the minds of young children are very frequently injurious; and from instances of disease in children which I have witnessed, I am forced to believe that the danger is indeed great, and that very often in attempting to call forth and cultivate the intellectual faculties of children before they are six or seven years of age, serious and lasting injury has been done both to the body and the mind.

Amariah Brigham, *1833,* Remarks on the Influence of Mental Excitement upon Health, *p. 15.*

Master Hills taught the North Grammar School, after it occupied its present site. I remember him in 1835; and I pause when I think of this teacher, and wonder if, in some other sphere, he remembers whipping a little girl to overcome her persistent denials of an accusation made against her, thereby forcing her to tell a lie. She was accused by one of her schoolmates of taking a one cent multiplication table from her desk, and tearing it in two. For this slight offence, he, a strong man, unheeding her denials of the charge, with a heavy strap, struck with his whole strength on the tender palm of the little hand of a child of scarcely ten years. He punished her till she could not see, for pain and terror, and then she gave in, *whipped into a lie,* and said she did it.

Harriet H. Robinson *describing school discipline in 1835,* Loom and Spindle, *p. 19.*

I have known Master Hills to go secretly behind a boy, who was playing at his desk, and strike him with a heavy strap across the back. Whipping was an every-day occurrence, and was done before all the children during school hours. A boy was made to lie across a chair, and was whipped in that position—not always through his clothing. Let us charitably hope that this cruel treatment of children was the fault of the times and of the arbitrary rule that was thought necessary to govern a community in those days. The day of children's rights had not yet dawned.

Harriet H. Robinson describing school discipline in 1835,
Loom and Spindle, *p. 20.*

These schools [in Wellfleet, Massachusetts] numbered nearly one hundred pupils each, ranging from six to twenty-five years of age. They were of a decidedly mixed character, and all gathered in one room, to be managed and taught without an assistant! In the "Back Side" school I had a whole ship's crew, including captain, mate, and cook. They had come home from a fishing voyage to spend the winter, and, having nothing else to do, they entered the school. . . .

The pupils were treated with attention and kindness, at all times and everywhere. Out of school hours I mingled familiarly with them, joined them in their sports, and sympathized with them in all their joys and sorrows. In their homes—where I frequently met them, by the way,—and on the playground we stood on a common level. In the schoolroom, however, I was recognized as master, and so complete was their loyalty—captain, mate and all—that I could punish, if need be, with severity, in the presence of the school, without the least opposition on the part of the offender.

Hiram Orcutt, teacher in Wellfleet, Massachusetts, between 1836 and 1841, Reminiscences of School Life, *pp. 57–59.*

Our district schoolhouse was at a crossing of the roads half a mile or less east of our home. It was of red brick, its walls were cracked, and kept from falling asunder by iron rods passing completely through, at a convenient height for boys to jump up to, and catch, and perform gymnastic feats on, in the dingy old entry, at recess. Grotesque methods of enforcing discipline among the pupils were in vogue in those days,—"sitting on nothing," with the back against the wall; "holding down a nail in the floor," with a forefinger, in a painfully stooping posture; standing with an arm outstretched and a pile of books in the hand; "licking jackets," when two boys who had quarreled received from the master each a stout switch, and were made to fight out their feud in the presence of the edified school, he himself putting in a cut for example when they were too tender of each other and did not hit hard enough. The school was ungraded and the methods of teaching were primitive, but there is this to be said of it, that the pupil that had a mind for self-improvement could get a fair common-school education under the worst teachers, and that some of these were far better than the system they represented.

John Townsend Trowbridge writing about his experience of school near Rochester, New York, ca. 1837,
My Own Story with Recollections of Noted Persons, *pp. 40–41.*

After I was thirteen I attended only the winter term of the school, my services being required on the farm in summer; but the teaching I missed was probably no loss to me when my mind had become independently aroused. In the hour's nooning with the books I loved, I have no doubt but I learned more than I should have done in the whole day's routine in school. I almost wonder now at the extent of my studies and readings while I was doing a boy's regular work on the farm.

John Townsend Trowbridge, who turned 13 in 1840,
My Own Story with Recollections of Noted Persons, *p. 47.*

I suppose I must have been a bad boy; at least I was mischievous. One day my brother, who was six, and I, eight, were playing with the Chaney boys, who were about our age. [Our teacher] sent one of the older children out and got a bundle of hazel switches—long and supple, just right for switching. She kept us boys after school and began using those switches. A Mrs. Starkey, living some forty rods from the school-house, heard us screaming, and ran over. Brother Alexander, who had started for home, also heard our cries and ran back and interfered.

The teacher was boarding at our house, and when we went home that night she told Father that Alexander had interfered with her correcting the younger children at school, and Father punished Alex for it.

Saturday night, when Becky Hedger, our hired girl, took us into the kitchen for the weekly bath, she called Father in to show him our backs and legs. The welts were there yet. Father cried, and the next day the teacher went back to town.

John McWilliams, who attended school in Griggsville, Illinois, and was eight in 1840, Recollections of John McWilliams, *p. 37.*

Parents, oftentimes, send their children to school before it can be of any essential benefit to them. In such cases, an injury is inflicted upon both the child and the school. The child is injured by being confined for several hours, upon the hard benches and the impure air of the house,—and the school is injured, by having a considerable portion of the instructor's time occupied in endeavoring to teach, and especially to govern, such children. . . . The proper order is, to begin with the education of the *body,* and then proceed to that of the *mind.* The practice of sending children, two or three years old, to school, to "get them out of the way," cannot be too much deprecated. Every teacher, it should be remembered, is employed to *give instruction,* not to *act the part of a nurse.*

Massachusetts Board of Education, 1840, in Carl F. Kaestle and Maris A. Vinovskis, "From Apron Strings to ABCs: Parents, Children, and Schooling in Nineteenth-Century Massachusetts," p. S60.

It was in the early autumn of [1841], at the age of sixteen, that I first stood before a class as their appointed teacher. The scene was the unceiled low room of the wagon-house loft on my father's farm. In my early years the free-school system had been adopted, and I was appointed teacher by the board of managers of my native township. . . .

Of the work in the schoolroom, I may say that such work would astonish and confound any young teacher of the present day [1907]. Arithmetic was "ciphered" individually, on slates, without any class instruction or the use of blackboards or charts, and the chief aim was to "get the answer," without much attempt at reasoning as to the processes employed to obtain it. In penmanship, the copies were "set" by the teacher's hand, at the top of each page of the copy-book, and without any aid from printed or engraved slips or copies. Steel pens, too, were not yet in common use; quill pens were almost universally employed. As teacher of the art of penmanship, I see myself now, walking about the small, low-ceiled room, criticising the forms of the letters, keeping the

pens mended, penknife in hand, with a bunch of new-made pens sticking behind my ear.

Edward Hicks Magill, who began teaching in 1841, Sixty-Five Years in the Life of a Teacher, 1841–1906, *pp. 8–9.*

I followed the usual practice of that time [1841–42], working on the farm in the summer, teaching only in the late fall and winter months, and closing in time for corn-planting and other farm work in the spring. From the opening of the school I engaged with my pupils in games of ball, snow-balling, etc., during the recess, just as one of them, but was careful to put on the serious and resolute schoolmaster's face when I rang the bell for them to reassemble. This acting a double part, as master and student, was made all the more difficult because my pupils were my own personal friends, relatives, and near neighbors, and a number of them, both boys and girls, were my seniors by several years.

Edward Hicks Magill, who first taught during the 1841–42 school year, when he was 16, Sixty-Five Years in the Life of a Teacher, 1841–1906, *pp. 10–11.*

Knowing, as we do, that the foundations of national greatness can be laid only in the industry, the integrity, and the spiritual elevation of the people, are we equally sure that our schools are forming the character of the rising generation upon the everlasting principles of duty and humanity? or, on the other hand, are they only stimulating the powers which lead to a base pride of intellect, which prompt to the ostentation instead of the reality of virtue, and which give augury that life is to be spent only in selfish competitions between those who should be brethren? Above all others, must the children of a republic be fitted for society as well as for themselves. . . . In a government like ours, each individual must think of the welfare of the State, as well as the welfare of his own family, and, therefore, of the children of others as well as his own. It becomes, then, a momentous question, whether the children in our schools are educated in reference to themselves and their private interests only, or with a regard to the great social duties and prerogatives that await them in after-life. Are they so educated, that, when they grow up, they will make better philanthropists and Christians, or only grander savages? For, however, loftily the intellect of man may have been gifted, however skillfully it may have been trained, if it be not guided by a sense of justice, a love of mankind, and a devotion to duty, its possessor is only a more splendid, as he is a more dangerous barbarian.

Horace Mann, "Challenges to a New Age," 1845, in Louis Filler, ed., Horace Mann on the Crisis in Education, *pp. 87–88.*

I was delighted at the idea of going to school—the place I had often heard about but never seen. My father went to the teacher of the district school, Mrs. Tunsil, who taught in what was called the Merryweather district. My brother Alfred and I went to this school for some time—indeed, until the school was closed. Mrs. Daniel Barton was next engaged to take charge of a colored school held in a house on the east side of the farm, which was built for my brother Samuel. The whole family attended this school for several sessions. I was next sent to the Brooklyn district school, to which I went for some considerable time. At length prejudice began to show itself on the part of the parents of some of the children, which was communicated to the trustees. Many of the parents of the children were perfectly willing that I should go to school with their children, but there were others who thought their children were too good to go to the same school with a colored person. The trustees thought it best, for peace sake, to have my parents withdraw me from the school. . . .

A school was opened immediately after this by a white lady exclusively for the benefit of colored children. I went to this school for six months, after which I was detained at home to attend to duties connected with the farm. During my absence from school I never forgot the instructions which I received while at school.

J. H. Magee, who attended school in Illinois, ca. 1845, The Night of Affliction and Morning of Recovery, *pp. 16–18.*

The dislike of school was so strong as to be a positive gain. The passionate hatred of school methods was almost a method in itself. Yet the day-school of that time was respectable, and the boy had nothing to complain of. In fact, he never complained. He hated it because he was herded with a crowd of other boys and compelled to learn by memory a quantity of things that did not amuse him. His memory was slow, and the effort painful. For him to conceive that his memory could compete for school prizes with machines of two or three times its power, was to prove himself wanting not only in memory, but flagrantly in mind. He thought his mind a good enough machine, if it were given time to act, but it acted wrong if hurried. School-masters never gave time.

In any and all its forms, the boy detested school, and the prejudice became deeper with years. He always reckoned his school days, from ten to sixteen years old, as time thrown away.

Henry Adams of Boston remembering the years 1848 through 1854 in his autobiography written in the third person, The Education of Henry Adams, *p. 38.*

New England School, a painting by Charles Frederick Bosworth, ca. 1852 *(Courtesy of the Massachusetts Historical Society)*

. . . [T]here is but one kind of public school established by the laws of Massachusetts. This is the general Public School, free to all the inhabitants. There is nothing in these laws establishing any exclusive or separate school for any particular class, whether rich or poor, whether Catholic or Protestant, whether white or black. In the eye of the law there is but *one* class, in which all interests, opinions, conditions and colors commingle in harmony—excluding none, comprehending all. . . .

The law contemplates not only that they shall all be taught, but that they shall be taught *all together.* They are not only to receive equal quantities of knowledge, but all are to receive it in the same way. All are to approach together at the same fountain. . . . since according to our institutions, all classes meet without distinction of color, in the school, beginning there those relations of equality which our Constitution and laws promise to all.

Charles Sumner arguing for school desegregation before the Massachusetts Supreme Court, 1849, in Robert Bremner, ed., Children and Youth in America: A Documentary History, *Vol. 1, pp. 531–34.*

In those days we were taught writing and each scholar had a writing book. It was a number of sheets of paper fastened together with a cover. At the top of each page was a written saying like "As the twig is bent the tree inclines." We were expected to copy this as well as we could on the lines below. The last line we wrote was usually much better than the first. Each day at a certain hour the writing books were passed out and at the end of the period gathered up and laid in the drawer of the teacher's desk.

Sarah Marie Moulton, who attended school in the 1850s, in Anne Gertrude Sneller, A Vanished World, *p. 113.*

I was determined to teach. . . .

At the beginning the school was small. Soon the larger boys came, and finally Sidney Ellis, weighing over two hundred. My heart sank within me. He was the leader in all mischief. He was ignorant, scarcely able to read or write his own name, but he was the hero and idol of the unruly. . . .

I talked with Mr. Bassett [of the school committee]. He said if Sidney did not behave to send him out of school. At the close of school, one day, after I had spoken to him several times on account of misbehavior, I told him what the committee man had authorized me to do, and said "You cannot come to school any more without his or my consent". He replied, "I'll see about that".

It was soon noised about that the boys were to carry the teacher out of doors the next morning. . . .

I was at the schoolhouse early; saw that the fire in the stove was all right, and that the old iron shovel was handy for all proper uses.

One thing was noticeable; generally the larger boys were not at school when it begun its session, but were straggling in all the forenoon. This morning they were all "present and accounted for", with Sidney among them.

Promptly at nine o'clock the school was called to order. [T]hey all had the benefit of the morning exercises, the reading of scriptures, excepting Ellis.

After this I walked, as calmly and coolly as the circumstances would permit, to the front of the desk where Ellis was sitting and said, "Sidney, I told you last night not to come to school again without permission". "Yes", he replied, "I believe you did", at the same moment winking to his friends and starting to rise. I sprang forward and dealt him a blow on the side of the head with my fist, with all the force and power I possessed. He fell partially forward and down. I seized him, with one hand hold of the long hair on the back of his head and neck, and with the other hand had hold of his chin whiskers, and, with great difficulty, dragged him across the floor to the door, where he tried to get hold of my legs and the door. I then let go my hold, and kicked him in the side of the head. The blood flew, but it ended the struggle. He was easily tumbled out and the door locked.

Not one of his friends moved from his seat; they looked frightened, and many of the children were crying.

Edgar Jay Sherman, who taught school in Bassettsville, Massachusetts, in 1853, Some Recollections of a Long Life, *pp. 14–18.*

[Henry Adams] finished with school, not very brilliantly, but without finding fault with the sum of his knowledge. Probably he knew more than his father, or his grandfather, or his great-grandfather had known at sixteen years old. Only on looking back, fifty years later, at his own figure in 1854, and pondering on the needs of the twentieth century, he wondered whether, on the whole, the boy of 1854 stood nearer to the thought of 1904, or to that of the year 1. . . . [He had] reasons for thinking that, in essentials like religion, ethics, philosophy; in history, literature, art; in the concepts of all science, except perhaps mathematics, the American boy of 1854 stood nearer the year 1 than to the year 1900. The education he had received bore little relation to the education he needed. Speaking as an American of 1900, he had as yet no education at all. He knew not even where or how to begin.

Henry Adams in 1906, reflecting on himself as a boy in 1854, The Education of Henry Adams, *p. 54.*

3 "Slave Young, Slave Long" 1619–1861

Frederick Douglass was a boy in Talbot County, Maryland, in the 1820s, when he watched a plantation overseer whip an enslaved woman. The punishment went on for a long time—it seemed to Douglass that it lasted half an hour. Blood poured from the woman's head as her children, who were witnesses as well, begged for her release.

Douglass had only dim memories of his own mother. She had been hired out to another master when he was less than 12 months old and forced to leave him in the care of his grandmother. She sneaked back to visit him four or five times during the first years of his life, always under cover of night. When he was about seven years old, she died.

Frederick Douglass's experiences were not unusual for a child growing up in slavery in United States. Children like Douglass were born into a social system in which the controlling majority viewed them—and their parents—as instruments of labor.

SLAVERY THRIVED IN THE SOUTH

Africans first arrived in the English colonies in North America on August 20, 1619, on a Dutch ship that docked at Jamestown, Virginia. Twenty in number, they were traded to the colonists for food. Initially the colonists treated these and other Africans brought to their shores as indentured servants and granted them freedom upon completion of four years' labor. A shortage of available workers caused white colonists to rethink the position of blacks in society, however, and laws were soon enacted that took away the rights of African settlers. In 1641, Massachusetts became the first colony to establish a legal basis for slavery; a 1661 Virginia law assigned African servants to their masters for the duration of their natural lives. According to laws such as these, which were in effect in every colony by 1750, the children of slave mothers would be themselves enslaved.

The population of enslaved Africans, which increased slowly in the 1600s, grew rapidly in the next century as slave labor became an integral part of the economy in the southern and middle colonies. It was less important in New England, where industry was to dominate. Already by 1804, seven northern states had passed legislation that began the gradual manumission of slaves. Slave traders carried approximately 250,000 Africans to the North American mainland in the colonial period, and another 100,000 to southern ports between 1783 and 1807, the year when the United States outlawed the importation of slaves. (The ban on importation took effect January 1, 1808.)

How many slaves a planter owned depended on his financial status and labor requirements. Most southern whites owned no slaves. Of those who did, nearly half were small farmers who owned fewer than five. In Maryland in 1860, for example, half of all slaveholders owned only one or two slaves. Roughly one-sixth of slaveholders operated plantations, the large farms that employed 20 or more slave laborers. By 1840, there were 46,000 plantations in the South upon which slaves raised a variety of crops: rice, tobacco, sugar, and especially cotton. Fully three-fourths of the 4 million enslaved people toiling in the southern United States in 1860 grew cotton.

Town and city residents owned slaves as well. In fact, 500,000 enslaved African Americans inhabited southern cities on the eve of the Civil War, working as servants, artisans, and factory hands. Enslaved men also processed tobacco and mined coal.

SLAVES WERE A COMMODITY

As the experience of Frederick Douglass shows, enslaved people had as little ability to keep their families intact as they did to choose their life's work. They were property that could be bought or sold, hired out to others, left to descendants in a will, or seized to satisfy an owner's debts. Although slaves of any age could find themselves on the auction block, most of those sold were teenagers or young adults. Many of the "solitaires," the young people put up for sale, were transferred from the Chesapeake region to points south and west, to work in cotton culture. In the 1820s and 1830s, as the New England textile industry increased its demand for raw fiber, between 350,000 and 450,000 slaves were transported from the upper to the lower South. Half of all laborers on the cotton and sugar plantations of the Deep South during this period are thought to have been under 17 years of age. Forced to leave their families behind, these young people formed new kinship groups based on a common heritage and fate rather than on blood ties.

As if to demonstrate an undying optimism, enslaved women and men continued to choose mates and reproduce. The birth rate among slaves was as high as, or higher than, it was among whites. Women began bearing children at about age 16 and gave birth to eight, 10, or more. It was not unusual for women in the Chesapeake region or on the Sea Islands off the coast of Georgia and South Carolina to have as many as 16 children.

Half of the children born in slave quarters in coastal areas died in the first years of life. Poor nutrition and hard work during pregnancy contributed to low birth weights, which reduced the chances of survival in infancy. An enslaved child was four times as likely as a white child to die of tetanus or an intestinal illness related to teething or weaning. Contaminated food and water caused many cases of diarrhea, dysentery, and intestinal worms as well. Plantation mistresses treated sick slaves with homemade remedies and called in a doctor when necessary. The slaves themselves employed traditional herbal cures learned from older generations.

In the 1830s, 72 percent of the enslaved children on one Savannah River plantation died before the age of five. The planter, James Henry Hammond, initially tried to reduce child mortality by using the heroic measures that Benjamin Rush recommended, such as applying leeches and administering purges. When those treatments failed to yield results, Hammond experimented with disease prevention. He ordered trash removed from the slave quarters and yard, supervised handling of the water supply, and allowed his slaves additional rest. The mortality of children age five and under dropped to 56 percent in the 1840s and 26 percent in the 1850s.

Planters' holdings increased when their slaves reproduced, so they encouraged their bondswomen to find mates. Women on small farms had to look beyond their owners' property to find single men to whom they were not related, and slave owners made this possible by permitting visits to neighboring farms. Husbands and wives with different owners lived apart, so many enslaved children saw their fathers just once or twice a week, when the men were permitted to visit.

Children born into slavery on a plantation became part of a kinship group that might include grandparents, aunts, uncles, and cousins. The family circle also took in people unrelated by blood. In a system where loved ones could be sold and bonds easily broken, people needed all the support they could get. Adults informally adopted the children of parents who died or were sold and children who had been purchased. For reasons not fully understood, young African Americans were taught to address all adults of their race as "Aunt" or "Uncle." It may be that these titles of respect forged ties that would aid children if they were to lose their parents. Alternatively, this practice might simply have been a sign of good manners: For anyone to refer to an African American as "Mr." or "Mrs." was not allowed.

Displaying good manners—especially when dealing with whites—was one of the survival skills for slavery that African-American parents taught their children. Children learned to be silent about happenings in the slave quarter when whites were in earshot or if whites tried to enlist them as spies. In preparation for

Several generations congregate outside a slave cabin in Fredericksburg, Virginia. *(Massachusetts Commandery Military Order of the Loyal Legion and the U.S. Army Military History Institute)*

life's labors and punishments, parents taught their children to work hard and even administered beatings. Children who misbehaved were also warned of witches roaming the earth by night and spirits dwelling in the surrounding forests. These stories were remnants of African culture that had been preserved by the children's ancestors.

Legends and folktales taught more than proper behavior. Gathered around a hearth, listening to their elders, children acquired a heritage to pass along to later generations. They gained factual knowledge as well, such as information about life in Africa and the exploits of African-American heroes such as Nat Turner, who led a violent slave rebellion in Southampton County, Virginia, in 1831; and Pierre Dominique Toussaint Louverture, leader of the Haitian Revolution of 1802. They learned news from neighboring plantations, what slavery was like in other states, and about the North and Canada, places where all African Americans were free.

THE NECESSITIES OF LIFE

Enslaved women gave birth inside the rude cabins where they lived. A slave cabin usually consisted of a single room with a dirt floor and openings in the walls for windows. In most parts of the South, this ramshackle structure was built of logs daubed with mud and sticks, a primitive mortar that washed away in the rain. Along the Georgia coast, the preferred construction material was "tabby," a plaster concocted from burned oyster shells, lime, and sand. Some slave cabins were made of brick, and some were divided into two or three rooms. Alternatively, on a number of plantations, all of the slaves lived together in barracks.

The tables, benches, and utensils that furnished a slave cabin were all homemade. A bed was a straw mattress lying on a framework of rope or boards. A child younger than three slept with a parent or other adult, while older children slept on trundle beds that could be pushed under the adults' beds during the day or on blankets piled on the floor.

The slave quarter at the Hermitage, home of President Andrew Jackson. This scene was photographed between 1900 and 1910. *(Library of Congress)*

The section of the plantation where the slaves' housing stood was known as the quarter. On a plantation of moderate size, the quarter was often built at a distance from the "great house," where the planter and his family lived, but close to sources of water and wood for fuel. A larger plantation might have two quarters: an "upper quarter" near the fields and a "lower quarter" close to the great house.

Slaves, like the whites who owned them, consumed a diet that was limited in variety and nutritional content. Not all slave children drank milk, and many of those who did enjoyed it in the spring and summer only, when the cows' milk supply was most abundant. The typical slave diet was chronically deficient in protein, B vitamins, vitamin D, and the calories needed for hard physical labor. Only a minority of slaveholders raised enough vegetables, fruit, and livestock for their families and their slaves, so the typical weekly allocation for an adult slave was one peck of corn and three to four pounds of bacon or salt pork. Rice was substituted for corn on Atlantic coastal plantations. A child's ration was half that of an adult until he or she entered the labor force, at which time the child received an adult's food allowance. Children's health therefore frequently improved when they started working.

There is evidence that a significant number of slaves developed rickets, a softening of the bones that results from a deficiency of vitamin D. Advertisements for runaway slaves frequently describe a missing person as having crooked legs, a common sign of this disease. In addition, slave children often exhibited the distended bellies that characterize kwashiorkor, a protein deficiency. Slave owners tended to misunderstand the children's appearance, believing it to be a sign that they were thriving. Most slaveholders did not deliberately starve the children they hoped to raise into workers, though, because to do so would make poor economic sense. Instead, they acted out of ignorance, thinking that the nutritional needs of blacks differed from those of whites. For example, it was commonly believed that people of African descent thrived on pork fat rather than on high-protein, lean cuts of meat.

Enslaved families supplemented their meager fare with sweet potatoes, watermelons, and other produce from garden patches that they tended after work. Men trapped small game and fished, and men and women alike stole chickens and corn from their owners. Some enslaved people raised their own poultry and pigs.

Mothers cooked for their children at night; during the day, while their parents were in the fields, the children ate from troughs. Using their hands (or seashells if they lived along the coast), they scooped up crumbled cornbread and vegetables that may or may not have been soaked in buttermilk. Former slaves stated that it was demeaning to be fed in this way, that they felt more like livestock than human beings.

Slaves' clothing, like their diet, was inadequate. Twice a year, women field hands received cloth, buttons, thread, and a needle—the materials for making two dresses. In the spring, male field workers were issued two cotton shirts and two pairs of pants; in the fall they were given two shirts, a pair of pants, and a woolen jacket. Young children wore long shirts or smocks made of rough, low-grade linen that scratched the skin when new. Children wore nothing but these garments until the time came for them to go to work. By then most girls and boys had experienced the growth spurt of adolescence, and the smocks of childhood did little to protect their modesty. House slaves, whom the owners and their guests saw every day, received better clothing than the field hands.

INTRODUCTION TO WORK

An enslaved woman was allowed minimal time off for childbirth. She continued her duties until the time of delivery and rested for about three weeks afterward before returning to work. New mothers toiled in the fields while their babies lay nearby in the shade and took breaks for nursing three or four times a day. Breastfeeding was often prolonged when measured by current American standards. For example, the Gullah women of the South Carolina and Georgia Sea Islands nursed their babies for two or three years, as mothers in West Africa did.

From Monday through Saturday, while their parents worked, young children remained in the quarter under the care of older siblings or elderly women no longer able to plant or harvest. To teach them good work habits and keep them out of mischief, most children were assigned small jobs by the age of eight. Children between eight and 12 carried water to the field hands, cleaned yards, fetched firewood, gathered eggs, churned butter, and fed chicken and pigs. Some had duties in the great house, such as washing dishes, building fires, running errands, and waving flies away from the table. At Thomas Jefferson's Monticello, an enslaved child's first task was to care for younger siblings. Girls between 10 and 16 spun thread, while boys that age made nails. Sixteen-year-olds went into the fields or learned a trade.

In the evenings, their parents had jobs for children to do as well. Sons and daughters helped cook the evening meal and washed and mended clothing alongside their mothers. They repaired furniture and tended the family's garden. With the chores complete, while their mothers put together a lunch to carry into the fields the next day, children visited their friends in neighboring cabins.

In this watercolor sketch by William Waud, old women care for many of the plantation's children. *(The Historic New Orleans Collection, accession no. 1977.137.4.10)*

When the time came for boys and girls to enter the field as laborers, they began by doing light work: pulling weeds, clearing away stones, collecting bits of cotton that the adult pickers had overlooked, and removing worms from tobacco leaves. Training could be harsh. More than one former slave recalled being forced to eat the worms that he or she had missed. Some young people started out as "three-quarter" hands, doing about 75 percent of the work required of an adult. They might be expected to hoe 12 rows or pick 30 pounds of cotton.

A field hand's day began well before sunrise, with the sounding of a bell or horn at 4:00 A.M. to awaken the workforce. People had to be out of their cabins and on their way to the fields by 4:30, and their workday would end at dusk. Fieldwork from sunup to sundown was the pattern of a plantation slave's life from youth until old age. An elderly man on one plantation summed up the life he had known when he said, "Slave young, slave long."

Slaves on small farms worked beside their owners in the fields. Everyone pitched in to finish all of the jobs necessary to run the farm, and the slaves' standard of living differed little from that of the farmer. White observers often insisted that slaves received better treatment on small farms than on plantations, although the slaves themselves made no such distinction.

A few boys were apprenticed to enslaved artisans to learn crafts such as carpentry, woodworking, or masonry. Other children, who were selected to be

While adults operate the cotton gin, it is the child's job to provide water. *(Library of Congress)*

house servants, cleaned the great house, worked in the kitchen, or waited on the planter and his family. House servants avoided the exposure to the sun and rain that field hands endured, and they received cast-offs from the family's closet and leftovers from the table. They also perceived other benefits. One girl, for instance, liked to dust in the great house because it gave her the chance to page through books and look at the illustrations. Yet house servants often envied the field hands' regular hours. Slaveholders expected the household staff to be available at all hours to respond to their needs and whims.

CHILDHOOD GAMES

Despite deprivation and early forced labor, many former slaves remembered childhood as a happy time. Without the demands of school, unsupervised for much of the day, they chased one another through the woods, climbed trees, and waded in streams. They tossed horseshoes, walked on stilts, and, in winter, slid across frozen ponds. Marbles was a favorite game among boys, who also engaged in contests of athletic skill and games played with a ball improvised from yarn wrapped in a stocking. Girls preferred ring games, which involved standing in a circle, clapping, and dancing. Girls also played with homemade dolls, jumped rope, played house, and pretended to host dances and parties like those held in the slave quarters on holidays or observed in the great house. Children of both sexes played games that helped them understand the adult world. They preached and baptized one another, and they held mock funerals and slave auctions. The opinion prevailed among planters that the children of slaves needed time for active play if they were to grow to be strong, healthy workers.

It was not uncommon for whites to treat the children among their slaves like cherished pets. Mistresses played with them and taught them Bible stories. Masters gave them candy, small presents, and rides on their horses. Some masters saved the choicest treats for the young slaves who were their own children. (The same children, however, might also have endured abuse from the mistress, who viewed them as a living reminder of her husband's unfaithfulness.)

On Sundays, and perhaps on Saturday afternoons, adults had time off from work, and children found pleasure in the company of friends and relatives. On these days, people indulged in singing, storytelling, and social calls. If a father lived apart from his family, Sunday was the day he was likely to visit. The adults on many plantations attended religious services on Sundays, but children were often excluded from public worship. Christmas was another day of leisure, when the enslaved people enjoyed a bountiful meal and gifts from their owners. Planters gave cash and bits of finery to the adults and candy and popcorn to the children. Christmas was a day for dancing in the slave quarters, a time when whippings were less frequent.

Enslaved children experienced a degree of social equality when they engaged in games with the white children of the plantation. Although some white parents feared that the bond servants might corrupt their young, others had no objection to their children playing with slaves. The offspring of planters and slaves usually divided themselves by sex rather than race when choosing companions, and close friendships were known to develop across racial lines, although black children generally viewed themselves as faster runners, higher jumpers, and keener inventors of games than the whites.

There were benefits to befriending a planter's children. Through games of hide-and-seek with the white children, young slaves learned to count, and many white boys and girls taught their black friends to read, defying their parents and the law. White children shared food with their black playmates and occasionally helped them avoid punishment. Just as often, though, black children were reprimanded for mischief when their white friends were the true culprits.

THE MOMENT OF TRUTH

Incredibly, many African Americans spent much of childhood ignorant of the fact that they were slaves. The truth dawned for some when the white children went off to school and they were sentenced to work in the house or the fields. White girls and boys now adopted a superior attitude toward them, and they were required to address their former playmates as "Young Massa" or "Young Missus." It was not uncommon, when a close bond had formed, for a black child to become the body servant of his or her white friend.

Realization could also be brutal. Children saw that their people were at the mercy of whites when they watched a slave being whipped for one of many infractions, such as stealing, being late for the fields, working too slowly, or acting with impertinence. Occasionally slaves attempted escape, and some succeeded. Between 1825 and 1860, an estimated 100,000 people, including Frederick Douglass, managed to escape slavery and settle in the North or in Canada. Those who failed—who were hunted down by the plantation overseer and his hounds—faced severe punishment. In addition to being flogged they might be mutilated, imprisoned in stocks, handcuffed, chained, or forced to wear a cowbell around the neck. Children themselves might be beaten if they lagged behind in their duties. A child might be spanked by the mistress with a wooden paddle, a leather strap, or a rope. He or she might instead receive a thrashing from the master, with the child's head held firmly between the master's knees.

Some enslaved children were shocked into awareness of their condition when a loved one was abruptly sold or hired out, or when they themselves were sold. A few southern states prohibited the separate sale of children under 10 years of age. In states without such a law, a master was considered humane if he waited until children were at least 10 years old before selling them away from their mothers. Many children younger than 10 were sold, however, and their family ties severed.

In 1861, as their workloads grew heavier and their rations became even scantier, young slaves gained a different kind of awareness. On April 15 of that year, Confederate forces had fired on Fort Sumter, a federal installation guarding the harbor of Charleston, South Carolina. Word spread from plantation to farm that the South and the North were at war. Many slaves had no idea what a war was until they overheard whites discussing it in angry or worried tones. The sight of planters' sons leaving to join the battle lines confirmed the rumors, and sometimes so did news of the young men's deaths. The war that brought sorrow to the great house brought hope to the slave quarter. Like their elders, young slaves felt confident that this war would make them free.

CHRONICLE OF EVENTS

1619

August 20: Twenty Africans who disembark at Jamestown, Virginia, are the first Africans to live in the English colonies of North America.

1619–1682

Slave traders transport approximately 250,000 Africans to North America.

1641

Massachusetts is the first state to establish a legal basis for slavery.

1661

A Virginia law assigns African servants to their masters for the duration of their natural lives; by law, the children of slave mothers are themselves enslaved.

1750

Slavery is now legal in every colony.

1783–1807

Slave traders carry 100,000 captured Africans to southern ports.

1802

Pierre Dominique Toussaint Louverture leads the successful Haitian struggle for independence.

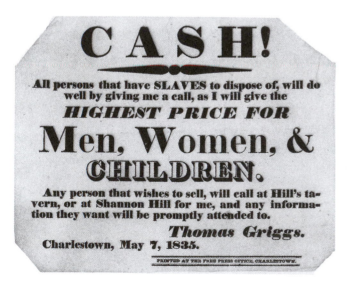

A notice informing planters that a slave trader is in town and eager to do business. *(Library of Congress)*

1804

The northern states begin the process of manumitting their slaves.

1807

The United States bans the importation of slaves.

1808

January 1: The ban on the importation of slaves takes effect.

1820–1839

Between 350,000 and 450,000 slaves are transported from the upper South to the Deep South.

1830s

Seventy-two percent of the enslaved children on the Savannah River plantation of James Henry Hammond die before age five.

1831

August 21: Nat Turner leads a violent slave rebellion in Southampton County, Virginia.

1840

There are 46,000 southern plantations employing slave labor.

1840s

Planter James Henry Hammond institutes preventive health measures; the death rate among children under age five on his plantation drops to 56 percent.

1850s

The death rate for children under five on the Hammond plantation drops further, to 26 percent.

1860

Four million slaves are held in the South; three-fourths of them farm cotton.

Five hundred thousand slaves live and work in southern cities.

1861

April 15: Confederate forces fire on Fort Sumter and touch off the American Civil War. Subsequently, enslaved children are forced to put up with a heavier workload and, because of wartime shortages, further deprivation.

EYEWITNESS TESTIMONY

My earliest employments were, to carry buckets of water to the men at work, and to hold a horse-plough, used for weeding between the rows of corn. As I grew older and taller, I was entrusted with the care of master's saddle-horse. Then a hoe was put into my hands, and I was soon required to do the day's work of a man; and it was not long before I could do it, at least as well as my associates in misery.

Josiah Henson, who spent his childhood in slavery in Charles County, Maryland, in the 1790s, An Autobiography of the Reverend Josiah Henson, *p. 19.*

. . . I grew to be a robust and vigorous lad. At fifteen years of age there were few who could compete with me in work or sport. I was as lively as a young buck, and running over with animal spirits. I could run faster, wrestle better, and jump higher than anybody about me, and at an evening shakedown in our own or a neighbor's kitchen, my feet became absolutely invisible from the rate at which they moved. All this caused my master and my fellow-slaves to look upon me as a wonderfully smart fellow, and prophecy the great things I should do when I became a man. My vanity became vastly inflamed, and I fully coincided in their opinion. Julius Caesar never aspired and plotted for the imperial crown more ambitiously than did I to out-hoe, out-reap, out-husk, out-dance, out-strip every competitor; and from all I can learn he never enjoyed his triumph half as much. One word of commendation from the petty despot who ruled over us would set me up for a month.

Josiah Henson, who was 15 years old in 1804, An Autobiography of the Reverend Josiah Henson, *p. 20.*

I slept in the same room with my master and mistress. This room was elegantly furnished with damask curtains, mahogany bedstead of the most expensive kind, and every thing else about it was of the most costly kind. And while Mr. and Mrs. Helm reposed on their bed of down, with a cloud of lace floating over them, like some Eastern prince, with their slaves to fan them while they slept, and to tremble when they awoke, I always slept upon the floor, without a pillow or even a blanket, but, like a dog, lay down anywhere I could find a place.

Austin Steward remembering his childhood in slavery ca. 1805–15, Twenty-Two Years a Slave, and Forty Years a Freeman, *pp. 26–27.*

My mother was the slave of a tobacco planter, who died when I was about four years old. My mother had several children, and they were sold upon master's death to separate purchasers. She was sold, my father told me, to a Georgia trader. I, of all her children, was the only one left in Maryland. When sold I was naked, never having had on clothes in my life, but my new master gave me a child's frock, belonging to one of his own children. After he had purchased me, he dressed me in this garment, took me before him on his horse, and started home; but my poor mother, when she saw me leaving her for the last time, ran after me, took me down from the horse, clasped me in her arms, and wept loudly and bitterly over me. My master seemed to pity her, and endeavored to soothe her distress by telling her that he would be a good master to me, and that I should not want anything. She then, still holding me in her arms, walked along the road beside the horse as he moved slowly, and earnestly and imploringly besought my master to buy her and the rest of her children, and not permit them to be carried away by the negro buyers; but whilst thus entreating him to save her and her family, the slave-driver, who had first bought her, came running in pursuit of her with a raw-hide in his hand. When he overtook us, he told her he was her master now, and ordered her to give that little negro to its owner, and come back with him.

My mother then turned to him and cried, "Oh, master, do not take me from my child!" Without making any reply, he gave her two or three heavy blows on the shoulders with his raw-hide, snatched me from her arms, handed me to my master, and seizing her by one arm, dragged her back towards the place of sale. My master then quickened the pace of his horse; and as we advanced, the cries of my poor parent became more and more indistinct—at length they died away in the distance, and I never again heard the voice of my poor mother. Young as I was, the horrors of that day sank deeply into my heart. . . . Frightened at the sight of the cruelties inflicted upon my poor mother, I forgot my own sorrows at parting from her and clung to my new master, as an angel and a saviour, when compared with the hardened fiend into whose power she had fallen.

Charles Ball recalling events occurring ca. 1808, Fifty Years in Chains, *pp. 9–11.*

The slave-boy escapes many troubles which befall and vex his white brother. . . . He is never chided for handling his little knife and fork improperly or awkwardly, for he uses none. He is never reprimanded for soiling the table-cloth, for he takes his meals on the clay floor. He never has the misfortune, in his games or sports, of soiling or tearing his clothes, for he has almost none to soil or tear. . . . To be sure, he is occasionally reminded, when he stumbles in the path of his master—and this he early learns to avoid—that he is eating his *"white bread,"* and that he will be made to *"see sights"* by-and-by. The threat is soon forgotten; the shadow soon passes, and our sable boy continues to roll in the dust, or play in the mud, as bests suits him, and in the veriest freedom. If he feels uncomfortable, from mud or from dust, the coast is clear; he can plunge into the river or the pond, without the ceremony of undressing, or the fear of wetting his clothes; his little tow-linen shirt—for that is all he has on—is easily dried; and it needed ablution as much as did his skin.

Frederick Douglass, who spent his boyhood in slavery in the 1820s, My Bondage and My Freedom, *in* Autobiographies, *pp. 144–45.*

. . . [M]y principal occupation was to nurse my little brother whilst my mother worked in the field. Almost all slave children have to do the nursing; the big take care of the small, who often come poorly off in consequence. I know this was my little brother's case. I used to lay him in the shade, under a tree, sometimes, and go to play, or curl myself up under a hedge, and take a sleep. He would wake me by his screaming, when I would find him covered with ants, or musquitos, or blistered from the heat of the sun, which having moved round whilst I was asleep, would throw the shadow of the branches in another direction, leaving the poor child quite exposed.

John Brown recalling his childhood in slavery in the 1820s, Slave Life in Georgia, *pp. 3–4.*

Our mistress Betty Moore was an old, big woman, about seventy, who wore spectacles and took snuff. I remember her very well, for she used to call us children up to the big house every morning, and give us a dose of garlic and rue [a bitter, medicinal shrub] to keep us "wholesome," as she said, and make us "grow likely for market." After swallowing our dose, she would make us run round a great sycamore tree in the yard, and if we did not run fast enough to please her, she used to make us nimbler by laying about us with a cow-hide. She always carried this instrument dangling at her side.

. . . It was painted blue, and we used to call it the "blue lizard."

John Brown recalling his childhood in slavery in the 1820s, Slave Life in Georgia, *p. 3.*

. . . [O]ur master was very cruel. I will give one instance of the fact. I and my little brother Curtis were sent up one day to the house. Passing through the grounds, where there was a large number of water-melons, they tempted us, we being very thirsty. So we took one and ate it. The value of it was not half a farthing. We did not know we were seen. [The master], however, was not far from us, and soon overtook us. He swore at us for thieving his property, and as I was the biggest, and had taken the fruit, he at once set to flogging me with the cow-hide, and continued doing so until he was tired out, and I could scarcely move. I did not get over that beating for a very long while.

John Brown recalling his childhood in slavery in the 1820s, Slave Life in Georgia, *pp. 12–13.*

There were several children in the [master's] family, and my first main business was to wait upon them. Another young slave and myself have often been compelled to sit up by turns all night, to rock the cradle of a little, peevish scion of slavery. If the cradle was stopped, the moment they awoke a dolorous cry was sent forth to mother or father, that Lewis had gone to sleep. The reply to this call, would be a direction from the mother, for these petty tyrants to get up and take the whip, and give the good-for-nothing scoundrel a smart whipping. This was the midnight pastime of a child ten or twelve years old. What might you expect of the future man?

Lewis Clarke, who spent his childhood in slavery in Kentucky in the 1820s, Narrative of the Sufferings of Lewis Clarke, *pp. 16–17.*

There were four house-slaves in this family, including myself, and though we had not, in all respects, so hard work as the field hands, yet in many things our condition was much worse. We were constantly exposed to the whims and passions of every member of the family; from the least to the greatest their anger was wreaked upon us. Nor was our life an easy one, in the hours of our toil or in the amount of labor performed. We were always required to sit up until all the family had retired; then we must be up at early dawn in summer, and before day in winter. If we failed, through weariness or for any other reason, to appear at the first morning summons, we were sure to have our hearing quickened by a severe chastisement.

Lewis Clarke, who spent his childhood in slavery in Kentucky in the 1820s, Narrative of the Sufferings of Lewis Clarke, *p. 17.*

Mrs. Banton, as is common among slave holding women, seemed to hate and abuse me all the more, because I had some of the blood of her father in my veins. There is no slaves that are so badly abused, as those that are related to some of the women—or the children of their own husband; it seems as though they never could hate these quite bad enough. My sisters were as white and good looking as any of the young ladies in Kentucky. It happened once of a time, that a young man called at the house of Mr. Campbell, to see a sister of Mrs. Banton. Seeing one of my sisters in the house and pretty well dressed, with a strong family look, he thought it was Miss Campbell, and with that supposition addressed some conversation to her which he had intended for the private ear of Miss C. The mistake was noised abroad and occasioned some amusement to young people. Mrs. Banton heard, it made her cauldron of wrath sizzling hot. . . .

She must wreak her vengeance for this innocent mistake of the young man, upon me. "She would fix me so that nobody should ever think I was white." Accordingly in a burning hot day, she *made me take off every rag of clothes, go out into the garden* and pick herbs for hours—in order to *burn* me black.

Lewis Clarke, who spent his childhood in slavery in Kentucky in the 1820s, Narrative of the Sufferings of Lewis Clarke, *pp. 20–21.*

My parents were not able to give any attention to their children during the day. I often suffered much from *hunger* and other similar causes. To estimate the sad state of a slave child, you must look at it as a helpless human being thrown upon the world without the benefit of its natural guardians. It is thrown into the world without a social circle to flee to for hope, shelter, comfort, or instruction. The social circle, with all its heaven-ordained blessings, is of the utmost importance to the *tender child;* but of this, the slave child, however tender and delicate, is robbed.

James W. C. Pennington, who spent his childhood in slavery in Maryland in the 1820s and 1830s, The Fugitive Blacksmith, *p. 2.*

There is another source of evil to slave children, which I cannot forbear to mention here, as one which early embittered my life,—I mean the tyranny of the master's children. My master had two sons, about the ages and sizes of my older brother and myself. We were not only required to recognise these young sirs as our young masters, but *they* felt themselves to be such; and, in consequence of this feeling, they sought to treat us with the same air of authority that their father did the older slaves.

James W. C. Pennington, who spent his childhood in slavery in Maryland in the 1820s and 1830s, The Fugitive Blacksmith, *pp. 2–3.*

. . . [W]hen between five and six years of age, I was assigned to the duties of housework, to wait on my mistress and to run errands. When she went out driving I had to accompany her in the capacity of a page, to open the gates and take down guard fences for her to drive through. That I might be found at night as well as by day my sleeping apartment was in her chamber on a truckbed, which was during the day time snugly concealed under her bedstead and drawn out at night for the reposing place of Isaac's weary body while he dreamed of days yet to come. I remained in this distinguished position until I was about fifteen years old. . . .

Isaac Mason describing his duties between 1827 and 1837, Life of Isaac Mason as a Slave, *p. 11.*

After various delays, the slave was put up to auction, at the end of the passage, near which four or five persons had by this time collected. There was a good deal of laughing and talking amongst the buyers, and several jests were sported on the occasion, of which their little victim took no more notice, than if he had been a horse or a dog. In fact, he was . . . a slender, delicate-looking youth, more yellow than black, with an expression every way suitable, I thought, with the forlorn situation in which he was placed—for both his parents, and all his brothers and sisters, he told me, had been long ago sold into slavery, and sent to the Southern States—Florida or Alabama—he knew not where!

Basil Hall, English traveler, describing a slave auction in the District of Columbia in 1828, Travels in North America, in the Years 1827 and 1828, *pp. 139–40.*

The slaveholders in [Maryland] often hire the children of their slaves out to non-slaveholders, not only because they save themselves the expense of taking care of them, but in this way they get among their slaves useful trades. They put a bright slave-boy with a tradesman, until he gets such a knowledge of the trade as to be able to do his own work, and then he takes him home. I remained with the stonemason until I was eleven years of age: at this time I was taken home. This was another serious period in my childhood; I was separated from my older brother, to whom I was much attached; he continued at his place, and not only learned the trade [of pump making] to great perfection, but finally became the property of the man with whom he lived, so that our separation was permanent, as we never lived nearer after, than six miles. My master owned an excellent blacksmith, who had obtained his trade in the way I have mentioned above. When I returned home at the age of eleven, I was set about assisting to do the mason-work of a new smith's shop. This being done, I was placed at the business, which I soon learned, so as to be called a "first-rate blacksmith." I continued to work at this business for nine years, or until I was twenty-one. . . .

> *James W. C. Pennington writing about the years 1828–40,* The Fugitive Blacksmith, *p. 4.*

. . . [T]he auctioneer was stopped by one of the buyers, a man whose features from the beginning had inspired me with horror, and who now, with the indifference and *sang-froid* of a real assassin, made the following observation: "The boy is good for nothing; he is not worth a day's feed. If I buy the mother, I will sell the brat immediately, at a cheap rate, to the first comer."

I cast a glance at the unfortunate mother, to observe what effect this barbarous expression might produce. She uttered not a word; but her countenance denoted profound grief and resignation. The little innocent child in her arms fixed his large dark eyes upon her, as if to ask, "Why do you weep, mother?" and then turned astonished towards those who witnessed this touching scene, with an expression which seemed to say, "What is the matter? What have ye done to my mother, since she is crying so bitterly?" I shall never forget this moment; it confirmed me for life in my former abhorrence of the traffic in human flesh.

> *Carl David Arfwedson, Swedish traveler,* The United States in 1832, 1833, and 1834, *pp. 329–30.*

Today, Tom, as we call him, entered our service. He is about fourteen years old, and we pay his master $4.50 a month. The little boy brings with him a blanket, which is all he ever had to sleep upon. He has but one shirt. Slavery is abominable in every respect.

> *Francis Lieber of Columbia, South Carolina, October 1835, in Herbert G. Gutman,* The Black Family in Slavery and Freedom, 1750–1925, *p. 600.*

My mother was very severe on me. She used to whip me nearly every night for the misdemeanors of the day. She would wait till I had undressed, and then attended to her loving boy as she used to call me.

Mothers were necessarily compelled to be severe on their children to keep them from talking too much. Many a poor mother has been whipped nearly to death on account of their children telling the white children things, who would then go and tell their mothers or fathers. My mother always told me what she was going to whip me for before commencing, and would talk to me while she was whipping me.

> *Elijah P. Marrs, who spent his childhood in slavery in Shelby County, Kentucky, in the 1840s,* History of the Rev. Elijah P. Marrs, *p. 11.*

The clothes that I wore did not amount to much, just a one piece dress or gown. In shape this was more like a gunny sack, with a hole cut in the bottom for me to stick my head thru, and the corners cut out for arm holes. We never wore underclothes, not even in the winter, and a boy was ten or twelve years old before he was given a pair of pants and a shirt to replace the sack garment. We never had more than one at a time, and when they had to be washed, we went naked until they had dried. When the garment had been worn until it would no longer hold together, or hold a patch, it was discarded and cut up for carpet rags, and another garment handed out. When one child outgrew a gown it was handed down to some one smaller. The fit was very immaterial, because there was no shape to these one piece garments, other than that of a sack. Some times old sacks were used to make these garments for the smaller children. One of these garments was made [to] last a year, and some times longer.

The cloth was of coarse home spun linen, and the thread ends and sticks in the cloth made my back sore. It had all the scratch of woolen underwear, but the scratching was worse, as the thread was more like the separate strands of a hemp rope. I always dreaded to put on a new dress—I suppose I should call it a dress—and used to ask my brother William, who was two years older than I, to wear mine for me and break it in so it wouldn't scratch so bad.

Robert Anderson, who spent his childhood in slavery in Kentucky in the 1840s and 1850s, From Slavery to Affluence, *pp. 7–8.*

Have lost another negro child. Did ever one poor mortal have so many deaths around him. For ten years I have been working hard, overwhelmed with anxiety and care and all I have made has been regularly swept off by death.... Great God what have I done. Never was a man so cursed! ... Thirteen deaths and 3 still births in 10 months in a population of 160 [slaves] is unparalleled. Ten percent. Good heavens they have been decimated. And so it has been for 10 long years.... It crushes me to the earth to see every thing of mine so blasted around me. Negroes, cattle, mules, hogs, every thing that has life around me seems to labour under some fated malediction.

James Henry Hammond, South Carolina planter, November 2, 1841, Sweet and Sacred, *pp. 78–79.*

I was only in the yard a short time before I was bought by one George Reid who lived in Richmond.... [His home] was surrounded with shrubbery, and was a pleasant country seat. But I did not like it here. I grieved continually about my mother. It came to me, more and more plainly, that I would never see her again. Young and lonely as I was, I could not help crying, oftentimes for hours together. It was hard to get used to being away from my mother. I remember well "Aunt Sylvia," who was the cook in the Reid household. She was very kind to me and always spoke consolingly to me, especially if I had been blue, and had had one of my fits of crying. At these times she would always bake me an ash cake for supper, saying to me: "My child, don't cry; 'Aunt Sylvia' will look after you." This ash cake was made of corn meal and water, a little salt to make it palatable, and was baked by putting it between cabbage leaves and covering it with hot ashes. A sweeter or more delicious cake one could not desire, and it was common upon the tables of all the Virginia farmers. I always considered it a great treat to get one of these cakes from "Aunt Sylvia."

Louis Hughes, who was sold to George Reid in the early 1840s, Thirty Years a Slave, *pp. 9–11.*

The earliest impressions that I can now recall, are of the slave quarters on the old plantation. This was where the slaves had their cabins, little one room log huts, for the most part, with the slaves housed in these huts pretty much as pigs in a pen, one family to a room, and some times two or three. There were few beds, the slaves sleeping for the most part on the floors on a pile of straw or a shuck mattress. There were no chairs and what few tables there were, were made of packing boxes or slabs. There were no luxuries, no conveniences, and no privacy. These conditions were so, not because my master was especially cruel, for he was not. It was merely the custom of the times, when it was thot that the colored race needed no more care than a hog or cow, and got considerably less than a horse.

Robert Anderson, who was born into slavery in 1843, From Slavery to Affluence, *p. 3.*

I remember, when I was but four years old, how I used to steal away from home and stay until the dark would drive me in. The white boys and colored boys would leave home soon in the morning and rove the woods through during the summer time.

We had the dog-fennel for our hiding-place, and often the whole family would be in an uproar to know where we were. We would get a flogging when we returned, but the next day we would be gone again.

Elijah P. Marrs, who was four years old in 1844, History of the Rev. Elijah P. Marrs, *pp. 9–10.*

Our folks were ... hired out to work in the tobacco factories at Keytesville [Missouri], except the old women, and such children as were too small to be put to work. I was left at this place with my mother and her younger children and was happy. I was too young to be put to work, and there being on the farm four or five boys about my age, spent my time with them hunting and fishing. There was a creek near by in which we caught plenty of fish. We made lines of hemp grown on the farm and hooks of bent pins. When we got a bite, up went the pole and quite often the fish, eight or ten feet in the air....

There was game in abundance, but our hunting was always for young rabbits and squirrels, and we hunted them with hounds.... I had never before seen so many squirrels. The trees there were usually small and too far apart for them to jump from tree to tree, and when we saw one "treed" by the dogs, one of us climbed up and forced it to jump, and when it did, in nine cases out of ten the dogs would catch it. We often got six or eight in a day's hunting.

Another sport which we enjoyed was gathering the eggs of prairie chickens. On account of the danger of snake bites, we were somewhat restricted in the pursuit of this pleasure, being forbidden to go far away from the cabins. Their eggs were not quite as large as the domestic hen's, but are of a very fine flavor.

H. C. Bruce remembering his activities in 1844, when he was eight years old, The New Man, *pp. 17–18.*

I was but a lad, yet I can remember well the cruel treatment I received. Some weeks it seemed I was whipped for nothing, just to please my mistress' fancy. Once, when I was sent to town for the mail and had started back, it was so dark and rainy my horse got away from me and I had to stay all night in town. The next morning when I got back home I had a severe whipping, because the master was expecting a letter containing money and was disappointed in not receiving it that night. . . .

Louis Hughes writing about an incident occurring ca. 1845, Thirty Years a Slave, *p. 19.*

About January 1, 1845, my mother and her children, including myself and those younger, were hired to one James Means, a brickmaker, living near Huntsville, Randolph County, Missouri. I remember the day when he came after us with a two-horse team. He had several children, the eldest being a boy. Although Cyrus was a year older than I, he could not lick me. He and I had to feed the stock and haul trees to be cut into wood for fire, which his father had felled in the timber. Mr. Means also owned a girl about fourteen years old called Cat, and as soon as spring came he commenced work on the brick yard with Cat and me as off bearers. This, being my first real work, was fun for a while, but soon became very hard and I got whipped nearly every day, not because I did not work, but because I could not stand it. Having to carry a double mold all day long in the hot sun I broke down. Finally Mr. Means made for my special benefit two single molds, and after that I received no more punishment from him.

H. C. Bruce, who was hired out to James Means in 1845, the year he turned nine, The New Man, *pp. 20–21.*

In January 1846, with my older brothers I was hired to Judge Applegate, who conducted a tobacco factory at Keytesville, Missouri. I was then about ten years old. . . . I was kept busy every minute from sunrise to sunset, without being allowed to speak a word to anyone. I was too young then to be kept in such close confinement. It was so prison-like to be compelled to sit during the entire year under a large bench or table filled with tobacco, and tie lugs all day long except during the thirty minutes allowed for breakfast and the same time allowed for dinner. I often fell asleep. I could not keep awake even by putting tobacco into my eyes. I was punished by the overseer, a Mr. Blankenship, every time he caught me napping, which was quite often during the first few months.

H. C. Bruce, who was hired out to Judge Applegate in 1846, the year he turned 10, The New Man, *pp. 21–22.*

After I became seven or eight years old I was made a dining-room boy. I remember how Brother Henry and I used to steal the biscuits off the plates while carrying them into the dining-room, and how they would burn us while hot in our pockets. In those days the colored people hardly knew the taste of wheat bread. The white boys used to make trades with the colored boys; for instance, I would have a marble he wanted; he would say to me, "I will give you a seldom for that marble." He meant that he would give me a biscuit with butter on it; that he would save a portion of what he was to eat to pay his debt.

Elijah P. Marrs, who was seven years old in 1847, History of the Rev. Elijah P. Marrs, *p. 10.*

I had been taught the alphabet while in Missouri and could spell "baker," "lady," "shady," and such words of two syllables, and Willie [Perkinson, the master's son] took great pride in teaching me his lessons of each day from his books, as I had none and my mother had no money to buy any for me. This continued for about a year before the boy's aunt . . . found it out, and . . . she raised a great row with our master about it. She insisted that it was a crime to teach a Negro to read, and that it would spoil him, but our owner seemed not to care anything about it and did nothing to stop it, for afterward I frequently had him correct my spelling. In after years I learned that he was glad that his Negroes could read, especially the Bible, but he was opposed to their being taught writing. . . .

Feb. 1866 – Laura M. Towne
Dick, Maria, Amoretta

As Union forces occupied Confederate territory during the Civil War, northern teachers traveled south to educate the former slaves. In 1862 Laura M. Towne founded a school for newly freed children on St. Helena Island, South Carolina. She is shown here with three students in 1866. *(From the Penn School Collection. Permission granted by Penn Center, Inc., St. Helena Island, S.C.)*

Willie Perkinson had become as one of us and regarded my mother as his mother. He played with the colored boys from the time he got home from school till bedtime, and again in the morning till time to go to school, and every Saturday and Sunday.

H. C. Bruce, who was transported from Missouri to Virginia in 1847 and befriended Willie Perkinson in that year, The New Man, *pp. 25–26.*

When my mother was sold, I had one brother, William, and three sisters, Silva, Agga, and Emma. . . .

When mother was taken from us, Emma was a baby three years old. Silva, the oldest of the children, was fourteen, and she was a mother to the rest of us children. She took my mother's place in the kitchen as cook for my boss. Working under the direction of the boss's wife, or "Missis" as we called her, my sister bought provisions, cooked the meals, knitted and sewed for the plantation. . . .

It was part of sister's work to run the spinning wheel and the loom to prepare the cloth, and to cut and sew the cloth into clothes for the plantation and for the boss'es family. My other sisters had to help with this work, but Silva, being the oldest, was forced to shoulder all the responsibility.

Silva would sit up until late hours of the night, working, and then would have to be up early in the morning to do the cooking for the family. Not only did she work, herself, but she made me work, too. Altho I was six years old when mother was taken away, she had taught me a number of things. My sister continued this education. She taught me how to patch my own clothes (such as I had), to piece quilts, to braid foot mats out of corn shucks, and to make horse collars stuffed with corn shucks.

Robert Anderson, who was six years old in 1849, From Slavery to Affluence, *pp. 5–6.*

Part of my duty as a child, working under the direction of my sister was to carry the food from the kitchen to the table. As our fare was always meager, and I was always hungry, I would some times shake the biscuit plate, or stump my toe an[d] let a biscuit fall on the ground or floor. After it had fallen on the floor, of course no one would eat it, and I would get it. I would carry them back to the kitchen and tell my sister what happened. I usually got my ears boxed, or got spanked, but I always got the biscuit.

Robert Anderson, who commenced working in the plantation kitchen in 1849, From Slavery to Affluence, *p. 9.*

We didn' have nothin' extra-ordinary in de way of play-things. De big boys make thread balls—wind balls of thread, you know—an' after dey play wid 'em a while an' dey git ter frazzlin', we little fellers would git 'em. We thought dey was fine. But most of de time, we didn' play wid things, we jes play; sing an' march aroun' an' pat an' clap hands dis-er-way:

"Oh, yes, we'll gain de day,
Oh, yes, we'll gain de day,
Oh, yes, we'll gain de day
Po' sinners, flockin' home!"

Sam Broach recalling his childhood in South Carolina in the 1850s, in George P. Rawick, ed., The American Slave: A Composite Biography, *Supplement, Series 1, Vol. 6,* Mississippi Narratives, Part 1, *p. 223.*

There were about 162 slaves on the plantation, and every Sunday morning, all the children had to be bathed, dressed, and their hair combed, and carried down to the Marster's for breakfast. It was a rule that all the little colored children eat at the great house every Sunday morning in order that Marster and Missus could watch them eat, so they could know which ones were sickly and have them doctored.

The slave children all carried a mussel shell in their hands to eat with. The food was put on large trays and the children all gathered around and ate, dipping up their food with their mussel shells, which they used for spoons. Those who refused to eat or those who were ailing in any way had to come back to the great house for their meals and medicine until they were well.

Mary Anderson of North Carolina describing her childhood in slavery from 1851, the year of her birth, through 1865, in Belinda Hurmence, ed., My Folks Don't Want Me to Talk about Slavery, *pp. 45–46.*

Ole mammy Lit wus mi'ty old and she lived in de corner uf de big yard an' she keered fur all de black chulluns while de old folks wurked in de fiel', an' de biggest chulluns had to help mammy Lit wid de lil'l ones. Mammy Lit wud spread a quilt on de gallery an' put de babies on de floor an' we had to keep de chaps frum gittin' off de pallet an' rollin' off de gallery. Mammy Lit smoked a pipe, an' I l'arnt to hide dat pipe, an' she wud slap me fur it, den sumtimes I wud run 'way an' go to de kitchen whar my mammy wus an' mammy Lit wud hafter cum fur me an' den she wud whup me er gin. . . .

Ebery day dar wus a pan uf milk poured in a big trough in frunt uf mammy Lit's house, under a shed, fur all uf de lil'l black chulluns; dat milk had bread crumbled in it. Ebery one uf us had a spoon an' we wud dip inter it an' see who cud git de most. Mammy Lit wud hit me ober de head an' tell me not to be so greedy an' eat it all up frum de udders.

Barney Alford, who spend the first 12 years of his life, 1853–65, enslaved in Mississippi, in George Rawick, ed., The American Slave: A Composite Biography, *Supplement, Series 1, Vol. 6,* Mississippi Narratives, Part 1, *pp. 39–40.*

My ole Mistess sot a big pan out in de yard wid potlicker and ash-cake and us got 'roun' hit and et and hit was "who shall, and who shan't, who got dare fust." Us was called shirt-tale fellows and dey was made at home and hung below our knees, outer orsanburg. Us had shoemakers too what killed cows and tanned de leather and when de seven months crop was laid by, de shoemaker made a pair shoes around. Fust I ever had was just as full of tacks and pegs as could be, but I had to have dem shoes, I was so skeered somebody'd show git 'em ef you left dem out, so I slept wid dem.

Abraham Chambers, who spent the first 11 years of his life, 1854–65, enslaved in Alabama, in George P. Rawick, ed., The American Slave: A Composite Biography, *Supplement, Series 1, Vol. 1,* Alabama Narratives, *p. 86.*

I used to steal sometimes,—sugar and coffee. I was the house boy and had to clean up the pantry storeroom. I would cut all the meats up for them to eat. They ate ham. The Negroes' meat was side and occasionally they would give us the shoulder meat. But ham was white folks' meat, and if you got any you would have to steal it; and I was good at that. They would put the hams up in the upper part of the pantry, and there was a hole up there about the size of a brick, and I would cut meat and cut ham and put them through this hole. . . .

A former slave, identified only as Charlie, recalling his life in Tennessee ca. 1855, when he was 12 years old, in Unwritten History of Slavery, *pp. 95–96.*

We lived in de house, in one room, wid Marster Cole, as mah mother was de nurse and housekeeper. We always had a good bed ter sleep in and good things ter eat. We would eat at de same table as Marster Cole and his family eat at, only after dey gits through eatin' first.

I was raised up wid de Cole chilluns and played wid dem all de time. We was all de time climbin' trees in de yard, and as I gits older, dey jest gradually puts more work and heavier work on me. Marster Cole started us out workin' by totin' in wood and kindlin' and totin' water and jest sech odd jobs. Den, later on, as we got older, we had ter feed de hogs, de cows, horses, goats, and chickens. All dis kind of work was fer boys too young fer heavy work. Of course, we had ter pick cotton every fall, as soon as we got big enough ter pick, and put de cotton in baskets. Dese baskets would hold 'bout seventy-five ter one hundred pounds. De little chilluns would pick and put de cotton in a basket wid some older person, so de older person could move de basket 'long.

Thomas Cole, who was a slave in Jackson County, Alabama, recalling his life ca. 1855–60, in James Mellon, Bullwhip Days, *pp. 55–56.*

I own a woman who cost me $400 when a girl, in 1827. Admit she made me nothing—only worth her victuals and clothing. She now has three children, worth over $3000 and have been field hands say three years; in that time making enough to pay their expenses before they were half hands, and then I have the profit of all half hands. She has only three boys and a girl out of a dozen; yet, with all her bad management, she has paid me ten per cent. interest, for her work was to be an average good, and I would not this night touch $700 for her. Her oldest boy is worth $1250 cash, and I can get it.

Unidentified farmer, 1858, in the Southern Cultivator, *in Wilma King,* Stolen Childhood, *p. 2.*

The early years of my life, which were spent in the little cabin, were not very different from those of thousands of other slaves. My mother, of course, had little time in which to give attention to the training of her children during the day. She snatched a few moments for our care in the early morning before her work began, and at night after the day's work was done. One of my earliest recollections is that of my mother cooking a chicken late at night, and awakening her children for the purpose of feeding them. How or where she got it I do not know. I presume, however, it was procured from our owner's farm. Some people may call this theft. If such a thing were to happen now, I should condemn it as theft myself. But taking

place at the time it did, and for the reason that it did, no one could ever make me believe that my mother was guilty of thieving. She was simply a victim of the system of slavery. I cannot remember having slept in a bed until after our family was declared free by the Emancipation Proclamation. Three children—John, my older brother, Amanda, my sister, and myself—had a pallet on the dirt floor, or, to be more correct, we slept in and on a bundle of filthy rags laid upon the dirt floor.

Booker T. Washington writing about his life ca. 1860, Up from Slavery, *pp. 8–9.*

I was small in slavery time, and played with the white chaps. Once [the master] saw me and some other chaps, white chaps, under a tree playing with letter blocks. They had the ABCs on them. Marster got awful mad and got off his horse and whipped me good.

Milton Marshall of South Carolina recalling an occurrence ca. 1860, in Belinda Hurmence, ed., Before Freedom, When I Just Can Remember, *p. 43.*

I was too small to work. They had me do little things like feeding the chickens and minding the table sometimes; but I was too small to work. They didn't let children work much in them days till they were thirteen or fourteen years old. We played base, cat, rolly hole, and a kind of baseball called 'round town. Marster would tell the children about Raw Head and Bloody Bones and other things to scare us. He would call us to the barn to get apples and run and hide, and we would have a time finding him. He give the one who found him an apple. Sometimes he didn't give the others no apple.

Isaac Johnson of North Carolina, born in 1855, recalling his life ca. 1860–65, in Belinda Hurmence, ed., My Folks Don't Want Me to Talk about Slavery, *pp. 21–22.*

We used to play a game we called "smut," but we would play it with corn spots instead of cards. We played it just like you would with cards only we would have grains of corn and call them hearts and spades, and so forth, and go by the spots on the corn. We would play marbles too, and . . . our biggest amusement was running through the woods, climbing trees, hunting grapes and berries and so forth. We would play peeping squirrel too. We would say, "Peep, squirrel, peep dibble, dibble, dibble; walk, squirrel, walk, dibble, dibble, dibble; then run, squirrel, run, dibble, dibble, dibble; and we would run after the squirrel (child)."

Unidentified former slave recalling games she played ca. 1861, when she was eight or nine years old, in Unwritten History of Slavery, *p. 15.*

The first cannon I heard scared me near about to death. We could hear them going boom, boom. I thought it was thunder, then Miss Polly [the mistress] say, "Listen, Sarah, hear them cannons? They's killing our mens." Then she begun to cry.

I run in the kitchen where Aunt Charity was cooking and told her Miss Polly was crying. She said, "She ain't crying 'cause the Yankees killing the mens; she's doing all that crying 'cause she scared we's going to be set free."

Sarah Debro of North Carolina, who was born in the 1850s, describing occurrences ca. 1864, in Belinda Hurmence, ed., My Folks Don't Want Me to Talk about Slavery, *p. 57.*

4

A National Crisis: The Civil War 1861–1865

Ten-year-old Dan Beard saw Abraham Lincoln in the closing weeks of 1860, when the president-elect visited Cincinnati, Ohio. Although his father had voted against the Republican, Dan stood with his mother, his Aunt Belle, and his cousin Tom to cheer Lincoln as he rode up Mound Street in an open carriage. Watching the tall, frock-coated man wave to the crowd, young Dan sensed that he was in the presence of a great human being. Soon Dan Beard was weaving through the throng of gleeful, shouting men who trotted alongside the barouche. As he worked his way to a spot from which he could view the future president's face, Lincoln turned and smiled down on him, and Dan dared to think that his father had supported the wrong candidate.

The excitement of Lincoln's visit allowed the people of Cincinnati to forget the issues of slavery and states' rights that were dividing their nation, if only for a little while. Soon seven southern states—South Carolina, Mississippi, Florida, Alabama, Georgia, Louisiana, and Texas—reacted to Lincoln's election by seceding from the Union and tearing the country in two.

To Lincoln, secession had no legal defense, yet in his inaugural address, delivered on March 4, 1861, he promised only to "hold, occupy, and possess" forts in the South that were still under Union control. War came quickly, though. Lincoln's effort on April 12 to resupply Fort Sumter, in the harbor of Charleston, South Carolina, led to a Confederate attack and the loss of that installation. Immediately, the president called for 75,000 volunteers. Meanwhile, four states— Virginia, Arkansas, Tennessee, and North Carolina—joined the seven that had already seceded.

The war fought to reunite the nation was a decisive event in U.S. history, affecting every person living in the North and South. Although the 20th century would bring wars of global proportions, for Americans they would be distant conflicts. The Civil War, however, was waged on native soil. American civilians witnessed the carnage firsthand and nursed the casualties of battle. Many—especially in the South—saw their homes, farms, and cities plundered or destroyed. At least 620,000 Americans died in the Civil War, more than in all 20th-century wars combined.

The U.S. population was young in 1861, when the Civil War began. One-third of the nation's people were children. These children actively participated in the war effort, both on the home front and on the battlefield.

THE FIRST HEADY DAYS

People south and north put on a show of optimism in the opening months of the war. When William H. Seward, Lincoln's secretary of state, predicted that the sectional dispute would be resolved within 60 days of the Inauguration, northerners took his words to heart. Southerners bragged that they would teach the Yankees a swift lesson.

Children and adults hurrahed and waved hats and flags as newly formed regiments paraded down Main Streets, ready to march off to war. Boys ran beside the recruits or scrambled up trees and lampposts for a broader view. Towns were transformed as trains packed with soldiers rolled through and army camps were hastily built nearby. One such spot, Camp Butler, training ground for thousands of soldiers during the four years of war, was located seven miles northeast of Springfield, Illinois. As soon as it opened in August 1861, it became a popular attraction. Springfield's children accompanied their parents to the camp—in family-owned carriages or on the omnibuses that now made regular trips to the training grounds—for a day of picnicking and watching military drills.

The war's impact became more direct for the thousands of children whose fathers, older brothers, and other male relatives enlisted in the armed forces. After the Union troops were put into flight in the First Battle of Bull Run, on July 21, 1861, and the North set out to raise a more substantial army, it was evident to people on both sides that the war would not be brief and that separations from loved ones were likely to be long.

The mail, which at best was unreliable, became the only link between men in the military and their wives and children. Children sent assurances that they were healthy and thriving and that things were fine at home. Many came to think of their fathers as remote, unseen figures whose missives contained not only reminiscences and words of affection but also instructions about proper behavior and work needing to be done. Fathers admonished children to study hard; they listed tasks to be performed to keep the family farm running. Men also tried to make their children understand their reasons for enlisting. They wrote about duty to their country, which in this time of crisis superceded their responsibilities at home.

Some fathers described the hard realities of army life—the hunger, weariness, and loneliness—and the horrors of the battlefield. One Union soldier trying to capture in words the scene following the battle at Shiloh, Tennessee, on April 7, 1862, wrote to his children about a field littered with corpses and dead horses. Similar letters home contained mementoes that children would treasure, such as spent bullets and bits of exploded shell.

BOYS IN UNIFORM

The armies of the North and South welcomed not only men but boys as well. The U.S. armed forces were permitted by law to accept recruits between the ages of 18 and 45, but boys younger than 18 were often able to slip in. Irregular record keeping in the 19th century, coupled with the absence of standardized personal identification, made it extremely difficult for recruiting officers to verify a candidate's age. Also, because a regiment needed a minimum number of men before it could be mustered into service, many officers never bothered to ask. There was no minimum age for musicians in the U.S. military until 1864, when the federal government required them to be at least 16, so a large number of youthful enlistees signed on as drummer boys. A boy named Edward Black joined the 21st Indiana Regiment as a musician when he was nine. The Union army enlisted more than 40,000 musicians, and the Confederates employed half as many.

The number of boys who served in uniform during the Civil War is unknown. According to some estimates, nearly 20 percent of all soldiers fighting for the Union and the Confederacy were under 18. A study published by the U.S. Sanitary Commission's Statistical Bureau in 1866 concluded that 1.5 percent of enlisted men and 3.33 percent of officers in the Union army were under 18 or over 45. Another study, this one conducted by U.S. Army statisticians after the war, matched available birth certificates with selected battalion rosters and determined that between 10 percent and 20 percent of soldiers included in the study were underage at the time of their enlistment.

No such surveys were conducted on the Confederate troops, so the number of underage soldiers in southern units is almost impossible to determine. Information about individual boy soldiers abounds, though. Charles T. Haigh of Fayetteville, North Carolina, was typical of many southern boys who enlisted. After learning of the Union victory at Gettysburg, Pennsylvania, in July 1863, he left the private military academy that he was attending and, although only 15, volunteered as a private in a North Carolina regiment. He survived the Battle of the Wilderness, which was waged on thickly forested land near Chancellorsville, Virginia, in May 1864, but died in a charge on the enemy at Spotsylvania Court House, Virginia, several days later. The youngest Confederate soldier may have been George S. Lamkin of Winona, Mississippi, who joined the army on August 2, 1861, when he was 11, and was badly wounded at Shiloh, Tennessee. Lamkin, who was exceedingly tall for his age when he enlisted, survived the war and attained an adult height of six feet, four inches.

If patriotism inspired many boys to enlist, so did the promise of adventure and the urge to escape the dulling routine of the farm. Boys soon learned that much of army life followed its own standard course as they spent hours drilling and days marching across the countryside. The realities of war confronted them abruptly, often in the form of gun and cannon fire, alarming in its loudness but not loud enough to awaken the dead men they came upon, lying where they had fallen in battle. With this first loss of innocence, many boys were sickened; they thought fondly of home and regretted having enlisted.

When they came under direct fire, though, there was no time for pity—for themselves or anyone else. Boy soldiers followed orders, shooting at the enemy and watching comrades fall. The battlefield hardened boys; seeing the dead became commonplace, and boys who once turned away in disgust from shattered corpses eventually scavenged among the dead for boots, uniforms, and equipment.

Drummers saw action too. It was their job to communicate orders to the soldiers on the field, and they served as markers, helping the fighting men keep track of their units. For these reasons, drummers frequently came under attack. They were also known to play an active role in combat, especially when casualties were heavy or enemy fire had damaged their drums. One of the most famous

Union drummer Johnny Clem *(National Archives)*

Union drummer boys, Johnny Clem, claimed to have fought with a musket in the Battle of Shiloh, although his participation in that conflict has never been verified. Clem had run away from home in May 1861, at age 10, and tagged along with an Ohio unit as its unofficial drummer. The regiment's officers chipped in to pay his wages.

Most drummers remained in their noncombat roles, though. In camp they curried horses, carried water to soldiers in their tents, collected firewood, trimmed beards, sharpened surgeons' instruments, and helped with cooking. In the aftermath of battle, they were assigned to the burial detail. The Civil War was the last armed conflict in which the United States employed drummers. Technological advances in weaponry would change the way soldiers fought in subsequent wars. As smaller fighting units and trench warfare became state of the art, drumming was deemed impractical and outmoded. The Civil War was also the last conflict in which a significant number of boys fought for the United States.

But because boys did fight in the Civil War, they were among those killed, wounded, and taken prisoner. Prison confronted boys with hunger, crowding, disease, and deprivation—further horrors of war. The most infamous Civil War prison was Andersonville, Georgia, a 40-acre death camp. Of more than 49,000 men and boys imprisoned at Andersonville between February 1864 and April 1865, at least 13,700 died in confinement. The death rate was highest in October 1864, when one of every two prisoners died of starvation, disease, or lingering battlefield wounds. Most soldiers imprisoned at Andersonville slept on the open ground without blankets or shelter. They were exposed to all kinds of weather, from blistering sun to torrential storms. Given almost nothing to eat and forced to drink contaminated water, prisoners became ill and resembled walking skeletons. Men were known to commit suicide by making brazen escape attempts so that the Confederate guards would shoot them on the spot.

With youth and strength on their side, some boys survived imprisonment by killing and eating rats or by trading brass uniform buttons and other negotiables to the guards for food. Priests and Sisters of Charity ministering to patients in the prison hospital at Andersonville paid special attention to the boys in their care, slipping them extra food and items of clothing.

A DISTANT CONFLICT

Most northern children experienced the war from afar. They sang patriotic songs in school and read about battles and troop movements in letters, newspapers, and illustrated weeklies. Ida M. Tarbell, who was born in November 1857, read about the war in *Harper's Weekly* and other magazines at her home in the oil region of Pennsylvania. The future muckraking journalist studied the facts, but the wider implications of wartime events eluded her. She wrote that "none of it went behind my eyes—none concerned me."

Children also accompanied their parents to community meetings, where they listened to political speeches. At home they attempted through play to master the information they were absorbing. Boys chose sides to reenact battle scenes, and boys and girls alike gave mock orations, mimicking the fine figures of speech heard in public forums.

Throughout the North, people in churches, schools, and homes made and collected goods for the men at the front. Children participated directly in the war effort by bringing gifts of food and blankets when they visited soldiers in camp. They knitted socks for the soldiers and scraped linen to create lint that would be used to pack battlefield wounds. (A zealous public that misunderstood the surgeon general of the army's call for lint also sent off hundreds of tons of cotton lint that could not be used and was discarded.)

Many children took part in fundraising fairs organized by the U.S. Sanitary Commission, a private organization dedicated to procuring supplies and medical care for the troops, improving the diet and hygiene of the men in uniform, and organizing army hospitals. Attending to the soldiers' health needs was a mammoth task, one that was beyond the ability of the federal government to accomplish.

Sanitary Commission fairs featured parades, entertainment, and the sale of handcrafted items, produce, beer, cider, and other refreshments. The fair held in Chicago in October 1863 was a gala event that shut down the city. Government offices, banks, and schools closed to let workers and children attend the festivities. Three hundred people could sit down at once in the fair's great dining hall, while others toured the art gallery and curiosity shop. The celebration reached a high point when the original manuscript of the Emancipation Proclamation was sold at auction. That one sale accounted for $3,000 of the $78,682.89 raised in Chicago to aid the fighting forces.

When the Sanitary Commission held a fair in New York City's Union Square Building in April 1864, an entire wing was designated the Children's Department. It contained booths and displays created by students from public and private schools and items made for sale by children from the Hebrew Orphan Asylum, the Deaf and Dumb Asylum, the Wilton Industrial School, and other institutions. Children orphaned by the war were on display, too.

Some children held neighborhood fairs to raise money for local regiments and specific hospitals. They set up patriotic displays on porch tables and sold fruit, cake, lemonade, and a variety of handcrafted items, such as pincushions, paper lanterns, embroidered towels, and dolls.

Few northern children experienced battle directly. The young people living in the crossroads town of Gettysburg, Pennsylvania, were among those who did. Gettysburg's children joined the other townspeople who lined up to greet the Union cavalry units that rode into town on June 30, 1863. Confederate troops—part of an invasion force led by General Robert E. Lee—had marched into Gettysburg four days earlier, having heard a false rumor that the town held a supply of shoes. Teenage boys eagerly sought out the Union camp and rode the soldiers' tired horses to a watering creek.

The next morning, children spilled outdoors to watch the day's fighting, but the first gunfire sent them scurrying home. As reinforcements arrived, it became clear that a major battle was taking shape. Many of Gettysburg's children spent the three days of conflict—July 1–3—sheltered in cellars. Some sat and cried, while others peered out windows for a glimpse of the action. An adventurous 13-year-old who lived at a safe distance watched the battle from a roof. The experience, he said, was "the sensation of a lifetime."

After the guns and cannons grew silent, Gettysburg's citizens emerged from their hiding places to witness a scene of death and suffering greater than anything they could have imagined. The bodies of soldiers and horses lay everywhere—in peach orchards, trampled wheat fields, and kitchen gardens. Ten-year-old Charles Curdy stepped outdoors to be shocked by the sight of bodies that had fallen beside the front porch of his home. Thousands of wounded men lay among the dead, moaning and calling for help. The people of Gettysburg moved the wounded from both armies into barns, sheds, and homes and cared for them as well as they could. Children brought water to the wounded soldiers, nursed them, and befriended them. They observed numerous amputations, as surgeons sawed off damaged limbs in an attempt to prevent infection.

Boys took paying jobs helping to bury the dead. More than 6,000 men had died in the battle, and more died every day from wounds or disease. The men who died in combat were buried where they lay, their names, if known, penciled on wooden markers thrust into the earth beside them. Enterprising children collected souvenirs of the battle to sell to the curious visitors who descended on the town. Tree branches containing embedded bullets were big sellers. Young people also gathered unexploded shells to sell; lead for making shells was in short supply.

One civilian, a woman, died in the Battle of Gettysburg. All of the town's children survived.

HARSHER CONDITIONS IN THE CONFEDERACY

Most Civil War battles were fought in the South, so Confederate children gained a more intimate knowledge of warfare than the young did in the North.

Throughout the war, the people of Charleston, South Carolina, endured almost constant shelling from the Union fleet. Many residents left the city; others moved out of range of the shells. In the meantime, the population that remained grew accustomed to the assault and attempted to live as normally as possible. A 15-year-old from a small town who visited his uncle in Charleston in November 1863 was astounded to see diners ignore the noise of shelling and continue to eat their meal.

To survive the 47-day siege of Vicksburg, Mississippi, which began on May 19, 1863, many families burrowed into the hills that lay to the north, east, and south of town. Some of the 500 newly dug earthen caves around Vicksburg had several rooms and were furnished with carpeting, beds, and rocking chairs lugged from home. A number of evacuees even brought slaves to serve them; still, life in this human "prairie-dog city" was anything but comfortable. Children learned to sleep through the deafening sounds of heavy bombardment, and they sweated in the damp darkness as the weather grew brutally hot in June.

Civilian deaths at Vicksburg numbered about 11, and three dozen civilians were injured in the fighting. Both totals included children. Children were shot dead while emerging from the caves or running to them for shelter. An African-American girl was severely injured when she picked up an unexploded shell that had fallen into a yard. A shell that burst in a cave wall buried another child under six feet of earth. Her mother and other adults dug out her head, pulled her free, and were grateful to see that her only injuries were minor ones.

The Confederacy became a nation of refugees as civilians sought safer locations in which to live out the war. People fleeing the besieged town of Fredericksburg, Virginia, in December 1862, headed for Richmond, joining the human stream flowing into that city from the surrounding countryside. In Georgia, farmers and villagers swarmed into Atlanta in July 1864, just as many residents were leaving to escape Union general William T. Sherman's army and heading for the southwestern part of the state.

Refugees from Arkansas and Louisiana who had abandoned their homes in advance of invading Union forces crowded towns in the eastern and coastal sections of Texas in 1862. The influx caused housing shortages, as towns such as Waco, Tyler, and Marshall doubled and tripled in population. In Houston's hotel, paying guests slept two to a bed. Well-to-do émigrés viewed Texas, a state of little strategic importance to the Union, as a safe haven for their families, but adults and children were repelled by the crude conditions of life there. Children complained about their makeshift accommodations; they openly pined for clean water for drinking and bathing and well-cooked, nutritious food. Like children throughout the South who were accustomed to the luxury of enslaved servants, young refugees in Texas learned to do many things for themselves. They swept porches, trimmed candles, and even dressed themselves for the first time.

The coarseness of the native Texans elicited children's comments. In imitation of their parents, young people looked with disapproval on women who

Southern whites pack up to flee the approaching Union army. *(Library of Congress)*

smoked cigars and tipped back in their chairs like men. But at least one young girl described the period she spent in Texas as an adventure, as one of the happiest times in her life.

The overcrowding in Texas intensified the shortages of food and consumer products that people were experiencing throughout the Confederacy. The agricultural South had long been a market for goods from the industrial North. Now the Confederates were unable to buy from northern producers, and a Union blockade of southern ports prevented European ships from docking. Blockade runners filled some of the demand in cities; nevertheless, throughout the South, meat, leather, soap, candles, ink, paper, cloth, and medicine were chronically in short supply. People learned to make bread from ground, dried peas, and coffee from sweet potatoes, peanuts, beans, cornmeal, and any number of inferior substitutes. A shortage of salt created problems in a society that preserved its meat by salting it. A number of families dealt with this dilemma by curing meat in the well-salted earth that they dug from the floors of smokehouses. The shortages became most apparent to children on the meager Christmas of 1863, when the gifts and treats that were so abundant in earlier years failed to appear. A significant number of children in the South and in the North who went without Christmas gifts during the Civil War, however, were motivated by patriotism: It seemed wrong to indulge in gift-giving when their countrymen were dying in battle.

SLAVERY BECOMES A CASUALTY

Shortages had a greater impact on the slaves, who were already surviving on an inadequate diet before the war. Despite the added hardship, large numbers of slaves remained hopeful that the war would result in their freedom.

With so many white men away in the army and women and children left in charge of plantations, the institution of slavery began to break down. Slaves refused to work as long or as hard as they had in the past, and they successfully resisted punishment. Slaves also were among the many refugees on the move in the South, although rather than running away from the invading Union forces, slaves ran toward them.

Union soldiers referred to the fugitive slaves who presented themselves for protection as contrabands, as if they were loot stolen from the enemy. The federal government first provided guidance for troops on the handling of fugitives with passage of the Confiscation Act of August 6, 1861. This law stated that any property used willingly and knowingly to aid the insurrection against the United States was lawful prize and capture. If the property in question was slaves, they were to be permanently free. Military units were often still at a loss about what to do with these people, though. Officers in Tennessee and Louisiana, for example, arranged for them to be hired by local planters. Elsewhere, the army paid male contrabands to build bridges and fortifications and repair roads.

The U.S. government permitted the enlistment of African Americans for military service with passage of the Militia Act of 1862 on July 17 of that year. The First Regiment of South Carolina Volunteers, the earliest African-American unit, was formed in November 1862 and commanded by a white officer, Thomas Wentworth Higginson. In all, 186,000 African-American soldiers—men from the North and the South—would serve in segregated regiments in the Civil War.

Many boys who fled slavery would find employment as drummers and officers' servants.

Following the Union victory at the Battle of Antietam, in rural Maryland, on September 17, 1862, Lincoln drafted the Emancipation Proclamation, a document granting freedom to slaves held in states or portions of states in rebellion, to become effective January 1, 1863. News of the proclamation filtered into the enslaved population, encouraging large numbers of people to resist bondage and flee at the earliest opportunity.

Men could be useful to the armed forces, but women and children were a burden and, to the soldiers' way of thinking, consumed precious resources. Army officers evicted nearly 400 women and children from Camp Nelson, Kentucky, and threatened to shoot anyone who refused to leave. U.S. soldiers in the South became accustomed to hungry African-American children coming to their tents and begging for food. In Louisiana a boy offered his puppy to a Massachusetts soldier in exchange for a loaf of bread. The soldier gave the boy food but let him keep his pet.

The federal government established camps to house the many displaced former slaves throughout the South at locations that included Natchez, Tennessee; De Soto, Louisiana; and Arlington, Virginia, the former home of Robert E. Lee. Most of the camps' inhabitants were children, women, and old men who endured miserable conditions. People lived crowded together in tents and muddy huts,

Lieutenant W. B. Sears of the 2nd Rhode Island Infantry with his contraband servant. *(Massachusetts Commandery Military Order of the Loyal Legion and the U.S. Army Military History Institute)*

and hunger and disease were rampant. According to an 1864 newspaper report, between 30 and 50 people died on an average day in the contraband camp at Young's Point, Louisiana; 75 people died in one dreadful day at the Natchez camp. Some desperate mothers hired out their children in order to have money for food.

U.S. forces frequently resented being ordered to guard contraband camps when they had come south to fight a war. There were civilians, though, who took an active interest in the welfare of the newly free African Americans. The American Missionary Association and other religious groups collected food and clothing to distribute among the contrabands. On September 17, 1861, the American Missionary Association opened a school for blacks in Hampton, Virginia, taught by Mary Smith Peake, an African American. This school would grow into the Hampton Institute (now Hampton University). The National Freedmen's Relief Association was formed in New York City on February 22, 1862, and similar secular organizations were soon founded in other northern cities. These groups sent several thousand teachers into places where slavery had fallen to prepare the black population for freedom. Thanks to the efforts of these individuals, a majority of children in contraband camps received some schooling and at least caught a glimpse of the great body of knowledge that had been hidden from them under slavery.

Although some African Americans taught in the freedmen's schools, the majority of teachers who ventured south were white. For many black children it was a new experience to encounter whites who valued them as individuals rather than as property. But in the Sea Islands and elsewhere, former slaves were required to work in exchange for the benefits of charity that they received. Children old enough to put in a day's labor frequently joined their parents in cotton fields to earn their schooling. True freedom and equality in American society would elude these children and their descendants for many generations.

THE WAR ENDS

On April 9, 1865, Robert E. Lee surrendered to Ulysses S. Grant, commander in chief of the Union forces, at Appomattox Court House, Virginia. The Confederate regiments remaining in the field quickly foundered, and the long, bloody war came to an end. Surviving soldiers returned home, frequently after long absences, and children in every northern and southern state were reunited with fathers changed by war or whom they were too young to remember. Children and parents worked to become reacquainted and build relationships.

Not every child would have the chance to see his or her father again. Approximately 620,000 men died in the Civil War of battlefield wounds or disease, leaving thousands of orphans or half-orphans (children with one parent—in these instances, a mother). The actual number of children left fatherless by the Civil War in unknown, but institutions that housed children saw their enrollment increase dramatically between 1861 and 1865. The number of boys seeking shelter at one such home, the New York Newsboys' Lodging House, doubled during these years. Other institutions noted a growing percentage of war orphans among their residents.

In the Union, public attention was drawn to the plight of orphans after a burial crew found a photograph of three children in the hand of a dead soldier

The Humiston children, whose father died clutching their photograph at Gettysburg, inspired a popular song, "The Children of the Battle Field." *(MS 92–25, Kantor Collection of U.S. Sanitary Commission and Civil War, Department of Special Collections, Ablah Library, Wichita State University)*

on the field at Gettysburg. The press launched a nationwide campaign to identify the children, and in November 1863, the public learned that they were the sons and daughter of Sergeant Amos Humiston and that they lived with their mother in Portville, New York.

The needs of fatherless children also concerned Abraham Lincoln. In his Second Inaugural Address, on March 4, 1865, Lincoln urged Americans "to care for him who shall have borne the battles, and for his widow, and his orphan." Protestant, Catholic, and Jewish groups, some stirred by Lincoln's words and some motivated by their own awareness of children's needs, opened orphan homes in the North and South. Wealthy individuals donated funds for new and existing homes, and African Americans established shelters for the orphans among the refugees from slavery. A number of state-supported homes also were constructed after 1865. The most famous Civil War orphanage was the National Homestead at Gettysburg, which was built with donations of private funds and opened in 1866.

Children living in public and private war orphanages included both orphans and half-orphans; although the federal government provided a pension to soldiers' widows and survivors, many women found it impossible to support all of their children without a husband's help. Children living in war orphanages were given housing, food, clothing, medical care, and education.

Some of these institutions continued to accept new residents and were still housing children in the early 20th century. One such orphanage, the Indiana Soldiers' and Sailors' Orphans' Home, which opened in 1865, ceased operations in 1904. Most Civil War orphanages had shorter life spans, however, closing after their residents reached maturity and the nation's need for orphanages diminished. The National Homestead at Gettysburg closed in 1877 after startling reports of embezzlement and child abuse by staff members became public. The home's matron was convicted, fined, and forced to leave town.

MOURNING A LEADER

For countless Americans, old and young, the assassination of President Abraham Lincoln on April 14, 1865, was a sad postscript to the Civil War. For the rest of their lives, Americans who were children in 1865 would remember where they were and what they were doing when they learned of Lincoln's death.

The nation grieved openly and visibly as Lincoln's casket was taken on a 16-day journey from Washington, D.C., to Springfield, Illinois, the slain president's former home. Children were in the crowds that turned out to pay their respects in cities where the procession stopped. They stood on packed sidewalks or peered from windows, for example, as 16 horses draped in black and adorned with ostrich feathers pulled Lincoln's hearse through Union Square in New York City.

Many children found personal ways to grieve and come to terms with the president's death. Some hung black cloth and ribbons in their homes, in imitation of the draping they viewed on the exteriors of houses and public buildings, while others reenacted the assassination in their play. For Ida Tarbell of Pennsylvania, now eight years old, the assassination was her "first realization of tragedy." It was the single occurrence from four long years of war to get behind her eyes, to sink into her mind and touch her emotions, and she could only wonder at the senselessness of this loss.

CHRONICLE OF EVENTS

1861

Children constitute one-third of the U.S. population.

March 4: Abraham Lincoln recites the Oath of Office and becomes the 16th president of the United States; seven southern states have adopted articles of secession.

April 12: An attempt is made to resupply Fort Sumter, a federal installation at Charleston, South Carolina; southern artillery opens fire on the fort.

April 15: Lincoln calls for 75,000 recruits to enforce the nation's laws; four additional states respond by seceding.

May: Johnny Clem, 10, runs away from home and tags along with an Ohio unit.

July 21: The Union suffers a defeat in the First Battle of Bull Run, fought near Manassas, Virginia.

August: Camp Butler opens near Springfield, Illinois.

August 1: Congress passes the Confiscation Act, stating that any property, including slaves, used willingly and knowingly to aid the insurrection is lawful prize and capture; slaves who are seized are to be permanently free.

August 21: George S. Lamkin, 11, of Winona, Mississippi, joins the Confederate army.

September 17: The American Missionary Association opens a school for African Americans at Hampton, Virginia.

1862

Refugees from Arkansas and Louisiana flood into Texas.

February 22: The National Freedmen's Relief Association is founded in New York City.

April 7: In Tennessee, the Battle of Shiloh ends in a victory for the Union.

July 17: The Militia Act of 1862 becomes law, permitting African Americans to be employed in military service.

November: The first African-American unit, the First Regiment of South Carolina Volunteers, is formed.

December 13–15: Fredericksburg, Virginia, is the site of a Civil War battle; residents flee to Richmond.

1863

May 19: The Union assault on Vicksburg, Mississippi, begins; many children wait out the siege in hillside caves.

June 26: Confederate regiments march into Gettysburg, Pennsylvania, looking for shoes.

June 30: Gettysburg's citizens, children as well as adults, turn out to greet arriving Union cavalry units.

July 1–3: Union and Confederate forces clash in Gettysburg; some children watch the battle from cellar windows and safe vantage points; the Confederate armies are forced to retreat and will never again venture into the North.

July 4: Children join the adult population to begin the massive job of caring for Gettysburg's wounded and burying the dead; Vicksburg falls to Union general Ulysses S. Grant.

July: A burial crew finds a photograph of three children in the hand of a dead Union soldier at Gettysburg; the children are identified as the sons and daughter of Sergeant Amos Humiston of Portville, New York.

Inspired by news of the battle at Gettysburg, Charles T. Haigh, 15, of Fayetteville, North Carolina, volunteers as a private in the Confederate army.

October: Business comes to a halt in Chicago while the population attends a U.S. Sanitary Commission fair.

Fall: Johnny Clem is promoted to sergeant.

December 25: Because of widespread shortages, children in the Confederacy do without gifts and treats at Christmas.

1864

For the first time, the federal government requires military musicians to be at least 16 years of age.

April: The U.S. Sanitary Commission fair held in the Union Square Building in New York City devotes an entire wing to its Children's Department.

May: Charles T. Haigh dies in a charge at Spotsylvania Court House, Virginia.

1865

March 4: Abraham Lincoln gives his Second Inaugural Address, calling on Americans to care for the orphans of war.

April 9: Confederate General Robert E. Lee surrenders to Ulysses S. Grant, commander in chief of the Union forces, at Appomattox Court House, Virginia, effectively ending the Civil War.

Residents and staff assemble outside the National Homestead at Gettysburg. *(William J. Little Collection at the U.S. Army Military History Institute)*

April 14: President Abraham Lincoln is assassinated at Ford's Theatre in Washington, D.C.

1866

The U.S. Sanitary Commission's Statistical Bureau concludes that 1.5 percent of enlisted men and 3.33 percent of officers in the Union army were under 18 or over 45.

The National Homestead at Gettysburg, the most famous Civil War orphanage, opens; it will cease operations in 1877.

EYEWITNESS TESTIMONY

I was too young in the fifties to appreciate political questions, but, even so, I saw the foreshadowing of trouble. The military spirit ran high and in 1858 there were three uniformed military companies in Talbot County. Added to these there were two companies of cadets, one at Trappe, commanded by George M. Jenkins, and one at St. Michaels, commanded by myself, then about thirteen years old. My company was very martial in spirit, though we were very juvenile, the members ranging in age from ten to fifteen years....

As war drew near feeling ran high in Maryland. Abolitionists were working among the slaves, persuading them to desert. During the year 1859 it is believed that John Brown was on the Eastern Shore secretly inciting the slaves to rise and attack the whites. At this time an excited slave confessed to her mistress that there was a plot to attack the whites that night. This news spread rapidly and precautions were taken at once by the men to protect their homes and families.

Our cadet company was called on to do duty and set to guard some of the roads. We were proud to undertake the task and on this occasion we were provided with real guns. I am glad to say there was no need of guns of any kind, as no attack was made.

Joseph B. Seth remembering events occurring in eastern Maryland in 1858 and 1859, in Joseph B. Seth and Mary W. Seth, Recollections of a Long Life on the Eastern Shore, *pp. 25–27.*

When rumors of secession arose I became of course alarmed, and was always ready to express my political views to any one who would listen. One of the experiments with me was to send me up to live with a farmer named Sheldon in Peterboro, N. H., who came to Fitchburg [Massachusetts] to drive me home with him. He was so much impressed by my political harangues that he stopped one or two neighbors and set me going so that they could see what a ready tongue a boy could have. He either got tired of it or thought I was not adapted to tending sheep, for after a few days he got me into his wagon again and drove me back to Fitchburg.

So when Sumter was fired on April 12, 1861, I was excited. I remember walking up and down the sitting room, puffing out my breast as though the responsibility rested on my poor little shoulders, shaking my fist at the south, and threatening her with dire calamities

which I thought some of inflicting on her myself. I joined the military company at the Orange country grammar school and took fencing lessons. As men began to enlist I wished I were older.

C. W. Bardeen, who was 13 in April 1861, A Little Fifer's War Diary, *pp. 17–18.*

With the fall of Sumter and Lincoln's call for 75,000 volunteers, the citizens of New York entered four years of political excitement. To a boy of nine who knew nothing at all about the why and the wherefore of the strife, the sight of a city going to war was most entertaining. I well remember the bustle about the armories as the militia regiments made haste to be off; the great ovation given the 7th Regiment as it marched down Broadway to the Jersey City ferry to entrain for Washington; the passage of the New England troops as they marched from the New York, New Haven and Hartford Railroad Station at Twenty-seventh Street and Third Avenue to the Jersey ferry; the great Sumter mass meeting around Union Square and the deafening cheers that rose . . . when the flag that waved over Sumter during the bombardment was held up to view; the calls for volunteers by private citizens eager to form companies, or battalions, or regiments; the recruiting stations, the fifers and drummers parading the streets and urging men to enlist; the display of flags everywhere.

John Bach McMaster describing Manhattan's response to the Civil War in 1861, when he was nine years old, in Eric F. Goldman, "Young John Bach McMaster: A Boyhood in New York City," p. 322.

We boys immediately got busy building Fort Sumters and firing on them. We made Fort Sumters of mud and wooden blocks, and we put up clothespins for soldiers, ruthlessly slaughtering them with shot from cannons made of old brass pistol barrels fastened to blocks of wood. When the charge of wadding and pebbles struck the clothespin soldiers the splinters flew and there was a terrible slaughter, but no bloodshed.

Next we began to hear talk about Jeff Davis. Poor old Jeff! We thought he was the worst criminal ever born. We made Jeffs of potatoes and put sticks in them for legs. We hung the desperate potato men by their necks and shot them with squibs from firecrackers.

Dan Beard describing his play in 1861, Hardly a Man Is Now Alive, *p. 151.*

. . . [W]hen here in Dansville we heard the news that Sumter had been fired upon and the blank walls were covered with calls for volunteers, our happy town seemed suddenly to grow grim and forbidding. We were far from the seat of strife, there was little danger from invasion, but all the same Dansville stepped into the arena and picked up her sword as defiantly as though the boom of battle was echoing from her protecting hills.

We ten year olds felt the shock keenly but met it bravely. While the fact remained uppermost in our minds that the nation was in danger, still we could not, brimming over with life and health as we were, help rising above the prevailing depression and being just boys. The quiet of our streets was broken by the inspiring strains of the fife and drum before the recruiting offices, young fellows we knew, were enlisting and awkward squads drilling on the public square. The war meetings were great fun for the boys, and we were always there, the serious aspect was not evident to us. . . .

H. W. De Long commenting on how children experienced the Civil War in Dansville, New York, in 1861, Boyhood Reminiscences, *pp. 56–57.*

Times with us are very dull—the prospect for a battle being exceedingly poor, in fact but few of our officers, are of the opinion that there will be a battle. . . . We have had good deal of sickness in our camp for the last few weeks. . . . The Measles has surrounded our camp. We are looking for some of the younger boys to take them daily. If we should get them we will have a hard time with them, having no conveniences & exposed to all kinds of weather. Our tents not having covers form but poor protection to shelter us from rain.

Langdon L. Rumph, age 16, of the 1st Regiment Alabama Volunteers, Warrenton, Florida, May 25, 1861, in Henry Eugene Sterkx and Brooks Thompson, eds., "Letters of a Teenage Confederate," p. 341.

There are over 100 with [measles] at the hospital. In all my life I never saw such a sickly time. Over 300 patients in the hospital, out of 90 men we never get out on parade more than 35 men,—so many sick in Camp & more will not go to hospital. . . . All hands are becoming monstrously tired of this hot climate, fleas flies & mosquitos.

Langdon L. Rumph, age 16, of the 1st Regiment Alabama Volunteers, Warrenton, Florida, July 25, 1861, in Henry

Eugene Sterkx and Brooks Thompson, eds., "Letters of a Teenage Confederate," p. 343. (Langdon L. Rumph died August 16, 1861, at Warrenton of typhoid fever or measles.)

Patriotism was pumped into us in school. Every morning after Bible reading, the young woman who presided at the piano would sing a war song, the boys joining in, and that done, a second and perhaps a third would follow. To teach the boys the words of a song, the teacher would read a line at a time and require them to repeat it over and over again until the words were committed to memory. In this manner we acquired quite a repertoire, made up of *Hail Columbia, The Star Spangled Banner, The Red, White, and Blue, John Brown's Body, In My Prison Cell I Sit, Tenting on the Old Camp Ground Tramp, Tramp, Tramp, The Boys are Marching, Marching Through Georgia, We are Coming, Father Abraham,* and, of course, *The Battle Hymn of the Republic.*

At home, with other members of the family, I scraped lint from old linen for use in the hospitals, in response to an appeal from the Surgeon General of the Army.

John Bach McMaster remembering his patriotic activities, 1861–65, in Eric F. Goldman, "Young John Bach McMaster: A Boyhood in New York City," p. 323.

Everybody was working for the soldiers. There was no Red Cross, but we had a Sanitary Commission to look after the hospitals and wounded men, and in every home and every school, parents, teachers and children were picking lint, which was carefully placed on a clean piece of paper and used by the field surgeons to stanch the blood. We also had Sanitary Fairs, held in the Fifth Street Market House, to which the ladies contributed quilts and fancywork.

I made a model of a saddlebag loghouse which was very realistic. The landscape and all was about three feet by a foot and a half, and I proudly carried that all the way to the Sanitary Fair. It was sold for seven dollars and a half, which was a severe blow to my artistic soul, because I really thought it was worth about fifty dollars.

Dan Beard on homefront activities in Cincinnati, Ohio, 1861–65, Hardly a Man Is Now Alive, *p. 152.*

The echoes of the Civil War, as they reverberated over the country, were but faintly heard by the children of our neighborhood. Our parents engaged in excited discussions with friends and neighbors and occasionally we saw women crying. Soldiers in uniform were constantly seen on the streets. We were told that there was a great war in the South. The negroes who now were slaves would be set free. That was our conception of the great war.

The sights and scenes about us found their reflex in child activity. The children donned paper caps in imitation of soldier caps, secured laths and sticks to represent guns and swords, and marched through the alleys and backyards singing: "Hang Jeff Davis on a sour apple tree." I had a little brother who shouted "Hurrah for Ding Dong." He was too small to pronounce the name of Lincoln.

On Sundays our parents took us on a visit to the several soldier camps located in the immediate outskirts of the city. I remember, too, as a small child something of the excitement manifested in our neighborhood when the news was spread that Abraham Lincoln had died at the hands of an assassin.

William George Bruce of Milwaukee summing up his experience of the Civil War, 1861–65, I Was Born in America, *pp. 26–27.*

. . . I was too young to know what it was all about when the Civil War began. I have a dim recollection of being held up by Father or Mother at the curb to see long lines of soldiers marching down streets—probably Broadway and Fifth Avenue—with flags waving and bands playing and crowds cheering, and it all seemed very fine; but a little later, when Father himself decided to go to the front, the war took on a different aspect. He had a wife and four children . . . and might very well have been excused if he had stayed at home; but many other family men were volunteering, Father was intensely patriotic and had the Irishman's love of a fight—and so he went.

Eddie Foy, who was six years old in 1862, when his father joined a New York regiment, Clowning through Life, *p. 9.*

While the battles for the Union were lost or won, while Lincoln lived in agony and Stonewall Jackson prayed and fought, our quiet life was not much disturbed. Our portions of sugar were reduced; we did not get so many clothes as formerly; all stuffs made of cotton soared in price, but we went to school as usual, hearing eagerly of our successes in the field and joining especially in helping, as far as we could, the success of

a great Fair held down near the wharf in Washington Avenue. Soldiers moved through the city in trains; we carried coffee and rolls to them, and cheered and heard various opinions of Burnside and Hancock and McClellan and Grant.

We learned, too, that Lincoln was by no means the idol of the people; that he had many critics; there seemed to be a party for McClellan and against him. The boys, however, with a curious insight, seemed always to believe in Lincoln, no matter what their parents thought; though there was a great deal of hysteria at times, there seemed to be little hatred; and the grey uniformed Confederates, when they passed through as prisoners, in the trains along Washington Avenue, were fed and assisted in every possible way.

Maurice Francis Egan recalling life in Philadelphia ca. 1862, when he was 10 years old, Recollections of a Happy Life, *pp. 46–47.*

Johnnie [Walker, age 12] is drummer for the band, and when they play at dress parade every evening lots of gentlemen and ladies come from the city to hear them play and see the little drummer and when we are marching, and the ladies see the little soldier-boy they always give him apples, cakes or something. . . . When we are marching Johnnie always keeps up with the big men, and is always singing and laughing but when he gets tired the big Colonel or Lieutenant Colonel or Adjutant will let Johnnie have his horse to ride. Everybody in the regiment likes Johnnie because he is a good little boy, is always pleasant and polite and not saucy like a great many boys. His mother sent him a suit of clothes made exactly like officer's clothes, and Lieutenant Baumman says he will get him a pair of shoulder straps with silver drum sticks upon them. Johnnie used to live in Racine and he has a half brother who is corporal in our company (but he is a mean bad man, don't take care of Johnnie, who lives with the Captain of Company B).

Private Harvey Reid of the 22nd Wisconsin Regiment writing to his brother Charles, 1862, in Bell Irvin Wiley, The Life of Billy Yank, *p. 297.*

I passed . . . the corpse of a beautiful boy in gray who lay with his blond curls scattered about his face and his hand folded peacefully across his breast. He was clad in a bright and neat uniform, well garnished with gold, which seemed to tell the story of a loving mother and sisters who had sent their household pet to the field of war. His neat little hat lying beside him bore the number of a Georgia regiment.... He was about my age.... At the sight of the poor boy's corpse, I burst into a regular boo-hoo and started on.

John A. Cockerill, 16, Union regimental musician, who arrived at Pittsburg Landing, Mississippi, in the aftermath of a battle, April 1862, in Emmy E. Werner, Reluctant Witnesses, *p. 25.*

A second cousin of mine was sent home from the front as a recruiting sergeant, and I went down to Boston to see him. He arranged the matter for me at once, and said I could learn to drum after I was enlisted. He even tried to enter me as a private to be detailed as a drummer, so that I could draw thirteen dollars a month instead of twelve. I had to undergo a medical inspection which I thought rather severe, taking off all my clothes and having among other tests to jump, to be sure I was sound in wind and limb; but I passed it, and on July 21, 1862, I became a Massachusetts soldier, assigned as musician to Co. D of the 1st Massachusetts infantry.

C. W. Bardeen, who joined the Union army on July 21, 1862, at age 14, A Little Fifer's War Diary, *pp. 18–19.*

... [My] shirt was of thick wool with wide seams, and when I turned over the first seam I felt as if I should faint. There they were, big and little and nits, a garrison of them. I had had blue days since I enlisted, but this was the first time I wished I had staid at home. Must I endure this sort of thing for three years? I made sure the present generation were extinct, and went back to camp a sadder and a wiser boy. I never got so that I could sit in front of my tent and do my (k)nitting as indifferently as a Spanish beggar cleans her daughter's head at the entrance to a cathedral, but I made my daily pilgrimages to secluded spots and reduced the infection to a minimum. Afterward when I tented alone I succeeded in tenting entirely alone except for now and then a straggler soon disposed of....

C. W. Bardeen of the First Massachusetts Infantry commenting on camp life in September 1862, when he was 15, A Little Fifer's War Diary, *pp. 38–39.*

... I was certainly scared. One shell had exploded near enough so that I could realize its effects, and the one thing I wanted was to get where no more shells could burst around me. This patriotic hero who had declared in front of campfires how he had longed for gore

would have liked to be tucked up once more in his little trundle-bed. Bomb-ague is a real disease and I had caught it.

There was no question of getting back to the regiment.... I could see that my division was preparing to march, and while I did not actually run I certainly walked fast to get to it. It is curious how little annoyances will keep themselves prominent even in time of danger. I had on thick woolen drawers which had somehow broken from the fastening that held them up. It was a warm day and as I hurried up the hill those drawers kept slipping down till they drove me almost distracted, disturbing my equanimity more than the danger did.

C. W. Bardeen, who saw combat at Fredericksburg, Virginia, December 12, 1862, A Little Fifer's War Diary, *p. 107.*

A small boy, with blood streaming from a wound in his leg, came running up to where Father and [General William T.] Sherman stood and reported that his regiment was out of ammunition. Sherman was directing that some attention be paid to his wound, when the little fellow, finding himself faint from loss of blood, gasped out, "Caliber 56!" as he was carried off to the rear. At this moment I observed that my father's eyes were filled with tears.

Frederick Dent Grant, who at 13 was with his father, General Ulysses S. Grant, during the attack on Vicksburg, Mississippi, recalling an event of May 22, 1863, in "General Fred Grant's Scare at Vicksburg," p. 900.

If ever I wished myself at home I did then. There I was, the only one of our family shut down in a damp, dark hole with crying children and a poor young soldier who had received three wounds which had not yet been attended to.... To know the rebels were in town, to hear the shells bursting and expecting every minute they would fall on the house, was indeed horrible.

Jennie McCreary, who at 17 spent July 1, 1863, in the cellar of a Gettysburg, Pennsylvania, neighbor, in Elizabeth Daniels, "The Children of Gettysburg," p. 100.

[The wounded] lay on the threshing floor, each on a single blanket, without covering of any kind. It was too early for organized relief. They had received no care and were a pitiful and dreadful sight.

Charles McCurdy describing a scene in a Gettysburg barn that he witnessed in July 1863, when he was 10, in Elizabeth Daniels, "The Children of Gettysburg," p. 105.

The battle was too big for a little boy. Had I realized that the noise and tumult, the confusion and excitement . . . meant that 140,000 [it was actually 160,000] men were trying to kill each other . . . my emotions might have been more in keeping with the great tragedy.

Charles McCurdy reflecting on his comprehension of the Battle of Gettysburg, which occurred in July 1863, when he was 10, in Elizabeth Daniels, "The Children of Gettysburg," p. 107.

One day mother and I were standing in the tent, she brushing my hair, when we heard the report of the mortar, heard the shell rattling over, and knew it was near. We looked at each other, and mother exclaimed, "That sounds very near; get into the cave." She did get in, but I had only time to jump into a small hole we children had dug out in the side of the hill when a piece of the shell came down into the tent, demolishing the wash-stand by which we had stood.

I felt the heat as it came down. Mother's face, white with anxiety for me, peeped out from the cave door. There I sat, stunned with fear.

L. McRae Bell, who as a child endured the Union attack on Vicksburg, spring 1863, "A Girl's Experience in the Siege of Vicksburg," p. 13.

Our provisions were becoming scarce, and the Louisiana soldiers were eating rats as a delicacy, while mules were occasionally being carved up to appease the appetite. Mother would not eat mule meat, but we children ate some, and it tasted right good, having been cooked nicely. Wheat bread was a rarity, and sweet-potato coffee was relished by the adults.

L. McRae Bell, who as a child endured the Union attack on Vicksburg, spring 1863, "A Girl's Experience in the Siege of Vicksburg," p. 13.

The morning of the 4th, how sad was the spectacle that met our gaze: arms stacked in the center of the streets, men with tearful eyes and downcast faces walking here and there; men sitting in groups feeling that they would gladly have given their life-blood on the battle-field rather than hand over the guns and sabers so dear to them! The drummer-boy of a Tennessee regiment, rather than give up his drum gave it to my brother, but it was very soon taken away from him. One poor fellow gave me his horse which was branded with the letters C. S., and my two brothers hid him in the yard;

but it was only a little while before a Federal solder came in and took him.

L. McRae Bell describing happenings in Vicksburg after the Union victory there, July 4, 1863, "A Girl's Experience in the Siege of Vicksburg," p. 13.

I remember with the utmost interest my life in camp, and with deepest affection the men whom I met in the army. Much of my time was spent among the private soldiers, who were never too tired or too worn out to comfort and pet the boy of thirteen—the son of "the Old Man." Young as I then was, my camp life was of such nature, I saw so much of the hardships, the self-denials, the sufferings and labors of both privates and officers, that my proudest moments are when I am recalling my associating with the old warriors of the Eastern and Western armies, the veteran comrades of my father.

Frederick Dent Grant, who was with his father, General Ulysses S. Grant, at Vicksburg in 1863, in "General Fred Grant's Scare at Vicksburg," p. 902.

I remember vividly a man who lifted me up to see Lincoln. This was opposite the Court House. The street was crowded with people leaving only enough room for him to pass on his horse. He would turn from side to side looking at the people on either side when he passed with a solemn face. He looked rather odd on such a small horse.

Annie Skelly, who was seven years old on November 19, 1863, when Abraham Lincoln delivered the Gettysburg Address, in Elizabeth Daniels, "The Children of Gettysburg," pp. 106–07.

I can recall a night of great commotion in a little cottage at La Porte City, in Blackhawk County, Iowa—a night when the entire family, my mother and five small children, were awakened by the barking of our watch-dog, a big, tawny Newfoundland. I can remember my mother unbolting and unlocking the door of the cottage and the entrance of a great figure of a man—a giant of a man, preceded by a bounding bundle of energy, the dog expressing his gratification at his master's return, with affectionate demonstration. The man was my father. He was as I have stated almost a giant in stature, towering more than six feet in height with long, bushy locks of black hair, inclined to curl, a full black beard, and bright blue, kindly eyes that sparkled with the joy of his welcome home. He spoke to my mother, and in subdued tones they talked for some minutes. He handed mother a legal looking paper. They read it together. It was an order for my father to report for military service at Dubuque. After several attempts to enlist in the army, followed by rejections because of some slight physical disability, the authorities in charge had at last accepted his tender of services. The time was January, 1864. The enlistment was with the artillery, and father had been assigned to the Third Iowa, or Dubuque, Battery, known better as Captain Hayden's Battery. The orders were to report at once at headquarters of the battery, then being reorganized at Dubuque. . . .

Mother was brave through her tears, and I can imagine my father going with a lighter heart because of her bravery and unfaltering courage. The parting was final. They were destined never to meet again.

George Gallarno remembering January 1864,
"How Iowa Cared for Orphans of
Her Soldiers of the Civil War,"
pp. 163–64.

No one, except he was there in the prison can form anything like a correct idea of our appearance about this time. We had been in prison nearly five months and our clothing was worn out. A number were entire naked; some would have a ragged shirt and no pants; some had pants and no shirt; another would have shoes and a cap and nothing else. Their flesh was wasted away, leaving the chaffy, weather-beaten skin drawn tight over the bones, the hip bones and shoulders standing out. Their faces and exposed parts of their bodies were covered with smoky black soot, from the dense smoke of pitch pine we had hovered over, and our long matted hair was stiff and black with the same substance, which water would have no effect on, and soap was not to be had. I would not attempt to describe the sick and dying, who could now be seen on every side.

Michael Dougherty, who joined the 13th Pennsylvania
Cavalry at age 16 and was imprisoned at Andersonville,
Georgia, in February 1864, Diary of a Civil War
Hero, p. 43.

Rained hard last night and is still raining. Our drinking water is thick with mud and filth. I sometimes think everything is coming us on to hurry us off. Well, probably the sooner out of such misery the better, but

I will keep up as long as there is a spark of life left in me. A great many get discouraged and die when they could prolong their lives with a little courage. But it is only a matter of time, as six months is considered a prisoner's life in a Confederate prison, although it has been eight months since I was captured. I am a mere skeleton.

Michael Dougherty, the only member of his company to
survive imprisonment at Andersonville, May 7, 1864,
Diary of a Civil War Hero, p. 89.

. . . [A] negro child has been lying dead at No. 81 Perdido Street . . . three days. Warm weather is coming on and it ought to be removed.

New Orleans Times, *April 8, 1864, in James Marten,*
The Children's Civil War, p. 132.

John Y. Mason Anderson, son of Confederate General Joseph R. Anderson, sporting a miniature Zouave uniform. Some Civil War units wore colorful uniforms in imitation of the Zouaves, Algerian infantrymen who served under the French. John Anderson died in 1866, soon after the war ended. *(Valentine Museum/Richmond History Center)*

. . . [W]hile the Confederates wore drab uniforms the color of dust, the Yankees wore blue and appeared better dressed. Among the latter I also observed occasionally a very gaudy one, especially one clothed in deeper blue with a roundabout [short jacket] scalloped on the edges and trimmed with gold lace. . . .

[S]ometime afterward my mother surprised me by dressing me in a deep blue suit with a roundabout gorgeous if not in gold lace yet with vivid yellow tape, and was not I proud and happy? I wandered around the house. I could not go out in front to display my fine feathers because the Yankee cavalry was passing along Main Street. So I went out into the chicken yard in the rear. When I noticed that a body of Yankee cavalry in a column of twos was coming down the alley to join the main body in Main Street, I posed for their benefit without being aware of the possible consequences. Presently, one of the Yanks, pointing toward me, said to his comrades, "That's my boy!" I was speechless with surprise and anger and humiliation. The idea that a hated Yankee should claim me filled me with disgust and loathing. I could not talk but I could make signs. A curling lip and my facial expression gave unmistakable signs of my feelings, for the entire cavalcade in sight, attracted by their comrade's exclamation, noticed my expression, [and] roared with laughter. . . .

Robert Hugh Martin, who was six years old in the spring of 1864, when the Union cavalry passed his home in Harrisonburg, Virginia, A Boy of Old Shenandoah, pp. 12–13.

From the front porch . . . I saw the ambulances speeding up the rather steep hill carrying their mangled and suffering human freight to the hospitals which were located at the north end of town. The horses drawing these vehicles were lashed mercilessly and continuously by the drivers and they aroused my compassion. . . . I heard the older folks say afterward that they could see the blood dripping from these vehicles but fortunately I did not see it or, if I did, I did not recognize it. I did see some gruesome sights of wounded men who were able to walk with the support of their comrades and especially one whose supporting companion held a hand over the wounded man's forehead. Removing his hand temporarily, I saw what looked like a cup-shaped wound in the middle of the forehead, all red and frightful, but it was probably only a surface wound. . . .

Robert Hugh Martin, who as a boy of six witnessed wounded soldiers returning from the Battle of New Market, Virginia, May 15, 1864, A Boy of Old Shenandoah, pp. 29–30.

One of the Women had the small pox, her face a perfect mass of Scabs, her children were left uncared for except for what they accidentally rec[eive]d. Another woman was nursing a little boy about 7 whose earthly life was fast ebbing away, she could pay but little attention to the rest of her family. Another was scarcely able to crawl about. They had no bedding. Two old quilts and a soldiers old worn out blanket comprised the whole for 35 human beings. I enquired how they slept, they collect together to keep one another warm and then throw the quilts over them. There is no wood for them nearer than half a mile which these poor children have to toat [sic] . . . hence they have a poor supply, and the same with Water. . . . [T]he only vessel they had to carry it in was a heavy 2 gallon stone jug, a load for a child when empty. . . . They were filthy and will all probably have the small pox and a number of them likely [will] die.

An agent for the Cincinnati Contraband Relief Commission describing conditions in the contraband camp at Davis Bend, Mississippi, spring 1864, in James Marten, The Children's Civil War, pp. 131–32.

Mother, with her brood of little ones all loaded in a big, lumbering wagon, was starting from our home for a visit with my grandparents at their farm in the country a few miles north of La Porte City [Iowa]. I can remember the youthful joy in anticipation of a day in the country. On the main street of the little village the horses were halted at the post office, and my mother entered to call for mail. When she came back to the wagon she was crying. The team was turned about and we were driven back to our home. Then I learned my mother had received a letter from Little Rock, Arkansas. It was an army letter, written by a comrade and bore tidings that my father was dead.

George Gallarno recalling events occurring in October 1864, "How Iowa Cared for Orphans of Her Soldiers of the Civil War," p. 164.

Remember the first time them Yankees come. I was sitting down in the chimney corner and my mammy was giving me my breakfast. Remember I been sitting there with my milk and my bowl of hominy, and I hear my old grandmammy come a-running in from out the yard and say all the sky was blue as indigo with the Yankees coming right there over the hill. Say she see more Yankees than could ever cover up all the premises about there.

Then, I hear my missus scream and come a-running with a lapful of silver and tell my grandmammy to bury and sew that up in the feather bed, 'cause them Yankees was mighty apt to destroy all they valuables. Old Missus tell all the colored people to get away, get away and take care of themselves, and tell we children to get back to the chimney corner, 'cause she couldn't protect us noways, no longer.

Hester Hunter of South Carolina recalling events ca. 1864, when she was 12, in Belinda Hurmence, ed., Before Freedom, When I Just Can Remember, *p. 15.*

As I walk'd home about sunset, I saw in Fourteenth street [Washington, D.C.] a very young soldier, thinly clad, standing near the house I was about to enter. I stopt a moment in front of the door and call'd him to me. I knew than an old Tennessee regiment, and also an Indiana regiment, were temporarily stopping in new barracks, near Fourteenth street. This boy I found belonged to the Tennessee regiment. But I could hardly believe he carried a musket. He was but 15 years old, yet had been twelve months a soldier, and had borne his part in several battles, even historic ones. I ask'd him if he did not suffer from the cold, and if he had no overcoat. No, he did not suffer from cold, and had no overcoat, but could draw one whenever he wish'd. His father was dead, and his mother living in some part of East Tennessee; all the men were from that part of the country. The next forenoon I saw the Tennessee and Indiana regiments marching down the Avenue. My boy was with the former, stepping along with the rest. There were many other boys no older. I stood and watch'd them as they tramp'd along with slow, heavy, regular steps. There did not appear to be a man over 30 years of age, and a large proportion were from 15 to perhaps 22 or 23. They had all the look of veterans, worn, stain'd, impassive, and a certain unbent, lounging gait, carrying in addition to their regular arms and knapsacks, frequently a frying-pan, broom, &c.

Walt Whitman, February 1865, Specimen Days, *in* The Whitman Reader, *pp. 311–12.*

President Lincoln, accompanied by Mrs. Lincoln and their youngest son, Tad, then a year or two older and considerably larger than I, came to City Point [Virginia, where General Ulysses S. Grant had his headquarters]. . . . Father rode at the head of his staff to the reviewing station, and at his side rode President Lincoln. Mother, Mrs. Lincoln, Tad, and I, had preceded them in an ambulance. Robert Lincoln, the President's eldest son, was on father's staff. The bands were playing and many of the staff horses, seasoned troopers though they were, were prancing. Father's horse, in particular, danced along with arching neck and curving body. But the horse President Lincoln rode walked calmly, almost as though conscious that his burden must be carried with anxious care, while the President sat stiffly erect, the reins hanging slack from his hands.

Father was but forty-two years old then, but I had always looked upon him as the largest, and, next to my Grandfather Dent, the oldest man in the world. But beside President Lincoln father looked small, and for the first time I saw him as a young man.

Jesse R. Grant, youngest child of Ulysses S. Grant, who was seven years old in March 1865, when Lincoln visited City Point, In the Days of My Father General Grant, *pp. 22–23.*

One morning in the spring of 1865 we boys were all busy at our tasks . . . when the bells down town began to ring a joyful peal and a boy came in and handed a note to Prof. Alva Dorris who had charge of the study room that day. Reading it he arose and said briefly, "Gentlemen, Lee has surrendered, you are excused." With a whoop we all started for town, some jumping through the open windows and others falling over their comrades down the front steps. Flags were waving, people were shaking hands and the bright April sun looked down on a perfectly happy Dansville and nation. It was a glorious day. . . . That night the rival torch light companies of the preceding fall election amicably joined forces making a tremendous procession.

H. W. De Long of Dansville, New York, remembering April 1865, Boyhood Reminiscences, *p. 66.*

It was the spring of 1865. Father was coming up the hill, mother and I were watching for him. Usually he walked with a brisk step, head up, but now his step was slow, his head dropped. Mother ran to meet him crying, "Frank, Frank, what is it?" I did not hear the answer; but I shall always see my mother turning at his words, burying her face in her apron, running into her room sobbing as if her heart would break. And then the house was shut up, and crape was put on all the doors, and I was told that Lincoln was dead.

From that time the name spelt tragedy and mystery. Why all this sorrow over a man we had never seen, who did not belong to our world—*my* world? Was there something beyond the circle of hills within which I lived that concerned me? Why, and in what way, did this mysterious outside concern me?

Ida M. Tarbell remembering how the news of Lincoln's assassination affected her family in April 1865, All in the Day's Work, *p. 11.*

Although I was but four and a half years old when Lincoln died, I distinctly remember the day when I found on our two white gateposts American flags companioned with black. I tumbled down on the harsh gravel walk in my eager rush into the house to inquire what they were "there for." To my amazement I found my father in tears, something that I had never seen before, having assumed, as all children do, that grown-up people never cried. The two flags, my father's tears, and his impressive statement that the greatest man in the world had died, constituted my initiation, my baptism, as it were, into the thrilling and solemn interests of a world lying quite outside the two white gateposts.

Jane Addams describing how she learned about Lincoln's death in April 1865, Twenty Years at Hull House, *p. 33.*

We hadn't been in Chicago long when the war ended, and a few days later President Lincoln was assassinated. Then came that long, strange railroad funeral journey, when they took his body to Baltimore, Philadelphia, New York, Buffalo, Cleveland, Chicago and a few other places en route, stopping almost everywhere to let the people see him in his coffin. When he lay in state in the Court House in Chicago we—my uncle's family and ours—were among the vast crowd that filed by his bier. . . . We had to stand in line a long time and I grew very tired and impatient; but finally we got in. When we reached the coffin, my uncle lifted me slightly so that I could look in and see his face, by then sallow and shrunken. I was tremendously impressed. . . .

Eddie Foy, who was nine years old in April 1865, Clowning through Life, *pp. 19–20.*

We all turn and look toward the road, and there. . . . is a soldier with a musket on his back, wearily plodding his way up the low hill just north of the gate. He is too far away for mother to call, and besides I think she must have been a little uncertain, for he did not so much as turn his head toward the house. Trembling with excitement she hurries little Frank into his wagon and telling Hattie to bring me, sets off up the road as fast as she can

draw the baby's cart. It all seems a dream to me and I move dumbly, almost stupidly like one in a mist. . . .

We did not overtake the soldier, that is evident, for my next vision is that of a blue-coated figure leaning upon the fence, studying with intent gaze our empty cottage. . . . His knapsack lay at his feet, his musket was propped against a post on whose top a cat was dreaming, unmindful of the warrior and his folded hands.

He did not hear us until we were close upon him, and even after he turned, my mother hesitated, so thin, so hollow-eyed, so changed was he. . . .

I could not relate him to the father I had heard so much about. To me he was only a strange man with big eyes and care-worn face. I did not recognize in him anything I had ever known.

Hamlin Garland describing his father's return to Wisconsin from the Civil War in 1865, A Son of the Middle Border, *pp. 2–3.*

July 4th, 1865, father and I walked to Wayland in the early morning, took an excursion train to Rochester and spent the day like a pair of school boys. We went to the best hotel and got dinner, rode to the lake and took an excursion on the steamer Norseman. Saw the great parade and witnessed the arrival of a regiment home from the war as they flocked from a train at the Erie depot to be gathered into the arms of waiting mothers, sweethearts and wives. Then we saw the fireworks on Crouch's island and about 2 a.m. started for home arriving in Wayland after daylight. We walked home and reached there O, so tired, and often comes to me the thought, will dad and I ever take another trip like that together?

H. W. De Long of Dansville, New York, remembering July 4, 1865, Boyhood Reminiscences, *p. 67.*

The first refuge for orphans [in Iowa] was known as the Lawrence Orphans Home, and it was in a large brick building, erected for a hotel, and located about one and a half miles from Farmington. This building was used for about two years, from 1864, and it is said the children were then removed to a building which was known as the Quaker Academy, near the town of Houghton, Lee County. . . .

As my mother lived in Blackhawk County, only twenty-three miles south of Cedar Falls, my two sisters, two brothers and myself were taken to that institution. There was no north and south railroad in Blackhawk County at that time. We were taken by stage to

Waterloo, and from there seven miles by railroad, over the Dubuque and Sioux City Railway, now the Illinois Central.

We were taken to the home in October, 1866, and my seventh birthday had been May 20 of that year.

George Gallarno remembering occurrences in October 1866, "How Iowa Cared for Orphans of Her Soldiers of the Civil War,"
p. 170.

In our district school the history books devoted at least a third of their contents to the Civil War and every battle was set down in detail, often with a map beside it. I sup- posed no generation after ours was required to learn and know the battles, generals, plans, armies, and achieve- ments of both sides as we were. The events were recited without bitterness and with a breath-catching thankful- ness that in the end the Union had been saved. There remained in our minds forever the rollcall of battle names: Shiloh and Shenandoah, Malvern Hill and Cold Harbor, the Wilderness and Island Number Ten. If the words were not beautiful in themselves, they became so to us by the splendor of association.

Anne Gertrude Sneller, who was born in Onandoga County, New York, in 1883, A Vanished World,
pp. 21–22

5

An Age of Contrasts
1860–1905

Americans anticipating modest, steady progress and quiet prosperity in the years following the Civil War entered a period of great economic and social change. Technology was advancing, factories were proliferating, and cities were experiencing unprecedented growth. Before the Civil War, the United States had been a nation of farmers. By 1870, although the output of agriculture still surpassed that of manufacturing, 3.5 million Americans held factory jobs. Industry was clearly displacing agriculture as the foundation of the economy. By 1900, industry's profits would beat out agriculture's by $8.3 billion, and U.S. factories would employ 14.2 million people.

The number of people living in U.S. cities tripled between 1860 and 1890, rising from 6,217,000 to 22,106,000. This growth was not limited to cities in the East. The population of Kansas City swelled from 60,000 to 132,000 in a single decade, the 1880s, and Omaha's population went from 30,500 to 140,000 during the same period. Crime was on the rise in cities, too. Chicago reported a 500 percent increase in homicides between 1881 and 1898.

The cities drew young job seekers from rural communities and immigrants from Europe. Thousands of Irish, Germans, English, and Scandinavians had come to the United States after 1840, and by the 1850s, many Germans and Scandinavians had moved on to the Midwest and even to the Far West. Beginning in the 1890s, the majority of immigrants were from southern and eastern Europe. In just nine years, 1892 to 1900, 3,127,245 immigrants arrived in the United States. These newcomers, many of whom spoke no English and lacked employable skills, settled largely in inner-city ghettoes, where rents were cheap and factories were within walking distance.

By 1870, one-fourth of the nation's children lived in cities, the breeding grounds of vice and social disorder, and that fraction would continue to grow. Yet Middle America was starting to emerge, with the typical American family becoming urban or suburban and middle class. How children experienced life in the decades of the Gilded Age depended greatly on their family's income and where their parents were born. The life of a child from a prosperous suburban home bore little resemblance to that of an immigrant boy or girl living in a tenement or a southern child toiling in a textile mill.

THE CHERISHED MIDDLE-CLASS CHILD

Middle-class parents, insecure about their own position in a changing nation, created a safe nest for their young children within the home. In the nursery, mothers attended closely to their children's care and development, believing that the foundation of a sound moral character was formed in the first years of life. Of course, there was a practical reason for setting aside a room for children's care and play: doing so protected the bric-a-brac that cluttered Victorian parlors from rough-and-tumble games.

With family size half of what it had been at the start of the 19th century, middle-class mothers had fewer household responsibilities than earlier generations of women did. Consequently, they had more time to devote to child rearing. Parents dressed their sons and daughters in clothing designed specifically for children: suits and dresses that reflected the perceived purity and innocence of childhood and children's declining role as workers within the family.

Adults filled their home nurseries with the many new items now being manufactured for children's use, including cribs, high chairs, perambulators, miniature tables and chairs, and toys. More efficient manufacturing methods and the proliferation of railroads had made toys more affordable and accessible to the middle class. As parents loaded up their children's toy chests in a materialistic display of status and wealth, children came to depend on toys to give focus to their play.

New toy shops opened in cities and towns across the United States after 1850, and existing ones expanded. Macy's in New York City was the first department store to sell toys, and by 1875 its toy department was doing a brisk business. The increasingly popular mail-order catalogs also spurred toy sales. In 1892, Marshall Field department store in Chicago produced a 36-page catalog devoted exclusively to toys.

At Christmastime, department stores decked their windows with displays of stuffed Santas in sleighs and mechanical toys, designed to attract crowds and move merchandise. Gift giving was now a holiday tradition, and the children of the middle class and well-to-do looked forward to unwrapping train sets, dolls, board games, mechanical tin fire engines with ringing bells, elephants with moving heads, and other glorious factory-made playthings.

Toy manufacturers continually brought out new items to tempt American consumers. In 1868, toy maker Milton Bradley introduced the Historoscope, a miniature theatrical stage on which to display panoramic scenes of the Civil War. Around 1880, the so-called safety bicycle was developed, and cycling became a popular activity for children and adults. The safety bicycle had wheels of nearly equal size and was operated by pedals that drive the rear wheel by means of gears and a chain. A drop-frame version, designed for women and girls in long skirts to ride, was soon

Clothing designed for the middle-class children of 1905 suggested innocence and leisure. *(Library of Congress)*

being built as well. Statistics on bicycle ownership in one U.S. city, Los Angeles, reflect the vehicle's popularity nationwide. There were 50 bicycles in Los Angeles in 1890; by 1899, 30,000 city residents owned bikes.

In 1889, factory production made possible the first major toy craze in the United States. On February 16 of that year, an advertisement appeared for Pigs in Clover, a puzzle toy invented by C. M. Crandall. Three weeks later, the Waverly Toy Works, manufacturer of Pigs in Clover, was producing 8,000 of the games a day. A player solved the popular puzzle by maneuvering marbles through a simple maze of pasteboard rings. The trick was to get all of the marbles—the "pigs"—into a central enclosure—the "pen"—at the same time.

With its abundance of toys, the nursery was a place where mothers raised boys and girls together, and brothers and sisters engaged in common play. Once middle-class children outgrew the nursery, however, at the age of six or seven, their experiences differed according to their sex. The family demanded less work of both boys and girls than it had in the past, leaving them with more free time; yet while boys looked to the wider world for adventure and sought companionship among their peers, girls remained tied to the home and interacted more closely with adults.

THE SEPARATE WORLDS OF BOYS AND GIRLS

Boys of earlier generations enjoyed a close familiarity with their fathers' work and frequently shared in it, whether their fathers farmed or plied a trade. Now many middle-class fathers held jobs in offices, keeping records and balancing accounts, doing abstract work to which boys could not relate. At the same time, the child-care experts of the day cautioned that excessive influence and attention from his mother would have a feminizing influence on a boy. Therefore, essentially cut off from the world of adults, boys formed close bonds with one another and created a subculture that fostered conventionally masculine traits. This subculture valued control of the emotions, especially fear, because fearfulness was associated with females. In fact, the term *sissy*, an affectionate nickname for one's sister, evolved after 1880 into a derogatory term for a timid boy or man.

Boys challenged one another to triumph over fear and spent much of their time outdoors, engaged in games of skill and competition. They wrestled, ran races, and swam; they played tug-of-war, leapfrog, blind man's buff, and settlers and Indians. The latter game was often loosely based on the real-life adventures of pioneering family members and acquaintances. Boys also sought excitement through hiking and exploring, and they founded secret societies. In an 1898 survey of more than 4,000 South Carolina schoolchildren, boys named baseball, football, and swimming as their favorite games, along with fox and geese, in which one child—the fox—tries to catch the others—the geese. Ball games of all kinds were the favorite pastimes of boys in Worcester, Massachusetts, who were surveyed for a study published in 1899. These boys also expressed preferences for marbles, sledding, skating, tag, and hockey. With so much time spent in the unsupervised company of their peers, boys' play became rougher and more violent. It was not uncommon for boys to abuse cats and other animals for sport or to damage property. They battled with sticks and bottles and went home injured.

Kansas girls with their dolls, ca. 1900
(*The Kansas State Historical Society, Topeka, Kansas*)

Dolls were the favorite playthings of most girls in Worcester, but like boys, girls also favored active games, including sledding, jumping rope, skating, and playing tag and hide-and-seek. The findings in South Carolina were similar, with girls there listing dolls, skipping rope, croquet, and games such as drop-the-hand-kerchief as their play of choice. (Drop-the-handkerchief is played in a circle. One player runs around the circle and drops a handkerchief behind another's back. That child then picks up the handkerchief and chases the first player, trying to tag her before she returns to her place.)

Adults encouraged girls under 13 to engage in active play, which was thought to develop strength and rationality, although girls who played outdoors stayed close to home and apart from boys. No one expected boisterous play to make girls courageous, but it was thought to prevent them from becoming too faint of heart. It is interesting to note that parents who dissuaded their sons from taking up the sedentary, homey pursuits common among girls out of concern that those activities might be feminizing seemed not to worry that vigorous "boys' games" would make their daughters too masculine.

While boys roamed their neighborhoods independent of adults, girls maintained close ties with their mothers and other women. Urban and suburban middle-class girls had less housework to do than their mothers and grandmothers did when they were young, and they had fewer siblings to watch. Increasingly, it was through doll play that they practiced their future roles as women. Girls used their dolls to act out such social rituals as teas, visits, and funerals. For the middle-class girl, the homemade, functional doll was a relic of an earlier age. Her dolls were purchased toys with extravagant wardrobes. She might own wind-up dolls that walked, cried, or crawled on their hands and knees like babies. There were dolls made of china or bisque, with their painted mouths closed or with their lips parted to reveal tiny teeth. Although dolls were more affordable than in years past, they were still beyond the budgets of most working-class families. In the 1880s, when 40 percent of industrial workers earned less than $500 a year, a doll with its accessories could cost $30 or more.

Middle-class parents of the late 19th century may have spent money on toys more freely than their elders did, but they still wanted their sons and daughters to learn the value of a dollar. Jacob Abbott, author of the most popular parenting manual of the period, *Gentle Measures in the Management and Training of the Young,* advocated the weekly allowance as a method for teaching thrift and good judgment. Parents apparently preferred children to earn their spending money, though. A survey conducted at the end of the 19th century among children in California determined that only 7 percent of girls and 10 percent of boys received an allowance. Girls more commonly were paid for doing housework or running errands for their mothers, while boys tended to find some kind of paid work outside the home. Rural children of both sexes (17 percent of girls and 12 percent of boys) were paid for doing agricultural work.

Abbott based the advice in his book on the latest research in human development and suggested that parental expectations not exceed the capabilities of the juvenile body and mind. Without using the 20th-century term *role model,* he stated that parents influence children more through the example of their actions than through their instructions. Abbott also gave advice about punishment, writing that it should never be cruel or vindictive; rather, punishment should be appropriate to the offense and teach a lesson in proper behavior that will promote future happiness. Spending quiet time in a corner and sacrificing a desired activity were examples of appropriate punishments, according to Abbott.

How carefully did parents follow these suggestions? According to an 1897 study by a researcher at Stanford University, nearly half of all boys questioned and more than one-fourth of girls reported being whipped. The study also found that children were frequently scolded and that girls were often confined or given extra work as punishment, while many boys were sent to bed early or deprived of a meal.

A HARD LIFE FOR THE WORKING CLASS

Middle-class parents viewed children as fundamentally guiltless and uncorrupted, even if they were slow to alter their child-rearing practices accordingly. Earlier attitudes about the role of children persisted in immigrant and working-class families, however. These families continued to be large, and children were expected to contribute to the financial well-being of the group.

According to the census of 1880, more than 1 million children between the ages of 10 and 15 lived in U.S. cities. Most of them worked in factories. The expansion of industry in the second half of the 19th century caused a labor shortage that encouraged manufacturers to employ child workers, and an economic depression in the 1890s induced many desperate parents to send their children out to work. The children of immigrants were more likely to work than those of native-born parents, because there was a higher incidence of poverty among immigrants, and their families needed the money. In the South, children replaced slaves in textile mills. Children, some as young as four, found jobs in southern flour mills, machine shops, shoe and garment factories, and tobacco-processing plants.

Some city children helped out in their parents' places of business, and a small number were still apprenticed to artisans. City children also sold newspapers, flowers, fruit, and other merchandise on the street. The average age of newsboys in 1900 was 12, but many were much younger. These boys had to be at work by 5:00 A.M., and if they sold an evening edition, they could be out past midnight. Children in the street trades were exposed to crime, bad weather, and tuberculosis. Standing on hard pavement all day damaged their growing bones. Young street workers who went to school were often too tired to pay attention; for some, school was nothing more than a place to catch up on sleep.

Piecework continued to attract poor families, and especially immigrants. In their tenement homes, which essentially were crowded, poorly ventilated fire-traps, whole families completed a single step in the manufacture of garments, artificial flowers, and other goods. The income from this kind of repetitive work was so low that a family could work from morning until night and still earn too little to pay their expenses.

Immigrant children were also working in Canada. Between 1868 and 1925, approximately 80,000 British children went to Canada as indentured laborers to be farm hands or domestic servants. Most were younger than 14—too young to

Bath time in a tenement in the early 20th century *(Library of Congress)*

quit school or work full-time under British law. One-third of these children were orphans; the rest had at least one parent living but crossed the ocean alone.

In the United States, it was not only poverty that set apart immigrant children in the late 19th and early 20th centuries. The newcomers from southern and eastern Europe were predominantly Roman Catholic, Orthodox, and Jewish in a nation that was largely Protestant. Most spoke little or no English, and their Old World ways—everything from the lunches they ate to the clothing they wore—subjected them to ridicule.

Although many immigrant parents expected their children to help support the family by working, many others placed a higher value on education. As a result, thousands of children from southern and eastern Europe enrolled in urban schools that were ill prepared to meet their needs. They were thrown into an environment where English was the only language spoken and were expected to adapt without assistance. The number of children forced to learn the ropes in this way was significant. For example, according to the U.S. census for 1890, nearly four-fifths of school-age children in two cities, New York and Chicago, had foreign-born parents.

By 1860, most urban schools had divided their student bodies into grades, according to age. Educators who were uncertain where to place foreign-born children now grouped them according to their knowledge of English, with the result that city classrooms came to resemble rural schoolhouses, where children of all ages learned together.

Urban schools strained to serve a burgeoning population by crowding 60 or more children into a single classroom and sometimes seating pupils two to a desk. At a school on Henry Street in lower Manhattan, in the heart of a Jewish neighborhood, 80 children tried to learn in a classroom meant for 40. In 1900 the superintendent of schools in Brooklyn, New York, discovered four classrooms in which a single teacher tried to cope with 140 students. Milwaukee and Boston housed classes in portable structures; Buffalo, New York, schools turned hallways, basements, and coat closets into classrooms; and 768 New York City children attended school upstairs from a live poultry market.

A number of urban schools coped with overcrowding by educating children in shifts. In 1893, Minneapolis children in grades one through three attended school for half a day; in 1905, pupils at 63 percent of the elementary schools in New York City attended only part time. Schools also denied children entry. In 1882, the Philadelphia school system turned away 60,000 children for whom there was no space. The previous year, more than 9,000 children in New York City had been denied admittance into school for the same reason.

In the 18th century, schools had been viewed as vehicles for bringing together diverse groups to create a unified American culture and value system. They had accomplished this task well; by the middle of the 19th century, white America considered itself homogenous. Then, when immigration threatened to alter the established way of life, the solution was to change the immigrants' attitudes and habits, to offer a crash course in being American. Once again, the job of unifying the population fell to the public schools.

With Americanization as their goal, school administrators and teachers offered a curriculum that emphasized the reading and writing of English and U.S. history and culture. The learning process was dull, concentrating on memorization and recitation, and it was not always painless. Although some

American-born teachers reached out to young immigrants, a significant number were hostile to all foreigners, including the ones in their classes. Like the teacher in Buffalo, New York, at the start of the 20th century who found Orazio Sapienza's name too bothersome to pronounce, teachers capriciously changed children's names. The Buffalo teacher told the young son of Sicilian parents that his name was now George, and for the rest of his life, he was George Sapienza to everyone who knew him. Nearly 500 miles away, on Manhattan's Lower East Side, schoolchildren had their mouths washed out with soap for speaking Yiddish. Jewish girls in home economics classes were forced to break the dietary rules of their faith.

Yet despite all of the obstacles, children learned. The national illiteracy rate for people over 10 years of age, which was close to 20 percent in 1870, declined about 3 percent per decade over the next 40 years.

SCHOOLS DIVERSIFY AND DEVELOP

Members of the Catholic clergy were troubled by the bias prevalent in the public schools that so many immigrant Catholic children attended. To give these children an alternative, Bishop John Hughes of New York, the founder of Fordham University, led efforts to create a parochial school system in his state. By the end of the 19th century, almost every New York diocese was running a small school. Parochial schools were established elsewhere as well. In Boston, a city with a large immigrant Catholic population, 8 percent of schoolchildren were attending parochial schools in 1888; by 1894, Catholic schools handled 15 percent of Boston's school enrollment. The student bodies of parochial schools tended to be ethnically homogenous, i.e., predominantly Irish, Italian, or Polish, reflecting the communities that they served.

Schooling became compulsory in most states in the last decades of the 19th century. In 1850, Massachusetts became the first state to pass a compulsory-education law that applied to working and nonworking children alike. Most of the other states passed similar laws between 1870 and 1900. These laws required children to attend school from the age of seven or eight until they reached 12, 14, 15, or 16 years of age. By 1907, only nine southern states lacked compulsory-education laws.

Because the new laws were weakly enforced, most working-class children attended school between the ages of eight and 13, stopping after the sixth grade. No U.S. city saw more than 60 percent of its school-age children enrolled in school during the late 19th century, and percentages for attendance were lower than those for enrollment. Although public high schools were built in most cities east of the Mississippi River by the end of the 19th century, few young people attended secondary school, public or private. Approximately 203,000 young people were enrolled in high school in 1890. The more financially well-off a family was, the longer its children stayed in school. As a rule, though, affluent boys left school before their sisters did, usually to enter business or go to college. Only Princeton University and the University of Wisconsin asked to see a diploma from an approved secondary school. All other colleges and universities looked instead at an applicant's score on an entrance exam. The typical high-school student in late 19th-century America, then, was female and middle-class.

At the same time that high schools were being constructed, kindergartens were gaining popularity in the United States. These classes, designed to provide mental stimulation and education to children between the ages of four and six, originated with the German educator Friedrich Froebel. Froebel had observed that young children had a strong instinct for self-development and that they educated themselves through play. In 1837 he opened a school in Blankenburg, Prussia, at which children could be nurtured "like flowers." Because he had a keen interest in botany, Froebel called his school a garden of children, or kindergarten.

Froebel's writings inspired Elizabeth Peabody, a teacher at an infant school in Concord, Massachusetts, to open a private kindergarten in Boston in 1860. In 1867, Peabody traveled to Europe to observe kindergartens on that continent and to study Froebel's educational philosophy. She returned to the United States to promote the kindergarten movement. Public kindergartens were established in Boston, Philadelphia, and St. Louis after the Civil War, and they slowly appeared in other locations. Those first American kindergartens offered a safe environment for learning and supervised play. They taught skills that would benefit children in their later school careers, including listening, punctuality, following directions, and self-control. They also took immigrant children off city streets and introduced them to American life.

As the kindergarten movement spread, teachers had trouble putting their hands on all of the blocks, paints, and other educational toys that their program required until toy manufacturer Milton Bradley came to their aid. Bradley, a firm believer in learning through play, worked in cooperation with Elizabeth Peabody to produce a variety of toys for use in kindergartens and Sunday schools, including the popular Kinder-Garten Alphabet and Building Blocks, first available in 1872. Sold in sets of 85 or 38, these blocks were decorated with letters of the alphabet, numbers, and pictures of animals.

Educators focused on children's mental development while municipalities addressed their health needs by seeking to improve the cleanliness and healthfulness of schools. In 1887, the New York Legislature passed the Health and Decency Act, which required school districts to provide separate privies or indoor toilet facilities for girls and boys. School trustees were now obligated to keep buildings clean; failure to do so could mean a loss of state financial aid. Hygiene improved in New York schools with enactment of the 1887 law, but because the state employed too few inspectors to monitor compliance, progress was slow. In the remaining years of the century, other states followed New York's example and passed sanitation codes of their own.

Philadelphia was the first U.S. city to promote fire prevention in its schools. An 1877 city ordinance required fireproof stairways in all public buildings, including schools. Soon all schools in Pennsylvania were required by law to have fire escapes. Baltimore's school board looked into fire safety in 1879, after fires had occurred in several schools, and found that children and teachers had rushed to converge on a single exit each time. In 1882, Baltimore schools conducted their first fire drills to ensure that any future evacuations would be orderly.

Schools became cleaner and safer, but the problem of foul air and poor ventilation persisted. Kentucky's superintendent of education reported in 1874 that putrid air permeated the state's schools; in Wisconsin, only 23 of 600 schools inspected by the Board of Health in 1879 were properly ventilated. An 1878

Massachusetts Board of Education report stated optimistically that schools in the state were being constructed with flues to conduct odors outdoors, but nine years later, the board discovered that 90 percent of Massachusetts schools depended on doors and windows for ventilation. An 1889 study ordered by the Boston City Council supported this finding. Of 163 Boston schools surveyed, 146 lacked an efficient, up-to-date ventilation system. The modern systems that had been installed in the remaining 17 schools were effective, according to the researchers, only "more or less."

Louisiana, the first state to establish a board of health (in 1855), was a leader in addressing this issue. Beginning in 1878, state public health and education officials cooperated to see that all new school buildings were adequately lit and ventilated. Throughout the nation, improvement was gradual. For example, a high school with a complete ventilation system was erected in Chester, Pennsylvania, in 1885 and 1886. Also, Chicagoans rebuilt their schools with ductwork after the fire of 1871 destroyed all but two school buildings. By 1900, the nauseating stench of the schoolhouse was nothing more than an unpleasant memory of the fading century.

CHRONICLE OF EVENTS

1860

The urban population of the United States is 6,217,000.

Most urban schools have separated their students into grades.

In Boston, Elizabeth Peabody opens the first private kindergarten in the United States.

1867

Elizabeth Peabody travels to Europe to study the kindergarten movement.

1868

Toy maker Milton Bradley introduces the Historoscope, a toy theater that displays panoramic scenes of the Civil War.

British children come to Canada as indentured laborers. By 1925, approximately 80,000 British children will have followed this route.

1870

About 3.1 million Americans, including thousands of children, hold factory jobs.

The national illiteracy rate for persons over 10 years of age is 20 percent; this rate will decline 3 percent per decade over the next 40 years.

1871

October 8: A fire starts in Chicago and quickly gets out of control; it will burn for 29 hours and destroy much of the city, including all but two schools; Chicagoans will rebuild their schools with ductwork for ventilation.

1872

Milton Bradley produces the Kinder-Garten Alphabet Building Blocks, the most popular of his educational toys designed for use in schools.

1874

The Kentucky superintendent of education reports that the air quality in state schools is poor.

1875

The toy department at Macy's in New York City becomes increasingly popular with shoppers.

1878

The Massachusetts Board of Education reports that schools in the state's cities are being constructed with ventilation flues.

Louisiana public health and education officials work to ensure that all new schools in the state are properly lit and ventilated.

1879

The Baltimore School Board investigates fire safety in schools.

Of 600 schools inspected by the Wisconsin Board of Health, only 23 are properly ventilated.

1880

The population of Kansas City is 60,000; the population of Omaha is 30,500.

The safety bicycle is developed at this time.

More than 1 million children ages 10 to 15 live in U.S. cities, according to the national census.

1880s

A fully accessorized doll can cost $30. Forty percent of industrial workers earn less than $500 a year.

1881

New York City schools turn away more than 9,000 children for whom there is no space.

1882

Philadelphia schools are forced to deny admission to 60,000 children.

Baltimore schools conduct their first fire drills.

1885–1886

A high school with a complete ventilation system is constructed in Chester, Pennsylvania.

1887

The New York Legislature passes the Health and Decency Act, requiring public schools to provide separate toilet facilities for girls and boys and obligating school trustees to keep schools clean.

A Philadelphia city ordinance makes fireproof stairways mandatory in public buildings, including schools.

The Massachusetts Board of Education finds that 90 percent of schools in the state use doors and windows for ventilation.

1888

In Boston, 8 percent of schoolchildren attend parochial schools.

1889

The population of Kansas City is now 132,000; the population of Omaha has reached 140,000.

The Boston City Council surveys 163 schools and finds that none are adequately ventilated.

February 16: An advertisement appears for the puzzle toy Pigs in Clover.

March: The Waverly Toy Works produces 8,000 Pigs in Clover puzzles a day.

1890

The urban population of the United States is now 22,106,000.

Four-fifths of school-age children in Chicago and New York have immigrant parents, according to the U.S. census.

There are 50 bicycles in Los Angeles.

Approximately 203,000 students are enrolled in U.S. high schools.

1890s

The majority of immigrants coming to the United States are from eastern and southern Europe.

Economic depression prompts many working-class families to send their children to work.

1892

The Marshall Field department store in Chicago distributes a 36-page toy catalog.

1893

Minneapolis children in grades one through three attend school half a day.

1892–1900

During these years, 3,127,245 immigrants arrive in the United States.

A Children's Day parade in Detroit's Belle Isle Park, ca. 1905–15 *(Library of Congress)*

1894

Fifteen percent of schoolchildren in Boston attend Catholic schools.

1897

Nearly half of boys and one-fourth of girls questioned by Stanford University researchers report being whipped as punishment.

1898

Chicago measures a 500 percent increase in homicides over 1881.

South Carolina boys who are surveyed name baseball, football, swimming, and fox and geese as their favorite kinds of play; girls name dolls, skipping rope, croquet, and games such as drop-the-handkerchief.

1899

There are now 30,000 bicycles in Los Angeles.

Among Worcester, Massachusetts, schoolchildren surveyed about their favorite forms of play, boys choose ball games, marbles, sledding, and skating; girls select dolls, sledding, jumping rope, and skating.

Most Catholic dioceses in New York State are operating small schools.

1900

Manufacturing in the United States employs 14.2 million people.

Industry's profits surpass those of agriculture by $8.3 billion.

The typical American family is urban and middle class.

The average age of newsboys is 12.

Most states have passed compulsory-education laws.

Teachers in four Brooklyn, New York, classrooms each have charge of 140 students.

1905

Children at 63 New York City elementary schools attend part time due to overcrowding.

EYEWITNESS TESTIMONY

I was named in a casual manner when I was a child, but father didn't like it. My mother's sisters were Anne and Mary, one wanted to call me Anna and one wanted to call me Mary, so they doubled the name. And mother said, "It would be all right if you call her Anna Mary, I do detest the name Mary Anne." But father didn't like the name, he always wanted me called Sarah after his sister, so I was called Sissy until I was about six years old. About that time, a man came into the yard one day and wanted to know what my name was, and what was my little brother's name. I said my name was Sissy and brother's name was Bubby. So I didn't know what a name meant up until that time. I told mother what this man had said, and she told me then what my name was.

You see, they didn't pay much attention to the kids. But they thought a lot of their kids anyway. . . . Mother didn't go to bed that she didn't go around to see that they were all sleeping and covered up, and father watched over us too.

Anna Mary Robertson Moses, who was born in 1860, Grandma Moses: My Life's Story, *pp. 10–11.*

The wicked boy could not resist the temptation to tie a bunch of firecrackers to a dog's tail, ignite the fuse, and watch the result with great glee. The dog, conscious of the fact that a batter of explosives attacked his rear anatomy, fled in a mad chase down the street in order to escape calamity. That was one of the wicked boy's Fourth of July diversions. For the rest of the year, he would tie a tin can to the dog's tail.

William George Bruce writing about his childhood in Milwaukee, ca. 1865–70, I Was Born in America, *p. 33.*

Mother was in advance of her time . . . in recognizing the individual rights of children. We had two bathrooms—then an unprecedented number for any house—a day nursery and a playroom. In the nursery we each had our own drawers for shoes, clothing, and toys, and we were expected to keep them in order. Some of us did and others didn't.

In the playroom each girl was given a doll house made out of a packing box and divided into three floors and closed with a door. We loved to dress up in "train" dresses, and to save her own skirts and sheets Mother had calico trained frocks made for all of us, and later fancy pink and blue cambric ones which rustled and shone like silk—or so we believed!

Addie Hibbard Gregory recalling early childhood in Chicago, ca. 1866, A Great-Grandmother Remembers, *pp. 32–33.*

A memorable feature of brick pavements was that on snowy days the best sliding places were made on them. "Making up" the slide was commenced by boys and girls, soon after the snow began to fall, and the perfect slide was only possible when the snow was neither too dry, nor too moist. By sliding a little further at every run the length was increased to thirty feet or more. Slippery as smooth ice, it took skill to maintain one's balance, particularly if you went backward, when you might take a fall, or you could go "little-woman" as it was called when the slider squatted down after the preliminary run. Collisions causing topsy-turvies brought shrieks of laughter from the children.

When in fine condition the boys never dared to leave the slide until the last call for supper, as on returning, even after a short absence, we would be sure to find some "meddlesome" housewife had sprinkled the glassy runway with hot ashes. Old timers, like myself, will remember with a thrill the late winter evenings they tarried to get in a few more solitary slides, after the kids who feared maternal wrath had gone home; when "all the air a solemn stillness held;" the flickering lamplight, the snow covered street and the long stretch of glistening slide!

Meredith Janvier recalling the winters of his childhood in the 1870s and 1880s, Baltimore Yesterdays, *pp. 5–6.*

I was a pretty boy with lovely long blond curls. This I know well because it kept me from playing with the other fellows of my age. They jeered at my curls and called me a girl or a "sissy boy" and were surprised when I answered with a blow. They were taken off their guard by my attack, but they recovered and charged in mass upon me, sending me home scratched, bleeding, torn, to my mother, to beg her to cut my hair. She would not. My father had to do it. One day when the gang had caught me, thrown me down, and stuffed horse-droppings into my mouth, he privately promised me relief, and the next morning he took me downtown and had his barber cut off my curls, which he wrapped up in a paper as a gift for my mother. How she wept over them! How I rejoiced over them!

Lincoln Steffens writing about his childhood in Sacramento, California, in the 1870s, The Autobiography of Lincoln Steffens, *Vol. 1, p. 9.*

. . . [P]aper dolls became the mere puppets of the imagination by which I enacted the blood-curdling melodramas of love and adventure which I didn't know how to spell so couldn't write.

These paper dolls . . . were not the prim and prissy paper dolls of ordinary paper-doll commerce, gaily lithographed creatures with eight or ten costumes apiece, both fronts and backs, but free-lance paper dolls as it were, filched at random from old magazines or current fashion plates.

Thus in a roomy cave under my father's desk, all the while that he worked quite undisturbed on his sermons and book reviews only a few inches above me, I, audibly and often vociferously, affianced the proudest scion of some tailor's catalogue to a vivid Red Riding Hood torn from a last year's picture-book; or with a hapless spinster coaxed from a Godley's Lady's Book, or a haughty Queen of England cut very adroitly from an English Christmas magazine with a brightly wrapped bottle of Gordon's Gin still practically intact upon her nether side, would instigate a screeching massacre by a bevy of half-naked savages whom I had just discovered in one of my father's missionary pamphlets. That these aforesaid savages bore unmistakable fragments of scriptural printings on their backs, alone relieved them of a dishabille of frontage not otherwise compatible with a Christian home.

Eleanor Hallowell Abbott, who was a child in Cambridge, Massachusetts, in the 1870s, Being Little in Cambridge When Everyone Else Was Big, *pp. 139–40.*

I was eight years old when I stepped out into society. A note in beautiful Spencerian handwriting, on pink paper with gilt edges . . . came to me, declaring: "Master Willie White is invited to be present at the birthday party of Miss Alice Murdock at their home on Star Street, March 23, 1876." And so I was dressed to kill in a little blue suit, bound in black braid with shiny little golden buttons, white stockings, and black shoes. My hair was wet and pasted down, and my neck washed even behind the ears. It was an afternoon party, bright and gay, and little Alice, with her spinal curvature, was the sunshine of it all. . . . We played games . . . and then went on the lawn, shot arrows at a target, and rather wickedly played hide-and-seek in the barn and had ice cream and cake and lemonade, sitting around like little angels eating their ambrosia.

William Allen White, who was eight years old in 1874, The Autobiography of William Allen White, *p. 10.*

His mother is reading to him every night while his father protests that she is spoiling him; reading the Dickens stories which he understands and the Cooper Indian stories which he loves, and *The Mill on the Floss* by George Eliot, which bothers him a little, and a story by George Sand about a dark pool, which scares him. He knows his Mother Goose by heart. His gospel hymns are engraved on his memory for life. He is going to four Sunday Schools for purely social reasons—because the boys are there and he is a gregarious kid. And, because his memory is a malleable tablet, he has learned hundreds of verses and, being a bit of a smarty, likes to show off.

William Allen White writing in the third person about himself as a child ca. 1876, The Autobiography of William Allen White, *pp. 13–14.*

I was three years old and saw my first Christmas tree. . . .

[It] was at the house of the German consul. He and his wife were young people recently married, and this tree celebrated their first Christmas in America, and so it was all a perfect German tree should be. . . . I can see the room still, in a typical rented suburban house, new

Christmas in the United States, 1897 *(Library of Congress)*

and tasteless, with stiff black-walnut furnishings, all throwing more strongly into relief the glory of the marvellous glittering tree towering to the ceiling, shining with threads of fine-spun gold, wreathed with chains and festoons of red and silver, hung with iridescent balls of gleaming metallic colors, with long icicles and toys and silver stars, and at the very top a snowy angel blowing on a tiny trumpet. Then my father and the consul began to light the candles. Real living flames, one by one they quivered into being like stars that are born at twilight, until the whole tree shimmered and breathed with their beauty.

Una Hunt, who was three years old in 1879,
Una Mary, pp. 9–10.

As Mamma put me to bed [on Christmas Eve] she told me about Santa Claus and read me "The Night before Christmas"—a poem sacred to many of my most precious memories. Then we all hung up our stockings around the fireplace in Mamma's room, and, sure enough, in the morning they were filled and overflowing in piles on the floor with presents for all of us, proving that the poem had been true and Santa Claus really had come down the chimney and galloped away with a much lightened sleigh. . . .

Christmas became the great day of the year, the day all the other days seemed merely shadows of, and Santa Claus was its spirit, the only person I associated with Christmas, for it was not until I was nine years old that I heard it was Christ's birthday.

Una Hunt remembering Christmases ca. 1879–85,
Una Mary, pp. 11–12.

In the block on which we lived, there were just five red brick, high stoop, four story private houses. . . . The remaining houses on the block . . . were tenements, and the house next door to ours was the worst of all. . . . This house and its inhabitants were a disgrace to the neighborhood and elicited constant, disgusted comments from the "better" people on the street, for drunken brawls and brutal fights occurred frequently there, and miserable derelicts of humanity often dragged themselves in and out of its doors. . . .

But there were good people and pleasant sights in that dreadful house as well: young mothers nursing their babies on the front steps; young fathers coming home with cheerful greetings to their families; little children playing, unconcerned with their environment, in the squalid yard. It was these children whom I was

not permitted to know, who were never invited into our yard, who had for me an uncanny fascination. I would watch them from the window of our extension sitting room, and sometimes I would call to them and they to me, but then mother usually came and closed the window.

One bright afternoon—it must have been in the late fall—my mother stood with me near the window looking over a large basket of apples that the cook had just purchased from a peddler. . . . [S]he heard the voices of the children in the yard next door and, leaning out of the window, she threw down an apple to them. One little boy deftly caught it, and now all the others began to clamor that they wanted apples too. This time mother took the basket to the window with her and threw out apples and still more apples until every child in the yard was supplied and the basket was three quarters emptied.

Meta Lilienthal recalling an autumn day in New York City,
ca. 1880, Dear Remembered World, pp. 46–48.

Mary Elizabeth and I were playing Dolls. We rarely did this on a pleasant day in Summer, Dolls being an indoor game, matched with carpets and furniture and sewing baskets rather than with blue sky and with the soft brilliance of the grass. But that day we had brought everything out in the side yard under the little catalpa tree, and my eleven dolls (counting the one without any face, and Irene Helena, the home-made one, and the two penny ones) were in a circle on chairs and boxes and their backs, getting dressed for the tea-party. There was always going to be a tea-party when you played Dolls—you of course had to lead up to something, and what else was there to lead up to save a tea-party? To be sure, there might be an occasional marriage, but boy-dolls were never very practical; they were invariably smaller than the bride-doll, and besides we had no mosquito-netting suitable for a veil. Sometimes we had them go for a walk, and once or twice we had tried playing that they were housecleaning; but these operations were not desirable, because in neither of them could the dolls dress up, and the desirable part of playing dolls is, as everybody knows, to dress them in their best.

Zona Gale remembering doll play ca. 1880,
When I Was a Little Girl, pp. 195–96.

Every Baltimore boy, in those days, had to be a partisan of some engine company, or, as the phrase ran, to go for it. The Hollins street boys went for No. 14, whose house was in Hollins street three blocks west of Union Square. Whenever an alarm came in a large bell on the roof of the engine-house broadcast it, and every boy within earshot reached into his hip-pocket for his directory of alarm-boxes. Such directories were given out as advertisements by druggists, horseshoers, saloonkeepers and so on, and every boy began to tote one as soon as he could read. If the fire was nearby, or seemed to be close to a livery-stable, a home for the aged, or any other establishment promising lively entertainment, all hands dropped whatever was afoot and set off for it at a gallop. It was usually out by the time we reached the scene, but sometimes we had better luck. Once we saw a blaze in a slaughter-house, with a drove of squealing hogs cremated in a pen, and another time we were entranced by a fire in the steeple of a Baptist church.

H. L. Mencken, Happy Days, 1880–1892, *pp. 125–26.*

The humor of the young bourgeoisie males of Baltimore, in those days was predominantly skatological. . . . The favorite jacosities had to do with horse apples . . . and small boys who lost control of their sphincters at parties or in Sunday-school; when we began to spend our Summers in the country my brother and I also learned the comic possibilities of cow flops. Even in the city a popular ginger-and-cocoanut cake, round in contour and selling for a cent, was called a cow flop, and little girls were supposed to avoid it, at least in the presence of boys.

H. L. Mencken, Happy Days, 1880–1892, *pp. 135–36.*

[My friend Harry and I] had two favorite games. One was to jump up and down in the centre of a large double bed, the springs sending us high in the air again at the end of each jump. It was blissful in itself, this effortless being shot straight up, like coming to the surface of the water after a dive; and then on coming down on the soft, bouncing mattress, to keep one's balance was almost as skilful as the circus rider's poise on the back of her horse. . . .

Our other game we only played when the family were all out. We felt it would not be approved. The servants certainly took that view of it, but, as they never told on us, we kept on playing it with a feeling of wickedness that was half its excitement. This was indoor coasting. We did it sitting on brooms or a tin tea-tray, down the front staircase in Harry's house—his stairs were steeper than ours. The broom was the safe

and conservative method, as the handle went in front and broke the fall at bottom; also it went more slowly; but my soul was only satisfied by the perils and joys of the tea-tray. I started at the top, collecting my small self and superfluous skirts as near the centre of the tray as possible, holding fast to the carpet until I was ready. Then I gave a push with both hands, and down through bumping, clattering space I tore with such impetus that I only stopped, when shot off the tray at the bottom step, by bumping into the front door at the opposite end of the hall.

Una Hunt describing her games of the early 1880s,
Una Mary, *pp. 22–23.*

The children I knew and played with during the eight years that I lived in Cincinnati were nearly all boys. There were a few girls—I remember them in the background—but boys cared for the things I liked. . . . [T]ogether we climbed every tree and shed in the neighborhood. I have always admired my mother's courage in allowing it, for I was often badly hurt, but after each fall, when vinegar and brown paper had been applied, her only comment was, "You must learn to climb better," and I did. Soon I could get to almost any roof by way of the waterspout and gutters.

Una Hunt describing her play in the early 1880s,
Una Mary, *pp. 24–25.*

. . . I slipped the screen from my window and leaned out in the dusk. The night, warm, fragrant, significant, was inviting me to belong to it, was asking me, even as bright day had asked me, what it had in common with the stuffiness and dulness of forever watching others do things. . . .

I ran blindly down the stairs where my Mother was helping to put away the supper dishes—in the magic of the night, helping to put away the supper dishes.

"Mother!" I cried, "Mother! Who made it so much harder to be a girl?"

Zona Gale recalling an event from the early 1880s,
When I Was a Little Girl, *pp. 208–09.*

. . . [W]e had just emerged from the age of discipline and there were reminiscences everywhere that a child soon learned to understand. It was the grand-parents you had to watch out for. Every family had a Great-Aunt Lizzie or a Grandma Smith with a thimble for knuckles and a withering voice, while the grandfathers, when they were not affectionate, looked through

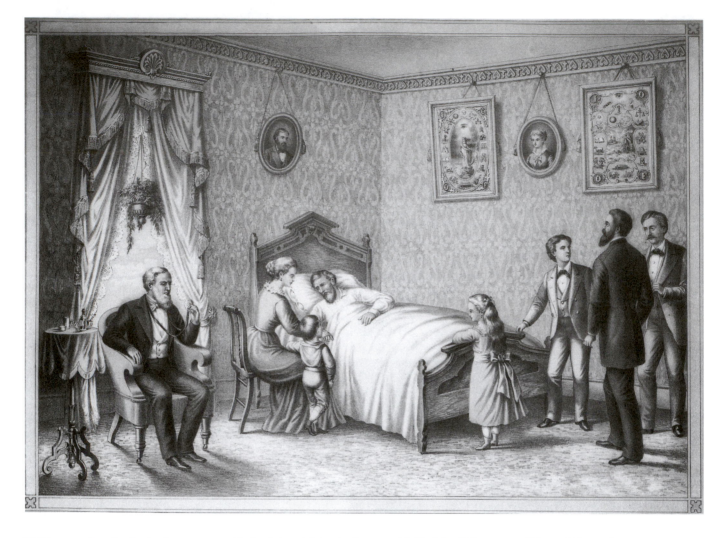

Children continued to be in close contact with the sick and dying in the second half of the 19th century. *(Library of Congress)*

children as if they were not there. Parents were by no means indulgent, yet they seemed usually to be secretly leagued with us to give the child a chance in the house.
Henry Seidel Canby, who grew up in Delaware in the 1880s, The Age of Confidence, *pp. 32–33.*

There was no "organized play," either athletic or otherwise. Any yard did for ball throwing, and one or two for crude tennis. When football swept in we took to the lots, but even at school it was mob work. The feminine influence could be felt in the shrubbery corners where the girls had their doll houses, and on rainy days sex distinctions were dropped in games of Stop and Hearts inside. There was always something to do and somewhere to do it.
Henry Seidel Canby recalling play in Delaware in the 1880s, The Age of Confidence, *p. 36.*

I had two favorite dolls, Elizabeth and Isabella. Isabella was made of French bisque china, as it was called, jointed at the shoulders and hips, had golden curls and eyes that shut. She was given to me by my uncle-to-be and was a person one could dress very fashionably, she had such innate style. . . .

My other favorite doll, Elizabeth, was bought one Christmas with money a cousin had sent me from California. . . . I selected her myself. She had a kid body, bisque head and hands—one finger was gone when I got her—and for hair there was pasted on her head some brownish lamb's wool. She was not beautiful. I knew that quite well. And she was broken. I saw that, too, and pitied her accordingly; and no amount of argument on the part of my mother and aunt, who were with me, could persuade me not to buy her. She appealed to something deep within me the instant I saw her lying there among the ringleted blond and brown haired beauties. She was as unlike a Real Doll as I was unlike a Real Girl; so we simply belonged together, and I loved her better than I did all the others, even more than I did my Big Doll brought to me from Paris, who was the size of a real child and the climax of all that Paris could achieve. The Big Doll was my great pride, but Elizabeth was my love.

Una Hunt, who played with Isabella and Elizabeth ca. 1885, Una Mary, *pp. 161–63.*

The schoolroom is a propaganda of contagion. The opening of schools in the autumn is the signal for the outbreak of contagious diseases rekindled from the still smoking embers of the last year's epidemic. There is no remedy, save in the formulation of discreet rules and their rigid enforcement by the authorities. Children come to the schoolroom from every sort of home, the unclean and the clean. Those wearing soiled clothing mingle with the neat and tidy. No schoolroom should have an odor, and no teacher should be employed whose olfactories are at all blunted. There is a prison smell, a hospital odor, a lying-in odor, etc., and there is a school odor, and wherever these exist there is disease and death. Right here is the place to begin the practical instruction in hygiene. Impressions made upon the growing mind are lasting for good or evil. It is very hard to convince people of the necessity of caring for their bodies after they have formed habits of uncleanliness. This is the reason that we meet with so much opposition in enforced sanitation. We shall never accomplish much in public hygiene until we commence with the school room. Wash-rooms, clothes-rooms, shoe-rooms, are necessary attachments to every schoolroom.

J. A. Larrabee, M.D., November 3, 1888, "The Schoolroom a Factor in the Production of Disease," pp. 613–14.

The school life, brief as it is, may reasonably be asked to furnish to the Republic loyal and obedient citizens; to the business world, men with a courage and a grip that will not easily let go in the pushing affairs of trade; to social life, an ease and grace of manners, a strength of self-reliance, which shall put each in possession of his full powers for his own up-building and for the advancement of his associates; and *to the home life of the nation,* men and women pure in heart, clear in conviction, strong in purpose, loving their children and loving to live with them.

Bettie A. Dutton, Cleveland, Ohio, educator, 1889, "Discipline in the Elementary School," in William A. Bullough, Cities and Schools in the Gilded Age, *p. 7.*

. . . [T]hough we feared to venture out of the building we did not lack amusement. Everything was new and interesting. To me it was pure pleasure just to stay in our own room and look and examine our new American furniture. . . .

A great part of the time we stayed out on the stoop. I was dazed by all there was to see. I looked with wonder at the tall houses, the paved streets, the street lamps. As I had never seen a large city and only had had a glimpse of a small one, I thought these things true only of America.

Rose Cohen, who was born in Russia in 1880 and immigrated to the United States ca. 1890, Out of the Shadow, *p. 71.*

. . . [F]ather came home at noon and took me along to the shop where he worked. We climbed the dark, narrow stairs of a tenement house on Monroe Street [New York City] and came into a bright room filled with noise. I saw about five or six men and a girl. The men turned and looked at us when we passed. I felt scared and stumbled. One man asked in surprise:

"Avrom, is this your daughter? Why, she is only a little girl!"

My father smiled. "Yes," he said, "but wait till you see her sew."

He placed me on a high stool opposite the girl, laid a pile of pocket flaps on the little narrow table between us, and showed me how to baste.

All afternoon I sat on my high stool, a little away from the table, my knees crossed tailor fashion, basting flaps.

Rose Cohen, who was introduced to piecework ca. 1890, Out of the Shadow, *p. 81.*

I liked my work and learned it easily, and father was pleased with me. As soon as I knew how to baste pocket-flaps he began to teach me how to baste the coat edges. This was hard work. The double ply of overcoat cloth stitched in with canvas and tape made a very stiff edge. My fingers often stiffened with pain as I rolled and basted the edges. Sometimes a needle or two would break before I could do one coat. Then father would offer to finish the edge for me. But if he gave me my choice I never let him.

Rose Cohen writing about the piecework she performed in the 1890s, Out of the Shadow, *p. 84.*

The Tenth Census [1880] gave our total foreign-born population as 6,679,943; but we must not forget their children of the first generation, who . . . present a more serious problem than their parents, the immigrants. This class numbered in 1880, 8,276,053, making a total population of nearly 15,000,000 which was foreign by birth or parentage. . . .

So immense a foreign element must have a profound influence on our national life and character. Immigration . . . furnishes the soil which feeds the life of several of the most noxious growths of our civilization. . . .

Let me hasten to recognize the high worth of many of our citizens of foreign birth, not a few of whom are eminent in the pulpit and in all the learned professions. Many come to us in full sympathy with our free institutions, and desiring to aid us in promoting a Christian civilization. But no one knows better than these same intelligent and Christian foreigners that they do not represent the mass of immigrants. The typical immigrant is a European peasant, whose horizon has been narrow, whose moral and religious training has been meager or false, and whose ideas of life are low.

Josiah Strong, 1891, in the best-selling book Our Country, *pp. 54–56.*

The piano struck up a march and from the hall we paraded into assembly—eyes straight ahead in military style. Mrs. Cutter [the teacher] was there on the platform, dominating the scene, her eyes penetrating every corner of the assembly hall. It was always the same. We stood at attention as the Bible was read and at attention as the flag was waved back and forth, and we sang the same song. I didn't know what the words meant but I sang it loudly with all the rest, in my own way, "Tree Cheers for de Red Whatzam Blu!"

But best of all was another song that we used to sing at these assemblies. It was a particular favorite of Mrs. Cutter's, and we sang it with great gusto, "Honest boys who never tread the streets." This was in the days when we not only trod the streets but practically lived in them.

Leonard Covello, Italian immigrant, who began attending school in Manhattan ca. 1892, The Heart Is the Teacher, *p. 27.*

With a weary expression my father glanced over the marks on the report card and was about to sign it. However, he paused with the pen in his hand.

"What is this?" he said. "Leonard Covello! What happened to the *i* in Coviello?"

. . ."From Leonardo to Leonard I can follow," he said, "a perfectly natural process. In America anything can happen and does happen. But you don't change a family name. A name is a name. What happened to the *i*?"

"Mrs. Cutter took it out," I explained. "Every time she pronounced Coviello it came out Covello. So she took out the *i*. That way it's easier for everybody."

. . . For a moment my father sat there, bitter rebellion building in him. Then with a shrug of resignation, he signed the report card and shoved it over to me.

Leonard Covello, Italian immigrant, recalling an event occurring ca. 1892, The Heart Is the Teacher, *pp. 29–30.*

In a Hester Street [New York City] house we found two little girls pulling basting-thread. They were both Italians and said that they were nine. In the room in which one of them worked thirteen men and two women were sewing. The child could speak English. She said that she was earning a dollar a week and worked every day from seven in the morning till eight in the evening. . . .

Even the crowding, the feverish haste of the half-naked men and women, and the litter and filth in which they worked, were preferable to the silence and desolation we encountered in one shop up under the roof of a Broome Street tenement. The work there had given out—there had been none these two months, said the gaunt, hard-faced woman who sat eating a crust of dry bread and drinking water from a tin pail at the empty bench. The man sat silent and moody in a corner; he was sick. The room was bare. The only machine left was not worth taking to the pawnshop. Two dirty children, naked but for a torn undershirt apiece, were fishing over the stair-rail with a bent pin on an idle thread. An old rag was their bait.

Jacob Riis, 1892, The Children of the Poor, *pp. 96–97.*

A clean face is the ticket of admission to the kindergarten. A clean or whole frock is wisely not insisted upon too firmly at the start; torn or dirty clothes are not so easily mended as a smudged face, but the kindergarten reaches that too in the end. . . . Once he is let in, the child is in for a general good time that has little of school or visible discipline to frighten him. He joins in the ring for the familiar games, delighted to find that the teacher knows them, too, and can be "It" and his "fair lady" in her turn. . . . After the game there are a hundred things for him to do that do not seem like work in the least. Between threading colored beads, cutting and folding pink and green papers in all sorts of odd ways, as boats and butterflies and fancy baskets; moulding, pasting, drawing, weaving and blowing soap-bubbles when all the rest has ceased to hold his attention, the day slips by like a beautiful dream, and he flatly refuses to believe that it is gone when the tenement home claims him again. Not infrequently he goes home howling, to be found the next morning waiting at the door an hour before the teacher comes. Little Jimmie's mother says that he gets up at six o'clock to go to the Fifty-first Street kindergarten, and that she has to whip him to make him wait until nine.

Jacob Riis, 1892, The Children of
the Poor, *pp. 176–78.*

It is the absolute helplessness of the human infant which challenges the maternal instinct to rush to his rescue, lest he should die at once. And to continue to study his manifestations of pleasure and discontent with obedient respectfulness, is the perfection of maternal nursing. But when the child has got so far as to know the simplest uses of its own body, and especially after it has learned enough words to express its simplest wants and sensations, even parents seem to think it can get on by itself, so that children from about two to five years of age are left to self-education, as it were; this virtual abandonment being crossed by a capricious and arbitrary handling of them—mind and body—on the part of those around them, which is even worse than the neglect; for when are children more unable, than between three and five years old, to guide their own thoughts and action? How would a garden of flowers fare, to be planted, and then left to grow with so little scientific

Anonymous American children, Lancaster, Pennsylvania, ca. 1890 *(Author's collection)*

care taken by the gardener, as is bestowed upon children between one and five years old?

... A kindergarten means a guarded company of children, who are to be treated as a gardener treats his plants; that is, in the first place, studied to see what they are, and what conditions they require for the fullest and most beautiful growth; in the second place, put into or supplied with these conditions, with as little handling of their individuality as possible, but with an unceasing genial and provident care to remove all obstructions, and favor all the circumstances of growth. It is because they are living organisms that they are to be *cultivated*— not *drilled* (which is a process only appropriate to insensate stone).

Elizabeth Peabody, 1893, Lectures in the Training Schools for Kindergartners, *in Sol Cohen, ed.,* Education in the United States: A Documentary History, *Vol. 3, p. 1793.*

A fairy godmother to us children was she who led us to a wonderful country called "uptown," where, in a dazzlingly beautiful palace called a "department store," we exchanged our hateful homemade European costumes, which pointed us out as "greenhorns" to the children on the street, for real American machine-made garments, and issued forth glorified in each other's eyes.

With our despised immigrant clothing we shed also our impossible Hebrew names. A committee of our friends, several years ahead of us in American experience, put their heads together and concocted American names for us all. Those of our real names that had no pleasing American equivalents they ruthlessly discarded, content if they retained the initials. My Mother, possessing a name that was not easily translatable, was punished with the undignified nickname of Annie. Fetchke, Joseph, and Deborah issued as Frieda, Joseph, and Dora, respectively. As for poor me, I was simply cheated. The name they gave me was hardly new. My Hebrew name being Maryashe in full, Mashke for short, Russianized into Marya (*Mar-ya*), my friends said that it would hold good in English as *Mary;* which was very disappointing, as I longed to posses a strange-sounding American name like the others.

Mary Antin, whose family came to Boston from Russia in 1894, when she was 13, At school in the Promised Land, *pp. 30–31.*

Father himself conducted us to school. He would not have delegated that mission to the President of the United States. He had awaited the day with impatience equal to mine, and the visions he saw as he hurried us over the sun-flecked pavements transcended all my dreams.

Mary Antin, Russian-Jewish immigrant, who began school in Boston in 1894, At School in the Promised Land, *p. 42.*

Pure air under all conditions of life is an absolute necessity; but when thirty, forty, fifty or even sixty children are shut up in a schoolroom, many of them coming from homes where the bathtub is a luxury unthought of, and often the garments are worn day and night, perhaps unwashed for weeks, only the most complete forced ventilation can keep the air decently pure.

The problem is intensified when we remember that to the impurities arising from the usual causes, we must add those from catarrhal breaths, diseased stomachs, decayed teeth and uncleanly persons. The chalk dust from the blackboards must not be forgotten. It is a very liberal allowance to say that in the average school of forty pupils where there is no ventilation the air is unfit to sustain vigorous life at the end of the first five minutes. You will find many a room twenty-eight by thirty-two by twelve heated by a vicious stove, or an equally vicious hot-air furnace, and absolutely with no means of ventilation, except by lowering the windows. This the teacher hesitates to do, because a blast of cold air slays like a sword.

I say, no means of ventilation. Possibly you will find a hole in the ceiling, seven by nine inches in size, or one of the same dimensions in the side near the chimney, which for ventilating purposes is of no practical value.

Henry Sabin, 1897, "Is Your Child in This School?" p. 95.

The mother who is made angry by the misconduct of her children, and punishes them in a passion, acts under the influence of a brute instinct. Her family government is in principle the same as that of the lower animals over their young. It is, however, at any rate, a *government;* and such government is certainly better than none. But human parents, in the training of their human offspring, ought surely to aim at something higher and nobler. They who do so, who possess themselves fully with the idea that punishment, as they are to administer it, is wholly remedial in its character—that is to say, is to be considered solely with reference to the future good to be attained by it, will have established in their minds a principle that will surely guide them into right ways, and bring them out successfully in the end. They will soon acquire the habit of never threatening, of never punishing in anger, and of calmly considering, in the case of the faults which they observe in their children, what course of procedure will be most effectual in correcting them.

Parents seem sometimes to have an idea that a manifestation of something like anger—or, at least, very serious displeasure on their part—is necessary in order to make a proper impression in respect to its fault on the mind of the child. This, however, I think, is a mistake. The impression is made by what we *do,* and not by the indications of irritation or displeasure which we manifest in doing it.

Jacob Abbott, 1899, Gentle Measures in the Management and Training of the Young, *p. 62.*

By the gentle measures . . . are meant such as do not react in a violent and irritating manner, in any way, upon the extremely delicate, and almost embryonic condition of the cerebral and nervous organization, in which the gradual development of the mental and moral faculties are so intimately involved. They do not imply any, the least, relaxation of the force of parental authority, or any lowering whatever of the standards of moral obligation, but are, on the contrary, the most effectual, the surest and the safest way of establishing the one and enforcing the other.

Jacob Abbott, 1899, Gentle Measures in the Management and Training of the Young, *p. 25.*

If a parent wishes to eradicate from the mind of his boy all feelings of delicacy and manly pride, to train him to the habit of obtaining what he wants by importunity or servility, and to prevent his having any means of acquiring any practical knowledge of the right use of money, any principles of economy, or any of that forethought and thrift so essential to sure prosperity in future life, the best way to accomplish these ends would seem to be to have no system in supplying him with money in his boyish days, but to give it to him only when he asks for it, and in quantities determined only by the frequency and importunity of his calls.

. . . [O]ne of the most important parts of the education of both girls and boys, whether they are to inherit riches, or to enjoy a moderate income from the fruits of their own industry, or to spend their lives in extreme poverty, is to teach them the proper management and use of money. And this may be very effectually done by giving them a fixed and definite income to manage, and then throwing upon them the responsibility of the management of it, with such a degree of guidance, encouragement, and aid as a parent can easily render.

Jacob Abbott, 1899, Gentle Measures in the Management and Training of the Young, *pp. 268–70.*

I cannot remember the time when my hands did not yearn for weapons. In my search for them I recapitulated the history of the race. I began by picking up rocks, clods, and chunks of coal and practicing on anything that came handy. A tin can would do, a bottle to smash was better, but something alive and on the run was greatly to be preferred. A large and prolific family of cats haunted our barn and feed-room and I kept them lean and wary for years by using them as targets. . . .

Armed with my beany [slingshot], I would plunge barefoot and stealthy into the jungle of cottonwood and button-willow about my grandfather's fish ponds, to spend a long afternoon stalking turtledoves and woodpeckers with the complete absorption of a savage. Once in a while I killed a bird and that was a satisfying triumph. If other games failed me I was not above stinging the rump of an unsuspecting horse or a cow and taking delight in its astonished capers. Once I went prowling in the back alleys of the town, taking shots at the pigeons that lived in eaves and cornices. It was not long before I smashed a window and had to sprint for cover.

Harvey Fergusson, recalling his amusements in Albuquerque, New Mexico, ca. 1900, Home in the West, *pp. 88–89.*

6

Growing Up on the Western Frontier
1840–1918

Cowboys, prospectors, and other colorful characters played memorable roles in the great drama of the American West, but the patient work of settling the land was accomplished by families. As parents and children put down roots, the land yielded homes, churches, and schools, which were the basis of communities. All family members, including the young ones, had essential work to do. Often it was the labor of children that made it possible for adults to clear and plow the land, tend ranch stock, and establish towns.

Americans had been cutting forests and building homesteads west of the Appalachians for as long as the United States had been a nation. Between 1840 and 1860, as many as 300,000 people followed overland trails to the Far West. Men traveling to the gold-mining region of California accounted for more than one-third of that total; young families with three or four children, on average, made up much of the balance. While a mindset formed in the culture of the East shaped the outlook and expectations of pioneering adults, children viewed the western landscape with fresh eyes. As they acquainted themselves with the wildlife and terrain, they made few comparisons with the world they had left behind. Growing up in this environment of unbroken plains and lofty mountains would set them apart from their parents. It would foster self-reliance and a perception of the future as a force to be shaped and controlled.

Men and women often moved west for the benefit of their children, to offer the young a better life and a chance to grow up with the country. To many adults, Oregon represented an ideal: free, fertile farmland and mild winters that would be kind to people and livestock alike. Similarly, the Utah desert symbolized religious freedom for 43,000 Mormon pioneers between 1847 and 1860.

Families also hoped to escape the diseases that plagued inhabitants of the Mississippi and Ohio River valleys, the original home of many settlers. Smallpox, influenza, and cholera were common in that region, although they also occurred throughout the United States.

Cholera is a bacterial illness that attacks the intestinal wall, causes a high fever, acute vomiting and diarrhea, and a quick death. It is spread through contact with victims, their clothing, and their bedding and by drinking contaminated water. Before 1883, when Robert Koch identified the microorganism that gives rise to cholera, its cause remained a mystery. People blamed it on heavy consumption of alcohol or exposure to moist night air. One scientist claimed that geology played a role; cholera occurred, he said, where the soil was rich in limestone.

Malaria claimed lives in the Mississippi and Ohio valleys as well. Because no one knew that it was transmitted by mosquitoes, malaria, like cholera, was impossible to prevent or avoid.

ON THE TRAIL

From beginning to end, a typical wagon train of the 1840s covered a mile of prairie. Forty covered wagons, pulled by oxen, carried families' provisions, clothing, bedding, tools, furniture, and kitchenware. Livestock—dairy cows, beef cattle, horses, and extra oxen—brought up the rear. The sight of a long, slow-moving wagon train reminded one despondent pioneer woman of a funeral procession.

Adults on the trail often dealt with homesickness, but children, who failed to comprehend the finality of the move they were making, immersed themselves in the present. For them the western environment inspired both wonder and fear. Children marveled at vast herds of grazing bison and bustling prairie dog villages. At night they listened to the howls of coyotes and wolves. The prairie became a frightening place for the young when intense thunderstorms swept over the land. Strong winds lifted tents off the ground, tore canvas from wagons, and even turned some vehicles over. Lightning and thunder caused oxen to bellow and cattle to panic and bolt.

Indians were another source of fear and amazement. Adults and children read horrifying tales in the press and popular literature of Indians attacking wagon trains, massacring settlers, and kidnapping pioneer children. Westward travelers sitting around nighttime campfires passed along these stories. Carried away by the sensational reports, adults panicked at the sight of Indians approaching their wagons to beg for food or offer advice. The frightening stories also made a strong impression on children, who frequently ran in terror upon first seeing the native people. One young girl demanded that her hair be cut short before she went west as protection against being scalped.

Such fears were largely unfounded, though. With the exception of the indigenous people in parts of the Southwest, who presented a threat until the late 19th century, Indians rarely instigated violence against emigrants. In fact, 462 Indians died at the hands of whites traveling west, while fewer emigrants—362— were killed by Indians. Many whites assaulted and cheated Native Americans; on more than one occasion, emigrants captured Native people and forced them to work as guides.

Indians were known to aid settlers traveling through their territory, offering water and food and escorting pioneers from one encampment to the next. In time, children's curiosity grew stronger than their anxiety, and they traded with the Indians, bartering nails and scrap metal for souvenirs.

Because the 2,400-mile trek from Missouri, the most frequent "jumping-off point," to the West Coast could take eight to 10 months, timing was crucial. A late-April or early-May departure ensured that there would be plenty of spring grass for the grazing animals. It also permitted emigrants to get over the western mountain ranges before the first blizzards of late autumn rolled in.

Of the several routes that the pioneers took, the most popular was the Oregon Trail. It followed the south bank of the Platte River across the Great Plains, then crossed the Rocky Mountains before branching. Oregon-bound pioneers traced the route of the Snake River, then traversed the Blue Mountains and Cascades to reach their destination. Those headed for California, meanwhile, veered south and crossed the Sierra Nevada range. The Mormon Trail ran parallel to the Platte River on its north bank, merged briefly with the Oregon Trail in Wyoming, then turned south to Utah. Rivers intersected the trails at several locations. If a river was shallow enough, people drove their wagons across. Otherwise they hoisted the wagons off their wheels and floated them to the far bank on rafts. Horses and cattle swam.

A day on the trail began well before sunrise. Pioneers woke at 4:00 A.M. to milk their cows, cook and eat breakfast, and pack up their tents and bedding. By 7:00 A.M., the wagons were ready to roll. A wagon train might cover 15 miles in a day. Some emigrants traveled along on horseback, but most walked. Small children rode in the wagons with their mothers or with older siblings who had been assigned to care for them. Once the train stopped for the night, women prepared an evening meal of beans, dried meat, and bread, or perhaps salt pork and flapjacks. Dinner was occasionally supplemented with fresh game or wild greens that the children had gathered along the trail. Many pioneer children first tasted exotic foods, such as antelope, bison calf, or nutritious weeds, on the way west.

Parents worried about losing children in accidents, and some did. Youngsters fell beneath the wheels of moving wagons; they drowned while playing beside muddy streams or riding in wagons that capsized in rivers. Yet it is interesting to note that life for the emigrants was not appreciably more dangerous than it was for most Americans in the mid-19th century. The overall death rate on the trail was 3 percent between 1840 and 1860, which was just slightly higher than the rate of 2.5 percent for U.S. society as a whole.

These migrants traveling west on the Arizona trail set up camp in Navajo country, ca. 1885. *(Ben Wittick, photographer; courtesy Museum of New Mexico; negative number 3083).*

A far greater danger than accidents was one that many people had hoped to leave behind: Disease accounted for 90 percent of the deaths that occurred on the trail. One case of a communicable disease such as smallpox, measles, typhus, or scarlet fever could spread rapidly to other travelers in a wagon train, but cholera was the principal killer. A cholera epidemic that affected the entire United States between 1850 and 1852 killed half of the people who would die on the trails from 1840 through 1860. Pioneers contracted cholera in camp, where they were exposed to refuse left by earlier wagon trains and water tainted with human waste. Accepting a new theory that beans caused cholera, some emigrants discarded their stores of beans when the dreaded disease broke out. Others simply put their faith in the Almighty.

A malady known as "mountain fever" plagued emigrants as they reached the Rockies. The term most likely was applied to several infectious diseases, including two that were tick-borne: Rocky Mountain spotted fever and Colorado tick fever. Mountain fever could be fatal, but children generally recovered.

Scurvy, caused by a deficiency of vitamin C, commonly appeared toward the end of the journey as well. Scurvy causes bleeding gums and swelling and severe pain in the legs. Without the addition of fresh fruits and vegetables to the diet, it is fatal.

Nineteenth-century children were more familiar with death than today's children are, but they found the necessarily abrupt nature of burial and grief on the trail particularly distressing. A loved one who died was placed in a shallow trailside grave with little formality, and then the wagon train moved on. As the trail became dotted with the graves of old and young, children worried about being buried and abandoned.

HARD WORK ON THE FRONTIER

Newcomers built log cabins in areas of the Far West where lumber was plentiful. Between 1850 and 1890, mining camps proliferated in the mountainous regions of California, Nevada, Idaho, Montana, South Dakota, Colorado, New Mexico, and Arizona. The Homestead Act of 1862 brought a large number of settlers into the Great Plains region by granting 160 acres of public land to heads of households who were over 21 and who were U.S. citizens or had applied for citizenship.

Before the Civil War ended in 1865, the pioneer population was largely white and native-born. After slavery was abolished, African Americans joined the move west. Their numbers were small at first; then, in 1879, the anti-black legislation and intimidation of the post-Reconstruction years caused many to flee the South. Kansas, a state with a strong history of abolitionism, was a popular destination. By 1880, 15,000 African Americans were residing in Kansas.

European immigrants came west after 1865 as well. The Central Pacific and Union Pacific railroads linked the East and West in 1869, and additional rail lines reached into western lands in the last decades of the century. The settlers who arrived by railroad included so many immigrants from northern Europe that in 1890 South Dakota became the state with the highest percentage of its population foreign born, 45 percent.

Because wood was scarce on the prairie, a family's first home was likely to be a dugout—a hole cut into the side of a hill with bricks of earth forming an

Members of the Shores family pose for a photographer outside their Nebraska sod house in 1887. Former slaves, the Shoreses moved west after the Civil War to obtain land and escape southern racism. *(Nebraska State Historical Society)*

outside wall. The family lived in the dugout for several months, until their free-standing sod house was ready. This rugged structure was made from blocks of prairie turf, each weighing 50 pounds, piled grass-side down in overlapping layers. A "soddy" had a frame roof if lumber was available; otherwise the roof, like the rest of the house, consisted of prairie grass and dirt.

Creating a life in the raw environment of the newly settled frontier required an enormous amount of labor, and adults who had left behind a support system of relatives and friends could not afford to let anyone be idle. While many children in the East were having their responsibilities lightened, western children had to do much of the day-to-day work that kept their families going. Children washed clothes, chopped wood, milked cows, cooked meals, churned butter, and made soap. They carried water from streams. On the plains, they collected cattle and bison dung, grass, hay, sunflower stalks, dried corncobs, and anything else that the family might burn for fuel. Before their farms were well established, frontier families survived by hunting and gathering, as the Indians of the region had done for countless generations. Young children harvested wild berries, onions, and greens, and their older siblings learned to shoot rabbits, deer, wild fowl, bison, and other game.

Sometimes boys did the traditional work of women, but more frequently girls did the traditional work of men. Children of both sexes cleared land, broke up the soil, planted crops, weeded, and harvested. Boys and girls living on cattle ranches learned to ride horses at an early age and helped to tend herds of cattle. Young people rode long distances on horseback to repair fences and hunt for stray calves. The work was hard and time-consuming, but children took pride in their ability to perform it well. Many girls faced a difficult adjustment, however, when they entered their teens and felt pressure to come in from the open range and devote themselves to such domestic duties as sewing, child care, cooking, and cleaning.

Children also did paying work to provide the cash that the family needed to buy staples such as sugar, coffee, and salt, and a small number of manufactured items. Most commonly, working children boarded at neighboring ranches to help with the herd during grazing season. Some children collected animal bones from the prairie and cashed them in at railroad stops. The bones would be shipped east to manufacturers of buttons, corset stays, and fertilizer. Other children chopped wood, drove wagons, or did laundry for money. Those living in towns could wait tables, sell newspapers, make deliveries, or go to work in a print shop, office, or sawmill. Western coal mines hired some boys to pick pieces of slate and stone from the coal and others to work underground.

PLAY AND COMMUNITY LIFE

Western children often relieved the monotony of work by turning it into a game. Picking vegetables or pulling weeds could easily be transformed into a contest to see who would be first to reach the end of a row. Children working on horseback raced one another, chased rabbits and other wild animals, and practiced trick riding.

Frontier children amused themselves in more traditional ways as well. Affluent youngsters living in towns and cities played with purchased toys, just as middle-class and well-to-do children in the East did. Most young people on the frontier, though, grew up with homemade toys. For girls, parents fashioned dolls from rags, wood, and cornhusks, while boys received miniature wagons crafted from spools, twine, bottles, and other items that might be at hand. When children got together with playmates, they favored active games such as tag. Those who

Children mingle with the crowd on Main Street in 19th-century Granite, Oklahoma. *(National Archives)*

lived far from other families sought the companionship of animals. Girls and boys raised puppies, kittens, lambs, fawns, and badger cubs. They also kept pigeons, prairie dogs, and ground squirrels as pets.

In the West, children interacted with adults to a greater degree than they did in the East. Lonely adults depended on their children for company, and families frequently spent evenings telling stories and singing. Whole communities turned out to watch children compete in spelling bees or march in parades. Children also took part in the dances that were popular in frontier towns, but they were welcomed primarily so that their mothers could be present; especially in mining communities, there was a shortage of women for dancing partners.

Eastern travelers often observed that young people living west of the Mississippi River behaved more like adults than children. Factors contributing to this outward bearing of maturity included the heavy workload that children shouldered and the frequent need to respond to crises. The death of a parent meant additional labor for many of the young. Children and teenagers also pitched in when drought or insects threatened crops or severe weather presented a risk to livestock.

There were other influences, though. Children in western towns hobnobbed with miners, gamblers, cowboys, and prostitutes, and social critics warned that their skill at using profanity and precocious knowledge of adult life would harm their development. Despite the dire predictions, there is no evidence that early exposure to vice had a widespread negative effect on the generations that came of age in America's frontier towns.

EDUCATING THE YOUNG

An immediate consideration for frontier parents was education. Mothers and fathers initially taught their children to read, write, and work with numbers, but they viewed home teaching as a necessary but temporary measure. As soon as they could, they organized schools.

The first western schools were financed by subscription, with families chipping in to hire a teacher. In the years following the Civil War, communities preferred male teachers, believing that men were better able to discipline the older boys in class. This was a genuine concern when the students in a one-room school might range in age from five to 20. The U.S. Commissioner of Education determined in 1871 that approximately half of the teachers in Kansas and Nebraska were men.

Qualified teachers could be hard to find. When westerners advertised for them in newspapers and magazines published in the East, the respondents tended to be young women who were eager for adventure or intent on bringing morality to the decadent frontier. The teaching force also included daughters of pioneer families attempting to escape domestic drudgery. Although they usually taught only for a year or two before marriage ended their employment, women gradually took over western teaching. In time, the percentages of male teachers declined significantly from what they were in 1871. A 1916 government survey found that just 18.7 percent of teachers in Kansas and 12.1 percent in Nebraska were men.

Teachers earned more in the West than they did in the East, but individuals' salaries varied widely. A teacher in a western town might receive as much as one dollar per week for each child taught, while another teacher, working in a sparsely populated region, might receive 50 cents per child per month. Men commanded higher salaries than women, although western teachers occasionally were paid in livestock or meat by cash-poor frontier parents.

Some communities raised enough money to build frame schoolhouses, but the majority established their schools in vacant sod houses, shacks, or space made available in private homes. The first school in Denver, Colorado, opened on October 3, 1859, in a log cabin with a flat roof that leaked in wet weather. A strip of canvas torn from a wagon cover served as the door.

School furnishings were primitive, and school supplies were scarce. Children sat with their classmates on wooden planks, or they supplied their own desks and chairs. They wrote their lessons in chalk on slates. Children also provided an eclectic assortment of reading material from home. Many families owned novels and volumes of poetry that they had carried on the journey west. Also, especially after 1880, it was not uncommon for westerners to subscribe to popular magazines such as *Harper's* and *Leslie's*.

For many parents, the need for their children's labor conflicted with the desire to see them educated. They generally kept their sons and daughters home from school from the planting season in early spring through harvest time in autumn. As a result, the school year was shorter in the West than it was in the East. By 1880, schools in two-thirds of Western states and territories were open for less than half the year. As late as 1910, one-fourth of the schools in Montana held classes during four months of the year at most.

Gradually, states and territories passed laws making education compulsory. Nebraska's 1887 law requiring children between the ages of eight and 14 to attend public or private school was typical. Like other western compulsory education laws, it contained no provision for enforcement and so had little impact on school attendance. The laws also standardized the curriculum. Reading, spelling, grammar, and arithmetic were always among the subjects to be studied; additional subjects varied from one jurisdiction to another, but they were likely to include penmanship, geography, physiology, history, and possibly bookkeep-

The first school to serve the Custer-Bonanza mining communities of Idaho. The teacher and students moved outdoors with all of their furniture and books in order to be photographed in the 1880s. *(Idaho State Historical Society, 73–215.1)*

ing and classical languages. States also began testing prospective teachers' mastery of academic subject matter and pedagogical techniques. Nevertheless, concern about teachers' lack of experience and training was a significant reason for the distribution of uniform textbooks in western states beginning in the 1890s, to replace the assorted schoolbooks provided from home.

Truancy was tolerated for practical reasons. Some school buildings would have been too small to hold all of the students if everyone were in attendance. Also, not only did children have work to do at home, but many lived several miles from school as well. Laws attempted to remedy the problem of distance; for example, North Dakota required a school to be established whenever 12 children lived more than 2.5 miles from an existing school. Montana required 10 children to be so situated. The population was so sparse in some regions, though, that a school district might cover 1,000 square miles.

Change came slowly. In Nebraska, 792 sod schoolhouses were still in use in 1890. In 1918, a survey conducted by the U.S. Bureau of Education determined that few rural schools on the northern plains had progressed from the 1840s. Children in Montana still attended school in 224 abandoned mining shacks and 54 ranch houses, and only 10 percent of schools in South Dakota had indoor plumbing.

INDIAN CHILDREN

By 1840, much of the Native American population lived west of the Mississippi River. The Indian peoples of the United States belonged to several hundred ethnic or cultural groups (or remnants of such groups), many of which had called the West home for centuries. Other groups had only recently arrived. Beginning in the colonial period, armed confrontations with white settlers had wiped out many of the eastern Native peoples or pushed them west of the Appalachian Mountains. Following the War of 1812, the federal government instituted a policy of Indian Removal, uprooting the Native Americans and driving them west again. As a result, some of the western Indians, such as the Cherokee and Creek, were actually displaced easterners.

Indians' ways of life varied according to the regions of the West that they inhabited. For example, the pastoral Navajo (Dineh) of the Southwest raised sheep, goats, cattle, and horses and excelled at such handcrafts as weaving blankets and making baskets, pottery, and silver jewelry. The Cheyenne and other hunting peoples of the Great Plains were nomads who followed the buffalo herds. The Wishram, Wasco, and other peoples of the Pacific Northwest fished and traded.

Although the specifics of growing up varied from one ethnic group to another, Native American children shared a number of experiences. They all participated in the work that was necessary to sustain the community. They all played with toys, and they engaged in competitive games. Finally, they were schooled in the beliefs and traditions of their culture by their parents and other relatives.

Certain tasks were traditionally performed by one sex or the other in Indian cultures; consequently, boys and girls did different work. Boys might learn to trap small animals, fish, build boats, and make weapons such as spears, bows, and arrows. In the Southwest, boys learned to watch sheep and to plant corn by making holes in the earth with a stick. Boys also hunted, often using miniature bows and arrows to kill frogs and small mammals. The Hopi boys of Arizona were taught to hunt in a group, surrounding a deer and shooting at it simultaneously from various directions. Some boys studied to be shamans, or prophets and healers, preparing to fill positions that belonged to men in most Indian cultures.

Women taught girls to cook and care for younger children. Girls growing up on the plains tanned buffalo hides, made leather garments and moccasins, and dried meat. Girls along the Pacific Coast dried fish, while those in the Southwest ground corn and made bread. Girls also practiced crafts, including embroidery, basketry, weaving, and pottery making.

Both boys and girls gathered food. Pine nuts, acorns, and agave grew in the Southwest; shellfish abounded along the Pacific; and wild carrots and onions, herbs, berries, and birds' eggs could be found everywhere. Children of all ages learned to ride ponies and horses while they were young. It was customary among some peoples to tie a child of two or three onto a gentle horse to get him or her used to being on horseback. A boy might have his own pony by the age of five or six.

In play, Indian children chased butterflies, rode stick horses, and spun wooden tops, as settler children often did. They walked on stilts, wrestled, and played cat's cradle. They also engaged in team sports, using balls made of leather and stuffed with animal hair. Sioux (Dakota, Lakota, Nakota) boys enjoyed a rough game played on horseback in which teams tried to wrestle their opponents to the ground.

Adults passed their knowledge of the culture's myths and rituals on to the young by word of mouth or by example. Specific beliefs varied, but all Native Americans perceived a spiritual side to nature. Adults therefore taught the children to worship the spirits that lived in the world around them and to perform traditional dances and songs. Because Native Americans interacted closely with the environment, children's education included lessons on the regional flora and fauna, the terrain, and the weather.

Most Indian parents avoided corporal punishment, which caused some white observers to remark that Indian children were undisciplined. Those impressions were not entirely correct, however. Native peoples preferred other methods, such as ridicule, for correcting the behavior of the young. If a Blackfoot boy of Montana or western Canada misbehaved, people shouted the details of his transgression from one tipi to the next. The youth had to remain out of sight until he had redeemed himself by performing a good deed. Sometimes parents threatened the young with supernatural punishment, warning of evil spirits in animal form that waited to carry off naughty children.

Prescribed rituals marked young people's coming of age. Boys on the cusp of manhood frequently withdrew from society to seek spiritual enlightenment or pass a test of endurance. Boys living on the plains retreated to a hilltop where they fasted in solitude for several days, waiting for an animal to appear to them in a vision. The kind of animal that a boy saw determined his adult name. Chiricahua Apache boys of the Southwest went alone into the wilderness to acquire survival skills. On the Columbia Plateau, girls as well as boys sought mystical visions. In most cultures, though, a girl entered a period of seclusion upon reaching puberty. She returned to society with an outward sign indicating her readiness for marriage, such as a tattoo or a particular kind of hairstyle or dress.

The demands of white settlement made it increasingly difficult for Native Americans to maintain their way of life in the late 19th century. Railroads cut across grasslands where the buffalo herds grazed, and they brought in hunters who slaughtered the animals for sport. In addition, thousands of bison were killed to meet the demand for their hides in the East. Habitat destruction and over-hunting, along with drought and diseases carried into the region by migrants' livestock, all but wiped out the herds that had blanketed the prairie before the period of settlement.

U.S. cavalry forces battled Indian war parties on the plains, and the Indians who survived were relocated to reservations. By 1877, most of the Sioux had sur-rendered to U.S. authorities or had been killed. The Indian Wars ended on December 29, 1890, when U.S. soldiers massacred more than 300 Sioux men, women, and children at Wounded Knee, South Dakota. A second struggle, to impose American culture on Indian children, would continue.

Religious groups had been educating young Indians since the 1600s, when the Spanish established Roman Catholic missions in the Southwest. The federal government and private philanthropists involved themselves in the re-education of Indian youth in the 1870s, primarily because of the efforts of Richard Henry Pratt. Pratt was a white officer serving on the frontier with the 10th Cavalry, an African-American unit, when he came to believe that the Indian population would die out unless its children left their environment and adopted the whites' way of life. At first no eastern boarding schools would accept Native Americans, because school administrators had been frightened by the dramatic Indian vic-tory at Little Bighorn, Montana, in 1876. In 1878, the Hampton Institute (now Hampton University) in Norfolk, Virginia, admitted 17 Indians who had been taken prisoner during the Red River War (1874–75). Nearly 1,400 Indians would attend the Hampton Institute, a school established for former slaves, over the next 45 years.

In 1879, Pratt opened a boarding school exclusively for Native Americans, the Carlisle Indian Industrial School, in abandoned army barracks at Carlisle, Pennsylvania. He recruited 60 boys and 24 girls from the Dakotas; together with 11 students from the Hampton Institute, they made up the original student body. In all, 1,000 children representing 70 Indian groups attended the school at Carlisle. Some parents sent their children to the school willingly, while others claimed to have been pressured.

Most of the young people spoke no English when they arrived in Penn-sylvania from the West, and many were terrified. One boy from the Dakota Territory was certain that the whites' only interest in Indian children was in killing them. Immediately, the children's traditional buckskin clothing was confiscated, and they were issued uniforms and dresses resembling those that the white population wore. The boys' long hair was cut, and everyone was given a new, non-Indian name. Students were expected to master academic subjects and to learn a useful trade, such as carpentry, masonry, sewing, or bookkeeping.

Stories of Carlisle students living happily ever after are regrettably few. Graduates complained of feeling adrift, at home in neither white nor Indian society. Some children contracted communicable diseases, such as tuberculosis and scarlet fever, and died before they could graduate. Several became deeply depressed, stopped eating, and died, ostensibly of homesickness. The Carlisle

Sioux boys in short hair and uniforms photographed at Carlisle, Pennsylvania, ca. 1880. *(National Archives)*

Indian Industrial School was the best known of dozens of Indian boarding schools that opened in the late 19th century. It operated until 1918, when the army responded to charges of student abuse by converting the Carlisle barracks into a hospital.

CHRONICLE OF EVENTS

1840
Most Native Americans reside west of the Mississippi River.

1840–1860
An estimated 300,000 people migrate overland to the Far West.

The death rate on the western trails is 3 percent; the overall U.S. death rate is 2.5 percent.

1847–1860
Forty-three thousand Mormon pioneers settle in Utah.

1848
January 24: Gold is found in the American River in California.

1849
Tens of thousands leave states east of the Mississippi River to prospect for gold in California.

1850–1852
A nationwide cholera epidemic kills half of all people who would die on the overland trails between 1840 and 1860.

1850–1890
Mining camps are established in the mountainous regions of the West.

1859
October 3: The first school in Denver, Colorado, opens in a log cabin.

1862
The Homestead Act of 1862 makes available 160 acres of public land to any head of household or any person over 21 who is a U.S. citizen or has applied for citizenship.

1865
Following the Civil War, African Americans begin to relocate to the West.

1869
May 10: The East and West Coasts of the United States are linked by rail as the Central Pacific and Union Pacific railroads join at Promontory Summit, Utah.

1871
A study by the U.S. Commissioner of Education finds that approximately half of the teachers in Kansas and Nebraska are men.

1878
The Hampton Institute admits 17 Indians, the first of nearly 1,400 to attend the school over the next 45 years.

1879
The Carlisle Indian Industrial School opens in Carlisle, Pennsylvania.

1879–1880
Fifteen thousand African Americans settle in Kansas.

1880
Two-thirds of schools in western states and territories are open for less than half the year.

Most of the Native Americans have surrendered to U.S. authorities or been killed.

1887
A Nebraska law requires children between the ages of eight and 14 to attend public or private school and standardizes the curriculum. This legislation is typical of western compulsory education laws.

1890
South Dakota, with 45 percent of its population foreign born, becomes the state with the highest concentration of immigrants.

In Nebraska, 792 sod schoolhouses are still in use.

December 29: U.S. soldiers kill 300 Sioux people at Wounded Knee, South Dakota, ending decades of warfare on the plains.

1890s
Uniform textbooks replace reading material brought from home in western schools.

1910
One-fourth of schools in Montana hold classes for a maximum of four months per year.

1916

A U.S. government survey determines that the percentages of male teachers in Kansas and Nebraska have declined sharply, to 18.8 percent and 12.1 percent, respectively.

1918

The U.S. Bureau of Education concludes that rural schools on the northern plains have shown little progress from the 1840s.

Montana continues to employ 224 abandoned shacks and 54 ranch houses as schools.

Ninety percent of schools in South Dakota lack indoor plumbing.

The Carlisle Indian Industrial School closes; the army opens a hospital in the Carlisle barracks.

EYEWITNESS TESTIMONY

I was seven years old when we started for Oregon. I can well remember what a hullabaloo the neighbors set up when father said we were going to Oregon. They told him his family would all be killed by the Indians, or if we escaped the Indians we would either starve to death or drown or be lost in the desert, but father was not much of a hand to draw back after he had put his hand to the plow, so he went ahead and made ready for the trip. He built a large box in the home-made wagon and put in a lot of dried buffalo meat and pickled pork. He had made over a hundred pounds of maple sugar the preceding fall which we took along instead of loaf sugar. He also took along plenty of corn meal. At Independence, Mo., he laid in a big supply of buffalo meat and bought more coffee. He also laid in a plentiful supply of home twist tobacco. Father chewed it and mother smoked it.

Benjamin Franklin Bonney describing his family's
departure from Illinois in 1845, in Fred Lockley,
Across the Plains by Prairie Schooner, *p. 2.*

One of the things I remember very vividly was a severe thunder storm that took place in the middle of the night. The thunder seemed almost incessant, and the lightning was so brilliant you could read by its flashes. The men chained the oxen so they would not stampede, though they were very restive. Our tents were blown down as were the covers off our prairie schooners and in less than five minutes we were wet as drowned rats. Unless you have been through it you have no idea of the confusion resulting from a storm on the plains, with the oxen bellowing, the children crying and the men shouting, the thunder rolling like a constant salvo of artillery; with everything as light as day from the lightning flashes and the next second as black as the depth of the pit.

Benjamin Franklin Bonney, who was a seven-year-old
Oregon-bound pioneer in 1845, in Fred Lockley,
Across the Plains by Prairie Schooner, *p. 3.*

Among the young children to be taken to Oregon was my sister, Ellen Francisco, who had been born at Sutter's Fort and who was only a few months old. There were no roads to Oregon, so the children had to go on horseback. An old Scotchman solved the problem by making pack saddles with arms fifteen inches high. He wove raw-hide strands around this framework, making a regular basket. Two children could be placed in each one of these pack saddles without any danger of their falling out. I will never forget the exciting forenoon we spent when we started from the fort. Many of the horses were not saddle broken and when the children were put in these high pack saddles the horses would run and buck. At first many of the children set up a terrible clamor, but when they found they were not spilled out, they greatly enjoyed the excitement. Their mothers were frantic.

Benjamin Franklin Bonney recalling events on
the trail to Oregon in 1846, in Fred Lockley,
Across the Plains by Prairie Schooner,
pp. 14–15.

After traveling a few days northward from Freemont's camp [in California] we came to a beautiful lake beside which was a clover meadow. We camped there for the night. The young man who took the horses out to pasture found near the lake an Indian girl about eight years old. The little girl was perfectly nude, her long black hair was matted and she was covered with sores from head to feet. She could only make a pitiful moaning noise. Dr. Truman Bonney, my uncle, examined her and said she was suffering from hunger and that the flies had almost eaten her up. Near by we could see where two tribes of Indians had fought. She had apparently crept to one side out of danger and had been left. She had been living on clover roots and grass. A council among the men was held to see what should be done with her. My father wanted to take her along; others wanted to kill her and put her out of her misery. Father said that would be wilful murder. A vote was taken and it was decided to do nothing about it, but to leave her where we found her. My mother and my aunt were unwilling to leave the little girl. They stayed behind to do all they could for her. When they finally joined us their eyes were red and swollen from crying and their faces were wet with tears. Mother said she had knelt down by the little girl and had asked God to take care of her. One of the young men in charge of the horses felt so badly about leaving her, he went back and put a bullet through her head and put her out of her misery.

Benjamin Franklin Bonney writing about events that
occurred in 1846 on the trail from California to
Oregon, in Fred Lockley, Across the Plains
by Prairie Schooner, *pp. 15–16.*

On the 25th day of December, 1849, on Canyon Creek, two miles from Georgetown, Placer county, California, the wife of William George Wilson gave birth to a twelve-pound boy baby. This was the first child born in the camp. Some miner of a jocular disposition at once started the story that Bill Wilson had found a twelve-pound nugget, the handsomest ever seen. The news of Bill's "big find" ran like wild fire up and down the canyon, where hundreds of men were at work. At once there was a grand rush to Bill Wilson's cabin. Every miner was anxious to see the twelve-pound lump.

Bill "dropped on" the joke at once. Taking the men, a few at a time, he introduced them into the room where his living nugget lay and proudly exhibited it as the best and biggest find ever made on Canyon Creek. The joke took at once with the miners. As each squad came out of the cabin every man solemnly asserted that Bill's nugget was the "boss," the finest ever seen. All went away, up and down the creek, spreading the news of the wonderful nugget. The joke was so well kept that the rush to Bill Wilson's cabin continued all day and far into the night. Indeed, the first day did not end the rush. Men came for two or three days and asked to be shown the nugget, some arriving from camps eight or ten miles distant....

Even after the joke about the "nugget" became known many men dropped in to see the child on its own merits. The miners were proud to be able to say they had a baby in camp.

William P. Bennett recalling events of Christmas 1849,
The First Baby in Camp, pp. 6–7.

Children were few in the mountains, so as a matter of course I came in for a large share of attention. Often the miners would take small nuggets of gold and ask me to guess the weight. "If you guess right, Martha, you can have it," was the usual offer, and in a short time I became so expert that I had accumulated a fair sized hoard of gold, and was in a fair way to make my fortune.

Martha A. Gentry, who spent the winter of 1849–50
in California mining camps, in Jennie E. Ross,
"A Child's Experience in '49," p. 402.

It was in Placerville that I found my first nugget. One day a miner gave me and the other children permission to dig on his claim, telling us we could have what we found. Diligently we set to work, and carefully scooped up the soft dirt and then washed it, just as we had seen the men do so many times. I was the luckiest one of the group, and found a nugget worth five dollars. With this I bought a pair of shoes, of which I was sorely in need, for the moccasins given me by the old Indian squaw were now worn out.

Martha A. Gentry, who spend the winter of 1849–50
in California mining camps, in Jennie E. Ross,
"A Child's Experience in '49," p. 403.

... [I]t was [near Coloma, California] that I met with a sad bereavement, for my sister took ill with a fever and died. Sickness of any kind was much to be dreaded in those days, for doctors were few and their services hard to secure. We had to send many miles for the one who attended my sister, and the fee, I remember, was fifteen dollars for the visit. There was no lack of nursing, for kind friends and neighbors proffered their services, but all efforts to save her life were unavailing.

Her death left me stranded and homeless, but a kind friend, Mrs. Steward, took me to her home, where I lived for some time. Domestic help of all kinds was very scarce. and even the services of a child were much sought after, as I was soon to find out.

Martha A. Gentry remembering the death of her sister
ca. 1849, in Jennie E. Ross, "A Child's
Experience in '49," p. 403.

In the year 1852 my father moved to the northern part of Iowa, and located in Chickasaw County, where he rented what was called a double-log house, which had been used as an Indian trading-post and here we spent part of the winter. There being no school within reach of us, we boys spent much of our time in hunting through the woods and over the prairies for the wild deer, turkey, prairie-hen, and rabbit.

We lived about one mile from the woods, where we got fuel for the house, which was drawn on hand-sleds that we boys made with our own hands. Sometimes we were half a day making the trip, but there being four or five of us together, we brought plenty of wood to keep the fire going.

Charles Wesley Wells, who was 11 years old in 1852,
A Frontier Life, p. 1.

He who has been brought up altogether in a prairie country knows nothing of the charm there is in the distant sound of a falling tree, and the echo of the woodman's ax mingling with the clarion notes of the

The Andrews family of Nebraska at the grave of Willie, son and brother, 1887. *(Nebraska State Historical Society)*

woodpecker, pecking on the dry trunk of a hollow tree. . . . Oh how my thoughts go back to the place where we used to fell the trees, and convert them into sawlogs, rails or cord-wood! The boy who has been raised exclusively in a prairie country knows nothing of the amount of labor there is in a timbered country. . . .

All hands working early and late, enough logs were soon brought together for a house. . . . The raising and covering of the house was the next thing to be done. As there were three or four men and as many boys at work on it, it was soon raised to a sufficient height, and the roof put on.

Charles Wesley Wells reminiscing about building a log cabin in northern Iowa in 1852, A Frontier Life, *pp. 3–4.*

We reached the Platte River, Cholera broke out, and Uncle Silas' family not being strong after measles, he was the first to take down with it and lived only a short time, we had to make a rough box from planks taken out of the wagons and we wrapped his body in bed clothes and buried him. It was so sad to see his family leave the lonely grave never to see it again.

We had traveled only a day or so, when two of his boys were stricken; we had an old doctor in the train but he would not allow them to have a drop of water and it was most distressing to hear their pitiful begging for water, and such suffering I hope I may never see again.

One little fellow died and we buried him as we did his father; but several miles apart; the other one lingered a few days longer and before death released him, he went blind.

Mary Jane Long, who crossed the plains in 1852, i n Robert L. Munkres, "Wives, Mothers, Daughters: Women's Life on the Road West," p. 194.

While eating William Belshaw and Charles Martin, 7 years of age, started to get a horse. William left Charles to return to the wagon. Charles could not see the wagon, he took the wrong road and got lost. We missed him in about 1/2 hour, made inquiry but could hear nothing of him.

Between 30 and 40 people were out hunting him, but no Charles to be found. Continued the search till sunset.

What agony did his parents endure during this time and what anxiety did his friends have until a man came to our wagon at sunset with the news that the child was safe in a camp nine miles from us. He followed the river 1/2 mile then struck out towards the road and came up to those wagons. They took him in and treated him kindly.

Maria A. Belshaw, who traveled from Lake County, Indiana, to Oregon by wagon train, June 22, 1853, "Diary Kept by Mrs. Maria A. Belshaw," p. 227.

One company just burying a boy 2 years old. It was just and right in the sight of God to take the child. The tender mother grieved bitterly to think she must leave her child in the cold and silent grave on the plains. Passed 2 dead cattle[,] one horse. Came down a valley. Crossed Rosser Creek again and camped on its bank 1/2 mile from the road on right. Very dusty and dry. Traveled 16 miles.

Maria A. Belshaw, who traveled from Lake County, Indiana, to Oregon by wagon train, July 26, 1853, "Diary Kept by Mrs. Maria A. Belshaw," pp. 235–36.

A long way down the Humboldt [River, in Nevada,] the train had to stop, for a child was born, a boy. The Indians were troublesome, so one of the men told them that the woman had smallpox, and they left in a hurry. Some of the women were much frightened. The mother of the woman who was confined cried and cried, fearing her daughter would die. Then the others followed suit. . . . We laid over one day, and then moved on. The mother and child did well, could not have done better anywhere else.

Lydia Milner Waters, "Account of a Trip Across the Plains in 1855," p. 73.

It was at Winona [Minnesota] that I saw my first Indian. I observed some red men coming up the river in a canoe and ran down toward them as they landed. When one of them arose to leave the craft he picked up a butcher knife and I, thinking that he meant to scalp me, took to my heels and never stopped running until I reached home.

Homer W. Wheeler recalling an event that occurred ca. 1858, when he was 10, Buffalo Days, p. 1.

We all had an idea that we were going to a farm, and we expected some resemblance at least to the prosperous farms we had seen in New England. . . . What we found awaiting us were the four walls and the roof of a good-sized log-house, standing in a small cleared strip of the wilderness, its doors and windows represented by square holes, its floor also a thing of the future, its whole effect achingly forlorn and desolate. It was late in the afternoon when we drove up to the opening that was its front entrance, and I shall never forget the look my mother turned upon the place. Without a word she crossed its threshold, and, standing very still, looked slowly around her. Then something within her seemed to give way, and she sank upon the ground. She could not realize even then, I think, that this was really the place father had prepared for us, that here he expected us to live. When she finally took it in she buried her face in her hands, and in that way she sat for hours without moving or speaking. For the first time in her life she had forgotten us; and we, for our part, dared not speak to her. We stood around her in a frightened group, talking to one another in whispers. Our little world had crumbled under our feet. Never before had we seen our mother give way to despair.

Anna Howard Shaw, whose family migrated from Massachusetts to Michigan in 1859, The Story of a Pioneer, pp. 24–25.

As a little child, it was instilled into me to be silent and reticent. This was one of the most important traits to form in the character of the Indian. As a hunter and warrior it was considered absolutely necessary to him, and was thought to lay the foundations of patience and self-control. There are times when boisterous mirth is indulged in by our people, but the rule is gravity and decorum.

After all, my babyhood was full of interest and the beginnings of life's realities. The spirit of daring was already whispered into my ears. The value of the eagle feather as worn by the warrior had caught my eye. One day, when I was left alone, at scarcely two years of age, I took my uncle's war bonnet and plucked out all its eagle feathers to decorate my dog and myself. So soon the life that was about me had made its impress, and already I desired intensely to comply with all of its demands.

Charles Eastman, a Santee Dakota Sioux, who was two years old in 1860, Indian Boyhood, pp. 10–11.

It is wonderful that any children grew up through all the exposures and hardships that we suffered in those days! The frail teepee pitched anywhere, in the winter as well as in the summer, was all the protection we had against cold and storms. I can recall times when we were snowed in and it was very difficult to get fuel. We were once three days without much fire and all of this time it stormed violently. There seemed to be no special anxiety on the part of our people; they rather looked upon all this as a matter of course, knowing that the storm would cease when the time came.

Charles Eastman, a Santee Dakota Sioux, recalling his childhood in the 1860s and 1870s, Indian Boyhood, p. 19.

. . . [W]e little boys scouted around and watched the hunters; and when we would see a bunch of bison coming, we would yell "Yuhoo" like the others, but nobody noticed us.

When the butchering was all over, they hung the meat across the horses' backs and fastened it with strips of fresh bison hide. On the way back to the village all the hunting horses were loaded, and we little boys who could not wait for the feast helped ourselves to all the raw liver we wanted. Nobody got cross when we did this.

Black Elk, Oglala Lakota Sioux Holy Man, remembering the hunts of his childhood, ca. 1870, Black Elk Speaks, p. 58.

When we played "hunting buffalo" we would send a few good runners off on the open prairie with a supply of meat; then start a few equally swift boys to chase them and capture the food. Once we were engaged in this sport when a real hunt by the men was in progress; yet we did not realize that it was so near until, in the midst of our play, we saw an immense buffalo coming at full speed directly toward us. Our mimic buffalo hunt turned into a very real buffalo scare. Fortunately, we were near the edge of the woods and we soon disappeared among the leaves like a covey of young prairie-chickens and some hid in the bushes while others took refuge in tall trees.

Charles Eastman, a Santee Dakota Sioux, describing play ca. 1870, Indian Boyhood, p. 73.

Occasionally, we also played "white man." Our knowledge of the pale-face was limited, but we had learned that he brought goods whenever he came and that our people exchanged furs for his merchandise. We also knew that his complexion was pale, that he had short hair on his head and long hair on his face and that he wore coat, trousers, and hat, and did not patronize blankets in the daytime. This was the picture we had formed of the white man.

So we painted two or three of our number with white clay and put on them birchen hats which we sewed up for the occasion; fastened a piece of fur to their chins for a beard and altered their costumes as much as lay within our power. The white of the birch-bark was made to answer for their white shirts. Their merchandise consisted of sand for sugar, wild beans for coffee, dried leaves for tea, pulverized earth for gunpowder, pebbles for bullets and clear water for the dangerous "spirit water." We traded for these goods with skins of squirrels, rabbits and small birds.

Charles Eastman, a Santee Dakota Sioux, describing play ca. 1870, Indian Boyhood, p. 73.

. . . [A]ll the boys from five or six years up were playing war. The little boys would gather together from the different bands of the tribe and fight each other with mud balls that they threw with willow sticks. And the big boys played the game called Throwing-Them-Off-Their-Horses, which is a battle all but the killing; and sometimes they got hurt. The horsebacks from the different bands would line up and charge upon each other, yelling; and when the ponies came together on the run, they would rear and flounder and scream in a big dust, and the riders would seize each other, wrestling until one side had lost all its men, for those who fell upon the ground were counted dead.

When I was older, I, too, often played this game. We were always naked when we played it, just as warriors are when they go into battle if it is not too cold, because they are swifter without clothes. Once I fell off on my back right in the middle of a bed of prickly pears, and it took my mother a long while to pick all the stickers out of me.

Black Elk, Oglala Lakota Sioux Holy Man, describing his play in the 1870s, Black Elk Speaks, p. 15.

May 7.—Several of us started for the bluff, 2 miles and a half. We found 11 new kinds of flowers. The prairie was covered with them. They are beautiful. We went to the top and found verbenas, geraniums, celery, sorrel and penny royal. Found the queerest stones—some like turtle shells. Brought some home. We found blackberry and gooseberry vines. Then we went on to Burnses, 2 miles above 12 mile creek. Had a splendid supper. On the way home we forded the river. Saw 4 snakes, 4 buffalo and ever so many antelope. We found yellow violets.

May 8.—Mamma and I waded the river and went over to our claim. We have peas, potatoes and pumpkins up in the buffalo wallows. We saw 5 buffaloes off on a hill about 2 miles. They were lying down. The men went after them. They killed one and broke the leg of another, which they finally killed after it ran down into the river. Then they got the team and cut up the buffaloes and brought them home. The buffaloes smell like skunk.

Luna E. Warner, May 7 and 8, 1871, in Venola Lewis Bivans, ed., "The Diary of Luna E. Warner, a Kansas Teenager of the Early 1870's," p. 283.

Tortoises were very common. I had one for a pet, and made him quite tame, so that I could open his mouth and put my finger inside without him biting. I used to amuse myself by getting him to draw a little sledge that I made. I bored two small holes in the shell at the back and put in some wire loops, and hitched him to the sledge with string. He used then to pull a little load of wood or anything else I put upon it. In the autumn he ran away to go torpid for the winter, as their manner is, but I found him again next spring, and of course recognised him by his wires.

I also had another queer "critter" for a pet. It was a sort of lizard, quite harmless, but decidedly ferocious in appearance. It was commonly called a "horned toad," though why I do not know; for although it had plenty of horns, it hadn't much toad about it.

Percy G. Ebbutt, whose family immigrated to the United States from England and settled on the Kansas prairie in 1871, when he was 11, Emigrant Life in Kansas, pp. 34–36.

"Cultivating" is rather pleasant work, not quite so heavy as ploughing, and requires a little skill to avoid injuring the growing corn. It always amuses me to contrast the method of ploughing in England with that practised in the States. In the old country it appears to be usual to take three horses, one behind another, a

small boy with a big whip to drive them, and a man to do the ploughing. Now in America a boy can run the whole thing. The reins are round his neck, the whip is fastened by a thong to his hand, the ploughs are made lighter, the three horses are worked abreast, and a great saving of labour is the result. I have ploughed acre after acre in this way from when I was twelve years old.

Percy G. Ebbutt, whose family immigrated from England and settled in Kansas and who was 12 years old in 1872, Emigrant Life in Kansas, p. 90.

My best loved toy was my bow, of choke-cherry wood, given me when I was four years old. My arrows were of buck-brush shoots, unfeathered. These shoots were brought in green, and thrust into the hot ashes of the fireplace; when heated, they were drawn out and the bark peeled off, leaving them a beautiful yellow. Buck-brush arrows are light, and I was allowed to shoot them in the lodge.

My uncle, Full Heart, a boy two years older than myself, taught me how to use my bow. In our lodge were many mice that nested in holes under the sloping roof, and my uncle and I hunted these mice as savagely as our fathers hunted buffaloes. I think I was not a very good shot, for I do not remember ever killing one.

Edward Goodbird of the Hidatsa people, who was four years old in 1873, Goodbird the Indian, pp. 22–23.

I can remember that at night my two younger brothers and I slept on the ground under a wagon sheet stretched over the tongue, which was held in a horizontal position by the neck yoke. We slept soundly although we had seen Father kill a huge rattlesnake beside the road one day. When we children got thirsty those hot days and the water jug was empty, Father would cut each of us a pieace of jerked buffalo meat to chew on. This was commonly sold in some of the markets, for the buffalo killers were still at work. The one highway marker on the roads then was the telegraph line, with its miles of poles all exactly alike stretching into the distance.

James K. Hastings, who was seven in 1875, when his family migrated to Trinidad, Colorado, "Boyhood in the Trinidad Region," p. 105.

Of the start of the journey [to Leadville, Colorado] I have no recollection, but I recall how jammed the train was with men and how we all left it together. There was a big white house where we spent the night. The next morning we were crowded into a stagecoach where Mother was the only woman and we three, the only children. A rough-looking man wept as he looked at little Harry in Mother's arms.

"Let me hold him for a minute," he pleaded. "He's the first baby I've seen in ten years. It was then I left mine back East."

Georgia Burns Hills, who was five in 1878, when she moved from Denver to Leadville, Colorado, "Memories of a Pioneer Childhood," p. 113.

A dreadful fear of the Indians was born and grown into me. As a child I had three gripping fears—starvation, Indians, and ghosts. Long after I had outgrown the fear of not having enough to eat, and the fear of a ghostly hand being laid upon my shoulder from behind, I still had horrible dreams of trying to hide from Indians; of running from them till my feet rose from the ground and I ran in the air—hundreds of times have I had this dream. This, no doubt, came from my mother's fear of them.

Anne Ellis, whose family migrated to the West in 1879, The Life of an Ordinary Woman, p. 11.

One of the most painful things in the Western States and Territories is the extinction of childhood. I have never seen any children, only debased imitations of men and women, cankered by greed and selfishness, and asserting and gaining complete independence of their parents at ten years old. The atmosphere in which they are brought up is one of greed, godlessness, and frequently of profanity. Consequently these sweet things seem like flowers in a desert.

Isabella Bird, 1879, A Lady's Life in the Rocky Mountains, p. 77.

Amongst the pupils in my class was a little girl whose father ran a saloon in the rear of which the family lived. . . . We stopped by for this child to go along with us [to school]. One morning when we stopped we were told that she was sick. A few days later it was announced in school that she had died. On the way home a group of us stopped by her home and asked if we might see the corpse. We were admitted and shown to the cot where the sheet-covered child lay ready for the coffin. Someone in the group suggested that we kiss her good-bye. We each did so, spilling our tears on the spotted face while the mother wept with us. . . .

When it turned out that she had died of scarlet fever, Mother went wild. In due course, Madgie and I both were taken with it. And, there being no way to keep the two younger children from being exposed to the disease, they, too, were attacked.

Georgia Burns Hills, who survived scarlet fever in the spring of 1880, "Memories of a Pioneer Childhood," pp. 118–19.

The greatest difference between our play and that of present day children was that we had almost no toys except those which we made for ourselves. The greatest treasure of the average Cross Timbers boy of the 1880's was his pocket knife. It was usually a Barlow knife with one blade. [My brother] George and I each had one, which we whetted to a razor-sharp edge on the sandstone that was abundant on our farm. To lose one's knife was a tragedy. Most little girls had only a doll and sometimes a set of little dishes.

Almost every boy also had a few marbles of various types. . . .

In addition to marbles and a pocket knife, I once received the gift of a small toy pistol and one box of caps. These were about the only "store bought" toys I ever owned. My sister Fannie, in Nebraska, sent us a Christmas box one year containing a bag of beautiful glass marbles for me and a harmonica, which we called a "French harp," for George. He was delighted with this and soon learned to play it very well. . . .

A good ball could be made from yarn obtained by unraveling an old hand-knitted woolen sock. When the yarn had been rolled up as tightly as possible into a ball, somewhat smaller than a baseball, it had to be thoroughly sewed with a needle and thread or it would unravel. Rubber balls could be bought at a store for from ten to twenty-five cents, but neither George nor I ever felt that we could afford to buy one, even if we had that much money, which was not often.

Edward Everett Dale describing the toys he owned in the 1880s in Texas, The Cross Timbers, pp. 81–82.

Several months after our arrival [in New Mexico] a weekly mail route was established. . . . If we hadn't done so before, we children certainly earned our bed and board then! In rain or shine, heat or cold, daylight or night-time, we made that twenty-mile round trip on horseback singly or in pairs every Monday of the world. With mail sacks flabby though never empty (for my mother was one of that species rapidly becoming extinct—a letter-writer) going to the post office, and bulging with mail coming back from it (we subscribed to innumerable papers and magazines), we children high-trotted back and forth, up and down that ten-mile stretch of Datil Canon, for more times than I probably would believe if count had been kept.

With icicles six inches long hanging from my pony's nostrils, and with frostbitten feet, I have made that trip in sub-zero weather, or, in midsummer, I have ridden it with the sun blasting down with all the force of a glass furnace. I have ridden it on easy-gaited horses, on rough-gaited horses, horses that were gentle and horses that were not: I have ridden it when I wanted to and when I didn't, when my excited imagination had Indians following me, and when I knew that coyotes were.

Agnes Mary Cleaveland, who grew up in Magdalena, New Mexico, in the 1880s, No Life for a Lady, *p. 47.*

Well, here I am at my first school. I realy wander if I'll like it. I arrived at the house about eight o'clock. It is a very pleasant looking place. I wander how I'll get along. My anticipations are great.—I am going to try to make rapid improvement. I hope the next three months will not be lost. And I trust they will not be if I continue with the effort I've made today. There is something in which I am bound to improve, and that is in speaking low (tho it is as natural for me, as it is to see). The Supt gave me *such a desperate* look while I was reading at the examination, that I resolved to "learn to read loud." I think if hollowing will do any good I'll overcome that fault entirely. I have a scholar that is some deaf, and I've "hollered" and talked today until my throat aches. I am among entire strangers, not knowing before I came here a single person.

DESCRIPTION.—The Country is right in the midst of the Blue Hills [Township], and is a very pleasant place. The school house is in a little valley, surrounded by hills. It is a small frame house, facing the South-west (or I guess it is, I can't tell one direction from another here.) It has three windows and a door. There is no benches, seats, black board or writing desks. I am now sitting on the floor with my paper on "the Teacher's chair," which is as high as my chin, (almost.) For seats we have two boards placed on rocks. I think if I had more scholars, and things more convenient I should like teaching very much.

Anna Webber, Kansas teacher, May 9, 1881, in Lila Gravall Scrimsher, ed., "The Diary of Anna Webber: Early Day Teacher of Mitchell County," p. 321.

It has been a novel sight, to watch a little girl about ten years old herding sheep near town; handling her pony with a masterly hand, galloping around the herd if they begin to scatter out, and driving them into the corral. I must add that I have also seen some fine looking cattle.

Frances I. Sims Fulton, who journeyed from Pennsylvania to Nebraska in 1883, To and Through Nebraska, *p. 42.*

A class of boys and girls from eight to twenty-five years of age, ignorant of every rule of school or society sits mute before you. The sad, homesick faces do not look encouraging. Everything is new and strange to them. The boys' heads feel bare without the long braids. The new clothes are not easy and homelike. They do not understand one word of your language, nor you of theirs, perhaps, but they are watching your every look and motion. You smile and say "Good Morning;" they return the smile in a hopeless kind of way, but not the "good morning." By a series of home-made signs, which they are quick to interpret, they are made to understand that they are to repeat your greeting, and you are rewarded with a gruff or timid "Good Monink," and thus another gate is opened to the "white man's road."

Cora Folsom, who taught Indian children at the Hampton Institute, 1884, in Daniel Wallace Adams, Education for Extinction, *p. 136.*

One day my brother and I ran away, off into the vast wilderness that surrounded three sides of our home. We were gone a long time, and my mother, in anticipation of our return, got down the old quirt [whip], which had done noble duty on many previous occasions, and sat down to her sewing to wait for us. . . . Finally she saw us. We were on our way home, trudging aimlessly along through the mesquite brush, and at the same instant that my mother saw us she saw something else. Coming along directly behind us was a big drove of cattle!

. . . [T]here wasn't anything that anyone, except my brother, could have done to save us, and strange to say he did it. He had human intelligence. He and I saw the herd coming behind us, and instead of trying to outrun the cattle, as I tried to do, he grabbed me by the arm and ruthlessly dragged me into the middle of a huge mesquite bush, where, with a million thorns puncturing us in every direction, we remained, while about the same number of cattle, eyes glazed and horns cracking, went thundering past.

I say "a million went thundering by," because, although it is probable there were only about fifteen hundred, and they were merely trotting, they were countless to me. . . . In her joy at having us restored to her, even though we were considerably damaged by thorns, my mother forgot all about the quirt, gathered us into her arms, wept over us, and treated us generally to an amount of love of which we were entirely unworthy. But later on, because my mother was always very just, she remembered that we had something coming to us, and so, but in a modified form, we got it before we retired.

Owen P. White remembering an incident that occurred in Arizona ca. 1885, A Frontier Mother, *pp. 91–93.*

[My father] was the leader of the 11th U.S. Infantry Band. . . .

Our first Army station in Arizona was at Fort Huachuca, where we arrived in the late 'eighties. Its location, miles and miles from urban civilization, its barren hills and bleak surroundings made it exceedingly unpleasant and undesirable for grown-ups but a paradise for a little boy. We could ride burros. Our playground was not measured in acres, or city blocks, but in miles and miles. We could do just about everything a little boy dreams of. We talked with miners and Indians. We associated with soldiers, and we learned to shoot even when we were so small the gun had to be held for us by an elder.

Fiorello H. La Guardia, who was a child in Arizona in the late 1880s, The Making of an Insurgent, *p. 19.*

Mining camp kids in the nineties didn't know what an allowance was. What we got to spend, we earned mostly. And many were the ways we earned it. How the rest of us envied Earl Lewis: he lived down near the red-light district and running errands for the girls was a better-paying proposition than any other job we could get. Almost as good but not so regular was carrying notes between the young blades and their enamoratas of the moment. Occasionally, there would be a case where the papa of some girl had an aversion for the swain of her choice so complete he would threaten to shoot the young man if he showed up around the place. Carrying notes between such a pair was hazardous employment and required some finesse in getting notes to and from the young lady without her parent catching on, so we always demanded a quarter for this service.

Edwin Lewis Bennett recalling childhood employment in the 1890s, Boom Town Boy in Old Creede, Colorado, *p. 48.*

Small-town children had a good deal of freedom and a wide range. Boys and girls played together and every generation produced a certain number of "tom-boy" girls who pushed their way into almost every masculine activity except football. . . . [B]ut for the girls it came completely to an end at a certain age. They then underwent a sudden and striking transformation. Their hair went up and their skirts went down. They played no more games with boys. They were suddenly enveloped in dry goods and mystery.

Harvey Fergusson, who spent his childhood in Albuquerque, New Mexico, in the 1890s, Home in the West, *p. 113.*

My job on the farm was to help out doors. The second year we bought a cow, and more cattle were bought as the years passed. As long as I was home with Father and Mother, my job was to milk the cows, churn the butter, wean the claves, and yoke the cattle to keep them from straying off as the fences were poor. At first, only one strand of barb wire was used for a fence but later two woven wires were used. For a long time, I milked from five to twelve cows every morning and night. When any cattle were sold, I rounded them up and started them out because when the buyers came, the animals would get scared and run and jump the fences. . . .

Brother and I worked at haying time, and in harvesting the grain. I helped haul in the hay from the meadow and stack it in the racks. One time the team ran away when we drove over a nest of bumble bees that swarmed up and stung the horses. I shocked the bundles of wheat in the field, helped scoop up grain into the wagons and haul it into the bins.

Fannie L. Eisele describing her work on an Oklahoma farm, from 1894, when she was 10 years old, through 1897, "We Came to Live in Oklahoma Territory," *p. 60.*

My brother, Herman, and I did the plowing. We would come in from the field in the evening at seven o'clock, and feed our horses. First, we would brush the horses and wash their shoulders. Then I milked the cows, while brother would look after the plows and get them

Alice Butcher, a "Nebraska Lassie," milking a cow. *(Nebraska State Historical Society)*

repaired for the next day. I drove three horses on a plow. It took six weeks to finish plowing 160 acres. Besides the grain crop, we would raise corn and use the cobs to burn in the stoves at the house as well as wood. Father fed corn to his hogs and we cured our own meat.

Fannie L. Eisele describing her work on an Oklahoma farm, from 1894, when she was 10 years old, through 1897, "We Came to Live in Oklahoma Territory," p. 61.

Gamblers and saloonkeepers were an important part of pioneer Western life, but they were never a reputable part of the community. . . .

My first attempt at applied mathematics—I must have been fourteen or fifteen then—was to figure out the percentage against the player in a crap game, a faro game and what was then called "policy," now known as "the numbers" and other fancy names as well as the old name "policy." Nearly every saloon in Prescott, Arizona, had its gambling department, mainly crap, faro and some Chinese game. There was, of course, a good deal of poker played—not under professional auspices. These games must have been exciting, according to the stories we kids would hear: the guns were laid on the table at easy reach, and of course the games were on the level.

Fiorello H. La Guardia recalling events of 1897, The Making of an Insurgent, *p. 24.*

I am sure there was not another schoolhouse in the whole country as primitive as this one. There couldn't have been. It was made of logs and had been built in a day by the men in the settlement. The dimensions were about fourteen by sixteen feet. The logs were chinked and daubed with adobe mud. In many places the mud had fallen out. If a child wanted to look at anyone passing, he would peek between the logs. . . . The floor was of unfinished boards and if a child dropped a pencil, he had learned to be quick to retrieve or it rolled through the cracks under the floor. At times we would have a general upheaval at the noon hour when the boys would take up the floor boards and reclaim the erasers, pencils, chalk, and various other articles the woodrat had hidden under there.

Nellie Carnahan Robinson, who taught school near Lavender, Colorado, 1897–99, in Michael B. Husband, ed., "The Recollections of a Schoolteacher in the Disappointment Creek Valley," p. 150.

The social event of the winter was a party given in the schoolhouse at the settlement twelve miles below us. All were invited and the children talked of little else at the noon hour for several days. The party was to be Friday night. We didn't have school on that day as it took the greater part of the afternoon to drive down there. . . .

The seats and desks were placed around the outer part of the room. In one corner some desks were arranged so as to make a bed for the babies. It was a friendly, happy gathering of neighbors. The dogs barked and at times the babies cried, but no one seemed to mind. The young people were soon dancing.

Nellie Carnahan Robinson, who taught school near Lavender, Colorado, 1897–99, in Michael B. Husband, ed., "The Recollections of a Schoolteacher in the Disappointment Creek Valley," pp. 154–55.

We didn't have any organized athletics or physical education; neither did we have any organized juvenile crime. The kids got their exercise walking to school and from our unorganized athletics such as One Hole Cat, Shinny, Duck-On-The-Rock and Barberoo, all games we could play without coaches, trainers, or supervision. We lived across the street, but some of the pupils had long walks. A few, who lived really far away, rode to school on their burros. The burro did not get called a Rocky Mountain Canary for no good reason whatever, so having them tied nearby was frowned upon by people who were not enthusiastic about their kind of singing. At that, they compared favorably with quite a few of the performers we tolerate on radio and TV now.

Edwin Lewis Bennett describing events ca. 1900, Boom Town Boy in Old Creede, Colorado, p. 68.

Very few of the next generation of Nebraskans will have the pleasure of attending school in a Nebraska sod schoolhouse. They might go to school in poorer buildings than the one built of sod, however, for it is as warm in winter and as cool in summer as any ordinary schoolhouse, although some of our lady teachers do object to the fleas and vermine that sometimes infest such a building. Many of our sod school houses are well finished, nearly all are floored and plastered, and many are finished around the doors and windows on the inside. Slate blackboards, patent desks, maps, charts, a school library, a globe and an international unabridged dictionary may be found in many of them. The better class of them have shingled roofs.

William K. Fowler, state superintendent of schools, Nebraska, 1902, in Richard E. Dudley, "Nebraska Public School Education, 1890–1910," p. 66.

7

Child Saving
1817–1922

On October 31, 1849, a divinity student named Charles Loring Brace led a prayer service at the almshouse on Blackwell's Island. Renamed Welfare Island in 1921 and Roosevelt Island in 1973, this narrow strip of land lies in New York's East River, between Manhattan and Long Island. In the 19th century, it was a repository for the city's unwanted, a place where cold, dark stone structures housed criminals, the mentally ill, and the poor. On that Halloween of more than 150 years ago, Brace preached to an assembly of typical almshouse residents that included drunkards, vagrants, the aged, and prostitutes with late-stage syphilis who had come to Blackwell's Island to die. Three and a half months later, Brace was still thinking about the people at the almshouse and about those who were destined to live there in the future. He had come to view New York as "an immense vat of misery and crime and filth," a place with "*ten thousand children* growing up almost sure to be prostitutes and rogues!"

Brace would pursue an uncommon ministry, one that centered on rescuing city children from poverty and vice. He would become one of the child savers, those 19th- and early 20th-century reformers who stepped into the lives of poor urban children and attempted to change things for the better. The child savers were predominantly white, middle-class Protestants whose idealized vision of childhood clashed with the realities of urban life. The threats to children's welfare that they observed were real, however, and they correctly perceived that society was ill equipped to remedy them. Boys roaming the streets joined gangs and committed crimes, while girls were drawn into prostitution. Orphaned and abandoned children were sleeping wherever they could find shelter, and long hours and mindless tasks were keeping working children out of school, putting their health at risk, and robbing them of the joys of youth.

State and municipal public-assistance programs did not yet exist, and the federal government would not provide citizens with financial support until the Great Depression of the 1930s. Although Americans traditionally had turned to their extended families in times of crisis, urbanization had weakened family ties and left people vulnerable. When illness, death, or job loss occurred, city residents fell into poverty.

AN ALTERNATIVE TO PRISON

The judicial system, as it existed throughout the United States in the early 19th century, also put children at risk. Children as young as seven could be sent to prison if the court determined that they were able to distinguish right from wrong and were deserving of blame. Children were even sentenced to death, and at least 10 prisoners under the age of 14 were executed. Children also died in prison as a result of accidents or disease. Juries sometimes acquitted young defendants, despite evidence pointing to their guilt, in order to protect them.

New York City's House of Refuge, one of the earliest efforts at social reform, was an attempt at compromise, allowing young people who were convicted of crimes to serve their sentences apart from hardened criminals. A Quaker group, the Society for the Reformation of Juvenile Delinquents, founded this institution, which began operations on January 1, 1825. Six boys and three girls were the first residents of the House of Refuge. By year's end, the inmates numbered 73: 54 boys and 19 girls. Their lives were less sheltered than the reformers had hoped, because according to the law, any boy under the age of 21 could be sent to the House of Refuge. This meant that young men experienced in the ways of crime served alongside youthful first offenders.

The House of Refuge was intended to serve as both prison and school, and it had features of each. If they broke the rules, children were disciplined like prisoners by being shackled to a ball and chain, handcuffed, locked in leg irons, or whipped. One girl was even given a purgative as punishment. Two hours a day were set aside for lessons in reading, writing, spelling, and arithmetic, taught according to the Lancasterian method.

The House of Refuge was also a workplace where children woke up early and put in a full day's labor. During its first year of operation, when the institution was housed in a former arsenal, the boys put up a new building. The girls planted a lawn in addition to practicing domestic skills. Once the new quarters were complete, the boys learned shoemaking, silver plating, tailoring, and other trades, while the girls washed and mended clothes for all of the inmates.

When the authorities determined that a child had been sufficiently reformed, they usually secured an apprenticeship for him or her. Boys generally were apprenticed to farmers, although some joined the crews of whaling ships. Most girls were placed as domestic servants. Boys were indentured until age 21 and girls until age 18.

By 1860, there were 20 such institutions for youthful offenders in the United States, and by 1885 there were 45. The proliferation of correctional institutions coincided with a dramatic increase in juvenile crime that occurred during the Civil War. When thousands of fathers and older brothers left home to join the army, many households experienced a breakdown in family discipline. At the same time, schools were forced to close in some regions of the South, and young people found themselves with time on their hands. In cities south and north, gangs of boys bullied passersby and committed petty crimes. Boys also engaged in vandalism, gambled, and tossed rocks at people, windows, and lamps. It became impossible in many communities to hold public gatherings and not have them disrupted by rowdy boys.

During the second half of the 19th century, the houses of refuge evolved into reformatories, or reform schools, which were designed to house first-time offenders, abandoned and neglected children, and those whose parents found them difficult to control. Reformatories directed their efforts at getting children out of the corrupting urban environment, exposing them to education and discipline, and then returning them to their families or placing them on farms as indentured servants. While some reformatories were privately run, many were

Scenes from the State Industrial School for Girls, Middletown, Connecticut. *Clockwise, from top:* school officials reason with a "vicious" girl; inmates learn the trade of making boxes; a cooking class; a well-mannered, well-groomed graduate *(Library of Congress)*

state institutions. Intended to offer training and discipline rather than punishment, they remained somber places nonetheless. Children committed to them lived cut off from the outside world; rules were strict, and punishment was severe.

Some state-run reformatories catered to subgroups within the institutionalized population, such as first-time male offenders age 16 to 25, or those age seven to 14. Most housed only boys, although some provided separate quarters for girls. The most common offense among reform-school girls was sexual precocity, which was usually described in case histories as "staying out late at night," or "running around with men." Girls tended to receive stiffer sentences than boys did, with the goal of keeping them sheltered until they were ready to re-enter society as respectable women. The first exclusively female reform school, the Massachusetts Industrial School for Girls, opened in 1854. Nearly all of its residents came from poor families. Thirty-five percent had fathers who had died or deserted their families, and the remaining 65 percent had fathers who were living but who for the most part were out of work or employed at menial jobs.

Following the Civil War, it was common for institutions of reform to enter into contracts with industry in order to raise needed funds. According to the contract terms, manufacturers set up shops within reformatories, and the inmates made umbrellas, brooms, and other items. Payment went to the institution and not to the workers. This practice came under attack from two sources, however, and was discontinued as a result. Organized labor protested because the young inmates took jobs away from union members, and some reformers complained that long hours spent at repetitive factory jobs did nothing to prepare the children for productive adult lives.

FROM THE ALMSHOUSE TO THE ORPHANAGE

While the courts were throwing young criminals into prison in the early 19th century, many orphaned and destitute children had nowhere to go but the local home for the poor. This establishment might be an almshouse, supported by charitable gifts, or a poorhouse, which was a public institution. Whether the home was publicly or privately funded, children shared cramped, filthy quarters with the aged, the ill, and the insane, and were cared for by these individuals. Babies sent to almshouses essentially received a death sentence: Very few lived to one year of age.

By mid-century, calls were coming from the public to remove children from almshouses and place them in orphanages. Churches, reformers, and philanthropists responded to the need, and the number of private orphanages in the United States grew rapidly, expanding from 77 in 1851 to 613 in 1880. Of course, many of these were built to house children orphaned by the Civil War. The Roman Catholic Church made a particular effort to construct orphanages after 1860, to accommodate homeless immigrant children.

State governments lagged behind the churches and private charities in their efforts to care for orphans. By the end of the 19th century, just one-fourth of the states had laws requiring children to be removed from almshouses and poorhouses. Most of these states moved the children to public asylums built especially to house them, but others, such as Indiana and New Jersey, placed the children in foster homes.

A large percentage of the children in orphan asylums—more than 50 percent in some instances—were half-orphans. In fact, the New Orleans Board of Prisons and Asylums reported in 1915 that a mere 15 percent of children in the care of the city's charitable organizations were without both parents. Many asylum residents were the sons and daughters of women who had been widowed or deserted by their husbands and who were unable to support their families. Often the only work available to these women was domestic servitude, which paid poorly and usually required them to live in their employers' homes without dependents. In the mid-19th century at least one institution, the Chicago Orphan Asylum, permitted parents to turn over their children for three months' care. The parents had to agree to surrender permanently all rights to their children if they were unable to provide a home at the end of that period.

Some children ended up in orphanages after losing one or both parents to workplace accidents or illness. The need for space in orphan asylums increased following cholera epidemics, such as one that swept through Chicago in 1849. Frightened city residents burned small packets of gunpowder in the hope that the resulting odor would counteract cholera's "noxious effluvia," yet every day the Board of Health published a long list of the dead. The Quakers of New Orleans had responded to a high death toll from yellow fever in the early 19th century by building a home for female orphans in 1817 and an asylum for orphaned boys in 1824. Nearly a century later, the influenza pandemic of 1918 also created many orphans. Entering an orphanage was a frightening experience for children. They frequently cried, vomited, and soiled their clothes.

Because 19th-century Americans commonly thought that poverty resulted from immorality, orphanages placed a heavy emphasis on its believed antidote,

Mealtime at the New York Foundling Hospital, ca. 1900 *(Museum of the City of New York; Byron Collection; 93.1.1.4997)*

religion. Staff members led the residents in morning and evening prayers, and attendance at religious services, which were sometimes held daily, was mandatory. Education also was made available, either within the institution or in the local public school. Children at the Chicago Orphan Asylum were taught reading, writing, arithmetic, and a trade. The curriculum at the Louisville Baptist Home included geography in addition to those subjects, but in 1915, administrators at the Louisville Home determined that they would save money by sending the orphans to public schools.

For most residents, the orphanage was a short-term home. They lived there until they could be returned to relatives or adopted, or until they ran away or died. Death rates were staggeringly high for babies in institutional care—sometimes reaching 90 percent or more. Administrators often endeavored to have children "placed out," or indentured to artisans or families so that they might learn a trade or be sent to school in return for their labor.

THE CHILDREN'S AID SOCIETY

Reform schools and orphanages were not without their critics. Many people insisted that locking children away in vast, impersonal structures merely got them out of the public view and that growing up in such an establishment stunted children's mental and emotional growth. Critics were fond of saying that even the worst home was better than the finest institution and that institutionalization should be considered only as a last resort. Furthermore, despite all the institution-building, homelessness among children continued to be a serious problem in cities. In 1872, Charles Loring Brace estimated that between 20,000 and 30,000 children were sleeping on the streets and sidewalks of New York on a regular basis. Brace was one of the most influential people to preach against institutionalization. He condemned the practice as a costly one that failed to prepare children for adulthood.

Between 1850, when he had lamented the fate of New York City's poor, and 1872, when he counted the homeless children, Brace had been to Europe to study charity work being conducted there. In New York, he and other ministers organized "Boys' Meetings" and preached to street youth, although they were occasionally rewarded with a shower of stones. In 1853, the ministers founded the Children's Aid Society, with Brace as its first secretary.

The principal activity of the Children's Aid Society was finding foster parents for homeless youngsters, children Brace called "street orphans." The agency sent children to live with families in rural communities where labor was in short supply. Initially children went to homes in upstate New York and New England, but in 1854, trains began carrying orphans to the Midwest. Forty-six children, most between the ages of seven and 15, made the first of these journeys, to Michigan. By 1860, the Children's Aid Society had placed more than 5,000 children in foster homes, and by 1884, the number passed 60,000. While orphan asylums and reform schools placed residents as indentured servants, the families taking in children from the orphan trains signed no articles of indenture. The children were free to leave whenever they wished.

Frequently the placements had happy outcomes, and in 1900 the Children's Aid Society boasted of an 87-percent success rate. There were failures, though. Some children suffered physical abuse at the hands of their foster parents, while others endured hunger, neglect, and overwork. The society's practice of placing siblings in separate homes caused many children distress.

Agencies in other cities, including Baltimore, Boston, and Philadelphia, also placed children in midwestern foster homes. Child-placement workers found justification for their activities in the Bible, quoting, for example, Psalm 68, which states that God is "A Father to the fatherless," who "setteth the solitary in families." Zealous about placing children in rural homes, these individuals were often careless in investigating potential foster parents, keeping records, and following up on the children who had been placed.

Not all of the children placed out were orphans, of course, and many left the city without their parents' permission. This knowledge weighed lightly on the consciences of Brace and his associates, because they believed that they were helping children by removing them from a harmful environment. Also, the public strongly supported placing-out programs and expressed little concern about the breakup of poor families. The most common criticisms of the Children's Aid Society and similar groups concerned the fact that Catholic children were regularly placed in Protestant homes and the possibility that troublesome city youth would fail to adapt to rural life.

Although the transplanted city children showed no greater inclination to break the law than local young people, Michigan enacted a law in 1887 restricting the placement of out-of-state children and in 1895 began requiring charitable agencies to post bond for any child placed in the state. Other midwestern and eastern states passed similar and sometimes stricter laws.

In addition to sending children west on "orphan trains," the Children's Aid Society operated five lodging houses for boys in New York City and one for girls. The best known of these was the Newsboys' Lodging House. When it opened in 1854, the Newsboys' Lodging House charged 6 cents a night for a bed and a bath and 4 cents for a hot meal. At first the boys were wary, suspecting that the lodging house was a ploy to lure them into religion classes, and some

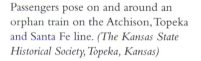

Passengers pose on and around an orphan train on the Atchison, Topeka and Santa Fe line. *(The Kansas State Historical Society, Topeka, Kansas)*

even plotted to destroy it before realizing that the Children's Aid Society was offering them a good deal. In time the lodging house did provide religious services as well as a night school and a savings bank for the newsboys, who were often self-supporting. (It is interesting to note that by the turn of the 20th century, mothers in the neighborhood would be objecting to the presence of the Newsboys' Lodging House, claiming that it encouraged their sons to stay away from home.)

Vocational training was another of the society's ventures. By 1892, the society sponsored 21 day industrial schools and 12 evening schools. In addition, there were classes in sewing, cooking, and housecleaning to prepare girls for future domestic work either as paid servants or as wives and mothers. There were also kindergartens, summer camps, and sanitariums.

PREVENTING CRUELTY TO CHILDREN

Reformatories, orphanages, and charitable groups such as the Children's Aid Society focused their efforts on children who had run afoul of the law or needed shelter. Before 1875, however, no social network existed to aid children living in abusive homes. The child savers had no authority to step between parents and their children.

Social policy toward abused and neglected children began to change in 1874, after a woman in New York City who was dying of tuberculosis told a missionary that she regularly heard cries from the next apartment, where a child was being beaten. Officials of the American Society for the Prevention of Cruelty to Animals (ASPCA) learned from the missionary about the case and took legal action against the abusive parents. The child, 10-year-old Mary Ellen Connolly, appeared in court with whip marks on her arms and legs and a scar running across her forehead, a permanent reminder of an assault with a pair of scissors by her adoptive mother. The presiding judge remanded Mary Ellen to an institution for dependent children, and Mrs. Connoly was later convicted.

Their success in the case of Mary Ellen Connolly inspired ASPCA members Elbridge Gerry and Henry Bergh to found, in 1875, the Society for the Prevention of Cruelty to Children (SPCC). The SPCC used the court system to prosecute parents suspected of abuse and gain custody of their children. Soon court officials began asking the SPCC to investigate cases of child neglect that came before them and to advise them on the most suitable placement of children removed from their homes. As a rule the court gave custody of such children to SPCC agents, who then placed them in institutions. The actions of the SPCC protected many children from physical harm, but the city's poor grew wary of the agency's power to intervene in family matters and nicknamed it "the Cruelty."

The SPCC also worked to help children in other ways. For example, the agency lobbied for enforcement of an 1877 law that allowed children caught begging in saloons, dance halls, or houses of prostitution, or found to be homeless and without means of support to be arrested and institutionalized. The SPCC endeavored to end the practice of girls selling flowers on city streets as a cover for prostitution and successfully battled the "padrone" system. A padrone was an individual who took children from Italian peasant families to the United States, promising to indenture them for three years and send their earnings to their parents in Italy. Instead, the padrone forced the children to entertain in bars and on street corners and to beg for money. Neither the children nor their parents received any income. Working closely with the Italian government, the SPCC arranged for the principal padrone operating in New York City to be taken into custody, and this system of child enslavement declined and soon disappeared.

THE ADVENT OF JUVENILE COURT

By 1880, agencies similar to the SPCC were active in 10 other cities. In 1899, lawmakers in Illinois came up with a new system for dealing with children who were neglected, abandoned, or dependent on public support, as well as those who came from unsuitable homes or who had been found peddling or entertaining on the streets. In that year the state legislature passed a law creating separate courts to handle all cases involving children under 16 years of age. Now, instead of convicting and punishing the young, judges in Illinois would strive to halt delinquency in individual cases by identifying the reasons for antisocial behavior and preventing it from being repeated.

With the goal of rehabilitation in mind, the juvenile court gathered as much information as possible about each child coming before it, examining the child's physical and mental health, home life, and school experience and looking into the financial status of his or her family. The atmosphere in family court was kept as informal and agreeable as possible; rather than handing down rulings from the bench, judges often engaged the young people in conversation.

The 1899 law required that children awaiting hearings be held in a detention home, apart from adult offenders. It also prohibited authorities from putting anyone younger than 12 in jail and required juveniles' court records to be kept confidential. The juvenile court relied on probation rather than incarceration to meet its ends, and the probation officer became the accused child's staunchest ally, assuming responsibility for the child who had been detained, representing him or her in court, and making home visits throughout the period of probation, whether the child was placed in a foster home or returned to his or her parents.

During the first two decades of the 20th century, all but a few states established juvenile courts modeled on the system in Illinois, and bureaucrats and judges spoke enthusiastically about their effectiveness. In 1902, the president of the New Jersey State Conference of Charities and Correction claimed that the crime rate had dropped significantly in his state and credited the use of probation in juvenile court. Two years later, the judge of the juvenile court in Indianapolis stated that 90 percent of the children placed on probation in his city avoided further trouble with the law, and in 1905, Judge Benjamin B. Lindsey of Denver boasted of a 95-percent success rate.

A federal survey of juvenile courts conducted in 1918 uncovered a number of problems within the system, however. The investigators learned that despite laws requiring separate detainment of children, 10 states provided no juvenile detention facility whatsoever. In 370 courts throughout the nation, children were regularly detained prior to their hearings in jails or almshouses. This meant that an original purpose of the juvenile courts—to keep children apart from adult criminals—was negated.

The federal study also found that courts were understaffed. Probation officers commonly handled more than 100 cases, and one overworked officer

Judge Benjamin B. Lindsey of the Denver Juvenile Court counsels young offenders in his chambers. Lindsey sits at the center, beneath the wall calendar. *(Library of Congress)*

carried a caseload of 156, although the limits allowed by law were much lower. Ten cities, for example, permitted probation officers to handle no more than 50 cases at a time. The personnel shortages resulted in shallow, perfunctory investigations and careless record keeping. In addition, juvenile courts lacked judges. Just 23 judges served full-time in the juvenile courts in 1918. Most of the nation's judges complained that juvenile-court cases presented no challenge and gave them little opportunity to use their legal expertise. They declined to serve permanently in this untested system and presided in juvenile court only on rotation.

By 1920, the juvenile court was well established in the United States, despite its shortcomings. It would improve steadily and remain the nation's dominant institution of juvenile justice throughout the 20th century.

SETTLEMENT HOUSES

While the courts attempted to steer delinquents toward responsible citizenship, social-settlement workers addressed urban problems at the community level to improve living conditions for all residents, including children, and possibly alter the environment that nurtured delinquent behavior.

The first social settlement in the United States was the Neighborhood Guild, later called the University Settlement, which was established in 1886 on the Lower East Side of Manhattan. Its founder, Stanton Coit, had been inspired to create a hub of culture and learning in the New York ghetto after visiting Toynbee Hall, a settlement in the slums of London. This settlement house was to be both a community center and a home for staff members who worked to improve the quality of neighborhood life and empower the local people to remedy social ills.

The settlement philosophy quickly gained popularity among U.S. reformers, and similar outposts appeared in cities throughout the nation. There were 100 settlement houses in the United States by 1900, and 400 by 1918. Nearly all were in impoverished, crowded immigrant communities. The movement attracted career-minded young women who had recently graduated from college but were denied entry into most fields dominated by men. Among the best-known settlements were Hull House, founded in 1889 in Chicago by Jane Addams and Ellen Gates Starr; and the Henry Street Settlement, established in 1893 in New York City by Lillian Wald.

The settlement houses offered such services as vocational training; health care; and classes in English, art, music, and drama. Settlements sponsored kindergartens and other classes for immigrants' children, after-school recreation, and playgrounds. Settlement houses also became centers of political activism as the resident reformers campaigned for safer tenements and better working and sanitary conditions. (Settlements continue to serve the public, although staff members no longer reside in them. The number of active settlements in the United States has risen and fallen since World War II, but it has remained between 400 and 800.)

In 1909, nearly 200 child-welfare advocates convened in Washington, D.C., for a White House conference on the care of dependent children. The experts advised President Theodore Roosevelt that whenever possible, children in need of assistance should be kept with their natural families. That conclusion persuaded lawmakers at the state level to provide widows' pensions, enabling many needy women to keep their families intact. The conference also urged the federal government to create a bureau specifically to investigate and report on child welfare. In 1912, President William Howard Taft appointed Julia Lathrop, a former Hull House resident, to head the U.S. Children's Bureau, a division of the Department of Labor and Commerce. The Children's Bureau studied such issues as birth rates, infant mortality, child health, and juvenile delinquency. It was this agency that conducted the 1918 study identifying problems in the juvenile courts.

THE CHALLENGE OF REGULATING CHILD LABOR

The Children's Bureau and settlement workers also investigated the conditions under which children labored, and they worked to secure and enforce state and federal child-labor laws. The child savers' concern for working children mirrored the evolving attitude of the middle class toward the young. While it was popularly held through much of the 19th century that work built character in children, that it developed such qualities as diligence and thrift, and that labor was preferable to idleness, reformers of the late 19th and early 20th centuries took a different view. To them, work robbed children of the time needed for play and normal physical and psychological development. Laboring children suffered by spending time in the workplace instead of at school, and they were exposed to an alarming number of health hazards.

Although the child savers previously had concentrated on the problems of urban youth and even relocated thousands of city children to farming regions, child labor was not confined to America's cities. Half of U.S. children lived on farms in 1900, and by age 12 the average farm boy or girl was spending more hours at work in the fields than in school. Between 1900 and 1920, sugar-processing companies began contracting with farmers, mostly in Colorado and Wisconsin, to grow sugar beets. Whole families worked together in the beet fields, especially in spring, when the young plants needed to be thinned, and again in fall, when it was time to pull the mature beets from the earth and lop off their leafy tops. In 1920, nearly all children in Colorado contracting families who were over age 10 labored an average of nine to 13 hours a day during the peak seasons. The work strained even young backs, and topping beets was a dangerous job done with a sharp, hooked blade.

Most child agricultural workers, including those in the beet business, worked for their parents without pay. Children working in the canneries and textile mills of the South earned low wages that were small compensation for labor's toll on their time, health, and intellectual growth.

Canneries along the Gulf Coast employed children as young as four or five to shell oysters and shrimp. Sharp oyster shells cut their fingers, and a corrosive chemical released by the shrimp made their hands bleed and peel. Adult workers taught the children to thrust their hands in alum, a harsh mineral salt, to stop the bleeding and toughen their skin. Because they were paid by the pot of cleaned shellfish rather than by the hour, children in canneries commonly started work before dawn and had little or no time for school.

The textile mills of the Piedmont region also kept children out of school and put them at risk. Child textile workers stood all day tending rows of spinning frames and darting their fingers into rapidly moving machinery to repair broken threads or replace empty bobbins. In 1890, there were 9,000 operatives age 14 or younger in southern textile mills; in 1900 there were 25,000. Most belonged to poor farming families that had migrated to mill towns in search of a steady, higher income.

Throughout the United States, the picture of child labor was grim. Boys working in the furnace rooms of glass factories in Pennsylvania and West Virginia were regularly exposed to temperatures of 100–130 degrees Fahrenheit. Balancing white-hot bottles on asbestos shovels, those employed as "carrying-in boys" ran repeatedly from the furnaces to the annealing ovens where the bottles were cooled. One activist observed a boy making this trip, covering a distance of 100 feet, 72 times an hour. In other kinds of factories, children inhaled fumes rich in toxins such as phosphorus and lead or filled in for fathers who had been injured while operating machinery. Boys employed in the risky business of coal mining were three times as likely to be injured as adult miners, but even children doing safe tasks, such as mounting snaps onto cards in home sweatshops, suffered from the dulling sameness of their work.

Child labor, like education, was left to the states to regulate. The SPCC lobbied for child-labor legislation in New York, and in 1886 the state legislature passed a weak factory act that prohibited children under 13 from working in rural manufacturing plants. By 1900, 15 states required children to be at least 14 years old to work, but children, parents, and employers frequently circumvented the poorly enforced age requirements.

In 1903, the Reverend Edgar Gardner Murphy, an Episcopal priest in Montgomery, Alabama, helped to get a law on the books in his state banning children under 12 from working in factories. He joined with northern activists in 1904 to form the National Child Labor Committee (NCLC), which worked to secure child-labor legislation state by state. NCLC members provided legislators with a model law that set a minimum age of 14 for employment in manufacturing and of 16 in mining. The model limited the workday of industrial laborers age 14 and 15 to eight hours, banned night work for anyone under 16, and required youthful workers to provide documentary proof of age.

Breaker boys, employees of the Woodward Coal Mines, Kingston, Pennsylvania, ca. 1890–1910. These boys spent from 10 to 12 hours a day separating slate from coal. *(Library of Congress)*

The NCLC also hired photographer Lewis Hine to travel throughout the United States and record the conditions of child labor with his camera. Between 1907 and 1918, Hine photographed barefoot children tending looms in textile mills, kindergarten-age cannery workers standing before mountains of oyster shells, and newsboys picking up their papers before dawn. Hine's photographs, distributed in pamphlets and on posters, raised public awareness of the dreary and dangerous conditions under which children worked and persuaded lawmakers to impose some control. By 1912, nine state had laws that met the criteria recommended by the NCLC; by 1914, 26 more states had enacted laws that complied with the NCLC model.

Southern textile manufacturers blocked passage of meaningful legislation in their states, however, and elsewhere enforcement of child-labor laws was erratic. For these reasons, the NCLC changed its approach and pushed for a federal child-labor law. The result was the Keating-Owen Act of 1916, which outlawed interstate shipment of goods produced in mines employing children younger than 16 and factories hiring laborers under 14, or where children of 14 or 15 worked more than eight hours a day, six days a week, or after 7:00 P.M. (Congress had the power to regulate interstate commerce but had no authority over business practices confined to a single state.) The 1916 law, which affected only a fraction of the nation's child laborers, was enforced by the Children's Bureau until the U.S. Supreme Court ruled in 1918 that it was an illegal extension of Congress's power to regulate trade among the states.

In 1919, Senator Atlee Pomerene of Ohio amended a revenue bill so that firms violating the terms of the defunct Keating-Owen Act would be taxed. The revenue bill became law, but in 1922, it too was declared unconstitutional. Americans would wait more than a decade, until they were in the midst of the Great Depression, for Congress to pass meaningful child-labor legislation.

In their efforts to end what one writer called in 1906 the "cruel and wasteful fungus" of child labor, the child savers largely failed. In 1920, just one-third of Americans age 14 to 17 were enrolled in school. Paid employment remained a way of life for many in this age group, especially the children of immigrants in the North and African Americans in the South.

CHRONICLE OF EVENTS

1817
The Quakers of New Orleans respond to outbreaks of yellow fever by opening an orphanage for girls.

1824
The Quakers of New Orleans open a home for male orphans.

1825
January 1: The House of Refuge begins operation in New York City. Founded by the Society for the Reformation of Juvenile Delinquents, this institution shelters young people convicted of crimes.

1849
A cholera epidemic in Chicago orphans many children.

1851
There are 77 private orphanages in the Unites States.

1853
Charles Loring Brace and other ministers found the Children's Aid Society, with Brace as secretary.

1854
The Massachusetts Industrial School for Girls, the first reform school in the United States for girls, is established.

The Children's Aid Society sends 46 children to Michigan to be placed with farm families.

The Children's Aid Society opens the Newsboys' Lodging House, offering beds, baths, and meals to self-supporting newsboys.

1860
There are 20 institutions for youthful offenders in the United States.

The Children's Aid Society has placed more than 5,000 children with farm families, most in the Midwest.

1872
Charles Loring Brace estimates the number of homeless children in New York City to be between 20,000 and 30,000.

1874
A dying woman in New York City complains to a missionary about a child being beaten in the next apartment; the Society for the Prevention of Cruelty to Animals (SPCA) intervenes in the case.

1875
ASPCA members Elbridge Gerry and Henry Bergh form the Society for the Prevention of Cruelty to Children (SPCC) to prosecute parents suspected of child abuse.

1880
Private orphanages in the United States now total 613.

Agencies similar to the SPCC are active in 10 other cities.

1884
The number of children placed in rural homes by the Children's Aid Society now exceeds 60,000.

1885
The number of institutions for youthful offenders in the United States has reached 45.

1886
Stanton Coit establishes the Neighborhood Guild, the first social settlement in the United States, on the Lower East Side of Manhattan.

New York State prohibits children under 13 years of age from working in factories in rural areas.

1887
Michigan restricts the placement of out-of-state children.

1889
Jane Addams and Ellen Gates Starr found Hull House, their Chicago settlement house.

1890
Southern textile mills employ 9,000 operatives age 14 or younger.

1892
The Children's Aid Society is sponsoring 21 day vocational schools and 12 evening schools.

1893
Lillian Wald establishes the Henry Street Settlement in New York City.

Girls at the Jewish Orphan Asylum, Cleveland, Ohio, learn the sewing and millinery trades, ca. 1900–1910. *(Western Reserve Historical Society)*

1895

Michigan requires charitable agencies to post bond for any child placed within the state.

1899

Illinois lawmakers create a juvenile-court system to handle cases involving children under 16 years of age.

1900

The Children's Aid Society claims an 87-percent success rate in placing out children.

There are approximately 100 settlement houses in the United States.

Half of U.S. children live on farms; the average 12-year-old farm child spends more hours working than in school.

Sugar companies begin contracting with U.S. farmers to grow sugar beets.

Twenty-five thousand children age 14 or younger work in southern textile mills.

Fifteen states require children to be 14 years of age to work.

1902

The president of the New Jersey State Conference of Charities and Correction credits the use of probation in the juvenile courts with a drop in the state's crime rate.

1903

The Reverend Edgar Gardner Murphy helps to secure a law prohibiting children younger than 12 from working in Alabama factories.

1904
The judge of the Indianapolis juvenile court claims that 90 percent of the city's young people who are placed on probation avoid further trouble with the law.

The National Child Labor Committee (NCLC) is formed.

1905
Judge Benjamin B. Lindsey of the Denver juvenile court boasts of a 95-percent success rate.

1907–18
The NCLC employs Lewis Hine to photograph child laborers.

1909
The White House Conference on the Care of Dependent Children recommends that children in need of assistance be kept with their natural families whenever possible.

1912
President William Howard Taft appoints Julia Lathrop to head the U.S. Children's Bureau.

Nine states have enacted child-labor laws that set minimum ages and maximum hours for working children as recommended by the NCLC.

1914
Child-labor laws in 35 states conform to the NCLC recommendations.

1915
The New Orleans Board of Prisons reports that 15 percent of children in city orphanages have lost both parents.

In an effort to cut costs, the Louisville Baptist Home stops teaching orphans within the institution and sends them to public school.

1916
The first federal child-labor law, the Keating-Owen Act, outlaws the interstate shipment of goods produced by underage workers.

1918
The U.S. Children's Bureau uncovers problems in the nation's juvenile courts that include improper holding of children being detained prior to hearings and understaffing.

Settlement houses in the United States total 400.

The Supreme Court finds the Keating-Owen Act to be unconstitutional.

1919
A revenue bill amended to tax companies violating provisions of the Keating-Owen Act becomes law.

1920
Most states now operate juvenile courts modeled on the Illinois system.

Nearly all children over age 10 in Colorado families contracted to grow sugar beets work between nine and 13 hours a day in the spring and fall.

One-third of Americans age 14 to 17 are enrolled in school; many in this age group hold paying jobs.

1922
The Supreme Court declares the 1919 revenue act to be unconstitutional.

EYEWITNESS TESTIMONY

For any one the least curious upon this subject, it will be easy to learn that the New-York House of Refuge has more features of a penitentiary than an asylum, and that its most characteristic name would be a *State Prison for Youthful Culprits;* or, A HIGH SCHOOL WHERE MERE VAGRANTS ARE INDUCTED INTO ALL THE MYSTERIES OF CRIME. Any boy over fourteen years of age, acquainted with the two institutions, would unhesitatingly prefer being sentenced to the penitentiary on Blackwell's Island, to a commitment to the House of Refuge.

Elijah Devoe, "Late Assistant Superintendent in the New-York House of Refuge," 1848, The Refuge System, *p. 9.*

Girls of any age over eight and under eighteen years are received into the [House of Refuge]. A very large majority of those over fourteen are committed for loose and dissolute conduct. When it is considered that these are suddenly checked in a career of voluptous, illicit pleasure, it will be easy to conceive in what manner the imagination will be affected by absolute restraint upon the passions. Vile thoughts and obscene language (when opportunity allows it utterance) are the monstrous offspring of ungratified desire; with those who, at the age of sixteen years, have become so familiar with the ways of vice that "No wonder 'waits them." And this impure state of mind betrays itself from the slightest temptations and in a hundred ways. Can the uncorrupted come in contact with such moral infection, and not imbibe the poison?

Will the syren song of pleasure, echoed with a thousand changes, leave the uninitiated without a dangerous curiosity?

Elijah Devoe, 1848, The Refuge System, *p. 11.*

The dietary of the House [of Refuge] has been much improved within the last four years. A good article of bread is furnished, baked fresh every day or two. The beef, which is generally served to the boys five or six times a week, is tolerable, though far from being of the first quality. The evening meal, for a considerable part of the year, consists of mush, served with molasses. Not many more than half of the boys taste of this article— preferring to do without supper rather than eat of it. Some complain that it is too relaxing to the bowels; others find it so unpalatable that they cannot eat it. The bread is baked out of the House. Mush, beef, potatoes,

and soups, are cooked on the premises by steam, which is conducted from the boiler directly into the cauldrons used for cooking. Mush boiled in this way is generally thin and slimy; and it is extremely difficult to "boil it done;" a part, at least, of the contents of each kettle will have a raw, crude taste.

Elijah Devoe, 1848, The Refuge System, *pp. 45–46.*

We took a little girl from the Orphan Asylum, three years ago last Nov, named Joanna Swenson; whom we call Anna Maria. . . . She has proved to be a girl of ordinary talents as far as developed. She reads in McGuffeys second reader, does not learn fast, though seems to have a good memory; is very pleasant and has as few bad traits as most children.

Seems perfectly at home with us, and really loves our two small children.

We do not say anything about her earlier years for we wish her to feel as though she had a right with us. General health has been good.

An adoptive father writing to the president of the Chicago Orphan Asylum, 1858, in Clare L. McCausland, Children of Circumstance, *p. 25.*

The child must have sympathy, individual management, encouragement for good conduct, pain for bad, instruction for his doubts, tenderness for his weakness, care for his habits, religious counsel and impulse for his peculiar wants. He needs, too, something of the robust and healthy discipline of every-day life. He ought to be tried; he ought to labor with a motive; he also should have something of the boundless hope which stimulates so wonderfully the American youth.

How can all this be got in an asylum or refuge?

Charles Loring Brace, 1859, The Best Method of Disposing of Our Pauper and Vagrant Children, *p. 11.*

If any portion of the inmates fail to become reformed, the failure is too often attributed to a defect in the system, or its improper management; but in making up a verdict, it should be borne in mind that the subject turned over to us have nearly all been pronounced *ungovernable, unmanageable* by their parents and their friends at home. This being the fact, can it reasonably be expected that *all these* shall be thoroughly purified and turned out models of excellence and propriety?

Trustees' report, State Industrial School for Girls at Lancaster, Massachusetts, 1862, in Barbara M. Brenzel, Daughters of the State, *p. 121.*

She is complained of for stubbornness and disobedience. For two years past, she has been in the habit of leaving home and returning at all hours of the night, and for the last six months, has been absent most of the time, sleeping in alleys and entries, wandering around the streets and saloons with bad boys, and has been in bad company generally.

Case 309, State Industrial School for Girls at Lancaster Massachusetts, 1863, in Barbara M. Brenzel, Daughters of the State, *p. 120.*

Traverse New York City in all its great business thoroughfares, its fashionable promenades, its parks, its by-lanes, its back-alleys, its outlets, and along by its great water-fronts, and everywhere you will find certain figures in the same foreground with yourself,—the figures of small, ragged, shoeless boys and girls. By twos and threes they go, mostly, in the more opulent quarters of the city. In the foul purlieus they swarm. Mackerelville—a pet name by which a certain quarter of the eastern district of the city is fondly known to its residents and to the police—teems with them. On the reeking wharves they settle thickly, as the local caterpillars do on the city trees when leaves are green. Sparse are the locusts of Algeria compared with these small Arabs of the streets, who, as they have no tents to fold, do not "silently steal away," but, on the contrary, illustrate their comings and goings with every variety of noise producible by the combined efforts of small human lips and small human lungs.

"The Small Arabs of New York," March 1869, p. 279.

Here is one who is a wonder to contemplate, and he may be taken as a fair specimen of his kind. He professes ignorance with regard to his age, but is adroit at catching copper coins that are jerked to him from a distance of two or three yards. Probably he is seven years old, but he is stunted and dwarfish for his age. As for clothes,—well, the newly emerged chicken, with some pieces of the egg-shell sticking to it, is about as dressy as that small Arab. A boiler was his bed last night. It has been his bed every night since the hard weather set in, and cold comfort must an iron boiler be when off the boil. He has a brother some years older than himself, and this brother does something for his living, and has a coat,—a real coat with sleeves and a tail, and possibly a button or two with which to loop it close,—and he shares it with the smaller shred of adversity, as

they huddle themselves together with other boys in the metal cylinder.

"The Small Arabs of New York," March 1869, p. 280.

The scene at some of the publication offices, during the distribution of papers, is a very curious and lively one. Most of the children who crowd the sidewalk, or jostle each other in the doorway, eager for their turns to come, are very small, and in summer time but few of them have shoes and stockings. Hats are absolutely exceptional, and the boys have their hair cropped very close. Remarkably loud-voiced for their size are these peripatetic promulgators of the news, and "rashly importunate" also; for should you stop a moment near a newspaper office when they are emerging from it, a dozen of them will assail you at once, vociferating the name of the paper in shrill chorus, and demanding that you buy a copy of it from each. Then they scurry off in various directions through the streets, and soon their shrill cries are to be heard in every quarter of the city. The boys will jump into the street cars, run along from rear to front, dropping a newspaper on the lap of each passenger, and then returning dash into the street again, having generally managed to dispose of several copies by this manoeuvre. Numbers of them cross over to the suburban cities by the ferryboats; and the stillness of Brooklyn Heights and the Teutonic serenity of Hoboken are alike startled by the piercing cries of small news-vendors from the lairs and dust-holes of New York.

"The Small Arabs of New York," March 1869, p. 283.

The smallest and raggedest specimens of New York's nomadic children are often to be met with in the most fashionable parts of the city. On a warm summer's day they may be seen even within the perfumed precincts of Fifth Avenue, chasing, perchance, the misguided butterflies that have fluttered over from their native meadows or suburban gardens and plunged recklessly into the dissipations and dangers of city life. Or a group of them will follow in the wake of an ice-wagon, watching it until a delivery of ice has been made at some house, when they will have a scramble for the few fragments dropped from the cart, which they suck with as much apparent relish as though all ice were ice-cream. In the autumn, when the small Arabs have obtained a few pence one way or another, a very favorite luxury with them is a slice of watermelon, which they can buy for a cent or two at some corner stall. The newsboys, especially, are much addicted to this juicy fruit,—a fact of which vendors frequently avail themselves, by setting out their tables just in front of some newspaper office to which the boys resort.

"The Small Arabs of New York," March 1869, p. 284.

One of the most touching facts to any one examining the lower strata of New York is the great number of young children toiling in factories and shops. With the children of the fortunate classes there are certain years of childhood which every parent feels ought to be freed from the burdens and responsibilities of life. The "struggle for existence," the labor of money-making, the toil for support, and all the cares and anxieties therewith, will come soon enough. And the parent is glad that the first years at least should be buoyant and free from care, with no shadow of after-life upon them. He knows how heavy the burden must be which the child will soon be forced to carry, and he is pleased that a few years can be left cheerful and happy and free from anxiety. But the father of the poor child can indulge in no such sentiments. He is compelled to harness the little one very early to the car of labor, or if he be not forced to this, he is indifferent to the child's natural growth and improvement, and believes that his boy ought to pass through the same hard experience which he had himself. He is struggling with poverty, and eager for every little addition which he can make to his income. The child's wages seem to him important, and, indeed, it requires a character of more disinterestedness and a mind of more scope of view than we usually find among the laboring class to be able to forego present profit for the future benefit of the little one.

Charles Loring Brace, August 1873, "The Little Laborers of New York City," p. 321.

On a given day in New York the ragged and dirty little ones are gathered to a central office from the streets and lanes, from the industrial schools and lodging-houses of the society, are cleaned and dressed, and sent away, under charge of an experienced agent, to seek "a new home in the West." When they arrive in the village a great public meeting is held, and a committee of citizens formed to decide on the applications. Farmers come in from twenty to twenty-five miles round, looking for the "model boy" who shall do the light work of the farm and aid the wife in her endless household labor; childless mothers seek for children that shall replace those that are lost; housekeepers look for girls to train up; mechanics seek for boys for their trades; and kind-hearted men, with comfortable homes and plenty of children, think it is their duty to do something for the orphans who have no fair chance in the great city. Thus in a few hours the little colony is placed in comfortable homes.

Charles Loring Brace describing the placing-out process, August 1873, "The Little Laborers of New York City," p. 330.

My name is Mary Ellen. My father and mother are both dead. I don't know how old I am. I have no recollection of a time I did not live with the Conollys. I call Mrs. Conolly mamma. I have never had but one pair of shoes, but I cannot recollect when that was. I have had no shoes or stockings this winter. I have never been allowed to go out of the room where the Conollys were, except in the night time and only in the yard. I have never had on a particle of flannel. My bed at night has been only a piece of carpet stretched on the floor underneath a window, and I sleep in my underclothes with a quilt over me. I am never allowed to play with any children or to have any company whatever. Mamma has been in the habit of whipping and beating me almost every day. She used to whip me with a twisted whip—a rawhide. The whip always left a black and blue mark on my body. I have now the black and blue marks on my head which were made by mamma, and also a cut on the left side of my forehead under my hair that was made by a pair of scissors. She often struck me with her scissors and cut me. I have no recollection of ever having been kissed by any one. I have never been taken on mamma's lap and caressed or petted. I never dared to speak to anybody, because if I did I would get whipped. I have never had any more clothing than I have at present to my recollection. I have seen stockings and other clothes in our room, but was not allowed to put them on. Whenever mamma went out, I was locked up in the bedroom. I do not know for what I was whipped. Mamma never said anything to me when she whipped me. I do not want to go back to live with mamma because she whips me so. I have no recollection of ever being on the street in my life.

The testimony of Mary Ellen Connolly as reported in the newspapers of 1874, in Frank Marshall White, "The Epoch of the Child," p. 215.

B——'s parents do not live together. The mother is an easy, shiftless kind of a person, and B—— is beyond her control and seems determined to have her own way. She has been away to Boston three times of late, and remained over night, and frequents places of bad repute. One time she was gone a week, and was then found at the Albany Depot, in company with a man forty years of age, waiting for the 3 P.M. train for New York where she was going with him. She refused to go home. Swears and fights her sister. Is very resolute, determined and high-tempered. "Will need watching or she will escape."

Case 885, State Industrial School for Girls, Lancaster, Massachusetts, 1875, in Barbara M. Brenzel, Daughters of the State, *p. 121.*

Now, the tenement house gives no sense of home. Anything like home life is almost an impossibility there. Enter one of those human hives on a summer's evening. There is no sign of privacy. The most anxious mother cannot preserve . . . [her children] from the contaminating influence of the most vicious adults. At an age when children should be innocent as lambs, they are too often steeped in the knowledge of every sort of vice and crime.

Editorial in the New York Times, *1875, in Joseph M. Hawes,* Children in Urban Society, *p. 130.*

The history of the poor-houses and alms-houses . . . is replete with instances of children who have been placed out in families or asylums after having been a long time in the poor-house, and have been afterward returned as incorrigible. If such a one be a girl her case is extremely hopeless. She may be placed out repeatedly in good families and as often returned. At length approaching maturity she chooses her natural associates, and in the end returns to the only refuge left where she may lay down her burden of sorrow and shame. If she goes out again it is alone and friendless to mingle with the unfortunate ones with whom her childhood has been spent. It is not strange that she should seek for society among this class, and however good her resolutions may be, her destiny shapes itself into the motherhood and frequently the grandmotherhood of a race of paupers or criminals.

William P. Letchworth, January 15, 1875, "Report on Pauper and Destitute Children," in Homes of Homeless Children, *p. 10.*

It takes something more than a farm of a hundred and sixty acres and well-filled granaries to constitute a good home. There may be all of these, and yet the elements of a good home be entirely wanting. The man may be vulgar, profane, intemperate, penurious, or tyrannical. Or the mistress may be slovenly, sickly, peevish, and an eternal scold. Or, if the parents are all right, there may be disagreeable, overbearing, hateful children; and a child placed in such a home would be living in the antipodes of a heaven on earth, while those who bound it out might complacently imagine that its life was a happy one.

Lyman P. Alden, superintendent of the Rose Orphan Home, Michigan, 1885, "The Shady Side of the 'Placing-Out System,'" in Robert H. Bremner, ed., Care of Dependent Children in the Late Nineteenth and Early Twentieth Centuries, *pp. 204–05.*

The great majority of all the children thrown upon the public for support are from the lower stratum of society. They have inherited tendencies to wrongdoing

The Humane Society of Washington, D.C., removed these children from the custody of their impoverished, alcohol-dependent mother and placed them in an orphan asylum (ca. 1890). *(Library of Congress)*

more or less marked, or have acquired habits, through neglect and a bad environment, that unfit them to enter a respectable family, especially when there are children. If sent out at once, they are soon returned; or, if they remain, the probability is that these bad habits will cling to them and grow stronger. Before being sent out to homes, they need something more than a change of clothes and a good bath.

Skilful training and considerable time are necessary to eradicate these habits and build up a new character. If the ordinary family is unable to cope with physical ailments, how much less is it able to cope with vastly more complicated maladies! Some of these children are too far gone to be reached either by institutional or home training. But it would be utter folly to send them out to homes. They are practically insane, and should be treated as such.

Lyman P. Alden, 1885, "The Shady Side of the 'Placing-Out System,'" in Robert H. Bremner, ed., Care of Dependent Children in the Late Nineteenth and Early Twentieth Centuries, *p. 205.*

Children should be bound out not longer than till eighteen years of age. No law but the law of love will hold them longer; and, at that age, they are competent to decide for themselves whether the home is a good one. Besides, their masters are more likely to treat them with consideration, and offer them inducements to remain. *As a matter of fact, of all those bound out till twenty-one, very few remain even till eighteen years of age.*

Lyman P. Alden, 1885, "The Shady Side of the 'Placing-Out System,'" in Robert H. Bremner, ed., Care of Dependent Children in the Late Nineteenth and Early Twentieth Centuries, *pp. 209–10.*

Contagion played havoc with the life. Ringworm of the scalp, trachoma (we youngsters called it "soreheads" and "sore-eyes") almost annually paid their mean visit—one or the other, and sometimes both. Such contagion would sweep through in wild fashion, making for prolonged quarantine in a most restricted way. Schooling was out; play could be enjoyed only under most limited conditions. It was a case of large groups at a time going into a kind of social shell hole. Nobody seemed to give a thought to the obvious need of compensating recreation for the isolated group. And to add to the depressing picture, closely shaven heads, topped with a miserable ointment unpleasantly visible, was the only treatment applied that I can recall. Occasionally,

there would be a dysentery attack going through the place like a swamping tidal wave, and at night the toilets would be the meanest kind of spectacle. . . .

Food was hardly a featured element of the day; breakfast and supper were alike: a couple of pieces of jelly bread with dubious coffee at breakfast and sickly looking tea at supper. An extra slice or two of bread was apportioned among the older children. The crust at the end of the loaf was always in demand. The noon luncheon had a show of heavily watered soup, a suggestion of meat, with a vegetable menu depending on the day of the week—an inflexible arrangement. There was a slight addition on Friday evening—in recognition of the Sabbath eve: a piece of herring broke the monotony of the bread and tea program.

Michael Sharlitt, who entered the orphanage of the Hebrew Sheltering Guardian Society of New York City in 1887, As I Remember, *pp. 20–21.*

We early learned to know the children of hard-driven mothers who went out to work all day, sometimes leaving the little things in the casual care of a neighbor, but often locking them into their tenement rooms. The first three crippled children we encountered in the neighborhood had all been injured while their mothers were at work: one had fallen out of a third-story window, another had been burned, and the third had a curved spine due to the fact that for three years he had been tied all day long to the leg of the kitchen table, only released at noon by his older brother who hastily ran in from a neighboring factory to share his lunch with him. When the hot weather came the restless children could not brook the confinement of the stuffy rooms, and, as it was not considered safe to leave the doors open because of sneak thieves, many of the children were locked out. During our first summer an increasing number of these poor little mites would wander into the cool hallway of Hull-House. We kept them there and fed them at noon, in return for which we were sometimes offered a hot penny which had been held in a tight little fist "ever since mother left this morning, to buy something to eat with."

Jane Addams describing the circumstances that led to the creation of a day nursery at Hull House in 1889, Twenty Years at Hull House, *p. 127.*

Here, as eleven o'clock strikes, is led in, stumbling from weakness, and half blind from a deep cut over the eye, a boy of ten. There is a cut on his head, too, about which the hair is matted, and bruises at every point where a bruise can show. "Michael Nevins," recites the officer to the waiting clerk. "Found on a grating in Ann Street, driven out by a drunken father after a beating. Father arrested and to answer to-morrow morning in the Tombs Court."

Down go name, age, etc., and a door opens at the end of the partition and the matron takes the boy's hand. A look from her is sufficient.

"Everything must be burned," she exclaims. "He is alive."

The "alive" means not the child, who truly seems half dead, but the vermin that a moment's inspection shows are swarming all over the wretched little figure.

"Sometimes it is possible to wash the clothing, but generally it goes at once into the furnace," says the attendant, and we follow for a moment and look into the bath-room, marble-lined half way to the ceiling, with porcelain-lined tubs, not a pipe concealed, and every precaution against either vermin or possibility of contagion provided for perfectly. Often the head must be shaved, and generally doused with larkspur tincture, the only effectual destroyer of the pests for head and body. . . .

Often this bath is the first the child has ever known, and, as the casing of dirt dissolves, the little bodies show strangely perfect and lovely, even with the hideous life that has been theirs from the beginning. But most frequently they are so scarred and marred with such pitiable bruises, cuts, and sores, that the tenderest handling is required. Wounds are dressed, bruises treated, and after as large a meal as is deemed good, the child, stupefied with wonder at the whole process, and often crying for joy, is put in one of the little white beds, and sleeps such sleep as it has never known. . . .

Helen Campbell describing the work of the Society for the Prevention of Cruelty to Children, 1895, Darkness and Daylight, *pp. 180–81.*

Some of these waifs are as fierce and wild as starved dogs, but for the most part they are silent, scared, trembling little wretches, covered with bruises, knowing no argument but the strap, and looking with feeble interest at the large collection, at the Society's headquarters, of whips, knives, canes, broomsticks, and all the weapons employed in torture, many of them still blood-stained or bent from the force of the blows given. There they hang on the wall of the inner room, a perpetual appeal to all who look, to aid in the work

of rescue and make such barbarity forevermore impossible.

Helen Campbell writing about the Society for the Prevention of Cruelty to Children, 1895, Darkness and Daylight, *p. 183.*

During the summer I was thirteen, I was asked one day to come to the office of the superintendent of the orphanage. The request was an unusual one and I remember complying with a high degree of curiosity as to what it might portend. The superintendent told me that he had just received a letter from a farmer in Kansas, Mr. Maxwell by name, asking if there were an older boy in the orphanage who would like to come out west and make his home with the Maxwell family. . . .

The superintendent said that he was sure, from everything he had learned, that it was a good opportunity, one which it would be worth considering. He asked me to think over the letter and let him know a little later what decision I made.

I was not long in deciding. To me the "West" meant cowboys and Indians, a chance to ride horses and to participate in all sorts of exciting adventures. Next day I told the superintendent that I would like to accept the opportunity that had been offered. . . .

One morning in early April the following spring [1899], I was told that the time for going west had arrived. With two other boys I was taken downtown to the Children's Aid Society in lower New York City. We found gathered there about fifty other boys about our age. We were told that the entire group was to start west that afternoon. . . .

Harry Colwell remembering events occurring in 1898 and 1899, "A New York Orphan Comes to Kansas," pp. 111–12.

The grated windows of the prison seen from afar, as the boy approaches the reformatory, the high walls of gray stone that surround it, the formidable gate-way at the entrance, through which, as he passes, he hears behind him the clash of bar and bolt, falling upon his ears like the sentence of an irrevocable doom, the passage onward through massive doors that swing heavily as they close behind him, till he finds himself at length in his little room, closed with a grated door and fastened with a massive bar and lock, in what seems to him a felon's cell, must powerfully affect the vivid imagination of the young, no matter how hardened he may be, and tend to break down pride of character and self-respect. The boy under such circumstances must feel that the world has turned its back upon him; that he has lost all; that every man's hand is against him, and that henceforth his hand must be against every man. The shock once over, and the mind of the boy accustomed to the terrible ordeal, what dread has Auburn or Sing Sing for him?

William P. Letchworth, 1903, Homes of Homeless Children, *p. 25.*

It gives us great, yes, very great satisfaction, to notice the general movement that is being made for better child labor laws. The newspapers, magazines, churches, and labor union organs, are bending their energies toward ridding the country of what is the greatest curse and disgrace that today rests on the fair name of America. It is like a brood of foul vultures hovering over their not quite dead prey. It is meet that the various state legislatures now in session should put forth their best efforts toward the enactment of more effective legislation for the protection of children against the inhumanity of man.

The Railway Conductor, *1903, in "Child Labor Regulation," p. 355.*

I shall never forget the first time this problem [of child labor] presented itself to me. I went to visit a mill village in my diocese and there stood up before me a class for "confirmation." As I looked at them it seemed to me that they were very small; rather young for the rite. After the services, when I was with the minister and his family in his own home, I said to him: "Weren't those very young children to be presented?"

He replied: "They were not young. Why do you think so?"

"They looked so small and puny."

Said he: "Ah, but that is not because they are so young, but because they have not had a chance to grow."

And then the wife went on to say that she was the teacher of a Sunday-school class of boys and girls, and among them were those fourteen and fifteen years old who could not read or write, and she added, "how can it be expected that they should?" And then she told me how, in that village, in the early morning, before daylight, the whole family in the house would be up, and after a hasty meal, father, mother, children, each and all of them, would go to the mill and were there until the evening. Then, in order to conform to the requirements of law, as to the education of children, an evening school was conducted where, for two hours, these little children, tired and fagged in mind and body, were gathered and the absurd pretense was made of teaching them something, when their brains were in no condition to take anything in.

William N. McVickar, Bishop of Rhode Island, 1905, in "Proceedings of the National Child Labor Committee," pp. 161–62.

Think of the deadly drudgery in these cotton mills [of the South]. Children rise at half-past four, commanded by the ogre scream of the factory whistle; they hurry, ill fed, unkempt, unwashed, half dressed, to the walls which shut out the day and which confine them amid the din and dust and merciless maze of the machines. Here, penned in little narrow lanes, they look and leap and reach and tie among acres and acres of looms. Always the snow of the lint in their faces, always the thunder of the machines in their ears. A scant half-hour at noon breaks the twelve-hour vigil, for it is nightfall when the long hours end and the children may return to the barracks they call "home," often too tired to wait for the cheerless meal which the mother, also working in the factory, must cook, after her factory-day is over. Frequently at noon and at night they fall asleep with the food unswallowed in the mouth. Frequently they snatch only a bite and curl up undressed on the bed, to gather strength for the same dull round to-morrow, and to-morrow, and to-morrow.

Edwin Markham, September 1906, "The Child at the Loom," pp. 482–83.

Look into one of the big glass-factories and see the place sprinkled with children. . . . In the center of the room stand the red-hot, reeking furnaces girdled with a circle of small doors. In front of these doors the glass-blowers and their boy minions are stationed. Sometimes as many as fifty boys are shuttling about the furnaces. With hollow iron blow-pipes the blower swabs up a little portion of the molten glass to blow into a globe. The globes are slapped and twirled on the bench, then thrust into molds, and blown farther into shape. A "cracker-off" boy deftly taps from the blower's pipe the "icicle" of glass dangling from the end. A "holding-mold" boy opens and shuts the molds. A "sticker-up" boy takes the unnecked ware and holds it to the "glory-hole" in the furnace to reheat it so that the "carry-in" boy can rush it to the finisher, where another boy races with it to the annealing oven to temper it for packing. Every motion is hurried; every boy is a darting automaton in his little rat-run of service. No halting, no lagging, no resting: nothing waits.

Edwin Markham, October 1906, "Child-Wrecking in the Glass-Factories," pp. 569–70.

A child of fourteen, a little old worker with seven years in the glass-works to his credit, was found recently by a school-teacher in Pittsburg, with his head buried in his arms, fast asleep on a doorstep. His hands and clothes were covered with factory burns. His home was far from the works, and the exhausted little fellow had been sleeping for hours out in the chill night. Another boy of twelve, in Pennsylvania, who can neither read nor write, has been a worker for years, and often does not go home at all after his night's work, but sleeps in any corner, and hangs around till time to work again. Such a boy is ripening, of course, for a common loafer or criminal.

Edwin Markham, October 1906, "Child-Wrecking in the Glass Factories," p. 573.

Shy brown eyes with deep amber shadows, and a sensitive, mobile face indicating an infinite capacity for suffering,—these tell Evelyn's story. It is written that all the pain and sorrow of life this child shall feel most acutely. You see what prompted her mother's heroism.

To spare her little daughter the acquaintance with grief that comes with the first knowledge of death, this woman counted no cost too great. She was a plain woman of the common people, but she paid a price of which only a great nature may be capable. With only a happy farewell, she has passed out into the great beyond. That no shadow of the parting should darken the young life she was leaving, she sweetly, smilingly effaced herself from the child's existence.

Six months ago this mother brought her little girl, to the Children's Aid Society in Philadelphia, and went away by herself to die. To the superintendent in his private office she explained that there were no relatives. There had been a comfortable home until her husband's death. Then, to support herself and the child, it had been necessary for her to go out to domestic service, taking the little girl with her. But the work was hard and she was a frail woman. Now, her health was gone. The doctors had told her there was not much time left. She had all the

arrangements made and was even now on her way to the hospital to await the end. Her strength was already so far gone that as she had come through the city streets, walking for lack of car fare, she had been compelled to sit down with the child on one doorstep after another before she had completed the journey. . . .

The Children's Aid Society is paying Evelyn's board in the country. Meantime they are looking for a permanent home for her. . . . She is offered for legal adoption.

"The Delineator Child-Rescue Campaign," November 1907, p. 717.

Bobby is a little boy given to the Illinois Children's Home and Aid Society by his father, who could no longer support him. His task was doubly hard because the home was without a mother.

Bobby does not understand why all this is so, for he is only a little boy. He knows that there are such things as mothers who have little boys in nice homes, and who love these little boys and spend lots of time in talking about all those things that little boys like. Bobby believes that some day he will have a mother just like others. . . .

Bobby is ready for adoption in any home in the United States. He must be taken on probation first, and if the term proves satisfactory to those concerned, Bobbie's adoption can be carried through according to the law of the State in which the home is found.

"The Delineator Child-Rescue Campaign," November 1907, p. 718.

The child who must be brought into court should, of course, be made to know that he is face to face with the power of the state, but he should know at the same time, and more emphatically, be made to feel that he is the object of its care and solicitude. The ordinary trappings of the courtroom are out of place in such hearings. The judge on a bench, looking down upon the boy standing at the bar, can never evoke a proper sympathetic spirit. Seated at a desk, with the child at his side, where he can on occasion put his arm around his shoulder and draw the lad to him, the judge, while losing none of his judicial dignity, will gain immensely in the effectiveness of his work.

Julian Mack, presiding judge of the Illinois juvenile court, 1909, in Robert E. Shepherd, Jr., "The Juvenile Court at 100 Years: A Look Back," p. 4.

... [T]he indications are that a new world for children has been discovered in this twentieth century of ours, just as truly as Columbus discovered a new continent in the fifteenth century. The work of exploration and conquest of this new child world by the [federal] children's bureau will not take so long as it took to make the American continent of real use to men. Homeless and neglected children are going to be better cared for because we are going to do more for all children as we begin to know more about the problems of childhood in general.

E. Leslie Gilliams, June 8, 1912, "Investigating the Child," p. 13.

The overworked street boy is a truant in the making. Premature toil encourages truancy in a double sense— breaking away from home as well as school. It starts the child on the road to vagrancy. Home desertion, while less known than school desertion, is even worse. The moment a boy becomes conscious of his ability to shift for himself, he assumes a false air of indepen-

dence and frequently leaves home. When the father who is aging begins to look to his son for contributions to the family budget, he gets no response. There is a strain on all natural ties. This new demand on the growing boy creates difficulties from which he is often only too glad to escape.

Philip Davis, 1915, Street-Land, *p. 169.*

The first process in [beet] harvesting is called "pulling." ...Walking between two rows and grasping the tops, a beet is pulled with each hand. Then the worker knocks the two beets together to dislodge the clinging soil, throws them into a pile nearby, and stooping again, pulls another pair. Although this is generally called "piling," most of the work is in the pulling, for a child must often exert his full strength, especially when the ground is "caked" or is very moist and sticky. . . .

The next process in harvesting is "topping," which is done at intervals, after a few rows of beets have been piled. Each worker provides himself with a huge knife about 16 inches long, having a sharp prong at the end

A poster created from Lewis Hine's photographs and used by the National Child Labor Committee to recruit members *(Library of Congress)*

by means of which the beet is lifted from the pile. A child holds the beet against his knee, and with a vigorous stroke, cuts off the top. The beet is fibrous and a sharp blow is required, and as the knee is not protected, children not infrequently hook themselves in the leg.

Edward N. Clopper and Lewis W. Hine, 1916, "Child Labor in the Sugar-Beet Fields of Colorado," in Dan Curry, ed., Children in the Fields, *pp. 183–84.*

A prosperous beet-raiser in the South Platte River district keeps his 6, 8 and 10-year-old children out of school to work in the fields although he owns more than two hundred acres of valuable land. Another family consisting of father, mother and two girls aged 9 and 10 years, who worked 40 acres of beets in 1915, own a good home in one of the large northern towns of the state; this home is boarded up for half the year while the family lives in a little shack "in the beets." An 11-year-old girl was found who, with her sister aged 7, is kept out of school to work in the beet fields although her family boasted that they made $10,000 last year from their farm. One parent declared to a school principal that his boy was worth $1,000 for work during the beet season but if he went to school he was nothing but an expense.

Edward N. Clopper and Lewis W. Hine, 1916, "Child Labor in the Sugar-Beet Fields of Colorado," in Dan Curry, ed., Children in the Fields, *p. 187.*

The ignorant and discouraged parent, weary of the desperate struggle with poverty, may be excused for wanting some help from the children he is trying to support, but the law should protect both child and parents by making it impossible for the child's future to be jeopardized in a fruitless attempt to meet the family necessities. "She might as well wear her shoes out going to work as going to school," said an overburdened mother who was insisting on putting an undeveloped child to work. "I've fed her for fourteen years and now that the law says she can help feed me and the other children, she's got to do it," was the bitter reply of an unemployed father to a request that his little girl might be allowed to stay in school until she was better fitted for work. "Do please find me a job, missus," was the plaintive request of a small boy of fourteen at the door of a friendly settlement. "My father says I can't come home if I don't get a job. He won't feed a bum, he says, 'No work, no eats.'" Such ignorant or desperate parents

need to be protected against themselves. They gain nothing in the end by being allowed to take their children out of school and see them grow into worthless men and women.

Edith Abbott and Sophonisba P. Breckinridge, 1917, Truancy and Non-Attendance in the Chicago Schools, *p. 330.*

... [T]he children who are most ambitious and industrious are the ones who will feel it their duty to leave school if it means lightening in the smallest degree the family burden..... Thus a little boy from an immigrant Italian family who asked for help in finding work reported that his father was dead and his mother could not leave the three small children to go to work, and he looked upon the finding of a "job" as an imperative duty. When he was told that he was too small and undersized to go to work, he burst into tears, asking, "Who's going to support the family if I can't work?" A similar situation was that of a small Hungarian boy who was found to be working under age. When he was told that his working papers would have to be canceled he, too, wept bitterly and asked over and over again, "Who'll pay the rent? Who'll take care of the children?"

Edith Abbott and Sophonisba P. Breckinridge, 1917, Truancy and Non-Attendance in the Chicago Schools, *p. 331.*

Cotton picking is the work of the entire family. One mother, when she puts "one at it," puts "them all at it." ... Many families take all the children to the field, even, as has been said, depositing the baby in a box under the trees at the end of the row. The cotton picker walks up and down between the rows, stooping over to pick the cotton and tossing it into a sack worn over the shoulder; when filled, the sack is emptied into a sheet spread out on the ground at the end of the row. Although cotton picking is light work requiring little strength, it has its bad features when the age of the children in the cotton fields is considered. There is exposure to sun and heat in the early part of the season; fatigue, due to long hours, monotony, and the stooping posture; and no small muscular strain from carrying the cotton—as much as 10, 15, or 20 pounds accumulates in the sack before it is emptied into the sheet. The pickers are also under some nervous strain, often racing one another to see who can pick the most in a day. Where they are working out for someone else, the pay is at piece rates—50 cents for every 100 pounds picked—which encourages speeding up.

Frances Sage Bradley and Margaretta A. Williamson, 1918, Rural Children in Selected Counties of North Carolina, *pp. 50–51.*

It is occasionally questioned if juvenile-court work, whether carried on by a separate tribunal or as part of the work of a domestic relations court, can ever be properly conducted by a judicial organ. But those persons who would give to administrative bodies the sole right to deal with children overlook the fact that in one way or another children are directly or indirectly affected by the determination of legal rights and legal obligations, on which only a judicial body can properly pass. The recognition that these cases must be dealt with separately, that the administration of justice is as much a matter of procedure as of rules, and that justice cannot be administered to children in the way that it is to adults, represents an advance in legal thought of which the juvenile court, conducted as a separate unit or as a part of a domestic relations court, is the only possible fruition.

Bernard Flexner and Reuben Oppenheimer, November 22, 1921, The Legal Aspect of the Juvenile Court, *p. 28.*

Some [boys] steal automobiles, some steal automobile accessories, others run away from school, still others run away from home. Some defy the cop just to see what he'll do about it; some upset the fruit stand and harvest the reddest of the apples while the owner shrieks in resounding Neopolitan what Judge Lindsey will do to them when he gets them into court....

What I understand first of all is that I must find means to keep these boys from repeating their offenses, and that any punishment which fails to get that result is likely to present society with a dangerous criminal. Reform can come about only through a change in the boy's way of thinking. He doesn't wilfully think wrong; he does it because the premises of his logic are incorrect. Change that and you change the boy; for direct, logical, free, and vigorous thinking, independent of adult conventions, is a peculiar gift of boyhood. A boy has a way of thought which is as deadly direct in its logic from an accepted premise as the path of a bullet from a rifle. If the boy misses it simply means that the rifle is sighted wrong, that's all; there is nothing wrong with the rifle itself.

Ben B. Lindsey, Judge of the Denver juvenile court, and Wainwright Evans, 1925, The Revolt of Modern Youth, *p. 25.*

Some people pitied me when I was made judge of the Juvenile Court, and I had letters from many and many of my friends. Almost all of them took the position, "Why did you give up the law? I suppose you thought you could be of some service, but wasn't it rather a pity to do that? Although, perhaps, if you can be of service it is all right." And I had a letter from one man who said to me, "I congratulate you on the position that you are given, because now you are standing at the gateway of life." And I think that all juvenile court judges, and all probation officers, and all of the great social workers in any community that have to do with children, and, more than all, the parents when they become parents for the first time, say in their hearts to themselves that they are standing at the gateway of life.

Frederick P. Cabot, justice of the Boston juvenile court, 1925, "The Detention of Children as a Part of Treatment," in The Child, the Clinic and the Court, *p. 249.*

8

The Era of the Adolescent
1900–1928

In 1909 G. Stanley Hall, president of Clark University, invited a Viennese neurologist to deliver a series of lectures at the Worcester, Massachusetts, school. The talks by Dr. Sigmund Freud were published in the *American Journal of Psychology* and did much to establish Freud's reputation in the New World. Freud, of course, went on to have a profound influence on 20th-century thought, while Hall receives only brief mention in history books. Today he is remembered principally as one of the first Americans to recognize the importance of Freud's thinking about the unconscious, dream interpretation, and child sexuality. Yet Hall was one of the leading psychologists of his day, and he hoped to be remembered as the "Darwin of the Mind."

Hall had put forth ideas about child development that were to affect how children were raised and taught in the first decades of the 20th century. Children at play, according to Hall, acted out the historical development of the human race. In other words, play was a process whereby children relived the stages through which humans passed as they adapted to and came to dominate the environment. A child's play might progress, then, from running and chasing to throwing rocks at a target and other hunting behaviors. Later the child might join others to form gangs or clubs, which resembled tribes. A boy between the ages of eight and 12, to Hall's way of thinking, was emotionally like a hunter-gatherer of a bygone age. In adolescence, he reached the emotional level of a man from the Middle Ages who was capable of idealistic and altruistic sentiments. As interest in the activities of one stage of development waned, those of another captured the child's attention. This process was necessary for normal psychological and physical development, Hall stated.

Hall based his thinking on the teachings of German biologist Ernst Haeckel (1834–1919). Haeckel, who was strongly influenced by Charles Darwin, popularized the concept that "ontogeny recapitulates phylogeny," suggesting that fetal growth mimics the evolutionary process that gave rise to Homo sapiens. Neither Haeckel's nor Hall's theories of human development had a sound scientific basis, but both were widely accepted in the early 20th century.

Hall did make a lasting contribution to the understanding of child development, however, with his 1904 book *Adolescence,* in which he defined the adolescent years as a transitional period between childhood and maturity, a time of emerging sexuality. The average person in this age group was larger at the start of the 20th century than in the past; the average boy of 15 in 1920 would be two inches taller and 15 pounds heavier than a boy of the same age in 1880. These bigger, healthier young people were drawing attention from psychologists and educators alike.

STAYING IN SCHOOL

Over the 30 years between 1890 and 1920, the elementary-school population grew 13 to 14 percent per decade. At the same time, the number of students in U.S. high schools increased tenfold, rising from 203,000 to 2.2 million. By 1920, most American children attended school. Children were remaining dependent on their parents longer than in the past, and the transition from youth to adulthood was becoming standardized. More and more young people shared the experience of graduating from high school, finding work, becoming self-supporting, and marrying and starting a family.

Why were more children remaining in school? For one thing, fewer jobs were available to them. For another, schools were tailoring courses of study to the perceived needs and interests of children and teenagers.

Technological progress had made many of the jobs traditionally performed by young people obsolete. Prior to 1900, it was not hard for a well-mannered teenager with limited education to find employment in an office or department store. Department stores relied on large crews of cash boys and cash girls to tote money, sales slips, and customers' purchases from the sales station to the cashier and wrapping department. In 1870, cash girls constituted one-third of the staff at Macy's in New York City, and by 1900, Marshall Field and other department stores employed more teenagers than any other type of business in Chicago. Then, in 1902, department stores introduced pneumatic tubes to carry money and paperwork and conveyor belts to move parcels, eliminating the need for youthful runners.

Similarly, thousands of young cigar makers were fired as tobacco factories installed cigarette-making machines in the 1880s; because fewer people sent messages by telegraph in the early 20th century as the telephone gained popularity, Western Union dismissed half of its child messengers. Even the notorious glass works mechanized some tasks that had long been done by hand. Child labor persisted, but the numbers of child laborers began to drop. The percentage of boys ages 14 to 18 who were employed declined from 43 percent in 1900 to 23 percent in 1920. The percentage of working girls in the same age group also diminished, falling from 18 percent in 1900 to 11 percent in 1920.

High schools appealed to a broader student body in the early 20th century by expanding the traditional academic curriculum of the 1800s and including vocational courses. One significant advocate of school-based vocational training was Calvin Woodward, professor of engineering at Washington University in St. Louis. Applying Hall's concept of adolescence to education, Woodward concluded that the physical and emotional changes of the adolescent years caused young people to crave activity and rebel against the lifelessness of the classroom. His remedy was to provide manual training for boys in high school and domestic instruction for girls. In 1911, George Strayer, a professor at the Teachers Col-

A cooking class at Armstrong High School, Richmond, Virginia, ca. 1925 *(Valentine Museum/Richmond History Center)*

lege of Columbia University, suggested that high schools offer separate courses of study for students planning to attend college and for those intending to work after graduation.

Vocational courses quickly gained popularity and enticed students to remain in school. In 1917, President Woodrow Wilson signed the Smith-Hughes Act, allocating federal funds for vocational training. A year later, the National Education Association stated that public secondary schools had a responsibility to offer courses in agriculture, clerical work, industrial arts, domestic science, and other vocational fields.

This move toward learning-by-doing also reflected the thinking of another influential American of the early 20th century, philosopher John Dewey. To Dewey, education was most effective when it involved experience. He counseled teachers to use children's existing interests as a basis for learning and to offer opportunities for thought and activity. According to Dewey, teachers best served children by acting as guides and partners in learning rather than as inquisitors and disciplinarians.

CONTROLLING AND SUPERVISING BOYS

Middle-class parents now felt a need to govern their children, especially boys, as they approached the critical age of 14, the time for entering high school but also the legal age in most states for leaving school and starting work. In addition, middle-class fathers worried that their sons were growing up soft, both physically and mentally. Urban life and prolonged schooling meant that boys spent more time pursuing sedentary activities than in years past, while the absence of fathers during working hours and the prevalence of women teachers meant that boys were exposed to feminine influences for much of the day.

Fathers' concerns that they held limited sway in their children's lives would be backed up by research in the 1920s. In one study, 10 percent of nine-year-old boys claimed to prefer their fathers to their mothers, while 76 percent claimed to prefer their mothers. The majority of nine-year-old girls surveyed also preferred their mothers. In addition, several investigators found that adolescents of both sexes were more likely to confide in their mothers than in their fathers, whom they viewed as the family breadwinners and figures of moral virtue.

The solution in many communities was to form clubs that placed previously unsupervised boys under the control of adults, especially men. By 1908 at least 124 independent boys' clubs were operating in cities throughout the United States. The largest organization for boys in the nation, the Boy Scouts of America, was founded in 1910 by woodsman and illustrator Daniel Carter Beard, naturalist and author Ernest Thompson Seton, Chicago publisher William D. Boyce, and others. It was modeled on the British Boy Scouts, which was established in 1908 by Robert Baden-Powell, a hero of the Boer War. Scouting attempted to exploit the perceived natural tribal behavior of adolescent boys by grouping members in tribelike units under adult male leadership.

The Boy Scouts strove to keep boys dependent and distract them from their emerging sexual urges, and yet to encourage manly behavior. Scouting stressed competition, with boys mastering skills and crafts and earning badges for achievement. Scouts also attended summer camps that took them away from female guardianship. Although boys between the ages of 12 and 18 were eligible to join the Boy Scouts, the organization's activities proved most appealing to those aged 12 to 14. In fact, throughout the 1920s there were very few scouts above the age of 15.

Older teens preferred the team sports and hobby clubs of another organization, the Young Men's Christian Association (YMCA). Established in England in 1844, the YMCA initially offered social and religious programs for young men. Branches of the YMCA opened in the United States and Canada in the 1850s

1912: Boy Scouts camping at Hunter's Island, New York, compose a letter to loved ones at home. *(Library of Congress)*

and accepted teenagers as full members. Separate junior departments were created in the 1870s and 1880s. By 1920 the YMCA had 243,050 junior members, and the Boy Scouts had 391,382 members.

Middle-class girls received less attention from club organizers prior to 1920 than their brothers did, because they generated less alarm among adults. Girls stayed in school longer than boys, on average, and they were less likely to frequent the streets. Nevertheless, two significant girls' organizations were established in the early 20th century. Juliette Gordon Low, a native of Georgia, founded the Girl Scouts of America in 1912; Luther Gulick and Charlotte Vetter Gulick formed the Camp Fire Girls in 1913. Ever conscious that they were molding future homemakers, the leaders of these organizations emphasized domestic skills as well as outdoor endeavors. Girl Scouts, for example, earned merit badges for housekeeping and laundry. In contrast to the Boy Scouts, which eschewed contact with females, the Girl Scouts and Camp Fire Girls encouraged coeducational activities, such as dances and hikes, as preparation for married life. The Camp Fire Girls, which admitted girls aged 12 through 15, surpassed the Girl Scouts in membership in the early years. The Girl Scouts, which admitted girls as young as 10, quickly caught up, however, growing from 5,000 members in 1915 to 50,000 in 1920. By 1930 the Girl Scouts would be the larger organization.

A TWENTIETH-CENTURY WAR

In 1917 and 1918, khaki-uniformed Girl Scouts and Boy Scouts marched in patriotic parades in cities and towns across the United States. They were among the millions of American children who took part in home-front efforts during World War I.

Like children living in the Union and Confederacy at the start of the Civil War, American children in 1917 attended rallies and heard speeches supporting the nation's cause. At movie theaters, concerts, and sporting events, they listened to Four-Minute Men—volunteers so-named because their pep talks filled the four minutes that a projectionist needed to change a reel of film—persuade the public to conserve resources and buy war bonds.

The federal government called on citizens of all ages to conserve food. Schoolchildren carried home information from the U.S. Food Administration on ways to stretch food supplies to ensure adequate provisions for the men overseas. The government also hoped to reduce the amount of freight carried to domestic markets so that trains could be diverted to wartime needs. Like their parents, children signed Food Pledge Cards, promising to eat less meat, sugar, and wheat. In spring and summer, whole families tended vegetable gardens. More than 3.5 million home gardens were planted in 1917, yielding an estimated 500 million quarts of canned vegetables and fruits for home consumption. Children helped to can this food in school and at home.

In July 1918, the U.S. Department of the Interior announced the creation of the United States School Garden Army. This organization enrolled 1.5 million schoolchildren, who cultivated more than 1.2 million vegetable patches, converting lawns, vacant lots, and golf and tennis courts into production.

Children collected scrap metal, tinfoil, leather, and paper for the government's Waste Reclamation Division, and they made items needed by soldiers and refugees. Girls sat beside their mothers at Red Cross meetings, sewing and knitting. Both girls and boys made things through the Junior Red Cross. Founded on September 3, 1917, this organization reached children through their schools and involved more than half of the U.S. school population. The children who belonged to the Junior Red Cross paid dues that were used to purchase yarn, cloth, wood, and other craft materials. From these the children fashioned a broad array of goods, such as towels, flannel shirts, and children's clothing; knitted caps, sweaters, scarves, mittens, and socks; surgical dressings, splints, and canes; and jigsaw puzzles and other toys.

In addition, children purchased war bonds. Most did so gradually, buying Thrift Stamps worth 25 cents apiece to paste on a card. A filled card was redeemed for a War Savings Stamp worth $5, and a filled War Savings Card was then turned in for a $50 Liberty Bond. Children's contribution to the war-bond drive was not insignificant: The schoolchildren of Maine bought more than $500,000 worth of Thrift Stamps in a one-year period, while the value of War Savings Stamps purchased by students in Chicago public schools in 1918 was $1,432,315.

The children of 1917 absorbed the prevailing anti-German sentiment, as Americans banished references to all things German from their vocabulary. "Liberty" served as the standard euphemism for "German"; dachshunds were now called Liberty hounds, frankfurters became Liberty sausages, and sauerkraut evolved into Liberty cabbage. Cities banned the teaching of German in public schools, insisting that the language of the enemy promoted its twisted ideals, namely despotism, inhumanity, and hatred. In the summer of 1918, Washington became the first of several states to ban the teaching of German in public schools.

Ohio Boy Scouts burn copies of a German-language newspaper, June 1918. *(National Archives)*

In many places the bias targeted not just the German language but the people who taught it as well. Teachers of German were branded as traitors, and many schools for the first time required employees to sign loyalty oaths. Parents and school officials pored over textbooks in a variety of disciplines, including history, literature, and economics, and they tossed out those that might even remotely have been viewed as pro-German. Meanwhile, New York legislators received so many complaints from the public about textbooks that they created a commission to process them.

The federal government presented its own viewpoint on the war to the nation's children. On April 13, 1917, exactly one week after the United States entered World War I, President Woodrow Wilson created the Committee on Public Information to educate citizens and unite them in the war effort. In 1918, the committee cooperated with the Bureau of Education and the National Board for Historic Service to draw up a war-study curriculum for the public schools. The government sought to temper local extremism while encouraging patriotism and honoring heroism and sacrifice.

Study guides distributed to teachers nationwide called for the topics of war and the current war effort to be presented in lessons in varied subjects, such as history, geography, and literature. Teachers were advised to contrast the autocratic German and democratic American forms of government and to assign readings on heroes from the Allied countries, especially Joan of Arc, the Marquis de Lafayette, William Pitt, and David Lloyd George. There were also to be semi-weekly lessons on patriotism beginning in the first grade.

Schools responded to the war not just by implementing the government's academic curriculum but by stressing physical training as well. Military leaders and the public had been dismayed by the wretched condition of the nation's draftees. Large numbers of potential soldiers were found to be poorly fed or to have physical or mental problems serious enough to exempt them from military service. During the three years prior to April 1917, the army was able to accept less than one-fourth of its 400,000 applicants; of 2.7 million men aged 21 to 31 who were examined during the first wartime draft, nearly half were rejected because they were physically or mentally unfit.

Before 1915, physical education was mandatory in only three states: North Dakota, Ohio, and Idaho. By 1918, some physical training was required in eight more states: Delaware, Maryland, Rhode Island, New York, New Jersey, Illinois, Nevada, and California. One in seven high school boys also underwent military training. The practice of making military drills part of the curriculum was largely confined to big-city school systems, and only one state, New York, made it compulsory for all boys ages 16 to 19.

Some schoolboys replaced farm laborers who had gone off to war. By mid-June 1917, more than 700 high school boys in Massachusetts had been released from school to help regional farmers plant their crops. Boys in New York, New Jersey, Illinois, and other states farmed as part of similar programs. In California the youthful laborers included the future novelist John Steinbeck, who was released from Salinas High School to work on nearby farms. Critics of these state-run programs protested that they were disorganized and pointed to examples of overworked and underpaid boys.

The nation's farmers needed the help, though, and therefore in 1917 the federal government established the Boys' Working Reserve, an agency that employed boys and young men ages 16 to 21 in agricultural work. Records show that the Boys' Working Reserve placed 7,200 boys and young men on farms in one state, Michigan, in 1918. These workers gathered fruit that otherwise would have fallen to the ground and rotted, and they saved the state's $5-million sugar-beet crop.

THE YOUTH PROBLEM

Throughout the period of U.S. involvement in World War I, from April 1917 through the signing of the Armistice on November 11, 1918, American young people were told—and largely believed—that the nation's armed forces were fighting to preserve peace abroad and at home. In the aftermath of the war, however, they experienced not peace but social strife and mob violence on a national scale.

One strike followed another in 1919 and 1920, as corporations resisted unionization among their employees. From New York to Chicago, there were strikes of clothing workers, coal miners, and cigar makers. In Boston even the police force struck. A strike by 35,000 Seattle shipyard workers on January 31, 1919, prompted 60,000 workers in other industries, on February 6, to walk off the job in support.

The Seattle strike seemed small, though, when compared with the Steel Strike of 1919. That industry-wide walkout, which began on September 22, involved as many as 279,000 of the nation's 350,000 steel workers and triggered violence. Confrontations between strikers and company guards in two localities—Buffalo, New York, and Farrell, Pennsylvania—each left two workers dead.

Before the steel strike ended in a failure for the union in January 1920, 30,000 African Americans had entered the steel mills as scabs. Most had recently left homes in the rural South, seeking greater freedom and an improved standard of living in the industrial North. They were part of a prodigious population shift known as the Great Migration, which would continue until about 1940 and involve 1.5 million people. Thousands went to Chicago, the city dubbed "the top of the world" by the *Defender*, an African-American newspaper. Returning white veterans not only reacted with alarm to this new African-American presence in northern cities and factories, they acted on their fears. Race riots made headlines in the summer of 1919, as whites clashed with blacks in Washington, D.C.; Omaha, Nebraska; and other cities. The July 27 drowning of an African-American boy swimming at a Lake Michigan beach sparked several days of fighting in Chicago that left 38 people dead.

While some World War I veterans roamed city streets looking for a fight, thousands of others, wounded and maimed, recovered in hospitals and homes. From December 1918 through spring 1919, approximately 18,000 wounded men returned from France to one port of entry, Hoboken, New Jersey. A significant number of them would survive with facial deformities and missing limbs. As they resumed their lives, children saw store clerks with artificial eyes, armless men operating newsstands, and farmers with prosthetic legs. There was another large group of veterans—nearly 70,000—scarred mentally by the war, whose lives were even more drastically changed.

The war and its aftermath had confronted the nation's youth with life's hard realities. Parents looked at their adolescent children and sighed that the young had lost their illusions and so lived only for momentary pleasure. Adults generally agreed that the generation coming of age in the 1920s was unlike any that had come before it. The young turned a deaf ear to the advice of those older and wiser, and they had no respect for social conventions.

In the 1920s, for the first time, a distinctive youth culture emerged in the United States. Teenage girls and young women rejected the corsets, long skirts, and ankle-hiding high shoes of their mothers' day, preferring short, shapeless dresses that showed plenty of leg. Those who were permitted (or dared) to do so bobbed their hair, rouged their cheeks, and took up smoking. Girls talked openly about sex and, contemplating a life different from that of their mothers, weighed the relative advantages of parenthood and a career. Young people of both sexes danced to jazz rhythms, drank gin, and took up the latest fads. They spent their money on yo-yos and roller skates; they bought sticks of chewing gum and competed to see who could stuff the most in their mouths.

A young woman smoking and exposing her legs: an ominous sight to the older generation in 1922 *(Library of Congress)*

Certainly a desire to forget the recent war promoted this early 20th-century generation gap, but it had other causes as well. One important contributing factor was the different life experiences of immigrant parents and their offspring born in the United States. Many girls and boys began to learn American ways while playing on city streets. Playing stickball or kick the can, they picked up English and some slang words from their friends. As these first-generation Americans grew older and entered high school or the workplace, they adopted the styles and mores of their peer group. Having money in their pockets gave them independence, allowing them to function in society as individuals, and they often felt ashamed of their parents' Old World ways.

The older generation also enjoyed the prosperity of the 1920s. "The business of America is business," President Calvin Coolidge observed in 1925, when industrial production was high and Americans were eager to share in its bounty. As young people spent on clothes, cosmetics, and entertainment, their parents bought furniture, washing machines, radios, and other appliances to save work and provide entertainment. Stores made buying easy, allowing customers to acquire merchandise on the installment plan. In addition, many Americans—as many as 1.5 million at any one time in the 1920s—invested in the stock market. They frequently did so on margin, borrowing most of the purchase price and intending to repay the loan from profits earned.

Consumerism contributed to the popularity of the family car, which increased the mobility of rural and suburban youth. Thanks to the automobile, the longstanding custom of paying calls, whereby a boy visited a girl under the watchful eyes of her parents, gave way to unchaperoned dating. Now boys picked girls up and took them to movie theaters, dance halls, and other public places of amusement. The automobile also offered privacy for kissing and petting.

THE EXPERTS WEIGH IN

The abundance of articles on the younger generation that appeared in newspapers and magazines in the 1920s attests to a high level of interest among the public. Some writers condemned young people for their pursuit of self-gratification and presented youthful sexuality as one sign of a decline in moral standards at all levels of society. They placed the blame for the behavior of the young squarely on parents who failed to control their children and instill old-fashioned values and on a culture that put temptation in the path of the immature. Other pundits presented the young as pioneers of a new society that would be free of hypocrisy, one in which sexuality was acknowledged and openly and honestly explored.

Preadolescent children also came under the scrutiny of experts. During the 1920s, colleges and universities devoted resources to the study of child development, and their graduates opened clinics to treat children thought to have psychological or emotional disorders. A newly identified syndrome, that of the problem child, served as a catchall diagnosis for children exhibiting a wide range of bothersome behavior, from bedwetting to fussy eating to thumb sucking. Children with undesirable personality traits also fell into the problem-child category. Thus, those who were highly imaginative, cried easily, or had trouble adjusting to school were candidates for treatment as well.

At the same time, psychologists, psychiatrists, and social workers advised parents on every aspect of rearing the healthy child. The authors of popular books

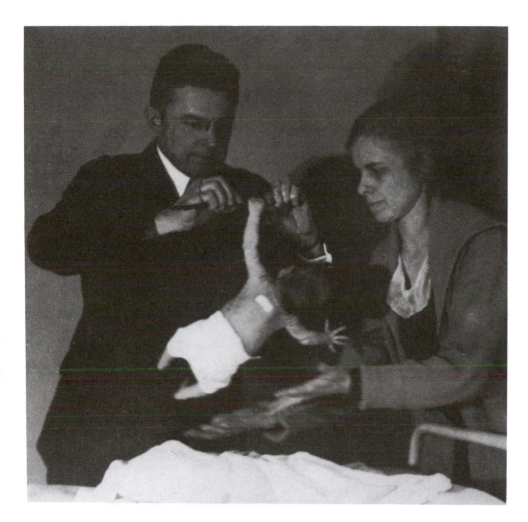

Ever the clinician, psychologist John B. Watson tests an infant's tonic grasp reflex. *(The Ferdinand Hamburger, Jr., Archives of the Johns Hopkins University)*

on the subject preached that scheduling was paramount. Children were to eat, sleep, and empty their bowels at set times, and toilet training was best accomplished early. These guidebooks reflected the teachings of John B. Watson, a psychologist who in 1913 defined his field as the science of behavior. In his own best seller, *Psychological Care of Infant and Child,* Watson counseled parents to let the clock govern a child's life. Parents were not to respond to cries for attention, even from a newborn; any wishes or feelings that the child expressed were to be ignored.

Rejecting the introspective methods of Sigmund Freud, Watson concentrated instead on actions and reactions, which can be observed and measured. He conducted experiments with children to prove that they learn through conditioning, like Pavlov's famous dog. In 1919, in a series of experiments with a baby boy whom he identified as Little Albert, Watson sought to induce a fear of animals. He exposed the child to animals and loud noises at the same time, and he predicted that eventually Albert would react with fear to the presence of an animal even if the sound were withheld. Although the results of the "Little Albert" experiment were inconclusive, Watson claimed that the same kind of conditioning and control could have more profound effects. He boasted that he could use the techniques of behaviorism to make any infant grow up to be a doctor, lawyer, artist, or thief.

CHRONICLE OF EVENTS

1844
The Young Men's Christian Association (YMCA) is founded in Great Britain.

1850s
Branches of the YMCA open in the United States and Canada and admit teenagers as full members.

1870
Cash girls constitute one-third of the staff at Macy's in New York City.

1870s
The YMCA forms its first junior divisions.

1880s
Cigarette-making machines replace many youthful workers in cigar factories.

1890
Approximately 203,000 students are enrolled in U.S high schools.

1900
Department stores employ more teenagers than any other type of business in Chicago.

Forty-three percent of boys and 18 percent of girls aged 14 to 18 are employed.

1902
Department stores start to install pneumatic tubes and conveyor belts, which eliminate the need for cash boys and cash girls.

1904
G. Stanley Hall, psychologist and president of Clark University in Worcester, Massachusetts, publishes *Adolescence,* defining that period of life.

1908
At least 124 independent boys' clubs are operating in U.S. cities.

Robert Baden-Powell establishes the British Boy Scouts.

1909
Sigmund Freud lectures at Clark University in Worcester, Massachusetts, at the invitation of G. Stanley Hall.

1910
A group of naturalists and businessmen founds the Boy Scouts of America.

1912
Juliette Gordon Low forms the Girl Scouts of America.

1913
Luther Gulick and Charlotte Vetter Gulick establish the Camp Fire Girls.

John B. Watson defines psychology as the science of behavior.

1915
Five thousand girls belong to the Girl Scouts of America.

Three states—North Dakota, Ohio, and Idaho—require physical education in schools.

1917
President Wilson signs the Smith-Hughes Act, making federal funds available to schools for vocational training.

American families plant more than 3.5 million home gardens; children help to can the food that is raised.

The federal government establishes the Boys' Working Reserve to employ boys and young men ages 16 to 21 in agriculture.

April 6: The United States enters World War I.

April 13: President Woodrow Wilson creates the Committee on Public Information to unite citizens in the war effort.

June: In Massachusetts, 700 boys are released from high school to work on regional farms.

September 3: The Junior Red Cross is founded and enlists children to make by hand items needed for the war effort; more than half of the U.S. school population will be involved.

1918
The National Education Association endorses vocational courses in the public schools.

Children in Chicago schools purchase War Savings Stamps worth $1,432,315.

Children in Washington, D.C., buy War Savings Stamps, 1918. *(Library of Congress)*

The Committee on Public Information, the U.S. Bureau of Education, and the National Board for Historic Service develop a war-study curriculum for U.S. schools.

Eight more states require some physical training in schools: Delaware, Maryland, Rhode Island, New York, New Jersey, Illinois, Nevada, and California.

Military training is compulsory for boys aged 16 to 19 who are enrolled in schools in New York State.

A massive exodus of African Americans from the rural South to the urban North begins; known as the Great Migration, this movement will involve 1.5 million people before slowing around 1940.

July: The U.S. Department of the Interior creates the United States School Garden Army, which will enroll 1.5 million schoolchildren to cultivate more than 1.2 million vegetable gardens.

Summer: Washington becomes the first state to remove German from the curriculum in schools.

November 11: An Armistice is signed, ending World War I.

December: Approximately 18,000 wounded soldiers returning from France disembark at Hoboken, New Jersey; wounded men will continue to arrive at this rate through spring 1919.

1919

January 31: In Seattle, 35,000 shipyard workers walk out on strike.

February 6: Another 60,000 workers employed in other industries strike in support of the shipyard workers.

July 27: The drowning of an African-American youth swimming in Lake Michigan touches off several days of fighting between blacks and whites in Chicago that leave 38 people dead; the Chicago riot is one of several incidents of racial violence to occur in the summer of 1919.

September 22: As many as 279,000 steel workers strike.

1920

Enrollment in U.S. high schools has increased tenfold from 1890, reaching 2.2 million.

Among those in the 14-to-18 age group, 23 percent of boys and 11 percent of girls are employed.

Junior membership in the YMCA is 243,050, while membership in the Boy Scouts of America is 391,382.

Membership in the Girl Scouts in America reaches 50,000.

John B. Watson uses conditioning in an attempt to induce a fear of animals in a baby identified as Little Albert.

January: The steel workers' strike ends in a defeat for the union.

The average boy of 15 is two inches taller and 15 pounds heavier than his 1880 counterpart.

1920s

Studies show that nine-year-olds who prefer one parent over the other tend to prefer their mothers and that adolescents are more likely to confide in their mothers than in their fathers.

Most Boy Scouts are age 15 or younger.

A distinctive youth culture emerges in the United States for the first time.

Colleges and universities expand their studies in child development.

1928

John B. Watson publishes *The Psychological Care of the Infant and Child,* a bestseller that instructs parents to impose rigid schedules upon their children and to ignore children's emotional appeals.

EYEWITNESS TESTIMONY

If you have the end in view of forty or fifty children learning certain set lessons, to be recited to a teacher, your discipline must be devoted to securing that result. But if the end in view is the development of a spirit of social cooperation and community life, discipline must grow out of and be relative to this. There is little order of the first sort where things are in process of construction; there is a certain disorder in any busy workshop; there is not silence; persons are not engaged in maintaining certain fixed physical postures; their arms are not folded; they are not holding their books thus and so. They are doing a variety of things, and there is the confusion, the bustle, that results from activity. But out of occupation, out of doing things that are to produce results, and out of doing these in a social and cooperative way, there is born a discipline of its own kind and type. Our whole conception of school discipline changes when we get this point of view. In critical moments we all realize that the only discipline that stands by us, the only training that becomes intuition, is that got through life itself.

John Dewey, 1899, The School and Society, *pp. 26–27.*

Life is the great thing, after all; the life of the child at its time and in its measure, no less than the life of the adult. Strange would it be, indeed, if intelligent and serious attention to what the child *now* needs and is capable of in the way of a rich, valuable, and expanded life should somehow conflict with the needs and possibilities of later, adult life. "Let us live with our children," certainly means, first of all, that our children shall live—not that they shall be hampered and stunted by being forced into all kinds of conditions, the most remote consideration of which is relevancy to the present life of the child.

John Dewey, 1899, The School and Society, *p. 67.*

It has long been observed that there are curious resemblances between babies and monkeys, between boys and barbaric tribes. Schoolboys administer law among themselves much as a tribal court does; babies sit like monkeys, with the soles of their little feet facing each other. Such resemblances led, long before the age of Darwin, to the speculation that children in developing passed through stages similar to those the race had passed through; and the speculation has become an accepted doctrine since embryology has shown how each individual before birth passes in successive stages through the lower forms of life.

Milicent Washburn Shinn, 1900, The Autobiography of a Baby, *pp. 6–7.*

Mothers do not like to think that the baby is at first an automaton; and they would be quite right in objecting if that meant that he was a mere machine. He is an automaton in the sense that he has practically neither thought, wish, nor will; but he is a living, conscious automaton, and that makes all the difference in the world. . . .

If mothers would only reflect how little developed a baby's mind is at a year old, after all the progress of twelve months, they would see that they rate the mental starting point altogether too high. And they miss thus the whole drama of the swift and lovely unfolding of the soul from its invisible germ—a drama that sometimes fairly catches one's breath in the throat with excitement and wonder.

Milicent Washburn Shinn, 1900, The Autobiography of a Baby, *pp. 37–38.*

I regard play as the motor habits and spirit of the past of the race, persisting in the present, as rudimentary functions sometimes of and always akin to rudimentary organs. The best index and guide to the stated activities of adults in past ages is found in the instinctive, untaught, and non-imitative plays of children which are the most spontaneous and exact expressions of their motor needs. . . . In play every mood and movement is instinct with heredity. Thus we rehearse the activities of our ancestors, back we know not how far, and repeat their life work in summative and adumbrated ways. It is reminiscent, albeit unconsciously, of our line of descent; and each is the key to the other.

G. Stanley Hall, 1906, Youth: Its Education, Regimen, and Hygiene, *p. 74.*

Adolescence is a new birth, for the higher and more completely human traits are now born. The qualities of body and soul that now emerge are far newer. The child comes from and harks back to a remoter past; the adolescent is neo-atavistic, and in him the later acquisitions of the race slowly become prepotent. Development is less gradual and more saltatory, suggestive of some ancient period of storm and stress when old moorings were broken and a higher level attained. The annual rate of growth in height, weight, and strength is increased and often doubled, and even more. Important functions, previously non-existent, arise. Growth of parts and organs loses its former proportions, some permanently and some for a season. Some of these are still growing in old age and others are soon arrested and atrophy. The old measures of dimensions become obsolete, and old harmonies are broken. The range of individual differences and average errors in all physical measurements and all psychic tests increases. Some linger long in the childish stage and advance late or slowly, while others push on with a sudden outburst of impulsion to early maturity. . . . . nature arms youth for conflict with all the resources at her command—speed, power of shoulder, biceps, back, leg, jaw—strengthens and enlarges skull, thorax, hips, makes man aggressive and prepares woman's frame for maternity.

G. Stanley Hall, 1906, Youth: Its Education,
Regimen, and Hygiene, p. 6.

Trousers should not be too tightly drawn up by suspenders, as boys are prone to do, but should be left loose and lax. They should be made ample, despite fashions often unhygienic. The irritation otherwise caused may be an almost constant stimulus. Undergarments for both sexes should be loose and well cut away, and posture, automatisms, and acts that cause friction should be discouraged. . . . Pockets should be placed well to the side and not too deep, and should not be kept too full while habitually keeping the hands in the pockets should be discouraged.

G. Stanley Hall, September 1907, "How and When
to Be Frank with Boys," in David Nasaw,
Schooled to Order, p. 89.

The dances of barbarous peoples (sometimes even their war dances) resemble the ring games of children. They are often of the merry, rollicking sort, strangely rhythmical, sometimes as graceful as the children's "ring around the rosy." The very songs they sing remind us of the meaningless ditties of childhood, when play and song are instinctive, the heart of a carefree life. The savage love of play is no more childish than their proverbial love of bright colors and their mania for crude ornamentation and display. . . . The savage's love of the dramatic, of story-telling, rhyming and chanting, are all very childlike, like their love for elementary colors.

George Walter Fiske, 1910, Boy Life and
Self-Government, p. 47.

The normal boy at the gang age—that is to say, between ten and sixteen—is a savage; he is passing through the stage in which his savage ancestors lived in the days of the mammoth. He likes to play at doing the things that they did perforce. He admires their virtues and makes them his—their courage, loyalty, cooperation, their sense of dependence on one another. With these he has also the savage vices; but, on the whole, he is laying the broad foundation of the primitive savage virtues on which, in later adolescence, he will support the civilized ones. Possibly Nature might make a civilized adult without making first a young barbarian. For some reason, possibly for a good one, she does not.

J. Adams Puffer, October 1911, "Boy Gangs
and Boy Leaders," pp. 679–80.

We have lived to see an unfortunate change. Partly through the growth of immense cities, with the consequent specialization of industry, so that each individual has been required to do one small specialty and shut his eyes to everything else, with the resultant perpetual narrowing of the mental horizon; partly through the decay of small farming, which would have offset this condition, for each mixed farm was a college of handicraft; and partly through the established forms of religion losing their hold, we see a very different type of youth in the country to-day. It is not the rule now for boys to be respectful to superiors and obedient to parents. It is exceptional when we see a boy who is handy with tools, and capable of taking care of himself under all circumstances. It is the rare exception when we see a boy whose life is absolutely governed by the safe old moral standards.

Ernest Thompson Seton, chief scout of the Boy Scouts of
America from 1910 to 1915, July 23, 1912,
"The Boy Scouts in America," p. 630.

. . . [C]hildren of the present time have no . . . need of Saturday. They write poems, and paint pictures, and read stories, and "act" them, and plant gardens, and even bake cake, as regular parts of their school routine. The schools are no longer solely, or even predominantly, academic. As for technicalities, where are they in the schools of to-day? As far in the background as the teachers can keep them. Children do not study grammar now; they are given "language work." It entails none of the memorizing of "rules," "exceptions," and "cautions" that the former study of grammar required. History would seem to be learned without that sometime laying hold of "dates." Geography has ceased to be a matter of the "bounding" of States and the learning of the capitals of various countries; it has become the "story of the earth." And arithmetic—it is "number work" now, and is all but taught without the multiplication tables. How could Saturday be to the children of to-day what it was to the children of yesterday?

Elizabeth McCracken, October 26, 1912,
"Going to School," p. 428.

It is for the sake of play that the great phenomenon of infancy exists; play is the positive side of that phenomenon. The reason the higher animals are born so helpless and unformed is in order that they may be finished by this method. The reason man is sent into the world the most helpless of them all—the most absurd, impossible phenomenon in a world of internecine competition—is in order that he above all the rest may be the playing animal, fashioned in obedience to the great play instincts. Play is, in sober truth, the very act and throe of growth. . . .

Play is thus the essential part of education. It is nature's prescribed course. School is invaluable in forming the child to meet actual social opportunities and conditions. Without the school he will not grow up to fit our institutions. Without play he will not grow up at all.

Joseph Lee, 1915, Play in Education, *pp. 5–7.*

The father's duty is to develop the very best that is in the boy. In many homes the fathers of boys fifteen and sixteen years old not only permit their sons to smoke tobacco, but actually make them presents at Christmas time of a pipe and can of tobacco. Can we as Scout Masters fight against this deplorable influence if [*sic*] some homes? Can we do any good for this boy under such conditions? I think not. I don't care how many churches there are or how many Y. M. C. A. buildings we may have, if that boy's home influence or environment is not what it should be we can do nothing. Our help will be temporary only, and not permanent.

H. G. Harper, scout master, Dove Troop, Poughkeepsie,
New York, January 15, 1914, "The Father's
Duty to a Scout," p. 5.

As [our German-born neighbor] came near, my sister and I moved slowly across the street side by side. Mr. Fenchel looked up and saw us moving toward him. We stopped in the gutter as he came by.

He broke into a smile and said, "Gut efning, Chon. Gut efning, Mary."

We stood stiffly side by side and we said in unison, "Hoch der Kaiser!"

I can see his face now, his startled innocent blue eyes. He tried to say something and then he began to cry. Didn't even try to pretend he wasn't. He just stood there sobbing. And do you know?—Mary and I turned around and walked stiffly across the street and into our front yard. We felt horrible.

John Steinbeck, who turned 15 in 1917,
East of Eden, *p. 670.*

. . . [T]he neat khaki uniform is a great incentive to joining [the Boy Scouts]. A boy of twelve would rather wear a uniform of some kind than eat turkey, and since scouts wore these strong soldier-like uniforms, my hesitation vanished and I applied for membership, and how proud I was the first time I wore my uniform. I couldn't help looking in the mirror a few times. Other less fortunate boys looking with envious eyes at my treasure and I, patronizingly telling them how many pockets it had, all about the dandy knapsack and about the strong belt and its hooks. It was rather childish, but such a treasure would make any boy of twelve a little stuck-up.

"A Real Boy," July 15, 1917, "Why I Joined the Boy
Scouts of America," p. 4.

The teacher of English can use much of the material of food economy as a basis for oral and written work in her class. Subjects like "Why must we conserve wheat? Sugar? Meat? etc." are very excellent for English composition work, both for the grades and for the high school. Supply the pupils with the necessary facts and make them use these facts as a basis of judgment of their own. Composition work of this kind will set the pupils to thinking intelligently in terms of community welfare and national necessity. Debates or essay contests between classes and schools can also be very conveniently arranged on such subjects, as was done in some school systems last year. A modern English teacher with sound pedagogical training will not fail to see the advantage of using such material to vitalize instruction. It gives the children food for thought and enables them to express such thought in definite, clear, and unmistakable terms.

Ping Ling, June 1918, "The Public Schools and Food
Conservation," p. 197.

I live in Highland Park, one of the suburbs of Los Angeles. It is a beautiful place, with its many flowers and delightful climate. In the distance are the mountains clothed in purple, nearer are the hills made green by the recent rains. The sunsets here are wonderful. I am sure you would become an ardent lover of nature as I am, if you lived in Southern California.

While we are not suffering from real want, we are denying ourselves to help feed the little French brothers and sisters of ours.

A schoolgirl writing to a French child "adopted" by her class, September 1918, in Ping Ling, "Moral Training of Children in War Time," pp. 296–97.

This year . . . we have a million and a half children in the United States who are members of the School Garden Army. We hope next year to increase this to 5,000,000. The work must be begun now if this end is to be reached. The President has taken such an interest in the matter that he has set aside a fund with which a propaganda can be carried on, but this is not sufficient to supply us with teachers, or with supervisors, except for a small group of supervising directors. It is work undoubtedly that you will be interested in,

Boy Scouts and Camp Fire Girls in Philadelphia tend a school garden. *(Library of Congress)*

because it takes care of our food needs, promotes the health of the children, makes each one study the problems of the war and become more thoroughly identified with the country, and exalts their spirit in our great adventure.

Secretary of the Interior Franklin K. Lane in a letter to the state councils of defense, October 19, 1918, in "The School Garden Army and the State Councils of Defense," p. 465.

For many reasons it is doubly important that the kindergartens be maintained and that as many children as possible be brought into them. Among these reasons the following may be mentioned.

1. The fathers of many young children have left home for the army or navy or for industries connected directly or indirectly with the war;
2. Many mothers have gone into service of some kind which takes them away from home during working hours;
3. Many families have moved from the country into cities or industrial towns, many of them new towns which have sprung up around munition plants, shipyards and other industries;
4. The high cost of living makes the intelligent care which kindergartens give to children and the help which they give to families more necessary than in normal times;
5. The unavoidable disorganization of society and tendencies toward juvenile delinquency which always accompany great struggles such as that in which we are now engaged.

Commissioner of Education P. P. Claxton, November 23, 1918, in "The Importance of Kindergartens in War Time," p. 617.

It is by furnishing wholesome outdoor and indoor activities under influences that tend to build sturdy character as well as sturdy bodies that the Girl Scouts are valuable in the educational work of the Nation, which we depend upon to develop the girls of to-day into sane, responsible women who will be capable of bearing intelligently the personal and social responsibilities that will come to them only a few years hence.

Juliette Low, 1919, Girl Scouts as an Educational Force, p. 8.

During the war we realized more keenly the number of foreign-born people in our midst, who, while not actively against us, were not actively "for us," because they did not know much about America or the language, customs, thoughts, and ideals of Americans. Most of the foreign people have children, and, like all parents, their first thought and consideration is for the welfare of their children. If America proves kind to their children, they will cheerfully live and die for America. Girl Scouts found a very special patriotic service in teaching through Girl Scout troop work the ideals of American citizenship to the children of foreign parents. Older scouts took great pride in starting troops in foreign settlements, training the tenderfoot scouts and teaching them about American citizenship.

Juliette Low, 1919, Girl Scouts as an Educational Force, *pp. 7–8.*

The work of the United States Boys' Working Reserve has been recognized as one of the big factors in helping to win the war; and the faithfulness of the boys, who worked long hours at unfamiliar tasks, and the uncompensated services of hundreds of Reserve Officers should be a matter of great pride to all citizens of Michigan. . . .

In some manner or form this work must continue, for it is worth a great deal to the future man to have the boy he knows is trained in practical agriculture, and no work in the world has a stronger tendency to develop a good human body than work on the farm. Many of the boys have caught the farm fever and intend to follow farming as their business in life. Many of them will go to the Agricultural College who would not have done so had it not been for one summer's experience in driving horses, milking cows, feeding pigs and poultry, helping plant and harvest grain, and really and truly associating with Nature and with God's noblemen—the farmers of Michigan.

L. B. W., January 1920, "The United States Boys' Working Reserve: Boy Soldiers of the Soil," pp. 285–86.

The most wasted years of life nowadays are commonly those six years between the ages of twelve and eighteen which civilization has taken from adult life and added to childhood. Yet they are the most spiritual, the least encumbered years of our whole lifetime. At that age we are nascent men and women. And so, being mature in rationality and emotion, untrammeled by binding obligations, childlike only

in instability and inexperience, we are fit for all nobilities and worthy of large opportunities. Moreover, having passed at twelve years old the tests for a sensible peasant, we are expected by civilization to gain in the next half-dozen twelve months all the delicate perceptions of a finely developed humanity. We must, as it were, cover in these brief six years the distance which the western world covered in the six hundred years between the fourteenth century and the twentieth.

Annie Winsor Allen, June 1920, "Boys and Girls," p. 796.

A keen interest in political and social problems, and a determination to face the facts of life, ugly or beautiful, characterizes us, as it certainly did not characterize our fathers. We won't shut our eyes to the truths we have learned. We have faced so many unpleasant things already,—and faced them pretty well,—that it is natural that we should keep it up.

Now I think that this is the aspect of our generation that annoys the uncritical and deceives the unsuspecting oldsters who are now met in judgment upon us: our devastating and brutal frankness. And this is the quality in which we really differ from our predecessors. We are frank with each other, frank, or pretty nearly so, with our elders, frank in the way we feel toward life and this badly damaged world.

John F. Carter, Jr., September 1920, "'These Wild Young People,' by One of Them," p. 303.

I know that we are a pretty bad lot, but has not that been true of every preceding generation? At least we have the courage to act accordingly. Our music is distinctly barbaric, our girls are distinctly not a mixture of arbutus and barbed-wire. We drink when we can and what we can, we gamble, we are extravagant. . . .

John F. Carter, Jr., September 1920, "'These Wild Young People,' by One of Them," p. 304.

Where I was brought up in Berkeley [California], the roaring twenties did not roar. It is true that the songs my older brother and sister sang around the piano puzzled and sometimes mildly shocked my parents: "Margie," "Ma, He's Making Eyes at Me," "Insufficient Sweetie." My sister had an all-out struggle with my father over wearing lipstick (she won). My parents stopped the *Chronicle* when it gave front-page treatment to the Fatty Arbuckle scandal, which grew out of a wild party in the St. Francis Hotel and gave rise to lurid accusations of rape and murder. Yet as I think back on the conversations I overheard, the way the house and furniture looked, the way we lived, what I remember is a massive sameness, a deep security troubled by a slight but growing sense of decline.

Henry F. May, who was born in 1915, recalling the 1920s, Coming to Terms, *p. 3.*

It is not because the girl is unsafe, or because she is less modest, that I am sorry to see the passing of the chaperon; it is because she is a little less refined. Going to a dance now is like eating at a lunch counter, where the food may be as varied and as savory as at a well-ordered and carefully served dinner, but where there are lacking the little refinements of napery and cutlery, and the little touches and attentions which mean quite as much as the food itself.

The unchaperoned girl gives an impression of strength and independence, it is true, but she seems cruder, less polished. Her laugh is louder than it used to be. She lacks a certain graciousness, an appealing finesse and poise which characterized her older sister. She is not quite a lady, as we were once wont to define the term. She has gained something, perhaps, but at the same time she has lost something.

Thomas Arkle Clark, April 1922, "The Passing of the Chaperon," p. 519.

By "our young people" is meant Americans of both sexes who are in the adolescent period, particularly those of secondary school and college age. That they are somehow different from the young people of "our generation" is a common remark of persons in middle age and beyond. As a rule, this difference makes us of the older generation uneasy. "Something ails" the youth of to-day. This opinion was in evidence for several years before the Great War, and since the War it has become an alarmed conviction.

George A. Coe, 1924, What Ails Our Youth?, *in Paula S. Fass,* The Damned and the Beautiful, *p. 13.*

I learned [from Helen, age 15] that one could go automobile riding at fifteen; that one could drink freely when one was eighteen; that love making could begin at any time. Kissing, petting, and other tentative excursions into sex experience, provided they were not too pronounced, were taken for granted by this sweet-faced girl as part of what she might properly look forward to long before she should be eighteen—if she could man-

age not to get found out. Such was her code, and such was the code of her friends and intimates.

Ben B. Lindsey, judge of the Denver Juvenile Court, and Wainwright Evans, 1925, The Revolt of Modern Youth, *pp. 25–26.*

I have in mind . . . a girl who has been in the charge of this court for the last two years because her parents have divorced and remarried, and do not properly look after her. She is very cynical and scornful of boys, but she is passionately fond of dancing. She uses boys as dancing partners; and her use for them stops right there. The dancing interests her; the boys do not. She, however, is enormously attractive to boys; and occasionally, she told me, she gives one of them a kiss because it's expected.

"But don't you resent the way they dance?" I asked.

"Oh, you mean the button shining?" she asked casually. "Not at all. Close dancing affects some girls, I know; but it never has any effect on me. In fact, I don't think it has on most girls."

"There is a common impression to the contrary," I observed.

"I know there is," she came back crisply. "All the old kill-joys and weeping willows in the country think the dirt that is in their own minds. That's the way *they'd* feel; so they think that's the way we feel; and how they do envy us the thoughts we don't think!"

Ben B. Lindsey, judge of the Denver Juvenile Court, and Wainwright Evans, 1925, The Revolt of Modern Youth, *pp. 57–58.*

Here in these United States in this post-war period, realizing that all is not right with our world, we have found the scapegoat which permits us to go about our business with a free mind. The name on its collar is 'The Younger Generation.' The absurdity of believing that the older generation is not responsible for shaping the conditions which have surrounded the younger, and that a world of mature men and women is being set topsy-turvy by young persons but recently emancipated from the nursery, seems to occur to no one. . . . As a matter of fact, whatever we may say of the individual of either generation, I think the responsibility of the older as a whole to the younger as a whole is—to use a liquid measure—just about in the ratio of dad's quart bottle to son's half-pint flask.

James Truslow Adams, November 1926, "Our Dissolving Ethics," p. 577.

The vocation your child is to follow in later life is not determined from within, but from without—by you—by the kind of life you have made him lead. If he has no bent toward any vocation, the reason is equally due to your method of handling him. . . .

This doctrine is almost the opposite of what is taught in the schools at the present time. Professor John Dewey and many other educators have been insisting for the last twenty years upon a method of training which allows the child to develop from within. This is really a doctrine of mystery. It teaches that there are hidden springs of activity, hidden possibilities of unfolding within the child which must be waited for until they appear and then be fostered and tended. I think this doctrine has done serious harm. It has made us lose our opportunity to implant and then to encourage a real eagerness for vocations at an early age.

John B. Watson, 1928, Psychological Care of Infant and Child, *pp. 39–40.*

If you expected a dog to grow up and be useful as a watch dog, a bird dog, a fox hound, useful for anything except a lap dog, you wouldn't dare treat it the way you treat your child. When I hear a mother say "Bless its little heart" when it falls down, or stubs its toe, or suffers some other ill, I usually have to walk a block or two to let off steam. Can't the mother train herself when something happens to the child to look at its hurt without saying anything, and if there is a wound to dress it in a matter of fact way? And then as the child grows older, can she not train it to go and find the boracic acid and the bandages and treat its own wounds? Can't she train herself to substitute a kindly word, a smile, in all of her dealings with the child, for the kiss and the hug, the pickup and coddling?

John B. Watson, 1928, Psychological Care of Infant and Child, *pp. 82–83.*

There is a sensible way of treating children. Treat them as though they were young adults. Dress them, bathe them with care and circumspection. Let your behavior always be objective and kindly firm. Never hug and kiss them, never let them sit in your lap. If you must, kiss them once on the forehead when they say good night. Shake hands with them in the morning. Give them a pat on the head if they have made an extraordinary good job of a difficult task. Try it out. In a week's time you will find how easy it is to be perfectly objective with your child and at the same time kindly. You will be utterly ashamed of the mawkish, sentimental way you have been handling it.

John B. Watson, 1928, Psychological Care of Infant and Child, *pp. 81–82.*

9

The Depression Alters Children's Lives
1929–1943

In spring 1930 Beverly Bunn of Portland, Oregon, found it painful to be near her despairing, unemployed father. Bunn, an eighth grader, wandered through department stores, although she had no money, rather than return to her sad, oppressive home. Sometimes she worried about the revolver and bullets stored in her parents' bedroom.

Eighteen hundred miles away, in Houston, Texas, seven-year-old Johnnie Lucille Collier sang in a kiddie show. Four years later, she would be supporting herself and her hearing-impaired mother by tap dancing in Hollywood, California, nightclubs—illegally, because she was underage.

Two American girls and two experiences of the Great Depression. This long period of economic adversity, the worst in American history, touched the lives of all children living in the United States to varying degrees and in myriad ways.

HARDSHIP REACHES HOME

The newsworthy events of October 29, 1929, were more meaningful to adults than to their children. On that date, investors lost more than $74 billion, as 16 million shares were traded on the New York Stock Exchange in a panic of selling that sent stock prices plummeting. Prices would reach their lowest levels on November 13, but the press and the public designated the last Tuesday in October, "Black Tuesday," as the start of the Great Depression.

The depression's root causes actually reached deeper into the past and farther around the world. They included the investment and lending practices of the 1920s, which dangerously inflated the value of stocks, and the loss of European markets for U.S. goods in the aftermath of World War I. Nevertheless, the stock market crash was immediate, causing more than 1 million ordinary Americans to lose their life's savings. People reacted by curbing their spending, and in the weeks and months that followed, production declined, workers lost their jobs, and countless banks and other businesses closed. Between 1929 and 1933 (when most economic indicators reached their lowest levels), the gross national product declined 29 percent, and the segment of the workforce that was unemployed rose from 2.9 to 24.9 percent. The number of unemployed reached 500,000 in Chicago and 1 million in New York City. In addition, thousands of people who kept their jobs were forced to accept cutbacks in pay or shortened hours.

The depression bore fruit in job loss and privation, which directly affected children's lives and made the crisis meaningful to them. For the majority of American families who belonged to the middle class, losing their regular source of income brought about a scramble to make ends meet and achieve stability as well as a shift in members' responsibilities and relative status. Real poverty and want primarily affected the urban lower classes and the rural population.

A STEP DOWN FOR THE MIDDLE CLASS

For middle-class Americans who had never suffered through hard times, the psychological trauma of being fired and losing one's position in the community could be profound. Suddenly parents faced the possibility that cherished hopes for their children's future might not be realized. Desperate to maintain a comfortable life to the extent that this was possible, families changed the way they procured goods and services, usually adopting cheaper, more labor-intensive methods. For example, they cooked beans instead of meat, canned vegetables and fruits, and did much of their own baking. People made clothing and patched or handed down garments that would have been discarded in better times. They took care of needed household repairs themselves rather than hire professionals. Children of both sexes took on part of this new workload, but because much of it was an extension of the housework usually performed by women, girls often shouldered a larger burden.

Traditionally, Americans had valued individualism. Just as success was perceived to result from an individual's hard work and persistence, failure was blamed on his or her shortcomings. Even in this time of economic crisis, the cult of the individual prevailed. For many members of the middle class, being fired amounted to a personal failure, and people went to great lengths to maintain a veneer of prosperity. They cashed in insurance policies and pinched pennies when shopping for food and other necessities in order to afford prestige items, such as automobiles. Frequently, the higher a family's income before the depression, the harder the adults struggled to maintain their standard of living following job loss.

Nevertheless, many children discovered that a changed appearance advertised a decline in status. Not only did they wear hand-me-downs and worn garments and shoes, but the need to conserve soap and hot water meant that people took fewer baths and laundered their clothes less frequently. Christmas could also be a painful reminder that family life was not what it once had been, especially when children saw some of their peers enjoying a bountiful holiday.

Once again, children and teens contributed to the family economically. They took after-school jobs selling newspapers, running errands, making deliveries, clerking in stores, and doing janitorial work. Some worked instead of going to school. Many women secured jobs when their husbands could not, albeit for less pay than a man would receive, and it was common for girls to care for younger siblings while their mothers worked.

Behind the solid doors of middle-class houses, family life changed. Working women made more of their families' decisions. Men accustomed to

Down and out in Dover, Delaware, July 1938 *(Library of Congress)*

providing for their wives and children felt powerless, and with no reason to get out of bed in the morning, it was not unusual for them to become clinically depressed. Meanwhile, financial pressures strained marriages. More children than before listened to their parents fighting or coped with the breakup of their families. Men unable to handle unrelenting financial pressure deserted their wives and children, and sometimes desperate parents gave up one or more of their offspring, either sending them to live with relatives or surrendering them to orphanages—temporarily, until the family's prospects improved, or permanently.

Even families that stayed together could not always manage to keep a roof over their heads. Joblessness forced hundreds of thousands of people out of their houses and apartments and into poverty. In New York City alone, there were nearly 200,000 evictions in 1931, and 60,000 in the first three weeks of 1932. People who could no longer afford to make payments left furniture bought on the installment plan at curbside. As always, children attempted through play to understand larger events, employing dolls and doll-houses in games of eviction. By night, many of those same children shared a bed with siblings or cousins, because their family had been forced to move in with kin. As poverty deepened, milk and fresh produce disappeared from children's diets.

Some people with nowhere to go took up residence in "Hoovervilles," which were makeshift communities named for President Herbert Hoover, a Republican who had been elected in 1928, at the close of the prosperous twenties. Across the nation, these clusters of shacks thrown together from scrap lumber, fruit crates, cardboard, and sheet metal clung to the outskirts of cities.

Local attitudes toward these newly made slums varied from hostility to compassion. Twice police set fire to a Hooverville constructed near the Seattle waterfront, and twice the residents rebuilt it. Meanwhile, curious visitors were invited to tour a Pittsburgh Hooverville in exchange for a contribution to the settlement's "community chest."

FARMERS LOSE THEIR LAND

Farmers were one group that had failed to prosper in the 1920s, a decade in which crop prices had been low. Many had borrowed against their land to tide them over the lean years, and now farm children saw their homes and property auctioned off after their parents had failed to make loan payments. In each week of 1932, a thousand families lost their farms through foreclosure. One social problem led to another in the rural parts of the nation. Farmers going bankrupt brought about a decline in real estate values that in turn reduced the property taxes that supported public schools.

Rural schools already depended on a smaller population base for support than urban schools did, because farmers tended to have larger families. In 1930, among the white population, there were 686 children under age 5 for every 1,000 women in rural America and 384 in cities. Among blacks, there were 799 children under 5 per 1,000 women in rural communities and 360 in cities. Country school districts therefore felt the loss of each taxpayer more keenly. Hardest hit were schools in southern and plains states, and in sections of Michigan, Ohio, and Montana.

By April 1, 1934, about 20,000 rural schools had been forced to close their doors to more than 1 million children and adolescents. Rural and urban school districts cut costs by dropping vocational programs, kindergartens, physical education, music instruction, and classes for the mentally retarded. Schools also shortened the term. During the 1933–34 academic year, schools in 21 states had terms shorter than six months; in 10 of those states, the term was shorter than three months. Of the nearly 300,000 rural teachers who earned less than $650 a year, 85,000 earned less than $450 a year.

The unprecedented conditions of the Great Depression widened the health gap that existed between rural and urban children. Even before the depression, rates of illness were higher among children in the country than those in cities and rural infant mortality rates were higher as well. Reliable statistics are unavailable, because many farming families lived far from the nearest physician and sought medical attention for their children only in cases of severe illness. Also, parents did not always inform physicians or public health officials when a child died. Frequently, small children were simply buried on private property.

Morbidity had declined in cities during the first decades of the 20th century as water and sewage treatment plants became operational and public health services were made available. These measures were lacking in farm country, and as a result the diseases that plagued the rural population, and its children in particular, were largely preventable. They included dysentery and gastroenteritis, which spread easily in places where people used outdoor privies, relied on wells and streams for water, and lived in proximity to livestock. A study conducted in 1933 determined that as many as 80 percent of children living in the West Virginia countryside had had dysentery at least once.

Especially in the South, rural children contracted hookworm by walking barefoot outdoors, and they frequently came down with malaria, which was spread by mosquitoes. Southerners had to wait for the development of DDT in 1939 for the threat of malaria to be eliminated. Pellagra, a disease caused by a deficiency of niacin, remained a worsening problem in the South until the time of World War II.

In the country and in cities, the poor went hungry. In 1933, according to the U.S. Children's Bureau, one in five American children received inadequate nourishment. Poor, hungry city children begged for food from neighbors and storekeepers and not infrequently snatched parcels out of the hands of customers emerging from grocery stores. Hunger had progressed to starvation in the cases of men, women, boys, and girls who combed city trash piles for edible scraps. In 1933, the New York City Welfare Council reported that 29 city residents had starved to death that year and that 110 others, most of them children, had died of conditions exacerbated by malnutrition.

THE GOVERNMENT'S PALTRY RESPONSE

President Hoover hesitated to involve the federal government in relief efforts. Not only did such intervention contradict his view, a conservative one, that government should avoid interfering with the economic cycle, but Hoover contended that such a step would undermine people's attempts to help themselves. He preferred to let municipal and private agencies assist the needy at the local level; he expected organizations such as the Boy Scouts to bolster young people's faith in the democratic process.

Alleviating the enormous distress of the Great Depression was beyond the scope of local charities, though. Conditions such as those that existed in Philadelphia in December 1931 illustrate why relief agencies were rapidly overwhelmed and depleted of funds. In that month, 43,000 Philadelphia families were collecting $3.93 a week in relief; but 283,000 of the city's workers were unemployed, and most of their families received no financial aid at all.

By that time Hoover had conceded that the federal government needed to act. On January 22, 1932, he signed a bill creating the Reconstruction Finance Corporation (RFC), an institution with the authority to pump $2 billion into banks and other businesses. This infusion of funds, in theory, would stimulate the economy from the top down, creating jobs and a demand for goods. Few ordinary Americans wound up with any money in their pockets as a result of RFC loans, however, and Hoover was perceived as a leader who put the interests of big business before the needs of working men and women.

THE NEW DEAL BENEFITS YOUTH

Hoover also called on Congress to increase spending for public works, but his efforts came too late and failed to go far enough. In the end, his political ideology cost him the presidency. In 1932, voters elected Franklin Delano Roosevelt, a Democrat, who initiated a broad legislative program known as the New Deal to resuscitate the economy. New Deal initiatives, to name just a few, included the Agricultural Adjustment Act (AAA, 1933), which subsidized farmers and stabilized crop prices; the National Industrial Recovery Act (NIRA, 1933), which set standards of fair competition in a variety of industries; and the Works Progress Administration (WPA, 1935), which employed 8.5 million adults on public works and cultural endeavors. While those enterprises had limited life spans, others, such as the Federal Deposit Insurance Corporation (1933), which insures bank deposits, have been continued indefinitely.

Some New Deal agencies specifically addressed the needs of youth. One of these was the Civilian Conservation Corps (CCC), which was created on March 31, 1933, with Roosevelt's signing of the Emergency Conservation Work Act. The aim of the CCC was to employ boys and young men between the ages of 17 and 28 on conservation and civil projects. (The maximum age for eligibility was later lowered to 24.) To participate, a young man had to be a U.S. citizen who was out of school, unemployed, and from a family on relief. He received $30 a month for the six to nine months that he was permitted to remain in the corps, but $23 to $25 of his monthly earnings went directly to his family. He needed very little cash during his term of service, however, because the government provided his food, shelter, equipment, transportation, and clothing. Prior to 1939, the enrollees wore denim work clothes, fatigues, or outdated army uniforms. In 1939, President Roosevelt approved the use of green CCC uniforms bearing the corps insignia.

The CCC brought together youthful workers from cities and rural communities and housed them in camps, many of which were situated in national forests and parks. Under the supervision of army officers, participants worked on approximately 200 kinds of projects. For example, they cleared streams, marked mountain trails, and built roads through the wilderness; they also combated forest fires and insect infestations, stocked streams, and built bird sanctuaries and wildlife shelters.

Although the CCC proved to be among the most popular New Deal programs, favored by 86 percent of people queried in one 1936 poll, it was not without critics. One such person was William Green, president of the American Federation of Labor, who said that the program smacked of "Hitlerism." Green was alluding to the *Hitlerjugend,* or Hitler Youth, a militaristic organization for young people that had been founded in Nazi Germany and was quickly attracting members. An estimated 250,000 German boys had joined the Hitler Youth by December 1932. Four years later, membership would reach 5 million to 6 million due to the absorption of other youth organizations and a government decree, issued on December 1, 1936, requiring all non-Jewish German young people to unite in the Hitler Youth. In fact, it was the existence of groups such as the Hitler Youth, which demonstrated the susceptibility of young people to extremism during difficult times, that had convinced Roosevelt of the need to aid teens and young adults.

The CCC relieved only a small fraction of the nation's joblessness, but it boosted the health and resolve of more than 3 million American boys and young men before being disbanded in 1942. During their months in the corps, they ate three nourishing meals a day. The menu served at Camp Rendell, Alabama, on March 26, 1934, was typical. Breakfast consisted of dry cereal and milk, sausages, bread, hominy grits, syrup, and coffee. For lunch the corps members ate pork and beans, bread, and apples, and for dinner they sat down to spareribs and sauerkraut, potatoes, greens, bread and butter, fruit, cocoa, and milk.

Many left CCC camps with better prospects for employment than when they entered, thanks to classes that had been provided. For the approximately 2.5 percent who entered the camps illiterate, there was instruction in reading and writing. Some participants obtained vocational training, and others earned high school diplomas. More than 40,000 completed the requirements for college degrees.

The National Youth Administration (NYA), which Roosevelt created by executive order on June 26, 1935, was another federal program that assisted young Americans. It helped those ineligible for acceptance into the CCC: girls and young women ages 16 to 25 and boys and young men who were unable to perform hard physical labor. The NYA also made funds available for student jobs, enabling many young people to complete high school or college. Between 1935 and 1943, when Congress denied the agency further funding, the NYA gave jobs to more than 600,000 young people of college age and more than 1.5 million of high school age.

Passage of the Social Security Act of 1935 marked a turning point in government policy. For the first time, a federal social welfare system was in place, and

A boy employed by the National Youth Administration in Washington, D.C., teaches younger children to sculpt in clay. *(National Archives)*

the government was providing financial assistance to segments of the population overlooked by other federal programs—groups such as the ill, the disabled, and the nation's children. Lawmakers had been alarmed to learn that 40 percent of relief recipients were children. The Social Security Act therefore established a program called Aid to Dependent Children (later Aid to Families with Dependent Children), which provided funds for needy children through state agencies. In addition, Title V of the Social Security Act made grants available to the states for the expansion of services for abused and neglected children.

Congress and the Roosevelt administration also protected child workers. The decline in child labor that had occurred in the early 20th century was reversed after 1932, as falling prices prompted manufacturers to replace adults workers with children. The National Industrial Recovery Act (NIRA) set a minimum age of 16 for employment in most industries and 18 in logging. The result was a 72-percent drop in the number of children under 16 working in industry—until the Supreme Court struck down this legislation on May 27, 1935. Within a year, the number of child laborers rose 150 percent.

Ultimately more successful was the Fair Labor Standards Act (FLSA) of 1938, which established a minimum wage for most workers regardless of age, making it no longer profitable to hire children instead of adults. Now 14- and 15-year-olds were permitted to work only if the job did not impinge on their schooling or health. It was also illegal for those under 18 to work in dangerous occupations such as logging and mining. The FLSA was an important step forward in the regulation of child labor, but its provisions applied to only 25 percent of working children. It gave no protection to children working for employers who did business exclusively within the boundaries of a single state or to children who sold newspapers or worked on farms. Nevertheless, the 1940 census revealed a 41-percent drop in the number of 14- and 15-year-olds with jobs and a 30 percent decline in working 16- and 17-year-olds. The census provided no data on working children between the ages of 10 and 13.

RIDING THE RAILS

When Americans of the 21st century think of the Great Depression, certain images repeatedly come to mind: out-of-work businessmen selling apples on sidewalks and breadlines stretching the length of city blocks. Another image of the depression decade that remains in the American memory is that of the hobo riding into town on a freight train, looking for a handout or a day's work. Hundreds of thousands of down-and-outers did indeed roam the country during the 1930s, among them many children. It is estimated that at the height of the depression, in 1932 and 1933, 250,000 teenagers were on the move in the United States. Most were boys, but girls also hitchhiked and hopped freight trains, although they often wore men's clothing as a protective disguise.

Young people took to the road for a variety of reasons. Some came from families that had broken under the weight of hardship, while others perceived that they were a burden to their parents and took off with dreams of finding a job and sending their earnings home. Steady work eluded them, but those young people who ran away for adventure found plenty of it. The railroads carried them across the Rocky Mountains to the shore of the Pacific Ocean, to places they might otherwise never have seen.

The hobo's life offered excitement, but it carried dangers as well. Contagious diseases spread rapidly among transients sharing boxcars, who had little opportunity to bathe and were often malnourished. Also, sexual predators targeted boys who were traveling alone.

The greatest risk, though, involved getting on and off moving trains. Thousands died or lost limbs after falling beneath rolling wheels. Hobos slid from the roofs of passenger cars, were crushed by animals in cattle cars, and wound up locked inside refrigerator cars. The Interstate Commerce Commission (ICC) reported than in one 10-month period, January through November 1932, 5,962 people were killed or injured while trespassing on property owned by the railroads. Of those, 1,508 were under 21. Looking at the entire depression decade, from 1929 to 1939, the ICC counted 24,647 trespassers killed and 27,171 injured on railroad property and estimated that minors accounted for one-third of those casualties.

Any transients found on trains and in railroad yards were quickly ejected. The Southern Pacific line removed nearly 700,000 people from its property in 1932, three-fourths of them between the ages of 16 and 25. Communities did not want hobos either, and local authorities either put them in jail or pressured them to leave town—on the same trains that had brought them in.

Child-development experts warned that young people who wandered for too long risked slipping permanently into the hobo's life. Such concerns were a key reason for the establishment, in May 1933, of the Federal Transient Relief Service (FTRS) to aid and shelter uprooted Americans. A year later, 283 transient camps and relief centers were up and running. The camps were intended for long-term stays, while the relief centers offered a bed for the night. A significant number of the people who received help from the FTRS were young. Workers at the Buffalo, New York, transient center, for example, estimated that one-third of the people whom they aided between December 1933 and August 1935 were between the ages of 15 and 24. The center that served the most young wanderers was located in Los Angeles, a city that was a popular destination for Americans on the move. Ten thousand males under 21 registered at that center between December 1933 and November 1934. FTRS doctors examined the registrants, and counselors urged them to return to their families. No one was made to go home against his or her will, because in such cases teens frequently climbed right back aboard a train and started traveling again. Those who did elect to go home were placed in a camp where they could work to earn their return fare.

DUST BOWL CHILDREN

No survey of the Great Depression in the United States can be complete without some discussion of the dust storms of the Southwest and the people who fled that region for California. Children were witnesses to and participants in this significant historical drama; sometimes they were its victims.

The drought that struck portions of Oklahoma, Texas, Kansas, New Mexico, and Colorado in 1931 could not have begun at a worse time. Overgrazing by livestock had stripped the protective plant coverings from large sections of the prairie, and poor farming practices had allowed wind and water to erode depleted fields. What was more, in 1930 state irrigation programs had run out of money and shut down.

Strong winds lifted the dry soil into the air, where it formed black clouds that blocked the sun. The clouds moved eastward with the wind currents, sometimes for hundreds of miles, and at last fell to earth as massive dust storms. A dust storm that began on May 9, 1934, and raged for three days swept 300 million tons of topsoil from the Great Plains and carried it across the Mississippi River to darken eastern cities.

The choking dust storms could be fatal to animals, adults, and children. A seven-year-old boy who wandered too far from home during one storm suffocated before his family could find him. Another time, two South Dakota children who became disoriented while walking home from school in a storm spent the night searching to find their way and at last died of exhaustion. "Dust pneumonia," a respiratory ailment caused by the inhalation of fine particles of soil, was potentially fatal as well. At the very least, dust worked its way into the seams of clothing and into eyes, mouths, and noses. For many children, clearing dirt from farm animals' nostrils was a daily task.

Thousands of families remained in this land of blowing, drifting soil and struggled to get by. Thousands of others packed up and abandoned their worthless fields. Estimates of the number of people who left the dust bowl during the Great Depression vary widely, from 1 million to 3 million. Whatever the actual total, historians agree that there has never been a larger movement of human

Elmer Thomas and his family prepare to leave their home near Muskogee, Oklahoma, and join the exodus to California. *(Library of Congress)*

beings in U.S. history. People moved north and west in search of a way to earn a living, with between 100,000 and 200,000 going to California, lured by the promise of jobs in agriculture. Large growers who owned thousands of acres of California farmland advertised throughout the drought-stricken region for workers. It did not matter that California already had an adequate agricultural labor force; bringing in more workers would create competition for jobs and allow the growers to reduce wages.

On ruined farms throughout the dust bowl, people tied whatever they could—mattresses, suitcases, dented pots and pans—onto old cars and trucks and headed west on the "Mother Road," Route 66. It often fell to the children to make sure that knots stayed secure and nothing was lost. The children and their parents cried tears of joy when they first viewed the green, fertile valleys of California, but most soon learned that this land of plenty had little to offer them and that hardship and hunger would be their way of life. Even if the adults were lucky enough to be hired to pick crops, they earned too little to feed or shelter their families. One grower might pay 25 cents an hour for picking cotton, another 20 cents an hour for digging potatoes.

Home for countless dust bowl refugees was a camp at the side of a highway, and children consumed a diet that was deficient in protein and vitamins. Many went without milk for weeks at a time. Diseases such as dysentery, tuberculosis, and pneumonia spread easily among these hungry, weakened people who had no access to clean running water or toilets. Some families moved into the shantytowns known as "Little Oklahomas" that grew near agricultural centers such as Bakersfield. From there they could send their children to school, and if they stayed long enough, they were eligible for public assistance.

Californians resented the migrants, whom they believed spread disease and used up community resources, and called them by derisive names such as "Okie." Some of the cruelest treatment was reserved for children at school. Their southwestern accents, dirtiness, and ragged clothing set the migrant children apart from their classmates and made them the targets of teasing. Their families' poverty and the months spent on the road had interfered with their education, and most lagged behind the local children academically. Teachers disliked the migrant children, too, and rather than give these pupils extra attention, they usually labeled them as stupid and ignored them.

The federal government addressed the homelessness and poverty in California by constructing migrant camps in the fertile San Joaquin Valley. The first two, at Marysville and Arvin, opened in late 1935. Reports of the number of government camps constructed in California between 1935 and 1941 vary from 12 to 17; the exact number is difficult to determine because some camps were temporary and others were mobile. The government camps substantially improved life for a small fraction of the refugee families. Camp residents could sleep in tents or cabins, shower, and wash their clothes. Parents could buy breakfast for their children for a penny a day. Also, children had the opportunity to attend classes in a setting where they would not be ridiculed.

The depression ended gradually as rains returned to the dust bowl and factories reopened. U.S. leaders, concerned about an observed buildup of military forces by two totalitarian powers, Germany and Japan, began in 1937 to increase spending for the production of weapons and machinery of war. By the time the

Children attend school at a camp for migrants in Caldwell, Idaho, 1941. *(Library of Congress)*

United States entered World War II in December 1941, severe unemployment had ended.

Beverly Bunn of Portland, Oregon, and the other American children who had weathered the Great Depression moved ahead with their lives. Bunn studied to be a librarian, married Clarence Cleary, gave birth to twins, and took up writing. As Beverly Cleary she became one of the most popular authors writing for children in the United States.

The hard times ended much sooner for Johnnie Lucille Collier and her mother than they did for most people. When she was 12, Johnnie Lucille lied about her age to get a part in a movie, changed her name to Ann Miller, and embarked on a long, successful film and stage career.

CHRONICLE OF EVENTS

1929

Unemployment affects 2.9 percent of the workforce.

March 4: Republican Herbert Hoover, who won the November presidential election, is inaugurated.

October 29: Approximately 16 million shares are traded on the New York Stock Exchange; investors lose more than $74 billion.

November 13: Stock prices reach their lowest level.

1929–1939

The Interstate Commerce Commission (ICC) counts 24,647 trespassers killed and 27,171 injured on railroad property; minors account for one-third of those totals.

1930

Southwestern states terminate irrigation projects because of a lack of funds.

1931

Nearly 200,000 evictions take place in New York City.

Drought conditions begin in the dust bowl.

December: In Philadelphia, 43,000 families each collect $3.93 per week in relief; 283,000 city workers are unemployed.

1932

The Southern Pacific Railroad removes almost 700,000 people from its property; three-fourths are between the ages of 16 and 25.

January: In New York City, 60,000 evictions occur in three weeks.

January 22: Hoover signs a bill creating the Reconstruction Finance Corporation.

January–November: The ICC reports that 5,962 people were killed or injured during this period while trespassing on railroad property; 1,508 were under 21.

December: An estimated 250,000 German boys belong to the Hitler Youth.

1932–1933

There are 250,000 transient teenagers in the United States.

1933

The gross national product has declined 29 percent since 1929.

Unemployment now affects 24.9 percent of the workforce.

Five hundred thousand workers in Chicago and 1 million workers in New York City are unemployed.

Dysentery affects about 80 percent of children living in rural West Virginia.

The U.S. Children's Bureau estimates that one in five American children is undernourished.

Twenty-nine New York City residents starve to death; 110 others, most of them children, die from causes exacerbated by malnutrition.

March 4: Democrat Franklin Delano Roosevelt is inaugurated.

March 31: Roosevelt signs the Emergency Conservation Work Act, creating the Civilian Conservation Corps (CCC). The CCC will give work to more than 3 million boys and young men. Additional New Deal programs initiated in 1933 include the Agricultural Adjustment Act; the National Industrial Recovery Act, which imposes regulations on child labor; and the Federal Deposit Insurance Corporation.

May: The Federal Transient Relief Service (FTRS) is established to aid wandering Americans.

December: One-third of all people assisted at the Buffalo, New York, transient center from this month through August 1935 are ages 15 to 24; between this month and November 1934, the Los Angeles transient center assists 10,000 males under 21.

1933–1934

Schools in 21 states are in session for less than six months of the year; schools in 10 of those states are open for less than three months of the year.

Nearly 300,000 rural teachers earn less than $650 a year; 85,000 earn less than $450 a year.

1934

April 1: Throughout rural America, approximately 20,000 schools have been forced to close, affecting more than 1 million students.

May: The FTRS is operating 283 camps and relief centers for transients.

May 9: A three-day dust storm beginning on this date carries more than 300 million tons of soil across the Mississippi River.

1935

May 27: The Supreme Court declares the National Industrial Recovery Act unconstitutional.

June 26: Roosevelt signs an executive order creating the National Youth Administration (NYA), which will employ more than 600,000 people of college age and 1.5 million of high school age. Additional New Deal measures enacted this year include the Works Progress Administration and the Social Security Act.

Fall: The federal government begins the construction of camps for migrant farm laborers in California.

1936

December 1: Germany's National Socialist government decrees that all non-Jewish young people must join the Hitler Youth; membership reaches 5–6 million.

1937

The federal government increases spending for defense manufactures.

1938

The Fair Labor Standards Act establishes a minimum wage for workers, permits 14- and 15-year-olds to work only if employment does not harm their health or schooling, and sets a minimum age of 18 for work in hazardous occupations.

1939

The development of DDT eliminates the threat of malaria in the South.

1940

The U.S. census reveals a 41-percent drop in the number of working 14- and 15-year-olds and a 30-percent decline in the number of working 16- and 17-year-olds.

1941

Dietary improvements lessen the incidence of pellagra in the South.

December 8: The United States enters World War II.

1942

The CCC is disbanded.

1943

Congress denies further funding for the NYA.

Children and adults, all members of a single family, work in bean fields owned by Seabrook Farms in summer 1941. *(Library of Congress)*

EYEWITNESS TESTIMONY

Mother came into the living room. "Daddy has lost his job," she said softly. "The bank is dismissing the employees it took over from the West Coast National and has given them two weeks' notice."

The Depression had come to us. Mother cleared the table and washed the dishes alone. I sensed she preferred solitude to help. I sat filled with anguish, unable to read, unable to do anything. When Dad finally emerged from the bedroom, I felt so awkward I did not know what to say or even how to look at him. To pretend nothing had happened seemed wrong, but seeing him so defeated and ashamed of defeat, even though he was not to blame, was so painful that I could not speak. How could anyone do such a thing to my father, who was so good, kind, reliable, and honest?

Beverly Cleary writing about events in 1930, A Girl from Yamhill, *pp. 173–74.*

A neighbor gave Mother an old pink woolen dress, which she successfully made over into a jumper for me. She contrived a cream-colored blouse from something found in a trunk in the attic. One of her friends, now married to an eastern Oregon wheat rancher, had a daughter older than I who passed on two nice dresses. In our neighborhood, no girl would dream of entering high school in half socks. I used hoarded nickels and dimes to buy silk stockings. Five dollars from my Arizona uncle bought a raincoat. . . .

We began admiring one another's clothes by saying, "Is it new, or new to you?"

Beverly Cleary, who entered high school in 1930, A Girl from Yamhill, *pp. 181–82.*

You leave home with good intentions and tell your folks you're going to come back a millionaire. You return with your head between your arms. You're broke and dirty and they see right away that you didn't make it. I'd stay a day or two and hit the road again.

I was never so desperate that I wanted to commit suicide but I often felt put down. I realized it would take a while to change things. "I'm going to keep going," I said. "I may not end up a millionaire but someday I will be able to face people I used to beg for food." If I hadn't had hope I would have starved to death by the time I was seventeen.

Arvel Pearson, originally from Spadra, Arkansas, who first hitched a ride on a freight train in 1930, at age 15, in Errol Lincoln Uys, Riding the Rails, *p. 88.*

A boy and an adult companion ride the rails in West Texas in May 1937. *(Library of Congress)*

There were nights I'd get homesick waiting for a train with nobody to talk to, sitting alone on a pile of ties under a water tank out in the middle of nowhere. You're only a kid and you get to dreaming about that warm bed back home and seeing the folks.

Arvel Pearson, originally from Spadra, Arkansas, who first hitched a ride on a freight train in 1930, at age 15, in Errol Lincoln Uys, Riding the Rails, *p. 85.*

If there was a national pastime I suppose it was hanging out, simply standing there on the street corner or on the beach waiting for something to appear around the bend. Evenings, before I had begun to feel embarrassed about any self-display, I'd be out there in front of Dozick's drugstore with half a dozen others singing the latest hits, sometimes in competition with anyone else who thought he sang better (for a couple of pennies you could buy pirated mimeoed lyrics of the newest songs). After I had turned fifteen these competitions seemed childish, but I continued as one of the star comics of the gang, improvising inanities, doing imitations of the Three Stooges, who even then were on the verge of our contempt as idiotic shadows of the

Marx Brothers. We always had a sandlot football team going, and one of our halfbacks, a giant with a heavy lower lip named Izzy Lenowitz, whom nobody dared tackle for fear of his bowling ball knees, would clap me on my thin back and implore me, "Oh, come on, Artie, enjoy us." And with sufficient encouragement I would ad-lib a monologue that with a little luck might stay airborne for five minutes or more.

Arthur Miller, who turned 15 in 1930, Timebends, *p. 119.*

From the early thirties on, the good times became fewer, the grimness and sadness more pervasive. Part of this, I well knew, was worry about money. Once my father, who usually dressed well, bought a badly made cheap suit that made him look foolish. For a while the house was for sale, and I was deeply troubled to see a For Sale sign on the lawn near the pepper tree. It didn't sell, and eventually the sign was taken down. We resigned from the country club and the tennis club. We got rid of the car, which had never been very important in our lives. In the thirties our standard of living was an odd one—a house full of elaborate furniture in a good neighborhood, an old maid who could not be fired, and no car. Only the level of the family meals was never cut—I don't think my mother really knew that there were any alternatives to the round of steaks and roasts. And behind everything, damping every family occasion, lurked the question, What would happen when all the money was gone? We were living, I later learned, on what remained of my father's investments. Even before the crash of '29, some of them were turning out badly.

Henry F. May, who was a teenager in Berkeley, California, in the early 1930s, remembering the depression years, Coming to Terms, *pp. 24–25.*

It was a deprived existence by today's standards. We didn't understand that. Nobody had any money. We had been through miserable times economically: businesses folded, the drought, soil dried up and blew away, no crops, mortgages foreclosed, there was just a lot of suffering. My family was never cold or hungry and we had clothes, so we were relatively all right. But we had nothing else. My dad never took a vacation, we never went out of the state, there was no travel at all. This little town was all you had. In many ways it was a marvelous life. We made kites; we'd buy a nickel orange crate and cut the lumber up and make model planes;

hiked; we swam in the old creeks around there. We were totally happy, but there was no money.

Hugh Sidey, who grew up in Greenfield, Iowa, in the 1930s, in Roy Hoopes, Americans Remember the Home Front, *p. 262.*

Rarely did I feel self-pity during the Depression. But one morning on my way to school I broke the tenth Commandment—"thou shalt not covet . . ." I stopped at a friend's house, and while he was getting dressed, I waited in the kitchen. Unwashed dishes still sat on the table where he had eaten breakfast. Big yellow bananas filled a bowl. A package of corn flakes stood nearby. And in all its white, glistening beauty stood almost a quart of fresh, cold milk from the dairy. For a fleeting minute I questioned why there wasn't enough fresh milk for everyone. It didn't seem fair for my friend to have a whole quart left at his plate while that same morning I had gagged on condensed milk and left it uneaten in my bowl.

Robert J. Hastings recalling his childhood in Marion, Illinois, in the 1930s, A Nickel's Worth of Skim Milk, *p. 5.*

Whatever was free was our recreation. This may have included playing records on our wind-up victrola or listening to the Atwater-Kent radio. You might watch a parachute jump at the airport or a free ball game at the city park, with perhaps a free band concert afterwards and the side attraction of a watermelon-eating contest (with your hands tied behind you). The band concerts survived only the first two years of the Depression.

Or you might go out to the airport hangar to watch the dance marathon, cringe at the risks taken by the Dodge-'Em cars at the fairgrounds on Labor Day, or attend a medicine show where the hawker peddled a single elixir said to cure everything from arthritis to zymosis. There were family dinners and picnics, and occasionally four or five families would pile into the back of Ted Boles' coal truck for an overnight camping-fishing trip to the Ohio River at Shawneetown or Metropolis.

Robert J. Hastings recalling his childhood in Marion, Illinois, in the 1930s, A Nickel's Worth of Skim Milk, *pp. 17–18.*

My boyhood diary shows that Dad sold iron cords from door to door, "worked a day in the hay," bought a horse to break gardens (a disaster!), rented an extra lot for a garden to be planted on the shares, picked peaches, raised and sold sweet potatoes slips, traded an occasional dozen of eggs at the grocery, and hung wallpaper.

He also "painted Don Albright's house for $5," picked up a day's work now and then at the Spillertown strip mines, cut hair for boys in the neighborhood, and sold coal orders. When he had to and could, he worked intermittently on WPA . . . or picked up an occasional "relief" (welfare) order of powdered milk, grapefruit, beans, meal, and flour.

Money being scarce, we learned to save back until we had the exact amount for a purchase. That explains why Mom asked me to get fifteen cents worth of lunch meat—rather than a half pound or so—since we might not know exactly how much that would cost. But fifteen cents worth of navy beans, a dime loaf of bread, or twenty cents worth of bananas meant exactly what you said!

Robert J. Hastings, who grew up in Marion, Illinois, in the 1930s, A Penny's Worth of Minced Ham, *p. 2.*

Kids improvised many toys in the thirties. We assembled our own kites out of brown paper and paste made of flour and water. We played street hockey with sticks and crushed tin cans and rode on homemade scooters with wheels salvaged from old roller skates. When we played marbles, we made sure no one shot with a "steelie," which in the hands of a sharpshooter could shatter and ruin the glass marbles.

Robert J. Hastings, who grew up in Marion, Illinois, in the 1930s, A Penny's Worth of Minced Ham, *p. 12.*

The happy days I had spent in my home, Clinton, Mass., were real good days until one sad day the factory or mill in which my father had worked gave a notice that their factory would only operate three days a week. My father came home that day planning of what to do, because of the notice given him and the employees of the factory. As the days passed one after another my father was still at his plan thinking of where he could get a better position to support our family. . . .

My little sister and I tried to help my father in a way which we thought best. My little sister thought of helping the lady next door by taking care of the lady's baby while the lady went shopping. Thus she earned fifty cents. I tried to help my father by having a paper route after school hours. Thus I received

my salary of one dollar and fifty cents per week. My little sister and I gave our salary to my father in order to help him and keep our home that we loved since we were very young. But now the factory only operated two days a week and our salary of two dollars a week wouldn't help my father any in buying our clothing and food.

A 13-year-old boy, 1931, "What Unemployment Has Meant to My Family," in Marion Elderton, ed., Case Studies of Unemployment, *pp. 390–91.*

A group of University of Chicago faculty members warns against the ravages of undernourishment among children in the public schools. It appears that principals and teachers in many schools have for several months been contributing from their salaries in order to provide free lunches for hungry children. Allowances have been made to the schools from the fund raised by the Governor's Commission on Unemployment, but the money has been insufficient to meet the need.

Meantime, the [Chicago] Board of Education announces that it has exhausted its fund for the payment of teachers and other educational purposes.

New York Times, April 8, 1931, in Sol Cohen, ed., Education in the United States, *Vol. 4, p. 2527.*

I remember the day the banks closed; I didn't understand it, but I reacted to the excitement in the air on that sunny March day. I knew young couples who had to postpone their marriages because the man couldn't find a job, or had been laid off. Boys who had been in college had to drop out and come home because their families couldn't afford to keep them in school any longer. They were happy to find work as water boys with a highway crew.

With little money to spend on entertainment, people learned to enjoy a simpler form of life than they'd known in the twenties. Dating couples spent the evening in the girl's living room, listening to the radio, or went for walks. There was a lot of walking in those evenings. We walked in the moonlight and in the dark of the moon; on warm summer nights and on hard cold winter ones; we walked in the mist and fog and light snow and even in drizzle. And we sat in the porch swing a lot too.

Emma Jane McKee Sepmeier recalling her teenage years, "Reminiscences of Life in Sheffield, Alabama, 1931–1934," p. 116.

Those were the days of the great depression. Bread was a nickel a loaf but everybody was scrambling for the nickel. When Chase and Sanborn coffee (to which I was partial because they sponsored Eddie Cantor's radio show) went up to .50 a pound, my mother switched to Maxwell House, which was still .35. The butcher would give you soup bones free. And we could afford lamb shoulder roasts on Sundays.

Emma Jane McKee Sepmeier recalling her teenage years, "Reminiscences of Life in Sheffield, Alabama, 1931–1934," p. 115.

. . . [W]hile we were at breakfast, the doorbell rang. Thinking it was the postman, I did not press the button which would open the outside door, but, as usual, went out to get the mail.

Instead of the postman, however, I was confronted by two children: a girl, as we learned afterward, of ten and a boy of eight. Not very adequate for the season and weather, their clothing was patched but clean. They carried school books.

"Excuse me, Mister," said the girl in a voice that sounded older than she looked, "but we have no eats in our house and my mother she said I should take my brother before we go to school and ring a doorbell in some house"—she swallowed heavily and took a deep breath—"and ask you to give us something to eat."

. . . The children were given food. The girl ate slowly; the boy quickly, greedily. He looked at no one and made no reply when Stella [Adamic's wife] or her mother asked him if he wanted more. When he got more food, he bolted it down rapidly.

The girl, however, answered every question directly, thoroughly, thoughtfully. Some of the information she volunteered. . . .

When her brother did not answer, she explained his silence. "He ate a banana yesterday afternoon, but it wasn't ripe enough or somethin', and it made him sick and he didn't eat anything since. He's always like this when he's hungry and we gotta ring doorbells."

. . . I studied the girl. She was tiny for her age, no doubt underweight, but appeared more an adult who had shrunk than a growing child. She was keen and knew more of the immediate world in which she found herself than people four times her age had known of the world they were living in before 1930.

Louis Adamic remembering a morning in January 1932, My America, pp. 279–80.

Even those with little imagination know how no employment or underemployment, the failure of banks and building and loan associations have affected many children whose parents faced the future self-reliant and unafraid a few years ago. In the millions of homes which have escaped the abyss of destitution fear of what may still happen is destroying the sense of security which is considered necessary for the happiness and well-being of children.

Great effort has been made to prevent suffering. Last year probably more than a billion dollars was expended by public and private agencies for the relief of the unemployed. Although this is probably some eight times as much as was spent for relief in normal times, no one who has been going in and out of the homes of the unemployed in large urban centres or in the single-industry towns and mining communities has reported that it has been adequate to insure shelter, clothes and reasonably adequate diet for all needy children.

New York Times, December 18, 1932, in Sol Cohen, ed., Education in the United States, Vol. 4, p. 2528.

They get used to the dangers and hardships; to the lack of opportunity for cleanliness; they overcome their abhorrence of begging. Their interest is in 'getting by,' and they come to make a game of beating the authorities. The danger is not only what is happening to them now, but they can easily become confirmed in the habit of vagrancy and become what is called the American hobo.

Grace Abbott, chief of the U.S. Children's Bureau, testifying before Congress on the problem of teenage vagrants, 1933, in Errol Lincoln Uys, Riding the Rails, p. 17.

There was a family that experienced a farm foreclosure. It was the first of March when they were forced off, and all their household goods were sold. Even family pictures. They went for five cents, ten cents a piece. Quite a few of the kids were brought there by their parents, partly by morbid fascination, partly by sympathy, partly—well, there was something going on. In those days of no TV, no radio in some places, an event was an event.

It was a hilarious thing for us kids. We got together, there were lots of new kids. . . . Gradually, I was aware, slightly, of the events. Overhearing the adults talk. The worry and the relief they expressed: it hadn't happened to them. The anticipation that it might . . . the fascination with catastrophe. I recall this undertone, horror, but also fascination. It dominated the conversation for weeks.

Slim Collier remembering a farm foreclosure that was held in Waterloo, Iowa, in March 1933, when he was nine, in Studs Terkel, Hard Times, *p. 97.*

Everybody was waiting for his ship to come in. It was a sad, bitter phrase used even by children to express the hopelessness of hoping. In the schoolyard we said, "When my ship comes in, I'm going over to New York and see the Yankees play." Meaning that we never expected to be rich enough to sit in the Yankee Stadium.

Russell Baker recalling life in Belleville, New Jersey, in 1933, Growing Up, *p. 134.*

We have learned from his parents that he has obtained a position as order and delivery clerk in a grocery store, averaging a salary of ten dollars per week. It is a permanent position. He seems to be readjusting himself to his home circle, and his parents say he appears to be quite happy and contented.

Report to the Federal Transient Relief Service on Nathan, a boy transient who returned from California to his home in New York, 1934, in George E. Outland, "Should Transient Boys Be Sent Home?" pp. 514–15.

Arthur is now living at home but is still unemployed. He is not attending school, nor is he in a Civilian Conservation Corps camp. Mrs. C. is greatly concerned about her son, for she feels that if he does not soon obtain some kind of work he will again go on the road.

Report to the Federal Transient Relief Service on Arthur C., a boy transient who returned from California to his home in Chicago, 1934, in George E. Outland, "Should Transient Boys Be Sent Home?" pp. 516–17.

The C—— family in Atlanta had always lived comfortably. The father was a foreman in a roller shop for 20 years, and for 9 years prior to losing his job in 1929 had made $55 a week. Unemployment came as a terrible shock. While they did not own their home they had savings amounting to $700. This was used up after a few months, and then Mr. C—— had to resort to anything he could find to do to earn a little money. He tried selling various articles, even papers on the streets, and finally started a delivery route for a dry-cleaning establishment on commission. At first he

made very little, but after about two years he began to average $15 a week, his present earnings. By cutting down drastically on food and clothes at the beginning of their difficulties and by moving from a house which rented at $25 to one which was only $9, they were barely able to get along for the first two or three years of the change. Their new car, bought in 1929, reverted to the company because of an unpaid balance of $100. They sold valuable furniture . . . and purchased nothing more except on cash basis. All of this was done very quietly, the mother said, and relatives and friends had no knowledge of the real circumstances. There was a time . . . when the family actually suffered for food and fuel, but they never thought of applying for relief because they were determined to come through somehow. By great sacrifice and extremely careful management they have been able to pay up the rent and doctor's bills which accumulated during the leanest period. . . . They have managed to keep their one boy, now 16, sufficiently well clothed so that he could continue in school.

Report on an Atlanta family studied by the U.S. Children's Bureau, fall 1934, in Katharine F. Lenroot, "Children of the Depression: A Study of 259 Families in Selected Areas of Five Cities," pp. 222–23.

. . . [I]n late 1934, I would guess, something began to happen. Some kind of psychological deterioration hit our family circle and began to eat away our pride. Perhaps it was the constant tangible evidence that we were destitute. We had known other families who had gone on relief. We had known without anyone in our home ever expressing it that we had felt prouder not to be at the depot where the free food was passed out. And, now, we were among them. At school, the "on relief" finger suddenly was pointed at us, too, and sometimes it was said aloud.

It seemed that everything to eat in our house was stamped Not To Be Sold. All Welfare food bore this stamp to keep the recipients from selling it. It's a wonder we didn't come to think of Not To Be Sold as a brand name.

Malcolm X, who was nine years old in 1934, The Autobiography of Malcolm X, *p. 14.*

I'll never forget my first Christmas in Hollywood in that dinky little one-room apartment. We had no tree, no presents, and nothing to eat. My mother had sold the car to pay our room rent and we lived on crackers for two days. Our landlady came by and brought a chocolate cake she had baked as our Christmas gift. I am sure she was not aware that we had no food in the house. . . .

I started to cry . . . because it was Christmas, our first Christmas away from our home in Houston, and because we were sad and homesick and broke and had nothing to eat after that chocolate cake was gone, and because it wasn't as easy for an eleven-year-old girl to take care of her mother as she thought it would be. . . .

That first Christmas day in Hollywood, when I was eleven, was the turning point in my life. It marked the end of my childhood, if I ever had one, [and] the beginning of adulthood long before I was ready. . . .

Ann Miller writing about Christmas 1934, Miller's High Life, *pp. 45–46.*

Anna, of Polish parentage, is only seventeen, and has had to leave school. She says, "I wanted to be a nurse, but I had to give up high school and help support the family because my Dad was out of work so long. I could get work and my father couldn't. I would like to work in a hospital, and I did apply at one or two, but couldn't get on." Anna managed to get a job breaking eggs for forty hours a week at $11.50.

Rachel Stutsman, 1934, What of Youth Today?, *p. 42.*

Dorothy, of native stock, the only child of a widowed mother, was accustomed to every luxury. She finished high school at sixteen and planned to take a business course in some college of Commerce and Finance. On account of reduced income, "my plans were all shot," she says, "the banks closed and we had oodles of bank stock and the rest in real estate." She is now nineteen and would like to get into newspaper work as she was good in English at school and feels that she can write well. Except for clerking in a gift shop during the Christmas holidays, she has never worked, and is not seriously looking for a position now. However, she says, "If I were trained for some type of work and could get a job, it would make things easier." Her home is pleasant and she has admirably adjusted herself to the changes consequent upon a smaller income. She says, "Our home life is much sweeter. I have been brought closer to my mother. I am not as selfish as I was three years ago. I do a great deal of the housework and part of the cooking. Three years ago I did absolutely nothing. . . ."

Rachel Stutsman, 1934, What of Youth Today?, *p. 19.*

I was born and reared in Saline Co., Missouri. At 16 years of age I enrolled in the CCC and was sent to Salisbury, Missouri. One crew or section as we were called worked in the 10 acre forest tree nursery weeding, watering, cultivating the small seedlings. As this was a soil erosion camp, our work was to prevent soil erosion in farmers' fields and meadows. Ditches were graded, bottoms and banks rounded and dams constructed of osage orange hedge, as we called it, by driving a double line of posts across and in the banks. The space between, we filled with smaller pieces of hedge, limbs, branches, etc. It was then packed tightly and bound tight to the posts on either side with heavy wire.

In late autumn we dug up the little locust seedlings, tied them in bundles and dug trenches and heeled them in for protection from freezing during the winter months. During the winter we went to the nearby river bottoms where there were thickets of small willows. We cut these from 1/2 to 1 1/2 in. diameter into approximately two foot lengths, tied them into bundles and stored them for the winter. In the spring we took the willows and the locusts to the ditches where we built the dams and planted the locusts along the banks. Then while there was mud in the bottoms we drove or pushed the willow sticks into the bottom hoping they would sprout and grow into trees to halt erosion.

George T. Nixon, a CCC enrollee in 1935 and 1936, in Perry H. Merrill, Roosevelt's Forest Army, *p. 104.*

. . . [T]he worst thing is that the boys may turn into bums. This year, already, they are tougher than they were last year. If hard times last much longer and nothing is done for these boys, things will be pretty bad for them. They won't get an education. They'll form the habit of getting by without working. They'll get used to going for days without taking their clothes off, and they'll learn stealing and vice from the old bums that are always on the road. Take it from me, an awful lot of young people in America are growing up to be criminals.

A federal inspector commenting on youthful transients, ca. 1935, in Kingsley Davis, Youth in the Depression, *p. 6.*

In our present economic distress (1933–35), the out-of-towner without money is not welcomed by the community. . . .

These men, and women too, or perhaps even better, these boys and girls, were forming a group which was at least unlike, if not opposed to, the accepted pattern of our society. Here was a mass of people who were close to becoming at least gypsies, if not bandits and criminals. They had had only a few years of being practically outcast. What will they be like when they have had a score of more in which to develop their unusual habit patterns and form their new allegiances?

Besides the fact that such a group may become a menace to society, there is the suffering and hardship which is occasioned whenever they fall into the hands of the predatory individual who uses such unfortunates for his own ends. The young boy may well become the vassal of some unscrupulous man who may make him beg and otherwise administer to his every wish. The case is perhaps even clearer for the girl who is without home and community.

Herman J. P. Schubert, 1935, Twenty Thousand Transients, *pp. 2–3.*

Please help us my mother is sick three year and was in the hospital three month and she came out but she is not better and my Father is peralised and can not work and we are poor and the Cumunity fun gives us six dollars an we are six people four children three boy 15, 13, 12, an one gril 10, and to parents. We have no one to give us a Christmas presents please buy us a stove to do our cooking and to make good bread.

A child whose family fled the drought-stricken Southwest, photographed near Shafter, California. *(Library of Congress)*

Please excuse me for not writing it so well because the little girl 10 year old is writing.

Letter to President Franklin D. Roosevelt from an anonymous Ohio girl, December 22, 1935, in Robert S. McElvaine, ed., Down and Out in the Great Depression, *p. 116.*

Picture how you would feel with two or three children headed for school, almost barefoot, with ragged or ill-fitting clothing. You see them going down the road with a paper bag in their hands, with two baking-powder biscuits, maybe, and some beans in-between. And if you were a little child, how would you feel going to school that way—and when it comes noon you sit down in your little bunch and drag out those two sandwiches full of beans, when the rest of the little ones are sitting around you there, children of more fortunate people? How do the children feel?

A dust bowl emigrant, a father, ca. 1935, in Jerry Stanley, Children of the Dust Bowl, *p. 39.*

This is a family of six; a man, his wife and four children. They live in a tent the color of the ground. Rot has set in on the canvas so that the flaps and the sides hang in tatters and are held together with bits of rusty baling wire. There is one bed in the family and that is a big tick lying on the ground inside the tent.

They have one quilt and a piece of canvas for bedding. The sleeping arrangement is clever. Mother and father lie down together and two children lie between them. Then heading the other way, the other two children lie, the littler ones. If the mother and father sleep with their legs spread wide, there is room for the legs of the children. . . .

The tent is full of flies clinging to the apple box that is the dinner table, buzzing about the foul clothes of the children, particularly the baby, who has not been bathed nor cleaned for several days. . . . There is no toilet here, but there is a clump of willows nearby where human feces lie exposed to the flies—the same flies that are in the tent.

Two weeks ago there was another child, a four year old boy. For a few weeks they had noticed that he was kind of lackadaisical, that his eyes had been feverish. They had given him the best place in the bed, between father and mother. But one night he went into convulsions and died, and the next morning the coroner's wagon took him away. . . .

They know pretty well that it was a diet of fresh fruit, beans and little else that caused his death. He had no milk for months.

John Steinbeck reporting for the San Francisco News *on dust bowl refugees in California, November 1936, in* Harvest Gypsies, *pp. 27–28.*

All German youth within the borders of the Reich are united in the Hitler Youth. All German youth, outside parents' homes and schools, are to be trained, bodily, mentally, spiritually and morally, in the spirit of national socialism for service to the nation and to the unified people.

Decree issued by the German government, December 1, 1936, as reported in the New York Times, *in W. Thatcher Winslow,* Youth: A World Problem, *p. 33.*

America has often been called the melting pot. It is now a double-boiler. The Civilian Conservation Corps is a smaller melting pot within the big one. We are thrown together in such a way that we have to get better acquainted whether or not we want to. Rustic farm lads mingle with Polish and Italian boys from back of the yards. Unlettered mountaineers from the west mingle with high-school graduates and college men from the centers of culture. Different races and nationalities look each other in the face, work and eat together for the first time. And it is a safe bet, we think, that this process many times results in the elimination of traditional prejudices based on ignorance and misinformation.

CCC enrollee C. W. Kirkpatrick, 1937, in A. C. Oliver. Jr., and Harold M. Dudley, This New America, *p. 66.*

According to Theodor Wilhelm and Gerhard Graefe [authors of *German Education Today* (Berlin, 1936)] . . . an "overemphasis of the intellect," a tendency "to identify life with knowledge," to believe "that education could be restricted to the development of the intellect, and . . . could only be effected through the medium of instruction," excluding feelings, will, soul, and emotions, caused German youth to revolt against "this theory of teaching and the kind of school which resulted." The young longed for "finite values." They did not want "merely to be instructed"; they wanted "to be led." Wilhelm and Graefe maintain that young Germans accepted the dictum of Hitler that "the German youth of the future must be slim and strong, as fast as a greyhound, as tough as leather, and as hard as Krupp steel."

German boys, members of the Hitler Youth, raise the Nazi flag. This organization attracted boys by offering uniforms, parades, camping trips, and hikes, just as the Boy Scouts did. *(Library of Congress)*

It is probable that the majority of the youth did not rationalize their feelings and desires to the extent these writers claim. Rather they were unemployed, dissatisfied, and frequently lacked the basic necessities of life. Faced by these difficulties they were critical and established institutions and grasped at any plan or program that promised better conditions.

Kenneth Holland, 1939, Youth In European Labor Camps, *p. 95.*

Patient, age eight months, was admitted to the Central Michigan Children's Clinic on 3–4–39, with the chief complaint of sweating and coughing for past week. The mother states that the patient has been perspiring markedly since December and was irritable when handled. The patient had not been taking formula well, had been getting some cod liver oil of a preparation of bulk cod liver oil. Had not taken any orange juice the past month. On admission the patient appeared to be an average nourished, acutely ill, white child. Physical examination found that the mouth hygiene was poor, lips scaled and cracked. Chest revealed scorbutic notching, heart was rapid, the buttocks were excoriated [peeling]. Examination of the extremities were painful on motion of legs.

Treatment was commenced and the baby seemed content as long as permitted to lie quietly, and when handled cried a great deal. The patient expired ten hours after admission. Post mortem examination was performed and it was found that there were numerous petechiae in the serous surfaces of the body [i.e., broken capillaries beneath the membranes sheathing the internal organs], the ribs definitely hemorrhagic and typically scorbutic in character [i.e., affected by scurvy] from gross examination.

Final Diagnosis: Scurvy
Secondary anemia
Malnutrition
Impetigo

. . . From the final diagnosis we feel had it had care just a few days earlier, its life need not have been lost.

A. Winnifred Golley, R.N., superintendent of the Central Michigan Children's Clinic, reporting on Case 1892, March 1939, in Joseph M. Hawes, Children Between the Wars, *pp. 108–09.*

10 World War II: Children on the American Home Front 1939–1945

On Sunday afternoon, December 7, 1941, Americans had their radios on. Some young people had tuned in to hear a football game: The New York Giants were playing the Brooklyn Dodgers. For others the radio provided background noise for the activities of life. They listened as they decorated the Christmas tree and set up the Lionel trains beneath it, accompanied their mother on a visit to a sick friend, or perhaps ate a midday dinner.

This ordinary day became noteworthy when broadcasters interrupted their programming with disastrous news. That morning, the fighting forces of Japan had attacked the headquarters of the U.S. Pacific Fleet—the naval base at Pearl Harbor, Hawaii. Japanese bombs had enfeebled or sunk mighty battleships and destroyed planes sitting on the ground. More than 2,000 people, both military personnel and civilians, had been killed. In homes across the United States, children saw their parents cry; they overheard adults losing their temper and vowing to destroy anything and anyone Japanese.

On Monday, December 8, children were among the millions of people who listened to a live radio broadcast from the U.S. Capitol, where President Franklin Delano Roosevelt had gone before Congress to request a declaration of war against Japan. As schoolchildren gathered in assemblies to hear the historic broadcast, even the most restive among them were silent. Three days later, on December 11, Germany and Italy declared war on the United States.

FEELING VULNERABLE

Americans reacted to news of their nation's entry into the Second World War not with clamor and parades but with tears, stunned silence, anger, and fear. The raid on Pearl Harbor had demonstrated that the United States was open to foreign attack, and across the land, children wondered when and where the next bombs would fall. They searched the skies for enemy planes and ran, frightened, to and from school. Young children felt particularly anxious about being separated from their parents during an air raid, but even teenagers were not immune from fear. A 16-year-old attending Regis High School in New York

City worried that he would be bombed while commuting to school by train from his home on Long Island.

Adults, too, feared enemy attack. On May 20, 1941, President Roosevelt had created the Office of Civilian Defense, headed by Fiorello La Guardia, mayor of New York City, to protect citizens and their property in the event of an air raid or invasion. Now, with the nation at war, more than 12 million people, including many parents and teachers, joined the Civil Defense Corps. These volunteers trained for such jobs as auxiliary police officers and firefighters; bomb, decontamination, and road-repair squad members; and air-raid wardens.

Wearing armbands and metal helmets, air-raid wardens patrolled residential streets during the nighttime drills known as blackouts. They made sure that all lamps had been turned off and that heavy blackout curtains had been drawn in every house to prevent light from escaping. A blackout, in theory, protected a community from enemy planes by making it disappear into the night. Radar had not yet come into use, so pilots relied on visual cues to locate targets on the ground.

Some young people found these drills to be fun, but for many children they were frightening. It was hard for small children to understand the concept of a drill, and many mistakenly believed that they were under attack. They panicked at the sound of an air raid siren or a plane overhead, and many were afraid of the dark. It was also not uncommon for children to fear that their own action—absentmindedly turning on a light, perhaps, or brushing against a blackout curtain—might signal the enemy.

During air raid drills at school, children crouched under their desks or filed into a hallway or basement and sat against a wall. In Hawaii, fear of a second bombing was so great that schools remained closed until February 1942. When children at last returned to class, civil defense personnel handed them gas masks and exposed them to tear gas during periodic drills. Concern about bombing raids was high in some mainland cities as well, especially on the West Coast, and officials there took added precautions. Children in San Francisco, for example, wore identification tags stamped with numbers that matched them to a master list of names held by the local civil defense office. The tags would help identify the children in the event that they were evacuated or became casualties.

Congress disbanded the Office of Civilian Defense in 1943, after concluding that an enemy attack was unlikely, but communities and schools held drills for the duration of the war.

FATHERS JOIN THE FIGHT

As children prepared for possible war at home, they said goodbye to older brothers, cousins, and uncles who had enlisted or been drafted to serve overseas. Few fathers entered the fighting force before October 1, 1943, the day the Selective Service System abolished its III-A classification, which protected men with dependents from induction. The Selective Service was so reluctant to draft fathers that it lowered the age of eligibility for single men and eased its physical and educational standards before taking this step. In October 1943, 13,300 fathers received their draft notices; in November, 25,700 fathers were drafted. In all, between October 1943 and December 1945, 944,426 fathers were drafted, accounting for 30.3 percent of the total for that period. Of course, not every father who served in World War II waited for his draft notice. Many responded to stirrings of patriotism and enlisted, sometimes in defiance of their wives' objections. This group included a large number of physicians who responded to the need for military doctors. Because of the long time that medical training required, physicians who enlisted tended to be above draft age and to have children.

Whether their fathers signed up or were drafted, children were likely to feel abandoned or bewildered by their departures. A child lived with the fear that his or her father might never return and possibly as well with an overwrought mother who was not only unable to provide reassurance but needed comforting herself. Many women were models of strength and optimism for their children, though, and kept father present in the children's memory by talking about him, showing them his photograph, and even baking a cake for his birthday.

As in earlier wars, mail linked men with their daughters and sons. Women wrote to their husbands about milestones and small accomplishments in their children's lives. Youngsters dictated letters or created their own missives and drawings for Daddy, who might have been at sea on a battleship or destroyer, among the allied forces liberating France or making advances in Italy in the summer of 1944, or stationed in Saipan or Guam in the Pacific. Children wrote that they missed their fathers and wanted them home. Fathers, in turn, encouraged their children to do well in school and to be helpful. They also sent home war souvenirs, such as Nazi insignia, which children brought to school to show-and-tell.

Beginning in 1942, to save space in wartime transport, letters could be written on forms available at the post office and then microfilmed by the Army Signal Corps for shipment overseas. Before delivery they were printed as 4-by-5$\frac{1}{2}$-inch Victory Mail, or V-mail, for delivery. American civilians and military personnel sent more than 1 billion pieces of V-mail during the years of World War II.

A father's departure often meant a change in residence as mother and children moved in with grandparents, aunts and uncles, or other relatives. This arrangement eased expenses for women who lacked the education and skill needed to earn enough money to maintain a household; it also allowed extended family members to care for children if their mother worked. Older men—grandfathers, neighbors, and family friends—commonly served as surrogate fathers for the children of absent servicemen, taking them to movies and sporting events or simply spending time with them in conversation.

Mental health professionals and many parents worried about the effect on children of war and a father's absence. The strict behavioral approach to child rearing that had been advocated by John Watson in the 1920s had fallen out of favor, and newer child-care manuals had replaced his book on parents' shelves. With titles such as *Babies Are Human Beings* (1938), they reassured mothers that it was all right to hug and caress their infants. Psychologists now placed importance on children's inner lives and studied how external events influenced the developing psyche. Professional journals and popular magazines delved into such topics as how children's understanding of war changed according to age and how day care affected children and their mother.

Many of the authors were influenced by studies of British children, who had been living in a nation at war since 1939. The noted psychoanalyst Anna

Freud, who studied British children evacuated from ports and inland cities to escape German bombing raids, had concluded that the children suffered worse trauma as a result of being separated from their parents than they would had they remained at home. Another study—this one of children in Bristol, England, who had survived air raids—found that the subjects reacted to the stress of war with psychological and psychosomatic symptoms, including frequent crying, chronic headaches and indigestion, bed wetting, and nosebleeds. These symptoms persisted in young children for weeks and months after the bombing had let up.

CHILDREN ON THE MOVE

World War II uprooted millions of American children, and not only the sons and daughters of fighting men. The U.S. Census Bureau has estimated that 15.3 million civilians—adults and children—moved during the war years and that nearly half of them crossed state lines.

One group of young people placed in new surroundings by the circumstances of war consisted of the children of women and men who went to work in defense plants. The manufacturing demands of World War II brought about the largest increase in factory production in U.S. history. Aircraft manufacturers enlarged existing plants, and companies that made items declared nonessential by the War Production Board, things like automobiles and refrigerators, now turned out tanks, generators, and weapons.

Most of the people who moved to take defense-related jobs left rural regions of Appalachia and the Deep South for urban manufacturing centers such as those in the Midwest and on the West Coast. This migration caused the population of industrial cities and suburbs to swell. The population of one such city, San Diego, more than doubled between 1940 and 1944, rising from 289,000 to 609,000. Over the same period, 583,000 people went to the San Francisco Bay area, and 518,000 moved to Los Angeles. (It is important to note that the defense-plant labor force included as many as 3 million workers aged 14 to 17. Desperate for employees, manufacturers ignored the child-labor provisions of the Fair Labor Standards Act, while many state child-labor laws were suspended during the war.)

Such large influxes created housing shortages. Families were forced to pay exorbitant rents for substandard units, such as trailers in the crowded, poorly maintained camps of suburban Detroit, where many people lived without heat, indoor toilets, and trash removal. The children in these communities attended overcrowded schools that were ill equipped to handle their burgeoning student bodies. Enrollment outpaced summer construction in many districts, so schools operated on half-day sessions. Educators in these districts faced other challenges as well. It was not unusual for students from the mountains and the South to enter their new schools with academic deficiencies. They came from regions where schools lagged behind the rest of the nation in quality, and the ordeal of moving had disrupted their education.

Much of urban life was new to these children. Many had never flipped a switch to turn on an electric light, poured a glass of water from an indoor faucet, or taken a ride on a school bus. These cultural differences set the newcomers apart from the local population and made them the victims of prejudice. Although teachers found the transplanted rural children polite and eager to please, they also believed them to be inherently backward. At the same time,

Children of defense-industry workers from Minnesota living in the Daniels Trailer Park near Detroit stand beside the park's toilet and trash facilities. *(Library of Congress)*

longtime residents taught their children to shun the young "hillbillies," who looked dirty, were sometimes allowed to smoke, and because of shoddy housing and poor nutrition, had higher rates of disease.

Whether they remained in their prewar residence, moved in with relatives, or relocated to a manufacturing center, millions of women went to work during World War II. In 1944, during the most intense period of the war, 2,690,000 women with dependent children held jobs in defense industries. Women had also taken over jobs that had been held by men currently in the armed forces. They drove buses, milk trucks, and taxis, and they wielded shovels in railroad yards. Working mothers were caught in a bind: They needed their salaries and the nation needed their labor, but society labeled them "maladjusted" and criticized them for neglecting their homes and children. Women fretted about their children, too, and tried to arrange for them to be cared for by people the children knew and loved. If both parents held factory jobs, they might work different shifts so that one of them was always at home. Relatives, friends, and neighbors also provided child care. Parents were reluctant, though, to put their children in day-care facilities. Professional day care could be expensive, and transportation to the center was an obstacle for some families. Also, remembering how British children suffered after being separated from their parents, mothers avoided leaving their own preschoolers in the hands of strangers, if only for part of the day.

Despite parents' best efforts, child-care arrangements often proved less than satisfactory, and this contributed to higher-than-average rates of absenteeism and job turnover among women with dependent children and slowed wartime production. The public grew alarmed at reports of children getting into trouble while left in a sitter's care. In one community, some of these children trampled gardens, broke windows, set fires, and flattened the tires of parked cars. People also objected to parents using movie theaters as drop-off child-care centers. The press fueled society's fears by reporting on children harnessed to posts or locked in cars all day or all night while their mothers worked. Teachers already burdened with large classes provided instruction to "door-key children" in home safety, food preparation, and personal hygiene.

Solving the child-care dilemma was problematic even for government. Officials of the U.S. Children's Bureau and the Office of Education opposed the opening of day-care facilities, believing that they weakened the bond between mother and child. The members of Congress heard these experts' concerns, but they listened more closely to business leaders. In July 1943, Congress appropriated funds for the Federal Works Agency to equip and staff day-care centers for the children of working women. By the end of the year, 2,065 federal day-care centers were in operation, and 58,682 children were enrolled. A few months later, in February 1944, there were 2,243 centers with 65,772 children attending. Fifty cents bought a full day's care for a child aged 2 to 5, the child's lunch, and morning and afternoon snacks. Defense manufacturers also operated their own daycare facilities for the children of employees. The Kaiser Shipyards of Portland, Oregon, for example, made funding for two child-care centers part of its federal contract.

Less controversial was the need for supervision of older children before and after school. In the fall of 1942, the federal government established Extended School Services (ESS), a program that employed college students, librarians, and others to lead children in organized recreation such as games, singing, storytelling, and arts and crafts, in the hours when their parents worked but school was not in session. According to the U.S. Office of Education, approximately 320,000 children were involved in ESS activities by June 30, 1943, the date when funding for the program expired and it was officially discontinued. ESS had proven so popular, though, that Kansas City, Cleveland, and other cities found the funding to keep it operating.

"SAVE, SERVE, CONSERVE"

On September 25, 1942, 4,000 children marched in Washington, D.C., to kick off Schools at War, a federal program that would enlist the school-age population in the war effort on the home front. A joint effort of the Office of Education and the Department of the Treasury, the program exhorted children to "save, serve, and conserve." The government asked children to save their money in the form of war stamps and bonds; to serve their schools, communities, and nation as volunteers; to eat all of the food on their plates, use school supplies sparingly, fix broken toys, and mend old clothing; and to collect scrap material that might be recycled and used for war purposes. Bacon grease, meat drippings, and other fats left over from cooking could be turned into glycerin for use in explosives. Scrap iron, tin cans, and used aluminum foil were the raw materials for guns, ammunition, tanks, ships, and planes. Old tires provided rubber for military vehicles, whereas worn silk stockings could be processed into parachutes.

More than 28,000 schools enrolled in the Schools at War program during its first year. Child participants lined up in classrooms to buy 10-cent war stamps to paste in their "Victory Books." A book of 187 stamps and a nickel could be exchanged for a $25 war bond that was redeemable in 10 years. Peer pressure was a strong incentive to buy stamps: No child wanted to be the only one in class without a dime to invest and be labeled unpatriotic. Children also sold millions of dollars in war stamps and bonds.

Girls and boys gave of their time to collect reading material for hospitalized veterans and to knit socks, sweaters, scarves, mittens, and afghans for the men and women in the armed forces. They baked cookies for the United Service Organization, or USO, which maintained recreational clubs for military personnel and arranged entertainment for troops stationed overseas. At Christmastime, children sent gifts and cards to "orphan soldiers," or military personnel who had no families, and throughout the year they wrote countless letters to people in the service. Not only did they write to relatives and friends, but as participants in letter-writing campaigns sponsored by schools and church groups, they wrote to young men in uniform whom they had never met.

When it came to collecting scrap, American children were indefatigable. Posters hanging in schools and other public buildings reminded them that one old shovel contained enough metal for four grenades and that a single radiator could be made over into 17 .30-caliber rifles. Children learned how to wash out cans, cut off the tops and bottoms, and stamp on the cylinders to flatten them. Many sacrificed toy cars and trucks, doll carriages, and other playthings

Students in Washington, D.C., weigh scrap paper that they have collected and brought to school. *(Library of Congress)*

made from metal and rubber. They carted the material they had collected to school in wagons and wheelbarrows. Children gathered scrap as participants in the Schools at War program and as members of the Boy Scouts, Girl Scouts, 4-H Clubs, and other youth groups. The Junior Commandos, a national organization founded by Harold Gray, creator of the "Little Orphan Annie" comic strip, enlisted thousands of children and adolescents in the war effort. Junior Commandos wore army-style caps and armbands and earned promotion in rank for collecting scrap and buying war stamps and bonds. Altogether, 30 million American children collected 1.5 million tons of scrap metal. On December 13, 1944, Congress formally thanked the nation's children for their generosity and hard work.

Living on the American home front during World War II meant putting up with shortages of manufactured goods and food. A significant amount of the food produced in the United States during World War II was shipped overseas to feed the troops and as lend-lease aid to allied countries. Beginning in January 1942, the U.S. Office of Price Administration issued ration books containing sheets of stamps with point values that consumers were required to use when shopping for sugar, coffee, and gasoline. Point rationing was extended in early 1943 to meat, fats and oils, cheese, and some processed foods, and later to shoes and nylon stockings. Other materials, although not rationed, became hard to obtain. For example, with the Japanese conquest of Southeast Asia in the spring of 1942, the United States lost its suppliers of rubber. Children wrote with pencils that had no erasers; girls wore underpants held up by drawstrings instead of elastic and suffered embarrassment if they fell down. Also, metal playthings such as roller skates, ice skates, sleds, and toy vehicles were unavailable throughout the war.

To offset wartime food shortages, adults and children planted vegetable gardens in backyards and vacant lots. Americans tended as many as 20 million Victory gardens in any one growing season during the war years. Novice gardeners read instructional brochures produced by the government and distributed free of charge or printed by seed companies and sold at nurseries to learn how to prepare soil, water and fertilize growing plants, and combat insect pests.

The War Invades Children's Leisure Time

Americans spent more time listening to the radio during World War II than in previous years. In 1942, children tuned in for six hours a day, on average. They listened to news broadcasts and to the president as he delivered "fireside chats," his talks on current issues delivered in an informal style. After dinner, children joined adults to hear such popular programs as "Edgar Bergen and Charlie McCarthy," "The Answer Man," and "The Kate Smith Hour." On weekdays, between 4:00 and 6:00 P.M., the networks broadcast programs intended primarily for children, including "Jack Armstrong: The All-American Boy," "The Green Hornet," "Red Ryder," "Terry and the Pirates," and "Captain Midnight." The content of these dramatic programs was likely to be war-related. Captain Midnight and his Secret Squadron, for instance, expended much energy tracking down Nazi agents, while Terry took a break from fighting pirates to combat the Japanese.

Movie attendance also rose dramatically during the war years. It has been estimated that 100 million people—in a nation with a home-front population of 135 million—went to the movies each week in 1942. Children were included in this number, both those dropped off at odd hours by working parents and those attending Saturday matinees.

It seems logical to think that movies offered an escape from thoughts of war, but films and short subjects continually reminded audiences of the world-wide conflict. For one thing, the newsreels that preceded feature films presented battle scenes that many children found frightening. For another, Hollywood studios were cooperating with the Office of War Information to produce films that would boost the public's morale and encourage a positive attitude toward the war effort. One-fourth of all commercial films released between 1941 and 1945 told idealized stories of combat. Even a Bugs Bunny cartoon might contain a wartime message, if only a reminder to buy bonds.

The war also infiltrated children's play. Influenced by the newsreels that they saw, boys and girls filled page after page with pictures of planes flying over enemy territory and bombs falling and exploding. They mimicked Adolf Hitler and Nazi soldiers by placing two fingers beneath their noses in imitation of the German leader's mustache, raising one arm in a stiff salute, and performing an exaggerated goose step.

Small boys ran across lawns, extending their arms and humming, pretending to pilot airplanes. At other times they shot at imaginary Japanese bombers with guns fashioned from cardboard or sticks. A clenched fist with one finger extended could also serve as a firearm, especially in games of combat. Boys regularly engaged in mock battles outdoors, while girls were more likely to stage armed encounters using dolls. To be welcomed into the boys' games, girls often had to agree to play the enemy—the Italians, the Germans, or the most hated foe of all, the Japanese.

FORCED EXCLUSION

Americans living through World War II directed more anger toward Japan than toward the other Axis nations, because Japan alone had directly attacked the United States, and because the Japanese were of a different race from most Americans. Many children heard their parents and other adults condemn all people of Japanese descent and watched them smash possessions that had been made in Japan. Some children learned at home that the Japanese differed from the rest of humanity—that they lacked normal human emotions. Stories spread that Japanese Americans' true loyalty was to the emperor of Japan and that some among them were involved in sabotage. It was rumored, for example, that Japanese Americans had created signals on the ground pointing enemy bombers toward strategic targets. (The rumors were unfounded: Not one Japanese American would be found guilty of committing espionage or treason during World War II.)

On the West Coast, where most Japanese Americans lived, the prejudice was older. Once the war began, white supremacists and western politicians pressured the federal government to remove all ethnic Japanese from the region. On February 19, 1942, despite warnings from U.S. Attorney General Francis Biddle that it was unconstitutional to forcibly confine U.S. citizens, President Roosevelt signed Executive Order 9066, which authorized the secretary of war and designated military commanders to declare any portion of the United States a military area and to exclude any and all persons from that area. This order resulted in all people of Japanese descent being evacuated from their homes in California, Oregon, Washington, and western Arizona and relocated to camps in remote western regions. In all, 120,000 Japanese-American civilians were imprisoned, including 77,000 U.S. citizens, 30,000 of whom were schoolchildren. (Unlike European immigrants, people who had left Japan to live in the United States were denied naturalization rights.) Orphans and foster children, some only

Japanese Americans in Salinas, California, board a bus that will take them to an assembly center. *(Library of Congress)*

six months old, were interned at the Children's Center at Manzanar, the largest relocation camp, 210 miles northeast of Los Angeles in the California desert.

The evacuation began on March 31, 1942. People had very little time—frequently just 24 hours—to dispose of their homes and businesses and most of their possessions. As a result, thousands of families suffered enormous financial setbacks. People were permitted to bring with them only as much as they could carry, and many children were upset at being forced to abandon beloved pets.

The people were bused first to fairgrounds and racetracks that had been converted into temporary assembly centers. These centers resembled prisons, surrounded as they were by barbed wire and soldiers with machine guns. For the approximately three months that they spent in the assembly centers, families were assigned to live in animals' stalls or flimsy barracks.

Conditions were no better at the permanent relocation camps that people entered in the summer and fall of 1942. These camps were situated in harsh, inhospitable places where shrill winds carried stinging sand and dust. Summer temperatures averaged 115°F at the Poston, Arizona, camp, and 100°F at Minidoka, Idaho, while winter nights at the camps in Wyoming and Colorado could be as cold as −30°F. In the two camps located in marshy Arkansas lowlands, residents coexisted with poisonous snakes.

Once again, Japanese Americans endured barbed wire, armed guards, crowding, and minimal privacy. At Manzanar, as at the other camps, residents were assigned to quarters according to family size. A family of four, for example, was allotted a 20-by-25-foot room in a drafty barracks. Two childless couples assigned to a similar space might hang sheets to divide the room. Barracks residents shared laundry and bathroom facilities and ate in a communal mess hall. Authorities issued each resident an army blanket, a cot, and a mattress casing to be stuffed with straw, and they confiscated hotplates, knitting needles, and any other items that might be considered dangerous.

Schoolrooms at the hastily organized relocation centers at first lacked furniture, textbooks, and teachers. In time, supplies arrived, and as Quaker volunteers conducted classes, children adjusted to camp life. They joined the scout troops and baseball teams that gradually took shape, and they signed up for music, dance, and acting lessons. Boys in the internment camps played at war, and just like boys throughout the United States, they pretended to defeat the Japanese. Some had male relatives in the Japanese-American 442nd Combat Team, which fought with distinction in Italy and France. The 442nd suffered more casualties and earned more decorations for bravery than any unit of comparable size with a similar length of service.

On December 17, 1944, Western Defense Command lifted the restrictions that prevented Japanese Americans from returning to their homes, and people picked up the broken threads of their lives. On July 2, 1948, President Harry S. Truman signed the Japanese American Evacuation Claims Act, giving those persons formerly detained the right to be compensated for lost property. In all the government paid about $37 million in claims, which equaled only a fraction of the real and personal property lost as a result of internment. Japanese Americans would wait until August 10, 1988, for a more meaningful government effort. On that date, President Ronald Reagan signed the Civil Liberties Act of 1988 and apologized to the Japanese Americans who had been imprisoned. The act entitled each of those individuals to symbolic compensation of $20,000. It also created the Civil Liberties Public Education Fund, to inform Americans about the interment of Japanese Americans; and the Office of Redress Administration, to track down people who qualify for compensation.

After seeing what had happened to Japanese-American youngsters, some children of German or Italian ancestry feared that they too might be imprisoned. They had reason to be concerned: U.S. residents born in Germany and Italy were the targets of government persecution, although to a lesser extent than Japanese Americans were. The FBI arrested 1,521 Italian Americans, for example, but released most of them after questioning. Of the 250 Italian Americans who were imprisoned in military camps, none were children. It was common, however, for German-American and Italian-American children to be taunted by classmates who viewed them as the enemy.

WAR ENDS, AND A NEW AGE BEGINS

The events of 1945 made unusual emotional demands on all American children—plunging them, in rapid succession, into hope, grief, euphoria, and uncertainty about the future.

The year began on a hopeful note because the Allies clearly were winning the war. Japan's position had weakened, and its navy was badly crippled. On March 16, the U.S. Marines secured the island of Iwo Jima, site of a Japanese air base. On April 1, the U.S. 10th Army landed at Okinawa, 310 miles from the Japanese island of Kyushu, and engaged in a lengthy fight.

The Germans were faltering as well. By February 1945, Allied troops were advancing into their nation. On April 11, the U.S. 9th Army crossed the Elbe River near Magdeburg, putting itself within 75 miles of Berlin. Several days earlier, the Soviets had launched a Berlin offensive.

Then came the grief. On April 12, 1945, children were among the first Americans to learn that the nation had lost its commander in chief. That evening, news bulletins interrupted three popular children's programs, "Tom Mix," "Captain Midnight," and "Wilderness Road," informing listeners that President Roosevelt had died of a cerebral hemorrhage at 3:35 P.M., central war time, while resting at Warm Springs, Georgia.

Word of the president's death spread rapidly, and by nightfall a benumbed nation mourned. Roosevelt had become president in 1933, before many of the children living through World War II had been born. These children had spent their lives hearing him speak familiarly in his fireside chats, and now they would miss him. As when Lincoln died, children took part in public expressions of sorrow. They were prominent in the crowds that came out to pay their respects as Roosevelt's funeral train proceeded from Warm Springs to Hyde Park, New York, where he was to be buried. When the train reached Charlotte, North Carolina, a Boy Scout troop led the assembled mourners in singing "Onward Christian Soldiers."

Adolf Hitler committed suicide in his Berlin bunker on April 30, and on May 7, General Alfred Jodl, representing the new German chief of state, Grand Admiral Karl Doenitz, signed an unconditional surrender. Japan surrendered three months later, on August 14, and only then did Americans celebrate. Noisy parties erupted spontaneously on city streets, while rural families marked the occasion with watermelon and ice cream. From the East to the West, towns staged patriotic parades.

Already, though, people were struggling to come to terms with the complicated issue of how the United States had defeated Japan: by dropping an atomic bomb equal in power to 20,000 tons of TNT on the city of Hiroshima on August 6, and a second atomic bomb on another Japanese city, Nagasaki, three days later. Movie newsreels and *Life* magazine confronted children with images of mushroom clouds and flattened city landscapes. Boys and girls old enough to read the newspaper digested articles speculating that humanity had created the instrument of its own destruction and predicting the damage that would be sustained by U.S. cities in the event of a nuclear attack. Eager to enter the atomic age, 750,000 children sent away for the atomic-bomb ring that was advertised on Kix cereal boxes, but such trinkets did little to assuage the anxiety that now pervaded society.

ABSENT FATHERS RETURN

Amid the celebrations and concerns for the future, the veterans came home. Children and their fathers worked at becoming reacquainted, and in many cases they reestablished close relationships. To do so required effort on the part of men and children alike, because both groups had changed during the long separation of war. Some children had been babies or toddlers when their fathers joined the armed forces or had been born while their fathers were overseas, and so were getting to know them for the first time.

Those children who had idealized their fathers now had to abandon the faultless images and accept the actual men. They had to overcome any fear that their fathers might leave again, and they also had to adjust to a father's presence and authority in the home. Sometimes the years spent apart remained a gulf that men and their children were never able to bridge.

No one knows how many of the 407,318 U.S. servicemen who died in World War II had minor children. The best estimate of the number of children left fatherless comes from the Department of Veterans Affairs, which paid benefits to more than 183,000 such children. These young people derived little joy from the soldiers' return, and those whose fathers were buried overseas, who attended no funeral and had no grave to visit, frequently nurtured fantasies that he was still alive and would one day come home. In the meantime, they and their mothers worked hard to secure a place in a society that valued the two-parent family.

CHRONICLE OF EVENTS

1941

May 20: President Franklin Delano Roosevelt creates the Office of Civilian Defense, headed by Fiorello H. La Guardia.

December 7: Military forces of Japan attack the U.S. naval base at Pearl Harbor, Hawaii; radio news bulletins inform the American public of the attack.

December 8: Roosevelt asks Congress to declare war on Japan.

December 11: Germany and Italy declare war on the United States.

1941–1945

One-fourth of commercial films released during these years have war-related plots.

1942

V-mail comes into use to save space in military transport vehicles.

The workday done, a woman greets her child and his playmate at the Lakeview Nursery School, Buffalo, New York. *(Library of Congress)*

The federal government establishes Extended School Services (ESS) to provide supervision of school-age children of working women.

The average child spends six hours a day listening to the radio.

January: The U.S. Office of Price Administration issues its first ration books.

February: Schools in Hawaii, which have been closed since the attack on Pearl Harbor, now reopen.

February 19: Roosevelt signs Executive Order 9066, which permits the removal of Japanese Americans from the West Coast.

March 31: The evacuation of Japanese Americans begins; 120,000 civilians will be imprisoned.

September 25: The federal government launches Schools at War, a program to involve children in patriotic home-front activities.

1943

Congress disbands the Office of Civilian Defense.

June 30: Although 320,000 children are participating, funding for ESS expires and the federal role in the program is discontinued.

July: Congress allocates funds for the Federal Works Agency to operate day-care centers for the children of working women.

October 1: The Selective Service System abolishes the III-A classification, which exempted men with dependents from military service.

December 31: Some 58,682 children attend 2,065 federally operated day-care centers.

1944

The population of San Diego has increased from 289,000 in 1940 to 609,000; the San Francisco Bay area has gained 583,000 people during the same period, and Los Angeles has gained 518,000.

Approximately 2,690,000 women with dependent children work in defense-related industries.

February: There are now 2,243 government-run day-care centers caring for 65,772 children.

December 13: Congress issues a statement thanking the nation's children for their efforts on the home front.

December 17: Western Defense Command lifts the restrictions preventing Japanese Americans from returning to their homes.

1945

April 12: Roosevelt dies at Warm Springs, Georgia.

May 7: Germany surrenders unconditionally.

August 6: The United States drops an atomic bomb on Hiroshima, Japan.

August 9: A second atomic bomb explodes over Nagasaki, Japan.

August 14: Japan surrenders; World War II ends.

December: Since October 1943, 944,426 fathers have been drafted.

1948

July 2: President Harry S. Truman signs the Japanese American Evacuation Claims Act, partially compensating Japanese Americans for the losses they suffered due to wartime detention.

1988

August 10: By signing the Civil Liberties Act of 1988, President Ronald Reagan offers a presidential apology to those Japanese Americans who were imprisoned. The act provides the Japanese Americans with financial compensation that is largely symbolic.

EYEWITNESS TESTIMONY

Conscientious mothers often ask the doctor whether it is proper to fondle the baby. They have a vague feeling that it is wrong for babies to be mothered, loved or rocked, and that it is their forlorn duty to raise their children in splendid isolation, "untouched by human hands" so to speak, and wrapped in cellophane like the boxes of crackers we buy.

C. Anderson Aldrich and Mary M. Aldrich, 1938,
Babies Are Human Beings, *p. 102.*

One of the first admonitions a young mother hears when she starts to bring up her baby is, "Now, don't spoil him!" Which usually means, "Don't fail to see that he gets plenty of firmness and discipline so that he will know that he cannot have everything he likes." This process of deliberate parental thwarting can never lead to a happy family relationship. Furthermore, such an attitude is superfluous since the world does not lack for opportunities in which he can learn to adjust to antagonistic and unpleasant requirements. . . .

In my experience most spoiled children are those who, as babies, have been denied essential gratifications in a mistaken attempt to fit them into a rigid regime. Warmth, cuddling, freedom of action and pleasant associations with food and sleep have been pushed out of the way to make room for a technique. The lack of these things is so keenly felt that by the time babyhood is past, such children have learned their own

These British children have boarded a bus that will take them to foster homes across Canada, where they will live for the duration of the war. Great Britain sent more than 16,000 children to Canada, the United States, and other nations to protect them from wartime dangers. *(Toronto Telegram Photograph Collection, York University Archives and Special Collections)*

efficient technique of whining and tantrums as a means of getting their desires.

C. Anderson Aldrich and Mary M. Aldrich, 1938,
Babies Are Human Beings, pp. 113–14.

[I] beg you not to let me go to Canada. . . . A) Because I don't want to leave Britain in time of war. B) Because I should be very homesick. . . . C) Because it would be kinder to let me be killed with you . . . than to allow me to drift to strangers and finish my happy childhood in a contrary fashion. D) I would not see you for an indefinite time, perhaps never again. Letters would simply redouble my homesickness. P.S. I would rather be bombed to fragments than leave England.

A letter from David Wedgwood Benn, age 11, to his parents, published in the London Times, July 1939, in Geoffrey Bilson, The Guest Children, p. 26.

I sat by our kitchen table, methodically turning the pages of a huge black leather-bound book whose cover carried the gold-embossed words: *The People's War Book and Atlas* [a history of World War I published in 1920]. It was early September, 1939. I was eight and one-half years old and I was doing what I had done so many times before—reading my favorite book. . . .

From the time I was old enough to turn its pages, I had literally devoured its pictures. It was a huge volume, some three inches thick, far too heavy for a child to manage, but it was so richly illustrated and romanticized that it thoroughly captured my imagination. Perhaps the scenes of conflict and destruction were in such contrast to the tranquil life I lived that I simply couldn't resist. In any case, when rumors of an impending war began to circulate and when the actual German invasion of Poland occurred on September 1, 1939, I was already highly sensitized to the meaning of war and to the villainous descriptions of Germany that the War Book portrayed. . . .

Our family was concerned about the invasion of Poland; but the immediate declaration of war by France and Great Britain seemed far more significant. It was clear that another Great War was in the offing—and there was no question of our sympathy for the Allied cause.

C. LeRoy Anderson, who grew up in the Snake River Valley of Idaho, recalling September 1939, in C. LeRoy Anderson, Joanne R. Anderson, and Yunosuke Ohkura, eds., No Longer Silent, pp. 4–6.

Every Sunday our family went to the movies, the matinee. Abbott and Costello was my father's favorite. I never could stand them, but nevertheless we would all go. On December 7 my mother and father and my two younger sisters and I were all in the car on the way to the movies when the announcement came over the radio that Pearl Harbor had been bombed.

"Oh, my God, we've got to go home," my dad says. . . .

The following week they closed down the schools in Berkeley, and everybody rushed around and bought blackout paper to glue over the windows to keep the light from showing. . . . People were panicking, my mother was crying that the end of the world was coming. It was exhilarating.

Barbara Norek, who was a child living in Berkeley, California, on December 7, 1941, in Mark Jonathan Harris et al., The Homefront, pp. 24–25.

In school, even before the war, a lot of us Japanese used to play handball together; we were a clique. And the reason we were in cliques is because we didn't feel that welcome with the whites. When Pearl Harbor was struck we tried to stick together because we didn't know what to do; we felt that in groups we would be stronger. In our classes, though, we didn't have those cliques. It was only on lunch breaks or before school. . . . [A] Filipino schoolmate of mine after the war started would bring in pictures of the Japanese planes being shot down and say, "Hey, howja like this?" And I would say, "Oh, that's great!" But you know, I felt kind of as if he was testing me out to see what my loyalty was.

Ben Takeshita, who was 11 years old in December 1941, in John Tateishi, And Justice for All, p. 242.

There was evidence at the Palermo School, Palermo, California, that primary children do not recognize a Japanese person as an object of hate. It was soon after Pearl Harbor. One morning before school, ten or a dozen first-grade boys came running around the corner of the schoolhouse, each with an eager, intent look in his eyes and a stick in his hand. One boy said, "Oh boy! are we gonna get them Japs!" Two of the boys were Japanese.

Pauline Jeidy reporting on an event occurring in December 1941, "Reactions of children of Different Age Levels to War and Their Implications for Teachers," p. 14.

For a boy living through the unsteady times of World War II in a small town in the United States, I remember the intense family togetherness mixed with feelings of sweet sadness, a hopeful yearning for a peaceful future, and the directive that permeated everything: WE HAD TO WIN THE WAR! As a youngster, I sought to emulate the fantasy comic book heroes I idolized like Captain Marvel, Superman, or Robin (Batman's sidekick), who were on the side of right and might and who had to destroy the putrid and evil common enemy. Idealistic to the extreme, that was the way we were; and as All-American kids we saw ourselves as good guys who were united against the bad and who fought for victory at all cost. To a child like myself much of the home front idea of combat seemed to be more akin to play. Since no real bombs ever fell on my hometown, it all appeared to my vivid imagination to be happening around me in some make-believe land of war that was offered up by the movies, the radio, the comics, or as some item you could buy at the Woolworth's toy counter for a dime. . . .

Robert Heide recalling his childhood in Irvington, New Jersey, 1941–45, in Robert Heide and John Gilman, Home Front America, *p. 23.*

To me as a child . . . the war never had any reality. It was like a story that someone was telling me. . . .

We lived in North Hollywood, and they had big searchlights on those hills, I guess to look for aircraft or something. I can remember going up and taking hot coffee to the soldiers in uniform. I was a member of the Civil Air Patrol, which was something they organized for kids. We bought WAC uniforms from the army surplus and were given wooden guns to drill with, and we were taught Morse code and the different kinds of airplanes to watch for. We were never actually used, but we did have a sense of being prepared for something, for some time in the future. That was the only time to me the war seemed real.

Anne Relph describing her home-front activities in California, 1941–45, in Roy Hoopes, Americans Remember the Home Front, *p. 264.*

The movies of those days were a great and dubious influence upon us; we were utterly seduced by them. On those Saturday afternoons at the Reel Theatre we were drawn into worlds of infinite possibility. Our taste ran to high adventure, and we cared much more for Sergeant York than for Mrs. Miniver, of course, but we devoured everything that came our way. . . . And we would not let go of the movies, but we lived in them for days afterward. I remember that after we had seen *The Black Swan*, there were sword fights in the streets, and we battered each other mercilessly. Most of the swords were flimsy affairs, curtain weights and yardsticks; but mine was a length of doweling that I had pushed through a gelatin mold; it was a superior weapon, and with it I terrorized the neighborhood.

N. Scott Momaday, who was born in 1934, remembering movies and play in the years 1941–45, The Names, *p. 89.*

Many of our games involved war themes. We made hideouts and plans (and alternate plans) in the event Long Beach would be invaded or bombed. My sister and I planned for situations in which we might be like the poor, starving children of Europe we saw in the newsreels, living without parents, in rags, in bombed-out buildings. We were convinced that if attacked only children would survive and all adults would be killed.

Sheril Janovsky Cunning describing her childhood games in Long Beach, California, ca. 1941–45, in Mark Jonathan Harris et al., The Homefront, *p. 69.*

Whistle while you work,
Hitler is a jerk,
Mussolini is a weenie,
And Tojo is a jerk.

A popular children's rhyme, ca. 1941–45, in William M. Tuttle, Jr., "Daddy's Gone to War," *p. 134.*

The fact is that children who awaken at night screaming in terror, though no real disaster has touched them, or who live in constant dread of Japs or Germans, Hitler or bombs, are, on the whole, the same children who yesterday might have peopled the darkness of the night with wholly imaginary phantoms of terror. A child does not change from being a happy-go-lucky, serene type of individual to one beset with nervousness and anxiety just because we are now at war. The mild anxieties that all children have and that escape notice because they are so slight may, it is true, become intensified in wartime so that parents can easily make the mistake of thinking them quite new. Furthermore, every child is affected when war enters his immediate life. The departure of a father or brother for the service never leaves even the most happy-go-lucky child untouched. His ways of showing that he is disturbed may vary anywhere from hypertension and irritability to more extreme forms of unruly behavior. But as long as his own life remains essentially the same, the child who is nervous in wartime would have been nervous also if the nation had remained at peace. The language would have been different, but the mood and apprehensiveness the same.

Anna W. M. Wolf, 1942, Our Children Face War, *p. 23.*

Boys and girls of America can perform a great patriotic service for their country by helping our National Salvage effort. Millions of young Americans, turning their energies to collecting all sorts of scrap, metals, rubber, and rags can help the tide in our ever increasing war effort. They will earn the gratitude of every one of our fighting men by helping them to get the weapons they need—now! I know they will do their part.

Franklin Delano Roosevelt, official letter to Boy Scouts and Girl Scouts, 1942, in Robert Heide and John Gilman, Home Front America, *p. 61.*

There is one front and one battle where everyone in the United States—every man, woman, and child—is in action, and will be privileged to remain in action throughout this war. That front is right here at home, in our daily lives, and in our daily tasks. Here at home everyone will have the privilege of making whatever self-denial is necessary, not only to supply our fighting men, but to keep the economic structure of our country fortified and secure during the war and after the war. . . .

Franklin Delano Roosevelt in a fireside chat, April 1942, in Phyllis Raybin Emert, ed., World War II: On the Homefront, *p. 22.*

On May 16, 1942 at 9:30 a.m., we departed . . . for an unknown destination. To this day, I can remember vividly the plight of the elderly, some on stretchers, orphans herded onto the train by caretakers, and especially a young couple with 4 pre-school children. The mother had two frightened toddlers hanging on to her coat. In her arms, she carried two crying babies. The father had diapers and other baby paraphernalia strapped to his back. In his hands he struggled with duffle bag and suitcase. The shades were drawn on the train for our entire trip. Military police patrolled the aisles.

Grace Nakamura remembering her departure, on May 16, 1942, for a wartime assembly center, in Personal Justice Denied, *p. 136.*

I had a job to do with my brothers, and I ran them like a drill sergeant. . . . I wouldn't let them be out after nine o'clock, I made them go to school, I made them study. . . . I had them help me scrub their clothes so that they would be clean. Then somewhere during that time I came to feel, well, we're going to show these people. We're going to show the world. They are not going to do this to me; nobody is going to make me feel this miserable. The United States government may have made me leave my home, but they're going to be sorry. . . . *I'm going to prevail, my will is going to prevail, my own life will prevail.*

Helen Murao, who entered the Minidoka internment camp in Idaho in August 1942 as a 16-year-old orphan responsible for two younger brothers, in John Tateishi, And Justice for All, *p. 46.*

With no exceptions, schools at the centers opened in unpartitioned barracks meant for other purposes and generally bare of furniture. Sometimes the teacher had a desk and chair; more often she had only a chair. In the first few weeks many of the children had no desks or chairs and for the most part were obliged to sit on the floor—or stand up all day. Linoleum laying and additional wall insulation were accomplished in these makeshift schoolrooms some time after the opening of school. At some centers cold waves struck before winterization could be started.

By the [end of 1942] . . . it was no longer necessary for many pupils to sit on the floor, but seating was frequently of a rudimentary character. Text books and other supplies were gradually arriving. Laboratory and shop equipment and facilities, however, were still lacking. No center had been able to obtain its full quota of teachers.

War Relocation Authority report on schools in the wartime relocation camps, 1942, in Personal Justice Denied, *p. 170.*

I recall sitting in classrooms without books and listening to the instructor talking about technical matters that we could not study in depth. The lack of qualified evacuee teachers, the shortage of trained teachers was awful. I remember having to read a chapter a week in chemistry and discovering at the end of a semester that we had finished one full years' course. There was a total loss of scheduling with no experiments, demonstrations or laboratory work.

An evacuee remembering his high school chemistry class in a wartime relocation camp, ca. 1942, Personal Justice Denied, *p. 171.*

Gasoline was the biggest problem for a teen-ager. We still had cars, and gasoline was our biggest worry of all the rationing. We'd always pick up our dates in sequence when we had gas, and you might end up not taking your date home if it would save gas for you to be dropped off first. You'd kiss your date goodnight in front of your house, not hers. Some guys you didn't trust very much, and you wondered if they might not be kissing your girl also, because they would drop their date before yours. You worried about such things, and there were certain guys you didn't double-date with because you didn't want them taking your girl home.

A man recalls how gasoline rationing altered dating customs among teenagers ca. 1942, in Archie Satterfield, The Home Front, *p. 179.*

When we were not playing war in the side lot, we were doing so on the playground of the Peter Vetal School, three blocks from my home [in Detroit]. At Vetal, there was a deep division between the middle-class children and the working-class children. In large part, we in the middle class lived on one side of the school, while blue-collar families, including recent arrivals from the southern Appalachians, lived on the other side. I got to know Tommy Fields, whose family had moved to Detroit from Kentucky. We were in the same class, and I visited his house on the other side of the school; I do not think he ever visited mine, but I never thought about it at the time.

William M. Tuttle, Jr., recalling the years 1942–45, "Daddy's Gone to War," *p. vii.*

. . . [T]he teachers would exhort us with shouts and occasional slaps to finish all of our weiners and sauerkraut or our bologna and blackeyed peas. It was our small contribution to the war effort, to eat everything on our plate. Once the third-grade teacher, known as the cruelest in the school, stood over me and forced me to eat a plateful of sauerkraut, which I did, gagging and in tears, wishing I could leave . . . and never come back.

Willie Morris remembering his childhood in Yazoo City, Mississippi, 1942–45, North Toward Home, *p. 20.*

The war itself was a glorious and incomparable thing, a great panorama intended purely for the gratification of one's imagination. I kept a diary on all the crucial battles, which I followed every day in the pages of the *Memphis Commercial Appeal* and the *Jackson Daily News,*

and whenever the Allies won one of them, I would tie tin cans to a string and drag them clattering down the empty sidewalks of Grand Avenue. We never missed the latest war film, and luxuriated in the unrelieved hatred exercised for the Germans and the Japs. How we hated the Japs, those grinning creatures who pried off fingernails, sawed off eyelashes with razors, and bayoneted babies! The Germans we also hated, but slightly less so, because they looked more like us. . . .

Willie Morris describing the war's impact on him as a child in Yazoo City, Mississippi, 1942–45, North Toward Home, *p. 35.*

In some ways, I suppose, my life was not too different from a lot of kids in America between the years 1942 and 1945. I spent a good part of my time playing with my brothers and friends, learned to shoot marbles, watched sandlot baseball and envied the older kids who wore Boy Scout uniforms. We shared with the rest of America the same movies, screen heroes and listened to the same heart-rending songs of the forties. We imported much of America into the camps because, after all, we were Americans. Through imitation of my brothers, who attended grade school within the camp, I learned the salute to the flag by the time I was five years old. I was learning, as best as one could learn in Manzanar, what it meant to live in America. But, I was also learning the sometimes bitter price one has to pay for it.

A Japanese American who spent the years 1942–45 at the Manzanar Relocation Center in California, in Personal Justice Denied, *p. 12.*

I was in the eighth grade of a Catholic girls' school at that time and we were taught in no uncertain terms that God was on our side. And the good sisters wouldn't lower their standards for anything. They still insisted that we wear long hose. To show a bare ankle would have caused so much sin in the community that you could even kill each other getting the hose; anything so long as you didn't turn some man on with a bare ankle. So our mothers would go downtown and stand in line so their daughters could have long hose and not go to hell or cause some poor man to go to hell for getting turned on by our bare legs. Isn't that something?

A woman remembers being in the eighth grade, ca. 1943, when stockings were rationed, in Archie Satterfield, The Home Front, *p. 184.*

The war acquires comparatively little significance for children so long as it only threatens their lives, disturbs their material comfort or cuts their food rations. It becomes enormously significant the moment it breaks up family life and uproots the first emotional attachments of the child within the family group. London children, therefore, were on the whole much less upset by bombing than by evacuation to the country as a protection against it.

Anna Freud and Dorothy T. Burlingham, 1943, War and Children, *p. 37.*

Hatred only perpetuates the causes of war for generations to come. Teaching children to hate means descending to the level of much German education, resorting to the methods of barbarism. If Americans schools adopt some of the worst features of the German methods, then that is a moral victory for Germany. War conditions may breed a callousness toward suffering and a contempt for human life; the schools must counteract this if one of the permanent values of civilization is to be maintained. The schools probably cannot effectively teach children to love their enemies but they can give them an understanding and appreciation of the lives of other children over the world. . . . One of the most practical applications of true internationalism exists in the place in school activities accorded to children of enemy alien descent, the second or third generation Italians, Germans and Japanese. As someone has put it, "What a loss for us if others should lose their ships but we should lose our hearts." We should not teach hatred.

David H. Russell, 1943, "The Elementary School Child and the War," p. 150.

The week he graduated from high school in June 1943, my older brother, Bradley, enlisted in the Air Force. . . .

That summer I did little more than hang around the house. I went outside only when my mother had had enough of me and wanted the house to herself for a few hours. In the evenings and on weekends I helped my father work on a little square of land behind the building that he'd designated as our "victory garden." We'd plant, hoe, water, and wait for mom to call us in for supper. We talked about Brad, where he was, and how the war was going. Brad had been offered a post as a flight instructor, but refused it. In September he was sent to Europe to fly fighter missions. That fall he sent

home a photo of himself in uniform standing in front of a P-47. I took the photo and showed it to the kids in school. . . .

I was in the lobby [of our apartment building], shortly after Christmas 1944, excited that I had a week off from school. I'd picked up our paper off the pile, tucked it under my arm, and was waiting for the elevator.

Mr. Lindblum, the building superintendent, came in. He was an old friend who sometimes let me run the elevator and use his workshop in the basement. He stopped by the telephone switchboard when he saw me.

"Dickie, I'm sorry. You know how I felt about Brad. I don't know what to say."

I stood there, staring at him. He didn't realize he was the first to tell me that Brad was dead. I took the newspaper from under my arm, opened it up, and held it in front of my face, pretending to read it. I didn't say anything. I kept turning the pages.

Dick Clark, who was 14 in June 1943, Rock, Roll and Remember, *pp. 14–16.*

There are a great many disruptions of homes . . . which are causing serious harm to the physical and mental health of children. I refer to those families in which fathers are away and the mothers are working in war factories. The children of all ages are left home without adequate supervision or general care. Mothers go home after 8 hours of work, 6 days a week, and often do the family washing and heavy housework. They are tired, and often cannot help being irritable toward their children.

Bert I. Beverly, July 1943, "Effect of War Upon the Minds of Children," p. 794.

Small children have no conception of war. To them Hitler is analogous to the "bogeyman" and other supernatural symbols. Their mental health depends upon the security they feel in their parents and home. When father is out of the home for long hours because of work or being away from home, their security depends upon mother's ability to take charge and make them feel that everything is all right. Those mothers whom I have observed are doing a remarkably fine job of managing their families without the aid of their husbands. . . .

Children of school age . . . are old enough to have a concrete conception of war. They think more about bombings and what may happen to them. Possible loss

The McLellands of Escambia Farms, Florida, inspect their victory garden on a Sunday in June 1942. *(Library of Congress)*

of home, less food and clothing, are of real concern to them. They are afraid that father who is in the army may be killed.

During the ages of 9 to 13 years there are fewer serious anxieties, according to the experience of the British, than in younger or older children. During this period youngsters like to dramatize events in life and thereby act out their feelings. In this way, a part of their tension is relieved. Although they are scared, the idea of war appeals to them.

Bert I. Beverly, July 1943, "Effect of War Upon the Minds of Children," pp. 794–95.

In the intermediate grades (grades four, five, and six) the children could think of many reasons for hating the Japanese as a nation or as an army. These reasons for hating Japan are indicated in some detail to show the vari-

ety of response in the list of answers to a test question, "Which enemy do you dislike most? Why?" The following reasons were expressed by some of the children:

Because of Pearl Harbor

They are uncivilized

They torture other men

They kill women and children

They burned Pearl Harbor—a sneak attack

Because they are the enemy

They do not fight fair

They cheat

Because they are hard

They are the cruelest and the most unjust. . . .

In response to the test question, "Which enemy do you dislike most? Why?" some of the children named Germany and gave these reasons:

Because they rob other nations

Because they starve and kill their conquered nations

Because they have captured more countries and kill people for doing nothing

Each block has a spy and children report on their own parents

Because they started it all

It is the source of Naziism

Because it is vile

Pauline Jeidy reporting on her research among California schoolchildren, August 1943, "Reactions of Children of Different Age Levels to War and Their Implications for Teachers," pp. 14–15.

Children feel what we think long before they can hear and understand what we say. Words used to cover true feelings do not deceive them for any length of time. To make the children feel secure and safe we must feel secure and safe in our souls. Under the circumstances that is easier said than done and yet, for the sake of the children, it must be done.

Don't distress yourself more than you can help. Listening to every report that comes over the air, one contradicting the other in fast succession, only makes one confused, and that feeling is passed on to the children and makes them afraid. To listen to the radio news once a day is sufficient. Usually the evening report is as close to the facts as we can get.

Angelo Patri, 1943, Your Children in Wartime, *p. 6.*

The children who suffer most during wartime are the adolescents. They are keenly alive to all that goes on about them. They miss nothing of the news, excitement, and drama of the day. They are sensitive and eager to know all about the battles and the men who fight them. Many of them want to get into the service and share the adventures so glamorously depicted on the radio and in the news. Many, indeed most of them, are frightened, and their excitement is hiding it even from themselves.

These children must be steadied by the quiet, strong assurance of their parents. Words alone will not accomplish this, but occupation that is useful will. Each older boy and girl should be kept busy at worthwhile work for the duration at least. Busy children are happy, and happy children have a hold on health that even a war fails to loosen.

Angelo Patri, 1943, Your Children in Wartime, *pp. 7–8.*

Even more serious throughout the whole country than the care of the infants whose mothers are at work is the protection of the school-age child, the "door-key children" who roam the streets by day and by night without parental supervision.

Mothers will make some sort of provision for the baby, however inadequate, but the fate of the school child was summed up for me by a woman taxi driver, "I have five children under 14 years of age. My mother takes care of the youngest, but the older ones go to school, so they have to take care of themselves."

Agnes E. Meyer, 1944, Journey through Chaos, *pp. 15–16.*

. . . [T]he schools at Inkster, Wayne, and other small villages already have two or three sessions daily of three hours each. In Ypsilanti, although there are no double sessions, there is overcrowding of 170 per cent. A new school of six rooms was constructed in the township which was immediately filled with over 400 pupils. Even with the best teaching, education under such conditions is a farce. In Inkster the stove in the colored school was defective. This school had to be closed during cold weather. The truancy rate in some districts has gone up 300 per cent.

Agnes E. Meyer describing school overcrowding in the Detroit suburbs, 1944, Journey through Chaos, *p. 36.*

Zoot-suiters can be found in most of the larger American cities . . . but they seem to be most numerous and most annoying to the authorities in Los Angeles and Detroit. The movement is not new. It has developed out of groups whose main objective was enjoyment of expressional orgies in the jitter bug dance, and for a large number of participants it still retains this meaning.

In some places this orgiastic tendency increased in vehemence and intensity. The original enjoyment of the dance was replaced by an interest in tough-guy behavior, in alcoholic excesses, in uninhibited and ostentatious sex behavior.

Agnes E. Meyer, 1944, Journey through Chaos, *p. 246.*

Two weeks after the enlistment of his 18 year old brother, [an] 11 year old boy, the third of seven children in the family, suddenly carried out his decision to transfer from parochial to public school. He attended the latter only two days before he began to cry whenever his mother tried to force him to go to school and defiantly stated that nobody could make him go. He

The zoot suit symbolized youthful rebellion during the years of World War II. The suit's long coattails and watch chain were designed to fly out from the wearer's body when he danced the jitterbug. *(Library of Congress)*

also threatened to run away, jump out of the window or kill himself. He had always been extremely fond of his enlisted brother whom the mother considered had taken the place of a good father to him, as the rather elderly father was always too tired or cross to be bothered to play with the children. The brother had spent a great deal of time with the boy and took much interest in his daily life. . . . During treatment when the psychiatrist first mentioned the brother's name, "the boy sat with tears streaming down his face, utterly lost in his misery. He gave the impression of being in a depressed state, was unable to answer questions or say anything, and kept on weeping for several minutes. When he finally dried his tears, he said simply that his brother had gone into the army. When the psychiatrist commented that he liked his brother very much, the boy began to cry again."

George E. Gardner and Harvey Spencer, January 1944, "Reactions of Children with Fathers and Brothers in the Armed Forces," pp. 37–38.

Since [the bombing of Hiroshima] I have hardly been able to smile, the future seems so utterly grim for our two little boys. Most of the time I have been in tears or near-tears, and fleeting but torturous regrets that I have brought children into the world to face such a dreadful thing as this have shivered through me. It seems that it will be for them all their lives like living on a keg of dynamite which may go off at any moment, and which undoubtedly will go off before their lives have progressed very far.

A mother of two small boys in a letter to radio news commentator H. V. Kaltenborn, August 13, 1945, in Paul Boyer, By the Bomb's Early Light, *p. 16.*

The war is over! Completely! Today is V-J Day. . . . Just think, nine days ago people were prepared for a long long war but that was before they discovered the Atom Bomb. It is a bomb about the size of a baseball[,] some say. . . . One of those bombs would completely destroy Elkhart. At least most of it. . . . Japan has unconditionally surrendered. . . . Daddy, Pat, Mother, Grandma, & I went downtown & everybody was going stark, raving, hysterically mad. The street was jammed. People were yelling, honking horns. . . . Everybody was happy . . . except the loved ones of those 152 Elkhart boys who sacraficed [sic] all they had. . . . We laugh and cry, we honk horns, yell and throw things, and we go to church and pray. The war is over. All wars are over[,] we hope.

Janet Sollet of Elkhart, Indiana, August 14, 1945, in William M. Tuttle, Jr., "Daddy's Gone to War," p. 214.

I was seven when my father came home. Because I had not really known him before he left for the Army, I could not tell how the war had affected him. My father for whom I am named was loud and regaled in storytelling; he liked to laugh, and I enjoyed him when he was having fun. Around him, however, I was usually very shy; I was an outgoing boy and very active, but I think he scared me. We had missed important years together, and we never bridged the gap.

William M. Tuttle, Jr., whose father returned from active duty in the fall of 1945, "Daddy's Gone to War," p. vii.

I always regret that my father was buried overseas. You need to know where a person is. If you are a child and you don't know where your father is, then he could be walking around anywhere. As a child, I always used to have this image that my dad would just come walking up the street and that he would have been a prisoner of war, gotten lost, or something.

Anna Moloney Black, whose father was killed in Germany in 1945, in Calvin L. Christman, ed., Lost in the Victory, *p. 15.*

11

The Baby-Boom Generation
1946–1970

The U.S. birthrate, which had been lower in the 1930s than in any other decade in history, began to rise in 1941. Each month, more babies were born than in the month before. More were born in September 1942 than in any previous month since February 1924, and in 1943 the yearly total of births reached 3 million for the first time.

The uncertainty of life in wartime was one reason for the increase. Men and women married and had children impetuously, not knowing if they would have a life together once peace returned or whether their babies might grow up fatherless. At least in the early months of the war, some young men sought parenthood as a way to avoid military service. Another reason for the increase was the improving economy: Women who had postponed childbearing because of the depression decided that they could afford to have babies in this period of full employment. Although they began to have children relatively late in life, many of these women went on to have large families.

The rise in the birthrate during World War II was just a preview of what would happen in peacetime. With the return of 16 million GIs, the U.S. marriage rate reached a high in 1946 of 118.1 per 1,000 unmarried females over age 14, and the number of births began to soar. In 1946, total births in the United States reached 3.4 million; in 1954 they hit the 4-million mark, and they would remain at that level through 1964. Men and women were marrying at younger ages than Americans did in previous years, and a healthy postwar economy permitted them to have more children than their parents or grandparents did. The result was a population anomaly known as the baby boom. More than 76 million Americans were born between 1946 and 1964—more than in any other 19-year period before or since. Social scientists and the media focused unprecedented attention on this enormous generation as it passed through childhood and adolescence. The baby boomers as a group were healthier, better clothed, and better housed than any previous generation. They profoundly influenced how and where Americans lived and how they spent their money—and they put their mark on American fashion, music, and politics.

235

THE GROWTH OF SUBURBIA

The most urgent need of millions of families formed in the aftermath of World War II was housing. The babies were arriving, and there was nothing for sale or rent. Six million young families moved in with relatives, as people had done during the depression, but couples eager to make children the focus of family life wanted houses with backyards on quiet streets where the young could breathe fresh air and where the neighbors were people much like themselves.

The U.S. government indirectly aided the housing industry when it made funds for mortgages available to the Federal Housing Administration and, as a provision of the Servicemen's Readjustment Act of 1944, created a mortgage program for returning GIs through the Veterans Administration. Astute building contractors saw an opportunity for big profits and went to work. Single-family housing starts rose from 114,000 in 1944 to 937,000 in 1946 and to 1,692,000 in 1950. Subdivisions in the suburbs of metropolitan areas accounted for most of the new construction (75 percent in 1955), and large companies put up most of those subdivisions.

No residential contracting firm of the postwar era achieved greater notoriety than that of Abraham Levitt and his sons William and Alfred, builders of housing for defense workers during the war. In 1946, William Levitt acquired 4,000 acres of farmland in Nassau County, Long Island. The company brought in bulldozers, construction crews, and truckloads of materials to build Levittown, New York, the largest private housing development in U.S. history.

The concrete-slab Cape Cod houses of Levittown went up with assembly-line precision, with crews assigned to perform tasks, such as roofing, painting, or laying asphalt tile. These crews completed 30 or more homes a day when operating at peak efficiency. Three hundred houses were ready for occupancy in October 1947; eventually there would be 17,447 houses that in 1960 sheltered 82,000 people. The development proved so successful that the Levitts built a second one near Philadelphia in the 1950s and a third near Willingboro, New Jersey, in the 1960s.

The three Levittowns and other subdivisions built following World War II appealed overwhelmingly to young, white families with small children. The Levitts refused to sell houses to African Americans through the mid–1960s, and realtors handling resales were quietly discriminatory. In 1960, not one African American lived in Levittown, New York.

Critics of suburban life faulted the subdivisions for the homogeneity of their population and for the "cookie-cutter" sameness of their architecture. There was minimal variation among the houses in one subdivision or among subdivisions nationwide. In the Northeast, Midwest, and Southwest, Americans were moving into nearly identical Cape Cods, ranches, and split-levels that the critics said stifled individuality.

Yet suburban mothers were being instructed to view their infants and toddlers as unique human beings with particular needs, to get to know their children as individuals, and to trust their own parental instincts when responding to a child's cries or demands. Millions relied on advice from a Connecticut pediatrician, Dr. Benjamin Spock. Spock's easy-to-read manual, *The Common Sense Book of Baby and Child Care,* first published in 1946, would outsell any other book in the United States except the Bible. By 1952,

Americans had bought 4 million copies of Spock's book; by 1980, sales world-wide would reach 30 million.

As he counseled parents on treating fevers and teaching babies to sleep through the night, Spock supported the move away from detached, schedule-driven child care and toward a relaxed, affectionate approach. He went a step further than C. Anderson Aldrich, the physician-author of the 1938 book *Babies Are Human Beings,* in cautioning that inflexible methods could cause psychological harm.

THREATS TO PHYSICAL WELL-BEING

Most parents of the postwar era would have agreed, though, that communicable diseases posed a more immediate threat to their children than neuroses or phobias. And no disease frightened these parents more than poliomyelitis, with its power to disable or kill. There was no remedy for this viral illness that destroyed nerve cells controlling muscle movement. Doctors and nurses could do little more than keep a patient's muscles relaxed and wait for the disease to take its course. Children undergoing treatment were separated from their families and endured a long convalescence. Those who survived might be left with paralysis; if the disease attacked nerves controlling respiration, they might be forced to live out their lives in an iron lung.

The United States experienced epidemics of polio before and during World War II, but the epidemics of the 1950s were more severe. More than 33,000 children contracted polio in 1950; 58,000 cases were reported in 1952. Parents felt powerless against this cruel disease, which seemed to choose its victims randomly. In summer, when the number of cases climbed, they kept their children away from swimming pools and movie theaters, hoping to avoid contagion.

In 1952, the American epidemiologist Jonas Salk and his research team developed a polio vaccine prepared from inactive virus. After wide-scale field testing showed the vaccine to be safe and effective, it was approved for use in the United States on April 12, 1955, and a program of mass inoculation began. By 1959, the number of new cases of paralytic polio reported in the United States had dropped to 3,190. Meanwhile, Albert Sabin, an American virologist, was perfecting an oral vaccine containing live virus. After Sabin's vaccine was licensed in 1963, it replaced the Salk vaccine as the standard method of immunization in the United States. By 1970, polio had been virtually eliminated throughout the nation.

The worst epidemics of measles in the United States and Canada also occurred among the children of the baby boom, simply because there was such a large young population lacking immunity. Measles swept across North America approximately every two years and usually in the winter and early spring, when children were cooped up together in classrooms. About 90 percent of Americans were infected with measles by age 20, and more than 400 children died from complications of the disease every year. The first measles vaccine was introduced in 1963, and once immunization was widespread, the number of new cases declined dramatically. Before 1963, U.S. public health officials received reports of approximately 400,000 cases of measles every year, but they suspected that most cases went unreported and that the actual total was closer to 4 million. In 1991, only 9,600 cases of measles were reported in the United States.

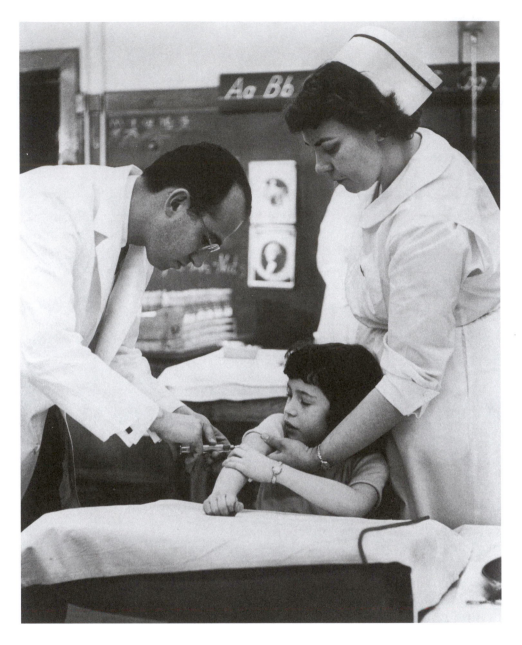

Jonas Salk inoculates a child at the Colfax School, Pittsburgh, with the polio vaccine that he developed. *(March of Dimes Birth Defects Foundation)*

IN THE SHADOW OF THE MUSHROOM CLOUD

Harder to wipe out than any childhood disease was a condition that was a legacy of World War II: anxiety about atomic weapons. With the end of the military conflict, the world had entered the era of the cold war, a period of intense rivalry that pitted the Soviet Union and nations in its sphere of influence against the United States and its allies. The conflict arose from the opposing and irreconcilable political, economic, and social goals of the two groups.

Americans worried about the possibility of nuclear war after the Soviets tested their first atomic warhead in 1949, the same year Communists gained control of mainland China. They continued to worry as communist and U.S. forces engaged militarily in the Korean War, which was fought between 1950 and 1953 and ended indecisively.

A decade later, in 1962, U.S. leaders learned that the Soviet Union had installed in Cuba nuclear-armed missiles that could reach much of the eastern United States. On October 22, President John F. Kennedy announced that he had ordered a naval blockade of Cuba and that U.S. forces would seize any additional weapons that the Soviets attempted to bring onto the island. On that date the world was closer to nuclear war than on any other day before or since. Children and adults waited tensely to learn how the standoff would end. At last, on October 28, Soviet Premier Nikita Khrushchev announced that his nation would halt construction of its Cuban missile sites and remove all of its missiles from Cuba.

The children of the 1950s and early 1960s listened for air-raid sirens as they lay falling asleep; they waited, even as they played, for the blinding flash of light that they knew, from the civil defense films shown in school, might be their only warning of a nuclear explosion. In classrooms, these children practiced a survival tactic called "duck and cover." Crouching under desks, they tucked in their heads and folded their hands over their necks as protection from flying debris.

SCHOOLS: NEW AND CROWDED

The schools where most children watched those black-and-white 16-millimeter civil defense films had been hastily built to accommodate them. Even in the emerging suburbs, the magnitude of the baby boom took community leaders by surprise when the first of these children registered for school. Nationwide, the class of children entering kindergarten in 1951 was 38 percent larger than the class preceding it. Fifty thousand additional classrooms were built by the following September, but they were too few to accommodate the 2 million children starting school that year.

Well into the next decade, school districts scrambled to keep up with the swelling school-age population. In California in the 1950s, one school opened each week, on average. By the mid-1960s, Los Angeles was budgeting more than $50 million a year for school construction. Still, 60 percent of classes in the United States were overcrowded. Students shared textbooks, and schools operated on split sessions so that two classes might use one classroom, one in the morning and the other in the afternoon. Teachers, too, were in short supply. In 1959, almost 100,000 of the 1.3 million teachers employed in public schools lacked the required credentials. Not until 1970 would enrollment in U.S. elementary and secondary schools peak at 51.3 million.

What were the children learning? Adults scrutinized the public-school curriculum after the Soviet Union launched two satellites in the fall of 1959. The first, *Sputnik,* was a 184-pound spiked ball that circled the earth every 1.5 hours; *Sputnik II* circled the earth and carried a dog. Shocked that their cold-war adversary had been first in space, Americans were desperate to catch up. People now looked to the schools to nurture future leaders in science and technology but feared that U.S. students had fallen behind their Soviet counterparts. Admiral Hyman G. Rickover, the engineer who developed the first atomic-powered submarine, accused the schools of failing to challenge the brightest young people and therefore putting the United States at a disadvantage in the cold war.

The federal government responded to this perceived emergency with the National Defense Education Act, which President Dwight D. Eisenhower signed on September 2, 1958. This law provided funding to strengthen instruction in science, mathematics, and modern foreign languages. The funds enabled educators to rely more heavily on audiovisual media to interest students in course content and to experiment with new ways of structuring traditional subject matter.

Perhaps the most controversial educational innovation of this era was "new math," which moved the focus of mathematical study away from solving problems and toward gaining a deeper understanding of mathematical concepts. Proponents of new math declared that it expanded students' capability for thought, whereas many parents complained about children who could define an integer but could not add, subtract, or multiply. New math also took some of the blame for the decline in Scholastic Aptitude Test (SAT) scores that occurred after 1963, as the baby boomers began graduating from high school. Scores on this exam, which many colleges consider important in granting admission, reached average highs in 1963 of 478 (verbal) and 502 (mathematics). (The highest possible score for either portion is 800.) Scores then dropped each year through 1979.

The causes of the declining scores were manifold and may not yet have been fully identified. It has been noted, for example, that during these years greater percentages of young people planned to go to college than in years past, and that the population taking the test therefore included a larger proportion of weaker students. Also, more minority students were striving for college, and the inferior schools that they often attended, coupled with culturally biased tests, placed them at a disadvantage.

Another culprit blamed for the decline was television. Most days, the average sixth grader of the 1950s spent 4.5 hours watching TV. As the number of television sets in U.S. households increased from 8,000 in 1946 to 15 million in 1952 and to 50 million in 1959, children spent less time reading and doing homework. Many sat in their living rooms with schoolbooks spread open in their laps and their eyes fastened to the television screen.

From the earliest years of television broadcasting, the networks were aware of the large number of potential viewers represented by the nation's children and developed programs specifically for them. Among the most enduring in the collective memory of the culture are *Howdy Doody, The Mickey Mouse Club,* and *Captain Kangaroo.* Also popular with children were situation comedies that presented an idealized picture of white, middle-class life, such as *The Adventures of Ozzie and Harriet* and *Father Knows Best,* and programs created for adults, which included westerns and police and detective dramas.

Television became the medium through which the children of the baby boom experienced major national and world events. All who were old enough in November 1963 to understand the significance of the assassination of President Kennedy remember where they were when they learned that the president had been shot. They also remember the key images of the next several days from television: Jack Ruby's murder of Lee Harvey Oswald; a dignified Jacqueline Kennedy in black dress and veil; three-year-old John F. Kennedy, Jr., stepping forward to salute his father's passing casket. Several years later, on July 20, 1969, children gathered with their families in front of the television to watch astronauts Neil Armstrong and Edwin "Buzz" Aldrin set foot on the moon.

Two New York City children watch television in 1950. Their father has tried to create a quiet space for reading. *(Library of Congress)*

Adults debated the possible harmful effects of TV viewing after studies began to show a link between exposure to violent programs and aggressive behavior, but the children kept watching. In this way they witnessed numerous fights, murders, and accidents, and by the time they turned 21, most had been exposed to 3,000 commercials.

CHILDREN AS CONSUMERS

The children of the baby boom started influencing the economy as soon as they were born. The diaper industry, which earned $32 million in 1947, was pulling in $50 million a decade later. Producers of children's clothing, baby food, milk, and other foodstuffs also saw their profits rise. It took very little time for manufacturers and the executives of Madison Avenue to recognize the baby-boom generation as a lucrative market. Toy manufacturers created products especially for children and appealed to them directly via television. Commercials persuaded children to insist that their affluent parents buy them Silly Putty, Remco Bulldog Tanks, Slinky toys, and Patty Playpal dolls.

The December 15, 1954, broadcast of the drama "Davy Crockett, Indian Fighter," on the *Disneyland* television show led to a retailing phenomenon: a brief but enormous demand from American children for coonskin caps like the one Crockett wore and other items identified with the TV character. Toy and department stores filled their shelves with Davy Crockett merchandise, including lunch boxes, pencil boxes, pajamas, sweatshirts, glassware, and more. A song recorded by Bill Hayes, "The Ballad of Davy Crockett," was a top-selling record of 1955. Another toy fad of this period was the Hula Hoop®, first produced by Wham-O in 1958. At the height of the craze, the company was manufacturing more than 20,000 of the plastic hoops daily, and 20 million children were twirling them on their hips.

By 1959, research showed that playing with dolls had lost some favor among girls and that it had become only their eighth favorite leisure activity. American girls now preferred such lively pursuits as jumping rope, bicycling, roller-skating, and dressing up. Nevertheless, Barbie, a fashion doll with an exaggerated woman's figure introduced by the Mattel Corporation in that year, was immediately popular. Mattel soon created dolls to interact with Barbie: a boyfriend, Ken; a little sister, Skipper; and a cousin, Francie. Over the next 20 years, Mattel sold 112 million copies of Barbie and the related dolls.

Ohio boys surveyed in 1959 named football as their favorite form of play. Throwing snowballs, bicycling, and playing hide and seek also received many votes. Baseball, the preferred pastime of boys queried in 1898 and 1921, had fallen to ninth in popularity with the Ohio boys. Yet throughout the United States, boys were playing baseball in record numbers. Although in previous years children had sorted themselves into teams and played spontaneous, unsupervised games, increasingly in the 1950s, children's baseball was organized and coached by adults. The 776 Little Leagues operating in the United States in 1950 had expanded by 1960 to 5,700, with more than 1 million teams.

Membership in scouting, another parent-controlled activity, surged as well. There were 766,635 Cub Scouts in 1949 and 1.6 million in 1956. The number of Girl Scouts, including Brownies, expanded from 1.8 million in 1950 to 4 million in 1960. Children's participation in such structured activities as instrumental music lessons and swimming and dance classes increased as well.

Parents oversaw more of their children's leisure, and children became dependent on them for transportation to both scheduled activities and informal gatherings with their friends. Most suburbs had been planned for reliance on the automobile, with schools, shopping centers, parks, and swimming pools located beyond walking distance from housing clusters. The absence of sidewalks made many suburbs unfriendly to walkers, and public transportation was often lacking. As more and more families relied on a second car, the station wagon, built to hold a passel of children and a week's groceries, became a common sight on suburban streets.

DISENCHANTED TEENS

A researcher who questioned young people in Levittown, New Jersey, in 1961, learned that a majority of the community's children—65 percent of sixth graders, for example—liked living there. Satisfaction dropped as children grew older, however, so that only 37 percent of 10th graders had good things to say about life in Levittown.

The opinions expressed in Levittown reflected the thinking of suburban youth nationwide. Subdivisions designed for families with small children failed to meet the needs of teenagers. Teens complained that they had no place to congregate with friends and that the lack of transportation made existing facilities accessible only to the minority with cars.

During the 1950s, the teenage population in the United States grew by 50 percent, increasing from 10 million to 15 million. As in the 1920s, several conditions favored the development of a distinctive youth culture. First, the decade's affluence meant that teenagers had money to spend on clothes, cosmetics, movie tickets, records, and cars. Second, like American-born children of immigrants 30 years earlier, these young people came of age in a different world from that of their parents. The hardships and dust clouds of the Great Depression held little meaning for them; they were growing up under a mushroom cloud. Third, with the majority remaining in high school through graduation, teens allied closely with their peer group and adopted its fashions and mores.

In this decade that valued uniformity and monogamy, girls in bobby socks and ponytails went steady with boys in crew cuts and letter sweaters. Teenagers with artistic inclinations and a need to assert their individuality found themselves ostracized. Many of these misfits identified with the Beats, those young adults living in cities such as New York and San Francisco who scorned the monotony and materialism of middle-class America. The Beats endeavored to live outside the system, to have few possessions, and to pursue intellectual and creative goals.

Despite the culture of conformity, the enduring image of the teen from the 1950s is of the malcontent, personified by the T-shirted, pompadoured James Dean in the film *Rebel Without a Cause* (1955). In that film, Dean played a misunderstood boy from a middle-class family who becomes involved with a gang of delinquents.

Another 1955 film, *Blackboard Jungle,* opened with the song "Rock Around the Clock" playing over the credits. The tune, as performed by Bill Haley and the Comets, had an insistent beat and an exuberance that appealed to youth.

In 1953, up-to-date teenage girls wore dog collars buckled over their socks. A collar worn on the left ankle indicated that a girl was going steady; a collar worn on the right meant that she was playing the field. *(Library of Congress)*

Teens bought 15 million recordings of the song and kept it at number one on the charts for two months, making it rock and roll's first big hit.

Bill Haley and the Comets were a white group, but the music that they played grew out of African-American culture. In 1951, a Cleveland disc jockey named Alan Freed had begun broadcasting rhythmic music by black artists that appealed to a young, white audience. Freed christened this music "rock and roll" and in 1954 brought his program to New York, where he reached more listeners. Radio stations in other U.S. cities were soon producing rock-and-roll programs of their own. Few white teens knew that *rock and roll* was a slang term for sex in the African-American community; they simply knew that they "dug" the music and their elders did not. Rock and roll united them as a generation. By 1956, they were also buying records by Chuck Berry, Little Richard, and other black rock-and-roll artists.

In 1961, Chubby Checker's recording of "The Twist" initiated a dance craze among teens that quickly spread to the adult population. A trend had begun: The young would learn the latest dance, which might be the mashed potato, the pony, or the swim, only to abandon it as soon as their parents picked it up.

Well before teenagers heard "Rock Around the Clock" or danced the twist, Sam Phillips, founder of Sun Records in Memphis, Tennessee, was convinced that a white singer who could duplicate the sound of black performers would become a major star. Phillips found the person he was looking for in Elvis Presley, a young man who had left him an audition tape. In 1954, Sun Records released four singles by Presley that gained him a sizeable following in the South. In 1956, Presley recorded "Heartbreak Hotel," "Don't Be Cruel," and "Love Me Tender," the first three in a string of hits for RCA Victor that made him a national sensation. Presley was a polarizing figure in American society. Young people loved—and mimicked—his greased hair, flashy clothes, and hip-swiveling stage manner, while more conservative oldsters pronounced him untalented, tasteless, and obscene. Presley influenced other rock-and-roll musicians of the 1950s as well as many of the rock and folk musicians who gained popularity in the 1960s. To the teenagers of the mid- and late 1960s, though, he was a relic.

On February 7, 1964, when a Liverpool club band boarded a plane for New York to begin a U.S. tour, young people understood that their music and their culture were being transformed. The hysteria that greeted the Beatles on their arrival was unprecedented in the history of American popular culture. The press labeled it Beatlemania. Crowds of fans—predominantly screaming adolescent girls—swarmed the four musicians wherever they appeared. The Beatles' shaggy hair and mod suits suddenly made the greasers' look passé.

As the Beatles sang innocently and optimistically about holding hands and falling in love, singer-songwriters such as Bob Dylan made young people more aware of racial injustice, the immorality of war, and the perceived hypocrisy of the generation in power. Young people who rejected the post-depression values of their parents came to view the majority of adults as acquisitive—people pursuing material comfort at the expense of self-satisfaction and fairness to others.

REBELS WITH A CAUSE

Because significantly more people were coming of age than in years past, unrest within the ranks of youth was bound to disrupt society. Rebellion began among college students, a group that was living out a prolonged adolescence. Borrowing a tactic from African Americans demonstrating for civil rights, students at the University of California at Berkeley staged a sit-in on October 1, 1964, to protest an arrest by campus police.

Demonstrations on other campuses followed. Many were inspired by university policies, but many more were held to protest U.S. involvement in the Vietnam War. From December 1961, when President Kennedy sent 400 uni-

April 15, 1970: Students hold an antiwar rally in Manhattan's Bryant Park. The coffin (center) represents the Americans who have died in Vietnam. *(AP/Wide World Photos)*

formed military personnel to South Vietnam to help that nation repel invaders from communist North Vietnam, the U.S. military presence in Southeast Asia grew steadily. In August 1964, after North Vietnamese torpedo boats reportedly attacked two U.S. destroyers in the Gulf of Tonkin, Congress passed a resolution calling for the United States to take all necessary measures to repel attacks against U.S. forces and to defend U.S. allies in Southeast Asia. Before Congress repealed the Tonkin Gulf resolution in 1970, Presidents Lyndon B. Johnson and Richard M. Nixon used it to justify redoubling the U.S. military presence in the region.

At the same time, because of the baby boom, more 18-year-olds were eligible for the draft than ever before in the history of the United States. There were 1.4 million eligible 18-year-olds in 1964 and 1.9 million in 1965. Although public-opinion polls showed that a majority of young Americans supported the war effort, a vocal and very visible minority objected to being called to serve, and possibly to die, in a war they believed the United States could not win and in which it did not belong. In one tumultuous year, 1968, there were 221 major demonstrations on U.S. college campuses involving close to 40,000 students. In Chicago, protests coinciding with the 1968 Democratic National Convention led to violent clashes between young demonstrators and police and National Guardsmen wielding clubs, tear gas, and mace. By the time the convention ended, on August 29, 668 protesters had been arrested and an undetermined number had been injured. Police records showed that 192 officers received injuries in the confrontations.

Antiwar protesting resulted in further bloodshed on May 4, 1970, when the National Guard fired on student marchers at Kent State University in Ohio, leaving four dead and nine wounded. Then, in the first minutes of May 15, 1970, two more young people were killed and 12 more wounded when police and the National Guard responded to student rioting at Jackson State College (now Jackson State University) in Jackson, Mississippi.

COME THE REVOLUTION

Whether or not they were politically active, millions of young adults and teenagers expressed their dissatisfaction with adult values by adopting an alternative way of life—becoming hippies and joining what came to be known as the counterculture. Young males and females alike wore long hair, beads, and bell-bottom jeans. Congregating in neighborhoods such as Haight Ashbury in San Francisco and Greenwich Village in New York City, the hippies rejected materialism and competition. They strove to freely express love for their fellow human beings and to expand their consciousness, largely through the use of illegal drugs. Marijuana use became as common among some segments of the youth population as alcohol use was among their parents.

By 1970, an estimated 8 million young Americans had smoked marijuana at least once, and students in high schools and junior high schools were experimenting with it. Although cannabis has since been shown to have addictive properties and to interfere with users' mental functioning, young people who used the drug in the 1960s considered it benign because it did not cause the hangover that followed heavy drinking. Many users, however, went on to experiment with other drugs that were clearly dangerous, especially lysergic acid diethylamide (LSD) and heroin. Negative experiences with the hallucinogen LSD brought on psychotic episodes that landed numerous users in hospital emergency rooms and precipitated some suicides. Heroin, in addition to being highly addictive, carried the risk of overdose and death. The most publicized death from heroin abuse in the years when hippie culture flourished was that of rock and blues singer Janis Joplin on October 4, 1970.

The young people of the counterculture spoke idealistically about an imminent social revolution that would transform the United States into a peaceable nation that met the basic needs of every individual and that took economic power away from large, uncaring corporations and gave it to small business owners.

Adults were deeply divided in their opinions of the younger generation. Some saw the hippie movement as a healthy correction to a society that had veered away from its moral foundation. One such person was Charles Reich, a professor at Yale University who wrote the best-selling book *The Greening of America* (1970). According to Reich, the young had achieved a new level of awareness, called Consciousness III, which embodied freedom, exploration of the self, the pursuit of meaningful goals, honesty, and responsibility. Consciousness III represented progress from Consciousness I, Reich's name for the rugged individualism of the nation's settlers, and Consciousness II, or the conformity of corporate America. Another enthusiast was Benjamin Spock, the pediatrician whose child-care manual had guided the mothers and fathers of many teens and young adults of the 1960s. Spock became active in the antiwar movement and was even arrested for demonstrating.

Spock also received blame for youth's unrest from some of the many critics of the young, who attributed their rebelliousness to permissive upbringing at the hands of parents following his advice. To the people whom President Nixon called the "silent majority," campus demonstrators were spoiled children who failed to appreciate the opportunities that were available to them, boys with long hair were effeminate, and the hippies were immoral and unclean. Some members of society considered antiwar protests to be a sign of disloyalty to the United States. In May 1970, construction workers in New York City responded to the demonstrations by marching in support of the Nixon administration's policies in Vietnam.

Was one adult outlook right and the other wrong? The Woodstock Music and Arts Fair, held on a dairy farm in the Catskill Mountains of New York on August 15, 16, and 17, 1969, made it seem, if only briefly, that the fabled revolution had arrived. Some 400,000 fans—tens of thousands more than had been expected—descended on the site for three days of music by such performers as Jimi Hendrix; Joan Baez; Janis Joplin; Country Joe and the Fish; and Crosby, Stills, and Nash. Throughout the rainy, muddy days of Woodstock, peace and brotherhood prevailed. There were two deaths, two births, and numerous drug arrests, but no violent crimes.

Four months later, on December 24, 1969, when about 300,000 people attended a concert by the Rolling Stones at the Altamont Raceway in Northern California, violence marred the pretty image established at Woodstock. An audience member attempting to reach the stage was stabbed to death by one of the Hell's Angels hired to guard the band.

THE "CULTURALLY DEPRIVED"

Like children in all periods of American history, those born in the postwar years had varied experiences of life in the United States. By 1960, educational researchers had affixed the label "culturally deprived" to children growing up in poverty in ghetto neighborhoods of major cities. These were children in minority groups, predominantly African Americans. Many were the sons and daughters of adults who had recently migrated to northern urban centers from the rural South and were living on public assistance because jobs had proven unobtainable.

Culturally deprived is a misleading term, because poor, young African Americans had a rich cultural heritage, albeit a different one from the white majority. They did lack books and other educational advantages enjoyed by the offspring of the middle class, however, and many had uneducated parents who were unable to help them do homework or prepare for college. These children usually attended inferior schools where they were subject to the prejudices of teachers and administrators. In addition, it often took so much energy for them to cope with poor housing, crime, and the other hardships of their environment that they had little left over for school.

For the majority of African-American children, life in the United States was not significantly better than it had been for black children a century earlier, when the enslaved population gained its freedom.

CHRONICLE OF EVENTS

1943

For the first time, 3 million babies are born in the United States in a single year.

1944

Congress creates a mortgage program for returning GIs through the Servicemen's Readjustment Act.

Construction begins on 114,000 single-family homes.

1946

The U.S. marriage rate is 118.1 per 1,000 unmarried females over 14.

Approximately 3.4 million babies are born in the United States.

Single-family housing starts total 937,000.

William Levitt purchases 4,000 acres in Nassau County, New York.

The Common Sense Book of Baby and Child Care, by Dr. Benjamin Spock, is published.

There are 8,000 television sets in U.S. households.

1947

Earnings in the diaper industry are $32 million.

October: Three hundred homes in Levittown, New York, are ready for occupancy.

1949

The Soviet Union tests its first atomic warhead.

Communists gain control of mainland China.

The Cub Scouts claim 766,635 members.

1950s

One school opens each week in California, on average.

A typical sixth grader spends 4.5 hours a day watching television.

The teenage population increases from 10 million to 15 million during this decade.

1950

Construction begins on 1,692,000 single-family homes.

More than 3 million U.S. children contract polio.

There are 776 Little Leagues in the United States.

Girl Scouts number 1.8 million.

1950–1953

The United States participates in the Korean War.

1951

Thirty-eight percent more children enter kindergarten this year than in 1950.

In Cleveland, Ohio, Alan Freed begins broadcasting lively, rhythmic music by African-American artists, which he christens *rock and roll.*

1952

Four million copies of Dr. Benjamin Spock's child-care manual have been sold.

Approximately 58,000 cases of polio are reported; at the same time, Jonas Salk develops a vaccine from inactive polio virus.

Television sets in U.S. households total 15 million.

1954

There are 4 million births in the United States.

Alan Freed brings his rock-and-roll radio program to New York.

Sun Records releases four songs by Elvis Presley that gain him a southern following.

December 12: The drama "Davy Crockett, Indian Fighter" is broadcast on television, creating a demand for Crockett paraphernalia among children.

1955

Suburban subdivisions account for 75 percent of new-home construction.

Top-selling records include "The Ballad of Davy Crockett" and "Rock Around the Clock."

April 12: The U.S. Food and Drug Administration approves Salk's vaccine for use in the United States; mass inoculation begins.

1956

There are now 1.6 million Cub Scouts.

Elvis Presley's recordings for RCA Victor make him a major star.

1957

The U.S. diaper industry earns $50 million.

1958

Wham-O introduces the Hula Hoop®.

September 2: President Dwight D. Eisenhower signs the National Defense Education Act, providing funding for education in mathematics, science, and modern foreign languages.

1959

The number of new polio cases is 3,190.

The Soviet Union launches two Sputnik satellites.

Nearly 100,000 U.S. teachers lack the required credentials.

There are now 50 million televisions in U.S. households.

The Mattel Corporation introduces the Barbie doll.

1960

In Levittown, New York, 82,000 people live in 17,447 homes; not one of these people is African American.

There are now 5,700 Little Leagues with more than 1 million teams.

Membership in the Girl Scouts reaches 4 million.

1961

Sixty-five percent of sixth graders questioned report that they like living in Levittown, New Jersey; only 37 percent of 10th graders express the same opinion.

The twist becomes a dance craze among teenagers and adults.

December: President John F. Kennedy sends 400 military personnel to South Vietnam.

1962

October 22: After learning that the Soviet Union has installed missiles in Cuba, President Kennedy orders a naval blockade of the island and threatens to seize any additional weapons that the Soviets attempt to bring into Cuba.

October 28: Soviet premier Nikita Khrushchev announces that all Soviet missiles will be removed from Cuba and that missile-base construction will cease.

1963

Albert Sabin's oral polio vaccine is approved for use in the United States.

The first measles vaccine is introduced.

Average SAT scores reach highs of 478 (verbal) and 502 (mathematics).

November 22: President Kennedy is assassinated in Dallas, Texas; children watch the ensuing events on television.

1964

Some 1.4 million 18-year-olds are eligible for the draft.

February 7: The Beatles leave England to tour the United States.

August: North Vietnam torpedoes two U.S. destroyers in the Gulf of Tonkin; Congress responds by passing a resolution calling for the United States to do whatever is necessary to repel enemy attacks and to defend allies in Southeast Asia.

October 1: Students at the University of California at Berkeley hold a sit-in to protest an arrest by campus police.

1965

For the first time since 1954, fewer than 4 million babies are born in the United States.

The number of draft-eligible 18-year-olds is 1.9 million.

1968

Nearly 40,000 college students hold 221 major demonstrations on U.S. campuses.

August: Young people demonstrating outside the Democratic National Convention in Chicago clash with police and the National Guard; 192 officers and an unknown number of demonstrators are injured.

1969

July 20: Astronauts Neil Armstrong and Buzz Aldrin walk on the moon as children watch on television.

August 15–17: The Woodstock Music and Arts Fair draws 400,000 people yet remains a peaceful event.

December 4: A member of the Hell's Angels motorcycle gang murders a disruptive fan at a concert by the Rolling Stones at Altamont Raceway in California.

1970

The threat of polio has been eliminated in the United States.

Enrollment in U.S. elementary and secondary schools peaks at 51.3 million.

Congress repeals the Gulf of Tonkin Resolution.

Approximately 8 million young Americans have tried marijuana.

In his best-selling book, *The Greening of America,* Charles Reich argues that the youth movement represents an emerging level of awareness, Consciousness III.

May: Construction workers march in New York City in support of the government's policies in Vietnam.

May 4: Members of the National Guard fire on protesting students at Kent State University in Ohio, leaving four dead and nine wounded.

May 15: The police and National Guard respond to turmoil at Jackson State College in Mississippi; two young people are killed and 12 are wounded.

October 4: Singer Janis Joplin dies of a heroin overdose.

EYEWITNESS TESTIMONY

The awesome flash of the atomic bomb has shocked thoughtful men into a realization of the social significance of science in a democratic culture. . . .

In the aftermath of war we have to take a second look at the moral constitution of man as embodied or prefigured in children. Here we get a warning glimpse of the race-made and man-made origins of evil. Children can be rude and aggressive. But it would be sadly gratuitous to infer that the failures of adult ways of life are due to the imperfections of children. Sound inheritance greatly reduces these imperfections; and wise management brings the others under control. . . .

A science of man, accordingly, becomes a most creative force in the atomic age. It will heighten and multiply human values. It will diffuse among peoples, among common men, and among leaders of state that increase of intelligibility which is necessary for mutual understanding. In a more sincerely sustained effort to understand children, men and women of maturity will better comprehend themselves and their fellows.

Arnold Gesell and Frances L. Ilg, 1946, The Child from Five to Ten, *pp. 453–54.*

With respect to future trends, it should be noted that epidemics of marriage, like those of measles, are inherently self-terminating. Both measles and marriage are highly immunizing events; and beyond a point, the epidemic dies out for lack of eligible subjects. Having made an extremely heavy drawing on the future's normal quota of eligibles, we are now coming to the end of the supply. Of course there will be a train of remarriages following a huge rise in divorces, for the war has resulted in a host of relatively light cases of matrimony. From the limited point of view of the number of births, however, this reshuffling of spouses is not very important. The avalanche of first births suggests that a large proportion of the war brides who will bear children have already had their first, and the rate of first births will inevitably drop. It is evident that only substantial increases in the higher orders of birth can prevent a sharp decline in the number of babies during the next few years.

Frank W. Notestein, June 1946, "The Facts of Life," p. 76.

Soon you're going to have a baby. Maybe you have one already. You're happy and excited, but if you haven't had much experience, you wonder whether you are going to know how to do a good job. Lately you have been listening more carefully to your friends and relatives when they talk about bringing up a child. You've begun to read articles by experts in the magazines and newspapers. After the baby is born, the doctors and nurses will begin to give you instructions, too. Sometimes it sounds like a very complicated business. . . .

Don't take too seriously all that the neighbors say. Don't be overawed by what the experts say. Don't be afraid to trust your own common sense.

Benjamin Spock, whose influential parenting manual was first published in 1946, Baby and Child Care, *p. 1.*

You'd think from what some people say about babies demanding attention that they come into the world determined to get their parents under their thumb by hook or by crook. This isn't true. Your baby is born to be a reasonable, friendly human being.

Don't be afraid to feed her when you think she's really hungry. If you are mistaken, she'll merely refuse to take much.

Don't be afraid to love her and enjoy her. Every baby needs to be smiled at, talked to, played with, fondled—gently and lovingly—just as much as she needs vitamins and calories. That's what will make her a person who loves people and enjoys life. The baby who doesn't get any loving will grow up cold and unresponsive.

Benjamin Spock, whose influential parenting manual was first published in 1946, Baby and Child Care, *p. 3.*

When the Goldschmidts bought their television in 1946, there were only seven thousand sets in use in the entire country, and theirs was the only one on our block. Within months, the number doubled when the Lubars' living room became the home of a nine-inch set with a slightly better picture, which became an irresistible attraction for all the children on the block. Almost every afternoon we would congregate on the Lubars' front stoop, waiting expectantly, and often vocally, for the invitation to enter, so we could sit cross-legged on the floor and watch the amazing parade of puppets, comedians, and cowboys which marched across their tiny screen.

It was only a matter of time, spurred by embarrassment at our imposition on the Lubars, before every family on our block had a set.

Doris Kearns Goodwin remembering when television came to her Long Island neighborhood in 1946, Wait Till Next Year, *p. 121.*

After breakfast, our energy at its height, we raced our bikes down the street, with playing cards clothespinned to the spokes to simulate the sound of a motorcycle, challenging one another to see how many times we could circle the block without holding on to the handlebars. Carelessly discarding bikes on the nearest lawn, skate keys dangling from multicolored lanyards around our necks, we zipped past each other on roller skates, throwing up our hands and shouting in the sheer exuberance of our performance. Then it was on to our endless games of hide-and-seek. . . .

Our days might have seemed shapeless to an adult, but to us, there seemed a definite rhythm to our activities. When we began to tire, we played potsy, a form of hopscotch, on the sidewalk, leisurely jumped rope, rolled marbles, played jacks, or flipped cards against the stoop to see who could come closest to the bottom stair without actually hitting it.

Doris Kearns Goodwin describing summer days in suburban Long Island ca. 1950, when she was seven, Wait Till Next Year, *p. 54.*

Richland Lane was untrafficked, hushed, planted in great shade trees, and peopled by wonderfully collected children. They were sober, sane, quiet kids, whose older brothers and sisters were away at boarding school or college. Every warm night we played organized games—games that were the sweetest part of those sweet years, that long suspended interval between terror and anger.

On the quiet dead-end side street, among the still brick houses under their old ash trees and oaks, we paced out the ritual evenings. . . . We are silent, waiting or running, spread out on the pale street like chessmen, stilled as priests, relaxed and knowing. Someone hits the ball, someone silent far up the street catches it on the bounce; we move aside, clearing a path. Carefully the batter lays down the bat perpendicular to the street. Carefully the hushed player up the street rolls the ball down to the bat. The rolled ball hits the bat and flies up unpredictably; the batter misses his catch; he and the fielder switch positions. Indian Ball.

Annie Dillard, who grew up in Pittsburgh in the 1950s, An American Childhood, *p. 123.*

The [nuclear] threat was part of our daily lives. We practiced for air raids in elementary school by going into the hallway, since all the classrooms were full of glass and facing out. The boys were instructed to stand against the walls and to arrange their hands and arms in such a way as to protect the face and eyes. The girls were to move to the center of the hall and drop to one knee beside the boys. I didn't know much, but I knew enough to know the probability of protecting us against an atomic bomb was on the order of slim to none. Nonetheless, I faithfully obeyed and took some pride in the protective role given to the boys.

Phil Woods writing about school air raid drills in Pueblo, New Mexico, in the 1950s, "Reciprocal Paranoia," in John Bradley, ed., Learning to Glow, *p. 63.*

We had all been caught up in the polio epidemic: the early neighbor boy who wore one tall shoe, to which his despairing father added another two soles every year; the girl in the iron lung reading her schoolbook in an elaborate series of mirrors while a volunteer waited to turn the page; my friend who limped, my friend who rolled everywhere in a wheelchair, my friend whose arm hung down, Mother's friend who walked with crutches. My beloved dressed-up aunt, Mother's sister, had come to visit one day and, while she was saying hello, flung herself on the couch in tears; her son had it.

Annie Dillard, who grew up in Pittsburgh in the 1950s, An American Childhood, *pp. 167–68.*

I was . . . both a cheerleader and a beatnik, and while the dissident persona chronologically followed the teen enthusiast during my high school years, they were never clearly separate. Glamor and dissidence, apparently contradictory, both drew me. I still wanted to go to the senior prom and to have all that entailed as I boarded the train for Greenwich Village on Sundays. Popularity mattered even as I donned my black tights. I browsed the makeup counter in Woolworth's evaluating lipstick and rouge and eyelash curlers. I was hedging my bets, searching for the gaps, exploring the cultural weak spots, trying to sort out what a girl was supposed to be or might be, constructing a feminine identity for the future.

Wini Breines, who was an adolescent in the 1950s, Young, White, and Miserable, *p. 165.*

Births are at a new high, and show little sign of decreasing. Demographers and sociologists are flabbergasted, as well they might be. For a long time it has been their theory that more prosperous and better-educated people do not have as many children as poorer and more ignorant people. . . .

[P]opulation changes have transformed the American market. There are, for example, 61 per cent more children under five than there were in 1941, and 45 per cent more between five and ten. Makers of children's goods have been feeling the hot wave of demand. Rarely has the toy industry had a summer season like this. It is expanding production and capacity far above previous estimates, and entrepreneurs are springing up like crab grass in August. And the increase in births is a major factor in the continuing demand for new and bigger houses.

Gilbert Burck and Sanford Parker, August 1953,
"The Changing American Market," p. 103.

The new suburbs are matriarchies, yet the children are in effect so dictatorial that a term like *filiarchy* would not be entirely facetious. It is the children who set the basic design; their friendships are translated into the mother's friendships, and these, in turn, to the family's. Fathers just tag along. . . .

Since the children have a way of playing where *they* feel like playing, their congregating areas have not turned out to be exactly where elders planned them to be; in the homes area the backyards would seem ideal, and communal play areas have been built in some of them. But the children will have none of them; they can't use their toy vehicles there and so they play on the lawn and pavements out front. In the court areas the children have amenably played in and around the interior parking bay out of traffic's way; the courts' enclosed "tot yards," however, haven't turned out to be as functional as was expected; in many courts the older children use them as a barricade to keep the younger children *out*.

It is the flow of wheeled juvenile traffic, then, that determines which is to be the functional door; i.e., in the homes, the front door; in the courts, the back door. It determines, further, the route one takes from the functional door; for when wives go visiting with neighbors they gravitate toward the houses within sight and hearing of their children and the telephone.

William M. Whyte, Jr., August 1953, "How the New
Suburbia Socializes," p. 122.

Children spent considerable time watching TV, but there is little evidence that TV has affected their scholastic attainment. Its effect on their use of other communications and entertainment media parallels the effect on their parents. Meals and bedtimes suffer disarrangement, but interest in other recreational and social activities does not appear to have been seriously affected. The "passive" nature of TV viewing and the content of crime and violence in TV programs have been of concern to observers. However, attitudes of both parents and children toward TV are definitely favorable, and parents see many more advantages than disadvantages in it for their children.

Thomas E. Coffin, 1955, "Television's Impact
on Society," p. 639.

Remember when Davy Crockett hit the theaters in 1955? I guess I was in third grade at the time. Suddenly the next day, everybody in my class but me was Davy Crockett. And because I didn't have my coonskin cap and my powder horn, or Old Betsy, my rifle, and the chaps, I was deemed the Mexican leader, Santa Anna. And everybody came after me with the butt ends of their flintlock rifles. And they chased me home from school until I got my parents to buy me a coonskin cap.

Steven Spielberg recalling the Davy Crockett craze of 1955,
in Chris Hayfield, "'1941': Bombs Away," p. 41.

. . . [E]ver since the end of the war, the American birth rate has undergone a metamorphosis which has left [demographers] only slightly less bewildered than the rest of the nation. Whereas it was once expected that the population would stabilize itself at about the 175 million mark, it seems now that by 1975 there will be 220 million Americans.

William Petersen, January 1956, "The New
American Family," p. 1.

The Hula Hoop® fad of 1958 takes over a parking lot. (*Hula Hoop®*
is a registered trademark of Wham-O, Inc.)

. . . [N]o matter what happens to the birth rate, 36 million babies have been born during the past decade. Barring a national calamity on the scale of an atomic war, the vast majority of these will grow to maturity. As they move up into adult life, they will disrupt, one after the other, institutions built to accommodate more modest numbers.

William Petersen, January 1956, "The New American Family," p. 5.

Children between the ages of eight and twelve are eligible to enter the lowest ranks of such organizations as the Girl Guides or the Boy Scouts, and many children become Cubs and Brownies around the age of eight or nine. These groups too are graded by age, and a highly developed and internationally accepted series of symbols marks the child's passing from one age grade to the next, stressing as criteria for progress, factual knowledge, motor skills, and social qualities.

In addition to participating in the institutional activities enumerated above, the five- to twelve-year-old must learn many individual and social skills. This is the age at which adults consider it desirable to begin instruction in piano or some other musical instrument, in figure skating, swimming, eurhythmics, dramatics, art, and, for girls, in dress and general appearance. It is not uncommon for a five-year-old to have had her first "permanent," and for slightly older girls to "plan" their clothes with their mothers.

What is noticeable in the life of the age group between five and twelve is not only the high degree of institutionalized activity at this level, but also the nature of the experiences to which children are introduced at this early age, despite the view, also part of the culture, that "the place for the small child is with his own mother in his own home."

John R. Seeley, R. Alexander Sim, and Elizabeth W. Loosley, who studied life in a new Canadian suburb, 1956, Crestwood Heights, *p. 99.*

The fault for neglecting our talented children lies in deep-seated national attitudes and in faulty educational theories and practices. Unless these are changed, the much-needed contributions of many potential scientists, engineers, or other professional persons will be lost. There are not enough young people with above-average minds and we cannot spare any of them. We must make special provision for our talented children. Every American has a legitimate concern with our educational system. Our children are the nation's hostages to the future. Both as parents and as citizens we have no more important job than to insure that all are given the very best education they are capable of absorbing. Never has this been more important than today when we are in danger of being outdistanced in technological developments by Russia.

Hyman G. Rickover, 1959, Education and Freedom, *pp. 111–12.*

The consequence of technological progress is that man must use his mind more and his body less. We still think in terms of a more primitive era; we overvalue physical prowess and undervalue intellectual competence. This has a profound effect on our attitudes toward education. The kind of school which prepares young people adequately for life in a less complicated environment is of little use today. Nor do we need schools that concentrate primarily on adjusting the children of immigrants to this new country; on helping them become Americans quickly and painlessly. Today we must have schools which develop in all children—talented, average, and below average—the highest level of intellectual competence of which they are capable; schools that help young people to understand the complex world of today and how it came to be what it is.

Hyman G. Rickover, 1959, Education and Freedom, *pp. 17–18.*

. . . I was raised in Texas, man, and I was an artist and I had all these ideas and feelings that I'd pick up in books, and my father would talk to me about it, and I'd make up poems and things. And, man, I was the only one I'd ever met. There weren't any others. There just wasn't *anybody,* man, in Port Arthur.

There were a couple of old ladies who used to do watercolors and paint still lifes, and that was it. And I'd look at these books of paintings and go, "Wow!" and I'd try and paint that free, to let it go. . . .

I remember when I read . . . in *Time* magazine about Jack Kerouac, otherwise I'd've never known. I said "Wow!" and split.

Janis Joplin, who was a high-school senior during the 1959–60 school year, in David Dalton, Piece of My Heart, *pp. 161–62.*

Slums in American cities today house families which hold a wide range of values and evidence a variety of behavior patterns. Some are households with female heads and are stable none-the-less; others may be ungrammatical but adhere to high moral standards; still others evidence all the attributes of middle-class behavior and are dedicated to its values, if not recipients of its rewards. All three groups have ambition and talent, but fight an uphill battle in maintaining respectability and achievement for themselves and their children.

Robert Weaver, May 1960, "Human Values of Urban Life," in Frank Reissman, The Culturally Deprived Child, *p. 4.*

I had no choice, it was either going to work or cracking up. I have another week of boring habits, then (when I get the car) I'll start living. I can get out of Levittown and go to other towns where I have many friends. . . . In plain words, a boy shouldn't live here if he is between the ages of 14–17. At this age he is using his adult mind, and that doesn't mean riding a bike or smoking his first cigarette. He wants to be big and popular and go out and live it up. I am just starting the life I want. I couldn't ask for more than being a senior in a brand new high school, with the best of students and teachers, and my car on its way.

A high school senior in Levittown, New Jersey, 1961, in Herbert J. Gans, The Levittowners, *p. 207.*

Levittown, New York: an aerial view *(Library of Congress)*

. . . [A] mother now has a pat answer to that frequent question of childhood, "Mom, what shall I do?" And the child himself more and more comes to use the medium [television] to bridge the gap between things that have to be done or things that he really wants to do, and to substitute for behavior that requires activity, initiative, and effort.

This is the schizoid side of television. It leads not toward human interaction, but rather toward withdrawal into private communion with the picture tube and the private life of fantasy. It is aimed less often at solving the problems of life than escaping from them. It is essentially a passive behavior—something a child surrenders himself to, something that is done to and for him, something that he doesn't have to work for or think about or pay for.

Wilbur Schramm, Jack Lyle, and Edwin P. Barker, 1961, Television in the Lives of Our Children, *p. 58.*

The previous evening's television programs provide an excellent common ground of shared experience for conversation at school. If you can't talk about the new programs or the new stars, you simple aren't up to date with your peer group; thus television has a direct social utility. Some children appear to be quite compulsive about television. They feel vaguely ill at ease when they miss a favorite program, sometimes even when the television set is out of commission for a few days, when one of their favorite performers is off the air for a time, or when they go away from television for a summer vacation. Asked to explain this, one girl said, "It's just as if they were your friends or your family. You miss them when you don't see them." Other children give vague explanations about feeling "out of things," "not doing what the gang's doing," or "missing what you're used to doing."

Wilbur Schramm, Jack Lyle, and Edwin P. Barker, 1961, Television in the Lives of Our Children, *p. 59.*

The Twist just went on and on. Everybody could do it. It took absolutely no artistic skill. All you needed was stamina. It was done at bar mitzvahs, weddings and supermarket openings. Duane Eddy did a Twist album. So did Keely Smith. Everybody jumped on the bandwagon.

People ask me, "What's the most significant period in contemporary music?" And I give them a very bizarre answer. I say it was the day the Twist took over. It had social significance. When the Twist happened, adults could go into drinking establishments and ask for old favorites like "Blue Suede Shoes" and dance unashamedly. Overnight, it was all right to be older and say you liked rock and roll.

Dick Clark reminiscing about the twist craze of 1961,
"How the Twist Discovered Bandstand," in Lynda Rosen
Obst, ed., The Sixties, *p. 43.*

A suburban pediatrician I know received a call from a mother who announced, "Doctor, I'm dreadfully worried about Susie." When the doctor tried to arrange an early appointment to check Susie, this proved to be complicated. "It turns out she can't make it Wednesday and can't make it Thursday," the doctor told me. "Would you know it? This 'dreadfully worried' mother can't bring Susie in for ten days!"

The case of ailing little Susie, who obviously was not sufficiently infirm to be cause for acute concern, spotlights two characteristics of her species. She is, for one thing, over-protected. She is, for another, over-organized and over-loaded with wholesome pastimes.

Peter Wyden, 1962, Suburbia's Coddled Kids, *p. 63.*

I am looked upon as an "odd-ball." I am shunned and derided because we do not do as others do. Our children walk. Their idea of a Sunday afternoon is to walk the three miles to a local shopping center to browse. In the rain they walk, properly outfitted with hats and coats. I neither take them to school nor drive them home. They each have home chores to do. My boys can cook and clean as well as the girls (for this they are labelled "kookies"). They are sternly punished for any and all infractions of the rules but are rewarded (simply, I assure you) for any and all jobs well done. As for grades in school, our attitude is not "get good grades and see what you get." Ours is, "Get poor grades and see what you get." The thing I am trying to ascertain is this . . . do you think that we are being old-fashioned?

A mother of seven living in a Michigan suburb, 1962,
in Peter Wyden, Suburbia's Coddled Kids, *p. 83.*

Fourth grade was the year of rationality, the calm before the storm. Boys still had cooties and dolls still tempted us. That was the year when I got my first Barbie. Perhaps they were produced earlier, but they didn't reach New Hampshire till late that fall, and the stores were always sold out. So at the close of our doll-playing careers there was a sudden dramatic switch in scale from lumpy, round-bellied Betsy Wetsys and stiff-legged little-girl dolls to slim curvy Barbie, just eleven inches tall, with a huge, expensive wardrobe that included a filmy black negligee, and a mouth that made her look as if she'd just swallowed a lemon. Barbie wasn't just a toy, but a way of living that moved us suddenly from tea parties to dates with Ken at the soda shoppe. Our short careers with Barbie, before junior high sent her to the attic, built up our expectations for teen-age life before we had developed the sophistication to go along with them.

Joyce Maynard, who was in the fourth grade in 1963,
Looking Back, *p. 23.*

I had been looking forward to watching my favorite noontime show on television, but now I realized "The Three Stooges" would be canceled. This was the first political event that I can remember which had any importance in my life. . . .

My mother was sitting with my two younger brothers on the living room rug before the television. She was crying. We all got on our knees and asked God to let the president live. The day the caisson went down Pennsylvania Avenue is now only fragments in my memory, but their aura haunts my mind. The day seemed cold, and I remember scuffing my shoes across frozen mud puddles as my family walked to a neighbor's house to watch the procession. The sky was a milky color and there was a scent of smoke from burning leaves. The streets were empty and the air was so still you could hear a dog barking a mile away. I can remember clearly the beat of muffled drums, and a horse caparisoned in black, churning and skittering past the crowds as a young soldier tried to rein it back, riderless and going out of control.

Richard Preston, who was in the fourth grade in November
1963, at the time of the assassination of John F. Kennedy,
"A Yearning for Great Teachers," p. C1.

The [Beatles' concert] at Carnegie Hall was an event like no one had ever witnessed before. The audience was well behaved, well mannered—it was Carnegie Hall and there was tradition to observe—but the screams must have penetrated to the tenth floor. The next day the lady who booked the hall said, "Mr. Bernstein, we would be very glad never to have you play here again." A year earlier, when she had asked me who the Beatles were, I'd said, "It's a phenomenon," never describing what this phenomenon was. She'd bought the explanation, probably thinking it meant a phenomenal violin player.

Sid Bernstein, manager and promoter of musical acts, recalling the Beatles' 1964 Carnegie Hall appearance, "The Beatles Take New York," in Lynda Rosen Obst, ed., The Sixties, *p. 114.*

Between the ages of about 10 and 20, I had fairly regular nightmares about the destruction of the world with nuclear weapons. These dreams almost always began with a flash of dazzling light, followed by a murky series of episodes in which I stumbled through rubble, always looking for someone—a friend, a member of my family, a pet—whom I could never find. Often I was chased by sinister figures, but my legs could hardly move. I would try to warn people that we were in great danger, but my mouth would be locked as if with tetanus.

Richard Preston, who was 10 years old in 1964, "A Yearning for Great Teachers," p. C3.

If I spent at the piano the hours I gave to television, on all those afternoons when I came home from school, I would be an accomplished pianist now. Or if I'd danced, or read, or painted. . . . But I turned on the set instead, every day, almost, every year, and sank into an old green easy chair, smothered in quilts, with a bag of Fritos beside me and a glass of milk to wash them down, facing life and death with Dr. Kildare, laughing at Danny Thomas, whispering the answers—out loud sometimes—with "Password" and "To Tell the Truth." Looking back over all those afternoons, I try to convince myself they weren't wasted. I must have learned something; I must, at least, have changed.

Joyce Maynard writing about her New Hampshire childhood in the mid-1960s, "An Eighteen-Year-Old Looks Back on Life," p. 4.

I hated elementary school. The teachers were narrow-minded. The questions they asked were mundane, uninspired. I wanted the universe and they gave me a rectangle with four sides. I could understand the space within the rectangle, but what about the space beyond the sides? I asked the teachers questions, but the answers they gave me were pat, solved: *Case closed.* I doubted pat answers.

I sat in the back of the class with the trouble-makers. They would make funny noises or throw erasers to disrupt the class and disturb the teacher. I would occasionally raise my hand to point out a mistake the teacher had made on the board. The trouble-makers would be momentarily silenced and the entire class would turn around to stare at me. Then the whole class would burst into hysterics. After about two weeks of this, my fifth-grade teacher called my parents in to tell them that I would never be able to handle abstract math. As my parents suspected, and I knew, it was the teacher who was having difficulties with abstract math. She stopped calling on me and passed me into the sixth grade.

John Aristotle Phillips recalling elementary school in North Haven, Connecticut, ca. 1965, Mushroom, *p. 24.*

Eighth grade was groovy. When I think of 1966, I see pink and orange stripes and wild purple paisleys and black and white vibrating to make the head ache. We were too young for drugs (they hadn't reached the junior high yet) but we didn't need them. Our world was psychedelic, our clothes and our make-up and our jewelry and our hair styles were trips in themselves. It was the year of the gimmick, and what mattered was being noticed, which meant being wild and mod and having the shortest skirt and the whitest Yardley Slicker lips and the dangliest earrings. (We all pierced our ears that year. You can tell the girls of 1966—they're the ones with not-quite-healed-over holes in their ears.)

Joyce Maynard recalling the fashions of 1966, when she was in the eighth grade, "An Eighteen-Year-Old Looks Back on Life," p. 7.

"Why?" asks the distraught father as he trudges through the Haight-Ashbury [section of San Francisco] searching for his runaway daughter. "Why?" ask the puzzled police and health authorities as they watch bright youngsters from good homes live together in filthy, vermin-infested pads in the slums of New York, Chicago and Boston. "Why? Why?" ask more and more middle-aged Americans as they see kids outfit themselves in bizarre trappings and spurn the customs and moral codes which have always been accepted as the very foundations of a healthy and stable society.

Why? The frequency of that question proves that there are no easy and simple answers. Obviously the nation's young are vastly dissatisfied with a great many aspects of the American scene, from its foreign policy to its moral values. Indeed, the glee or sympathy with which most young people have accepted hippies, even when they have withstood the lure to join them, suggests that some kind of social change may be in the making.

Judson Gooding, "Revolution or Revival?" 1967, in Joe David Brown, ed., The Hippies, *p. 191.*

Children, it cannot be too often said, want their parents to be parents, not *pals.* They expect and want discipline. They want as firm a "Nay" as a "Yea." They want guidance, not a debating society in which everyone is equal. Children want parents to whom they can look up, not on whom they can look down. They want parents whose judgments they can respect and whose examples they can follow. . . . Too many parents are really afraid of their children. They are so afraid of doing the wrong thing that they do what is most pleasing, in their view, to the child. What is most pleasing to the child may be extremely undesirable for his healthy development as a human being.

Ashley Montagu, 1967, The American Way of Life, *pp. 215–16.*

Teen-agers have virtually declared their independence of the adult world. And in all this they are encouraged by a catering agent of the adult world, the world of business. The teen-ager is very big business. . . .

Such phenomena as James Dean, the Beatles and their innumerable imitators, Joan Baez, and Bob Dylan would be impossible without the support of teen-agers. The magazines that cater to the needs of teen-agers constitute a very profitable industry, and a large number of TV programs are designed for the same market. So while the adult world of parents criticizes teen-agers on the one hand, the business world, on the other, gives them all the support and encouragement they need to go on doing all that the world of parental figures disapproves.

The truth is that teen-agers are the scapegoats of adults. Adults expect teen-agers to be problems, and so they specify the conditions and the behavior they expect them to exhibit, in a self-fulfilling prophecy, and that is exactly what they get.

Ashley Montagu, 1967, The American Way of Life, *pp. 222–23.*

We were all stoned, really stoned. And this girl friend of mine had O.D.'d on something, and no one knew what it was. So someone called the hospital, and while we were waiting for the ambulance and police to come, I was sitting there trying to hold her. I remember thinking, Oh, my God, the insanity, the absolute insanity.

A Los Angeles woman remembering a high school drug party in the late 1960s, in Landon Y. Jones, Great Expectations, *p. 113.*

I was walking in Golden Gate Park in San Francisco, around the museums and aquariums which form the borders of an ornate square. In the middle of the square is a fancy fountain encircled by a small wall. The summer's tourists—in golf-hat, sun-visor, camera-and-light-meter uniform—were taking in the sights. Suddenly three figures jumped up on the wall of the fountain and began to dance rhythmically around it in time to the melody played by one of the members of the troupe on his flute. The tourists tried to figure out the sexes of the three minstrels. Their children pointed out that the one in jeans with shoulder-length hair was a girl, while the one with hair down to his waist, and the flutist with a water gourd around *his* waist, were boys. The cameras, which had been mostly idle before, started clicking—not at the edifices, not at the alligator holes or porpoises and turtles in the aquarium, but at the weird kids around the fountain. Now there was really something to show the folks back home!

Mark Gerzon, 1969, The Whole World Is Watching, *p. 56.*

This generation finds it difficult to be satisfied with the meaning derived from traditional cultural orientations and goals. The number of young men who are choosing jobs simply because of the size of the salary has diminished greatly. Young people today ask for some inherent value in their work, not just for monetary reimbursement. They know they personally can have enough money to live satisfactorily, and so they must find other criteria besides the size of the paycheck for selecting an occupation.

Mark Gerzon, 1969, The Whole World Is Watching, *p. 19.*

When I was about fifteen, I began to realize that with my parents, everything was for show. They knew the titles of all the books and the names of all the great composers and their works, and one day I realized they never read the books and seldom listened to the music. The more I became conscious of how they really lived, the more I hated it. Both mother and dad are afraid to grow old, and each fights it in his own irrational way. I didn't want to be like that. I started reading like mad. . . . I listened to a lot of music. And I got so I really wanted to feel and hear and sense everything, and in high school I started using pot. Later, I got onto LSD. . . .

Steve Winston, a 22-year-old college student, 1969, in Robert C. Albrook, "Parenthood Today Is No Bore!" p. 117.

There is a revolution coming. It will not be like revolutions of the past. It will originate with the individual and with culture, and it will change the political structure only as its final act. It will not require violence to succeed, and it cannot be successfully resisted by violence. It is now spreading with amazing rapidity, and already our laws, institutions and social structure are changing in consequence. It promises a higher reason, a more human community, and a new and liberated individual. Its ultimate creation will be a new and enduring wholeness and beauty—a renewed relationship of man to himself, to other men, to society, to nature, and to the land.

This is the revolution of the new generation. Their protest and rebellion, their culture, clothes, music, drugs, ways of thought, and liberated life-style are not a passing fad or a form of dissent and refusal, nor are they in any sense irrational. The whole emerging pattern, from ideals to campus demonstrations to beads and bell bottoms to the Woodstock Festival, makes sense and is part of a consistent philosophy. It is both necessary and inevitable, and in time it will include not only youth, but all people in America.

Charles A. Reich, 1970, The Greening of America, *p. 4.*

. . . [O]ur kids, I think, on the whole, constitute a marvelous generation. . . .

We disavow, and criticize, and oppose our youngsters because of the way they comb their hair, and the way they dress. Well, I think we've got to go deeper than that, and look and see what's in their hearts and minds and souls, and not judge them on their exterior appearances.

. . . I also believe it's quite likely that these youngsters are the finest patriots we've ever had. Now this may shock a few of the older generation. But these youngsters of ours, I believe, do genuinely care about this country. They really care about what it's going to look like, and what its status is in the world, and what our political institutions are, and how they're going to thrive and endure.

For example, these kids care about us, they care about each other, they care about their fellow man. They have heard us talking about the brotherhood of man, and they bought it. And now they're pointing to us and saying to us elders, "All right, we believe you. We believe all you've said about the brotherhood of man. Now how about you living up to the code that you've been talking about?"

Chet Huntley, 1970, in David Frost, The Americans, *pp. 185–86.*

12

Hearts and Minds: African-American Children Face Challenges
1865–1990

The Thirteenth Amendment to the Constitution, ratified on December 6, 1865, outlawed slavery and involuntary servitude in the United States. It gave the former slaves full responsibility for themselves; they now had the right to choose where they would live and what kind of work they would do, and to make decisions regarding the welfare of their children.

The slaves greeted freedom with laughter and tears, dancing and song, but as the celebrations wound down, the foremost task for many men and women became locating sons and daughters who had been sold away from them. People traveled the country on foot inquiring about their children or advertised for them in newspapers. Some searches proved fruitful, while others met with less success. Many parents discovered that trails had gone cold or children had died, and they had to content themselves with faith in a heavenly reunion.

Vengeful whites hampered search efforts by demanding money for children or refusing to relinquish them to their biological parents until they reached maturity. Slave marriages had been performed without legal sanction, and any children born to such unions could therefore be considered orphans under the law. Wasting no time, some planters bound young African Americans into apprenticeships in order to retain them as laborers.

Throughout the South, thousands of African-American children were apprenticed in the months following the Civil War. Most were between the ages of 10 and 13, old enough to be valued as workers. Parents correctly viewed these apprenticeships as an extension of slavery. Not only did many employers fail to provide the wages, clothing, and schooling called for in apprenticeship contracts, but they subjected the children to brutal punishments as well.

A great many frustrated parents sought assistance from the Freedmen's Bureau, a federal agency formed in March 1865 to help African Americans make the transition from slavery to freedom. The Freedmen's Bureau found shelter for people who were displaced in the aftermath of war, negotiated labor contracts for workers formerly enslaved, and distributed food and medicine to the needy. With no clear directive from Washington on the issue of parental rights, though, bureau agents hesitated to interfere in disputes between parents and plantation owners. It was their job to represent the interests of the ex-slaves, but they were also under pressure to keep African Americans employed and minimize vagrancy. Apprenticeship frequently seemed a better alternative than returning young people to parents who might be unable to support them.

Like private agencies such as the American Missionary Association, the Freedmen's Bureau established schools for African Americans in the South. These schools held classes in the daytime, at night, or on Sundays, offering academic or industrial courses. The bureau acquired and furnished school buildings but relied on northern religious and charitable groups to supply teachers. By 1869, there were 9,503 teachers at work in southern freedmen's schools, most of them young white women. In 1870, when the Freedmen's Bureau discontinued its educational activities due to a lack of funds, 4,329 of its schools were serving 247,333 students. The 66 freedmen's schools in Texas had provided at least some instruction to 20,000 people.

This student body represented just a fraction of the nearly 2 million young blacks living in the United States who were eager for education. Because many parents thirsted for knowledge as well, mothers and fathers at times sat beside their children in classrooms. It was not unusual, too, for youngsters to bring along baby sisters and brothers in their care in order to be present for lessons.

The pupils' ability to learn surprised white teachers who had been taught that science classified people of African descent below whites in intelligence. Between 1860 and 1870, the literacy rate of African Americans increased from 10 percent to 25 percent, in large part because of the work accomplished in these schools. The freedmen's schools also performed the important job of training African-American teachers to take over the instruction of children when the white volunteers returned home.

USING TERROR TO MAINTAIN CONTROL

Southern whites, striving to maintain their antebellum way of life, considered the education of African Americans a dangerous undertaking. These whites feared that too much learning would make African Americans less willing to remain subordinate, especially when northern teachers employed the Emancipation Proclamation and abolitionist tracts as reading texts. Limiting access to education was one reason for the formation of white supremacist organizations such as the Ku Klux Klan, Knights of the White Camelia, and White Brotherhood. These groups used guns, swords, and threats to intimidate any African American who dared to step out of his or her second-class role.

Lynching was another, more horrifying, tool that some southern whites used to keep blacks in line. The exact number of these public murders committed in the second half of the 19th century is unknown. The National Association for the Advancement of Colored People (NAACP) counted 3,324 reported lynchings in the United States between 1889 and 1918; the victims in 2,522 instances were African Americans whose alleged crimes ranged from homicide and felonious assault to insulting a white person. Time and again, law-enforcement officers and the judicial system looked the other way: Between 1880 and 1905, not one person was convicted for taking part in a lynching.

Between 1865 and 1867, southern states enacted "Black Codes"—laws that enforced economic and social segregation. Black Codes specified where African Americans could live and limited their right to testify in court to cases involving members of their own race. Black Codes also included strict vagrancy laws that compelled African Americans to work for menial wages. For that reason, for the rest of the 19th century, many people had no choice but to perform agricultural labor—the only work they had been trained to do—on land owned by whites.

In the years following the Civil War, a black man earned between $9 and $15 a month from a white farmer, and a black woman received between $5 and $10. Children, who frequently helped their parents in the fields, earned less. Share-cropping soon emerged as the predominant method of agriculture in the South, because many landowners lacked cash to pay their workers. Sharecropping families farmed land owned by whites and were paid in a share of the crop that they raised. They were entitled to one-fourth to one-half of the cotton, corn, or tobacco, which they were free to sell. Sharecroppers became indebted to white landowners at the start of the growing season for seed and other supplies, with the understanding that they would satisfy the loan with profits from the harvest. All too often, though, families were left with little cash reserve after paying off what they owed, or they remained in debt.

On the heels of the Black Codes came the "Jim Crow" laws. In 1875, Tennessee was the first southern state to adopt these statutes, which were designed to minimize interaction between the races. Jim Crow laws called for separate public facilities for whites and blacks—separate railroad cars, waiting rooms, restaurants, and schools. Public libraries, such as the one in Jacksonville, Florida, could now require African Americans to sit in their own reading room, away from whites. The U.S. Supreme Court upheld this kind of segregation in 1896 in deciding the case *Plessy v. Ferguson*. The Court specified that facilities for the two races were to be "separate but equal," but nowhere in the South did a community spend on its black population what it did on whites.

Expenditures for white students were consistently higher than for blacks as segregated public school systems were established throughout the South in the early 20th century. In 1916, according to data gathered by the U.S. Bureau of Education, southern school districts spent an average of $10.32 per year on each white student and $2.89 on each black student. There were other inequities in education as well. Communities provided wood-frame or brick schoolhouses for their white children, but black schools were often located in private homes, abandoned cabins, or structures used for other purposes, such as lodge halls and churches. High school in most parts of the South was for whites only; because students were required to complete the eighth grade before moving on to high school, schools for African Americans usually offered no classes beyond grade seven.

EDUCATION: THE GREAT DEBATE

At the turn of the 20th century, African-American thinkers discussed very publicly how education could best serve their race. Booker T. Washington, who in 1881 established the Tuskegee Institute (renamed Tuskegee University in 1985), advocated training in trades and manual skills that would make African Americans useful to whites and therefore more able to gain a place in society. Only then, Washington said, did it make sense for African Americans to pursue professional careers or intellectual or artistic endeavors. At Tuskegee, Washington had put his philosophy into practice. The school offered courses in such trades as carpentry, food preparation, mattress making, and gardening. Washington caused a stir in black intellectual circles in 1895 when, in a speech at the Atlanta Exposition, he said that economic integration might coexist with social segregation. In a statement viewed as an effort to appease the whites in his audience, Washington said that in society blacks and whites could remain "as separate as the five fingers. . . ."

Leading the opposition to Washington's line of thinking was W. E. B. Du Bois of Atlanta University. Du Bois asserted that academic education was essential to racial progress, if only to provide teachers for African-American schools. Du Bois favored educating the brightest young African Americans, whom he called the "Talented Tenth," to serve as community leaders and role models.

As the debate went on, African-American children continued to receive a substandard education in deteriorating schools in the South and in the public-school systems of the North, which practiced segregation by custom rather than by law. Of 2,330 African Americans enrolled in Indianapolis schools in 1909, all but 50 attended segregated schools. At the same time, school administrators in Philadelphia kept African Americans in separate schools for expediency, to more efficiently provide them with an education suited to their perceived aptitudes and limited job potential.

It was not only whites in the North who desired school segregation, however. Many practical middle-class blacks favored the system because the teachers and administrators employed in the African-American schools came from their ranks. But even caring, fair-minded educators wrestled with difficult questions: Was it a disservice to prepare African Americans for careers they would never be permitted to pursue? Would children not be happier with an education that took into account their modest prospects for professional and social advancement?

THE GREAT MIGRATION

Schools for blacks in the North may have been inferior to schools for whites, but they were better than anything the South had to offer. The chance for their children to receive an education, then, was one factor that lured African Americans from the rural South to the urban North in the population shift known as the Great Migration.

People also moved to escape the oppressive racism of the South and exercise their rights as citizens. The principal causes of the Great Migration, though, were economic. An infestation of Mexican cotton boll weevils that began in Texas in 1892 and would spread to North Carolina by 1922 was destroying the sharecroppers' livelihood. At the same time, northern factories were desperate for workers. The outbreak of World War I in Europe had created a demand for American-made munitions, but it had eliminated industry's main source of cheap labor, the immigrants who had been coming in large numbers to northern manufacturing centers.

In a two-year period beginning in 1916 and ending in 1918, 400,000 African Americans—an average of 500 per day—left the South for such cities as Chicago, New York, and Pittsburgh. Chicago's black population rose 148 percent between 1910 and 1920, and Detroit's increased by 611 percent. People traveled by train, bus, and automobile. Frequently, one family member went first to find a job and

In this undated photograph, people newly arrived from the South stand on the stoop of their Philadelphia row house. In the early 20th century, most of Philadelphia's African Americans lived in crowded, dilapidated housing. *(Urban Archives, Temple University, Philadelphia, Pennsylvania)*

prepare a home for the others. A kinship group commonly migrated to the same northern city, so for children the move north included a joyful reunion with cousins, uncles, and aunts.

Conditions in the North seldom matched newcomers' expectations. Excluded from many neighborhoods, they congregated in communities such as the South Side of Chicago and Harlem in New York City. They were forced to live in crowded, rundown housing that often lacked adequate plumbing, and they paid higher rents than whites did for comparable dwellings. It was not uncommon for a family to take in a lodger, usually a single person who was new in town. In cities such as Cleveland, Ohio, where housing was particularly scarce, African-American families occupied abandoned railroad cars, condemned buildings, and empty shacks. Because northern factories hired African-American men almost exclusively for low-level unskilled jobs with no opportunity for advancement, many women had to help support their families. Most did domestic work, which kept them away from home for long periods and left their children unsupervised.

Children alone at home were at risk for injury, but the greatest danger to African-American children in northern cities in the early 20th century was illness. Meager food, inadequate clothing, and crowded conditions facilitated the spread of tuberculosis, pneumonia, and other contagious diseases. Poverty and a lack of good medical care caused the infant mortality rate to be significantly higher among blacks than among whites. Between 1915 and 1919, 150 black babies died for every 1,000 born, while 92.8 white babies died per 1,000 born. Babies commonly succumbed to "summer complaint," or chronic diarrhea caused by consuming contaminated milk or food; whooping cough; pneumonia; and other communicable diseases.

The racial violence that erupted throughout the United States in the late 19th and early 20th centuries affected children as well. Three children died, for example, on February 22, 1898, when a white mob set fire to their Lake City, South Carolina, home and shot at the escaping family. The children's father, who also died, was the town's African-American postmaster. In May 1905, at a time when racial tension was high in Chicago because management had hired nonunion black workers during a teamsters strike, an African American fatally shot an eight-year-old white boy and sparked a week of fighting. The July 27, 1919, stoning and subsequent drowning of Eugene Williams, an African-American youth swimming in Lake Michigan, precipitated the Chicago riot that left 38 people dead.

Because most parents successfully sheltered their children from the fighting, the main effect of the riots on black youngsters' lives was indirect. As fear engendered by the racial violence occurring in the aftermath of World War I strengthened whites' resolve to live apart from blacks, middle-class whites who could afford higher real estate prices left cities for the surrounding suburbs. White immigrant groups that remained in urban areas resisted more strongly than ever attempts by African Americans to move onto their blocks. African Americans who rented or bought homes in white neighborhoods now had their windows and porches smashed, their fence posts pulled out of the ground, and their garages set on fire. In 1926, whites dynamited the house of an African-American physician who had moved into a suburb of Cleveland, hoping to frighten him into relocating. The strategy failed, but it made other African Americans less inclined to move to unfamiliar territory. Thus, partly because of the race riots of the early 20th century, African-American children in the North would grow up in segregated inner-city ghettoes for generations to come.

THE DEPRESSION TOUCHES BLACK AMERICA FIRST

By the late 1920s, many African Americans felt removed from mainstream American life by economic as well as neighborhood boundaries. While much of white America was sailing smoothly on a current of prosperity, black America was encountering the first choppy waters of recession. Black workers were the first to lose their jobs as businesses cut expenses.

Throughout the 1930s, higher percentages of black workers than whites were jobless in every U.S. city. By 1934, the government considered 38 percent of blacks incapable of supporting themselves in any occupation. (Seventeen percent of whites fell into the same category.) African Americans had always earned less than whites, on average, and therefore had been less able to accumulate savings. Many had nothing in reserve when their incomes disappeared. Furthermore, because charitable and relief organizations often served whites only, the distress and deprivation that African-American families experienced could be severe.

African-American sons and daughters, like millions of other children, did whatever they could to earn money and support their families. They were less likely than young whites, however, to withdraw from school. Black families placed a high value on education, and they apparently preferred to do without basic necessities rather than sacrifice their children's schooling. Still, according to one survey conducted in New York City in the 1930s, 21 percent of African

Americans between the ages of 16 and 21 held full-time jobs. Their younger brothers and sisters sold newspapers, shined shoes, and sometimes resorted to theft. Across the nation, African-American juveniles were disproportionately represented in arrest totals during the depression.

Larger percentages of African-American parents also appeared in court on charges of child neglect. The core problem in most cases was not a lack of parental concern but destitution. Nevertheless, the courts committed growing numbers of African-American children to the handful of children's shelters that accepted members of their race. One such place was New York City's Colored Orphan Asylum, which was founded in 1836 by Quaker women. The Colored Orphan Asylum took in boys as old as 14 and girls as old as 12. Like similar shelters, it was filled to capacity by the early 1930s, and it was housing more children who had been exposed to tuberculosis, who were malnourished, or who had emotional or psychological problems than it had done in the past.

Religious and charitable groups that had been founded in earlier decades to assist African Americans now aided children to the extent that their limited finances permitted. Churches and missions opened nursery schools and day care centers for the sons and daughters of working people, served lunches, and organized social activities. In Harlem the Urban League sent children to summer camp and handed out emergency food, clothing, and rent money. The Children's Aid Society had always cared for African Americans, and it continued to do so now, although its services were segregated. In 1932, the Children's Aid Society undertook to feed the 100 hungriest children in Harlem. The society also provided medical and dental care and sponsored Boys' and Girls' Clubs. The Harlem Boys' Club offered training in trades that were open to African Americans, such as cooking, waiting tables, tailoring, and custodial work. The club's officials limited instruction in this way not because they believed that African Americans should remain in traditional occupations but because in this time of economic emergency they wanted to give boys the best possible chance of finding a job. Together these organizations reached only a fraction of the African-American children needing help, but for those children they were a lifeline.

New Deal programs also benefited black youth. Both the National Youth Administration (NYA) and Civilian Conservation Corps (CCC) enrolled African Americans in proportion to their numbers in the population if not to their suffering. Ten percent of the young people employed in the NYA's student programs and 13 percent in its other programs were African American. Approximately 200,000 African-American boys and young men worked for the CCC between 1933 and 1942, although the corps's camps were racially segregated. Other government agencies that helped African-American children and their families included the U.S. Housing Authority (later called the Federal Public Housing Authority), which subsidized the construction of housing projects nationwide, and the Public Works Administration, which built playgrounds, hospitals, and other needed public facilities in African-American neighborhoods.

The institutions that deteriorated most in African-American communities during the depression were schools. Southerners continued to spend less to educate black children than to educate white children. In the school year that began in September 1935, 10 southern states spent an average of $37.87 per white child and $13.09 per black child. African-American schools were forced to let many teachers go; those who kept their jobs saw their salaries sharply reduced. A government study conducted during the late 1930s found that African Americans in many rural areas still had no opportunity to continue their education beyond elementary school.

The schools that African Americans attended in the North were often inferior as well. Only after Harlem exploded in a race riot in March 1935 did the mayor's office look into conditions in New York City's largest black community. The investigators reported on schools that were crowded, rundown firetraps lacking playgrounds and cafeterias. At that time the city had applied for federal funds to build 168 schools, but none were planned for Harlem. As a result of the investigators' report and petitions submitted by parents, the New York City Board of Education allocated money in 1936 for four new schools in Harlem and for repairs to existing school buildings. These measures eased but did not eliminate the shortcomings in the educational system.

CHILDREN AND CIVIL RIGHTS

African-American children in many parts of the United States were still attending second-rate schools in the 1950s, but by then they—and their parents—had begun to seek equality in the federal judicial system.

On May 17, 1954, the U.S. Supreme Court announced its unanimous opinion in the landmark case *Brown v. Board of Education*. Reading the historic decision, Chief Justice Earl Warren stated that "School segregation by law causes a feeling of inferiority in black children." It "inflicts damage to their hearts and minds that may never be undone." The doctrine of "separate but equal," which had been the law of the land since 1896, now had no place in the field of public education.

The court actually had considered collectively six cases involving school segregation. One, of course, was the suit brought by Oliver Brown against the Topeka, Kansas, Board of Education for requiring his daughter Linda to take a long and dangerous walk to a school for black children, when another elementary school—one that admitted whites only—was closer to her home. The other cases were similar: Students at R. R. Moton High School in Farmville, Virginia, for example, had filed a lawsuit asking for improvements to their school and the desegregation of all schools in Farmville. The parents of Spottswood Thomas Bolling, Jr., who had been denied admission to Sousa Junior High School in Washington, D.C., because of his race, had begun legal proceedings as well.

Children were central to this significant legal victory and to other achievements of the civil rights movement of the 1950s and 1960s. They also numbered among the movement's martyrs. Few incidents of injustice have touched the emotions of Americans, black or white, as deeply as the murder of Emmett Till. In August 1955, the 14-year-old Chicagoan was visiting relatives in Money, Mississippi. Egged on by his cousins and friends, he made comments to a white woman that were considered inappropriately forward for a black youth in the South. That night the woman's husband and brother-in-law kidnapped Till from his uncle's home, beat him, shot him behind the ear, smashed his head, and threw him into the Tallahatchie River with a 150-pound cotton-gin fan tied around his neck. Till's mutilated body was returned to Chicago, where his mother insisted it be placed in an open casket for the world to see. His killers were tried in September 1955, but despite clear evidence of their guilt, an all-white jury acquitted them.

Children, many of whom depended on public transportation to get to school, were among the black residents of Montgomery, Alabama, who gave up riding city buses for 13 months beginning in December 1955. Two African-American ministers, Martin Luther King, Jr., and Ralph David Abernathy, organized the boycott after a local woman, Rosa Parks, was arrested on a Montgomery bus for refusing to surrender her seat to a white passenger. In Montgomery and other southern cities, not only were whites given priority in seating, but African Americans had to step off the bus after paying their fare and re-enter through the rear door.

The boycotters were resolved to stay off the buses until the municipal government and the bus company met their three demands: that all passengers be treated with respect; that passengers be seated without regard to race; and that black drivers be hired for routes on which a majority of riders were black.

The months of the boycott were a dangerous time to be black in Montgomery. Bombs exploded at the homes of King and other protest leaders, and neither adults nor children felt safe. Meanwhile, a group of city residents filed suit in federal court, claiming that bus segregation violated rights protected by the Fourteenth Amendment. The court ruled in their favor, and although lawyers for the city appealed to the Supreme Court, the justices declined to review the case. Segregation on public transportation was now illegal. King, Abernathy, and their associates formed an organization, the Southern Christian Leadership Conference (SCLC), to continue working for nonviolent social change.

Nine African-American teenagers made headlines on September 3, 1957, when they tried to integrate Central High School in Little Rock, Arkansas. Across the South, many school districts had taken steps to comply with the May 1954 Supreme Court ruling, but many others had resisted. In Little Rock a white mob harassed the nine students, and National Guardsmen, bayonets raised, blocked the school's doors. The menacing crowd assembled again two weeks later when the black teenagers made a second attempt to enter Central High. This time the principal dismissed all of the students, ostensibly for their safety.

It became necessary for President Eisenhower to order federal troops to Arkansas to protect the black teens, who became known as the Little Rock Nine. Each of the three boys and six girls had a soldier of the 101st Airborne Division responsible for him or her, escorting that student to classes. The soldiers' presence failed to deter some white students from tripping their black classmates in hallways and calling them names. The African Americans had ink poured on their clothes and water pistols squirted in their faces. In class, teachers repeatedly ignored their raised hands and called on whites instead. At home, the Little Rock Nine received late-night telephone calls threatening that some of the water pistols would soon contain acid. A bomb exploded at the residence of one black student, Carlotta Wells. Another girl, Minniejean Brown, was expelled after she responded to taunts in the school cafeteria, but the other eight stuck out the school year. On May 27, 1958, Ernest Green became the first African American to graduate from Central High School. The following fall, Arkansas governor Orval Faubus closed the school rather than allow integration to continue.

The city of Birmingham, Alabama, employed a similar tactic in the early 1960s in response to a federal order to integrate public facilities, and closed

Young protesters arrested during the Birmingham, Alabama, Children's Crusade approach the police vans that will take them off to jail. *(The Birmingham News. Reprinted with permission.)*

swimming pools, golf courses, parks, and playgrounds. In spring 1963 the children of Birmingham played a significant role in the SCLC's campaign to end segregation in their city.

The circumstances that made Birmingham a worthy target for civil rights demonstrations also made many African Americans reluctant to take part. Some members of the city's police and fire departments had ties to the Ku Klux Klan and felt no qualms about using violence to intimidate blacks. They were not the only ones: Between 1957 and 1963, 18 bombs had been exploded in African-American sections of the city. As the protest marches began, Police Commissioner Eugene "Bull" Connor ordered his forces to use nightsticks and dogs to break them up. Large numbers of people were jailed, including King and Abernathy, and adults began to fear that being arrested might cost them their jobs.

For that reason, the SCLC called on the city's young people, who had no jobs to lose. On May 2, more than 900 teenagers and children, some as young as six, gathered in Birmingham's Sixteenth Street Baptist Church, where the Children's Crusade was to begin. The children filed out of the church singing "We Shall Overcome," and the police descended to make arrests. As parents watched from Kelly Ingram Park, across the street from the church, children were handcuffed and carted off to jail in police vans and school buses.

The next day, more than 1,000 children stayed home from school in order to march for their rights. This time the opposition employed another weapon: fire hoses. The force of the water pouring from these hoses was enough to press children against brick walls, knock them down, and roll them along the street. Seeing their children mistreated in this way, many parents decided that they had no choice but to involve themselves in the campaign.

As the tension escalated, Governor George Wallace sent 500 state troopers to Birmingham to prevent further violence. On May 10, the municipal government and business leaders, weary of the negative press that their city was receiving, announced a desegregation plan. Parks, playgrounds, and other facilities would be open to people of all races, and downtown department stores would hire African-American salespeople.

A few months later, on August 28, 1963, children attended the historic March on Washington for Jobs and Freedom at which 250,000 people gathered in the nation's capital for a peaceful demonstration in support of racial equality. Then, on September 15, 1963, the civil rights movement claimed more young martyrs. Four girls died when a bomb exploded in Birmingham's Sixteenth Street Baptist Church. They were Denise McNair and Cynthia Wesley, both 13, and Addie Mae Collins and Carole Robertson, 14.

SERIOUS CHALLENGES REMAIN

In 1964, President Lyndon Johnson signed a Civil Rights Act that gave the U.S. attorney general the power to protect citizens' right to equality in voting, education, and the use of public facilities. The act also required school districts to desegregate or present workable plans for desegregation in order to receive federal funding. This provision, coupled with lawsuits filed in federal court, drastically reduced segregated schooling over the next several years. Although in 1965, only 6 percent of African-American schoolchildren in the 11 states of the former Confederacy were enrolled in desegregated schools, by 1970, more than 90 percent of southern school districts had been classified as desegregated.

De facto school segregation persisted in the North, largely because of housing patterns. During the 1970s and 1980s, the federal courts tried to achieve a racial balance in northern urban schools by ordering children to be bused to different neighborhoods. Racial hostility came to the fore in Boston in June 1974, after a federal judge mandated busing to achieve school integration there. Both black and white students were harassed in their new schools, but none more than the blacks bused into white, blue-collar South Boston, where schools had to be closed one or two days each week because of racial tension. Irate adults gathered in the streets of South Boston to hurl insults at the African-American students and throw stones at their buses. African-American children commonly returned home with glass in their hair.

When mandatory busing was ended in Boston in 1987, the racial makeup of the public-school population had changed markedly. In 1975, the population was 39 percent black and 49 percent white. The remainder was Hispanic and Asian. In 1987, the population was 49 percent black, 26 percent Hispanic, and 15 percent white. A significant number of white families had enrolled their children in private schools or moved to suburbs rather than permit their children to be bused.

By 1980, 81 percent of African Americans lived in metropolitan areas, and they constituted a majority in 15 cities. As whites fled to the suburbs, industry followed, and black adults in inner-city neighborhoods increasingly found themselves without access to jobs. Despite passage of the Fair Housing Act of 1968, which outlawed racial discrimination in the sale or rental of housing, African

Americans attempting to move into white suburbs continued to be threatened or shut out.

Increasingly, education led to prosperity as opportunities opened for African Americans to attend college and graduate school and embark on professional careers. At the same time, though, millions of others remained trapped in poverty, and families broke down. Three-fourths of African-American families were headed by two parents until the 1960s, when the number of households headed by single women began to increase. By 1990, more than half of all black children lived in such homes, and two-thirds of them were poor. Similarly, some 3.8 million African-American children lived in poverty in 1979; by 1990, that number had risen to 4.6 million. Black children were more than three times as likely as white children to live without either parent (to live with a grandparent or other relative or to be in a foster home); one-third of the American children in foster care in 1990 were black.

As the 20th century dew to a close, African-American children continued to face an increased risk of illness and premature death. In 1982, exposure to lead paint in old, substandard housing resulted in elevated blood levels of lead in one of every eight African-American children under age six. That same year, African-American children were five times as likely as white children to contract tuberculosis. In 1990, half of all reported cases of AIDS in children under 13 occurred in African Americans.

Low birthweight, defined as weighing less than 5.5 pounds at birth, affected nearly one in seven African-American babies born in 1989. Low-birthweight babies are 40 times more likely to die in the first year of life than more robust infants, and in 1990, there were 18 deaths in the first year of life per 1,000 live births among African Americans, contrasted with 9.2 deaths per 1,000 live births in the population as a whole.

Inner-city life exposed children to drug abuse, gang activity, and violence. One study published in 1990 found that 72 percent of fifth graders in an economically deprived section of New Orleans had seen weapons being used. Another study determined that 75 percent of African-American boys aged 10 to 19 surveyed in Chicago had witnessed a murder or other violent crime. All too often, children themselves were the victims of these crimes. The homicide rate for African-American children of all ages was six times higher than it was for white children in 1990; for boys aged 15 to 19, it was 10 times higher. In 1987, homicide took the lives of roughly 85 of every 100,000 black males in this age group, and gunshots caused 80 percent of these deaths.

The guns killed hope and incentive as well. Psychologists teach that adolescents who repeatedly attend the funerals of brothers, cousins, and friends come to believe that someday they will be the one laid out in the casket—that they have no future and in fact are already dead.

CHRONICLE OF EVENTS

1860
The literacy rate among African Americans is 10 percent.

1865
March: The U.S. Freedmen's Bureau is formed to help former slaves make the transition to freedom.

December 6: The Thirteenth Amendment to the Constitution is ratified; slavery and involuntary servitude are now illegal throughout the United States.

1865–1867
Southern states enact "Black Codes" to enforce economic and social segregation.

1870
The Freedmen's Bureau discontinues its educational activities; 4,329 bureau schools are serving 247,333 students.

The literacy rate among African Americans is now 25 percent.

1875
Tennessee is the first state to pass "Jim Crow" laws, which call for separate public facilities for blacks and whites.

1880–1905
Not one person is convicted for taking part in a lynching.

1881
Booker T. Washington founds the Tuskegee Institute, the famous vocational school for African Americans, in Alabama.

1892
An infestation of Mexican cotton boll weevils begins in Texas; it will reach farms in North Carolina by 1922.

1896
In deciding the case *Plessy v. Ferguson,* the U.S. Supreme Court upholds racial segregation in instances where facilities for the two races are "separate but equal."

1898
February 22: Three children die in Lake City, South Carolina, when a white mob burns their home and shoots at their family.

1905
May: The fatal shooting of a white child by an African American touches off a week of racial violence in Chicago.

1909
Of 2,330 African Americans enrolled in Indianapolis schools, only 50 attend classes with whites.

1915–1919
The infant mortality rate among African Americans is 150 per 1,000 births; among whites it is 92.8 per 1,000 births.

1916
Southern school districts spend an average $10.32 per white child per year and $2.89 per black child per year.

1916–1918
Approximately 400,000 African Americans leave the South for northern cities. They represent the first wave of the 1.5 million who will have moved north by 1940 in the Great Migration.

1918
A reported 3,324 lynchings have occurred in the United States since 1889; the victims in 2,522 cases were African American.

1919
July 27: A black youth is attacked while swimming in Lake Michigan and drowns; this incident in Chicago triggers the most violent riot of the summer of 1919.

1920
The African-American population of Chicago has increased 148 percent since 1910; that of Detroit has increased 611 percent over the same period.

1926
When an African-American physician moves to a suburb of Cleveland, whites dynamite his house.

Washington, D.C., schoolchildren tour the Library of Congress, 1899. *(Library of Congress)*

1930s

According to one survey, 21 percent of African Americans age 16 to 21 hold full-time jobs.

New York's Colored Orphan Asylum and other shelters for African-American children are full.

In many parts of the South, African Americans have no opportunity to attend high school.

1932

The Children's Aid Society feeds the 100 hungriest children in Harlem.

1933–1942

About 200,000 African Americans are employed by the Civilian Conservation Corps.

1934

The U.S. government classifies 38 percent of blacks and 17 percent of whites as incapable of supporting themselves.

1935

The New York City mayor's office finds schools in Harlem to be in deplorable condition.

1935–1936

During this school year, 10 southern states spend an average $37.87 per white child and $13.09 per black child.

1935

The New York City Board of Education allocates funds for four new schools in Harlem and repairs to existing buildings.

1954

May 17: The Supreme Court announces its decision in *Brown v. the Board of Education;* school segregation is now illegal in the United States.

1955

August: Teenager Emmett Till is murdered by whites while visiting relatives in Money, Mississippi.

September: An all-white jury finds Till's accused murderers not guilty.

December: The Montgomery bus boycott begins; African-American children join adults in refusing to ride the city buses for 13 months, until demands for equal treatment are met.

1957

September 3: Nine African-American teenagers attempting to integrate Central High School in Little Rock, Arkansas, are prevented from entering the building.

President Eisenhower orders federal troops to Little Rock to protect the nine students.

1957–1963

Eighteen bombs explode in African-American sections of Birmingham, Alabama.

1958

May 27: Ernest Green becomes the first African American to graduate from Central High School.

1963

May 2: Nine hundred children participate in the Children's Crusade in Birmingham; many are arrested.

May 3: One thousand children stay home from school to be part of the Children's Crusade; police officers attack them with fire hoses.

May 10: Birmingham's government and business leaders agree to integrate public facilities in the city.

August 28: An estimated 250,000 people gather for the March on Washington for Jobs and Freedom; among them are many children.

September 15: Four teenage girls die when a bomb explodes in the Sixteenth Street Baptist Church in Birmingham.

1964

President Johnson signs the Civil Rights Act of 1964; among other provisions, this law requires school districts to desegregate in order to receive federal funding.

1965

Six percent of schoolchildren in 11 southern states attend desegregated schools.

1968

The Fair Housing Act outlaws racial discrimination in selling or renting homes.

1970

More than 90 percent of southern school districts are classified as desegregated.

1974

June: A federal judge mandates busing to achieve school integration in Boston.

1975

Boston's public-school population is 39 percent black and 49 percent white.

1979

Roughly 3.8 million African-American children live in poverty.

1980

Eighty-one percent of African Americans live in urban areas; they constitute a majority in 15 cities.

1982

Elevated blood levels of lead are found in one of every eight black children under age six who are tested.

African-American children are five times as likely as whites to contract tuberculosis.

1987

Court-ordered busing in Boston ends; the city's public-school population is now 40 percent black, 26 percent Hispanic, and 15 percent white.

Homicide claims approximately 85 of every 100,000 black males aged 15 to 19.

1989

Low birthweight affects nearly one in seven African-American babies born this year.

1990

More than half of African-American children live in homes headed by single women; two-thirds of these children are poor.

The number of African-American children living in poverty has reached 4.6 million.

One-third of the children in foster care are black.

Half of all cases of AIDS reported in children under 13 occur in African Americans.

The infant mortality rate is 18 per 1,000 live births in African Americans and 9.2 per 1,000 live births in whites.

In one New Orleans neighborhood, 72 percent of fifth graders have seen weapons being used.

In Chicago, 75 percent of African-American boys aged 10 to 19 have witnessed a violent crime.

The homicide rate for African-American children is six times higher than it is for white children; among boys aged 15 to 19, it is 10 times higher. Gunshots cause 80 percent of these deaths.

EYEWITNESS TESTIMONY

Information Wanted, of Caroline Dodson, who was sold from Nashville, Nov. 1st, 1862, by James Lumsden to Warwick, (a trader then in human beings), who carried her to Atlanta, Georgia, and she was last heard of in the sale pen of Robert Clarke, (human trader in that place), from which she was sold. Any information of her whereabouts will be thankfully received and rewarded by her mother.

Advertisement placed by Lucinda Lowery in the Colored Tennessean, *August 12, 1865, in Leon F. Litwack,* Been in the Storm So Long, *p. 232.*

. . . [I] have bin to Mr tilor about my children and he will not let me have them an he say he will Beat me to deth if i cross his Plantasion A Gain an so i dont now what to do About it an i wish if you Pleas that you wood rite Mr Joseph tilor A lettor an let him Give me my childrin . . . i want my childrin if you Pleas to Get them for me i have bin after them an he says i shall not have them and he will not Pay me nor my childrin ether for thar last year work and now want let me have my childrin nother. . . .

Letter from Hulelah Tyler to the Freedmen's Bureau, June 10, 1866, in Rebecca Scott, "The Battle Over the Child: Child Apprenticeship and the Freedmen's Bureau in North Carolina," p. 105.

Neither my father nor mother had taught me directly anything about race. Naturally, I gained some impressions and picked up some information. Many things I would have learned much sooner had I not been restricted in play. My vague, early impressions constituted what might be called an unconscious race-

The Zion School for Colored Children, Charleston, South Carolina, was founded in December 1865 with an African-American administrative and teaching staff. In December 1866, when this illustration appeared in *Harper's Weekly,* the school had 13 teachers and 850 students. *(Library of Congress)*

superiority complex. All the most interesting things that came under my observation were being done by colored men. They drove the horse and mule teams, they built the houses, they laid the bricks, they painted the buildings and fences, they loaded and unloaded the ships. When I was a child, I did not know that there existed such a thing as a white carpenter or bricklayer or painter or plasterer or tinner. The thought that white men might be able to load and unload the heavy drays or the big ships was too far removed from everyday life to enter my mind. There were yet some years for me to live before I would feel the brutal impact of race and learn how race prejudice permeated the whole American social organism.

James Weldon Johnson, who was a child in Jacksonville, Florida, in the 1870s, Along This Way, *pp. 31–32.*

Since emancipation a good deal has been done to educate the negro. Many schools in which a superior education is afforded have been maintained by benevolent Northerners. . . . For the education of the masses a public school system has been started in all the States, of which the blacks have a fair share. Owing, however, to financial difficulties these schools are extremely imperfect, being open but a small portion of each year—in some States as little as two months, and in none, I believe, more than about four months on an average. However, this is better than nothing. The negroes show a laudable zeal for education, and upon the whole I think that as much has been done as could be expected under the circumstances.

George Campbell, English traveler in the United States, 1879, White and Black, *pp. 130–31.*

Too often the educational value of doing well what is done, however little, is overlooked. One thing well done prepares the mind to do the next thing better. Not how much, but how well, should be the motto. One problem thoroughly understood is of more value than a score poorly mastered. One language well learned is of more value than six of which we only have a smattering. . . .

Hitherto the education of the Negro has too largely failed to produce special men for special work. The Jacks-of-all-trades are too numerous.

Give the youth a training that will fit him to do one thing well—better than anybody in the community—and you put his services in demand.

Booker T. Washington addressing the Alabama State Teachers' Association, April 11, 1888, in E. Davidson Washington, ed., Selected Speeches of Booker T. Washington, *p. 19.*

My daddy put me to plowin the first time at nine years old, right after my mother died. I remember the first plowin he put me to doin. She died in August and he put me to plowin in October, helpin him plow up sweet potatoes. . . . In October that year the weather was warm and the gnats was awful bad. And doggone it, the gnats looked like they would eat me up and I was just nine years old. So I would fight the gnats and my daddy got mad with me for that and he come to me and he picked me up by the arm and he held me up and he wore out a switch nearly on me, then dropped me back down. That was the first whippin he ever give me bout plowin. I just wasn't big enough for the job, that's the truth.

And that country where we was livin was rough and rocky. And he . . . put me to plowin a regular shift at twelve, thirteen years old. And I had to plow barefooted on that rocky country; anything liable to skin up my feet.

Nate Shaw, an Alabama sharecropper's son, who was nine years old in 1894, in Theodore Rosengarten, All God's Dangers, *p. 15.*

. . . [T]he black boy of the South moves in a black world—a world with its own leaders, its own thoughts, its own ideals. In this world he gets by far the larger part of his life training, and through the eyes of this dark world he peers into the veiled world beyond. Who guides and determines the education which he receives in his world? His teachers here are the group-leaders of the Negro people—the physicians and clergymen, the trained fathers and mothers, the influential and forceful men about him of all kinds; here it is, if at all, that the culture of the surrounding world trickles through and is handed on by the graduates of the higher schools. Can such culture training of group leaders be neglected? Can we afford to ignore it?

W. E. B. Du Bois, 1903, "The Talented Tenth," in The Negro Problem, *pp. 61–62.*

These early 20th-century children smile and pose for the camera, but harvesting cotton was hard work at any age. *(Library of Congress)*

group and community in which he works, liberally trained teachers and leaders to teach him and his family what life means; the second is to give him sufficient intelligence and technical skill to make him an efficient workman; the first object demands the Negro college and college-bred men—not a quantity of such colleges, but a few of excellent quality; not too many college-bred men, but enough to leaven the lump, to inspire the masses, to raise the Talented Tenth to leadership; the second object demands a good system of common schools, well-taught, conveniently located and properly equipped.

W. E. B. Du Bois, 1903, "The Talented Tenth," in The Negro Problem, *pp. 62–63.*

What shall we do with the negro? Certainly the system of education suited to the white child does not suit the negro. This has been demonstrated by forty years of experience and the expenditures of more than three hundred millions of dollars in the southern states. It was natural and quite reasonable, immediately after the civil war, especially by those who had made but a superficial study of the negro, to expect that freedom, equal educational facilities and the example and precept of the white man would have the effect of improving his morals and make a better man of him generally. But it has not, I am sorry to say. As a race, he is deteriorating morally every day.

James Kimble Vardaman, governor of Mississippi from 1904 through 1908, speaking in 1909, in Horace Mann Bond, The Education of the Negro in the American Social Order, *p. 101. (The dollar amount that Vardaman cites is a gross exaggeration. Historians have estimated that between 1865 and 1908, the southern states spent at most $140 million to educate African Americans.)*

I am an earnest advocate of manual training and trade teaching for black boys, and for white boys, too. I believe that next to the founding of Negro colleges the most valuable addition to Negro education since the war, has been industrial training for black boys. Nevertheless, I insist that the object of all true education is not to make men carpenters, it is to make carpenters men; there are two means of making the carpenter a man, each equally important: the first is to give the

To keep us out of mischief, my mother often took my brother and me with her to her cooking job. Standing hungrily and silently in a corner of the kitchen, we would watch her go from the stove to the sink, from the cabinet to the table. I always loved to stand in the white folks' kitchen when my mother cooked, for it meant that I got occasional scraps of bread and meat; but many times I regretted having come, for my nostrils would be assailed with the scent of food that did not belong to me and which I was forbidden to eat. Toward evening my mother would take the hot dishes into the dining room where the white people were seated, and I would stand as near the dining-room door as possible to get a quick glimpse of the white faces gathered around the loaded table, eating, laughing, talking. If the white people left anything, my brother and I would eat well; but if they did not, we would have our usual bread and tea.

Watching the white people eat would make my empty stomach churn and I would grow vaguely angry. Why could I not eat when I was hungry? Why did I always have to wait until others were through? I could not understand why some people had enough food and others did not.

Richard Wright, whose mother took a job as a cook in Memphis, Tennessee, in 1914, when he was six years old, Black Boy, *p. 17.*

On my visits to the country schools in [southern] states I have seen some very pathetic sights. In some of the so-called school buildings the roofs leak, the winds blow up through the cracks of the floor and down through the ceilings. I have seen in many of these schools five little boys and girls trying to study out of

Learning to repair shoes in Junction City, Kansas, 1915 *(Joseph J. Pennell Collection, Kansas Collection, Spencer Research Library, University of Kansas)*

the same book. In some cases two children would occupy the front seat with the book between them, with two others peeping over their shoulders and a fifth trying to peep over the shoulders of the four.

Booker T. Washington writing in the New York Age, *1915, in Carole Marks,* Farewell—We're Good and Gone, *pp. 76–77.*

... [H]ere I was, a high-school graduate, eighteen years old, principal in a two-teacher school with 132 pupils ranging from beginners to eighth graders, with no teaching experience, a schoolhouse constructed of boards running up and down, with no slats on the cracks, and a fireplace at one end of the room that cooked the pupils immediately in front of it but allowed those in the rear to shiver and freeze on their uncomfortable, hard, back-breaking benches. ...

The board walls had been nailed up before the boards had been properly dried and I remember how on chill and damp days the wind often howled through the cracks between them. And the wind blowing down the chimney would send the smoke spiraling back into the room.

I had the older children, roughly the fifth, sixth, seventh and eighth grades. The other teacher had those through the fourth. But my pupils in the seventh and eighth grades and some of those, even, in lower ones, were most erratic in their attendance, for they were old enough to work in the fields. They didn't come in until the cotton had been picked, and often it was Christmas and sometimes even January before all the cotton was gleaned. To add to this difficulty, most of these children had to stop school in early spring to begin preparing the fields for the new crop. Naturally, the attendance varied greatly from day to day.

Septima Poinsette Clark, who became principal of a school for African Americans on Johns Island, South Carolina, in 1916, Echo in My Soul, *pp. 38–39.*

[N]ow the best classes of colored men in the south are still here but are making preparation to come north and are not particular about coming to Chicago. ... I have been living here in New Orleans only seven years I formerly live in the country but owing to bad conditions of schools for my children I sold my property and moved here I didnt think there was any justice in my paying school taxes and had no fit school to send by children to. I have been employed here as night eatchman [*sic*] for the last four years and are still working at

it but my wajes are so small the high cost of living leaves very little for traveling expenses but never the less I have a boy sixteen years old as soon as school closes I will take him north with me hoping to find work for him and I during vacation.

A reader in New Orleans writing to the Chicago Defender, *May 5, 1917, in Emmett J. Scott, "Additional Letters of Negro Migrants of 1916–1918," p. 433.*

My earliest recollection of racial problems relates to discussions I heard in my grandfather's house when I was only six or seven. I heard real fear in the voices of my cousins and my aunt when they talked about the "race riots" in progress on U Street, just one short block north of our house at 11th and T. The voices warned me not to approach U Street for any reason whatever while the riots were taking place. I do not recall just what the disturbance was about—something to do with jobs and the return of troops from overseas service during World War I—but I do know that the ominous term "race riot" was indelibly lodged in my consciousness from that time on.

Benjamin O. Davis, Jr., recalling the summer of 1919 in Washington, D.C., Benjamin O. Davis, Jr.: American, *p. 7.*

Our parents had filled us with love and a staunch Methodist religion. We were poor, though I did not know it at the time; the rich soil surrounding our clapboard house had yielded the food for the family. And the love of this family had eased the burden of being black. But there were segregated schools and warnings to avoid white neighborhoods after dark. I always had to sit in the peanut gallery (the Negro section) at the movies. We weren't allowed to drink a soda in the drugstore in town. I was stoned and beaten and called "nigger," "black boy," "darky," "shine." These indignities came so often I began to accept them as normal. Yet I always fought back.

Gordon Parks, who was a child in Kansas in the 1920s, A Choice of Weapons, *p. 2.*

Public education in Harlem has been ... long and grossly neglected. The facts are notorious.

Dirt and filth and slovenliness have no more educational value for our children than for yours. ... New school-houses with ample grounds and appropriate modern facilities are urgently needed to supplement or replace overcrowded and outmoded structures, to provide for the large increase in our population during the past decade or more. . . .

Teachers, principals and superintendents are needed who have abiding faith in our children and genuine respect for the loins and traditions from which they have sprung. . . .

So far as public education is concerned, we beg you to dispel by concrete action the widespread conviction that this region is neglected because its people are comparatively poor in this world's goods and in social and political influence, because many of them are of African descent.

> *Petition submitted to the New York City Board of Education by Harlem residents, March 1935, in Cheryl Lynn Greenberg, "Or Does It Explode?" p. 190.*

The school plant as a whole is old, shabby . . . in many instances not even sanitary or well-kept and the fire hazards . . . are great. The lack of playgrounds and recreational centers . . . is all the more serious when it is considered that some of the schools are surrounded by . . . corrupt and immoral resorts of which the police seem blissfully unaware. Four of the schools lack auditoriums: one endeavors to serve luncheons to 1,000 children when there are seats for only 175. Most of all, no elementary school has been constructed in Harlem in 10 years. . . .

Prejudicial discrimination appears from the fact that the Board of Education, asking funds from the federal government for 168 school buildings, asked for but one annex for Harlem.

> *Conclusion of the Mayor's Commission on Conditions in Harlem, April 1935, in Cheryl Lynn Greenberg, "Or Does It Explode?" p. 189.*

The white school [near Shelby Post Office, Virginia] has three large rooms, three teachers, ninety children, with four buses to bring them to school. The equipment inside is excellent, with desks, and small tables and chairs for special activities. . . .

The colored school has one room, one teacher, fifty-three children, who must walk if they get to school. The children have to sit on uncomfortable homemade benches. With no equipment whatever, the teacher was trying to do a progressive job of teaching. On a rickety table in one corner of the room were some dishes and bowls, for which the teacher apologized, because it was lunch time, and she was trying to

give the children hot lunches. A well had been dug four years ago, but efforts to get a pump put in had failed, and the school was getting its water from a neighbor's spring.

> *"'Equal' Schools in Virginia," November 1936, p. 333.*

A typical Harlem school is like a prison, and a badly run one at that. Even the most diligent scrubbing cannot really clean a building built in the 70's or 80's; that there is not diligent scrubbing the odor of ages in the lunchrooms and the rubbish accumulated under benches testify. The children have none of the *joie de vivre* popularly associated with their age, and tuck their rachitic legs under benches too small for them in rooms unadorned, bleak and dingy. Teachers, trying to cope with classes whose numbers average slightly more than even those in other overcrowded sections, with children who have eye defects and toothaches and empty stomachs, suffer from frayed nerves and give way to harsh-voiced impatience.

Few teachers would make a Harlem appointment first choice. The Board has a ruling that new teachers will not be granted transfers until three years after appointment, and the inexperienced undergo a three years' purgatory at the expense of pupils who need the most experienced. Some bring with them indifference, some prejudice. Discriminatory practices are supposedly dealt with by the authorities; yet one teacher who snapped, "How dare you talk like that to a white woman?" was still teaching in the same school weeks after the incident.

> *Edith M. Stern, July 1937, "Jim Crow Goes to School in New York," pp. 201–02.*

. . . [T]he Florida Negro realizes that the money spent on the public education of all children in Florida is just about one-half of the average for the country, [and] that the money spent in Florida for Negro public education is just one-sixth of the general state average. This means to the Florida Negro that roughly one-twelfth as much money is spent to educate his child as is spent on the average child in the country. . . .

[T]here are 1,494 school buildings for white children in the state, with an assessed valuation of seventy million dollars. The 1,029 buildings for Negroes have cost the good folk who spend education money only five million. If the white school buildings are such that several local politicians are elected each year by promis-

In January 1939 a Transylvania, Louisiana, mother teaches her children letters and numbers at home. *(Library of Congress)*

ing to improve them, imagine the shacks the Negroes must go to school in!

Martin D. Richardson and Le Roy M. Washington, September 1937, "A Picture of Florida's Schools," p. 270.

Richard Claxton Gregory was born on Columbus Day, 1932. A welfare case. You've seen him on every street corner in America. You knew he had rhythm by the way he snapped his cloth while he shined your shoes. Happy little black boy, the way he grinned and picked your quarter out of the air. Then he ran off and brought himself a Twinkie Cupcake, a bottle of Pepsi-Cola, and a pocketful of caramels.

You didn't know that was his dinner. And you never followed him home.

Dick Gregory, who grew up in St. Louis in the 1930s,
Nigger, *frontispiece.*

I wonder about my Momma, who walked out of a white woman's clean house at midnight and came back to her own where the lights had been out for three months, and the pipes were frozen and the wind came in through the cracks. She'd have to make deals with the rats: leave some food out for them so they wouldn't gnaw on the doors or bite the babies. . . .

I wonder how she felt telling those white kids she took care of to brush their teeth after they ate, to wash their hands after they peed. She could never tell her own kids because there wasn't soap or water back home.

I wonder how my Momma felt when we came home from school with a list of vitamins and pills and cod liver oils the school nurse said we had to have. Momma would cry all night, and then go out and spend most of the rent money for pills. A week later, the white man would come for his eighteen dollars rent and Momma would plead with him to wait until tomorrow. She had lost her pocketbook. The relief check was coming. The white folks had some money for her. Tomorrow.

Dick Gregory, who grew up in St. Louis in the 1930s, Nigger, *p. 40.*

As a young child I was just told what to do, but as I grew older I began to wonder why I couldn't go in restaurants downtown and couldn't go to the public parks and playgrounds on the other side of the tracks. I was curious about these things and had difficulty accepting them, because even at an early age I could see that there was more to get out of life. But my parents explained to me that there were limits—in other words, blacks had a place and they had to stay in it.

Sybil Lewis remembering her childhood in Sapulpa, Oklahoma, ca. 1940, in Mark Jonathan Harris et al., The Homefront, *p. 38.*

When I was a kid, I used to hear folks talking about "colored people," and that dark-skin people were Negroes, so I just concluded that I was one too. I don't remember an incident, but I had several experiences of being told I couldn't do things because I was a Negro. I remember one ride on a bus I had to Alexandria [Virginia] where the driver told me I couldn't sit where I wanted to because I happened to be a Negro. It happened before a bus load of white people and they laughed and smiled. I almost cried and I tried to hide in the seat I was in. I felt hurt and embarrassed and was so sorry it fell my luck to be born a Negro.

A 15-year-old boy living in Washington, D.C., 1940, in E. Franklin Frazier, Negro Youth at the Crossways, *p. 79.*

Pity the poor colored child who walked past the schoolhouse when [the poor white boys] were outside. There would be cries of "coon" or "nigger baby," followed by a barrage of rocks and dirt clods. When I was a grown man, and saw the deputy sheriffs and the mobs pummeling Negro demonstrators on television, I needed no one to tell me they had been doing the same thing since the age of eight.

Willie Morris, who was eight years old in 1942 and grew up in Yazoo City, Mississippi, North Toward Home, *pp. 22–23.*

Like countless other Black families in the forties and fifties, we fell victim to . . . indifference and corruption when we moved to Oakland. It was as difficult then as it is now to find decent homes for large families, and we moved around quite a bit in my early years in search of a house that would suit our needs. The first house I remember was on the corner of Fifth and Brush streets in a rundown section of Oakland. It was a two-bedroom basement apartment, and much too small to hold all of us comfortably. The floor was either dirt or cement, I cannot remember exactly; it did not seem to be the kind of floor that "regular" people had in their homes. My parents slept in one bedroom and my sisters, brothers, and I in the other. Later, when we moved to a two-room apartment at Castro and Eighteenth streets . . . I slept in the kitchen. That memory returns often. Whenever I think of people crowded into a small living space, I always see a child sleeping in the kitchen and feeling upset about it; everybody knows that the kitchen is not supposed to be a bedroom. That is all we had, however. I still burn with the sense of unfairness I felt every night as I crawled into the cot near the icebox.

Huey P. Newton, who was three years old when his family moved from Louisiana to Oakland, California, in 1945, Revolutionary Suicide, *pp. 15–16.*

. . . I was aware that the people across the street were different—without yet being able to trace their alien nature to the color of their skin. What made them different from our neighbors in the projects was the frown on their faces, the way they stood a hundred feet away and glared at us, their refusal to speak when we said "Good afternoon." An elderly couple across the street, the Montees, sat on their porch all the time, their eyes heavy with belligerence.

Almost immediately after we moved there the white people got together and decided on a border line between them and us. Center Street became the line of demarcation. Provided that we stayed on "our" side of the line (the east side) they let it be known we would be left in peace. If we ever crossed over to their side, war would be declared. Guns were hidden in our house and vigilance was constant.

Angela Davis, whose family moved to a racially mixed neighborhood of Birmingham, Alabama, in 1949, when she was four years old, Angela Davis, *p. 78.*

I was in the bathroom washing my white shoelaces for Sunday School the next morning when an explosion a hundred times louder than the loudest, most frightening thunderclap I had ever heard shook our house. Medicine bottles fell off the shelves, shattering all around me. The floor seemed to slip away from my feet as I raced into the kitchen and my frightened mother's arms.

Crowds of angry Black people came up the hill and stood on "our" side, staring at the bombed-out ruins of the Deyaberts' house. Far into the night they spoke of death, of white hatred, death, white people, and more death. But of their own fear they said nothing. Apparently it did not exist, for Black families continued to move in. The bombings were such a constant response that soon our neighborhood became known as Dynamite Hill.

Angela Davis recalling a Saturday evening in spring 1949,
Angela Davis, *p. 79.*

When the boycott started, I just couldn't wait for morning to come because I wanted to see what was happening. I walked to school. As the buses passed me and my schoolmates, we said, "Nobody's on the bus! Nobody's on the bus!" It was just a beautiful thing. It was a day to behold to see nobody on the bus.

Joseph Lacey, who was 13 years old in December 1955, when the Montgomery bus boycott began, and who walked to school every day until it ended, in Ellen Levine,
Freedom's Children, *p. 27.*

The very basis of our individual rights and freedom rests upon the certainty that the President and the executive branch of Government will support and insure the carrying out of the decisions of the federal courts even, when necessary, with all the means at the President's command.

Unless the President did so, anarchy would result.

There would be no security for any except that which each one of us could provide for himself.

The interest of the nation in the proper fulfillment of the law's requirements cannot yield to opposition and demonstrations by some few persons.

Mob rule cannot be allowed to overrule the decisions of our courts.

President Dwight D. Eisenhower addressing the nation on his decision to send federal troops to Little Rock, Arkansas, September 24, 1957.

. . . [Y]ou were subjected to all kinds of taunts, someone attempting to trip you, pour ink on you, in some other way ruin your clothing, and at worst, someone physically attacking you. . . . I got hit with water guns. We got calls at all times of the night—people saying they were going to have acid in the water guns and they were going to squirt it in our faces. . . .

You'd be crazy not to have fear. You kept fear in the back of your mind at all times, a fear that somebody was going to come over and physically harm you, and that nobody would come to your rescue. But we had to be nonviolent. . . . We were nine students out of a couple of thousand.

Ernest Green, one of the nine teenagers who integrated Central High School in Little Rock, Arkansas, in 1957, in Ellen Levine, Freedom's Children, *pp. 45–46.*

Behind the shouting and the newspaper demands that we stop the inequities of Southern school segregation, there is often hidden the fact of Northern segregation. Here, the separation of the "nice" white children from the poor white and Negro children is accomplished both by the enlargement of private and parochial school systems, and by the move to the suburbs—a move for which the family's main reasons are usually the better suburban schools and the fact that the children will associate with more desirable playmates than would be the case in the city. In the white suburbs the children are supposed to enjoy better cultural opportunities. These opportunities, strangely enough, are no longer equated with being close to the cultural facilities that an urban center offers, but rather with lawns and trees, though historically cultural advances have been tied to urban and not to rural life.

Bruno Bettelheim, October 1958, "Sputnik and Segregation," p. 332.

I still remember the day of the march how I looked into the [reflecting] pool and saw all of the different faces of people and how their reflections made it appear like these people were looking up at me. Some people sat at the edge of the pool and soaked their feet in the cool water. . . .

I also remember a lot of children there, some younger than me, sitting on the shoulders of their fathers. Babies were cradled in their mothers' arms. I had never seen that many people in my life.

I don't remember any of the speeches. I don't remember hearing King's speech—my mother read it to me later. I do remember people's reactions. I especially remember the clapping; it sounded like thunder.

Raymond Greene, who as a child attended the August 28, 1963, March on Washington for Jobs and Freedom, in Belinda Rochelle, Witnesses to Freedom, *pp. 68–69.*

I was a friend of Denise McNair [one of the girls killed in the bombing of the Sixteenth Street Baptist Church]. I knew her grandfather. He owned a cleaners, and I knew her from there. I was a flower girl for her funeral. Three of the funerals were held at the same time. There was nothing like seeing those three families there, and the three coffins. I was just trying to understand how somebody could do this to children. . . .

I wasn't angry because you were taught not to be. You were taught to forgive people. Things were happening so fast during that time, you didn't know what to expect next. Anger and sorrow were just a part of trying to get accomplished what you wanted.

Bernita Roberson, who was a child in Birmingham, Alabama, in 1963, in Ellen Levine, Freedom's Children, *p. 91.*

I wish that I could have a better block than I have Now. My landlord said that He was going to put Swings in my back yard. how can He do that When the backyard is junky I do not like people throw junk and I demand a Pretty good houses and more food to eat thats What I demand and I better get it.

Rhonda, age 7, of New York City, 1969, in Stephen M. Joseph, ed., The Me Nobody Knows, *p. 65.*

I wish they will stop killing people around My block. . . . I keep dreaming that I will get hurt. But that is not true. I keep saying to my mother I don't want to go out. But my mother says it is sunny out. I said that is not what's wrong. I'm scared that someone will hurt me.

Lorraine, age 7, of New York City, 1969, in Stephen M. Joseph, ed., The Me Nobody Knows, *p. 65.*

I live in a block which is a bad block. It has dope pushing and pot smoking. In my building there are fights, killings and shootings. A man raped a woman on the roof and killed her. Another man stole a t.v., a hi-fi and some money; 500,000.00 dollars in cash. A cop ran after them. He fired three times in the air, then he said, "Stop! in the name of the law!" Then he shot the man in the arm, but they got away.

Two men stole some furniture out of a truck and they got away.

A boy fell off a roof and he died and his mother cried because he didn't listen to her when she said, "Don't fly your kite on the roof," but he didn't listen to her.

Charles B., age 16, of New York City, 1969, in Stephen M. Joseph, ed., The Me Nobody Knows, *p. 83.*

to day I saw a very butiful pigen. It white and grey. It landed on top of a fence I tried to grab it with my hand but it flew befor I could grasp it. I saw it fly off and it look butiful.

A. P., age 14, of New York City, 1969, in Stephen M. Joseph, ed., The Me Nobody Knows, *p. 76.*

At 15th and Kedvale three boys are lagging pennies on a sidewalk. . . . Their ages are nine, ten and twelve. Younger aged boys are playing softball in the streets, and shouting and darting around the passing cars which momentarily disrupt their game. A group of little girls are skipping rope near a two story frame house, whose wooden shingles have begun to corrode from years of neglect. In the backyard a fat woman, wearing a tight bathrobe that pinches her body, is hanging the morning laundry. In front of the corner tavern, two old men begin arguing over a bottle of wine. The boisterous voices of other men can be heard inside. A teenage youth enters and after a few minutes comes out with a small brown bag which fails to cover the neck of a quart beer bottle he has tucked under his arm. A small boy, age four, dashes across the street and a speeding car comes to a screeching halt, inches away from the undisturbed child. A police squadron pulls over to the curb and two officers get out, guns in hand, and enter a four story building. A few people mill around the squadron and some of the kids begin to play with the spotlight on the vehicle. The officers finally return with a young adult male, his wrists handcuffed behind him, and immediately leave before more people arrive.

It is a summer morning in North Lawndale and the streets are active as usual.

Eugene Perkins describing life in an African-American neighborhood of Chicago, 1975, Home Is a Dirty Street, *pp. 17–18.*

Our children are in imminent danger. Millions of them are engulfed in a morass of drugs and violence and are falling in staggering numbers to some of the most virulent social ills plaguing America. Gang warfare, a bustling cocaine trade, child abuse, premature parenthood and illiteracy are among the urban cancers eating away at today's Black youth. So fatal and far-reaching are these malignancies that even some of our best and brightest young minds are at risk.

Charles Whitaker, August 1988, "A Generation in Peril," p. 34.

Gangs—trafficking in the deadly but cheap cocaine derivative known as crack—have become a particular menace. Skirmishes between warring street gangs, each vying for control of the billion-dollar crack trade, have come to resemble the conflict in the Middle East, complete with Uzis and Soviet-made AK-47 assault rifles. Decked out in identifying regalia, gang members have taken to driving through enemy territory and unloading their automatic weapons on rival gang members. In the process, hundreds of innocent bystanders also have been brutally gunned down.

Charles Whitaker, August 1988, "A Generation in Peril," p. 36.

When I was growing up in rural, segregated South Carolina, the ugly messages of segregation were counteracted by the nurturing voices of positive parental and community expectation and pride. Black adults in our families, churches and community made children feel valuable. While life was often very hard and resources were scarce, we always knew who we were and that the measure of our worth was inside our heads and hearts and not on our backs or in other people's minds. We were told—and believed—that being black and poor was no excuse for not achieving. As a result of our elders' attention and support we never lost hope, as so many black children have today.

Marian Wright Edelman, March 31, 1990, "Why America May Go to Hell," p. 314.

13

An America Inhospitable to Children
1971–2001

In 1984, Jerry Steinberg, a teacher of English as a second language in Vancouver, British Columbia, founded No Kidding!, a club for adults like himself who have decided not to have children. People join No Kidding! to make friends who respect the choice that they have made and with whom they have the common bond of childlessness. In 2001, No Kidding! had 60 chapters in North America.

Thirteen million adults born in the United States during the baby boom are childless, many deliberately so. Some see themselves as a minority whose rights society fails to protect. They are offended by prying questions from family members, friends, and coworkers. They are angered by employee benefits that apply specifically to workers who are parents, and they are sometimes openly antagonistic toward children, calling them ankle biters, crib lizards, or brats.

Do American children inhabit a hostile world? Recent survey data indicate that they do. In 1999, 53 percent of adults questioned by Public Agenda, a non-profit public-opinion research organization, used words such as lazy, irresponsible, and wild to characterize the current generation of children; 71 percent applied these and similar terms to teens and volunteered that they seldom encounter teenagers who are friendly and helpful. Respondents placed most of the blame for this sad state of affairs on parents. Yet parents complain that society offers them little in the way of support and guidance. They claim—with some justification—that environmental factors such as drugs and violence make it hard for them to do their job well.

Today's youth are growing up in a nation that is different in many ways from the one that their parents knew as children. And although adults may view them with alarm, a majority of young people report that they have strong relationships with their parents and other adults and that they have caring, trustworthy friends.

THERE IS NO TYPICAL CHILD

Children living in the United States at the start of the 21st century are more ethnically and economically diverse than any preceding generation. In 1998, 65 percent of American children were white and 15 percent were black. For the first time, as a result of immigration from Central America and Mexico, children of Hispanic heritage slightly outnumbered African Americans, while 4 percent of U.S. children were classified Asian or Pacific Islander.

The strong economy of the 1990s significantly reduced unemployment. Job growth occurred in technical fields requiring highly skilled workers in which salaries are high and in service occupations in which wages traditionally are low. Meanwhile, corporations cut mid-level jobs paying average salaries. These trends have created economic polarity in the United States, increasing the ranks of the wealthy and poor and shrinking the middle class.

As in earlier periods, the economy affects how children live. In affluent Falls Church, Virginia, for example, mothers recently raised $90,000 to build a neighborhood playground. In nearby Springfield, parents spent $60,000 to throw a graduation party for the high school's class of 2000. Children in such communities are commonly cared for by live-in nannies when they are small and drive to school in their own luxury cars as teens.

Elsewhere, often just a short drive from places like Falls Church and Springfield, children live without adequate medical care, shelter, and food. In 1991, 12.5 percent of American children younger than 12 were chronically undernourished. Children who do not have enough to eat miss more school than those who are well fed, and they also have more colds, ear infections, headaches, fatigue, and dizziness. Poor children are also less likely to attend high-quality preschools and day-care centers than their wealthier counterparts. They are more apt to fall behind in school, drop out, or, if they are girls, get pregnant. In 1991, one-fifth of American children were living in poverty, a 21-percent increase since 1970, and 330,000 were homeless.

Families headed by single women are most liable to be living below the poverty line, and in 1988, 45 percent of such households with children under 18 were classified as poor. The number of these households is on the rise, because the divorce rate is high and because more teenage girls and young single women who become pregnant are raising their babies alone rather than marrying or relinquishing infants for adoption.

THE PREVALENCE OF DIVORCE

In 1976, approximately one marriage in three ended in divorce. In 2001, it was estimated that 50 percent of couples marrying for the first time would divorce within 10 years and that 60 percent of second marriages would end in divorce. Until recently, the majority of child-development specialists held the opinion that children fared better if their parents divorced than if they remained unhappily married. It was thought that divorce created a temporary crisis in children's lives but that once their parents were happier, children would be happier as well. Now, long-term studies reveal that the sadness, stress, and anxiety caused by divorce can be profound and enduring.

A small percentage of divorced parents share the physical custody of their children; in a growing number of cases, fathers are granted sole custody. Most of the time, though, the children of divorced parents live with their mothers. These children see their fathers according to an agreed-upon schedule, but it often happens that fathers' visits gradually become irregular and infrequent. In 1991, 42 percent of divorced fathers failed to see their children at all. Having little or no contact with their fathers has been linked to poor school performance and pre-cocious sexuality in children and adolescents.

Divorce also has financial consequences for children and adults, principally because the standard of living of custodial mothers frequently declines. About 40 percent of divorced fathers pay nothing toward the support of their children even if they are legally obligated to do so, and those who do pay child support usually contribute less toward the expenses of raising their children than they did before their marriages ended.

If a divorced mother works, she is likely to earn less than her former husband. According to the U.S. Department of Labor, women earned an average 72.2 cents in 1999 for every dollar earned by men. The post-divorce drop in income may disrupt children's lives by necessitating a move to more affordable housing and forcing their mother to be at work and therefore out of the home for longer periods. It takes about five years, on average, for divorced women and their children to return to their previous standard of living.

The most reliable and expedient route to economic recovery is remarriage, which demands further adjustments of the children involved. In 1991, approximately one in five U.S. households comprising a married couple and children under 18 was a stepfamily; that is, at least one of the children lived with one biological parent and the parent's spouse, who was unrelated to the child.

SEXUAL ACTIVITY AMONG THE YOUNG

Births to teenage girls are an issue of public concern, but the percentage of girls aged 15 to 19 giving birth has actually been declining. Births in this age group fell 16 percent between 1991 and 1996, and this drop was accompanied by a 22-percent fall in the teen abortion rate. In 1999, the teen birthrate was 49.6 per 1,000 girls aged 15 to 19, the lowest since 1940, when records were first kept. But because declines in fertility have been even greater in older women, births to women under age 20 account for a larger share of all births than they did in the past.

Nevertheless, 19 percent of teenage girls surveyed in 1995 reported having sex before age 15, compared with 11 percent of girls in 1988. No similar increase was observed among boys. According to a study published in the *Journal of the American Medical Association* in 1997, 17 percent of seventh and eighth graders nationwide had engaged in sexual intercourse.

The reasons for the trend toward early sexual activity have not been identi-fied with certainty, but popular culture gets most of the blame. Contemporary parents, who might recoil at the exposure of 19th-century children to the dying and dead, allow their own sons and daughters access to television programs, movies, music videos, and websites with explicit sexual content. Other sug-gested causes for precocious sex include the rising divorce rate; inadequate atten-tion from adults; earlier onset of puberty; and the availability of condoms. Also, health professionals who work with adolescents speculate that boys in their late teens are choosing younger, inexperienced girls as partners to reduce their own risk of contracting a sexually transmitted disease (STD). Yet becoming sexually active at an early age makes it more likely that a girl will be exposed to HIV or another STD, because as a rule those who start younger have more partners than those who wait.

FAMILIES ARE SMALLER

In every era of U.S. history, economics has influenced family size. In the early national period, for example, when sons and daughters were active members of a working family unit, couples produced large numbers of offspring. During the Great Depression of the 1930s, when each child was another hungry mouth for destitute parents to feed, the birthrate plunged. The decline was reversed in the prosperous years following World War II, as couples confidently welcomed a third, fourth, or even fifth child, although children seldom became economically productive until their late teens or early twenties.

Demographers predicted that there would be a rise in births—an echo of the baby boom—as girls born between 1946 and 1964 entered their 20s, but it never happened. By 1974, the number of births in the United States was 3.1 million, a total significantly lower than the 1957 record of 4.3 million, and the demographers began to wonder whether the birthrate would remain permanently low. In 1997, 3.8 million babies were born in the United States, or 14.5 for every 1,000 people. (The 1957 total represented 16.7 births per 1,000 people.)

Economics is a big reason for the persistently low birth rate. Raising a child in the United States has become a costly undertaking. The U.S. Department of Agriculture has estimated that a child born in 1999 will cost his or her parents between $117,390 and $233,850 for food, shelter, and other necessities by the time he or she turns 18. In 1981, the Department of Agriculture projected that it would cost between $58,200 and $153,700 to raise a child born in that year. A particular family's final cost is determined by several variables, including socioeconomic status and the mother's employment. Other reasons for the continuing low birth rate include more effective birth control and a greater number of agencies providing family-planning services to the poor.

MORE MOTHERS WORK

American women have always sought paid employment, but in the 1970s the teachings of the women's liberation movement, combined with high inflation and the proliferation of female-headed households, propelled women into the work force as never before. In 1976, 54 percent of married women and 37 percent of women with children of preschool age worked outside the home. Over the next 12 years, as the U.S. labor force grew 26.5 percent, the number of working women rose 40.4 percent. As a result, more American children then ever before spent significant amounts of time in the early years of life in day care, either in a caregiver's home or at a community child-care center. Girls and boys of school age attended after-school child-care programs or became "latch-key kids" who went home to an empty house in the afternoon and stayed alone until a parent returned from work.

As working parents worried that they were neglecting their children and struggled to meet the demands of home and workplace, many employers accommodated their needs. Benefits and options introduced by Corning Glass Works in 1988 were typical of those offered by many large corporations. They included on-site child care, job sharing, and a parenting resource center. In 2001 the Marriott Corporation provided day care at its Maryland headquarters at the approximate cost of $5,000 per child.

The federal government protected the jobs of adults who needed time off to care for children and other relatives with the Family and Medical Leave Act, which became effective August 5, 1993. This law allows 12 weeks of unpaid leave in a 12-month period for an employee to attend to a new baby or a child placed in the home through adoption or foster care; to take care of a child, spouse, or parent with a serious health condition; or to be treated for a serious illness. To be eligible for the unpaid leave, a person must work for a company that employs 50 or more people within a 75-mile radius. He or she must have been employed by the company for the previous 12 months and have worked 1,250 hours within that year.

CHILDREN'S HEALTH

By some measurements, American children are healthier than in years past. Thanks to immunization, epidemics of once-common childhood diseases such as measles and chikenpox no longer occur in the United States and Canada. Also, mortality rates are falling for children in most age, racial, and ethnic groups. The change has been most dramatic in African-American children ages one to four. In 1996, the mortality rate was 67.6 per 100,000 in this group. A year later, it had fallen to 59.2 per 100,000. That figure, however, was significantly higher than the rate for white youngsters in the same age group, which was 31.5 per 100,000. Finally, there is another hopeful sign: Fewer young people of all races are dying from gunshot wounds. In 2000, the Children's Defense Fund determined that for the first time since 1988, the number of children and teenagers killed by bullets dropped below 4,000.

By other measurements, children's health has declined. For example, African-American infant mortality remains a problem. In Montgomery County, Maryland, an affluent county near Washington, D.C., African-American infant mortality worsened in 1999, reaching 17.4 deaths per 1,000 live births. The infant mortality rate for whites in Montgomery County in 1999 was 4.1 per 1,000 live births. Low birthweight is still a concern as well. In 1997, 7.5 percent of babies born in the United States weighed less than 5.5 pounds. This was the highest rate of such births in more than 20 years, although the increase was due in part to a rise in multiple births.

At the start of the 21st century, more American children are overweight than ever before. According to the National Center for Health Statistics, in the years 1971 to 1974, 4 percent of children ages six to 11 and 6 percent of adolescents ages 12 to 19 were overweight or obese (20 percent above their ideal weight). In 1999, 13 percent in the six-to-11 age group and 14 percent of those 12 to 19 were overweight or obese. Although heredity and some health conditions can play a role in weight gain, the principal causes are too much food and too little exercise. Children now consume more fast-food meals, soft drinks, and high-calorie snacks than youngsters did in the past. They frequently are driven from place to place and therefore do less walking, and they engage more often in sedentary activities, such as watching television and playing computer games. Television viewing remains a favorite individual and family activity. In fact, in one-third of American homes, the TV is left on all afternoon, during the dinner hour, and through the evening.

In 1993, 2 million cases of child abuse and neglect were reported to child-protection agencies in the United States, more than three times the number reported in 1975, and more than 1,000 of the children died from the injuries they received. In 80 percent of these cases, the abuser was a parent. Rates of adolescent suicide and homicide also remain high.

Some of the health problems that have been diagnosed frequently in children and adolescents since the 1970s, such as attention-deficit–hyperactivity disorder and the eating disorders anorexia nervosa and bulimia, were uncommon in earlier years, and their causes and treatment remain controversial. In addition, physicians now see many children with headaches, stomachaches, and other ailments linked to stress.

CHILDREN ADJUST TO A CHANGED WORLD

It would be gratifying to end this history of childhood in America with a description of young people who, although wise beyond their years, are able to put aside adult worries and gather in parks and playgrounds to shoot baskets and jump rope, but such a closing would be simplistic. Events that occurred on

Like many American children of the early 21st century, Kyle and Bonnie McNee of Wilton, Connecticut, spend much of their free time in organized activities. Kyle plays baseball and football as well as lacrosse. Bonnie is a cheerleader, a Brownie, and a ballet student. *(John Reef)*

September 11, 2001, and in the following weeks have necessitated a qualified conclusion.

On the morning of Tuesday, September 11, two hijacked airliners struck and felled the Twin Towers of the World Trade Center in New York City. A third hit the Pentagon, just outside Washington, D.C., and a fourth crashed in Pennsylvania, its intended target unknown. More than 3,000 people died in the attacks, which the FBI soon linked to the Saudi-born terrorist leader Osama bin Laden, who was operating from Afghanistan. On October 7, the United States initiated a war against terrorism by launching air strikes against Afghanistan's Taliban regime.

A small number of children were among the terrorists' victims. For example, three Washington, D.C., sixth graders were aboard American Airlines Flight 77, which hit the Pentagon. Hundreds more children became victims indirectly when they lost parents and other relatives in the burning, tumbling skyscrapers. One of those children, an 11-year-old Connecticut boy, spent the day calling a cell-phone number, hoping to awaken his father from unconsciousness in the rubble of the Twin Towers. A classmate of this boy told his own parents that he would have done the same thing.

Especially on the East Coast, most children were already in school when the attacks occurred. More than 5,000 children and teenagers at six schools in Lower Manhattan saw the second plane crashing into the towers, desperate people jumping to their death, or the buildings collapsing. Many fought their way through smoke and falling debris as they evacuated their schools. The lives of hundreds of these young people and their smaller siblings were disrupted further when their families had to move from neighborhoods such as Battery Park City and TriBeCa.

Elsewhere in New York City on that day, schools remained open. Some stayed open late to shelter children whose parents might be caught in the confusion downtown. School telephones rang constantly with calls from worried fathers and mothers, and parents swarmed schools, eager to take their children home. Most schools in and around Washington, D.C., kept regular hours, although those in Prince George's County, Maryland, closed two hours early.

Children throughout the United States watched the terrorist strikes and their aftermath on television. Researchers from the RAND Corporation and the University of California at Los Angeles (UCLA) reported that the average American child watched 3.1 hours of televised disaster coverage and that more than half of 18-year-olds watched at least five hours of special news programming. This viewing was associated with increased symptoms of stress, including sleep disturbances, irritability, headaches, stomachaches, and disruptive behavior.

Of course, television was not the only stressor. Muslim children had the added worry that their peers would link them with the terrorists and blame them for the devastation.

Nearly all of the parents questioned in the RAND Corporation–UCLA survey said that they had spoken to their children about the attacks. These and other parents struggled to decide how much information to share and how much to withhold. In the days ahead, parents who were reservists or on active duty in the military had the added burden of explaining mobilization to the children they would leave behind.

Caring adults did what they could to help children through this difficult time. Psychologists volunteered to counsel schoolchildren and their parents in the New York and Washington, D.C., metropolitan areas. Nationwide, teachers involved children in activities that helped them feel in control. Students collected money for the American Red Cross; in neighborhoods as diverse as inner-city Indianapolis and upscale Springfield, Virginia, they responded to a request from President George W. Bush and contributed dollars to buy food and medicine for the children of Afghanistan. Teachers used writing and drawing exercises to help children master their fears, understanding that drawing is useful for young children who lack the verbal skills needed to express themselves. In schools, on playgrounds, and at home, the nearly unthinkable images of September 11 became the subject matter of drawings, compositions, and games.

In the meantime, Americans faced a second terrorist threat as letters that would test positive for anthrax arrived at the offices of journalists and lawmakers, including NBC news anchor Tom Brokaw and Senate Majority Leader Tom Daschle. The first anthrax-laden letters were postmarked September 18; by October 31, four people had died of inhalation anthrax and others, including a seven-month-old boy, had been treated for the inhaled and cutaneous (skin) forms of the disease. A fifth victim, a 94-year-old Connecticut woman, died November 2. As an estimated 10,000 people acquired antibiotics as a precautionary measure, the source of the anthrax remained mysterious.

Parents looked with suspicion on the contents of their mailboxes, and children asked questions: Who would put deadly germs in envelopes? Were they or their families going to catch this disease? Children's fears mirrored those of adults, but the young were less able than their elders to separate fantasy from reality or to gauge their safety.

At the start of the 21st century, American children were adapting to a way of life that had already been labeled the "new normal." Their nation had become a place where people hesitate to visit large cities or board jets and where citizens buy gas masks and medicines, fearing a chemical or biological attack. Yet in all probability, American children retain the capacity for joy. In time, they will once again find it easy to dream and hope.

CHRONICLE OF EVENTS

1971–1974
Four percent of children ages six to 11 and 6 percent ages 12 to 19 are overweight or obese.

1974
Births in the United States total 3.1 million.

1976
One-third of marriages end in divorce.

Fifty-four percent of married women and 37 percent of mothers of preschoolers work outside the home.

1981
The cost of raising a baby born in this year to age 18 is estimated to be between $58,200 and $153,700.

1984
Jerry Steinberg of Vancouver, British Columbia, founds No Kidding!, a social club for childless adults.

1988
Eleven percent of teenage girls surveyed have had sex by age 15.

Corning Glass Works offers such family-friendly benefits as on-site child care, job sharing, and a parenting resource center.

1991
More than 12 percent of American children are chronically undernourished.

One-fifth of American children are poor; 330,000 are homeless.

Forty-two percent of divorced fathers have no contact with their children.

One in five U.S. households comprising a married couple and children under 18 is a stepfamily.

1993
Two million cases of child abuse and neglect are reported to child-protection agencies, more than 1,000 of them fatal; in 80 percent of the cases, the abuser is a parent.

August 5: The Family and Medical Leave Act becomes effective. This law permits workers to take unpaid leave to care for a new or sick child or a seriously ill spouse or parent or to be treated themselves for a serious illness.

1995
Nineteen percent of teenage girls surveyed have had sex by age 15.

1996
Births to girls aged 15 to 19 have fallen 16 percent since 1991; the teen abortion rate declined 22 percent in the same period.

The mortality rate for African-American children ages one to four is 67.6 per 100,000.

1997
Seventeen percent of seventh and eighth graders have had sexual intercourse.

The U.S. birthrate is 14.5 per 1,000 people; 3.8 million babies are born in the United States.

The mortality rate for African-American children ages one to four is 59.2 per 100,000; the rate in white children of the same age is 31.5 per 100,000.

Of babies born in the United States, 7.5 percent weigh less than 5.5 pounds.

1998
Sixty-five percent of U.S. children are white, 15 percent are African American, another 15 percent are Hispanic American, and 4 percent are Asian or Pacific Islander.

1999
Fifty-three percent of adults surveyed by Public Agenda describe children as lazy, irresponsible and wild; 71 percent use the same words to describe teenagers.

For every dollar that a man earns, a woman earns 72.2 cents.

The teen birthrate is 49.6 per 1,000 girls aged 15 to 19, the lowest since 1940.

The cost of raising a baby born in this year to age 18 is estimated to be between $117,390 and $233,850.

In Montgomery County, Maryland, the infant mortality rate for African Americans is 17.4 per 1,000 live births; the rate in whites is 4.1 per 1,000 live births.

Thirteen percent of children ages six to 11 and 14 percent ages 12 to 19 are overweight or obese.

2000

Parents in Springfield, Virginia, spend $60,000 on a party for the town's high school graduating class.

The number of U.S. children and teens to die from gunshot wounds falls below 4,000 for the first time since 1988.

2001

There are 60 No Kidding! chapters in North America.

Fifty percent of couples marrying for the first time are expected to divorce; an estimated 60 percent of second marriages will end in divorce.

The Marriott Corporation spends $5,000 per child for on-site day care at its Maryland headquarters.

A television is on throughout the afternoon and evening in one-third of U.S. homes.

September 11: Two hijacked airliners hit the Twin Towers of the World Trade Center in New York City; the towers collapse; a third hijacked plane strikes the Pentagon, and a fourth crashes in Pennsylvania. More than 3,000 people are killed.

September 18: Anthrax-laden letters are mailed to members of the government and the media.

October 7: The United States launches the first air strikes against Afghanistan, the refuge of Osama bin Laden, the terrorist leader who is widely believed to have ordered the September 11 attacks.

October 31: Inhalation anthrax has killed four people; several others, including a seven-month-old-boy, have contracted cases of anthrax from which they will recover.

November 21: A 94-year-old Connecticut woman dies of anthrax.

Eyewitness Testimony

I'm really worried about my brother and sister. I have to set them a good example so they'll be good. That means I have to be good. They fight all the time since my parents broke up. I try to stop that and teach them to talk instead of hitting. I'm also worried about my mom. Since Dad left she cries every day when she comes home from work. I try to comfort her and also to warn her about her new boyfriend. I think that he'll hurt her feelings even more.

> *Karen James, an 11-year-old child of divorced parents, 1971, in Judith Wallerstein et al.,* The Unexpected Legacy of Divorce, *p. xiv.*

Seven-year-old Philip has a strange family doctor. . . .

Philip's family doctor is the emergency clinic at Jackson Memorial Hospital, in Miami. Few of the 33,000 children treated there yearly are accident victims. Most are sick youngsters whose mothers have nowhere else to turn.

There's a doctor three blocks from Philip's home and a private clinic a mile away. But they charge $10 cash in advance, plus the cost of lab tests and prescriptions, which the family can't afford on the father's $100-a-week take-home pay. So when Philip or either of his two sisters suffers a scrape, fever, diarrhea or any ailment short of a true emergency, his mother heads for the county hospital—eight miles, two buses and one

Children at play, Long Island, New York, ca. 1970 *(Author's collection)*

hour away. Most of her 30-odd visits over the last three years have been in the middle of the night; at other hours, she has found, the waiting can take the better part of a day.

Ours is a two-class medical system. First class is for those who can pay directly or with insurance, for private care. The others, like young Philip, rely on a subsystem of emergency rooms, "free clinics" manned by volunteers, and federally funded neighborhood health centers—or get infrequent health care or none at all.

Lester Velie, May 1974, "The Shocking Truth About Our Children's Health Care," pp. 170–71.

It is interesting to realize that the 16-year-olds of 1976 were born in 1960. Their development years were probably quite different from those of young people who reached this age in 1966. The latter were likely to have experienced a childhood of considerable security and conventionality, but as teenagers they may have been caught up in the social movements of the 1960's and experienced the disintegration of these movements. They probably had to struggle with parents and other adults to win their personal freedoms in the new mode; for them, "alternative lifestyles" may have been an exciting discovery and a symbol of their growing autonomy.

In contrast, the 16-year-olds of 1976 grew up as children in chaotic, confusing times. They probably became individually aware of the larger society in the early 1970's, a time of widespread disillusionment with Government, business, and industry. It is unlikely that they have needed to fight much with their parents for personal freedoms because there has been a large shift in the attitudes of adults as well as youth. Because adolescents need to search for their personal identities and values and separate themselves from their parents, will their search take them in more conservative, traditional directions or on to new explorations of individual self-expression as young men and women?

Catherine S. Chilman, 1979, Adolescent Sexuality in a Changing American Society, *p. 90.*

No matter what philosophy of life we espouse, it is important to see childhood as a stage of life, not just as the anteroom to life. Hurrying children into adulthood violates the sanctity of life by giving one period priority over another. But if we really value human life, we will value each period equally and give unto each stage of life what is appropriate to that stage.

A philosophy of life, an art of living, is essentially a way of decentering, a way of looking at our lives in perspective and of recognizing the needs and rights of others. If we can overcome some of the stresses of our adult lives and decenter, we can begin to appreciate the value of childhood with its own special joys, sorrows, worries, and rewards. Valuing childhood does not mean seeing it as a happy innocent period but, rather, as an important period of life to which children are entitled. It is children's right to be children, to enjoy the pleasures, and to suffer the pains of a childhood that is infringed by hurrying. In the end, a childhood is the most basic human right of children.

David Elkind, 1981, The Hurried Child, *pp. 199–200.*

A typical day in school for me is to go to school, go out in the smoking area, and hope to get high. I usually do. I'll proceed to art, then sociology, then biology, and next to English. After English I go out to the smoking area, smoke a butt, then go either into the bathroom or outside to smoke a bowl.

Occasionally, I may do some speed or other minor drugs. After lunch I go to study hall, next to history, and last to study hall. After school I hop on the bus and head for home. We usually get high on the bus, too.

A 16-year-old girl living in Vermont, 1982–83 school year, in Glenbard East Echo, *comp.,* Teenagers Themselves, *p. 15.*

I remember when I was 11, I was playing catch (baseball) in front of my house with my friend. This girl, who lives next door to me, was about 13 then, and she really had a thing for me. She asked me to come in front of her house to keep her some company.

At first I said no, but she convinced me to come anyway. When I came to the porch, she asked me to kiss her, but I had never kissed a girl before. So I told her no because I feel that when I'm going to have sex, I'm going to do it with good intentions.

Brian Turner, 14, of Chicago, 1982–83 school year, in Glenbard East Echo, *comp.,* Teenagers Themselves, *p. 126.*

My parents are divorced, and I've been depressed since it happened. I noticed a change in my personality during the months that my parents were fighting over custody in court. I would sit up in bed for most of the night, and when I did fall asleep, I would have awful dreams. I figured that this was just a normal reaction to the divorce and once it was decided who would get custody of me these problems would go away. But I still have these symptoms of depression even though the custody case has been settled and I know I am to live with my mother. Normally I'd go to my mother with this problem. But she's not in any better shape than I am.

"Troubled Teen," 1984, in Bobby Simpson,
Dear Bobby Simpson, *pp. 155–56.*

The reality is that we're creating a new generation and that many of them are not being supervised, cared for, loved and nurtured. Society has to change. There must be ways of working and caring for children so that we will raise secure, emotionally complete individuals.

Linda Jefferson, California teacher and mother of two, 1990, in Ruth Sidel, On Her Own, *p. 193.*

Every night it's the same old thing. We go to the church for dinner, walk home to our one bedroom apartment and go in bed for a night full of bad dreams. In the morning we walk around town looking for food in garbage cans. We find cereal boxes with a little cereal left in it and a rotten apple. At six o'clock we start walking to the church for our dinner. I made a poem that expresses my feelings about the way my day crawls by:

Cereal and a rotten apple for breakfast
Nothing for lunch
A dinner at the Baptist church
And that's the way my day goes by.
Cathy, a fifth grader living in New Mexico, 1991, in Clifford M. Johnson et al., Child Poverty in America, *p. 17.*

As far as this thing about teen suicide, if a kid's really disturbed and if his parents aren't bright enough or don't care enough to pick up on it, then it's partly their responsibility, too. What's so funny is that if a kid's listening to a heavy metal record and he kills himself, they blame it on the music. But, you're telling me, with

the suicide rate the way it is for teenagers in this country, that all these kids listen to heavy metal?

Reggie, age 17, 1996, in Jeffrey Jansen Arnett, Metalheads, *p. 111.*

Four or five times a week I drive through a pretty little town surrounded by green fields. Its houses are mostly modest and crisply painted, and their lawns are broad and kempt, and trees and flowerbeds flourish. The speed limit for the occasional car is 25 miles an hour. Crime is unknown. Nothing about the town has changed since 1950, or possibly 1900, except that it seems to have been abandoned. Its sidewalks are empty. Its silence is broken only by birdsong. Once or twice a week I see a middle-aged citizen taking a mandated walk. On a Saturday I may see a bicycle, but it's always ridden by an adult male in helmet and spandex, looking determined. Never a child. Five years ago there were still some old signs saying Children At Play, but someone's taken them down.

I know from the statistics that this town is fairly bursting with children and its elementary school bulging out of its classrooms. It's slightly sinister to think that hundreds and hundreds of children can be so effectively hidden, as if they might all be locked in the basements. They aren't, of course; people around here are most particularly tender and careful of their children. Either they're safely in their rooms facing television or computer, or they're off being safely supervised on softball or soccer field, or in karate or gymnastics classes or basketball clinic at the community center, or practicing with the under-eight swim team. Anywhere but loose.

Barbara Holland, 1999, Wasn't the Grass Greener? *p. 205.*

Morning brings the invitations. The casual ones. So routine are they that she hardly thinks about them, just waves them away like gnats. Today, for example, a boy came up to her in the hall and asked, "When are you going to let me hit that?" "That means, like, intercourse," the girl explains, with a sort of gum-popping matter-of-factness. She is 13.

Liza Mundy, July 16, 2000, "Sex and Sensibility," p. 17.

What should we think about five Bethesda [Maryland] eighth-graders standing at a picnic, saying that each of them knows a classmate who has had sex? "My mom doesn't know this goes on," says one. "She thinks we don't even kiss. I don't tell my parents anything. I don't want to tell them. They wouldn't understand. They'd think I was retarded."

Liza Mundy, July 16, 2000, "Sex and
Sensibility," pp. 18–19.

As the mother of two young sons and as a writer on work-life issues, here's what I see when I look at the world: parents who are stressed. Workplace policies that try to ease that stress but can go only so far. Airplane attendants who used to be nicer to children than they are now. The cost of child care and summer camp and orthodontics, which makes it tough to save for tomorrow's cost of college. Drivers who don't slow down on side streets. Louts who wear obscene T-shirts that my kids can read and curse at baseball games where my kids can hear.

Lisa Belkin, July 23, 2000, "Your Kids Are
Their Problem," p. 32.

. . . [E]very day that I go to school, I am exposed to sex talk and cuss words. I also have been exposed to such things on TV, although it was at a young age and at that time it pretty much went over my head. Starting in middle school, health classes teach about HIV and AIDS. My 8-year-old brother had a "drug unit" in his elementary school. . . .

I hope parents will listen when I say that maybe they should examine their child's real world. . . .

Alexandra De Armon, an eighth-grade student living in
Frederick, Maryland, in a letter to the Washington Post,
March 17, 2001, p. A20.

There is 8-year-old Liam Galloway and his sister, Kiera, 9, fleeing with their parents, who were dropping them off at school. A black cloud of smoke, debris from the burning buildings, a "black avalanche," overcomes them. They fall to the ground, holding hands, waiting for the cloud to pass them by. Later, once they had evacuated to New Jersey, their dad tells them, "Nothing in your life is going to be as scary as that. You handle that, you can get through anything."

Then there is Lucas Tatarsky, 9 years old today, who looked out the window of his fourth-grade class and witnessed the second crash. As he puts it, the hole made by the plane was "shimmering and it looked so cool." He talks about this, analyzing the shape and size of the hole, describing it all, his voice racing a little

ahead of itself as though he's reciting a book report. But as he tells his story, he's staring ahead, his eyes just a little glazed. . . . Finally, Lucas stops his recitation and admits, to a reporter, "It's too much for my brain to tolerate."

Teresa Wiltz, September 15, 2001, "Terror Doesn't Spare
Young," p. A10.

Like many little girls, Mallory O'Bryan is usually preoccupied with rainbows, stuffed animals, butterflies and the animals she sees on television. Her crayon and pencil drawings reflect an innocent focus.

But on the morning after terrorists destroyed the World Trade Center, the 7-year-old had something else on her mind.

As her mother chatted on the phone, Mallory drew a picture of a flaming skyscraper under jet attack, complete with a screaming stick-woman pedestrian and a howling child face in a top-floor window.

"She said, 'Look mommy,'" her mother, Dana, recalled. "I stopped my entire conversation. I didn't know what to say."

Mary Macdonald, September 21, 2001,
"How Kids Cope," p. C1.

Five days after the attacks, New York psychotherapist Myrna Lewis counseled a little boy who was having trouble sleeping. His bedroom faced the World Trade Center. Every night before the attacks, he'd count the windows across the way and when he got to 23 or 24, he'd fall asleep. Now the windows are gone and the family has been evacuated from their apartment. He has to find a new routine to fall asleep.

Abigail Trafford, October 9, 2001, "A New Kind of
Normal," p. F1.

Adolescents are fragile. We try to protect them from unbearable realities because they are impulsive, unpredictable, inexperienced, without perspective. Should we go on now as if the events raging outside the classroom could be left "out there"? Could we keep the school atmosphere inviolable? Ultimately, the shock waves were too palpable. We had to let the world into the classroom.

Jane Danaher, seventh-grade English teacher
at Thoreau Middle School, Vienna, Virginia,
November 11, 2001, "A Change in
Course," p. 39.

. . . K]ids started making little jokes to me about my family being involved, about my culture and my religion. They'd say things like, "Hey, where's your family hiding Osama bin Laden?" or, "Which one of your cousins crashed that plane?" I didn't say anything; I tried to act like it didn't bother me. But after a time it started making me feel bad. I mentioned it to our principal, and he said this type of stuff is going to happen and we've just got to get through it.

Haroon Rasheed, senior at H-B Woodlawn High School, Arlington, Virginia, November 11, 2001, "A Test in Tolerance," p. 41.

The third week after the attacks, the sentence, "Have you visited the twin towers at the World Trade Center?" popped up in the middle of a set of grammar exercises. Before I could form a response, the kids were wild with laughter. The laughter rose, almost hysterically, for a minute or two, and then subsided, not out of disrespect, but as a desperate release. On one level, I thought, these kids are untouched by the tragedy of the terrorist attack. But on a deeper level they also know that life has changed forever in America. They are kids; they will revel in the emotional peaks and valleys of adolescence as before, but the comforting background of peace has shifted, and they know it.

Jane Danaher, seventh-grade English teacher at Thoreau Middle School, Vienna, Virginia, November 11, 2001, "A Change in Course," p. 40.

APPENDIX A
Documents

1. Extract from a letter from John Adams to his son John Quincy Adams (1767–1848), March 16, 1777
2. Extract from a letter from John Adams to his daughter Abigail Amelia Adams (1765–1813), March 17, 1777
3. Extracts from "A Bill for the More General Diffusion of Knowledge," presented by Thomas Jefferson to the Committee of Revisors of the Virginia Assembly, June 18, 1779
4. Extracts from Noah Webster's introduction to *A Grammatical Institute, of the English Language,* 1783
5. Extract from "A Plan for Establishing Public Schools in Pennsylvania, and for Conducting Education Agreeably to a Republican Form of Government," presented by Benjamin Rush to the legislature and citizens of Pennsylvania, 1786
6. Extracts from the Massachusetts school law of 1789
7. Article of indenture, April 26, 1802
8. Albert Gallatin, "Manufactures, April 19, 1810"
9. Extracts from *An Act* to *incorporate the Society for the Reformation of Juvenile Delinquents,* in the city of New York, March 29, 1824
10. "Rules for the Enforcement of Discipline in the New York House of Refuge," ca. 1825
11. An Act to amend the laws in relation to slaves and free persons of color, passed by the South Carolina Legislature, 1834
12. The Massachusetts Compulsory School Law of 1850
13. A notice on the decline in the price of Negroes, *Richmond South,* December 14, 1857
14. Letter to Charles Loring Brace from the Reverend E. P. S. of Pepperell, Massachusetts, December 14, 1859
15. Letter from Mary Lewis, age 17, to her father, Captain Andrew Lewis of the 40th Regiment of Pennsylvania Volunteers, August 13, 1861
16. The Emancipation Proclamation, January 1, 1863
17. Extracts from the instructions issued to principals of Pennsylvania's soldiers' orphan schools, October 13, 1866
18. Extracts from "The Indian School at Carlisle Barracks," a report to the U.S. commissioner of education, 1880
19. Extracts from the First Annual Report of the Factory Inspectors of Illinois, 1893
20. The 25 leading amusements of Worcester, Massachusetts, schoolchildren as reported in *Pedagogical Seminary,* September 1899

21. Extract from a paper read by J. J. Kelso, superintendent of the Department of Neglected and Dependent Children of Ontario, at the annual meeting of the American Humane Association, held in Boston, November 12–14, 1907

22. Extracts from a letter to the president of the United States embodying the conclusions of the Conference on the Care of Dependent Children held in Washington, D.C., January 25 and 26, 1909

23. The stages of childhood as charted by George Walter Fiske, 1910

24. Extract from *An Act To establish in the Department of Commerce and Labor a bureau to be known as the Children's Bureau,* April 9, 1912

25. Letter from Theodore Roosevelt to William E. Hall, national director of the Boys' Working Reserve, September 4, 1917

26. Extract from *Outline of an Emergency Course of Instruction on the War,* distributed to schools by the Committee on Public Information, 1918

27. Form submitted by Indiana farmers to the state director of the U.S. Boys' Working Reserve, 1918

28. Extracts from the Delaware law relating to the interstate placement of dependent children, 1921

29. Extracts from Emergency Conservation Work: An Act, March 31, 1933

30. Extract from Unemployed Youth of New York City, a report published by the U.S. Bureau of Labor Statistics, February 1937

31. Extracts from Executive Order 9066, February 19, 1942

32. Extracts from Protection of School Children During Air Raids: A Fact Sheet, Office of Civilian Defense Publication 5222, April 1943

33. House Concurrent Resolution 104, December 13, 1944

34. Extracts from the opinion of the U.S. Supreme Court in *Brown et al. v. Board of Education of Topeka et al.,* 1954

35. Dress Right, January 24, 1956

36. Extracts from *An Act To grant family and medical leave under Certain circumstances,* February 5, 1993.

1. Extract from a Letter from John Adams to His Son John Quincy Adams (1767–1848), March 16, 1777

Philadelphia March 16. 1777

My dear Son

There is an observation, which I wish you to make very early in Life because it may be usefull to you, when you grow up. It is this, that a Taste for Literature and a Turn for Business, united in the same Person, never fails to make a great Man. A Taste for Literature, includes the Love of Science and the fine Arts. A Turn for Business, comprehends Industry and Application as well as a faculty of conversing with men, and managing Affairs.

I hope you will keep these two Objects in View all your Lifetime. As you will not have Property to enable you to pursue your Learning alone, you must apply yourself to Business to procure you the Means of subsistence. But you will find Learning of the utmost Importance to you in Business, as well as the most ingenious and elegant Entertainment, of your Life. . . .

I am your affectionate Father.

2. Extract from a Letter from John Adams to His Daughter Abigail Amelia Adams (1765–1813), March 17, 1777

Philadelphia March 17. 1777

My dear Daughter

I hope by this Time, you can write an handsome Hand; but I wish you would, now and then, send a Specimen of it, to Philadelphia to your Pappa, that he may have the Pleasure of observing the Proficiency you make, not only in your Hand Writing, but in your turn of Thinking, and in your Faculty of expressing your Thoughts.

You have discovered, in your childhood, a remarkable Modesty, Discretion, and Reserve; I hope these great and amiable Virtues will rather improve, in your riper Years. You are now I think, far advanced in your twelfth Year—a Time when the Understanding generally opens, and the Youth begin to look abroad into that World among whom they are to live—To be good, and to do good, is all We have to do. . . .

I am with inexpressible Affection, your Father.

3. Extracts from "A Bill for the More General Diffusion of Knowledge," Presented by Thomas Jefferson to the Committee of Revisors of the Virginia Assembly, June 18, 1779

Whereas it appeareth that however certain forms of government are better calculated than others to protect individuals in the free exercise of their natural rights, and are at the same time themselves better guarded against degeneracy, yet experience hath shewn, that even under the best forms, those entrusted with power have, in time, and by slow operations, perverted it into tyranny; and it is believed that the most effectual means of preventing this would be, to illuminate, as far as practicable, the minds of the people at large, and more especially to give them knowledge of those facts, which history exhibiteth, that, possessed thereby of the experience of other ages and countries, they may be enabled to know ambition under all its shapes, and prompt to exert their natural powers to defeat its purposes; And whereas it is generally true that that people will be happiest whose laws are best, and are best administered, and that laws will be wisely formed, and honestly administered, in proportion as those who form and administer them are wise and honest; whence it becomes expedient for promoting the publick happiness that those persons, whom nature hath endowed with genius and virtue, should be rendered by liberal education worthy to receive, and able to guard the sacred deposit of the rights and liberties of their fellow citizens, and that they should be called to that charge without regard to wealth, birth or other accidental condition or circumstance; but the indigence of the greater number disabling them from so educating, at their own expence, those of their children whom nature hath fitly formed and disposed to become useful instruments for the public, it is better that such should be sought for and educated at the common expence of all, than that the happiness of all should be confided to the weak or wicked:

Be it therefore enacted by the General Assembly, that in every county within this commonwealth, there shall be chosen annually, by the electors qualified to vote for Delegates, three of the most honest and able men of their county, to be called the Aldermen of the county; and that the election of the said Aldermen shall be held at the same time and place, before the same persons, and notified and conducted in the same manner as by law is directed for the annual election of Delegates for the county. . . .

The said Aldermen on the first Monday in October, if it be fair, and if not, then on the next fair day, excluding Sunday, shall meet at the court-house of their county, and proceed to divide their said county into hundreds, bounding the same by water courses, mountains, or limits, to be run and marked, if they think necessary, by the county surveyor, and at the county expence, regulating the size of the said hundreds, according to the best of their discretion, so as that they may contain a convenient number of children to make up a school, and be of such convenient size that all the children within each hundred may daily attend the school to be established therein, distinguishing each hundred by a particular name; which division, with the names of the several hundreds, shall be returned to the court of the county and be entered of record, and shall remain unaltered until the increase or decrease of inhabitants shall render an alteration necessary, in the opinion of any succeeding Aldermen, and also in the opinion of the court of the county. . . .

At every of these schools shall be taught reading, writing, and common arithmetick, and the books which shall be used therein for instructing the children to read shall be such as will at the same time make them acquainted with Graecian, Roman, English, and American history. At these schools all the free children, male and female, resident within the respected hundred, shall be intitled to receive tuition gratis, for the term of three years, and as much longer, at their private expence, as their parents, guardians or friends, shall think proper. . . .

Every teacher shall receive a salary of   by the year, which, with the expences of building and repairing the schoolhouses, shall be provided in such manner as other county expences are by law directed to be provided and shall also have his diet, lodging, and washing found him, to be levied in like manner, save only that such levy shall be on the inhabitants of each hundred for the board of their own teacher only.

And in order that grammar schools may be rendered convenient to the youth in every part of the commonwealth, Be it farther enacted, that on the first Monday in November, after the first appointment of overseers for the hundred schools, if fair, and if not, then on the next fair day, excluding Sunday, after the hour of one in the afternoon, the said overseers appointed for the schools . . . shall meet . . . and shall fix on such place in some one of the counties in their district as shall be most proper for situating a grammar school-house, endeavouring that the situation be as central as may be to the inhabitants of the said counties, that it be furnished with good water, convenient to plentiful supplies of provision and fuel, and more than all things that it be healthy. . . .

In these grammar schools shall be taught the Latin and Greek languages, English grammar, geography, and the higher part of numerical arithmetick, to wit, vulgar and decimal fractions, and the extraction of the square and cube roots. . . .

Every overseer of the hundred schools shall, in the month of September annually, after the most diligent and impartial examination and enquiry, appoint from among the boys who shall have been two years at the least at some one of the schools under his superintendance, and whose parents are too poor to give them farther education, some one of the best and most promising genius and disposition, to proceed to the grammar school of his district; which appointment shall be made in the court-house of the county, on the court day for that month if fair, and if not, then on the next fair day, excluding Sunday, in the presence of the Aldermen, or two of them at the least, assembled on the bench for that purpose, the said overseer being previously sworn by them to make such appointment, without favor or affection, according to the best of his skill and judgment, and being interrogated by the said Aldermen, either on their own motion, or on suggestions from the parents, guardians, friends, or teachers of the children, competitors for such appointment; which teachers shall attend for the information of the Aldermen. On which interrogatories the said Aldermen, if they be not satisfied with the appointment proposed, shall have right to negative it; whereupon the said visiter may proceed to make a new appointment, and the said Aldermen again to interrogate and negative, and so toties quoties until an appointment be approved.

Every boy so appointed shall be authorised to proceed to the grammar school of his district, there to be educated and boarded during such time as is hereafter limited; and his quota of the expences of the house together with a compensation to the master or usher for his tuition, at the rate of twenty dollars by the year, shall be paid by the Treasurer quarterly on warrant from the Auditors.

A visitation shall be held, for the purpose of probation, annually at the said grammar school on the last Monday in September, if fair, and if not, then on the next fair day, excluding Sunday, at which one third of the boys sent thither by appointment of the said overseers, and who shall have been there one year only, shall be discontinued as public foundationers, being those who, on the most diligent examination and enquiry, shall be thought to be of the least promising genius and disposition; and of those who shall have been there two years, all shall be discontinued, save one only the best in genius and disposition, who shall be at liberty to continue there four years longer on the public foundation, and shall thence forward be deemed a senior.

The visiters for the districts which, or any part of which, be southward and westward of the James river, as known by that name, or by the names of Fluvanna and Jackson's river, in every other year, to wit, at the probation meetings held in the years, distinguished in the Christian computation by odd numbers, and the visiters for all the other districts at their said meetings to be held in those years, distinguished by even numbers, after diligent examination and enquiry as before directed, shall chuse one among the said seniors, of the best learning and most hopeful genius and disposition, who shall be authorised by them to proceed to William and Mary College, there to be educated, boarded, and clothed, three years; the expence of which annually shall be paid by the Treasurer on warrant from the Auditors.

4. EXTRACTS FROM NOAH WEBSTER'S INTRODUCTION TO *A GRAMMATICAL INSTITUTE, OF THE ENGLISH LANGUAGE,* 1783

To attack deep rooted prejudices and oppose the current of opinion, is a task of great difficulty and hazard. It commonly requires length of time and favourable circumstances to diffuse and establish a sentiment among the body of the people; but when a sentiment has acquired the stamp of time and the authority of general custom, it is too firm to be shaken by the efforts of an individual: Even errour becomes too sacred to be violated by the assaults of innovation.

But the present period is an era of wonders: Greater changes have been wrought, in the minds of men, in the short compass of eight years past, than are commonly effected in a century.

Previously to the late war, America preserved the most unshaken attachment to Great-Britain: The king, the constitution, the laws, the commerce, the fashions, the books, and even the sentiments of Englishmen were implicitly supposed to be the *best* on earth: not only their virtues and improvements, but their prejudices, their errours, their vices and their follies were adopted by us with avidity. But by a concurrence of those powerful causes that effect almost instantaneous revolutions in states, the political views of America have suffered a total change. She now sees a mixture of profound wisdom and consummate folly in the British constitution; a ridiculous compound of freedom and tyranny in their laws; and a few struggles of patriotism, overpowered by the corruptions of a wicked administration. She views the vices of that nation with abhorrence, their errours with pity, and their follies with contempt.

While the Americans stand astonished at their former delusion and enjoy the pleasure of a final separation from their insolent sovereigns, it becomes their duty to attend to the *arts of peace,* and particularly to the interests of *literature;* to see if there be not some errours to be corrected, some defects to be supplied, and some improvements to be introduced into our systems of education, as well as into those of civil policy. We find Englishmen practicing upon very erroneous maxims in politics and religion; and possibly we shall find, upon careful examination, that their methods of education are equally erroneous and defective.

The British writers remark it as one of the follies of their nation, that they have attended more to the study of ancient and foreign languages, than to the improvement of their own. The ancient Greek and Roman languages, and the modern French and Italian, have generally been made a necessary part of a polite or learned education; while a grammatical study of their own language, has, till very lately been totally neglected. This ridiculous practice has found its way to America; and so violent have been the prejudices in support of it, that the whispers of common sense, in favour of our native tongue, have been silenced amidst the clamour of pedantry in favour of Greek and Latin.

The consequence is, that few attempts have been made to reduce our language to rules, and expunge the corruptions that ignorance and caprice, unguided by any standard, must necessarily introduce. It is but a short time since we have had a grammar of our own tongue, formed upon the true principals of its Saxon original: And those who have given us the most perfect systems, have confined themselves chiefly to the two last two branches of grammar, Analogy and Syntax. In the two first, Orthography and Prosody, that is, in the spelling and pronunciation of words, we have no guide, or none but such as lead into innumerable errours. The want of some standard in schools has occasioned a great variety of dialects in Great-Britain and of course, in America. Every county in England, every State in America and almost every town in each State, has some peculiarities in pronunciation which are equally erroneous and disagreeable to its neighbors. And how can these distinctions be avoided? The sounds of our letters are more capricious and irregular than those of any alphabet with which we are acquainted. Several of our vowels have four or five different sounds; and the same sounds are often expressed by five, six or seven different characters. The case is much the same with our consonants: And these different sounds have no mark of distinction. How would a child or a foreigner learn the different sounds of *o* in these words, *rove, move, dove* or of *oo* in *poor, door?* Or that *a, ai, ei,* and *e,* have precisely the same sound in these words, *bare, laid, vein, there?* Yet these and fifty other irregularities have passed unnoticed by authors of Spelling Books and Dictionaries. They study the language enough to find the difficulties of it—they tell us that it is impossible to reduce it to order—that it is to be learnt only by the ear—they lament the disorder and dismiss it without a remedy.

Thus the pronunciation of our language, tho' the most important and difficult part of grammar, is *left* to parents and nurses—to ignorance and caprice—to custom, accident or nothing—Nay to something worse, to coxcombs, who have a large share in directing the *polite taste* of pronunciation, which of course is as vicious as that of any other class of people. And while this is the case, every person will claim a right to pronounce most agreably to his own fancy, and the language will be exposed to perpetual fluctuation.

This consideration gave rise to the following little system, which is designed to introduce uniformity and accuracy of pronunciation into common schools. It cost me much labour to form a plan that should be both *simple* and *accurate.* The one here adopted seems to unite these two articles; at least so far as to prevent any material errours. A more accurate method might have been invented; but it must have been too complicated to be useful. The rules for ascertaining a just pronunciation are so simple and concise, that I flatter myself they

fall within the comprehension of the most indifferent capacity. Some may possibly be too indolent to study them; and others, from a principle of self-sufficiency, may affect to despise them. The former will be modest enough neither to approve nor condemn what they deem beneath their attention; and I would inform the latter that after I had devoted nine years to the acquisition of knowledge, three or four of which were spent in studying languages, and about the same period in teaching the English, I was astonished to find myself a stranger to its principal beauties and most obvious faults. Those therefore who disdain this attempt to improve our language and assist the instructors of youth, must be either much more or much less acquainted with the language than I am. The criticisms of those who know more, will be received with gratitude; the censure or ridicule of those who know less, will be inexcusable.

The principal part of instructors are illiterate people, and require some easy guide to the *standard* of pronunciation, which is nothing else but the customary pronunciation of the most accurate scholars and literary Gentlemen. Such a standard, universally used in schools, would in time, demolish those odious distinctions of provincial dialects, which are the objects of reciprocal ridicule in the United States. . . .

The author wishes to promote the honour and prosperity of the confederated republics of America; and chearfully throws his mite into the common treasure of patriotic exertions. This country must in some future time, be as distinguished by the superiority of her literary improvements, as she is already by the liberality of her civil and ecclesiastical constitutions. Europe is grown old in folly, corruption and tyranny—in that country laws are perverted, manners are licentious, literature is declining and human nature debased. For America in her infancy to adopt the present maxims of the old world, would be to stamp the wrinkles of decrepid age upon the bloom of youth and to plant the seeds of decay in a vigourous constitution. American glory begins to dawn at a favourable period, and under flattering circumstances. We have the experience of the whole world before our eyes; but to receive indiscriminately the maxims of government, the manners and the literary taste of Europe and make them the ground on which to build our systems in America, must soon convince us that a durable and stately edifice can never be erected upon the mouldering pillars of antiquity. It is the business of *Americans* to select the wisdom of all nations, as the basis of her constitutions,—to avoid their errours,—to prevent the introduction of foreign vices and corruptions and check the career of her own,—to promote virtue and patriotism,—to embellish and improve the sciences,—to diffuse an uniformity and purity of *language,*—to add superiour dignity to this infant Empire and to human nature.

5. Extract from "A Plan for Establishing Public Schools in Pennsylvania, and for Conducting Education Agreeably to a Republican Form of Government," Presented by Benjamin Rush to the Legislature and Citizens of Pennsylvania, 1786

Before I proceed to the subject of this essay, I shall point out, in a few words, the influence and advantages of learning upon mankind.

I. It is friendly to religion, inasmuch as it assists in removing prejudice, superstition and enthusiasm, in promoting just notions of the Deity, and in enlarging our knowledge of his works.

II. It is favourable to liberty. Freedom can exist only in the society of knowledge. Without learning, men are incapable of knowing their rights, and where learning is confined to a few people, liberty can be neither equal nor universal.

III. It promotes just ideas of laws and government. "When the clouds of ignorance are dispelled (says the Marquis of Beccaria) by the radiance of knowledge, power trembles, but the authority of laws remains immoveable."

IV. It is friendly to manners. Learning in all countries, promotes civilization, and the pleasures of society and conversation.

V. It promotes agriculture, the great basis of national wealth and happiness. Agriculture is as much a science as hydraulics, or optics, and has been equally indebted to the experiments and researches of learned men. The highly cultivated state, and the immense profits of the farms in England, are derived wholly from the patronage which agriculture has received in that country, from learned men and learned societies.

VI. Manufactures of all kinds owe their perfection chiefly to learning—hence the nations of Europe advance in manufactures, knowledge, and commerce, only in proportion as they cultivate the arts and sciences.

For the purpose of diffusing knowledge through every part of the state, I beg leave to propose the following simple plan.

I. Let there be one university in the state, and let this be established in the capital. Let law, physic, divinity, the law of nature and nations, œconomy, &c. be taught in it by public lectures in the winter season, after the manner of the European universities, and let the professors receive such salaries from the state as will enable them to deliver their lectures at a moderate price.

II. Let there be four colleges. One in Philadelphia; one at Carlisle; a third, for the benefit of our German fellow citizens, at Lancaster; and a fourth, some years hence at Pittsburg. In these colleges, let young men be instructed in mathematics and in the higher branches of science, in the same manner that they are now taught in our American colleges. After they have received a testimonial from one of these colleges, let them, if they can afford it, complete their studies by spending a season or two in attending the lectures in the university. . . .

III. Let there be free schools established in every township; or in districts consisting of one hundred families. In these schools let children be taught to read and write the English and German languages, and the use of figures. Such of them as have parents that can afford to send them from home, and are disposed to extend their educations, may remove their children from the free school to one of the colleges.

By this plan the whole state will be tied together by one system of education. The university will in time furnish masters for the colleges, and the colleges will furnish masters for the free schools, while the free schools, in their turns, will supply the colleges and the university with scholars, students and pupils. The same systems of grammar, oratory and philosophy, will be taught in every part of the state, and the literary features of Pennsylvania will thus designate one great, and equally enlightened family. . . .

6. Extracts from the Massachusetts School Law of 1789

Every town or district within this Commonwealth, containing *fifty* families, or householders, shall be provided with a School-Master or School-Masters, of good morals, to teach children to read and write, and to instruct them in the English language, as well as in arithmetic, orthography, and decent behaviour, for such term of time as shall be equivalent to *six months* for one school in each year. And every town or district containing *one hundred* families, or householders, shall be provided with such School-Master or School-Masters, for such term of time as shall be equivalent to *twelve* months for one school in each year. And every town or district containing *one hundred and fifty* families, or householders, shall be provided with such School-Master or School-Masters, for such term of time as shall be equivalent to *six months* in each year; and shall, in addition thereto, be provided with a School-Master or School-Masters, as above described, to instruct children in the English language, for such term of time as shall be equivalent to *twelve months* for one school in each year. And every town or district containing *two hundred* families, or householders, shall be provided with a grammar School-Master, of good morals, well instructed in the Latin, Greek and English languages; and shall, in addition thereto, be provided with a School-Master or School-Masters, as above described, to instruct children in the English language, for such term of time as shall be equivalent to *twelve months* for each of said schools in each year. . . .

[N]o youth shall be sent to such grammar schools unless they shall have learned, in some other school or in some other way, to read the English language, by spelling the same; or the Selectmen of the town where such grammar school is, shall direct the grammar School-Master to receive and instruct such youth. . . .

[N]o person shall be allowed to be a Master or Mistress of such school, or to keep the same, unless he or she shall obtain a certificate from the Selectmen of such town or district where the same may be kept, or the Committee appointed by such town, district or plantation, to visit their schools, as well as from a learned Minister settled therein, if such there be, that he or she is a person of sober life and conversation, and well qualified to keep such school. And it shall be the duty of such Master or Mistress, carefully to instruct the children, attending his or her school, in reading (and writing, if contracted for) and to instil into their minds a sense of piety and virtue, and to teach them decent behaviour. And if any person shall presume to keep such school without a certificate as aforesaid, he or she shall forfeit and pay the sum of *Twenty Shillings,* one moiety thereof to the informer, and the other moi-ety to the use of the poor of the town, district or plantation where such school may be kept. . . .

No person shall be permitted to keep, within this Commonwealth, any school described in this Act, unless, in consequence of an Act of naturalization, or otherwise, he shall be a citizen of this or some other of the United States. And if any person who is not a citizen of this or some one of the United States, shall presume to keep any such school within this State for the space of one month, he shall be subjected to pay a fine of *Twenty Pounds,* and a proportionable sum for a longer or shorter time; the one half of which fine shall be to the use of the person who shall sue for the same, and the other half thereof to the use of this Common-wealth.

7. Article of Indenture, April 26, 1802

Biddy Dougherty, with the advise and consent of her mother Catherine of the City of Philadelphia, was bound apprentice to Arthur Howell of the City of Philadelphia, Tanner and Currier, to him, his heirs and assigns for and during the term of seven years, to be taught domestic work, to be provided with meat and drink, clothing, lodging, working, fitting for an apprentice during the said term of seven years, to have four quarters half days schooling and when free to have two suits apparel, one whereof to be new.

8. Albert Gallatin, "Manufactures, April 19, 1810"

Returns have been received of eighty-seven mills, which were erected at the end of the year 1809; sixty-two of which (forty-eight, water, and fourteen, horse, mills) were in operation, and worked, at that time, thirty-one thousand spindles. The other twenty-five will all be in operation in the course of this year, and, together with the former ones, (almost all of which are increasing their machinery) will, by the estimate received, work more than eighty thousand spindles at the commencement of the year 1811.

The capital required to carry on the manufacture, on the best terms, is estimated at the rate of one hundred dollars for each spindle; including both the fixed capital applied to the purchase of the mill-seats, and to the construction of the mills and machinery, and that employed in wages, repairs, raw materials, goods on hand, and contingencies. But it is believed that no more than at the rate of sixty dollars for each spindle is generally actually employed. Forty-five pounds of cotton, worth about 20 cents a pound, are, on an average, annually used for each spindle; and these produce about thirty-six pounds of yarn, of different qualities, worth, on an average, one dollar and twelve and a half cents a pound. Eight hundred spindles employ forty persons, viz: five men and thirty-five women and children. On those data, the general results for the year 1811, are estimated in the following table:

Persons employed

Mills	Spindles	Men	Women and children	Total
87	80,000	500	3,500	4,000

The increase of carding and spinning of cotton by machinery, in establishments for that purpose, and exclusively of that done in private families, has, therefore, been fourfold, during the two last years, and will have been tenfold in three years.

9. EXTRACTS FROM *AN ACT TO INCORPORATE THE SOCIETY FOR THE REFORMATION OF JUVENILE DELINQUENTS,* IN THE CITY OF NEW YORK, MARCH 29, 1824

WHEREAS, by the petition of several inhabitants of the city of New York, it is represented, that they are desirous of establishing a Society and House of Refuge for the Reformation of Juvenile Delinquents, in the said city, and have prayed to be incorporated: Therefore,

I. *Be it enacted by the people of the State of New York, represented in the Senate and Assembly,* That all such persons as now are or hereafter shall become subscribers to the said association pursuant to the by-laws thereof, shall be, and hereby are constituted a body corporate and politic, by the name of "The Managers of the Society for the Reformation of Juvenile Delinquents in the City of New York," and by that name they shall have perpetual succession, and be in law capable of suing and being sued, defending and being defended, in all courts and places, and in all manner of actions and causes whatsoever, and may have a common seal, and change the same at their pleasure, and shall be capable in law by that name and style of purchasing, holding and conveying any estate, real or personal, for the use of said corporation: *Provided,* That such real estate shall never exceed the yearly value of ten thousand dollars, nor be applied to any other purposes than those for which this incorporation is formed. . . .

IV. *And be it further enacted,* That the said Managers shall have power in their discretion to receive and take into the House of Refuge to be established by them, all such children as shall be taken up or committed as vagrants, or convicted of criminal offences in the said city, as may in the judgment of the Court of General Sessions of the peace, or of the Court of Oyer and Terminer, in and for the said city, or of the Jury before whom any such offender shall be tried, or of the Police Magistrates, or of the Commissioners of the Alms House and Bridewell [Prison] of the said city, be proper objects; and the said Managers shall have power to place the said children committed to their care, during the minority of such children, at such employments and to cause them to be instructed in such branches of useful knowledge as shall be suitable to their years and capacities; and they shall have power in their discretion to bind out the said children with their consent, as apprentices or servants during their minority, to such persons and at such places, to learn such proper trades and employments as in their judgment will be most for the reformation and amendment, and the future benefit and advantage of such children: *Provided,* That the charge and power of the said Managers upon and over the said children, shall not extend in the case of females beyond the age of eighteen years. . . .

VI. *And be it further enacted,* That the said managers under this act, may from time to time make by-laws, ordinances and regulations relative to the management and disposition of the estate and concerns of the said Corporation, and management, government, instruction, discipline, employment and disposition of the said children while in the said House of Refuge, or under their care, not contrary to law, as they may deem proper, and may appoint such officers, agents and servants as they may deem necessary to transact the business of the said Corporation, and may designate their duties; *and further,* That the said Managers shall make an annual report to the Legislature, and to the Corporation of the city of New York, of the number of children received by them into the said House of Refuge, the disposition which shall be made of the said children by instructing or employing them in the said House of Refuge, or by binding them out as apprentices or servants; the receipts and expenditures of said Managers, and generally all such facts and particulars as may tend to exhibit the effects, whether advantageous or otherwise, of the said Association. . . .

10. "Rules for the Enforcement of Discipline in the New York House of Refuge," ca. 1825

I.—Tell no lies.

II.—Always do the best you can.

III.—The boys and girls are divided into four grades, according to conduct.

Grade 1—Includes the best behaved and most orderly boys and girls; those who do not lie, nor use profane language; who are neat and tidy in their persons, and cleanly in their habits; who do not wilfully or carelessly waste, injure, or destroy property belonging to the House, and who are always respectful to the officers.

Grade 2—Embraces those who are fair in conduct, but not entirely free from faults mentioned above.

Grade 3—Consists of those whose conduct is not so good as those in Grade 2. The first Grade of a boy or girl is always 3.

Grade 4—Is the lowest, and one of disgrace, it is only given in cases of continued or gross misconduct; a former inmate returned for fault is placed in Grade 4.

IV.—For violation of rules, boys and girls are degraded from 1 to 2, from 2 to 3, and from 3 to 4; for improvement in conduct they are raised in Grade from 4 to 3, from 3 to 2, and from 2 to 1. Any boy or girl continuing for thirteen weeks in succession in Grade 1, is advanced to the Class of Honor, and wears an appropriate badge.

V.—The Grades are determined every Saturday evening, in the presence of the whole division, according to the marks made during the week.

VI.—Five marks lower the Grade one step; four leave it the same as the previous week; less than four are forgiven.

VII.—In the Second Division, punishment with the strap degrades to 4; except when the subject is in the Class of Honor, in which case it degrades to 2.

VIII.—Boys and girls gain their release from the Refuge by retaining Grade 1 for fifty-two weeks in succession, and by attaining to the highest class in school—and they are discharged from the House when a proper place is provided for them.

IX.—No applications from parents or friends of children will be entertained by the Indenturing Committee, until the individual applied for shall have been in Grade 1 at least six weeks next preceding the time of application, and shall have reached at least the third class in school.

X.—When an inmate has been degraded to 4, an addition of four weeks' continuance in Grade 1, required by the foregoing rule, will be made, before an application for discharge can he heard; and two weeks more are added for every other Grade of 4 received.

XI.—Grades can be changed only by the Assistant-Superintendent, in case of boys, and by the Matron, in case of girls, for offences committed out of school; and by the Principal for offences occurring in school.

XII.—Any officer in charge of boys or girls may give, for disorderly conduct, not to exceed two marks during any one week, provided the marks given, added to those already imposed by others during the same week, do not exceed four.

XIII.—Before any marks are given, the boy or girl must be required to tell the number of marks already received, and the statement must be taken and noted.

XIV.—In case an inmate makes a false statement, which will be discovered at "Badge call," the offender shall be degraded at least two Grades, or may be punished according to the discretion of the officer in charge. In the latter case the Grade will be 4.

XV.—When the aggregate marks for the week amount to four, and other offences are counted, the boys out of school must be reported to the Assistant-Superintendent, and the girls to the Matron; and all cases in school, either boys or girls, must be reported to the Principals. After a report is made to the Assistant-Superintendent, Matron, or Principal, no marks can be altered or cancelled except by their approval; nor can these officers cancel any marks legitimately given by the subordinate officers previous to the report.

XVI.—When the Grade is determined at the calling of the badges at the close of the week, it cannot be changed except by the consent of the Superintendent.

11. An Act to Amend the Laws in Relation to Slaves and Free Persons of Color, Passed by the South Carolina Legislature, 1834

If any person shall hereafter teach any slave to read or write, or shall aid or assist in teaching any slave to read or write, or cause or procure any slave to be taught to read or write, such person, if a free white person, upon conviction thereof, shall, for each and every offense against this Act, be fined not exceeding one hundred dollars, and imprisoned not more than six months; or if a free person of color, shall be whipped, not exceeding fifty lashes, and fined not exceeding fifty dollars, at the discretion of the court of magistrates and freeholders before which such free person of color is tried; and if a slave, to be whipped at the discretion of the court, not exceeding fifty lashes; the informer to be entitled to one half of the fine, and to be a competent witness. And if any free person of color or slave shall keep any school, or other place of instruction, for teaching any slave or free person of color to read or write, such free person of color or slave shall be liable to the same fine, imprisonment and corporal punishment, as are by this Act imposed and inflicted on free persons of color and slaves for teaching slaves to read or write.

12. THE MASSACHUSETTS COMPULSORY SCHOOL LAW OF 1850

Section 1.

Each of the several cities and towns in this Commonwealth is hereby authorized and empowered to make all needful provisions and arrangements concerning habitual truants, and children not attending school, without any regular and lawful occupation, growing up in ignorance, between the ages of six and fifteen years; and also all such ordinances and by-laws, respecting such children, as shall be deemed most conducive to their welfare, and the good order of such city or town; and there shall be annexed to such ordinances, suitable penalties, not exceeding, for any one breach, a fine of twenty dollars: *provided,* that said ordinances and by-laws shall be approved by the court of common pleas for the county, and shall not be repugnant to laws of the Commonwealth.

Sec. 2.

The several cities and towns, availing themselves of the provisions of this act, shall appoint, at the annual meetings of said towns, or annually by the mayor and aldermen of said cities, three or more persons, who alone shall be authorized to make the complaints, in every case of violation of said ordinances or by-laws, to the justice of the peace, or other judicial officer, who, by said ordinances, shall have jurisdiction in the matter, which persons, thus appointed, shall alone have author-

ity to carry into execution the judgments of said justices of the peace or other judicial officer.

Sec. 3.

The said justices of the peace, or other judicial officers, shall in all cases, at their discretion, in place of the fine aforesaid, be authorized to order children, proved before them to be growing up in truancy, and without the benefit of education provided for them by law, to be placed, for such periods of time as they may judge expedient, in such institution of instruction or house of reformation, or other suitable situation, as may be assigned or provided for the purpose, under the authority conveyed by the first section of this act, in each city or town availing itself of the powers herein granted.

13. A NOTICE ON THE DECLINE IN THE PRICE OF NEGROES, *RICHMOND SOUTH,* DECEMBER 14, 1857

Heavy Decline in Slaves! *The Dispatch* on Friday last, for the benefit of "country readers," on what it no doubt thinks reliable authority gave the price of the slaves in this market. To show that the prices given in the *Dispatch* are not to be had, and slightly artificial, and must be above what slaves are bringing, and to prevent owners and sellers of slaves from being misled, I request that you publish the sale of seven, made on Thursday by the leading house here. . . . : A No. 1, field hand, black, 22 years old, $620. No. 2, a woman, stout and healthy, a good cook, $475. No. 3, a No. 1 brown, fancy woman, 26 years, good seamstress, $530. No. 4, man and wife, 40 and 30, man slightly unsound, taken in at $670 for the pair. No. 6, a man, about 27, $416. Little niggers, from 5 to 7 years, so slow that they are generally sold in lots or by the dozen.

14. LETTER TO CHARLES LORING BRACE FROM THE REVEREND E. P. S. OF PEPPERELL, MASSACHUSETTS, DECEMBER 14, 1859

My dear Brace—Four children of your Society have been transplanted in our town. Two of them have grown up to womanhood, have acquired a good common-school education, and give evidence that they have entered upon a Christian life. A third, a lad who had his early training in the Half-Orphan Asylum, was thoroughly dishonest, and gave no little trouble to all his new friends. After taking a fresh start in seven different homes, and being despaired of by all, he is at last established, and for two years has been doing well. The fourth, an Irish orphan girl of fifteen, is the only one who has committed crime. She came to us from Brooklyn street-life and the city prison. Entirely untaught (except that she had learned the alphabet in the Mission Sunday-school), and unused to the least restraint, she found our quiet, regular country life becoming intolerable, and watching her opportunity, stole money from the house for her fare, and ran away to New York I sent a constable for her, but she was hard and sullen, and left me no alternative but to have her sent to the County House of Correction for six months. There she showed genuine penitence, and won the affection and commendation of the matron. At the expiration of her sentence we found another home for her in New Hampshire, but it was not a suitable place, and she returned to us. There was great prejudice here against her, and it was not till after a long search that we found a family who were willing to shelter the girl till we could get a home for her. But while they were waiting for us to take her away, they become interested in her case, and decided to keep her, and for eighteen months past she has been repaying their kindness with affection and faithful service. They would not part with her now, and she has no desire to return to her former life.

Our little experience with these children has deepened the feeling that it is not safe to despair of human nature when God is so willing to help and bless every honest effort.

Yours for the friendless children, Rev. E. P. S.

15. Letter from Mary Lewis, Age 17, to Her Father, Captain Andrew Lewis of the 40th Regiment of Pennsylvania Volunteers, August 13, 1861

Ebensburg [Pennsylvania]
Aug 13 1861

Dear Father

As this is the first time I hav ever wrote a letter and as I think for my first beginning I cant find one more worthey then my one dear Papa I will attempt to scribble a few lins to you to let you know that we are all well at least as far as helth is conserned but our minds are never easy on your account nor never will be untill your safe return Dear Papa it is so loansom here with out you O when will this dreadfull war be over and when will we have you home with us never to leave us again I have just herd that Lousa Myers is ded Mr J Myers youngest daughter She died of somthing like scarlet fever We were so fread Jackey will get it Poor little Jackey wants to see you so bad

All of our friends here sends love to you We are so sorry we have nothing nice to send you now Papa I want you someday to write me a letter Mamma Jackey and myself sends love to you And now dear Papa for to take good care of yourself is the prayer of your loving daugther Mary

Mary F. Lewis
to her dear father
Andrew Lewis

16. The Emancipation Proclamation, January 1, 1863

By the President of the United States of America:
A Proclamation.

Whereas on the 22d day of September, A.D. 1862, a proclamation was issued by the President of the United States, containing, among other things, the following, to wit:

"That on the 1st day of January, A.D. 1863, all persons held as slaves within any State or designated part of a State the people whereof shall then be in rebellion against the United States shall be then, thenceforward, and forever free; and the executive government of the United States, including the military and naval authority thereof, will recognize and maintain the freedom of such persons and will do no act or acts to repress such persons, or any of them, in any efforts they may make for their actual freedom.

"That the executive will on the 1st day of January aforesaid, by proclamation, designate the States and parts of States, if any, in which the people thereof, respectively, shall then be in rebellion against the United States; and the fact that any State or the people thereof shall on that day be in good faith represented in the Congress of the United States by members chosen thereto at elections wherein a majority of the qualified voters of such States shall have participated shall, in the absence of strong countervailing testimony, be deemed conclusive evidence that such State and the people thereof are not then in rebellion against the United States."

Now, therefore, I, Abraham Lincoln, President of the United States, by virtue of the power in me vested as Commander-in-Chief of the Army and Navy of the United States in time of actual armed rebellion against the authority and government of the United States, and as a fit and necessary war measure for suppressing said rebellion, do, on this 1st day of January, A.D. 1863, and in accordance with my purpose so to do, publicly proclaimed for the full period of one hundred days from the first day above mentioned, order and designate as the States and parts of States wherein the people thereof, respectively, are this day in rebellion against the United States the following, to wit:

Arkansas, Texas, Louisiana (except the parishes of St. Bernard, Plaquemines, Jefferson, St. John, St. Charles, St. James, Ascension, Assumption, Terrebonne, Lafourche, St. Mary, St. Martin, and Orleans, including the city of New Orleans), Mississippi, Alabama, Florida, Georgia, South Carolina, North Carolina, and Virginia (except the forty-eight counties designated as West Virginia, and also the counties of Berkeley, Accomac, Northhampton, Elizabeth City, York, Princess Anne, and Norfolk, including the cities of Norfolk and Portsmouth), and which excepted parts are for the present left precisely as if this proclamation were not issued.

And by virtue of the power and for the purpose aforesaid, I do order and declare that all persons held as slaves within said designated States and parts of States are, and henceforward shall be, free; and that the Executive Government of the United States, including the military and naval authorities thereof, will recognize and maintain the freedom of said persons.

And I hereby enjoin upon the people so declared to be free to abstain from all violence, unless in necessary self-defense; and I recommend to them that, in all cases when allowed, they labor faithfully for reasonable wages.

And I further declare and make known that such persons of suitable condition will be received into the armed service of the United States to garrison forts, positions, stations, and other places, and to man vessels of all sorts in said service.

And upon this act, sincerely believed to be an act of justice, warranted by the Constitution upon military necessity, I invoke the considerate judgment of mankind and the gracious favor of Almighty God.

17. Extracts from the Instructions Issued to Principals of Pennsylvania's Soldiers' Orphan Schools, October 13, 1866.

The object of the State in taking charge of the destitute orphans of her dead soldiers is to provide for their education and maintenance. This is to be done in a manner at once worthy of her and useful to them. In carrying out this intention, it is to be kept in view, that, while education and maintenance are both to be provided in proper degree, the one is subordinate to the other; for inasmuch as the soul is the nobler and more valuable, its wants are to be preferred to those of the body. Neither, however, is to be neglected or stinted.

Education, in its full sense, embraces proper habits of body and development of conscience as well as instruction of mind. All are indispensable to the formation of right character. All are, therefore, to be provided for and promoted in these schools to the fullest extent of which their officers and teachers are capable. But, inasmuch as in this complicated process there must be a starting-point and a department of instruction to which all the others are to be in a certain sense subsidiary, and inasmuch as the wisdom of the world and the custom of our ancestors have decided the instruction of the mind to be that starting-point in the general education of youth,—

I. *The regular education of these orphans in the school-room is hereby recognized as and declared to be that department, in their general instruction, which is to have precedence in, while it is at the same time to be, as far as practicable, promotive of all their other necessary studies, pursuits, exercises, and employments.* It is in nowise and at no time to be curtailed or interfered with, either for profit in employment, for the ease of instructors, under pretext of pleasure or exercise for pupils, or for any other cause, except sickness and those periodical intermissions and vacations which are the right of youth.

This rule is to be without exception. And when it is considered that only five hours' work in the school-room, during five of the seven days in the week, are required of the pupil, and that consequently all the rest of the time is left for physical labor and recreation, for eating, rest, and sleep, and for religious instruction, exercises, and worship; it cannot with truth be asserted that an undue draft is thereby made, either upon the pupil's time, energies, or patience, or that the teacher's labor and professional skill are unduly taxed by devoting eight hours to the school-room.

The nature of these schools—in which industrial instruction and employment are to be connected with intellectual, moral, and religious training—renders an additional fundamental principle or rule imperative; and that is,—

II. *That every pupil shall have an equal duration and opportunity of school-room instruction with all the others, and that such instruction shall be adapted to his or her intellectual condition and wants.* Therefore, neither is any larger pupil to be detained from the school-room for the purposes of labor when the time for attendance has arrived or during such time (except in regular turn to which all shall be subject), nor is any junior pupil to be curtailed in the number or duration of lessons, under pretext of the superior or more pressing wants of the elder. Each is to have the degree of instruction and attention proper for his or her age and state of advancement, and a sufficient force of teachers is to be provided to effect this object.

The rights of children in matters of sleep, rest, and play are as well founded in reason as those of mental or moral instruction. They cannot be violated without injury as well as injustice. Therefore:

III. *Rising before daylight, in a school or institution for children at least, is neither promotive of health, comfort, study, nor economy.* The damp air of the morning and the cheerless rooms of the school before either sun or fire has rendered them pleasant, are as unwholesome as they are comfortless and unpropitious to mental effort. The same candle-light wasted in the dark hours of the morning, or rather of the latter part of the night, if properly employed during two or three hours after sunset, will effect much more in the way of study. While the school-room is yet warm in winter or begins to be cool in summer, and while the studies of the day are still fresh in the memory and their accompanying instructions recent, as much may be effected in the evening as in double the time during the dark and probably chill morning hours; or if miscellaneous reading and voluntary improvement be the work of these hours, as they should mainly be, the body, the mind, and the spirits will all be in better condition for effort in the latter part of the day than at any other time. Accordingly, that kind of early rising, which is really getting up and performing or attempting to perform the first duties of the day in the dark, is to be avoided.

IV. *As rest, play, and exercise are also rights of childhood, so they are to be not only allowed in due quantities, but so regulated as to promote moral and physical improvement.* It is, therefore, the duty of instructors to regulate without improperly restraining the amusements of the pupils, and to see to it that, while cheerfulness and relaxation prevail, nothing detrimental to health or good morals is practised.

Soldiers' orphans, like all other children, are subject to evil influences, and will occasionally be guilty of improper conduct. Those influences are, as far as possible, to be corrected and this improper conduct punished. In cases in which no other corrective is found to succeed, corporal punishment is to be administered. But, in order to prevent the abuse of this power,—

V. *Every instance of corporal punishment, whether it be the application of the rod, confinement to the room, or exclusion from meals, shall be entered in a book kept for that purpose, by the Principal of the school, with the name of offender, cause, and kind of punishment, and date. And all corporal punishments shall be inflicted by the Principal of the school himself, and not by any of the teachers or other employees.*

General Distribution of Time.

In order to methodize all the operations of the schools and obtain due time for sleep, food, care of the person, study, work, worship, and play, the following hours will be observed:

1st. Pupils will rise about five o'clock in April, May, June, July, August, and September; and about six o'clock in October, November, December, January, February, and March, except such details in succession as may be required earlier to attend to special duties, such as making fires, cooking, feeding animals, &c. These hours, however, may be varied, according to the month, within the above limits.

2d. The first thirty minutes after rising shall be devoted to washing the face, neck, teeth, and hands, combing the hair, and arranging the clothing, &c., for inspection; the next fifteen minutes to inspection of the person and clothing by the proper officer, and the last fifteen minutes of the hour before breakfast to morning worship.

3d. Breakfast shall be on the table and the pupils called to it at six o'clock in the summer half year, and at seven o'clock in the winter; and the pupils shall be allowed a full half hour for the meal.

4th. The time between breakfast and the opening of school shall be allowed for play the whole year round, except in haytime and harvest, when the pupils shall be permitted to aid in the light and pleasant labors of the season till the regular school hour.

5th. The school shall open with the calling of the roll, at fifteen minutes before eight o'clock in the morning, and continue till fifteen minutes of twelve o'clock, with fifteen minutes of recess at ten o'clock.

6th. Dinner shall be on the table at twelve o'clock, and the pupils shall have a full half hour at table.

7th. The time between dinner and the opening of school shall be for play, except for such pupils as, in their turn, shall be detailed for special duty.

8th. The school shall reopen at one o'clock P.M., and continue till fifteen minutes of five o'clock P.M., with a recess of fifteen minutes at three o'clock.

9th. The first half hour after close of school shall be devoted to military drill by the boys and proper physical exercise by the girls, and the remaining time till supper to play, except by pupils specially detailed for work in their regular turn.

10th. Supper shall be served and pupils called to it at six o'clock, all the year round, and a half hour allowed for the meal.

11th. The half hour between supper and seven o'clock shall be for play.

12th. From seven to eight o'clock in summer, and to nine o'clock in winter, shall be spent in the main study-hall and under the eye of the Proprietor of the school himself, in exercises of vocal music, declamation, reading essays, writing essays and letters, familiar lectures, miscellaneous readings, &c.; an evening, or part of an evening in each week, as the Principal shall direct, being devoted to each of these, or other similar employments.

13th. After family worship, in the study-hall, the pupils shall retire to their rooms at eight o'clock in summer and nine o'clock in winter, and all lights in bed-rooms shall be extinguished at the end of fifteen minutes from those hours, respectively. . . .

Food.

Wholesome, sufficient, and regular food is all that is needed for childhood. Rich dishes and dainties are prejudicial. Of course an occasional treat of this kind will be greatly enjoyed, would do little harm if partaken of in moderation, and is not forbidden.

The following, for the present, are the regulations on this subject. It being understood that a sufficiency for all pupils, of at least one of the articles in each of the numbered lists, shall be on the table at the respective meals:

Breakfast: 1. Bread. 2. Butter, sauce, or molasses. 3. Coffee, tea, chocolate, or sweet milk, the latter to be warm or cold at the option of the pupil. 4. One or more of the following articles: Fried mush, fried potatoes, with or without onions, fried bread, fried or boiled eggs, gravy, boiled potatoes, with skins, tomato sauce, milk gravy, mackerel or other fish, hash, or any other warm meat preparation.

Dinner: 1. Bread. 2. Beef, pork, mutton, veal, poultry, or other meat. 3. One or more of the following articles: Potatoes, cabbage, parsnips, turnips, carrots, green beans, green corn, green peas, hominy, beans, rice, stewed onions, stewed beets, or any other vegetable stewed or boiled, vegetable or other soup, boiled or baked pot-pie, tomato sauce, green apple sauce, salad.

Supper: 1. Bread. 2. Butter or molasses. 3. Coffee, tea, or milk. 4. One or more of the following articles: Cold meat, hash, stewed fruit, potatoes, onions, pone or other corn bread, potato soup.

Sunday dinner to consist of cold meat, bread, cakes, pies, stewed fruit, &c.

Fruit to be given at any meal, when in season, and grown on the premises.

Clothing.

These children are to be plainly but comfortably clad, and their clothes kept in good repair by the seamstresses, assisted by the female pupils.

Such of the garments as can shall be made at the schools, by the seamstresses, with the assistance of the girls; and a reasonable compensation will be allowed to the Proprietor of the school for his trouble and care in the matter, and for the cutting out and labor by the seamstresses. All the articles worn by the girls, except shoes, stockings, cloaks, and head dresses, and all those of the boys except their parade dresses, winter suits, and overcoats, and their shoes, stockings, hats, and caps will be made in the schools. . . .

Inspection of New Pupils and Care of Sick.

No orphan is to be excluded from the school on account of any degree of destitution, or of any disease merely temporary and not in itself dangerous. The opposite course would defeat the very purpose of the institutions, which are for the improvement of the physical condition as well as intellect. Still, due means are to be adopted to prevent the spread of any contagious disease or other unpleasant condition in the school from a new pupil thus afflicted.

So in case of sickness of pupils while members of the school, the duty of providing for their wants and cure is even more incumbent than that of promoting their comfort in health. Accordingly,—

1. Two infirmary rooms shall be set apart in each school, one for the boys and the other for the girls; and each shall be provided with the furniture and appliances necessary.

2. A nurse shall be employed to take charge of all new pupils and keep them apart from the others, till examined by the physician and pronounced free from all cutaneous and other contagious diseases; and also to have the care of all sick pupils.

3. It shall be her duty to attend upon all diseased pupils, and administer to them such medicines and remedies as shall be prescribed by the physician, and also to see that their rooms are kept well ventilated and clean and their garments often changed; and that the inmates have such food as their cases may require.

4. No pupil, either newly arrived or previously in the school, shall be discharged from the infirmary till so directed by the physician. . . .

Correspondence with Home.

The manifest design of the State, in the establishment of these schools, is not to destroy the home feeling, but to act as a father to the fatherless. Correspondence with the mother and other relatives is therefore a right of each of these orphans; and it is to be as frequent as may be consistent with other duties, and not to be in any way restrained except for abuse. Therefore,—

Each pupil is to be permitted to write home at least once a month, if so desired by him or herself. Neither the letters sent nor received are to be subject to examination by the Principal or any other authority in the school, except after ascertained violation of truth by the pupil, in former letters sent, or disturbing sentiments in letters received.

In such cases, but no other, the right of unrestricted correspondences shall be forfeited and that of examining letters exercised; but all such cases shall be reported to the State Superintendent, or one of his officers, at the next visit.

Visits of Mothers.

Frequent visits of parents to their children, while at boarding-school, are not desirable in any case. These schools are no exemption from the disturbing practice. Therefore,—

1. Mothers are not to visit the schools oftener than once in each quarter of a year, and not to prolong their visits beyond one day, except in cases of sickness, when the visits may be of such frequency and duration as shall be necessary.

2. A mother's room shall be provided in each school, and comfortably furnished with two beds, &c.

3. Mothers shall eat at the table with the pupils, and shall not be charged anything for their accommodations, unless their stay be prolonged without such reason as that of sickness, &c.

Vacations.

There shall be one vacation annually in all the schools of this grade, from the last Friday in July till the end of five weeks from the following Tuesday. During this time all studies and labor shall cease in the schools, except the work necessary to carry on the domestic operations.

During, but not to exceed this period, leaves of absence to visit relatives may be granted by the Principal, to such pupils as shall have deserved it, and have a comfortable and proper home to visit. . . .

THOMAS H. BURROWES,
LANCASTER, Oct. 13, 1866.   Supt. Soldiers'
                                                      Orphans.

18. Extracts from "The Indian School at Carlisle Barracks," a Report to the U.S. Commissioner of Education, 1880

. . . The barracks stand west of the town, on a well drained piece of land belonging to the Government. . . .

The buildings occupy the sides of a grassy square used for parade ground, &c. One row is occupied by the superintendent and his staff, another by the teachers' and female pupils' dormitories, a third by the boys' dormitories. Other buildings conveniently placed are used as chapel, school-house, refectory, infirmary, gymnasium, stable and coach-house, trade schools, &c. There is ample accommodation for double the actual number of pupils.

Lieutenant Pratt has at present under his charge about 110 boys and 44 girls, from several tribes. It was found impossible to obtain as many girls as boys, because the labor of the girls is so useful under the present ideas and social arrangements of the Indians.

A few of the older pupils had received some instruction and training before coming to this school. . . . More than a hundred of them, however, were last October utterly without any civilized knowledge or training whatever. "They had never been inside of a school or a house," said one of the employes. They were brought to the barracks filthy, vermin covered, and dressed in their native garb. When they were assigned to their sleeping quarters "they lay down on the veranda, on their bellies, and glared out between the palings of the railing like wild beasts between the bars of their cages." The first thing to do was to clean them thoroughly and to dress them in their new attire. Baths are compulsory thrice a week. The vermin have been suppressed, all the more easily because the boys have allowed their hair to be cut in the fashion of white people. Everything except swallowing, walking, and sleeping had to be taught; the care of person, clothing, furniture, the usages of the table, the carriage of the body, civility, all those things which white children usually learn from their childhood by mere imitation, had to be painfully inculcated and strenuously insisted on. In addition to this, they were to be taught the rudiments of an English school course and the practical use of tools.

. . . . .

Three and a half mouths have passed, and the change is astonishing. The present condition of affairs can be told best by resuming the account of the day's work. . . .

The Schools

We entered one room after another. The first was one in which a number of the younger children were being exercised in the use of a vocabulary and in the formation of English sentences. On the teacher's desk was a large number of small familiar objects, drinking glasses, balls, cups, &c. The children successively were asked to name an object; the teacher phonetized the name into its sound elements and the children repeated it in the same way. Then the teacher placed one object on the top of another and the child made a sentence on the following model: "The cup is on the book."

In another room a class of boys was reciting a lesson in geography. One boy pointed out and named the continents, another the countries in North America, a third the oceans, a fourth the seas of Europe, and so on. . . .

The Dormitories

We next visited the quarters assigned to the pupils. Each child has a separate cot bedstead with sheets, blankets, and white counterpane. The lavatories were sufficient and in good order. The number of beds in each room on the boys' side was eleven; this may be thought too many for the size of the room (about 20 feet square it seemed to me); but it was explained that these Indians of their own accord sleep with the windows open all night. Indeed, as one of the employes remarked, "They would never shut even a door if it depended on their sensations." Each room is in charge of an older boy, who is squadmaster, and responsible for the behavior of the others and for the care of the bedding and other furniture.

The Shops

We found some of the girls learning how to sew, others cooking, others mending clothes. Some of the boys were cobbling shoes, some were in the carpenter's shop, where a pinewood table was being finished by one pupil, while another was making tongues and grooves on the edges of boards, apparently for the top of another table; a third was working on table and chair legs. Two other boys were at a blacksmith's forge working away industriously. Three of the older boys had been apprenticed to a wagonmaker in Carlisle; one of these is painting wagons, another is making or putting together the parts of wheels and other woodwork; the third devotes his attention to the iron parts. I understood that these young men propose when they return home to pursue wagonmaking in partnership. The pupils are said to learn the use of tools as readily as white children do. There is a master blacksmith, master carpenter, and a shoemaker in the corps of instruction.

Dinner

At half past twelve we went to the refectory, where the pupils' dinner was in progress. The bill of fare for the day was roast beef, sweet and Irish potatoes, tomatoes, and wheat bread. I tasted each, and found it palatably cooked. All except the very smallest children managed their own knives and forks, of course with varying degrees of skill and grace. I thought the girls in general more successful in this than the boys. The supply seemed abundant and the appetites good. The attendance on table was done by a detail of girls.

Physical Exercise

. . . [T]he boys are supplied with a good sized and sufficiently appointed gymnasium. I think that an instructor in this branch would prove of great use. . . .

The personal appearance of the pupils is generally satisfactory; there is some coughing, particularly among the boys, but no more than would be heard among an equal number of white boys. Whenever from admixture of blood the skin was pale enough to show the color of the blood, the cheeks were more or less rosy. Most of them are straight; nearly all walk in the usual ungraceful Indian fashion with no divergence of the toes. The teeth of most seemed in good condition.

The Infirmary

There is only one patient at the present time. Those who had not been vaccinated at the agencies were vaccinated on their reception. There have been two deaths since the opening of the school; in both cases the superintendent objected to the admission of these pupils, but was overruled by various considerations. . . .

CHARLES WARREN,
Chief Clerk

Hon. JOHN EATON,
Commissioner of Education.

19. EXTRACTS FROM THE FIRST ANNUAL REPORT OF THE FACTORY INSPECTORS OF ILLINOIS, 1893

Child labor.—Among the first work of the inspectors was a careful canvass of the sewing, metal-stamping, woodworking, book-binding, box, candy, tobacco, and cigar trades, and the discharge of a large number of children under fourteen years of age.

The requirement that an age affadavit be filed in the workshop or factory, before a child is employed, has already made it a general practice on the part of employers to hand to every child applying for work an affadavit blank to be filled by the parent. Children who cannot get such blanks filled because not yet fourteen years old, apply at one shop after another until they either find some unscrupulous employer, or grow dis-couraged and give up the quest for work. Although some affadavits are undoubtedly false, hundreds of parents have withdrawn their children from work rather than forswear themselves.

Principally to meet the contingency of perjury, the inspectors have required health certificates of children markedly undersized, as well as of those who are diseased or deformed. . . .

Where the child was found able to continue at work, it was granted a health certificate. In a large majority of cases, however, the examining physician endorsed upon the age affadavit the following formula:

"It is my opinion that this child is physically unfit for work at his present occupation."

The employer was then notified to discharge the child.

It soon transpired that some occupations were more injurious than others; sweat-shops, tobacco, cutlery and stamping works being worse, for instance, than candy-packing rooms. On the other hand, the lightest occupations are rendered injurious by long hours of work. Therefore the prohibition of work for delicate children has been rarer in factories having good sanitary conditions, and known absolutely to obey the eight-hour section of the law, than in factories concerning which there was any doubt upon this point. . . .

The medical profession and the law.—The value of this provision of the law [i.e., the medical certificate clause], however, depends upon the intelligent cooperation of the medical profession. For if the certificates are granted merely *pro forma,* upon the representation of the employer of the child, the object of the law is nullified. The physician who grasps the situation and appreciates the humane intent of the law, will always find time to visit the factory and see under what conditions the child is working. Otherwise his certificate may be worse than valueless, and may work a positive injury to a child whom the inspectors are trying to save from an injurious occupation.

Thus a healthy child may wish to enter a cracker bakery, and unless the physician visits it, and sees the dwarfish boys slowly roasting before the ovens, in the midst of unguarded belting and shafting (a danger to health which men refuse to incur), he may be inclined to grant the certificate, and thereby deprive the child of the only safeguard to his health which the State affords him. Similar danger exists in regard to tobacco, picture-frame, box, metal-stamping and woodworking factories.

Unfortunately the law does not require that the physician shall visit the workshop or factory, and see the child at work, and certificates have in some instances been granted in a disgracefully reckless manner.

A delicate looking little girl was found at work in a badly ventilated tailor shop facing an alley, in the rear of a tenement house. The bad location and atmosphere of the shop, and the child's stooping position as she worked, led the inspector to demand a health certificate. Examination at the office revealed a bad case of rachitis [rickets] and antero-posterior curvature of the spine, one shoulder an inch higher than the other, and the child decidedly below the standard weight. Dr. Milligan endorsed upon the age affadavit: "It is my opinion that this child is physically incapable of work in any tailor shop." The employer was notified to discharge the child. A few days later she was found at work again in the same place, and the contractor produced the following "certificate," written upon the prescription blank of a physician in good and regular standing:

(Dated.) Dr. M. Meyerovitz, 179 W. 12th st., cor. Jefferson.

"This is to certify that I examined Miss Annie Cihlar, and found her in a physiological condition.

(*Signed*,) "MEYEROVITZ."

A test case was made, to ascertain the value of the medical certificate clause, and the judge decided that this certificate was void, and imposed a fine upon the employer for failure to obtain a certificate in accordance with the wording of the law. The child then went to another physician, and was given the following:

(Dated.) Dr. Frank J. Patera, 675 W. Taylor st.

CHICAGO, November 26, 1893

"To whom it may concern:

"This is to certify that I have this day examined Annie Cihlar, and find her, in my opinion, healthy. She is well developed for her age, muscular system in good condition, muscles are hard and solid; the lungs and heart are normal; the muscles of right side of trunk are better developed than upon the left side, which has a tendency to draw spine to that side, as a result of greater muscular activity upon that side. I cannot find no desease [*sic*] of the spine."

(*Signed*,) "F. J. PATERA, M.D."

The sweater, taught by experience, declined to re-engage this child until this certificate was approved by an inspector. The inspector of course declined to approve it. . . .

Physical deterioration. . . . The human product of our industry is an army of toiling children undersized, rachitic, deformed, predisposed to consumption if not already tuberculous. Permanently enfeebled by the labor imposed upon them during the critical years of development, these children will inevitably fail in the early years of manhood and womanhood. They are now a long way on the road to become suffering burdens upon society, lifelong victims of the poverty of their childhood and the greed which denies children the sacred right of school life and healthful leisure.

Illiteracy.—The enforcement of Section Four of the law brings to light a deplorable amount of illiteracy among working children. Thus, in the first case prosecuted, that against Gustav Ravitz for employing a girl under fourteen years of age in his tailor shop, it was shown in court that this child had been brought thirteen years before to Chicago from Poland, yet she could not read or write in any language, nor speak English. Neither she nor her mother knew the year of the child's birth, and an interpreter was required in speaking with them both.

A little girl thirteen years of age found at 120 West Taylor street (Baumgarten's knee-pants shop), sewing on buttons in the bedroom of the sweater's family, was discharged. She is a Russian Jewess three years in this country, and does not know her letters. She was taken bodily to the Jewish Training School and entered as a pupil.

Greek, Italian, Bohemian, Polish and Russian children are constantly encountered who speak no English, hundreds of whom cannot read nor write in any language. Children who cannot spell their name or the name of the street in which they live are found at work every day by the deputies.

Where these children are under fourteen years of age, they are turned over to the compulsory attendance officer of the board of education, but for those over the age of fourteen the state prescribes no educational requirement, and unless they look deformed, undersized, or diseased, the inspectors have no ground upon which to withdraw them from their life of premature toil. . . .

20. The 25 Leading Amusements of Worcester, Massachusetts, Schoolchildren as Reported in *Pedagogical Seminary*, September 1899

The Twenty-Five Leading Amusements.

Total, 1,000 Boys, 929 Girls.

BOYS.					GIRLS.			
	Mentioned by Boys.	Favorite with Boys.	Mentioned by Girls.	Favorite with Girls.		Mentioned by Girls.	Favorite with Girls.	Mentioned by Boys.	Favorite with Boys.
1. Ball,	679	241	409	67	1. Dolls,	621	356	39	6
2. Marbles,	603	115	130	21	2. Sled,	498	69	555	10
3. Sled,	555	110	498	69	3. Jump Rope,	480	60	13	1
4. Skates,	538	168	412	113	4. Tag,	442	93	356	73
5. Football,	455	157	1		5. Hide and Seek,	427	132	241	74
6. Tag,	356	73	442	93	6. Skates,	412	113	538	168
7. Relievo,	336	126	194	48	7. Ball,	409	67	679	241
8. Hockey, Polo, Shinney,	313	53	8		8. Play House,	365	54	59	5
9. Checkers,	277	87	189	34	9. Jackstones,	341	63	28	2
10. Hide and Seek,	241	74	427	132	10. Play School,	257	32	69	1
11. Wagon, Express,	188	35	7		11. Doll Tea Set,	242	73	8	
12. Dominoes,	185	42	133	26	12. Doll Carriage,	233	80	5	
13. Top,	176	28	11		13. Relievo,	194	48	336	126
14. Play Horse,	166	26	47	3	14. Checkers,	189	34	277	87
15. Cards,	163	34	151	51	15. Hop Scotch,	154	21	16	
16. Bicycle,	160	78	86	45	16. Cards,	151	51	163	34
17. Snow Balling,	123	14	98	3	17. Croquet,	148	52	62	3
18. Swimming,	119	26	15	2	18. Dominoes,	133	26	185	42
19. Kite,	107	5	12		19. Marbles,	130	21	603	21
20. Black Tom and Black Jack,	102	26	97	14	20. Leaves,	112	6	75	2
21. Horse Cobbles,	88	5	7		21. Hoop,	110	14	71	3
22. Books, Reading,	87	7	108	22	22. Books, Reading,	108	22	87	7
23. Fishing,	80	19	7	1	23. Flowers,	102	1	32	1
24. Boat,	78	18	27	4	24. Drop the Hand-kerchief,	101	11	22	2
25. Leaves,	75	2	112	6	25. Snow Balling,	98	3	123	14

21. EXTRACT FROM A PAPER READ BY J. J. KELSO, SUPERINTENDENT OF THE DEPARTMENT OF NEGLECTED AND DEPENDENT CHILDREN OF ONTARIO, AT THE ANNUAL MEETING OF THE AMERICAN HUMANE ASSOCIATION, HELD IN BOSTON, NOVEMBER 12–14, 1907

Supervision of Children.

In Ontario, when the children's protection act was passed in 1893, it was recognized that if home-finding work was to be extensively adopted, subsequent supervision of the children placed out would be essential to success. Therefore our system provides that all children's aid societies should be branches of one organization having its center in a government office known as the Department of Neglected and Dependent Children. There are at the present time 60 of these societies covering the different districts of the Province, and each year about 300 children are placed in foster homes in a territory over 500 by 800 miles in extent. Whenever a child goes to a foster home through one of these societies the full particulars are at once reported to the central office on a form provided for the purpose. The child then passes under the supervision of the government office, and I, as a general superintendent, assume its future care. Its name is entered both in a supervision book and on a card index, the latter for division into towns, cities, and counties, so as to facilitate visiting, and from that time on every reasonable effort is made to insure its proper treatment. This plan has been in operation over 14 years and there are about 4,000 children on the books. In addition, two or three of the orphanages report the children placed out by them and they are entered and visited, though this is not compulsory. The local society or institution is expected to keep up a friendly interest in the child, and this can be done without any clashing with the central scheme of visitation. Some societies are faithful in remembering the children once under their immediate care, others inquire about them occasionally, while some organizations are content to leave it all to the central office. The great importance of having all placed-out children properly reported and recorded has been demonstrated over and over again. The smaller societies pass out of existence, there are frequent changes of secretaries or managers and if the children were not on record they would in many cases be completely forgotten and lost sight of. State supervision provides for continuity and permanency, and whether the local society exists or not the children are looked after, helped, encouraged, and protected until there is no doubt that they are of age.

The children recorded in the central office are visited once each year, some twice, some several times, according to the special need. Typewritten reports of these visits are furnished without expense to the society holding the guardianship. A very mild supervision is exercised over those children who are adopted in infancy and who have become fully incorporated as members of the family. We have many cases on our books where after the first visit an entry is made "Very little supervision necessary," although we do not entirely give up oversight of any child, owing to the fact already stated that home conditions are liable to change at any time and do as a matter of fact change. Those who require special attention are the boys and girls taken at 8, 10, and 12 years of age, where the consideration of work is likely to enter. Great care is needed to see that they receive a fair amount of schooling and are not overworked.

With a system such as ours there is always some one available to be sent on short notice to visit a child, no matter how great the distance, and once all the circumstances of each child are fully understood this preparation for instant action prevents neglect and carelessness. This point is worth emphasizing. We keep four persons constantly on the road, three gentlemen and a lady, and in addition there are six other persons who have the oversight of certain districts. Catholic children are visited by a Catholic inspector, and this is a wise and reasonable rule to follow. We have also at least 15 or 20 persons who can be called in for special visiting or reporting on children in their district, and through these various agencies we believe we are looking fairly well after the young people whose names are on our books. We do not take names off our records. Often a friendly visit is paid to young women long after they have married and settled in life. We are then better able to judge the results of our work and the visits are appreciated and welcomed. . . .

22. EXTRACTS FROM A LETTER TO THE PRESIDENT OF THE UNITED STATES EMBODYING THE CONCLUSIONS OF THE CONFERENCE ON THE CARE OF DEPENDENT CHILDREN HELD IN WASHINGTON, D.C., JANUARY 25 AND 26, 1909

Hon. Theodore Roosevelt,
    President of the United States,
SIR:. . . The proper care of destitute children has indeed an important bearing upon the welfare of the

Nation. We now know so little about them as not even to know their number, but we know that there are in institutions about 93,000 and that many additional thousands are in foster or boarding homes. As a step, therefore, in the conservation of the productive capacity of the people and the preservation of high standards of citizenship, and also because each of these children is entitled to receive humane treatment, adequate care, and proper education, your action in calling this conference and your participation in its opening and closing sessions will have, we believe, a profound effect upon the well-being of many thousands of children, and upon the Nation as a whole.

Concerning the particular objects to which you call attention in the invitation to this conference, and the additional subjects brought before us by the executive committee, our conclusions are as follows:

Home Care.

1. Home life is the highest and finest product of civilization. It is the great molding force of mind and of character. Children should not be deprived of it except for urgent and compelling reasons. Children of parents of worthy character suffering from temporary misfortune, and children of reasonably efficient and deserving mothers who are without the support of the normal breadwinner should, as a rule, be kept with their parents, such aid being given as may be necessary to maintain suitable homes for the rearing of the children. This aid should be given by such methods and from such sources as may be determined by the general relief policy of each community, preferably in the form of private charity rather than of public relief. Except in unusual circumstances the home should not be broken up for reasons of poverty, but only for considerations of inefficiency and immorality.

Preventive Work.

2. The most important and valuable philanthropic work is not the curative but the preventive; to check dependency by a thorough study of its causes and by effectively remedying or eradicating them should be the constant aim of society. Along these lines we urge upon all friends of children the promotion of effective measures, including legislation to prevent blindness; to check tuberculosis and other diseases in dwellings and work places, and injuries in hazardous occupations; to secure compensation or insurance so as to provide a family income in case of sickness, accident, death, or invalidism of the breadwinner; to promote child-labor

reforms, and, generally, to improve the conditions surrounding child life. To secure these ends we urge efficient cooperation with all other agencies for social betterment.

Home Finding.

3. As to the children who for sufficient reasons must be removed from their own homes, or who have no homes, it is desirable that if normal in mind and body and not requiring special training, they should be cared for in families whenever practicable. The carefully selected foster home is for the normal child the best substitute for the natural home. Such homes should be selected by a most careful process of investigation, carried on by skilled agents through personal investigation and with due regard to the religious faith of the child. After children are placed in homes, adequate visitation, with careful consideration of the physical, mental, moral, and spiritual training and development of each child on the part of the responsible home-finding agency, is essential. . . .

State Inspection.

6. The proper training of destitute children being essential to the well-being of the State, it is a sound public policy that the State, through its duly authorized representative, should inspect the work of all agencies which care for dependent children, whether by institutional or by home-finding methods and whether supported by public or private funds. Such inspection should be made by trained agents, should be thorough, and the results thereof should be reported to the responsible authorities of the institution or agency concerned. The information so secured should be confidential, not to be disclosed except by competent authority. . . .

Facts and Records.

8. The proper care of a child in the custody of a child-caring agency, as well as the wise decision as to the period of his retention and ultimate disposition to be made of him, involve a knowledge of the character and circumstances of his parents, or surviving parent, and near relatives, both before and at the time the child becomes dependent, and subsequently. One unfortunate feature of child-caring work hitherto is the scanty information available as to the actual careers of children who have been reared under the care of charitable agencies. This applies both to institutions, which too frequently lose sight of the children soon after they leave their doors, and

home-finding agencies, which too frequently have failed to exercise supervision adequate to enable them to judge of the real results of their work. It is extremely desirable that, taking all precautions to prevent injury or embarrassment to those who have been the subjects of charitable care, the agencies which have been responsible for the care of children should know to what station in life they attain and what sort of citizens they become. Only in this manner can they form a correct judgment of the results of their efforts. . . .

Physical Care.

9. The physical condition of children who become the subjects of charitable care has received inadequate consideration. Each child received into the care of such an agency should be carefully examined by a competent physician, especially for the purpose of ascertaining whether such peculiarities, if any, as the child presents may be due to any defect of the sense organs or to other physical defect. Both institutions and placing-out agencies should take every precaution to secure proper medical and surgical care of their children and should see that suitable instruction is given them in matters of health and hygiene. . . .

Undesirable Legislation.

11. We greatly deprecate the tendency of legislation in some States to place unnecessary obstacles in the way of placing children in family homes in such States by agencies whose headquarters are elsewhere, in view of the fact that we favor the care of destitute children, normal in mind and body, in families, whenever practicable.

We recognize the right of each State to protect itself from vicious, diseased, or defective children from other States by the enactment of reasonable protective legislation; but experience proves that the reception of healthy normal children is not only an act of philanthropy, but also secures a valuable increment to the population of the community and an ultimate increase of its wealth. . . .

Federal Children's Bureau.

13. A bill is pending in Congress for the establishment of a Federal children's bureau to collect and disseminate information affecting the welfare of children. In our judgment the establishment of such a bureau is desirable, and we earnestly recommend the enactment of the pending measure. . . .

Yours very respectfully,
Hastings H. Hart,
Edmond J. Butler,
Julian W. Mack,
Homer Folks,
James E. West,
Committee on resolutions.

23. THE STAGES OF CHILDHOOD AS CHARTED BY GEORGE WALTER FISKE, 1910

Stage	Duration	Culmination	Characteristics	Favorite Plays And Games
1. "Root and Grub"	1st to 5th year	3d year	Mouth as criterion of everything.	Biting and tasting plays.
2. Hunting and Capture	4th to 12th year	7th year	Fear of strangers; stalking methods; indifference to pain; hero-worship; cruelty.	Bo-peep (stealth, stalking, approach, ambush, surprise); Hide and Seek; Black Man; Prisoner's Base (pursuit, attack; mimic sieges, wars, assaults; gangs).
3. Pastoral	9th to 14th year	10th year	Fondness for pets; desire to have something "for his own."	Keeping and feeding pets; building huts; digging caves, etc.
4. Agricultural	12th to 16th year	12th year	Development of foresight; passion for gardening.	Watching weather signs; gardening, digging up seeds "to see if they're growing!"
5. Shop and Commercial	14th to 40th year	18th to 20th year	Demanding pay for services; recognition of value and sense of arithmetic.	Swapping, selling, trading, exchanging, bargaining.

24. Extract from *An Act To Establish in the Department of Commerce and Labor a Bureau to be Known as the Children's Bureau,* April 9, 1912

Be it enacted by the Senate and House of Representatives of the United States of America in Congress assembled, That there shall be established in the Department of Commerce and Labor a bureau to be known as the Children's Bureau.

Sec. 2. That the said bureau shall be under the direction of a chief, to be appointed by the President, by and with the advice and consent of the Senate, and who shall receive an annual compensation of five thousand dollars. The said bureau shall investigate and report to said department upon all matters pertaining to the welfare of children and child life among all classes of our people, and shall especially investigate the questions of infant mortality, the birth rate, orphanage, juvenile courts, desertion, dangerous occupations, accidents and diseases of children, employment, legislation affecting children in the several States and Territories. But no official, or agent, or representative of said bureau shall, over the objection of the head of the family, enter any house used exclusively as a family residence. The chief of said bureau may from time to time publish the results of these investigations in such manner and to such extent as may be prescribed by the Secretary of Commerce and Labor. . . .

25. Letter from Theodore Roosevelt to William E. Hall, National Director of the Boys' Working Reserve, September 4, 1917

OYSTER BAY
LONG ISLAND, N.Y.
September 4, 1917

My dear Mr. Hall:–

I wish to express my hearty and unreserved support of what you are doing. You are now actually engaged in meeting the shortage of labor on the farm by the creation of the Working Reserve, to include the boys between the ages of sixteen and twenty-one who ordinarily would not be in productive labor, and who can be turned into workers on the farm. You have shown, and the farmer has been prompt to recognize the fact, that the strong healthy boy is a tremendous help at this time and that if this patriotism is appealed to, they will stick to the farm where the need is great, in spite of the offer of higher wages in the City. The training of boys to prepare for some essential industry where they can take the place of a man called to the front is going to be of great benefit to the country.

One of the great benefits you confer is that of making a boy realize that he is part of Uncle Sam's team; that he is doing his share in this great War, that he holds his services in trust for the Nation, and that although it is proper to consider the question of material gain and the question of his own desires, yet that what he must most strongly consider at this time is where his services will do most good to our people as a whole. I earnestly wish you every success in your wise and patriotic effort.

Faithfully yours,
Theodore Roosevelt

Mr. William E. Hall,
National Director,
Boys' Working Reserve, U.S.A.
Washington, D.C.

26. Extract from *Outline of an Emergency Course of Instruction on the War,* Distributed to Schools by the Committee on Public Information, 1918

COURSE FOR GRADES ONE AND TWO

Instruction on the war in the first two grades should take the form of:

I. Stories of War Incidents.
II. Celebrations of Special Holidays.
III. Talks on the War and the Children's Relation to It.

I. Stories of War Incidents.

True incidents of the war, illustrating the three ideas of *patriotism, heroism,* and *sacrifice,* should be selected and told the children. So far as possible, incidents centering about the actions of children in France, Belgium, and other invaded countries should be selected. The stories should by no means be limited to those about children, however, as children take a very real interest in the actions of grownups—brave soldiers, self-sacrificing mothers, and the like. Besides inculcating an admiration for the virtues of patriotism, heroism, and sacrifice, these stories should incidentally give the children some notion of life "over there."

The treatment throughout should be informal. Pupils should not be held for "facts." Informal conversations should be encouraged, but the children should not be required to retail stories nor to answer questions about them.

II. Celebrations of Special Holidays.

Columbus Day. Thanksgiving Day. Lincoln's Birthday. Washington's Birthday. Liberty Day (anniversary of April 6, 1917). Memorial Day. Flag Day. Fourth of July. Bastille Day.

These celebrations should be treated from a national and international rather than from a personal point of view. For example, on Columbus Day emphasize the relations of the Old World with the New, and of our country with the countries of Latin America; in connection with Lincoln emphasize the preservation of our country and the freeing of the slaves rather than the personal characteristics of Lincoln; on Flag Day discuss the meaning of the flag rather than the story of Betsy Ross. Dramatics should form a part of most holiday celebrations in lower grades.

The celebration of each of these holidays should center about its relation to the present war. Washington founded this Nation and Lincoln saved it; so that today we may do our part toward establishing liberty and democracy for the world. Flag Day should serve as an occasion for reference to the flags of our associates in the war.

III. Talks on the War and the Children's Relation to It.

A. Reasons why father, brother, uncle, cousin, had to go to war: (1) To protect the people of France and Belgium from the Germans, who were burning their homes and killing the people, even women and children; (2) to keep the German soldiers from coming to our country and treating us the same way.

B. How little children can help:

1. Save pennies for thrift stamps.
2. Eat less of things the soldiers and the people of the allied countries need.
3. Eat less candy and sweet cakes.
4. Do not waste food. (The "clean plate" idea.) Remind brothers and sisters not to waste.
5. Do not waste water. Faucets left running mean wasted coal at the pumping station.
6. Be careful of health. Doctors and nurses are needed just now for more important work than curing children's ailments that are the result of carelessness.
7. Be careful of shoes and clothes. We need all the cloth and leather we can spare for the soldiers. . . .
8. Save labor by not giving other people extra work. Avoid—
   a. Throwing paper about the streets.
   b. Breaking windows or otherwise destroying or defacing property.
   c. Carelessness with school books and other public property.
9. Try to be better boys and girls, so that older folks will not be troubled or worried about you and so can work harder. . . .

27. Form Submitted by Indiana Farmers to the State Director of the U.S. Boys' Working Reserve, 1918

Name........................Postoffice Address....................
County.....................Township.................................
Nearest Railroad Station.......Name of Railroad.........
Telephone.....................Nearest town........................

Without definitely obligating myself, but rather to give you some indication as to what I anticipate in the way of labor requirements next spring and summer, I hereby notify the U. S. Department of Labor, through the State Council of Defense for Indiana, that I probably can use.....boy or boys, 16 to 21 years of age, whom I shall need.......(date). I am willing to pay........dollars per week with board. I am willing to pay........dollars per week without board.

In consideration of the service they are going to render me, I shall gladly co-operate with them in their efforts to succeed and will be patient and considerate of them. I realize that their presence on my farm will be indicative of the patriotism they possess and therefor deserving of an equal amount of patriotic effort on my part to build of them fine, up-standing citizens, equipped for the man's job which of necessity they now must shoulder.

28. Extracts from the Delaware Law Relating to the Interstate Placement of Dependent Children, 1921

It shall be unlawful for any person, association, or corporation to bring or send, or cause to be brought or sent into the State of Delaware, any dependent child for the purpose of placing such child in any home in this State, or for the purpose of procuring the placing of such child in any home by indenture, adoption, boarding or otherwise, without first obtaining the written consent of the State board of charities, and giving bond, as hereinafter provided. . . .

Before any child shall be brought into this State for any of the purposes provided in . . . this article, the person, association, or corporation desiring to bring or send any such child into this State, or the individual desiring to receive a child or both as the State board of charities may require, shall execute a bond to the State of Delaware in the penal sum of $3,000 to be approved by the State board of charities, and to be with surety, if the said State board of charities shall so require. The condition of said bond shall be substantially that such person, association, or corporation shall not bring or send, or cause to be brought or sent, or receive, into this State any child that is incorrigible, that is of unsound mind or body, or is mentally subnormal; and that such person, association, corporation, or individual shall abide by all rules laid down by the State board of charities. . . . If any such child shall become a public charge, or be convicted of any crime or misdemeanor before reaching the age of 21 years, such person, association, or corporation responsible for such child, shall, within 30 days after written notice given by the State board of charities, remove such child from the State and shall pay to the State, county, or municipality such sum as may have been expended in the care or prosecution of such child. . . .

The State board of charities shall examine the proceedings of societies for securing homes for children, and whenever satisfied that a child has been placed by such society in an improper home, it may order its transfer to a proper one or its removal from the State; and if said order is not obeyed within 30 days, it shall itself take charge of the child, returning it to the society responsible, or otherwise providing for it. Any society failing to remove a child after such notice shall at once pay to the State such sum as the State may have expended in the care, maintenance, or transportation of such child. . . .

That any person, association, or corporation, or any officer, agent, or employee thereof, who shall violate any of the provisions of the foregoing sections . . . shall be guilty of a misdemeanor and upon conviction thereof shall be fined not less than $50 or more than $100, and any such person, association, or corporation, or officer, agent or employee thereof who shall continue to disregard any of the provisions of the said sections for a period of 10 days after notification from the State board of charities shall be guilty of a new, separate, and distinct offense and misdemeanor, and upon conviction thereof shall be fined for each such offense not less than $100 or more than $1,000. . . .

29. Extracts from Emergency Conservation Work: An Act, March 31, 1933

For the relief of unemployment and through the Performance of useful public work, and for other purposes.

Be it enacted by the Senate and House of Representatives of the United States of America in Congress assembled, That for the purpose of relieving the acute condition of widespread distress and unemployment now existing in the United States, and in order to provide for the restoration of the country's depleted natural resources and the advancement of an orderly program of useful public works, the President is authorized, under such rules and regulations as he may prescribe and by utilizing such existing departments or agencies as he may designate, to provide for employing citizens of the United States who are unemployed, in the construction, maintenance and carrying on of works of a public nature in connection with the forestation of lands belonging to the United States or to the several States which are suitable for timber production, the prevention of forest fires, floods and soil erosion, plant pest and disease control, the construction, maintenance or repair of paths, trails and fire-lanes in the national parks and national forests, and such other work on the public domain, national and State, and Government reservations incidental to or necessary in connection with any projects of the character enumerated, as the President may determine to be desirable: *Provided,* That the President may in his discretion extend the provisions of this Act to lands owned by counties and municipalities and lands in private ownership, but only for the purpose of doing thereon such kinds of cooperative work as are now provided for by Acts of Congress in preventing and controlling forest fires and the attacks of forest tree pests and diseases and such work as is necessary in the public interest to control floods. The President is further authorized, by regulation, to provide for housing the persons so employed and for furnishing them with such subsistence, clothing, medical attendance and hospitalization, and cash allowance, as may be necessary, during the period they are so employed, and, in his discretion, to provide for the transportation of such persons to and from the places of employment. That in employing citizens for the purposes of this Act no discrimination shall be made on account of race, color, or creed; and no person under conviction for crime and serving sentence therefor shall be employed under the provisions of this Act. . . .

Sec. 2. For the purpose of carrying out the provisions of this Act the President is authorized to enter into such contracts or agreements with States as may be necessary, including provisions for utilization of existing State administrative agencies, and the President, or the head of any department or agency authorized by him to construct any project or to carry on any such public works, shall be authorized to acquire real property by purchase, donation, condemnation, or otherwise. . . .

30. Extract from Unemployed Youth of New York City, a Report Published by the U.S. Bureau of Labor Statistics, February 1937

A heavy incidence of unemployment among young people 16 to 24 years of age, in New York City, was disclosed by a recent study made by the Welfare Council of that city, with the assistance of the Works Progress Administration. The study, made in 1935, though based upon a sample of the city's youth population and therefore not furnishing a complete census of the unemployed youth of the city, gives a basis for estimating the total numbers of young persons of each sex and of different ages who were unemployed. It also supplies information regarding education and previous work experience which is essential for the guidance of public and private agencies planning for unemployed youth. Any program, at least for New York City, set up with a view to providing training and work for this segment of the unemployed population should take account of the following findings:

1. Unemployed youth—that is, young persons 16 to 24 years of age who were out of school, able to work and desirous of employment but unable to obtain it—constituted one-third of the total sample of the youth population of that city.

2. The unemployed group contained almost as many girls (47 percent) as boys (53 percent).

3. A larger proportion of the Negro than of the white youth was unemployed and seeking employment (43 percent as compared with 33 percent), so that the unemployed group contained a disproportionate number of Negroes.

4. Unemployed youth exhibited wide variations in degree of maturity, in educational achievement and vocational training, and in work experience. Almost one-fifth were found to be under 18, about two-fifths 18 to 20, and about two-fifths 21 to 24 years of age. One-fourth had left school on finishing the eighth grade, and one-fifth on graduating from high school; one-tenth had not completed even the eighth grade, while, on the other hand, almost as many had had from 1 to 7 years of college or university training. The unemployed young men and women who had never had work had a better education, measured in terms of school-grade attainment, than the others who were without jobs. As to work experience, half of the group under 21 years of age, compared with about one-seventh of those 21 years of age or older, comprising altogether over one-third of the total, had never had a job of any kind. The other two-thirds had had work experience of varying lengths covering many types of employment, with about half in semiskilled and unskilled occupations and about two-fifths in clerical and kindred occupations.

These variations point to the necessity of a varied program in education, work projects, and other organized outlets for youthful energy, and also to the need of individualized treatment for many through the provision of counseling and other types of adjustment service.

5. The unemployed youth had been out of school for from a few weeks' time to 10 years or more. The average for those who had never had employment was between 1 and 2 years, and for those with work experience about 5. Almost all who had never had work, and a large proportion of the others, had left school at a time when they must have been faced with the fact of scant likelihood of their getting a job. Even so, three-fourths had left without completing high school. It seems likely therefore that programs emphasizing a return to school for regular high-school or college courses would be acceptable in comparatively few cases.

6. Of the unemployed youth with some work experience half had had no work for at least 1 year, and half had had at least 2 years' unemployment since

leaving school. More than half had been idle at least half the time since they left school. This takes no account of the boys and girls who had been unable to obtain any employment, though out of school, on an average, between 1 and 2 years. What such facts as these may mean in the dissipation of youthful energies and the undermining of youthful enthusiasm cannot be measured, but they must be considered in the formulation of programs for unemployed youth, both from the point of view of rehabilitating those who morale has suffered from protracted idleness, and also on the preventive side through the provision of abundant facilities for the use of the enforced leisure.

7. Unemployed young persons who were themselves in receipt of relief or who were members of relief households (the group specially served by the National Youth Administration), who constituted one-fourth of the total unemployed, are seen, when compared with unemployed youth not on relief, to have had a more limited education and training, to have left school earlier, to have been out of work longer, and to have spent a larger proportion of their working lives without employment. The problem presented by this group is therefore more serious than that of unemployed youth as a whole and as such will require especially careful and thorough attention in all its aspects, if the singling out of this group for special observation and treatment is to be continued. . . .

31. EXTRACTS FROM EXECUTIVE ORDER 9066, FEBRUARY 19, 1942

AUTHORIZING THE SECRETARY OF WAR TO PRESCRIBE MILITARY AREAS

WHEREAS the successful prosecution of the war requires every possible protection against espionage and against sabotage to national-defense material, national-defense premises, and national-defense utilities. . . .

NOW, THEREFORE, by virtue of the authority vested in me as President of the United States, and Commander in Chief of the Army and Navy, I hereby authorize and direct the Secretary of War, and the Military Commanders whom he may from time to time designate, whenever he or any designated Commander deems such actions necessary or desirable, to prescribe military areas in such places and of such extent as he or the appropriate Military Commanders may determine, from which any or all persons may be excluded, and with such respect to which, the right of any person to enter, remain in, or leave shall be subject to whatever restrictions the Secretary of War or the appropriate Military Commander may impose in his discretion. The Secretary of War is hereby authorized to provide for residents of any such area who are excluded therefrom, such transportation, food, shelter and other accommodations as may be necessary, in the judgment of the Secretary of War or the said Military Commander, and until other arrangements are made, to accomplish the purpose of this order. . . .

I hereby further authorize and direct the Secretary of War and the said Military Commanders to take such other steps as he or the appropriate Military Commander may deem advisable to enforce compliance with the restrictions applicable to each Military area hereinabove authorized to be designated, including the use of Federal troops and other Federal Agencies, with authority to accept assistance of state and local agencies.

I hereby further authorize and direct all Executive Departments, independent establishments and other Federal Agencies, to assist the Secretary of War or the said Military Commanders in carrying out this Executive Order, including the furnishing of medical aid, hospitalization, food, clothing, transportation, use of land, shelter, and other supplies, equipment, utilities, facilities and services. . . .

FRANKLIN D. ROOSEVELT
February 19, 1942

32. EXTRACTS FROM PROTECTION OF SCHOOL CHILDREN DURING AIR RAIDS: A FACT SHEET, OFFICE OF CIVILIAN DEFENSE PUBLICATION 5222, APRIL 1943

School Authorities Responsible

School authorities are responsible for the safety, during school hours, of all children entrusted to their care. During a time of war this responsibility takes on an added, grave significance.

American schools are not exempt from enemy attack. A high school in Honolulu was burned during the Japanese attack on Pearl Harbor. Recent Nazi bombings of British schools and the death of many school children are grim reminders of the constant danger which our American children face.

There is no single, magic formula for safeguarding our children from bombing. Each school has to consider its particular situation in order to find the best possible shelter, all things considered, within the shortest time possible. In deciding what procedure will assure maximum safety to pupils and teachers during an air raid, a school administrator has to keep certain factors in mind. Two important questions must be answered:

The Time Factor

(1) *How much time will probably be available* to get the children to shelter?

(2) *What is the best shelter available* in the time allowed?

The local commander of the Citizens Defense Corps can help answer the first question. *The thing to remember is that the time factor is decisive.* Any effective plan for evacuation of children should be based on the assumption that *the time will always be short*—seldom more than three minutes, usually less than fifteen. The actual time available in an air raid will be affected by many unpredictable circumstances and may vary in different localities.

Neighborhood Hazards

The problems of each school building have to be related to the general hazards of the neighborhood. These include:

(1) Nearness to prime industrial targets, such as war plants or large freight terminals.

(2) Nearness to non-fireproof structures, or to congested areas that constitute an extreme fire hazard.

(3) Proximity to landmarks such as rivers, harbors, bridges, or hills.

Each school system should examine its individual schools, taking into account neighborhood as well as individual building hazards. There can be no blanket rule governing all schools. Some cities have placed schools in two main categories: (a) schools from which children should be sent home (b) schools in which children should remain. Other cities have made the mistake of basing categories on types of building alone, or on date of construction, without taking into account neighborhood hazards and protection assets.

Building Hazards

Each building has its own particular features which may constitute hazards in time of air raid. For example, a single stairway made unusable by explosion or fire, would cut off all escape from upper floors. Wall-bearing construction (brick, stone, wood frame, or stuccoed building, lacking a structural steel "skeleton") is subject to collapse from explosion. Non-fireproof construction may be wiped out by incendiaries. Revolving doors without alternative exits have proven extreme hazards.

Glass presents a serious hazard. One of the greatest dangers in classrooms comes from flying glass and fragments. A study should be made of the amount of glass in each building, including glass partitions. Some glass areas can be covered with boards, or replaced by a flexible substitute, or treated to prevent shattering. In general, school corridors are much safer than classrooms as a place of shelter, but children should not stand near the doors. Basements offer special hazards from broken water, gas, or steam lines. The top floor is subject to more danger from direct hits of light incendiaries. Any intervening floors offer greater safety.

Each building must be studied carefully as to its special construction and traffic hazards. Every favorable feature should be utilized, every hazard eliminated or reduced to a minimum.

School Shelters

It is the obligation of school authorities to get each child into the best available shelter when the need arises, within the known time limit. The best available shelter will often be found in the school building. In some instances a building in the immediate neighborhood, a store or apartment house of structural steel and reinforced concrete type, or the nearby homes of children may offer the best shelter.

Any cover is better than no cover at all. When school authorities have to decide between general hazards of location and special building dangers, they will find it better to keep the children under orderly, centralized control than to take a chance of having them outdoors when an actual attack begins. *It is no solution to evacuate children from a poor building to a good shelter too far away to reach within the known time limit. This would expose them to bombing out-of-doors, and to the tons of shell fragments from anti-aircraft fire, and traffic.*

When to Evacuate

On the other hand, where building hazards are exceptionally serious and better shelter is easily available within close walking distance, it is better to evacuate, provided evacuation can be accomplished within the time limit allowed. Remember, the time is always short.

If a school is evacuated, children should never be sent unescorted. In no case should children be dismissed from the building and sent home, unless complete arrangements have been made for an alternative place of refuge in case parents are not at home.

Air Raid Drills

The only safe step is to provide for air raid drills. Air raid drills, like fire drills, are insurance against panic. They build up in the child trust in his teacher, and a feeling of confidence in himself because he knows what to do next. *Failure to institute and perfect drills verges on criminal negligence.*

Cooperation of Parents

Parents should be informed of the protection program of the school. Their cooperation is needed to help give the child confidence. They must be made to realize why, in the event of an air raid, they must not telephone or come to the school.

Personal contact with parents is an essential factor in a school's protection program.

Technical Problems

The problem of protecting school children from air raids has many technical aspects which require the advice of experts. The U.S. Office of Civilian Defense has established a Nationwide Technical Auxiliary Service, through which the best qualified architects and engineers may be organized and trained for service in their own communities, *where the lives of their own children may be at stake.* Schools should seek this service first through their local Defense Council. If not yet organized they may obtain advice from the local building inspector, municipal and school architects and engineers, if these men have qualified for such service by attending special courses of instruction, such as those given at the War Department Civilian Protection Schools in various universities.

Legal Responsibility

School authorities are held responsible for "exercising due care" in protecting children entrusted to their custody against the results of air raid attacks. The exact interpretation of what this legal responsibility entails will depend upon local law....

Neglect of precautionary steps possible to assure the safety of children is to invite tragedy—and a public accounting.

33. House Concurrent Resolution 104, December 13, 1944
IN THE HOUSE OF REPRESENTATIVES
December 13, 1944
Mr. Dirksen submitted the following concurrent resolution; which was referred to the Committee on the Library

Concurrent Resolution

Whereas the children of the Nation by their enthusiastic and wholehearted participation in the salvage campaigns for the collection of waste paper, fats and greases, tin cans, scrap metal, and other commodities, and by their many other war activities, have made an indispensable contribution to the victory effort; and

Whereas this generous effort on their part is so eminently deserving of official recognition and of an expression of the Nation's gratitude: Therefore be it

Resolved by the House of Representatives (the Senate concurring), That the Congress of the United States, in behalf of a grateful Nation, hereby recognizes the important contributions to the victory effort being made by the Nation's children and extends its thanks for their generous and indispensable participation in the cause of freedom.

34. Extracts from the Opinion of the U.S. Supreme Court in Brown et al. v. Board of Education of Topeka et al., 1954

These cases come to us from the States of Kansas, South Carolina, Virginia, and Delaware. They are premised on different facts and different local conditions, but a common legal question justifies their consideration together in this consolidated opinion.

In each of these cases, minors of the Negro race, through their legal representatives, seek the aid of the courts in obtaining admission to the public schools of their community on a nonsegregated basis. In each instance, they had been denied admission to schools attended by white children under laws requiring or permitting segregation according to race. This segregation was alleged to deprive the plaintiffs of the equal protection of the laws under the Fourteenth Amendment. In each of the cases other than the Delaware case, a three-judge federal district court denied relief to the plaintiffs on the so-called "separate but equal" doctrine announced by this Court in *Plessy v. Ferguson,* 163 U.S. 537. Under that doctrine, equality of treatment is accorded when the races are provided substantially equal facilities, even though these facilities be separate. In the Delaware case, the Supreme Court of Delaware adhered to that doctrine, but ordered that the plaintiffs be admitted to the white schools because of their superiority to the Negro schools.

The plaintiffs contend that segregated public schools are not "equal" and cannot be made "equal," and that hence they are deprived of the equal protection of the laws. Because of the obvious importance of the question presented, the Court took jurisdiction. Argument was heard in the 1952 Term and reargument was heard this Term on certain questions propounded by the Court.

Reargument was largely devoted to the circumstances surrounding the adoption of the Fourteenth Amendment in 1868. It covered exhaustively consideration of the Amendment in Congress, ratification by the states, then-existing practices in racial segregation, and the views of proponents and opponents of the Amendment. This discussion and our own investigation convince us that, although these sources cast some light, it is not enough to resolve the problem with which we are faced. At best, they are inconclusive. The most avid proponents of the post-War Amendments undoubtedly intended them to remove all legal distinctions among "all persons born or naturalized in the United States." Their opponents, just as certainly, were antagonistic to both the letter and the spirit of the Amendments and wished them to have the most limited effect. What others in Congress and the state legislatures had in mind cannot be determined with any degree of certainty.

An additional reason for the inconclusive nature of the Amendment's history, with respect to segregated schools, is the status of public education at that time. In the South, the movement toward free common schools, supported by general taxation, had not yet taken hold. Education of white children was largely in the hands of private groups. Education of Negroes was almost nonexistent, and practically all of the race were illiterate. In fact, any education of Negroes was forbidden by law in some states. Today, in contrast, many Negroes have achieved outstanding success in the arts and sciences as well as in the business and professional world. It is true that public school education at the time of the Amendment had advanced further in the North, but the effect of the Amendment on Northern States was generally ignored in the congressional debates. Even in the North, the conditions of public education did not approximate those existing today. The curriculum was usually rudimentary; ungraded schools were common in rural areas; the school term was but three months a year in many states; and compulsory school attendance was virtually unknown. As a consequence, it is not surprising that there should be so little in the history of the Fourteenth Amendment relating to its intended effect on public education....

In approaching this problem, we cannot turn the clock back to 1868 when the Amendment was adopted, or even to 1896 when *Plessy v. Ferguson* was written. We must consider public education in the light of its full development and its present place in American life throughout the Nation. Only in this way can it be determined if segregation in public schools deprives these plaintiffs of the equal protection of the laws.

Today, education is perhaps the most important function of state and local governments. Compulsory school attendance laws and the great expenditures for education both demonstrate our recognition of the importance of education to our democratic society. It is required in the performance of our most basic public responsibilities, even service in the armed forces. It is the very foundation of good citizenship. Today it is a principal instrument in awakening the child to cultural values, in preparing him for later professional training, and in helping him to adjust normally to his environment. In these days, it is doubtful that any child may reasonably be expected to succeed in life if he is denied the opportunity of an education. Such an opportunity, where the state has undertaken to provide it, is a right which must be made available to all on equal terms.

We come then to the question presented: Does segregation of children in public schools solely on the basis of race, even though the physical facilities and other "tangible" factors may be equal, deprive the children of the minority group of equal educational opportunities? We believe that it does....

We conclude that in the field of public education the doctrine of "separate but equal" has no place. Separate educational facilities are inherently unequal. Therefore, we hold that the plaintiffs and others similarly situated for whom the actions have been brought are, by reason of the segregation complained of, deprived of the equal protection of the laws guaranteed by the Fourteenth Amendment. . . .

35. Dress Right, January 24, 1956

Board of Education
Buffalo, New York
School-Community Coordination
Recommendations of the Inter High School Student Council for Appropriate Dress of Students in High School

BOYS
ACADEMIC HIGH SCHOOLS AND HUTCHINSON-TECHNICAL HIGH SCHOOL

Recommended:
1. Dress shirt and tie or conservative sport shirt and tie with suit jacket, jacket, sport coat, or sweater
2. Standard trousers or khakis; clean and neatly pressed
3. Shoes, clean and polished; white bucks acceptable

Not Recommended:
1. Dungarees or soiled, unpressed khakis
2. T-shirts, sweat shirts
3. Extreme style of shoes, including hobnail or "motorcycle boots"

VOCATIONAL HIGH SCHOOLS

Recommended:
1. Shirt and tie or sport shirt and tie
2. Sport shirt with sweater or jacket
3. Standard trousers or khakis; clean and neatly pressed
4. Shoes, clean and polished; white bucks acceptable

Not Recommended:
1. Dungarees or soiled, unpressed khakis
2. T-shirts, sweat shirts
3. Extreme styles of shoes, including hobnail or "motorcycle boots"

Note: The apparel recommended for boys should be worn in standard fashion with shirts tucked in and buttoned, and ties tied at the neck. Standard of dress for boys, while in school shops or laboratories, should be determined by the school.

GIRLS
ACADEMIC AND VOCATIONAL HIGH SCHOOLS

Recommended:
1. Blouses, sweaters, blouse and sweater, jacket with blouse or sweater
2. Skirts, jumpers, suits or conservative dresses
3. Shoes appropriate to the rest of the costume

Not Recommended:
1. V-neck sweaters without blouse
2. Bermuda shorts, kilts, party-type dresses, slacks of any kind
3. Ornate jewelry
4. T-shirts, sweat shirts

36. Extracts from *An Act to Grant Family and Temporary Medical Leave under Certain Circumstances*, February 5, 1993

SEC 2. *Findings and Purposes.*

(a) Findings.—Congress finds that—

(1) the number of single-parent households and two-parent households in which the single parent or both parents work is increasing significantly;

(2) it is important for the development of children and the family unit that fathers and mothers be able to participate in early childrearing and the care of family members who have serious health conditions;

(3) the lack of employment policies to accommodate working parents can force individuals to choose between job security and parenting;

(4) there is inadequate job security for employees who have serious health conditions that prevent them from working for temporary periods;

(5) due to the nature of the roles of men and women in our society, the primary responsibility for family caretaking often falls on women, and such responsibility affects the working lives of women more than it affects the working lives of men; and

(6) employment standards that apply to one gender only have serious potential for encouraging employers to discriminate against employees and applicants for employment who are of that gender.

(b) Purposes.—It is the purpose of this Act—

(1) to balance the demands of the workplace with the needs of families, to promote the stability and economic security of families, and to promote national interests in preserving family integrity;

(2) to entitle employees to take reasonable leave for medical reasons, for the birth or adoption of a child, and for the care of a child, spouse, or parent who has a serious health condition;

(3) to accomplish the purposes described in paragraphs (1) and (2) in a manner that accommodates the legitimate interests of employers;

(4) to accomplish the purposes described in paragraphs (1) and (2) in a manner that, consistent with the Equal Protection Clause of the Fourteenth Amendment, minimizes the potential for employment discrimination on the basis of sex by ensuring generally that leave is available for eligible medical reasons (including maternity-related disability) and for compelling family reasons, on a gender-neutral basis; and

(5) to promote the goal of equal employment opportunity for women and men, pursuant to such clause.

TITLE 1—General Requirements for Leave

SEC. 101. Definitions. . . .

(2) Eligible employee.—

(A) In general.—The term "eligible employee" means an employee who has been employed—

(i) for at least 12 months by the employer with respect to whom leave is requested under section 102; and

(ii) for at least 1,250 hours of service with such employer during the previous 12-month period. . . .

SEC 102. Leave Requirement.

(a) In General—

(1) Entitlement to leave. . . . [A]n eligible employee shall be entitled to a total of 12 workweeks of leave during any 12-month period for one or more of the following:

(A) Because of the birth of a son or daughter of the employee and in order to care for such son or daughter.

(B) Because of the placement of a son or daughter with the employee for adoption or foster care.

(C) In order to care for the spouse, or a son, daughter, or parent, of the employee, if such spouse, son, daughter, or parent has a serious health condition.

(D) Because of a serious health condition that makes the employee unable to perform the functions of the position of such employee. . . .

APPENDIX B
Biographies of Major Personalities

Abbott, Edith (1876–1957) *social worker, educator, author*

Born in Grand Island, Nebraska, Abbott was strongly influenced as a child by her mother's fervent belief in women's rights. She graduated from the University of Nebraska at Lincoln in 1901 and subsequently earned a Ph.D. degree from the University of Chicago. In 1906, she continued her studies in London at University College and the London School of Economics and Political Science. In 1924, Abbott became the first dean of the School of Social Services at the University of Chicago, a position she held until 1942. As a social scientist, she studied working women, child labor, and immigration. As an educator, she advocated field work as training for social workers. She advised the federal government on relief programs during the Great Depression and was an adviser to the International Office of the League of Nations. Her books include *Women in Industry* (1910), *Historical Aspects of the Immigration Problem* (1926), and several works written with her close friend and associate, Sophonisba Breckinridge. Abbott died in Grand Island, the town of her birth, in 1957.

Abbott, Grace (1878–1939) *social worker, second person to head the U.S. Children's Bureau*

The sister of Edith Abbott, Grace Abbott earned a master's degree in political science from the University of Chicago in 1909. In 1908, she became a resident of Hull House, the settlement house founded by Jane Addams and Ellen Gates Starr; there she headed the Immigrants' Protective League. Her writings on immigration were collected in the 1917 book *The Immigrant and the Community*. In 1917, Abbott joined the U.S. Children's Bureau to administer the federal child-labor law that was enacted in 1916. In 1919, President Warren G. Harding appointed her to succeed Julia Lathrop as head of the Children's Bureau. In that position she distributed funding for more than 3,000 child and maternal health centers that were established nationwide in the 1920s. From 1922 to 1934 she was a delegate to the League of Nations Advisory Committee on the Traffic in Women and Children. She joined the faculty of the University of Chicago School of Social Service Administration in 1934, and in 1938 she published *The Child and the State,* a compilation of documents pertaining to child welfare and public policy.

Abbott, Jacob (1803–1879) *writer, educator, clergyman*

Abbott was born in Hallowell, Maine. He entered Bowdoin College at age 14 and graduated in 1820. He earned a master's degree from Bowdoin in 1823 and completed a course of study at Andover Theological Seminary in 1824. From the 1820s through 1835, Abbott moved from one teaching or ministerial job to another. He taught mathematics and natural philosophy at Amherst College between 1824 and 1828; he then opened the Mount Vernon School for Young Ladies, an experimental school, in Boston. In 1834, he was appointed minister of the Eliot Congregational Church in Roxbury, Massachusetts, but he resigned the following year to write. He entered the field of education once more in 1843, when he founded the Abbott Institute, a school in New York City. He ran the institute with his brothers, John Abbott and Gorham D. Abbott, until 1851. Most of the approximately 200 books that Abbott wrote or co-wrote were for children. His first novel, *The Young Christian,* was published in 1832. Other popular works include the 28-volume Rollo series (e.g., *Rollo Learning to Read* [1835]; *Rollo at School* [1839]) and a parenting guide, *Gentle Measures in the Management and Training of the Young* (1899).

Adamic, Louis (1899–1951) *author, journalist*

Adamic left his native Slovenia for New York City at the age of 13. He worked for a Slovenian newspaper before joining the army in 1916 and became a U.S. citizen in 1918. In the 1920s, Adamic translated stories by eastern European writers into English and wrote for *American Mercury* magazine. His first book, *Dynamite,* about labor violence, was published in 1931. Subsequent works include *Laughing in the Jungle* (1932), an autobiography; *The Native's Return* (1934), a best-selling account of a visit to Slovenia; and *My America* (1938), a collection of short, impressionistic writings. In 1940 Adamic became editor of *Common Ground,* a magazine that explored race and culture in the United States. In the same year, he published *From Many Lands,* a book on immigration. His last books, *My Native Land* (1943) and *The Eagle and the Roots* (1952), concern Yugoslavian politics. Marshall Josip Tito awarded Adamic the Yugoslavian Order of National Unity in 1944.

Adams, Henry Brooks (1838–1913) *historian, writer*
The grandson of President John Adams, Henry Adams was born in Boston. Following his graduation from Harvard University in 1858, he traveled in Germany and Italy and studied at the University of Berlin. Adams spent the years 1861 through 1868 in London, serving as secretary to his father, Charles Francis Adams, who was minister to England. He took up journalism upon returning to the United States and wrote for *The Nation* and other periodicals. Some of these writings were collected in *Chapters of Erie and Other Essays* (1871). Between 1870 and 1876, Adams was editor of the *North American Review.* In 1870 he also was appointed professor of medieval history at Harvard. He resigned in 1877 to edit the papers of Albert Gallatin. Adams authored several works of biography and history, including *The Life of Albert Gallatin* (1879), *John Randolph* (1882), the nine-volume *History of the United States of America During the Administrations of Thomas Jefferson and James Madison* (1889–91), and *Mont-Saint-Michel and Chartres* (1904), a study of medieval culture. He is known best for his autobiography, *The Education of Henry Adams* (1906), for which he was posthumously awarded a Pulitzer Prize in 1919.

Adams, John (1735–1826) *second president of the United States*
Adams, who was born in Massachusetts Bay Colony, was educated at Harvard College and pursued a career in law. His outspokenness on political issues earned him a reputation as a leading patriot. He was a delegate to the First and Second Continental Congresses (in 1774 and 1775–76). During the American Revolution he held diplomatic posts in France and Holland. He was instrumental in drafting the Massachusetts Constitution of 1780, and his *Thoughts on Government* (1776) influenced the constitutions of Virginia and North Carolina. In 1782 and 1783, Adams helped to negotiate the Treaty of Paris, ending the war with Great Britain. From 1785 through 1788, he was diplomatic envoy to Great Britain. Adams was the first U.S. vice president, serving under President George Washington from 1789 until 1797, and he succeeded Washington as president. He presided during a period of difficult relations with France, and he faced opposition from the Hamilton Federalists within his administration. Adams served one term as president, losing the election of 1800 to Thomas Jefferson. He spent the last 25 years of his life in retirement and wrote extensively.

Adams, John Quincy (1767–1848) *sixth president of the United States, congressman from Massachusetts*
Adams, the oldest son of President John Adams, was born in Braintree, Massachusetts. At age 12 he accompanied his father, then a diplomat, to Europe. He was his father's secretary during the treaty negotiations with Great Britain that followed the American Revolution. Adams graduated from Harvard College in 1790, whereupon he began to practice law. In 1802, the voters of Massachusetts elected him to the U.S. Senate. In 1808, President James Madison appointed him minister to Russia. As secretary of state under President James Monroe between 1817 and 1824, Adams helped to formulate the Monroe Doctrine, a declaration of U.S. opposition to European intervention in the Americas. In 1824, in an election decided in the House of Representatives, Adams won the presidency. As president he proposed ambitious plans for highways, canals, education, and research, but hostility in Congress prevented him from executing his programs. He lost the election of 1828 to Andrew Jackson, but he returned to government when Massachusetts voters elected him to the House of Representatives in 1830; there he became an outspoken opponent of slavery. In 1848, he suffered a stroke on the floor of the House and collapsed. He died two days later.

Addams, Jane (1860–1935) *social reformer, pacifist, Nobel laureate*
Addams was born in Illinois and educated at the Rockford Female Seminary (now Rockford College),

graduating in 1881. While in Europe in 1887 and 1888, she was inspired by the social reform movement. In 1889 she and college classmate Ellen Starr founded Hull House, a social welfare center, or settlement house, in an immigrant neighborhood of Chicago. The Hull House staff was active in child labor reform and education. The settlement provided the community with a day nursery and a gymnasium, among other services. Addams became chairperson of the Woman's Peace Party in 1915. That same year she also chaired the International Congress of Women at The Hague, Netherlands. She traveled in Europe at the start of World War I, urging peace through mediation. Her pacifism following U.S. entry into the war, however, earned her criticism at home. In 1931, she shared the Nobel Peace Prize with American educator Nicholas Murray Butler. Her 10 books include *Democracy and Social Ethics* (1902), *The Spirit of Youth and the City Streets* (1909), and *Twenty Years at Hull House* (1910).

Alcott, Amos Bronson (1799–1888) *educator, philosopher, writer*
Alcott was born near Wolcott, Connecticut. The oldest of eight children, he helped to support his family. Between 1819 and 1823, he worked as a peddler in Virginia and the Carolinas. In 1823 he returned to New England and embarked on a teaching career. Wherever he taught—in Connecticut, Massachusetts, or Pennsylvania—Alcott employed a controversial method, eschewing corporal punishment, using conversation to stimulate thought, and developing students' physical and imaginative capabilities. With the opening of a school in Boston's Masonic Temple in 1834, Alcott's approach became more radical. He encouraged students to think freely about religion and introduced sex education. Protests from the community forced him to close the school. In 1837, Alcott moved with his family to Concord, Massachusetts, and joined the transcendentalist circle. He was a founder of a short-lived utopian community, Fruitlands, in 1844. Although best remembered as the father of Louisa May Alcott, Bronson Alcott was himself the author of several books, including *Observations on the Principles and Methods of Infant Instruction* (1830), the two-volume *Conversations with Children on the Gospels* (1836–37), and *Sonnets and Canzonets* (1882).

Baker, Russell Wayne (1925–   ) *journalist, author*
Baker, who was born in Loudoun County, Virginia, was five years old when his father died. His mother raised Baker and one of his sisters in a series of homes in Virginia, Maryland, and New Jersey. In 1947, Baker graduated from Johns Hopkins University. He was employed by the *Baltimore Sun* between 1947 and 1954, serving as London bureau chief in 1953 and 1954. In 1954, he joined the staff of the *New York Times.* His column "Observer" first appeared in the *Times* in 1962. In 1979, he received the Pulitzer Prize for commentary. Baker won a second Pulitzer Prize, for biography, for *Growing Up* (1982), his memoir of childhood and youth during the Great Depression. A sequel, *The Good Times,* was published in 1989. His other works include a novel, *Our Next President* (1968), and several collections of his newspaper columns. He edited *The Norton Book of Light Verse* (1986). In 1993, Baker replaced Alistair Cooke as host of television's *Masterpiece Theater.*

Beard, Daniel Carter (1850–1941) *illustrator, writer, founder of the Boy Scouts of America*
Beard was born in Cincinnati, Ohio, and studied at the Art Students League in New York City. He illustrated numerous books and articles, including the first edition of Mark Twain's *A Connecticut Yankee in King Arthur's Court* (1889). Beard became interested in working with boys and published his best-known book, *The American Boys' Handy Book,* in 1882. In 1905, he started the first scouting organization for boys in the United States, the Sons of Daniel Boone. This club became part of the Boy Scouts of America, which was founded in 1910. Beard was made national scout commissioner and held that position for life. He wrote many articles on nature study and outdoor living as well as several other books, including his autobiography, *Hardly a Man Is Now Alive* (1939).

Beecher, Lyman (1775–1863) *theologian*
Because his mother died shortly after his birth, Beecher was adopted by an aunt and uncle. He grew up in Connecticut, learned farming and the blacksmith's craft in his youth, and attended Yale College. After graduating in 1798 and pursuing an additional year of study, he was ordained in the Presbyterian Church. He first preached in East Hampton, Long Island, where he observed the harm caused by alcohol among the Montauk Indians and was inspired to be active in the temperance movement. In 1810, Beecher moved to the Congregational Church in Litchfield, Connecticut. He gained a reputation throughout

New England as an inspirational preacher, and in 1826 he became minister of Boston's Hanover Street Church. During the 1820s he helped found the American Society for the Promotion of Temperance, the Domestic Missionary Society, and the American Bible Society. In 1832, he was appointed president of Lane Theological Seminary and minister of the Second Presbyterian Church in Cincinnati. Beecher expressed liberal views that offended his conservative congregation. For example, he endorsed the concept of free will rather than the orthodox belief in predestination. He was charged with heresy and brought to trial by the local presbytery but was acquitted. He resigned from the pulpit in 1834 and from Lane Theological Seminary in 1850. After a stroke left him partially paralyzed, he lived in Brooklyn, New York, with a son, the influential preacher Henry Ward Beecher. Lyman Beecher was also the father of Harriet Beecher Stowe, author of *Uncle Tom's Cabin* (1852).

Bergh, Henry (ca. 1811–1888) *advocate of animal and child welfare*
Bergh, a shipbuilder's son, was born in New York City. He attended Columbia College but did not graduate. Instead, he went to Europe to travel and write plays. He returned to the United States in 1836 and joined his brother at shipbuilding. The Bergh brothers sold the family business upon the death of their father in 1843, and Henry settled with his wife in Europe and resumed writing. In 1861, President Abraham Lincoln appointed Bergh to the American Legation in Russia. Bergh was distressed by the brutal treatment of horses and donkeys that he witnessed in Europe, and once back in the United States he spoke out about the need to protect animals. In 1866, the New York legislature passed laws punishing mistreatment of animals and chartered the American Society for the Prevention of Cruelty to Animals (ASPCA). ASPCA agents were empowered to arrest anyone violating the state's anticruelty law. Bergh was the society's president from 1866 until his death. Working with Elbridge T. Gerry, legal counsel to the ASPCA, he helped to secure federal legislation against cruelty to animals in interstate transport. In 1874 he and other ASPCA personnel rescued a child, Mary Ellen Connolly, from an abusive home and brought her case to trial. Bergh was a founder, in 1875, of the Society for the Prevention of Cruelty to Children.

Bettelheim, Bruno (1903–1990) *psychologist*
As a Jew in Nazi-occupied Austria, Bettelheim was imprisoned in a concentration camp in 1938. He immigrated to the United States upon his release in 1939 and was hired as a research associate at the University of Chicago. He was an associate professor at Rockford College in Illinois from 1942 to 1944. The 1943 article "Individual and Mass Behavior in Extreme Situations," based on his concentration-camp observations, gained him wide recognition. In 1944, Bettelheim joined the psychology faculty at the University of Chicago and became director of the university's Sonia Shankman Orthogenic School for emotionally disturbed children. He retired from academic life in 1973. His writings based on his work with children include *Love Is Not Enough* (1950); *The Empty Fortress* (1967), on autism; and *The Uses of Enchantment* (1976), on the value of fairy tales in emotional development. Bettelheim's death was a suicide. It was subsequently revealed that his claim to have earned a doctorate from the University of Vienna was false. In addition, former students at the Sonia Shankman School claimed that he had physically abused them.

Black Elk (Hehaka Sapa, Ekhaka Sapa) (1863–1950) *Oglala Lakota holy man*
Black Elk was born near the Little Powder River in present-day Wyoming. He had mystical visions as a child and came to believe that it was his mission to preserve the religion of the Sioux (Dakota, Lakota, Nakota). Black Elk fought at Little Bighorn in June 1876. After the U.S. Army achieved victories over the Sioux later that year, his family traveled with Crazy Horse, an Oglala chief who was a leader in the Indian resistance to white invasion of the northern plains. In May 1877, the family followed Sitting Bull, leader of the Sioux nation, into Canada. Meanwhile, Black Elk gained a reputation as a shaman. From 1886 through 1889 he toured the eastern United States and Europe with Buffalo Bill's Wild West Show. While in England, he appeared before Queen Victoria. After returning to the United States, Black Elk lived at the Pine Ridge Indian Reservation in South Dakota. He converted to Roman Catholicism and was baptized in 1904. In 1930 he dictated his life story to poet John G. Neihardt, and it was published in 1932 as *Black Elk Speaks*. He also advised anthropologist Joseph E. Brown, author of the 1953 book on Sioux ritual and religion *The Sacred Pipe*.

Brace, Charles Loring (1826–1890) *social reformer, child-welfare advocate*

Brace was born in Connecticut and educated at Yale College. A devout Christian, he entered Yale Divinity School in 1847 but soon decided he was unsuited for the traditional ministry. In 1848, he moved to New York City to continue his studies and work among the poor. In January 1853, Brace became the first secretary of the Children's Aid Society, a position he held for the rest of his life. He worked unceasingly to help New York's poor children and find homes for destitute children in rural communities. A fervent abolitionist, Brace wrote many newspaper articles during the Civil War advocating emancipation. His books include *The Dangerous Classes of New York* (1872) and *Gesta Christi; or a History of Humane Progress under Christianity* (1882), a work influenced by the ideas of Charles Darwin.

Breckinridge, Sophonisba Preston (1866–1948) *educator, social reformer*

Breckinridge was born into a prominent Lexington, Kentucky, family. She graduated from Wellesley College in 1888 and took a job as a high school mathematics teacher in the District of Columbia. In 1892, she was the first woman admitted to the bar in Kentucky, but Chicago would become her permanent home. Breckinridge earned a master's degree in political science from the University of Chicago in 1897 and a Ph.D. in 1901. In 1904, she was the first woman to graduate from the University of Chicago Law School. In that year she also joined the faculty of the University of Chicago. In 1920, she helped to found the university's School of Social Service Administration. Breckinridge spent 14 summers at Hull House. She was a founder of the Immigrants' Protective League (1907) and the Chicago branches of the National Association for the Advancement of Colored People (1911) and the National Urban League (1915). In addition, she served on a commission investigating the Chicago race riot of 1919. With her friend and colleague Edith Abbott, Breckinridge began publishing the *Social Service Review* in 1927. In 1933, she represented the United States at the first Pan American Conference. Breckinridge wrote or co-wrote 12 books, including *The Delinquent Child and the Home* (1912) and *Women in the Twentieth Century* (1933). She stopped teaching in 1942.

Canby, Henry Seidel (1878–1961) *educator, editor, critic*

Canby, who was born in Delaware, attended Yale University, earning a bachelor's degree in 1899 and a Ph.D. in English literature in 1905. While teaching at Yale from 1900 to 1916, he introduced courses in American literature. Between 1911 and 1920, he was assistant editor of the *Yale Review,* although he interrupted his work to serve in Europe under the British Commission of War Information during World War I. Canby was editor of the *Literary Review* from 1920 to 1924; in 1924 he founded, with Christopher Morley, the *Saturday Review of Literature,* and was its editor until 1936. Canby was also chairman of the board of the Book-of-the-Month Club from 1926 to 1955. He went to Australia and New Zealand during World War II with the U.S. Office of War Information. Canby wrote 32 books, including textbooks on grammar, composition, and literature. He also wrote three books of literary biography: *Thoreau: A Biography* (1939); *Walt Whitman, an American: A Study in Biography* (1943); and *Turn West, Turn East: Mark Twain and Henry James* (1951). In addition, he was an editor of the *Literary History of the United States* (1948), for many years a standard reference work. His autobiography, *American Memoir,* was published in 1947.

Child, Lydia Maria Francis (1802–1880) *abolitionist, writer*

Lydia Francis, born in Medford, Massachusetts, was 22 when she published her first novel, *Hobomok* (1824), concerning the marriage of a white woman and a Pequot Indian man. It was followed by a short-story collection and a second novel. In 1825, she began publishing *Juvenile Miscellany,* a magazine for children. In 1828, she married David Lee Child, a lawyer and a founder of the New England Anti-Slavery Society. Over the next several years, she wrote a series of books on home and family management, including *The Frugal Housewife* (1829) and *The Mother's Book* (1830). She next published *An Appeal in Favor of that Class of Americans Called Africans* (1833), in which she demanded an immediate end to slavery. Lydia Child continued working to further abolitionist goals and became editor of the *National Anti-Slavery Standard,* the journal of the American Anti-Slavery Society, in 1840. She withdrew from the society in 1843 to protest the call by its president, William Lloyd Garrison, for "no union with slaveholders." Her later writings include *The Freedmen's*

Book (1865), containing writings for and about African Americans; and *An Appeal for the Indians* (1868).

Clark, Richard Wagstaff (1929–   ) *television performer, producer*
Dick Clark grew up in Mount Vernon, New York, and graduated from Syracuse University in 1951. He began his career as a radio announcer in New York and Pennsylvania. He is best known for his association with the television program *American Bandstand,* which he hosted from 1956 until 1989. Other programs that he hosted include *Where the Action Is, Dick Clark's Rock 'n Roll Revue, Miss Teenage America,* and *TV Bloopers and Practical Jokes.* In 1957, he founded Dick Clark Productions; since then he has produced more than 500 hours of television programming. The recipient of numerous awards, including six Emmys, Clark is also the author of several books. His autobiography, *Rock, Roll and Remember,* written with Richard Robinson, was published in 1976.

Cleary, Beverly (1916–   ) *writer best known for her novels for children*
The author of more than 30 novels for children, Cleary has received three Newbery Medals and numerous other literary awards. Her books have sold millions of copies and have been translated into 14 languages. She was born Beverly Bunn in McMinnville, Oregon, and grew up in Portland. She graduated from the University of California at Berkeley in 1938 and studied library science at the University of Washington in 1939. She worked as a librarian in Yakima, Washington, in 1939 and 1940, and at an army hospital in California between 1943 and 1945. In 1940, she married Clarence T. Cleary. Beverly Cleary's first book, *Henry Huggins,* was published in 1950. Other notable works include *The Mouse and the Motorcycle* (1965), *Ramona the Pest* (1968), and *Dear Mr. Henshaw* (1983). Cleary has also written two memoirs, *A Girl from Yamhill* (1988) and *My Own Two Feet* (1995).

Clem, John Lincoln (1851–1937) *Civil War soldier*
In June 1861, Clem ran away from home and followed the Third Ohio Regiment as it marched toward battle. Another unit then took him in and allowed him to act as its drummer. He was officially mustered into service as a musician with the 22nd Michigan Regiment on May 1, 1863. He took part in the Battle of Chickamauga in September 1863, wounding a Confederate

officer and taking him prisoner. Clem in turn was captured by the Confederates in October 1863 and held for two months. Upon his release, he served as a courier for George H. Thomas, commander of the Army of the Cumberland, and was wounded twice in the Atlanta campaign. He was discharged on September 19, 1864, having reached the rank of lance sergeant. Some events of Clem's Civil War service are unsubstantiated. He said, for example, that he picked up a musket and fought in the Battle of Shiloh, a claim that was never proved but earned him the nickname Johnny Shiloh. After the Civil War, he applied to the U.S. Military Academy at West Point but lacked the necessary schooling to be accepted. In 1871, he was commissioned as a second lieutenant and assigned to the 24th Infantry, an African-American unit. He retired from duty in 1916 as a major general.

Clinton, George (1739–1812) *first governor of New York, fourth vice president of the United States*
Clinton was born in Little Britain, New York. He served in the French and Indian War from 1756 to 1763 and was elected to the provincial assembly of New York in 1768. In 1775, he became a delegate to the Continental Congress, but military service in the American Revolution prevented him from signing the Declaration of Independence. He was elected governor of New York in 1777 and held that office until 1795 and again between 1801 and 1804. Clinton's political views were antifederalist. He strongly supported state sovereignty but failed to persuade the 1788 state convention to vote against ratification of the constitution. Clinton was twice elected vice president, in 1804 and 1808, serving under Thomas Jefferson and James Madison, respectively. He died shortly before completing his second term, becoming the first vice president to die in office.

Coit, Stanton (1857–1944) *settlement house founder, exponent of Ethical Culture*
Coit, the son of a Columbus, Ohio, dry goods merchant and a spiritualist, earned a bachelor's degree in philosophy from Amherst College in 1879. In 1881, he moved to New York City to attend Columbia University and study Ethical Culture. He entered the University of Berlin in 1883 and earned a Ph.D. in philosophy in 1885. Before leaving Europe he visited Toynbee Hall, the world's first settlement house, in London. In 1886, he founded the Neighborhood

Guild, a settlement house on the Lower East Side of Manhattan. The following year he became minister of the South Place Chapel in London, where he promoted Ethical Culture. He directed the New York City settlement house, now called University Settlement, from 1892 until 1894, when he returned to England. He became a British subject, and in 1909 he established the Ethical Church in London. Coit published an English translation of *Ethick* by the German philosopher Nicolai Hartmann in 1932. He was the author of *Neighborhood Guilds* (1892), on settlement houses, and several books on religious topics.

Colwell, Harry (1885–1969) *orphan, teacher, social worker*
When his father died in 1888, Colwell's mother surrendered him and his brother Frank to the Half Orphan Asylum in New York City. After their mother died in 1890, Harry and Frank were moved to an orphanage on Riverside Drive in Manhattan. In November 1894, the Children's Aid Society placed Frank Colwell with a family in Coffeyville, Kansas, and the brothers lost touch with each other. The Children's Aid Society found Harry Colwell a home with the Maxwell family of Leonardville, Kansas, in 1899. Colwell worked on the Maxwell farm and attended the local school through the eighth grade. In 1903, he completed a four-week teacher-training course and was hired to teach in Baldwin Creek, Kansas. In January 1905, he entered Kansas State Agricultural College and completed two years of study before returning to teaching and farming. In 1916 he took a job as teacher and counselor at the Graham School, an orphanage north of New York City. He earned a bachelor's degree from Columbia University and, in 1920, a master's degree from the Teachers College at Columbia. From 1920 until his retirement, Colwell did social work at children's homes in Saco, Maine, and Randolph, New York.

Crandall, Prudence (1803–1890) *teacher who attempted to educate African-American girls in the 1830s*
Crandall was born into a Quaker family in Hopkinton, Rhode Island. She was educated at the New England Friends' Boarding School in Providence and briefly taught school in her home state. In 1831, she moved to Canterbury, Connecticut, and opened a girls' boarding school. In 1833, she admitted an African-American student who wished to train as a teacher. Following strong community protest, Crandall closed her school,

reopened it as a school for African-American girls, and recruited students throughout New England. The town of Canterbury responded by outlawing the education of any African American from outside Connecticut. Crandall was arrested, tried, and convicted of violating this law, but the conviction was reversed on appeal in July 1834. Local opposition to the school continued, and in September 1834 mob violence forced Crandall to close her school permanently. She moved with her husband, the Reverend Calvin Philleo, to Illinois. Following Philleo's death, she lived with her brother in Elk Falls, Kansas.

Davis, Angela Yvonne (1944–) *militant African-American activist, academic*
Davis, the daughter of schoolteachers, grew up in Birmingham, Alabama. She studied in Frankfurt, Germany, and Paris before earning a bachelor of arts degree from Brandeis University in 1965. She was a doctoral candidate at the University of California at San Diego when she joined the Communist Party and Black Panthers in 1968; her political views caused the California Board of Regents to refuse renewal of her teaching appointment. In the late 1960s, Davis befriended George Jackson, a prisoner at California's Soledad Prison, and worked to free the Soledad Brothers, a group of African-American prisoners that included Jackson. Davis was suspected as an accomplice in a failed escape and kidnapping that occurred on August 7, 1970, at the Hall of Justice in Marin County, California. Four people died in the attempt, including the trial judge and Jackson's brother Jonathan. Davis fled, and her name was added to the FBI's Most Wanted list. She was arrested in New York City in October 1970. A Free Angela Davis movement gained followers in the United States and overseas who worked for her acquittal in 1972. Davis soon resumed an academic life at San Francisco State University. In 1994, she was appointed to a presidential chair at the University of California at Santa Cruz, where she is currently on the faculty. Her books include *If They Come in the Morning* (1971), an essay collection; *Angela Davis: An Autobiography* (1974); *Women, Race and Class* (1981); and *Women, Race and Politics* (1989).

Davis, Benjamin Oliver, Jr. (1912–) *first African-American general in the U.S. Air Force*
Davis was raised in Washington, D.C., and at the Tuskegee Institute in Alabama, where his father, Ben-

jamin O. Davis, Sr., the only black officer in the U.S. Army, taught military science. (Benjamin O. Davis, Sr., would become the nation's first black general in 1940.) The younger Davis was one of the first African Americans to attend the U.S. Military Academy at West Point, where he was socially ostracized because of his race. He graduated as a second lieutenant in 1936 and was assigned to Fort Benning, Georgia. During World War II he organized the 99th Pursuit Squadron, the first African-American flying unit, which saw combat in North Africa and Italy. In 1943 he commanded the 332nd Fighter Group, known as the Tuskegee Airmen. Davis also commanded a fighter wing in the newly desegregated armed forces in the Korean War. His career decorations include two Distinguished Service Medals and a Silver Star. Promoted to colonel during World War II, Davis was made a brigadier general in 1954 and the nation's first black major general in 1959. He was promoted to lieutenant general in 1965. Davis retired from the military in 1970 and went to work for the U.S. Department of Transportation. As director of civil aviation security, he worked to end a rash of airliner hijackings. In 1998, Davis was honored with a fourth general's star. His autobiography, *Benjamin O. Davis, Jr.: American,* was published in 1991.

Dewey, John (1859–1952) *philosopher, educator*

Dewey earned a bachelor's degree from the University of Vermont in 1879 and a doctorate from John Hopkins University in 1884. From 1884 until his retirement, he taught at the University of Michigan (1884–88; 1889–94), the University of Minnesota (1888–89), the University of Chicago (1894–1904), and Columbia University (1904–31). Dewey gained national recognition as a philosopher while at Chicago. He viewed human beings as creatures of the natural world who must seek life's meaning in their present surroundings. He recognized truth as any idea that works in practical experience. He contributed to *Studies in Logical Theory* (1903), an essay collection that marked the appearance of the Chicago school in philosophy. In 1896 Dewey established the Laboratory School at the University of Chicago to experiment with teaching methods, especially those that actively involved students. His work led to a shift in teaching practices in the early 20th century, as educators focused on students' needs and interests. Dewey was politically active and favored progressive, even radical approaches to international and economic issues. His many books

include *The School and Society* (1899), *Democracy and Education* (1916), *Human Nature and Conduct* (1922), *Art as Experience* (1934), and *Problems of Men* (1946).

Dillard, Annie (Annie Doak) (1945–) *writer*

Dillard was born Annie Doak in Pittsburgh and grew up in a wealthy family. She attended Hollins College in Virginia, earning a bachelor of arts degree in 1967 and a master of arts degree in 1968. Her first two books, both published in 1974, were *Tickets for a Prayer Wheel,* a collection of poems; and *Pilgrim at Tinker Creek,* a meditation on nature based on observations made in the Roanoke Valley of Virginia. In 1975, Dillard received the Pulitzer Prize for general nonfiction for *Pilgrim at Tinker Creek.* She was an editor at *Harper's Magazine* from 1973 through 1975, and she pursued an academic career as well. She was scholar in residence at Western Washington University in Bellingham from 1975 through 1979; she joined the faculty of Wesleyan University in Middletown, Connecticut, in 1979. Dillard published *Holy the Firm,* which attempts to reconcile religious faith with human suffering, in 1978. *Living by Fiction,* a book of literary criticism, was published in 1982. In that year Dillard was part of a U.S. cultural delegation to China. That experience inspired the book *Encounters with Chinese Writers* (1984). Subsequent works include a memoir, *An American Childhood* (1984); and a novel, *The Living* (1992).

Douglass, Frederick (Frederick Augustus Washington Bailey) (1817–1895) *abolitionist, orator, writer*

Frederick Augustus Washington Bailey was born into slavery in Tuckahoe, Maryland, and separated from his mother in infancy. He learned to read while working as a house servant in Baltimore. He escaped from slavery in 1838 and made his way to New Bedford, Massachusetts, where he changed his name to Frederick Douglass. In 1841, he was asked to speak about his life in slavery at an abolitionist meeting; his eloquence impressed members of the Massachusetts Anti-Slavery Society, and he became an agent of that organization. Douglass published his autobiography, *Narrative of the Life of Frederick Douglass,* in 1845. Because he had identified his former owner in the book, he embarked on a two-year speaking tour of Great Britain and Ireland to avoid recapture. Between 1847 and 1860, Douglass lived in Rochester, New York, and published the *North Star,* an abolitionist newspaper. He actively supported the Union in the Civil War by advising President Abraham Lincoln and helping to raise two African-American regiments, the Massachusetts 54th and 55th. In later life he served the District of Columbia as U.S. marshal (1877–81) and recorder of deeds (1881–86). From 1889 until 1891, he was U.S. minister to Haiti. A revised version of Douglass's autobiography, *Life and Times of Frederick Douglass,* was published in 1882.

Du Bois, William Edward Burghardt

(1868–1963) *scholar, writer, a founder of the National Association for the Advancement of Colored People (NAACP)*

Du Bois was born in Great Barrington, Massachusetts, and educated at Fisk and Harvard Universities and the University of Berlin. In 1895 he became the first African American to earn a Ph.D. from Harvard. From 1897 to 1910, he taught history and economics at Atlanta University. He emerged as a spokesperson for African Americans in the early 20th century when he objected in print to Booker T. Washington's advocacy of manual training for young blacks. Du Bois called instead for education of the "Talented Tenth" of his race to serve as leaders in the African-American community. Du Bois led the Niagara Movement, a group that first met in Niagara Falls, Canada, in 1905 to demand an end to racial inequality. After the NAACP was formed in 1910, he served as director of publications. He also edited *The Crisis,* the journal of the NAACP. After World War I, Du Bois organized several pan-African conferences. He worked again with the NAACP from 1944 to 1948. In 1959, the Soviet Union awarded him the Lenin Peace Prize, and in 1961, he joined the Communist Party and moved to Ghana. His 20 books include *The Philadelphia Negro* (1899) and *The Souls of Black Folk* (1903). He died before completing his final project, *Encyclopedia Africana.*

Eastman, Charles (Hakadah, Ohiyesa)

(1858–1939)

Native American physician, writer

Hakadah was born on the Santee Dakota reservation near Redwood Falls, Minnesota. His mother died when he was born. He was renamed Ohiyesa in 1862, the year his grandmother and uncle took him first to the Dakota Territory and then to Canada to elude federal troops responding to an Indian uprising in Minnesota. Ohiyesa was reunited with his father in 1873 and went to live with him on a homestead in North Dakota. Adopting the name Charles Eastman, he attended several schools established for Indian children. In 1857 he graduated from Dartmouth College. He went on to study medicine at Boston University and earned his degree in 1890. Eastman began his medical career at the Pine Ridge Reservation in South Dakota, where he treated people injured in the army attack at Wounded Knee on December 29 of that year. Between 1894 and 1897, he established 32 branches of the YMCA for Native Americans. He was later active in founding the Boy Scouts of America. In 1900, Eastman was hired as a physician at the Crow Creek Reservation in South Dakota. He also worked for the federal government on behalf of the Indian population, helping to secure the land rights of the Sioux peoples during the administration of President Theodore Roosevelt (1901–09) and serving as Indian inspector from 1923 to 1925. His writings include nine books of Indian history, folklore, and autobiography, most notably *Indian Boyhood* (1902), *The Soul of the Indian* (1911), and *From the Deep Woods to Civilization* (1916).

Edelman, Marian Wright (1939–) *lawyer, civil rights activist, founder of the Children's Defense Fund*

A native of Bennettsville, South Carolina, Edelman graduated from Spelman College in Atlanta in 1960 and the Yale University Law School in 1963. She worked on voter-registration drives in Mississippi before becoming a staff attorney for the Legal Defense and Educational Fund of the NAACP. In 1964 Edelman was the first African-American woman admitted to the Mississippi bar. She headed the NAACP Legal Defense and Education Fund office in Jackson, Mississippi, from 1964 to 1968. She then moved to the nation's capital, where she founded the Washington Research Project, forerunner of the Children's Defense Fund, the advocacy group for children's rights established in 1973 of which she is the head. From 1971 to 1973, Edelman directed the Center for Law and Education at Harvard University. In 1996, she formed a second children's rights organization, Stand for Children. Edelman's many awards include the Albert Schweitzer Humanitarian Prize, a MacArthur Foundation Fellowship, and the Presidential Medal of Freedom.

Egan, Maurice Francis (1852–1924) *writer, diplomat*

Egan began his literary career at 17 with the publication of an essay in *Appleton's Journal.* He earned a bachelor's degree from La Salle University in his home-town, Philadelphia, in 1873. In 1875, he commenced studying and teaching philosophy at Georgetown University in Washington, D.C. He published a steady stream of articles and poems and in 1878 he joined the editorial staff of *Magee's Weekly* in New York City. In 1881, he was hired by the *Freeman's Journal.* Egan returned to academia in 1888 as a professor of literature at Notre Dame University. In 1896, a professorship at Catholic University brought him back to Washington. In 1907, President Theodore Roosevelt appointed him minister to Denmark. Egan negotiated the purchase of the Dutch West Indies in 1916, but ill health caused him to resign from diplomatic service in 1918. In 1919, King Christian of Denmark made Egan a commander of the Order of Danebrog, and in 1923, Egan was the first American to receive the Danish Medal of Merit. Egan's account of his time abroad, *Ten Years Near the German Frontier* (1919), was one of his most popular books. He followed it with *Confessions of a Book Lover* (1922) and *Recollections of a Happy Life* (1924), his autobiography.

Eisenhower, Dwight David (1890–1969) *Allied supreme commander during World War II, 34th president of the United States*
Born in Texas, Eisenhower grew up in Abilene, Kansas. He attended the U.S. Military Academy at West Point and was commissioned an infantry officer upon graduation in 1915. He commanded a tank corps training center during World War I. His service in World War II began with an assignment in Washington, D.C. He commanded the Allied forces that landed in North Africa in 1942 and was supreme commander of the Allied invasion of France on June 6, 1944. In December 1944, Eisenhower was promoted to general of the army and given overall responsibility for the Allied forces. He became president of Columbia University in 1948 but left in 1951 to be supreme commander of the North Atlantic Treaty Organization. He was elected president of the United States in 1952. As president he worked to reduce cold war tensions and maintain world peace. In September 1955, he sent troops to Little Rock, Arkansas, to ensure compliance with court-ordered school desegregation. Eisenhower was elected to a second term as president in 1956. In 1960, he accepted responsibility for a U-2 spy-plane flight over the Soviet Union, an event that strained relations between the United States and the USSR.

Fergusson, Harvey (1890–1971) *writer of novels with western settings*
Fergusson was born and raised in Albuquerque, New Mexico. In 1911, after graduating from Washington and Lee University in Lexington, Virginia, he worked briefly as a ranger at Kit Carson National Forest in New Mexico. In 1912, he returned to the East and worked as a reporter for newspapers in Washington, D.C.; Savannah, Georgia; Richmond, Virginia; and Chicago. He was also assistant to columnist Frederic H. Haskin. Beginning in 1923, he earned his living as a freelance writer. He wrote 14 books, most notably novels set in the West. These include *The Blood of the Conquerors* (1921), *Wolf Song* (1927), and *In Those Days* (1929), which form the trilogy *Followers of the Sun. Home in the West,* an autobiography, was published in 1945. Between 1931 and 1942, Fergusson was a screenwriter.

Fiske, George Walter (1872–1945) *theologian, educator, author*
Fiske was born in Holliston, Massachusetts, and graduated from Amherst College in 1898. He continued his studies at Amherst (master of arts, 1898; doctor of divinity, 1925), the Hartford Theological Seminary (bachelor of divinity, 1898), and Boston University (Ph.D., 1919). He was a congregational minister from 1898 to 1907, serving at churches in Massachusetts and Maine. In 1907, he became a professor at the Oberlin Graduate School of Theology in Ohio. He retired from Oberlin in 1937. In 1937 and 1938, he taught at the Near East School of Theology and at the American University in Beirut. Fiske wrote a number of books on religious topics as well as *Boy Life and Self Government* (1910), on boyhood.

Foy, Edwin Fitzgerald (1856–1928) *comedian*
Foy was born in New York City, but his mother moved the family to Chicago in 1865 after his father, a Civil War veteran, was committed to a mental institution. As a child Foy performed on city streets to support his family, and as a young man he entertained in western mining camps and cattle towns. He returned to Chicago in 1888 to star in musicals and revues. In 1904, he was acting in the play *Mr. Bluebeard* in Chicago when fire broke out in the theater and killed 600 audience members. From 1904 to 1913, Foy performed on the New York stage in *Piff! Paff! Pouf!* and other musical comedies. In 1913, he and his children

first appeared together in vaudeville as Eddie Foy and the Seven Little Foys. The popular family act made one motion picture. Foy retired from the stage in 1923 but returned to work in 1927.

Freed, Alan (1922–1965) *disk jockey who popularized rock and roll*

Freed played the trombone in a swing band while in high school in Salem, Ohio. In 1942, he took the first of several broadcasting jobs that he would hold in Pennsylvania and Ohio. In July 1951, he began broadcasting rhythmic music by African-American artists, which he called rock and roll, on WJW radio in Cleveland. A live rock-and-roll show he was to host at the Cleveland Arena in March 1952 had to be cancelled when 20,000 people tried to attend. Freed moved his radio show to WINS in New York City in 1954. He staged several live rock-and-roll shows in New York, but some were marred by audience violence. He also appeared in *Rock Around the Clock* (1955) and other films. As Freed moved from one broadcasting job to another over the next several years, disputes with management and accusations of payola damaged his career. In December 1962 he pled guilty to two counts of bribery and was fined $300. In 1965, Freed died in Palm Springs, California, of complications of alcoholism. He was one of the first people inducted into the Rock and Roll Hall of Fame in 1986.

Freud, Anna (1895–1982) *psychoanalyst noted for her work with children*

As a child in Vienna, Austria, Anna Freud became interested in the work of her father, Sigmund Freud. She trained to teach elementary school, but she soon left the classroom to pursue child psychology. She worked closely with her father after he was first treated for cancer in 1923; from 1925 through 1928, she chaired the Vienna Psycho-Analytic Society. Anna Freud established her own credentials with the publication of *The Ego and Mechanisms of Defense* (1936). In 1938, the Freuds, who were Jewish, secured permission to leave Nazi-occupied Austria and settle in Great Britain. Anna Freud worked at a London nursery school until 1945. During World War II, she and her American-born colleague, Dorothy Burlingham, studied the effects of wartime family separation on children. They published their results in *War and Children* (1943) and other works. Freud founded the journal *Psychoanalytic Study of the Child* in 1945 and the Hampstead Child

Therapy Course and Clinic in 1947. She was director of the clinic from 1952 until 1982. She summarized her contributions to psychoanalysis in *Normality and Pathology in Childhood* (1968).

Froebel, Friedrich Wilhelm August (1782–1852) *German educator, founder of the first kindergarten*

Froebel, son of a Lutheran minister, was born in Oberweissbach, Saxony (now part of Germany). In his youth, Froebel acquired an extensive knowledge of plant life. He drifted from one occupation to another, working as a forester, surveyor, and architect before becoming a teacher. He also studied briefly in Jena, Gottingen, and Berlin. From 1806 to 1810, he worked at a school run by the Swiss educator Johann Pestalozzi. Between 1813 and 1815, he served in the Prussian army and supervised the mineralogical museum at the University of Berlin. In 1816, Froebel founded the Universal German Educational Institute, where he developed his program for educating preschool children. In 1827, he opened a school for young children at Blankenburg, Thuringia, which he called a *Kindergarten,* or children's garden. The Prussian government banned kindergartens in 1851, suspecting that Froebel held radical political ideas; the ban was lifted in 1860. Froebel's writings include *The Education of Man* (1826) and *Mother Play and Nursery Songs* (1843).

Gale, Zona (1874–1938) *novelist, playwright*

A native of Portage, Wisconsin, Gale decided in childhood to be a writer. After graduating from the University of Wisconsin in 1895, she spent six years as a reporter, first for the *Evening Wisconsin* and then for the *Milwaukee Journal.* She continued her studies in the meantime and earned a master's degree in literature from the University of Wisconsin in 1899. In 1901, she moved to New York City to write for the *Evening World;* two years later, she embarked on a freelance career and was soon selling short stories to magazines. Several were set in a fictional village resembling Portage. Her novel *Romance Island* was published in 1906. After winning a literary prize from *Delineator* magazine, Gale returned to Portage to live. She became involved with the Women's Trade Union League and other progressive groups, and she was a pacifist during World War I. She also continued to write. The novel *Miss Lulu Bett,* about a small-town spinster's attempts to take control of her life, appeared in 1920. Gale's dramatization of this novel won her the Pulitzer Prize for drama in 1921. Other significant works include the novels *Birth* (1918), *Faint Perfume* (1923), and *Preface to Life* (1926), and an autobiography, *When I Was a Little Girl* (1913). From 1923 to 1929, Gale sat on the board of regents of the University of Wisconsin.

Gallatin, Abraham Alfonse Albert (1761–1849) *statesman, financial expert*
The Swiss-born Gallatin was educated at the University of Geneva. He immigrated to the United States in 1780 and worked first as a merchant and then as a tutor at Harvard College. He also bought land in Virginia and Pennsylvania on speculation. Gallatin served in the Pennsylvania legislature from 1790 until 1792 and in the U.S. House of Representatives from 1795 until 1801. As a congressman he helped to organize the Finance Committee (now the House Ways and Means Committee) and earned praise for his understanding of financial matters. President Thomas Jefferson appointed him secretary of the treasury in 1801; he held that post until 1814. As treasury secretary, Gallatin reduced the public debt and created a budget surplus. He opposed the War of 1812, worked to end the hostilities, and helped negotiate peace with Great Britain and draft the Treaty of Ghent. He was minister to France from 1816 to 1823 and minister to Great Britain from 1826 to 1827. Gallatin retired from government service in 1827 and between 1831 and 1839 served as president of a New York City bank. He was a founder and first president of the American Ethnological Society and, from 1843 until his death, president of the New-York Historical Society.

Garland, Hannibal Hamlin (1860–1940) *writer whose youth on the frontier inspired his most successful work*
Garland was born on a farm in West Salem, Wisconsin. His family migrated west during his childhood, first to Iowa and then to the Dakotas. In 1884 Garland moved to Boston and embarked on a literary career. His first book was *Main-Travelled Roads* (1891), a collection of short stories critical of life on the plains. Another book of short stories and three novels followed. In 1917, Garland published the memoir *A Son of the Middle Border* to critical acclaim. A sequel, *A Daughter of the Middle Border,* was published in 1921 and earned the Pulitzer Prize for biography in 1922. Garland also wrote *Crum-*

bling Idols (1894), a book on art and literature; and *The Mystery of the Buried Crosses* (1939), on psychic research.

Gerry, Elbridge Thomas (1837–1927) *lawyer, children's advocate*
Gerry graduated from Columbia University in 1857 and was admitted to the bar in New York in 1860. In 1867, he was a delegate to the constitutional convention of New York State. He served as legal counsel to the American Society for the Prevention of Cruelty to Animals and was a founder in 1874 of the New York Society for the Prevention of Cruelty to Children. He became president of the society in 1879. In 1886 Gerry chaired a commission to determine the most humane method of execution; the group advised the New York legislature to adopt electrocution instead of hanging. In 1889, he chaired the committee that planned the centennial celebration of the U.S. government, and in 1892 he investigated the care of the insane in New York State. Gerry moved to Rhode Island and was admitted to the bar in that state in 1889; by 1896, though, he had largely retired from the practice of law.

Goodwin, Doris Kearns (1943–   ) *historian, writer, political analyst*
A child of the Long Island suburbs, Doris Kearns attended Colby College in Maine, graduating in 1964. Four years later she earned a Ph.D. degree from Harvard University. She began her career in Washington, D.C., as a congressional intern, in 1965. She subsequently worked in the Department of Health, Education, and Welfare and the Department of Labor. In 1968, she became a special assistant to President Lyndon Johnson. She taught government and politics at Harvard beginning in 1969 and served as a special consultant to President Johnson from 1969 to 1973. In 1972, she hosted the show *What's the Big Idea* for WGBH-TV, Boston, and was a political analyst for WBZ-TV, Boston. She continues to appear as a commentator on television and radio. In 1976, Doris Helen Kearns published a highly acclaimed authorized biography, *Lyndon Johnson and the American Dream*. Her second book, published under her married name, was *The Fitzgeralds and the Kennedys: An American Saga* (1987). Goodwin is the author as well of *No Ordinary Time: Franklin and Eleanor Roosevelt: The Home Front in World War II* (1995, Pulitzer Prize for History) and *Wait Till Next Year* (1997), a memoir of growing up as a fan of the Brooklyn Dodgers.

Grant, Frederick Dent (1850–1912) *army officer, civil servant, diplomat*

Frederick Grant first tasted army life when he accompanied his father, General Ulysses S. Grant, during the 1863 Vicksburg campaign in the Civil War. He attended the U.S. Military Academy at West Point, and despite charges that he was involved in the hazing of the first African-American cadet and that he enjoyed special treatment because his father was president, Grant graduated in 1871 and was commissioned as a second lieutenant in the Fourth Cavalry. Military service took him to Europe with General William T. Sherman, to Texas, and to Chicago. He took part in expeditions exploring the American West in 1873 and 1874, and he fought in the Bannock Indian War of 1878. He toured Asia with his parents in 1879 and resigned from the army in 1881 to enter business. He also served as his father's assistant until General Grant's death in 1885. Frederick Grant was minister to Austria-Hungary from 1889 to 1893 and a New York City police commissioner from 1895 to 1897. He returned to active military duty in 1898, receiving a commission as brigadier general in 1901. He served in Puerto Rico and fought in the Philippine insurgency (1899–1902). Thereafter his duties were limited to appearances at military, civic, and social functions.

Greeley, Horace (1811–1872) *newspaper editor, antislavery activist, politician*

Greeley was born in Amherst, New Hampshire, and apprenticed to a printer in East Poultney, Vermont, at age 14. In 1831, he moved to New York City, where he edited the *New Yorker,* the *Jeffersonian,* and then the *Log Cabin.* He also published pamphlets supportive of the Whig Party and promoted progressive government policies. In 1841, he founded the *New York Tribune,* which he edited for 31 years. His high journalistic standards made him the leading newspaperman of his day. In the pages of the *Tribune,* Greeley advocated free public education for all children, westward migration, and the development of agriculture. Greeley vigorously opposed slavery and spoke out against the U.S.-Mexican War and the Kansas-Nebraska Act, because he viewed both as means for extending slavery in the West. He criticized Lincoln for delaying the freeing of slaves during the Civil War and angered many northerners after the war when he signed a bail bond for Jefferson Davis. In 1872, Greeley was the newly formed Liberal Republican Party's candidate for president. He

received more than 40 percent of the popular vote but died before the Electoral College met. His electoral votes went to minor candidates, and the incumbent, Ulysses S. Grant, was determined to have won the election.

Gregory, Richard Claxton (1932–) *comedian, civil rights activist, promoter of healthful living*

Dick Gregory was raised in poverty in St. Louis. An athletic scholarship enabled him to enter Southern Illinois University in 1951, but he left school in 1953 to join the army. After performing at the Chicago Playboy Club in 1961, he became a popular television and nightclub comedian whose routines dealt with such serious issues as poverty and discrimination. Gregory was active in the civil rights movement and was arrested during several demonstrations. His strong political convictions impelled him to run for mayor of Chicago in 1966 and president of the United States in 1968. Soon afterward, he gave up performing to devote his energy to social and health issues. On numerous occasions he fasted to protest human rights abuses. He became an expert in nutrition and in 1984 formed Dick Gregory Health Enterprises, Inc., to market weight-loss products. He launched the Campaign for Human Dignity in 1992 to combat crime in St. Louis. In 1996 he returned to the stage in a one-man show, *Dick Gregory Live!* Gregory is the author of several memoirs as well as books on politics and nutrition.

Hall, Granville Stanley (1844–1924) *psychologist, educator*

Hall was a native of Ashfield, Massachusetts. Over an 11-year period, from 1868 to 1878, his interest shifted from theology to philosophy and then to psychology. He spent a year at Union Theological Seminary in New York City, pursued further study in Germany, and taught at Antioch College. In 1878, at Harvard University, he earned the first Ph.D. in psychology granted in the United States. In 1883, he joined the faculty of Johns Hopkins University and founded one of the nation's earliest psychology laboratories. He began publishing the *American Journal of Psychology* in 1887, and in 1888 he was a founder of Clark University in Worcester, Massachusetts. He also served as the school's first president. Hall promoted the study of child development, and he defined the term *adolescence.* He established the *Pedagogical Seminary* (later the *Journal of*

Genetic Psychology) in 1893 and was one of the first Americans to recognize the importance of psychoanalysis. In 1909, he arranged for Sigmund Freud and Carl Jung to visit Clark University. Hall's 489 written works include *Adolescence* (1904), *Youth* (1906), *Senescence* (1922), and *Life Confessions of a Psychologist* (1923).

Hammond, James Henry (1807–1864) *politician, planter, slaveholder*
Hammond was born in Newberry District (now Newberry County), South Carolina, and attended South Carolina College (now the University of South Carolina), graduating in 1825. He spent his early career as a teacher and journalist, and in 1828 he was admitted to the bar. Hammond founded a newspaper in support of nullification, or a state's right to refuse to enforce federal law. He represented South Carolina in Congress as a Nullifier from March 1835 until February 1836, when he resigned due to ill health. He then spent two years in Europe, returning to pursue a planter's life. His marriage to a wealthy woman allowed him to increase his holdings significantly. He was governor of South Carolina from 1842 to 1844 and a U.S. senator from South Carolina between 1857 and 1860, when he retired. Hammond was a staunch proponent of slavery who had a complicated attitude toward his own slaves. He instituted progressive measures to reduce illness and mortality among them, yet he fathered several slave children.

Hine, Lewis Wickes (1874–1940) *photographer who documented immigration and child labor*
Hine attended the state normal school in his hometown of Oshkosh, Wisconsin, and spent a year at the University of Chicago. He began his first and only teaching job, at the Ethical Culture School in New York City, in 1901. In 1904, he started taking pictures of immigrants arriving at Ellis Island, becoming one of the first U.S. photographers to document social history. In 1907, Hine began a project that would occupy 11 years: photographing conditions of child labor for the National Child Labor Committee. His pictures of children working on city streets and in coal mines, textile mills, and canneries persuaded legislators in many states to pass child-labor laws. In 1919, Hine documented Red Cross relief efforts in Europe in the aftermath of World War I. The American worker became his subject after he returned to the United States, and he made more than 1,000 photographs of laborers constructing the Empire State Building. He published a collection of his industrial photographs, *Men at Work,* in 1932.

Hoover, Herbert Clark (1874–1964) *thirty-first president of the United States*
Hoover, who was born into a Quaker family in rural Ohio, studied geology and mining at Stanford University. He began his career managing mining properties in Western Australia and China. He performed relief work during World War I, arranging transportation home for 120,000 American tourists stranded in Europe and securing food for war-torn Belgium. Following the war, he headed the American Relief Administration, which distributed food, clothing, and medical supplies in Eastern Europe. Between 1921 and 1928, he was secretary of commerce under presidents Warren G. Harding and Calvin Coolidge. Hoover, a Republican, was elected president in 1928. Although he took unprecedented steps to combat the Great Depression, sanctioning government spending for public works and federal loans to businesses through the Reconstruction Finance Corporation, the public perceived him as insensitive to their distress. Franklin D. Roosevelt defeated him in the 1932 election. Hoover headed commissions under Presidents Harry S. Truman and Dwight D. Eisenhower to streamline the executive branch of the federal government. He was the author of *American Individualism* (1922), *Challenge to Liberty* (1934), and the three volume *Memoirs* (1951–52).

Howells, William Dean (1837–1920) *novelist, critic*
As a child in Ohio, Howells learned the printing trade from his father. He worked as a typesetter and later as a journalist. During the presidential campaign of 1860, he wrote a brief biography of candidate Abraham Lincoln. Following the election, President Lincoln appointed Howells U.S. consul in Venice, Italy. In 1866, Howells returned to the United States and worked for the *Atlantic Monthly*. He was editor in chief from 1871 through 1881. In 1909, he became the first president of the American Academy of Arts and Letters; he held that position until his death. Howells was one of the most influential literary personages of his time. He wrote more than 30 novels, many of which offer insightful descriptions of American life. They include *A Modern Instance* (1882), *The Rise of Silas Lapham* (1885), *Annie Kilburn* (1888), *Through the Eye of the Needle* (1907), and *A Hazard of New Fortunes* (1890).

Howells also published several volumes of literary criticism. He furthered the careers of such promising young American writers as Stephen Crane, Mark Twain, Henry James, and Paul Laurence Dunbar, and he introduced American readers to Leo Tolstoy, Emile Zola, Henrik Ibsen, and other European authors.

Hughes, John Joseph (1797–1864) *Roman Catholic bishop who promoted parochial education*
Hughes, an Irish immigrant, settled in Pennsylvania in 1817. He entered St. Mary's Seminary in 1820 and was ordained a priest in the diocese of Philadelphia in 1826. In 1837, he was appointed coadjutor bishop of New York, where he was made bishop in 1842. Throughout his career, Hughes responded publicly to critics of Catholicism, including such distinguished ones as John Quincy Adams and Samuel B. F. Morse. His strongly worded writings in the press earned him the nickname Dagger John. In the 1840s, his protests against the use of the King James Bible in public schools furthered the secularization of public education. Meanwhile, his objections to perceived anti-Catholic rhetoric in the public school curriculum caused him to support the development of parochial schools. In 1840 Hughes founded St. Joseph's Seminary and in 1841 St. John's College (now Fordham University), both in the Bronx. He also helped to establish the Pontifical North American College at Rome in 1859. In 1850, when the archdiocese of New York was established, Hughes became archbishop. In 1858 he supervised the start of construction of St. Patrick's Cathedral at Fifth Avenue and 50th Street in New York City. He traveled in Europe in 1861 and 1862 at the request of President Abraham Lincoln to enlist support of the union cause from Catholic heads of state, such as Emperor Napoleon III of France.

Huntley, Chester Robert (1911–1974) *radio and television news commentator*
Chet Huntley was born in Caldwell, Montana, and graduated from the University of Washington in 1934. He began his broadcasting career with radio station KPCB in Seattle while still in college. He then worked at stations in Spokane and Portland, Oregon, before joining CBS in Los Angeles in 1939 as a newscaster and analyst. In 1951 he joined ABC in Los Angeles, and in 1955 he moved to New York to work for NBC. In 1956, he teamed with David Brinkley to cover the Republican and Democratic National Conventions for NBC television. Huntley and Brinkley hosted a nightly news program on NBC, with Huntley broadcasting from New York and Brinkley commentating from Washington, D.C., until Huntley retired in 1970 and returned to Montana. Huntley received George Foster Peabody Awards for excellence in broadcasting in 1942 and 1954.

Janvier, Meredith (1872–1936) *book dealer, photographer*
Janvier was born in Albemarle County, Virginia, but raised in Baltimore, the city that would be his lifelong home. In 1894, he received the Sandow Award, named for bodybuilder Eugen Sandow, for excellence in physical development. He earned a law degree from the University of Maryland in 1896 but gave up the practice of law in 1903 to become a photographer. He specialized in making portraits of prominent Baltimoreans. Janvier was also a collector of books and prints, and in 1913 he issued a catalog and began to trade in these items. He made many trips to Europe to find books, and his customers included H. L. Mencken and Christopher Morley. Janvier was the author of *Baltimore in the Eighties and Nineties* (1933) and *Baltimore Yesterdays* (1937).

Jefferson, Thomas (1743–1826) *third president of the United States, principal author of the Declaration of Independence*
Jefferson grew up on a Virginia plantation and attended the College of William and Mary. He was admitted to the bar in 1857 and elected to the Virginia House of Burgesses in 1859. Throughout his life, Jefferson was a voracious reader and a prolific writer. He wrote the *Summary View of the Rights of British America* for the Virginia delegates to the First Continental Congress in 1774. In June 1776, he drafted the Declaration of Independence for the Second Continental Congress. He was governor of Virginia from 1779 until 1781. Jefferson had many interests, including architecture and agriculture. He devoted much time and energy to designing and building his Virginia estate, Monticello, and he was an enthusiastic farmer. His interest in the people, politics, and commerce of his home state inspired him to write *Notes on the State of Virginia*. Jefferson was minister to France from 1784 to 1789 and the first U.S. secretary of state from 1789 to 1794. He was a candidate for president in the election of 1796; because he received the second largest number of

votes, he became vice president under John Adams, the victor, in accordance with the electoral system in use at the time. The presidential election of 1800 resulted in a tie between Jefferson and Aaron Burr, which the House of Representatives decided in Jefferson's favor. As president, Jefferson was responsible for the Louisiana Purchase, which significantly increased the territory of the United States. Upon completion of his second term as president, in 1809, Jefferson retired to Monticello. He founded the University of Virginia in 1819.

Johnson, James Weldon (1871–1938) *writer, civil rights leader*
Johnson began his education in Jacksonville, Florida, under the tutelage of his mother, a teacher. He earned a bachelor of arts degree from Atlanta University in 1894. He spent four years as principal of Staughton High School in Jacksonville and was admitted to the Florida bar. In 1898 he went to New York City and formed the successful songwriting team of Cole and Johnson Brothers with his brother, composer J. Rosamond Johnson, and performer Bob Cole. He also began publishing poetry in magazines. In 1906, Johnson was appointed U.S. consul at Puerto Cabello, Venezuela, and from 1909 to 1913 he was U.S. consul at Corinto, Nicaragua. In 1916, he became field secretary of the NAACP; from 1920 to 1930 he held the position of executive secretary. As a writer Johnson is associated with the Harlem Renaissance. His works include *Fifty Years and Other Poems* (1917); a novel, *Autobiography of an Ex-Coloured Man* (1927); a collection of African-American sermons in verse form, *God's Trombones* (1927); an autobiography, *Along This Way* (1933); and anthologies of African-American poetry and spirituals.

Joplin, Janis Lyn (1943–1970) *rock and blues vocalist*
An artistic misfit in her hometown of Port Arthur, Texas, Joplin attended Lamar State College of Technology and the University of Texas at Austin. She left school in 1963 to pursue a singing career. In 1966 she became lead singer for Big Brother and the Holding Company, a San Francisco band. With this band Joplin recorded two of her best known songs, "Piece of My Heart," and "Ball and Chain." Joplin left the group in 1968 and briefly joined the Kozmic Blues Band. In 1970, despite worsening heroin addiction, she formed a new musical group, the Full Tilt Boogie Band. She

was recording the album *Pearl* (1971) at the time of her death from a heroin overdose. In 1995 Joplin was inducted into the Rock and Roll Hall of Fame.

Kennedy, John Fitzgerald (1917–1963) *35th president of the United States*
Kennedy graduated from Harvard University in 1940; his expanded senior thesis, *Why England Slept,* was published in the same year. In August 1943, he was commanding a navy PT boat that was rammed and sunk by a Japanese destroyer off the Solomon Islands. Kennedy, severely injured, led the surviving crew members to safety. Massachusetts voters elected him to the U.S. House of Representatives as a Democrat in 1946 and to the Senate in 1952. Kennedy wrote *Profiles in Courage* (1956) while recovering from back surgery. In 1960, Kennedy was elected president. In December 1961, he sent the first U.S. military personnel to South Vietnam to help that country repel invaders from communist North Vietnam. In October 1962, he responded to the installation of Soviet missiles in Cuba with a naval blockade of the island and forced the Soviets to remove their weapons. Many Americans, young and old, closely watched on television the events following Kennedy's assassination on November 22, 1963.

La Guardia, Fiorello Henry (1882–1947) *lawyer, politician, mayor of New York City*
La Guardia was born in New York City, the son of a U.S. Army bandmaster, and grew up on a military post in Arizona where his father was stationed. When he was 16, La Guardia moved with his mother to Hungary. He served in the American consulates at Budapest and at Trieste and Fiume in Italy. He returned to the United States in 1906 and supported himself as an interpreter at the Ellis Island immigration station while studying law at New York University. He was admitted to the bar in 1910. In 1914, he became deputy attorney general of New York State, and in 1916 he was elected to the House of Representatives as a Republican. He interrupted this term in Congress to serve as a pilot with the U.S. Air Service in World War I. After being president of the New York City board of aldermen in 1920 and 1921, he was elected to the second of his six terms in the House. La Guardia was elected mayor of New York City in 1933. During his three terms in office, he earned a reputation for honesty. He was a progressive mayor who fought political corruption and organized crime and significantly improved public

services. President Franklin D. Roosevelt appointed him director of the U.S. Office of Civilian Defense in 1941 and director general of the United Nations Relief and Rehabilitation Administration in 1946.

Lancaster, Joseph (1778–1838) *British educator who perfected the monitorial system of education*
Lancaster attended school only briefly before leaving his London home at age 14 and joining the navy. Friends secured his discharge, and in 1798, he began teaching children in the home of his father, a sieve maker. He soon moved his school to roomier quarters and, to cut expenses, enlisted older students to teach the younger ones. From this beginning he developed a complex monitorial system of instruction, order, and discipline. Lancaster traveled throughout Great Britain to promote his method and won converts in North and South America. Lancasterian schools were first established in Canada in 1814. In 1818, financial difficulties and scandal forced Lancaster to leave England and settle in the United States. His health declined, and in 1820 he moved to Venezuela. In 1828 he lived in New York; he moved in 1829 to Montreal, where he opened a school. He endeavored to publish the *Gazette of Education and Friend of Man* in 1830 but produced only one issue. Soon afterward, he closed his school because of a lack of funds. Lancaster returned to New York, where he died in 1838 after being run over by a breakaway horse.

Larcom, Lucy (1824–1893) *writer, teacher*
Larcom was born in Beverly, Massachusetts, the ninth of 10 children. Her father, a merchant and sea captain, died when she was six. Her mother then moved the family to Lowell, Massachusetts, where she supervised a dormitory for female mill workers. Larcom joined the girls working in the mills at the approximate age of 10. Her textile-mill experience inspired her best-known work, the memoir *A New England Girlhood* (1889), and the book-length narrative poem *An Idyl of Work* (1875). Her published works also include four collections of verse. In 1846, Larcom moved to Illinois, where she taught school and attended the Monticello Seminary. Following graduation in 1853, she returned to Massachusetts and accepted a teaching job at the Wheaton Female Seminary. Between 1865 and 1873, she edited *Our Young Folks,* a children's magazine. In the 1870s, she collaborated with the poet John Greenleaf Whittier to compile several poetry anthologies.

Lathrop, Julia Clifford (1858–1932) *social worker, first director of the U.S. Children's Bureau*
Lathrop was born in Rockford, Illinois, and attended Rockford and Vassar Colleges, graduating in 1880. Strongly interested in social reform, she moved to Chicago in 1890 to join the staff of Hull House. From 1893 to 1901, and again from 1905 to 1909, she served on the Illinois Board of Charities and undertook to investigate almshouses throughout the state. During that period she worked for the creation of a juvenile court in Illinois and was a founder of the Immigrants' Protective League. In 1903, she helped to found the Chicago Institute of Social Science (renamed the Chicago School of Civics and Philanthropy). She was also the first director of the school's research department, which she helped to establish. In 1912, President William Howard Taft appointed Lathrop to be the first head of the U.S. Children's Bureau of the Department of Commerce and Labor, a position she held until 1922. She also served as president of the National Conference of Social Work from 1918 to 1919. Between 1925 and 1931, she was an advisory member of the Child Welfare Committee of the League of Nations.

Levitt, William Jaird (1907–1994) *developer of Levittown*
Levitt was born in New York City. He entered New York University in 1924 but withdrew before graduating. In 1927 he went to work for his father, Abraham Levitt, an attorney. With his father and brother, Alfred, he formed Abraham Levitt and Sons, a construction company, which built its first house in 1929. In 1941, the firm was awarded a contract to build 2,350 homes for defense workers in Norfolk, Virginia. William Levitt was a Navy Seabee during World War II. In 1947, he acquired 4,000 acres of Long Island farmland on which Abraham Levitt and Sons constructed more than 17,000 homes. The community, originally called Island Trees, soon acquired the name Levittown. Between 1951 and 1956, Levitt built a second Levittown in Bucks County, Pennsylvania, and, beginning in 1958, a third one in New Jersey. By 1968 the firm had built more than 140,000 houses worldwide. In that year Levitt sold the company to the ITT Corporation for $92 million in ITT stock. In the 1970s, Levitt was involved in construction projects in Africa, South America, and the Middle East, but business setbacks caused him to fall into debt.

Lincoln, Abraham (1809–1865) *16th president of the United States, U.S. leader during the Civil War, author of the Emancipation Proclamation*

Lincoln grew up in the wilderness of Kentucky, Indiana, and Illinois and had little formal education. As a young man he worked at a variety of occupations; he piloted a Mississippi River flatboat, clerked in a store, and was a surveyor. He also fought as a captain in the Black Hawk War of 1832. Lincoln studied law on his own and was admitted to the bar in 1836. Over the next 20 years, he was recognized as one of the most sucessful lawyers in Illinois. He pursued a political career as well, serving in the Illinois legislature from 1834 until 1840. In 1840, he was elected to the U.S. House of Representatives, serving one term. In 1858, he was the Republican candidate for the Senate from Illinois, challenging the incumbent, Stephen A. Douglas. Lincoln spoke against slavery during the campaign and gained national recognition, but he lost the election. In 1860, as the Republican nominee for president, he defeated two Democrats and one candidate from the Constitutional Union Party. Support for Lincoln was virtually nonexistent in the Deep South, and following his election seven southern states seceded from the Union. Four others would secede as well. When Lincoln attempted to relieve forces stationed at Fort Sumter in South Carolina, in April 1861, the Confederates fired on the fort and touched off the Civil War. On January 1, 1863, Lincoln issued the Emancipation Proclamation, freeing slaves in regions held by the Confederates. He advocated passage of a constitutional amendment outlawing slavery that was ratified December 6, 1865. Lincoln was re-elected on November 1864 and assassinated on April 14, 1865, just days after the Confederate surrender.

Lindsey, Benjamin Barr (1869–1943) *judge of the Denver juvenile court*

Lindsey was born in Jackson, Tennessee, and spent much of his childhood on the plantation owned by his mother's family. In 1886, he moved to Denver, where his father was a telegrapher with the Denver and South Park Railway. His father's suicide the following year left Lindsey financially responsible for his mother and brother. The strain of trying to study law while supporting his family drove Lindsey to attempt suicide himself, but the gun's failure to discharge restored his resolve; he persevered in his studies and was admitted to the Colorado bar in 1894. He then spent several years as a litigator and was the first lawyer to persuade a judge to admit X-rays as evidence in a trial. In 1899, he was appointed public guardian and administrator; in 1901, he became a judge in Arapahoe (now Denver) County. Lindsey took an interest in reforming juvenile offenders and established an informal juvenile court. When the Colorado juvenile court was officially founded in 1907, he was its first judge. He resigned from the court in 1927 following a political dispute, and his enemies succeeded in having him disbarred in 1929. In 1930, Lindsey moved to Los Angeles, where he served as a judge and was active in children's causes. Colorado readmitted him to the bar in 1935, but he remained in California, where he founded the Children's Court of Conciliation in 1939. Lindsey wrote three books: *The Beast* (1910), about corruption; *The Revolt of Modern Youth* (1925); and *The Companionate Marriage* (1927), an argument in favor of trial marriages.

Locke, John (1632–1704) *English philosopher*

Locke was born to Anglican parents in Wrington, Somerset, and educated at Oxford. From 1661 to 1664, he lectured to undergraduates on Greek, rhetoric, and moral philosophy. He went on to hold a series of government appointments. As one of his official duties, he wrote a constitution for the Carolina Colony in 1669, but it was never adopted. From 1675 until 1678, Locke lived in France. He spent the years 1683 through 1688 in Holland because he opposed Roman Catholicism, the faith of the British monarchy at that time. He returned to England after the Glorious Revolution of 1688 brought William of Orange to the throne and Protestantism was restored to favor. In 1689, Locke published the *Essay Concerning Human Understanding,* in which he compared a newborn's mind to a *tabula rasa,* or blank slate, on which knowledge is recorded as a result of experience. In the same year he also published *Two Treatises of Government,* which included an attack on the theory of the divine right of kings and the assertion that power resides in a nation's people. Many of the ideas Locke put forth, such as the duty of government to protect people's rights and the right of the majority to rule, influenced the writers of the U.S. Constitution. King William III appointed him to the Board of Trade in 1696, but he resigned in 1700 because of ill health. Locke's writings also include *Some Thoughts Concerning Education* (1693) and *The Reasonableness of Christianity* (1695).

Low, Juliette Gordon (1860–1927) *founder of the Girl Scouts of America*
Juliette Gordon was born in Savannah, Georgia, and educated at private schools in Virginia and New York. She was married to William M. Low, a wealthy Georgia native, from 1886 until his death in 1905. Throughout their marriage, the couple resided in England. In 1911, Juliette Low met Robert and Agnes Baden-Powell, founders of the Boy Scouts and Girl Guides in Great Britain. Low organized several troops of Girl Guides in Scotland and London before returning to Savannah in 1912 to establish the first American troop of Girl Guides. Scouting quickly became popular among girls in the United States as a result of Low's promotional activities. The Girl Scouts of America (GSA) was established in 1913 and incorporated in 1915. Low served as president of the organization until 1920, when she was granted the title of founder. In 1919, she represented the GSA at the first International Council of Girl Guides and Girl Scouts. In 1926, she helped to establish an international Girl Scout camp in the United States. Low died of cancer on January 17, 1927; she was buried in her Girl Scout uniform.

Malcolm X (Malcolm Little, El-Hajj Malik El-Shabazz) (1925–1965) *African-American leader*
Malcolm X, who was born Malcolm Little, had a hard childhood in Lansing, Michigan. White supremacists burned down the Littles' home, and Malcolm's father was murdered. The family endured poverty during the depression, and Malcolm's mother was hospitalized for mental illness. Malcolm was arrested for burglary at age 20. While in jail, he learned about the Nation of Islam, or Black Muslims. He joined a Black Muslim temple in Detroit following his release from prison in 1952 and took the name Malcolm X. He rose to become the organization's leading spokesperson, condemning white exploitation of African Americans. In 1964, he made a pilgrimage to the Islamic holy cities of Mecca and Jiddah and renounced his racist teachings. Following his return to the United States, he founded a black nationalist group, the Organization of Afro-American Unity, and adopted a new name, El-Hajj Malik El-Shabazz. Assassins connected with the Nation of Islam murdered him while he was addressing a gathering in New York City.

Mann, Horace (1796–1859) *champion of public education*
Mann was born into a poor family in Franklin, Massachusetts. He attended school irregularly during childhood but studied independently at the Franklin library. He graduated first in his class at Brown University and continued his education at Litchfield Law School, Litchfield, Connecticut. Mann was admitted to the bar in 1823 and served in the Massachusetts House of Representatives from 1827 to 1833. As a representative, he worked to open the nation's first hospital for the insane at Worcester, Massachusetts. In 1835, he was elected to the Massachusetts Senate. Mann left the senate in 1837 to become the first secretary of the Massachusetts Board of Education. In this position he lobbied for improved schools and teaching methods and the establishment of normal, or teacher-training, schools. His speeches and writings influenced trends in education throughout the United States. Mann resigned from the board of education in 1848 to take the seat in the U.S. Senate left empty by the death of former president John Quincy Adams. In 1853, he became president of Antioch College, a new institution in Yellow Springs, Ohio, and held that position until his death.

Maynard, Daphne Joyce (1953–) *writer*
Joyce Maynard began writing as a child in Exeter, New Hampshire. She first had a story appear in *Seventeen* magazine in 1970. Her article "An Eighteen-Year-Old Looks Back on Life" was published in the *New York Times Magazine* in 1972, while she was a freshman at Yale University. Maynard left school to develop her article into the memoir *Looking Back* (1973), which caused her to be considered a spokesperson for her generation. She also engaged in a nine-month affair with the reclusive author J. D. Salinger, a relationship she chronicled in her 1998 book, *At Home in the World.* Maynard worked as a freelance journalist and a radio commentator before publishing her first novel, *Baby Love,* in 1981. Her novel *To Die For* (1991) was later made into a motion picture. Maynard has been a regular contributor to *McCall's, Newsweek,* and other periodicals. In 1992, she started *Domestic Affairs,* a newsletter devoted to motherhood and family issues.

McGuffey, William Holmes (1800–1873) *educator, textbook author*
McGuffey began teaching on the Ohio frontier at age 13. He attended Washington College (now Washington and Jefferson College) in Pennsylvania and in 1826 joined the faculty of Miami University in Oxford, Ohio, where he taught languages. In 1836, he was

appointed president of Cincinnati College (now Cincinnati University), and in 1839 he became president of Ohio University. In 1845, he accepted a professorship in mental and moral philosophy at the University of Virginia, and he held that position for the rest of his life. McGuffey is best remembered for compiling a series of readers for American schoolchildren. Published between 1835 and 1857, the McGuffey readers progressed in difficulty from basic exercises to excerpts from English and American classics. They were widely used in classrooms throughout the United States for half a century.

McMaster, John Bach (1852–1932) *historian*
McMaster grew up in New York City and studied civil engineering at the City College of New York, graduating in 1873. He was employed briefly as an engineer in Virginia and Chicago, and after spending time as a tutor in New York City, he became assistant professor of civil engineering at Princeton University in 1877. He led an expedition to the western United States in 1878. Soon afterward he began to write the work for which he is best remembered, the eight-volume *History of the People of the United States from the Revolution to the Civil War.* The first volume was published in 1883; the eighth appeared in 1913. In 1883, McMaster left Princeton for the Wharton School of Finance and Economy at the University of Pennsylvania, where he would teach until his retirement in 1919. In 1891, he helped to establish the University of Pennsylvania's School of American History, the first such school in the United States. McMaster's books include *Benjamin Franklin as a Man of Letters* (1887); *School History of the United States* (1912), a popular textbook; and *A History of the People of the United States during Lincoln's Administration* (1927).

Mencken, Henry Louis (1880–1956) *journalist, critic, essayist*
A lifelong resident of Baltimore, Maryland, Mencken attended Baltimore Polytechnic. He joined the *Baltimore Morning Herald* as a reporter in 1899, and in 1906 he went to work for the *Baltimore Sun.* He would write for the *Sun,* off and on, for most of his life. From 1914 to 1923, Mencken and drama critic George Jean Nathan edited *The Smart Set,* a satirical magazine. In 1924 the two men founded another periodical, *American Mercury,* which Mencken edited until 1933. Mencken was an influential literary and social critic

who adopted a curmudgeonly persona in his reviews and essays. These collected writings fill the six-volume *Prejudices* (1919–27). He made an important contribution to the study of American English with *The American Language,* a three-volume work published between 1936 and 1948. He also wrote three autobiographical books: *Happy Days* (1940), *Newspaper Days* (1941), and *Heathen Days* (1943).

Miller, Ann (Johnnie Lucille Collier) (1923–   )
dancer, singer, actress
Miller was born in Houston, Texas, and began performing as a small child. She moved to Hollywood, California, with her mother in 1934. Her motion picture career began with *New Faces of 1937,* in which she tap danced. Notable films in which she appeared include *You Can't Take It With You* (1938), *Room Service* (1938), *Easter Parade* (1948), *On the Town* (1949), and *Kiss Me Kate* (1953). She also performed on Broadway in *George White's Scandals* (1939–40), *Mame* (1969–70), and *Sugar Babies* (1979–82). She was nominated for a Tony award for her work in *Sugar Babies.*

Miller, Arthur Asher (1915–   ) *dramatist, one of the most important playwrights of the 20th century*
The son of a prosperous garment manufacturer, Miller was born in New York City. When the senior Miller suffered severe financial losses in the Great Depression, the family moved to Brooklyn, New York. Miller worked his way through the University of Michigan, where he studied drama and journalism. In 1937, while still a student, he shared the Theatre Guild Bureau of New Plays Award with Tennessee Williams. Upon graduating in 1937, he returned to New York, where he wrote radio plays. He continued to write for the stage as well, and in 1945 he published a novel entitled *Focus.* He soon completed two significant dramatic works: *All My Sons* (1947) and *Death of a Salesman* (1949), generally considered his greatest achievement. *The Crucible* (1953), a story of the Salem witch trials, was an attack on the House Un-American Activities Committee. Miller himself appeared before the committee in 1956. His refusal to cooperate earned him a conviction for contempt, but it was later reversed. Miller's later dramas include *A View from the Bridge* (1955), *After the Fall* (1963), and *The Price* (1968). He wrote a screenplay, *The Misfits* (1960), for his second wife, actor Marilyn Monroe. His autobiography, *Timebends,* was published in 1987.

Momaday, N. Scott (1934–   ) *Native American writer, educator*

Momaday was born in Lawton, Oklahoma, and grew up on Indian reservations in the Southwest. He attended the University of New Mexico and did graduate work at Stanford University, earning a master's degree in 1960 and a Ph.D. in 1963. He taught English and comparative literature at Stanford and at the University of California at Berkeley. He currently is on the faculty of the University of Arizona. Momaday writes poetry, fiction, and nonfiction, drawing heavily on the oral tradition of the Kiowa people. In 1969, he was awarded the Pulitzer Prize for Fiction for *A House Made of Dawn*. Momaday is the founder and chairman of the Buffalo Trust, a foundation dedicated to preserving and protecting the cultural heritage of Native Americans. Since 1970 he has been a consultant to the National Endowment for the Arts. His memoir, *The Names,* was published in 1976.

Montagu, Montague Francis Ashley (1905–1999) *anthropologist, author*

Born Israel Ehrenberg in London, Montagu began educating himself in social philosophy as a teenager. He studied physical anthropology at the University of London and continued his studies at the University of Florence and Columbia University, from which he received a Ph.D. in 1937. From 1949 to 1955, Montagu chaired the Department of Anthropology at Rutgers University. His assertion that race was a social construct without biological foundation gained him widespread attention. He helped to draft the United Nations' "Statement on Race" (1950), which developed this idea. The most talked about of Montagu's more than 60 books was *The Natural Superiority of Women* (1953), in which he argued that evolution has given women biological advantages over men. This was a highly controversial opinion in the years before feminism. Montagu wrote books on a wide range of topics with popular appeal, including human aggression; the significance of touch; American culture; and Joseph Merrick, the "elephant man" of Victorian England.

Moses, Anna Mary Robertson (Grandma Moses) (1860–1961) *artist*

Anna Robertson was born on a farm in Washington County, New York, and had very little schooling. As a child she drew and painted with berry juice. She worked as a hired girl from age 12 until her marriage in 1887 to Thomas Moses, who farmed at Eagle Bridge, New York. After Thomas died in 1927, she continued to farm with the help of a son. In 1936, she retired and went to live with a daughter. At that time she again took up painting and created scenes of rural 19th-century American life in a primitive style. The art world became interested in Grandma Moses after a collector purchased several of her works in 1939. In that year, three of her paintings were exhibited at the Museum of Modern Art in New York City. At age 80 she had her first one-woman show. She completed 25 paintings in her last year of life, and her work continues to be widely shown. Among the best known of her more than 1,500 paintings are *Catching the Thanksgiving Turkey* (1943), *A Fire in the Woods* (1947), and *A Country Wedding* (1951). Her autobiography, *My Life's Story,* was published in 1952.

Murphy, Edgar Gardner (1869–1913) *clergyman, reformer*

Murphy was born in Fort Smith, Arkansas, and grew up in Texas. He studied at the University of the South, in Tennessee, and at General Theological Seminary in New York City. He was ordained a priest in the Episcopal Church in 1893. In 1900, while assigned to a parish in Montgomery, Alabama, he founded a church for African Americans, oversaw construction of YMCA and YWCA buildings, and persuaded Andrew Carnegie to donate a public library to the city. In 1900, Murphy also organized a conference on racial and social problems in the new South. He established the Alabama Child Labor Committee in 1901 and was a founder of the National Child Labor Committee (NCLC) in 1904. He left the NCLC in 1907 to protest the committee's support of federal child-labor legislation, which he considered unconstitutional. Murphy resigned from the ministry in 1903 to devote all of his time to social activism. From 1903 to 1908, he was secretary of the Southern Education Board. In 1908, when illness forced him to retire from activism, Murphy took up astronomy. His writings include the *The Problems of the Present South* (1904). He also wrote *A Beginner's Star Book* (1912), under the pseudonym Kelvin McKready.

Newton, Huey Percy (1942–1989) *militant African-American activist, founder of the Black Panther Party*

Newton graduated illiterate from an Oakland, California, high school, taught himself to read, and enrolled in Merritt College in Oakland. He also studied at the San Francisco School of Law. In 1966, with friend and fellow student Bobby Seale, he founded the Black Panthers to improve conditions for African Americans—by force if necessary. The party engaged in several armed conflicts with police, and in 1967 Newton was convicted of voluntary manslaughter in the death of a police officer. The conviction was later overturned. In 1971 Newton announced that the Black Panther Party would pursue nonviolent goals and aid African Americans in their communities. Nevertheless, in 1974 he was accused of another murder; he spent three years in Cuba avoiding arrest before returning to the United States to face charges. His two trials ended in hung juries. In 1980 Newton earned a Ph.D. in social philosophy from the University of California at Santa Cruz. Two years later, the Black Panther Party was disbanded. In August 1989, Newton was found dead of a gunshot wound on an Oakland street.

Parks, Gordon (1912–   ) *photographer, writer, composer*
Parks was born in Fort Scott, Kansas, but moved to Minnesota at 15 and went to high school in St. Paul. He worked at odd jobs as a young man while experimenting in art, writing, and music, and joined the Civilian Conservation Corps (CCC) in 1933. Later, while working as a railroad porter, he discovered photography as an artistic medium. In 1942, he was hired as a correspondent for the U.S. Farm Security Administration. From 1943 to 1945, he was a correspondent for the U.S. Office of War Information. In 1948, he became the first African-American staff photographer at *Life* magazine and soon earned an international reputation. Some of his best known documentary work explores the experiences of such young people as a Harlem, New York, gang leader and a boy from an impoverished family in Brazil. Parks has published a number of books, including an autobiography, *A Choice of Weapons* (1966); poetry; and books on photographic technique. He has directed and scored several motion pictures.

Peabody, Elizabeth Palmer (1804–1894) *New England educator who promoted kindergartens in the United States*
Peabody was born in Billerica, Massachusetts, and educated at a school operated by her mother in Salem. Peabody herself taught at the Salem school before establishing a school in Brookline, Massachusetts, with her sister Mary. She was a founding member of the Transcendentalist Club in 1837. Soon afterward she operated a bookstore in Boston from which she published *The Dial,* a transcendentalist journal, from 1842 until 1843. In 1860, Peabody opened a kindergarten in Boston, the first in the United States. She traveled to Europe in 1867 to learn more about the kindergarten movement and returned to the United States to write and lecture on the subject. Her writings include *Kindergarten Culture* (1870) and *Letters to Kindergartners* (1886). She published the *Kindergarten Messenger* from 1873 to 1875, and in 1877 she became founder and first president of the American Froebel Union.

Pratt, Richard Henry (1840–1924) *army officer, educator of Native Americans*
Pratt was born in Rushford, New York, but grew up in Logansport, Indiana, where he was apprenticed to a tinsmith. He enlisted in the Union army in 1861 to serve in the Civil War and rose to the rank of lieutenant. He re-enlisted in 1867 and was assigned to the 10th Cavalry, an African-American unit stationed on the western frontier. In 1875, Pratt was assigned to escort Native American prisoners of war to Fort Marion in St. Augustine, Florida. At Fort Marion he developed a program of education for the Indian prisoners that emphasized vocational training. Some of the prisoners were sent to the Hampton Institute in Virginia in 1878, and Pratt went there to teach. He was at Hampton until 1879, when the War Department authorized him to establish and supervise the first federally funded boarding school for Indian youth, located in abandoned barracks at Carlisle, Pennsylvania. The school served as a model for other Indian boarding schools. Pratt resigned from the army in 1903; in 1904 he was removed as supervisor of the Carlisle school for speaking out against the reservation system and the U.S. Indian Bureau. He continued to work on behalf of Indian education and to promote assimilation of Native peoples into mainstream American life.

Presley, Elvis Aron (1935–1977) *rock-and-roll singer, actor*
Presley was born into poverty in Tupelo, Mississippi. He taught himself to play guitar as a teenager living

in Memphis, Tennessee, and he started singing at church services and revival meetings. In 1954 and 1955, he recorded several songs for the Memphis label Sun Records that gained him a southern following. Three songs recorded for RCA Victor in 1956 ("Heartbreak Hotel," "Don't Be Cruel," and "Love Me Tender") made him a national sensation. Presley was drafted into the army in 1958 and was stationed for two years in Germany. Upon returning to the United States, he starred in *Blue Hawaii* (1961), the first of more than 30 motion pictures in which he acted and sang. He continued to release records as well. In the 1970s, Presley was a popular live performer, but he spent much of his free time at his Memphis mansion, Graceland, having become addicted to prescription drugs. His drug habit contributed to a fatal heart attack at age 42.

Reich, Charles Alan (1928–   ) *attorney, educator, writer*
Reich, who was born in New York City, graduated from Oberlin College in 1949 and Yale University Law School in 1952. He was admitted to the bars of New York in 1952, the District of Columbia in 1954, and the U.S. Supreme Court in 1958. He was a practicing attorney from 1952 until 1960, when he joined the faculty of Yale University. After getting to know his students at Yale, Reich wrote *The Greening of America* (1970), in which he postulated that the youth movement of the 1960s was leading humanity to a new level of consciousness. Reich resigned from Yale in 1974 to write full time. His autobiography, *The Sorcerer of Bolinas Reef,* appeared in 1976. A second book on social trends, *Opposing the System,* was published in 1995.

Rickover, Hyman George (1900–1986) *naval officer, engineer who developed the nuclear-powered submarine*
Rickover came to the United States from Russia as a child. He grew up in Chicago and moved east to attend the U.S. Naval Academy, graduating in 1922. He earned a master's degree in engineering from Columbia University in 1929. Rickover served aboard submarines and a battleship, the U.S.S. *New Mexico,* before assuming command of a minesweeper, the U.S.S. *Finch,* in 1937. During World War II he was assigned to the Electrical Station of the navy's Bureau of Ships in Washington, D.C. In 1946 and

1947, Rickover was in Oak Ridge, Tennessee, for training in nuclear science through the Manhattan Project, the operational unit that developed the atomic bomb. Subsequently he supervised the planning and construction of the U.S.S. *Nautilus,* the first nuclear-powered submarine, which was launched in 1954. Rickover attained the rank of rear admiral in 1953 and was promoted to vice admiral in 1959. In the late 1950s, he was an outspoken critic of U.S. schools. He discussed perceived flaws in the educational system and their remedies in books such as *Education and Freedom* (1959). He was promoted to admiral in 1973 and retired in 1986. He spent a record 63 years on active duty because Congress had exempted him from mandatory retirement at the standard age for senior admirals. In 1980 President Jimmy Carter presented Rickover with the Medal of Freedom.

Riis, Jacob August (1849–1914) *social reformer, writer, photographer*
Riis immigrated to the United States from Denmark at age 21. He settled in New York City and in 1873 became a police reporter for the *New York Tribune,* assigned to cover the Lower East Side. In 1888, he was hired by the *New York Evening Sun.* Riis used flash photography to record the interiors of tenement buildings, and the illustrations in his 1890 book on slum life, *How the Other Half Lives,* were based on these photographs. The deplorable conditions shown in this popular book shocked readers and caught the attention of New York Police Commissioner Theodore Roosevelt, who later worked with Riis on social reforms, such as improvements in tenement housing and schools and the creation of playgrounds and parks in urban neighborhoods. Riis's many books include *The Children of the Poor* (1892); *Out of Mulberry Street* (1896); and his autobiography, *The Making of an American* (1901).

Robinson, Harriet Jane Henson (1825–1911) *activist for women's rights, writer*
Following the death of Harriet Henson's father, a carpenter, in 1831, her family left New Hampshire for the mill town of Lowell, Massachusetts, where her mother operated a boardinghouse. Harriet went to work in a textile mill at age 10. The following year, she led several coworkers in a short-lived strike. In 1848, she married William Stevens Robinson, a jour-

nalist and abolitionist. After the Civil War, the Robinsons devoted themselves to the cause of woman suffrage; Harriet Robinson continued to write and speak on this subject after she was widowed in 1876. She helped to form the National Woman Suffrage Association of Massachusetts and testified before a committee of the U.S. Senate in 1882. Robinson also was a proponent of women's clubs and a founder of the General Federation of Women's Clubs. Her writings include *Massachusetts in the Woman Suffrage Movement* (1881); *Captain Mary Miller* (1887), a novel; *The New Pandora* (1889), a play in verse form; and *Loom and Spindle* (1898), a memoir of her years in the mill.

Roosevelt, Franklin Delano (1882–1945) *32nd president of the Untied States*
The only child of wealthy parents, Roosevelt spent his early life in New York City and Hyde Park, New York. He graduated from Harvard University in 1904, and after studying law at Columbia University, he was admitted to the New York State bar in 1907. In 1905 he married a distant cousin, Eleanor Roosevelt. His political career began with his election to the New York State Senate in 1910. President Woodrow Wilson appointed him secretary of the navy during World War I. In 1920, Roosevelt was the Democratic candidate for vice president, sharing the ticket with James M. Cox, but Cox lost the election to Warren G. Harding. Although an attack of poliomyelitis in 1921 left Roosevelt unable to walk, he was elected governor of New York in 1928. In 1932, he defeated the incumbent, Herbert Hoover, in the presidential election. He would be elected to an unprecedented four terms. During his first three months in office, Roosevelt prevailed on Congress to pass legislation to combat the economic instability and unemployment of the Great Depression. Among the programs established by New Deal legislation were two to provide work for young people. The Civilian Conservation Corps (1933) employed teenage boys and young men on conservation and public works projects. The National Youth Administration (1935) gave jobs to young women and students. The second crisis of Roosevelt's presidency was World War II. He asked Congress to declare war following the December 7, 1941, Japanese attack on Pearl Harbor, Hawaii; he died in 1945, before the United States and its allies achieved victory.

Rumph, Langdon Leslie (1844–1861)
Confederate soldier
Rumph was born in Alabama, the son of Dr. James David Rumph. He attended the Perote Institute, a private school, and was part of a company known as the Perote Guards. This unit was absorbed into the First Regiment Alabama Volunteers in February 1861 and stationed at the Warrington Navy Yard in Florida. Rumph died of disease in a military hospital in August 1861 at the age of 16.

Rush, Benjamin (1746–1813) *physician, statesman*
After graduating from the College of New Jersey (now Princeton University) in 1760, Rush spent six years as a physician's apprentice. He continued his studies in Europe, earning a medical degree from the University of Edinburgh in 1768. Rush returned to America in 1769 and was appointed professor of chemistry at the College of Philadelphia. In 1770, he published *Syllabus of a Course of Lectures on Chemistry,* the first American chemistry text and the first of many scientific and medical books that he would write. Rush gained a reputation as a leading American physician. He taught a great many apprentices and students, and his lectures attracted crowds. He is remembered as the father of American psychiatry because he pushed for humane treatment of the mentally ill. He also advocated bloodletting and purging as remedies for a wide range of ailments, however, and was largely responsible for the continued use of those treatments in the United States after European doctors had cast doubt on their value. He was a member of the Continental Congress in 1776–77 and a signer of the Declaration of Independence.

Sabin, Albert Bruce (1906–1993) *physician, virologist who developed the oral polio vaccine*
Sabin and his parents immigrated to the United States from Poland in 1921, and Sabin became a U.S. citizen in 1930. In 1931 he received an M.D. degree from New York University, where he had begun research on poliomyelitis. He practiced medicine for two years at Bellevue Hospital in New York City before attending the Lister Institute for Preventive Medicine in London. In 1935 he joined the Rockefeller Institute for Medical Research in New York City. There he successfully grew the polio virus in human nerve tissue outside the body. In 1939, Sabin became a professor and researcher at the University of Cincinnati College of Medicine;

he also headed the division of infectious diseases at the Children's Hospital Research Foundation. In Cincinnati he proved that polio enters the body through the digestive tract. He also isolated strains of the disease that were too weak to cause disease but strong enough when ingested to stimulate antibody production. From these he developed the Sabin oral polio vaccine. The U.S. government approved the vaccine for use in 1960. The Sabin vaccine is now the principal defense against polio worldwide. Sabin also developed vaccines for sandfly fever and dengue, and he studied the role of viruses in cancer and in diseases of the nervous system. He retired from the University of Cincinnati in 1971. From 1974 to 1982, he conducted research at the University of South Carolina at Charleston.

Salk, Jonas Edward (1914–1995) *physician and medical researcher who developed the first safe, effective polio vaccine*
Salk, who was born in New York City, received an M.D. degree from New York University in 1939. In 1942 he joined the faculty of the University of Michigan School of Public Health and participated in research on immunization against influenza. In 1947 he moved to the University of Pittsburgh School of Medicine, where his research on poliomyelitis led him to isolate three strains of the polio virus and demonstrate that killed polio virus stimulated antibody formation in monkeys. Large-scale field tests of the vaccine in humans, conducted in 1954, demonstrated its safety and efficacy. The vaccine was approved for use in the United States on April 12, 1955. In 1963, Salk became director of the Institute for Biological Studies in San Diego, California (later the Salk Institute). President Jimmy Carter awarded him the Medal of Freedom in 1977.

Seton, Ernest Thompson (1860–1946) *naturalist, illustrator, writer, founder of the Boy Scouts of America*
Ernest Evan Thompson was born in South Shields, Durham, England. His family immigrated to Canada in 1866 and settled on an Ontario farm. In 1870, they moved to Toronto, where Ernest's father worked as an accountant. Ernest showed a talent for drawing and in 1876 began studies at the Ontario School of Art. In 1879, he went to London to continue his studies, but ill health forced him to return to Canada in November 1881. Following his recovery, he moved to Manitoba in May 1882; there he studied the wildlife of the Cana-

dian prairie and began to contribute illustrations and articles to Canadian journals of natural history. The quality of his work persuaded a U.S. publisher, Century Company, to hire him to make 1,000 illustrations of animals for the *Century Dictionary* (1889–91). Thompson also illustrated works by the noted ornithologist Frank M. Chapman. Around 1900, he changed his name to Ernest Thompson Seton to reflect his genealogical link to the Setons of English nobility. Living and working in New York City, he began to write and illustrate his own works of natural history, which include the two-volume *Life Histories of Northern Animals* (1909) and the four-volume *Lives of Game Animals* (1925–28). For the latter work Seton was awarded the John Burroughs Medal (1926) and the Daniel Giraud Elliott Medal (1928). In 1902, Seton founded the Woodcraft Movement, a coeducational scouting group. He chaired the committee that established the Boy Scouts of America in 1910, and he wrote the first Boy Scout manual. From 1910 until 1915 he was the first chief scout. An intrepid adventurer, Seton traveled through much of the wilderness of western North America. In 1907, he completed a 2,000-mile canoe trip that brought him close to the Arctic Circle. In 1930, he became a U.S. citizen and relocated to New Mexico, where he built a 30-room mansion to house his many books, paintings, drawings, and natural specimens.

Slater, Samuel (1768–1835) *founder of the American cotton-textile industry, pioneer of the factory system*
Slater, who was born in Belper, Derbyshire, England, was apprenticed at age 14 to Sir Richard Arkwright, inventor of cotton-spinning machinery. In 1789, at a time when Great Britain prohibited textile workers from leaving the country, Slater traveled to the United States in disguise. He had memorized techniques of textile manufacture and machine specifications, which enabled him to build and operate spinning and carding machines based on Arkwright's designs. In 1790, he formed a partnership with the Rhode Island firm of Almy and Brown and opened the first important spinning mills in the United States at Pawtucket, Rhode Island. In 1798, he established his own firm, Samuel Slater and Company, at Rehoboth, Massachusetts. He also founded the town of Slatersville, Rhode Island. At the time of his death, Slater operated mills in Massachusetts, Rhode Island, Connecticut, and New Hampshire.

Spielberg, Steven (1947–   ) *motion picture director and producer*
Interested in filmmaking even as a child, Spielberg was already winning prizes for his films while a student at California State College (now University) in Long Beach. He began his professional career with Universal Studios, directing episodes of television series and television films such as *Duel* (1971). The first film that he directed for release in theaters, *The Sugarland Express* (1974), was followed by *Jaws* (1975), one of the highest-grossing films ever made. Spielberg went on to direct numerous films, most of them commercial successes. They include *Close Encounters of the Third Kind* (1977), *Raiders of the Lost Ark* (1981), *E.T.: The Extraterrestrial* (1982), *The Color Purple* (1985), and *Schindler's List* (1993; Academy Award for best picture, 1994). He won Oscars for best director for *Schindler's List* in 1994 and *Saving Private Ryan* in 1999. He was also executive producer of many other successful films. In 1987, the Academy of Motion Picture Arts and Sciences presented Spielberg with the Irving G. Thalberg Memorial Award, which honors achievement in directing. In 1994, with film-studio executives David Geffen and Jeffrey Katzenberg, Spielberg formed a film and television production company, DreamWorks SKG.

Spock, Benjamin McLane (1903–1998) *pediatrician, author*
Spock grew up in New Haven, Connecticut. He attended Yale University and in 1929 graduated first in his class from the College of Physicians and Surgeons at Columbia University. From 1933 until 1947, he practiced and taught pediatrics at New York Hospital and Cornell Medical College. The first edition of his parenting manual, *The Common Sense Book of Baby and Child Care,* was published in 1946. Spock revised this book throughout his life, producing seven editions in all. More than 30 million copies were sold between 1946 and 1976, and the book has been translated into 42 languages. In 1955, Spock joined the faculty of Western Reserve University (now Case Western) in Cleveland, Ohio. He resigned in 1967 to protest full-time against U.S. involvement in the Vietnam War. In 1968, he was arrested, tried, and sentenced to two years in prison for counseling draft evasion, but the conviction was overturned on appeal. Spock was the People's Party candidate for president in 1972 and received 75,000 votes. In later years, he protested nuclear proliferation. His 13 books include *Dr. Spock Talks with Moth-*

ers (1961), *Dr. Spock on Vietnam* (1968), *Raising Children in a Difficult Time* (1974), and *Spock on Spock: A Memoir of Growing Up with the Century* (1989).

Steffens, Joseph Lincoln (1866–1936) *muckraking journalist*
Steffens was born in San Francisco and raised in Sacramento, California. After graduating from the University of California in 1889, he spent three years studying psychology in Germany and France. Between 1892 and 1901, he did newspaper work in New York City. He spent the next nine years writing about corruption in business and municipal government for three periodicals: *McClure's, American,* and *Everybody's* magazines. These articles were collected in such books as *The Shame of the Cities* (1904), *The Struggle for Self-Government* (1906), and *Upbuilders* (1909). Steffens published his autobiography in 1931.

Steinbeck, John Ernst (1902–1968) *Nobel Prize–winning novelist who documented the lives of displaced southwesterners in the 1930s*
Steinbeck, a California native, started writing in his teens. He entered Stanford University in 1920 but did not earn a degree. *Cup of Gold* (1929), his first novel, was followed by many others. *In Dubious Battle* (1936) is a fictional account of a strike among migrant farm workers; *Of Mice and Men* (1937) is a short, tragic tale of itinerant ranch hands. Steinbeck reported on the dust bowl migrants for the *San Francisco News*. He captured the nation's attention with *The Grapes of Wrath* (1939; Pulitzer Prize 1940), a stark portrayal of an Oklahoma family's efforts to survive in California during the Great Depression. Steinbeck's other works include *East of Eden* (1952), which interweaves his own family history with the saga of the fictional Trask family; and *Travels with Charley in Search of America* (1962), a nonfiction account of a road trip with his dog. Steinbeck reported on World War II from Europe for New York's *Herald Tribune;* he spent six weeks in Southeast Asia in 1966 and 1967, covering the Vietnam War for the Long Island newspaper *Newsday.*

Sumner, Charles (1811–1874) *U.S. senator, opponent of slavery*
Sumner was born in Boston and educated at Harvard University. He was an outspoken critic of the Compromise of 1850, a series of federal laws designed to reconcile the factions in Congress that were for and

against slavery. The citizens of Massachusetts elected him to the U.S. Senate in 1851; he held his seat until his death. In 1854, Sumner used the Senate floor to denounce both the Kansas-Nebraska Act, which permitted the territories of Kansas and Nebraska to decide whether to allow slavery, and its authors, Senators Andrew P. Butler and Stephen A. Douglas. Butler's nephew, Congressman Preston S. Brooks of South Carolina, retaliated by entering the Senate and severely beating Sumner with a cane. Sumner spent three years recovering from his injuries. From 1861 until 1871, Sumner was chairman of the Senate Committee on Foreign Relations. He strongly favored the impeachment of President Andrew Johnson and later clashed with President Ulysses S. Grant on foreign policy. He blocked Senate approval of Grant's plan to annex Santo Domingo.

Tarbell, Ida Minerva (1857–1944) *investigative journalist, leader of the muckraking movement*
Tarbell was born in Erie County, Pennsylvania, and grew up amid the tanks and wells of the fledgling oil industry. She attended Allegheny College in Meadville, Pennsylvania, and taught school for a short period before being hired as an editor for the Chautauqua Literary and Scientific Circle. In 1891, she went to Paris to study at the Sorbonne. While abroad, she wrote articles for U.S. magazines. Tarbell returned to the United States and in 1894 became associate editor of *McClure's Magazine*. From 1906 until 1915, she was editor of *American Magazine*. Tarbell wrote several books, most notably *The History of the Standard Oil Company* (1904), a two-volume study of a monopolistic trust. Her writings also include biographies of Napoleon Bonaparte (1895) and Abraham Lincoln (1900) and *All in the Day's Work: An Autobiography* (1939).

Timrod, Henry (1829–1867) *poet*
A lifelong resident of South Carolina, Timrod has been called the poet laureate of that state. He attended Franklin College (now the University of Georgia) for two years beginning in 1845 and briefly studied law. By the 1850s, he was reporting for Charleston, South Carolina, newspapers, and in 1857 he began publishing poems and essays in local periodicals. His book, *Poems,* appeared in 1860. Timrod covered the Civil War for the *Charleston Mercury* in 1861. He joined the Confederate army, and before being discharged for poor health, he was with the forces that retreated from Shiloh, Tennessee, in April 1862. In 1864, he became editor of a Columbia newspaper, the *Daily South Carolinian*. He died of tuberculosis in Columbia in October 1867. In poems such as "The Cotton Boll" and "Ethnogenesis," Timrod romanticized Confederate ideals. Other lyrical poems, including "Our Willie" and "A Mother's Wail," explore complex emotions on a personal level.

Trowbridge, John Townsend (1827–1916) *writer, editor*
Trowbridge was born on a farm near Rochester, New York. Although he attended a country school for six months of the year until age 14, he was largely self-taught. At 16 he began to publish poetry and prose in rural journals. After trying his hand at teaching and farming, he moved to New York City at age 19 to live as a writer. He sold some pieces but was unable to support himself on his earnings. He relocated to Boston in 1848 and, using the pseudonym Paul Creyton, sold literary sketches to local periodicals. In 1853, he published *Father Brighthopes,* the first of more than 40 novels. While in France in the summer of 1855, Trowbridge wrote one of his most successful books, *Neighbor Jackwood.* This novel presents a realistic picture of 19th century New England life. In 1856, he dramatized *Neighbor Jackwood* for the Boston stage. Trowbridge was one of the first contributors to the *Atlantic Monthly* and consulting editor of *Our Young Folks,* a magazine for children, from 1865 until 1870, when he was made managing editor.

Vardaman, James Kimble (1861–1930) *Mississippi politician*
The son of a farmer who fought for the Confederacy, Vardaman studied law in Carrollton, Mississippi, and was admitted to the bar in 1881. He practiced law and edited two local newspapers, first in Winona and then in Greenwood, Mississippi. He served as a Democrat in the state legislature from 1890 until 1896; he was speaker of the house for the 1894–95 session. During the Spanish-American War of 1898, he held the rank of captain. Campaigning on a racist platform, Vardaman lost more elections than he won. He was governor of Mississippi from 1904 until 1908 and a U.S. senator from 1913 until 1919. As governor he established the state department of agriculture and commerce.

Wald, Lillian D. (1867–1947) *nurse, social worker*
Wald spent her childhood in Cincinnati, Ohio, and Rochester, New York. In 1891, she graduated from the New York Hospital Training School for Nurses and went to work as a nurse at the New York Juvenile Asylum. In 1892, while studying at the Women's Medical College, she taught a course in home nursing on the Lower East Side of Manhattan and observed the bleak conditions of tenement life. She left medical school the following year and moved to the Lower East Side to work as a visiting nurse. In 1895, with another woman, Mary Brewster, she opened the Nurses Settlement, which grew into the Henry Street Settlement, offering community services as well as nursing and nursing education. Wald worked tirelessly on behalf of children, persuading New York City officials to place nurses in the public schools in 1902, and she was a founder of the National Child Labor Committee in 1904. In 1912, she founded the National Organization for Public Health Nursing and became its first president. She was awarded the gold medal of the National Institute of Social Sciences in the same year. She headed the committee on home nursing for the Council of National Defense during World War I and the Nurses' Emergency Council during the influenza epidemic of 1918 and 1919. Wald wrote two books: *The House on Henry Street* (1915) and *Windows on Henry Street* (1934).

Warren, Earl (1891–1974) *14th chief justice of the U.S. Supreme Court*
The son of a Los Angeles railroad worker, Warren studied law at the University of California at Berkeley. He began his career in public service in 1925 as attorney general of Alameda County, California. He was attorney general of California from 1939 to 1943 and governor of California from 1943 until 1953. He was the running mate of Republican Thomas E. Dewey, who ran unsuccessfully against Harry Truman in the 1948 presidential election. In 1953, President Dwight D. Eisenhower nominated Warren to be chief justice of the Supreme Court. A notable court decision during Warren's tenure was the 1954 ruling in *Brown v. Board of Education,* in which the court determined that school segregation was inherently unequal and therefore unlawful. In 1966, the Warren court ruled in *Miranda v. State of Arizona* that criminal suspects must be informed of their rights prior to questioning. On November 29, 1963, President Lyndon B. Johnson appointed Warren to head a commission investigating the assassination of President John F. Kennedy. In *The Warren Report,* submitted in September 1964, the commission concluded that a single assassin was responsible for the president's death and that no evidence of a conspiracy existed. Warren retired from the court in 1969.

Washington, Booker Taliaferro (1856–1915) *educator, founder of the Tuskegee Institute, spokesperson for African Americans*
Washington, who was born a slave in Franklin County, Virginia, moved with his family to Malden, West Virginia, following the Civil War. There, from the age of nine, Washington worked in a salt furnace and in coal mines. In 1872, he enrolled in the Hampton Normal and Agricultural Institute in Virginia. He taught for two years in Malden after graduating in 1875, and then entered the Wayland Seminary in Washington, D.C. He returned to the Hampton Institute to teach in 1879. In 1881, the institute's director, Samuel Chapman Armstrong, chose Washington to head the recently established Tuskegee Institute, a trade school for African Americans in Alabama. Washington's advocacy of vocational training and temporary social inferiority for African Americans persuaded whites to recognize him as a spokesperson for his race. Although many black Americans accepted Washington's line of thinking, his opinions brought criticism from other African-American leaders, most notably the scholar W. E. B. Du Bois. Washington's books include *The Future of the Negro* (1899); his autobiography, *Up from Slavery* (1901); *Life of Frederick Douglass* (1907); *The Story of the Negro* (1909); and *My Larger Education* (1911).

Waterhouse, Benjamin (1754–1846) *physician who pioneered smallpox vaccination in the United States*
Waterhouse was raised in a Quaker household in Newport, Rhode Island, and apprenticed to a local physician at age 16. In 1775, he went to Europe to study medicine. His studies took him to London, Edinburgh, and Leiden. He returned to the United States in 1782. The following year he became one of the first faculty members at Harvard Medical School. In 1799, Waterhouse read about British physician Edward Jenner's success in protecting people against smallpox by inoculating them with the milder disease cowpox. After receiving a sample of cowpox virus from England, Waterhouse inoculated his son Daniel, age 5,

and other family members and servants. He became an advocate of vaccination in the United States, but his efforts—and his arrogance—brought him into conflict with colleagues. In 1812, he lost his post at Harvard. Waterhouse next served as medical superintendent of U.S. military bases in New England during the War of 1812. His writings include *A Prospect of Eliminating the Smallpox* (1800) and *A Journal of a Young Man of Massachusetts* (1816), a popular book about a ship's surgeon during the War of 1812.

Watson, John Broadus (1878–1958) *behavioral psychologist*

Watson, who was born and raised near Greenville, South Carolina, earned a Ph.D. in experimental psychology from the University of Chicago in 1903. He spent five additional years in Chicago before becoming professor of psychology at Johns Hopkins University in 1908. In 1913, he published an article titled "Psychology as a Behaviorist Views It," in which he defined psychology as the science of behavior. From behavioral research on animals Watson progressed in 1918 to conditioning experiments with infants. In 1920, he was involved in a sensational divorce; as a result he resigned from Johns Hopkins and discontinued his research. He began a career in advertising in 1921 and continued to write on psychological topics. His books include *Behavior* (1914), *Psychology from the Standpoint of a Behaviorist* (1919), *Behaviorism* (1925), and the popular parenting guide *The Psychological Care of Infant and Child* (1928).

Webber, Anna (Anna Webber Gravatt) (1860–1948) *Kansas teacher*

Webber was born in Breckenridge (now Lyon) County, Kansas. She passed the state teachers' examinations in spring 1881 and was hired to teach in the Blue Hills, Kansas, district school for the three months of its term, May through July. She taught in the Kansas and Nebraska public schools through the 1880s, and in 1890 was hired by the Kansas Industrial School for Girls in Beloit, where she taught sewing. In 1891, she married Robert H. Gravatt of Talmadge, Nebraska.

Webster, Noah (1758–1843) *lexicographer, educator*

Webster, who served in the American Revolution, graduated from Yale College in 1778. He was admitted to the bar in 1781 but soon was hired as a teacher

in Goshen, New York. In 1782, he embarked on his life's work: standardizing and cataloguing American English. Between 1783 and 1785, he published *A Grammatical Institute of the English Language,* consisting of *The American Spelling Book,* a grammar book, and a reader. An estimated 60 million copies of the *Grammatical Institute* were sold over the next 100 years. In 1793, Webster moved to New York City and founded two newspapers: a daily, the *Minerva;* and a semiweekly, the *Herald.* Both supported the Federalist Party. He was living in New Haven, Connecticut, in 1806, when he published the *Compendious Dictionary of the English Language.* From 1812 until 1822, Webster lived in Amherst, Massachusetts. He was a founder of Amherst College, which opened in 1821. In 1828, he published *An American Dictionary of the English Language,* containing 70,000 definitions, approximately half of which were appearing in a dictionary for the first time. To prepare this work, Webster had gained familiarity with 20 languages and traveled to France and England to use research materials unavailable in the United States. An enlarged edition was published in 1840.

White, William Allen (1868–1944) *journalist known as the Sage of Emporia*

White was born in Emporia, Kansas, and attended the University of Kansas. He left college in 1890 to work for a Kansas newspaper, the *El Dorado Republican.* From 1892 to 1895, he wrote editorials for the *Kansas City Star.* In 1895, he purchased the *Emporia Gazette,* which he would edit until his death. Under his stewardship, this small-town newspaper gained widespread recognition and influenced national events. For example, an editorial written by White is thought to have helped William McKinley win the 1896 presidential election. White's editorials were collected in volumes such as *Forty Years on Main Street* (1937). He also wrote novels, including *A Certain Rich Man* (1909). *The Autobiography of William Allen White* (1946), which earned White the Pulitzer Prize for biography posthumously in 1947, was completed by his son, William Lindsay White.

Whitman, Walter, Jr. (1819–1892) *influential poet whose book* Leaves of Grass *celebrated the individual and the unity of all life*

Walt Whitman was born on a Long Island farm but spent his youth in Brooklyn, New York. He attended school until age 12, when he was apprenticed to a printer. He was subsequently employed as a teacher, newspaperman, and carpenter. In 1855, he published the first edition of *Leaves of Grass,* a landmark volume of poetry that broke with literary conventions in terms of meter, form, and subject matter. Whitman spent the rest of his life expanding and revising *Leaves of Grass,* and he published numerous editions of the book. He spent the Civil War years in Washington, D.C., working for the federal government and nursing sick and wounded soldiers in army hospitals. The war was the subject of his 1865 poetry collection, *Drum-Taps.* This slim book also contained two poems written in memory of Abraham Lincoln, "When Lilacs Last in the Dooryard Bloom'd," and "O Captain! My Captain!" After a stroke in 1873 left him partially paralyzed, Whitman went to live with his brother George in Camden, New Jersey. In 1884, he purchased his own house in Camden, and he lived there until his death. Whitman's prose writings include *Democratic Vistas* (1871), a series of essays on democratic government, and *Specimen Days* (1882), a book of memoirs and observations of nature.

Wright, Richard Nathaniel (1908–1960) *writer best known for his books on African-American subjects*
Wright was born into a poor family in Natchez, Mississippi. The Wrights moved to Memphis, Tennessee, when Richard was six years old. He and his brother spent a brief period in an orphanage after his father deserted the family. Wright attended school for several years and held various jobs before relocating to Chicago in 1927. There he worked with the Federal Writers' Project and became affiliated with the Communist Party. In 1937, he left Chicago for New York, where he was an editor for both the *Daily Worker* and a literary magazine. A story collection, *Uncle Tom's Children,* appeared in 1938. Two years later, Wright published the novel *Native Son,* which many critics call his most important work. His first volume of autobiography, *Black Boy,* was published in 1945. After severing his ties with communism, Wright moved with his family to Paris in 1946 and became a French citizen in 1947. He continued to produce works of fiction and nonfiction. He also traveled widely in Europe, Asia, and Africa. A book of his poetry, *Haiku: This Other World,* was published posthumously in 1998.

BIBLIOGRAPHY

Abbott, Edith and Sophonisba P. Breckinridge. *Truancy and Non-Attendance in the Chicago Schools.* Chicago: University of Chicago Press, 1917.

Abbott, Eleanor Hallowell. *Being Little in Cambridge When Everyone Else Was Big.* New York: D. Appleton-Century Co., 1936.

Abbott, Grace. *The Child and the State.* Vol. 1: *Legal Status in the Family, Apprenticeship and Child Labor.* Chicago: University of Chicago Press, 1938.

Abbott, Jacob. *Gentle Measures in the Management and Training of the Young.* New York: Harper and Brothers, 1899.

"Account of a Visit to an Elementary School." *American Journal of Education* 4, no. 1 (January and February 1829), pp. 74–76.

Adamic, Louis. *My America.* New York: Da Capo Press, 1976.

Adams, David Wallace. *Education for Extinction: American Indians and the Boarding School Experience, 1875–1928.* Lawrence: University Press of Kansas, 1995.

Adams, Henry. *The Education of Henry Adams.* Franklin Center, Pa.: The Franklin Library, 1980.

Adams, James Truslow. "Our Dissolving Ethics." *Atlantic Monthly* 138, no. 6 (November 1926), pp. 577–583.

Addams, Jane. *Twenty Years at Hull House.* New York: Signet, 1961.

Albee, John. *Confessions of Boyhood.* Boston: The Gorham Press, 1910.

Albrook, Robert C. "Parenthood Today Is No Bore!" in *Youth in Turmoil.* N.p.: Time-Life Books, 1969.

Alcott, Bronson. *The Journals of Bronson Alcott.* Vol. 1. Edited by Odell Shepard. Port Washington, N.Y.: Kennikat Press, 1938.

Aldrich, C. Anderson and Mary M. Aldrich. *Babies Are Human Beings.* New York: Macmillan Co., 1938.

Allen, Annie Winsor. "Boys and Girls." *Atlantic Monthly* 125, no. 6 (June 1920), pp. 796–804.

America's Children and Their Families: Key Facts. Washington, D.C.: Children's Defense Fund, 1982.

Anderson, C. LeRoy, Joanne R. Anderson, and Yunosuke Ohkura, eds. *No Longer Silent: World-Wide Memories of the Children of World War II.* Missoula, Mont.: Pictorial Histories Publishing Co., 1995.

Anderson, Robert. *From Slavery to Affluence: Memoirs of Robert Anderson, Ex-Slave.* Hemingford, Neb.: Hemingford Ledger, 1927.

Antin, Mary. *At School in the Promised Land.* Boston: Houghton Mifflin Co., 1912.

Arfwedson, Carl David. *The United States and Canada in 1832, 1833, and 1834.* Vol. 1. London: Richard Bentley, 1834.

Ariès, Philippe. *Centuries of Childhood: A Social History of Family Life.* New York: Alfred A. Knopf, 1962.

Arnett, Jeffery Jansen. *Metalheads: Heavy Metal Music and Adolescent Alienation.* Boulder, Colo.: Westview Press, 1996.

Ashby, Le Roy. *Endangered Children: Dependency, Neglect, and Abuse in American History.* New York: Twayne Publishers, 1997.

———. *Saving the Waifs. Reformers and Dependent Children, 1890–1917.* Philadelphia, Pa.: Temple University Press, 1984.

Baker, Russell. *Growing Up.* New York: Signet Books, 1982.

Ball, Charles. *Fifty Years in Chains, or, the Life of an American Slave.* Indianapolis: Dayton and Asher, 1858.

Bardaglio, Peter. "The Children of the Jubilee: African American Childhood in Wartime," in *Divided Houses: Gender and the Civil War,* edited by Catherine Clinton and Nina Silber. New York: Oxford University Press, 1992.

Bardeen, C. W. *A Little Fifer's War Diary.* Syracuse, N.Y.: C. W. Bardeen, 1910.

Barton, Michael, ed. "The Civil War Letters of Captain Andrew Lewis and His Daughter." *Western Pennsylvania Historical Magazine* 60, no. 4 (October 1977), pp. 371–390.

Baruch, Dorothy W. "Child Care Centers and the Mental Health of Children in This War." *Journal of Consulting Psychology* 7, no. 6 (November–December 1943), pp. 252–266.

Baur, John E. *Growing Up with California: A History of California's Children*. Los Angeles: Will Kramer, 1978.

Beard, Dan. *Hardly a Man Is Now Alive: The Autobiography of Dan Beard*. New York: Doubleday, Doran and Co., 1939.

Becker, Jo. "Montgomery Finds Racial Gap in Child Health Care." *Washington Post* (March 14, 2001), pp. B1, B8.

Beecher, Lyman. "Future Punishment of Infants Never a Doctrine of the Calvinistic Churches." *The Spirit of the Pilgrims* 1, no. 2 (February 1828), pp. 78–95.

———. "Future Punishment of Infants Not a Doctrine of Calvinism." *The Spirit of The Pilgrims* 1, no. 1 (January 1828), pp. 42–52.

Belkin, Lisa. "Your Kids Are Their Problem." *New York Times Magazine* (July 23, 2000), pp. 30–63.

Bell, L. McRae. "A Girl's Experience in the Siege of Vicksburg." *Harper's Weekly* 56, no. 2894 (June 8, 1912), pp. 12–13.

Belshaw, Maria A. "Diary Kept by Mrs. Maria A. Belshaw," in *New Spain and the Anglo-American West*. Vol. 2: *The Anglo-American West*. Lancaster, Pa.: Lancaster Press, 1932, pp. 215–243.

Bennett, Edwin Lewis. *Boom Town Boy in Old Creede, Colorado*. Chicago: Sage Books, 1966.

Bennett, Lerone, Jr. *Before the Mayflower: A History of Black America*. New York: Penguin Books, 1988.

Bennett, William P. *The First Baby in Camp*. Salt Lake City: The Rancher Publishing Co., 1893.

Bettelheim, Bruno. "Sputnik and Segregation." *Commentary* 26, no. 4 (October 1958), pp. 332–339.

Beverly, Bert I. "Effect of War Upon the Minds of Children." *American Journal of Public Health* 33, no. 7 (July 1943), pp. 793–798.

Billington, Ray Allen and Martin Ridge. *Westward Expansion: A History of the American Frontier*. 5th ed. New York: Macmillan, 1982.

Bilson, Geoffrey. *The Guest Children: The Story of the British Child Evacuees Sent to Canada During World War II*. Saskatoon, Saskatchewan: Fifth House, 1988.

Bird, Isabella L. *A Lady's Life in the Rocky Mountains*. London: John Murray, 1879.

Bivans, Venola Lewis, ed. "The Diary of Luna E. Warner, a Kansas Teenager of the Early 1870's." *Kansas Historical Quarterly* 35, no. 3 (autumn 1969), pp. 276–311.

Black Elk. *Black Elk Speaks: Being the Life Story of a Holy Man of the Oglala Sioux*. New York: William Morrow and Co., 1932.

Blank, Barbara Trainin. "Settlement Houses: Old Idea in New Form Builds Communities." *New Social Worker* 5, no. 3 (summer 1998). URL: *http://www.socialworker.com/settleme.htm*. October 24, 2000.

Blassingame, John W. *The Slave Community: Plantation Life in the Antebellum South*. New York: Oxford University Press, 1979.

Bleser, Carol. *Sweet and Sacred: The Diaries of James Henry Hammond, a Southern Slaveholder*. New York: Oxford University Press, 1988.

Bodman, Frank. "War Conditions and the Mental Health of the Child." *British Medical Journal* (October 4, 1941), pp. 486–488.

Bond, Horace Mann. *The Education of the Negro in the American Social Order*. New York: Octagon Books, 1966.

Boyd, Julian P., ed. *The Papers of Thomas Jefferson*. Vol. 2: *1777 to 18 June 1779*. Princeton, N.J.: Princeton University Press, 1950.

Boyer, Paul. *By the Bomb's Early Light: American Thought and Culture at the Dawn of the Atomic Age*. New York: Pantheon Books, 1985.

Brace, Charles Loring. *The Best Method of Disposing of Our Pauper and Vagrant Children*. New York: Wynkoop, Hallenbeck and Thomas, 1859.

———. "The Little Laborers of New York City." *Harper's New Monthly Magazine* 47, no. 279 (August 1873), pp. 321–332.

Brace, Emma, ed. *The Life of Charles Loring Brace*. New York: Charles Scribner's Sons, 1894.

Bradley, Frances Sage and Margaretta A. Williamson. *Rural Children in Selected Counties of North Carolina*. Washington, D.C.: Government Printing Office, 1918.

Bradley, John. *Learning to Glow: A Nuclear Reader*. Tucson: University of Arizona Press, 2000.

Breines, Wini. *Young, White, and Miserable: Growing Up Female in the Fifties*. Boston: Beacon Press, 1992.

Bremner, Robert H., ed. *Care of Dependent Children in the Late Nineteenth and Early Twentieth Centuries*. New York: Arno Press, 1974.

———. *Children and Youth in America: A Documentary History*. 3 Vols. Cambridge, Mass.: Harvard University Press, 1970.

Bremner, Robert H. and Gary W. Reichard, eds. *Reshaping America: Society and Institutions, 1945–1960.* Columbus: Ohio State University Press, 1982.

Brenzel, Barbara, Cathy Roberts-Gersch, and Judith Wittner. "Becoming Social: School Girls and Their Culture Between the Two World Wars." *Journal of Early Adolescence* 5, no. 4 (winter 1985), pp. 479–488.

Brenzel, Barbara M. *Daughters of the State: A Social Portrait of the First Reform School for Girls in North America, 1856–1905.* Cambridge, Mass.: MIT Press, 1983.

Brigham, Amariah. *Remarks on the Influence of Mental Excitement and Mental Cultivation upon Health.* 2nd ed. Boston: Marsh, Capen, and Lyon, 1833.

Brown, D. Clayton. "Health of Farm Children in the South, 1900–1950." *Agricultural History* 35, no. 1 (January 1979), pp. 170–187.

Brown, Joe David, ed. *The Hippies.* New York: Time Incorporated, 1967.

Brown, John. *Slave Life in Georgia.* London: W. M. Watts, 1855.

Bruce, H. C. *The New Man: Twenty-Nine Years a Slave, Twenty-Nine Years a Free Man.* York, Pa.: P. Anstadt and Sons, 1895.

Bruce, William George. *I Was Born in America.* Milwaukee, Wis.: Bruce Publishing Co., 1937.

Bullough, William A. *Cities and Schools in the Gilded Age: The Evolution of an Urban Institution.* Port Washington, N.Y.: Kennikat Press, 1974.

Burck, Gilbert and Sanford Parker. "The Changing American Market." *Fortune* 48, no. 2 (August 1953), pp. 98–198.

Burton, Warren. *The District School as It Was.* Edited by Clifton Johnson. Springfield, Mass.: Johnson's Bookstore, 1928.

Butterfield, L. H., ed. *Adams Family Correspondence.* Vol. 2: *June 1776–March 1778.* Cambridge, Mass.: The Belknap Press, 1963.

Butts, R. Freeman. *Public Education in the United States: From Revolution to Reform.* New York: Holt, Rinehart and Winston, 1978.

Campbell, Edward D. C., Jr., ed. *Before Freedom Came: African-American Life in the Antebellum South.* Richmond: The Museum of the Confederacy, and Charlottesville: University Press of Virginia, 1991.

Campbell, George. *White and Black: The Outcome of a Visit to the United States.* New York: R. Worthington, 1879.

Campbell, Helen. "Child Labor and Some of Its Results." *Chautauquan* 10, no. 1 (October 1889), pp. 21–24.

———. *Darkness and Daylight; or, Lights and Shadows of New York Life*. Hartford, Conn.: Hartford Publishing Co., 1895.

Canby, Henry Seidel. *The Age of Confidence*. New York: Farrar and Rinehart, 1934.

Carpenter, Seymour D. *Genealogical Notes of the Carpenter Family*. Springfield, Ill.: Illinois State Journal Co., 1907.

Carter, John F., Jr. "'These Wild Young People,' by One of Them." *Atlantic Monthly* 126, no. 3 (September 1920), pp. 301–304.

Cavallo, Dom. "Social Reform and the Movement to Organize Children's Play During the Progressive Era." *History of Childhood Quarterly* 3, no. 4 (spring 1976), pp. 509–522.

Censer, Jane Turner. *North Carolina Planters and Their Children*. Baton Rouge: Louisiana State University Press, 1984.

Channing, Steven A. *Confederate Ordeal*. Alexandria, Va.: Time-Life Books, 1984.

Channing, William Ellery. "Dissertation on the Sinfulness of Infants." *Christian Disciple* 2, no. 8 (August 1814), pp. 245–250.

Cherlin, Andrew J., ed. *The Changing American Family and Public Policy*. Washington, D.C.: Urban Institute Press, 1988.

"Child Labor Regulation." *Gunston's* 24, no. 4 (April 1903), pp. 355–357.

Child, Lydia M. *The Mother's Book*. New York: Carter, Hendee and Babcock, 1831.

The Child, the Clinic and the Court. New York: New Republic, 1925.

Christman, Calvin L., ed. *Lost in the Victory: Reflections of American War Orphans of World War II*. Collected by Susan Johnson Hadler and Ann Bennett Mix. Denton, Tex.: University of North Texas Press, 1998.

Clark, Dennis. "Babes in Bondage: Indentured Irish Children in Philadelphia in the Nineteenth Century." *Pennsylvania Magazine of History and Biography* 101, no. 4 (October 1977), pp. 475–486.

Clark, Dick and Richard Robinson. *Rock, Roll and Remember*. New York: Thomas Y. Crowell, 1976.

Clark, Septima Poinsette. *Echo in My Soul*. New York: E. P. Dutton and Co., 1962.

Clark, Thomas Arkle. "The Passing of the Chaperon." *Atlantic Monthly* 129, no. 4 (April 1922), pp. 516–519.

Clarke, Lewis. *Narrative of the Sufferings of Lewis Clarke.* Boston: David H. Ela, 1845.

Clay, George R. "Children of the Young Republic." *American Heritage* 11, no. 3 (April 1960), pp. 46–53.

Cleaveland, Agnes Morley. *No Life for a Lady.* Lincoln: University of Nebraska Press, 1969.

Clement, Priscilla Ferguson. "Children and Charity: Orphanages in New Orleans, 1817–1914." *Louisiana History* 27, no. 4 (fall 1986), pp. 337–352.

Cochrane, Willard W. *The Development of Agriculture: A Historical Analysis.* Minneapolis: University of Minnesota Press, 1979.

Coffin, Thomas E. "Television's Impact on Society." *American Psychologist* 10, no. 10 (October 1955), pp. 630–641.

Cohen, Rose. *Out of the Shadow.* New York: George H. Doran Co., 1918.

Cohen, Sol, ed. *Education in the United States: A Documentary History.* 5 vols. New York: Random House, 1974.

Colwell, Harry. "A New York Orphan Comes to Kansas." *Kansas History* 8, no. 1 (spring 1985), pp. 110–123.

Covello, Leonard with Guido d'Agostino. *The Heart Is the Teacher.* New York: McGraw-Hill Book Co., 1958.

Cress, Gary. *Kids' Stuff: Toys and the Changing World of American Childhood.* Cambridge, Mass.: Harvard University Press, 1997.

Cross, Herbert J. and Randall R. Kleinhesselink. "The Impact of the 1960s on Adolescence." *Journal of Early Adolescence* 5, no. 4 (winter 1985), pp. 517–531.

Croswell, T. R. "Amusements of Worcester School Children." *Pedagogical Seminary* 6, no. 3 (September 1899), pp. 265–371.

Culin, Stewart. "Street Games of Boys in Brooklyn, N.Y." *Journal of American Folklore* 4, no. 14 (July–Sept. 1891), pp. 221–237.

Curry, Dan, ed. *Children in the Fields.* New York: Arno Press, 1975.

Dale, Edward Everett. *The Cross Timbers: Memories of a North Texas Boyhood.* Austin: University of Texas Press, 1966.

Dalton, David. *Piece of My Heart: The Life, Times and Legend of Janis Joplin.* New York: St. Martin's Press, 1985.

Danaher, Jane. "A Change in Course." *Washington Post Magazine* (November 11, 2001), pp. 18–40.

Daniels, Elizabeth. "The Children of Gettysburg." *American Heritage* 40, no. 4 (May/June 1989), pp. 97–107.

Davis, Angela. *Angela Davis: An Autobiography.* New York: Random House, 1974.

Davis, Benjamin O., Jr. *Benjamin O. Davis, Jr.: American.* Washington, D.C.: Smithsonian Institution Press, 1991.

Davis, Kingsley. *Youth in the Depression.* Chicago: University of Chicago Press, 1935.

Davis, Philip. *Street-Land: Its Little People and Big Problems.* Boston: Small, Maynard and Co., 1915.

"The Delineator Child-Rescue Campaign." *Delineator* 70, no. 5 (November 1907), pp. 715–718.

De Long, H. W. *Boyhood Reminiscences.* Danville, N.Y.: F. A. Owen Publishing Co., 1913.

Demos, John. *Past, Present, and Personal: The Family and the Life Course in American History.* New York: Oxford University Press, 1986.

Devoe, Elijah. *The Refuge System, or Prison Discipline Applied to Juvenile Delinquents.* New York: John R. M'Gown, 1848.

Dewey, John. *The School and Society.* Chicago: University of Chicago Press, 1899.

Dillard, Annie. *An American Childhood.* New York: HarperPerennial, 1988.

Dougherty, Michael. *Diary of a Civil War Hero.* New York: Pyramid Books, 1960.

Douglass, Frederick. *Autobiographies.* New York: The Library of America, 1994.

Dow, Neal. *The Reminiscences of Neal Dow.* Portland, Me.: Evening Express Publishing Co., 1898.

Drake, Daniel. *Pioneer Life in Kentucky.* Cincinnati, Ohio: Robert Clarke and Co., 1870.

Dudley, Richard E. "Nebraska Public School Education, 1890–1910." *Nebraska History* 54, no. 1 (Spring 1973), pp. 65–90.

Duffy, John. "School Buildings and the Health of American School Children in the Nineteenth Century," in Charles E. Rosenberg, ed., *Healing and History: Essays for George Rosen.* Kent, England: William Dawson and Sons, 1979.

Dwight, Theodore, Jr., *The Father's Book.* Springfield, Mass.: G. and C. Merriam, 1834.

Dyer, Heman. *Records of an Active Life.* New York: Thomas Whittaker, 1886.

Eastman, Charles A. *Indian Boyhood.* Garden City, N.Y.: Doubleday, Page, 1910.

Ebbutt, Percy G. *Emigrant Life in Kansas.* London: Swan Sonnenschein and Co., 1886.

Edelman, Marian Wright. "Why America May Go to Hell." *America* 162, no. 12 (March 31, 1990), pp. 310–314.

Egan, Maurice Francis. *Recollections of a Happy Life.* New York: George H. Doran Co., 1924.

Eggen, Dan and Victoria Benning. "Pampered and Privileged." *Washington Post* (March 13, 2001), pp. B1, B4.

Eisele, Fannie L. "We Came to Live in Oklahoma Territory." *Chronicles of Oklahoma* 38, no. 1 (spring 1966), pp. 55–65.

Elder, Glen H., Jr. *Children of the Great Depression.* Chicago: University of Chicago Press, 1974.

Elderton, Marion, ed. *Case Studies of Unemployment.* Compiled by the Unemployment Committee of the National Federation of Settlements. Philadelphia: University of Pennsylvania Press, 1931.

Elkind, David. *The Hurried Child: Growing Up Too Fast Too Soon.* Reading, Mass.: Addison-Wesley, 1981.

Ellis, Anne. *The Life of an Ordinary Woman.* Boston: Houghton Mifflin, 1929.

Ellis, Edward Robb. *A Nation in Torment: The Great American Depression, 1929–1939.* New York: Kodansha International, 1995.

Emert, Phyllis Raybin, ed. *World War II: On the Homefront.* Carlisle, Mass.: Discovery Enterprises, Ltd., 1996.

"'Equal' Schools in Virginia." *Crisis* 43, no. 11 (November 1936), p. 333.

Erdoes, Richard. *The Rain Dance People.* New York: Alfred A. Knopf, 1976.

Espenshade, Thomas J. *Investing in Children: New Estimates of Parental Expenditures.* Washington, D.C.: The Urban Institute Press, 1984.

Fass, Paula S. *The Damned and the Beautiful: American Youth in the 1920's.* New York: Oxford University Press, 1977.

Fergusson, Harvey. *Home in the West: An Inquiry into My Origins.* New York: Duell, Sloan and Pearce, 1945.

Filler, Louis, ed. *Horace Mann on the Crisis in Education.* Yellow Springs, Oh.: Antioch Press, 1965.

Finkelstein, Barbara. "In Fear of Childhood: Relationships Between Parents and Teachers in Popular Primary Schools in the Nineteenth Century." *History of Childhood Quarterly* 3, no. 3 (winter 1976), pp. 321–335.

Fiske, George Walter. *Boys Life and Self-Government.* New York: Young Men's Christian Association Press, 1910.

Flexner, Bernard and Reuben Oppenheimer. *The Legal Aspect of the Juvenile Court.* Washington, D.C.: Government Printing Office, 1921.

Folwell, William Watts. *The Autobiography and Letters of a Pioneer of Culture.* Edited by Solon J. Buck. Minneapolis: University of Minnesota Press, 1933.

Forum on Child and Family Statistics. *America's Children 1999.* URL: *http://childstats.gov/ac1999/highlight.asp.* March 25, 2001.

Foster-Home Care for Dependent Children. Washington, D.C.: Government Printing Office, 1924.

Foy, Eddie and Alvin F. Harlow. *Clowning through Life.* New York: E. P. Dutton and Co., 1928.

Franklin, John Hope and Alfred A. Moss, Jr. *From Slavery to Freedom: A History of Black Americans.* 6th ed. New York: McGraw-Hill, 1988.

Frazier, E. Franklin. *Negro Youth at the Crossways: Their Personality Development in the Middle States.* Washington, D.C.: American Council on Education, 1940.

Freud, Anna and Dorothy T. Burlingham. *War and Children.* New York: Medical War Books, 1943.

Frost, David. *The Americans.* New York: Stein and Day, 1970.

Fuller, Wayne E. "Country Schoolteaching on the Sod-House Frontier." *Arizona and the West* 17, no. 2 (summer 1975), pp. 121–140.

Fulton, Frances I. Sims. *To and Through Nebraska.* Lincoln, Neb.: Journal Company, 1884.

Furstenberg, Frank F. and Andrew J. Cherlin. *Divided Families: What Happens to Children When Parents Part.* Cambridge, Mass.: Harvard University Press, 1991.

Gaines, Donna. *Teenage Wasteland: Suburbia's Dead End Kids,* Chicago: University of Chicago Press, 1998.

Gale, Zona. *When I Was a Little Girl.* New York: Macmillan Co., 1913.

Gallarno, George. "How Iowa Cared for Orphans of Her Soldiers of the Civil War." *Annals of Iowa* 15, no. 3 (January 1926), pp. 163–193.

Gans, Herbert J. *The Levittowners: Ways of Life and Politics in a New Suburban Community.* New York: Pantheon Books, 1967.

Gardner, George E. and Harvey Spencer. "Reactions of Children with Fathers and Brothers in the Armed Forces." *American Journal of Orthopsychiatry* 14, no. 1 (January 1944), pp. 36–43.

Garland, Hamlin. *A Son of the Middle Border.* New York: Macmillan, 1917.

"General Fred Grant's Scare at Vicksburg." *Literary Digest* 44, no. 17 (April 27, 1912), pp. 898–902.

Genovese, Eugene D. *Roll, Jordan, Roll: The World the Slaves Made.* New York: Vintage Books, 1974.

Gerard, Margaret W. "Psychological Effects of War on the Small Child and Mother." *American Journal of Orthopsychiatry* 13, no. 3 (July 1943), pp. 493–496.

Gerzon, Mark. *The Whole World Is Watching: A Young Man Looks at Youth's Dissent.* New York: The Viking Press, 1969.

Gesell, Arnold, and Frances L. Ilg. *The Child from Five to Ten.* New York: Harper and Brothers, 1946.

Gilliams, E. Leslie. "Investigating the Child." *Harper's Weekly* 56, no. 2894 (June 8, 1912), pp. 13–14.

Glenbard East Echo, comp. *Teenagers Themselves.* New York: Adama Press, 1984.

Goldman, Eric F. "Young John Bach McMaster: A Boyhood in New York City." *New York History* 20, no. 3 (July 1939), pp. 316–324.

Goldrick, O. J. "The First School in Denver." *Colorado Magazine* 6, no. 2 (March 1929), pp. 72–74.

Goodbird, Edward as told to Gilbert L. Wilson. *Goodbird the Indian: His Story.* New York: Fleming H. Revell Co., 1914.

Goodwin, Doris Kearns. *Wait Till Next Year.* New York: Simon and Schuster, 1997.

Graebner, William and Jacqueline Swansinger. *The American Record: Since 1941.* New York: McGraw Hill, 1997.

Graff, Harvey J. *Conflicting Paths: Growing Up in America.* Cambridge, Mass.: Harvard University Press, 1995.

————, ed. *Growing Up in America*. Detroit, Mich.: Wayne State University Press, 1987.

Graham, Patricia Albjerg. *Community and Class in American Education, 1865–1918*. New York: John Wiley and Sons, 1974.

Grant, Jesse R. *In the Days of My Father General Grant*. New York: Harper and Brothers, 1925.

The Great Migration: African Americans Journey North. Upper Saddle River, N.J.: Globe Fearon, 1998.

Greeley, Horace. *Recollections of a Busy Life*. New York: J. B. Ford and Co., 1868.

Greenberg, Cheryl Lynn. *"Or Does It Explode?" Black Harlem in the Great Depression*. New York: Oxford University Press, 1991.

Greenfield, Jeff. *No Peace, No Place: Excavations Along the Generational Fault*. Garden City, N.Y.: Doubleday and Co., 1973.

Gregory, Addie Hibbard. *A Great-Grandmother Remembers*. Chicago: A. Kroch, Publisher, 1940.

Gregory, Dick with Robert Lipsyte. *Nigger*. New York: E. P. Dutton and Co., 1964.

Gutman, Herbert G. *The Black Family in Slavery and Freedom, 1750–1925*. New York: Pantheon Books, 1976.

Hall, Basil. *Travels in North America in the Years 1827 and 1828*. Vol. 2. Philadelphia, Pa.: Carey, Lea and Carey, 1829.

Hall, G. Stanley. *Youth: Its Education, Regimen, and Hygiene*. New York: D. Appleton and Co., 1906.

Hallowell, Benjamin. *Autobiography of Benjamin Hallowell*. Philadelphia, Pa.: Friends' Book Association, 1883.

Hargreaves, Mary W. M. "Rural Education on the Northern Plains Frontier." *Journal of the American West* 18, no. 4 (October 1979), pp. 25–32.

Harper, H. G. "The Father's Duty to a Scout." *Scouting* 1, no. 18 (January 15, 1914), p. 5.

Harper, Keith. "The Louisville Baptist Orphan's Home: The Early Years." *Register of the Kentucky Historical Society* 90, no. 3 (summer 1992), pp. 236–255.

Harries, Meirion and Susie Harries. *The Last Days of Innocence: America at War, 1917–1918*. New York: Random House, 1997.

Harris, Mark Jonathan, Franklin D. Mitchell, and Steven J. Schechter. *The Homefront: America During World War II*. New York: G. P. Putnam's Sons, 1984.

Hart, Jeffrey. *When the Going Was Good! American Life in the Fifties.* New York: Crown Publishers, 1982.

Hastings, James K. "Boyhood in the Trinidad Region." *Colorado Magazine* 30, no. 2 (April 1953), 104–109.

Hastings, Robert J. *A Nickel's Worth of Skim Milk: A Boy's View of the Great Depression.* Carbondale, Ill.: University Graphics and Publications, 1972.

———. *A Penny's Worth of Minced Ham: Another Look at the Great Depression.* Carbondale: Southern Illinois University Press, 1986.

Hawes, Joseph M. *Children Between the Wars: American Childhood, 1920–1940.* New York: Twayne Publishers, 1997.

———. *Children in Urban Society.* New York: Oxford University Press, 1971.

Hawes, Joseph M. and N. Ray Hiner, eds. *American Childhood: A Research Guide and Historical Handbook.* Westport, Conn.: Greenwood Press, 1985.

Hayfield, Chris. "'1941': Bombs Away." *Rolling Stone* (January 24, 1980), pp. 37–42.

Heide, Robert and John Gilman. *Home Front America: Popular Culture of the World War II Era.* San Francisco: Chronicle Books, 1995.

Henson, Josiah. *An Autobiography of the Reverend Josiah Henson.* Reading, Mass.: Addison-Wesley Publishing Co., 1969.

Hewlett, Sylvia Ann. *When the Bough Breaks: The Cost of Neglecting Our Children.* New York: Basic Books, 1991.

Hills, Georgia Burns. "Memories of a Pioneer Childhood." *Colorado Magazine* 32, no. 2 (April 1955), pp. 110–128.

"Hints with Regard to the Management of Very Young Children." *American Journal of Education* 1, no. 1 (January 1830), pp. 28–33.

Hoffert, Sylvia D. *Private Matters: American Attitudes toward Childbearing and Infant Nurture in the Urban North, 1800–1860.* Urbana: University of Illinois Press, 1989.

Holland, Barbara. *Wasn't the Grass Greener? A Curmudgeon's Fond Memories.* New York: Harcourt Brace and Co., 1999.

Holland, Kenneth. *Youth in European Labor Camps.* Washington, D.C.: American Council of Education, 1939.

Holloran, Peter C. *Boston's Wayward Children.* Rutherford, N.J.: Fairleigh Dickinson University Press, 1989.

Holt, Marilyn Irvin. *The Orphan Trains: Placing-Out in America.* Lincoln: University of Nebraska Press, 1992.

Hoopes, Roy. *Americans Remember the Home Front: An Oral Narrative.* New York: Hawthorn Books, 1977.

Howells, William Dean. *Years of My Youth.* New York: Harper and Brothers, 1916.

Hughes, Louis. *Thirty Years a Slave: From Bondage to Freedom.* Milwaukee, Wis.: South Side Printing Co., 1897.

Hull, Susan R. *Boy Soldiers of the Confederacy.* New York: Neale Publishing Co., 1905.

Hunt, Gaillard. *Life in America One Hundred Years Ago.* New York: Harper and Brothers, 1914.

Hunt, Una. *Una Mary: The Inner Life of a Child.* New York: Charles Scribner's Sons, 1914.

Huntington, Susan. *Memoirs of the Late Mrs. Susan Huntington, of Boston, Mass.* Boston: Crocker and Brewster, 1829.

Hurmence, Belinda, ed. *Before Freedom, When I Just Can Remember.* Winston-Salem, N.C.: John F. Blair, 1989.

———. *My Folks Don't Want Me to Talk about Slavery.* Winston-Salem, N.C.: John F. Blair, 1984.

Husband, Michael B., ed. "The Recollections of a Schoolteacher in the Disappointment Creek Valley." *Colorado Magazine* 51, no. 2 (spring 1974), pp. 141–156.

"The Importance of Kindergartens in War Time." *School and Society* 8, no. 204 (November 23, 1918), pp. 617–618.

Isaacs, Mareasa R. *The Impact of Community Violence on African American Children and Families.* Arlington, Va.: National Center for Education in Maternal and Child Health, 1992.

Jackson, Kenneth T. *Crabgrass Frontier: The Suburbanization of the United States.* New York: Oxford University Press, 1985.

Jantzen, Steven. *Hooray for Peace, Hurrah for War: The United States During World War I.* New York: Alfred A. Knopf, 1971.

Janvier, Meredith. *Baltimore Yesterdays.* Baltimore, Md.: H. G. Roebuck and Son, 1937.

Jarrell, Anne. "The Face of Teenage Sex Grows Younger." *New York Times,* April 2, 2000, section 9, pp. 1 and 8.

Jefferson, Thomas. *Notes on the State of Virginia*. Edited by William Peden. Chapel Hill: University of North Carolina Press, 1955.

Jeidy, Pauline. "Reactions of Children of Different Age Levels to War and Their Implications for Teachers." *California Journal of Elementary Education* 12, no. 1 (August 1943), pp. 12–21.

Jenkins, Henry, ed. *The Children's Culture Reader*. New York: New York University Press, 1998.

Jeter, Jeremiah Bell. *The Recollections of a Long Life*. Richmond, Va.: The Religious Herald Co., 1891.

Johnson, Clifford M., Leticia Miranda, Arloc Sherman, and James D. Weill. *Child Poverty in America*. Washington, D.C.: Children's Defense Fund, 1991.

Johnson, Clifford M., Andrew M. Sum, and James D. Weill. *Vanishing Dreams: The Economic Plight of America's Young Families*. Washington, D.C.: Children's Defense Fund, 1992.

Johnson, James Weldon. *Along This Way*. New York: The Viking Press, 1933.

Jones, Landon Y. *Great Expectations: America and the Baby Boom Generation*. New York: Coward, McCann and Geoghagan, 1980.

Jones, Louis C., ed. *Growing Up in Cooper Country: Boyhood Recollections of the New York Frontier*. Syracuse, N.Y.: Syracuse University Press, 1965.

Joseph, Stephen M., ed. *The Me Nobody Knows: Children's Voices from the Ghetto*. New York: World Publishing Co., 1969.

Kaestle, Carl F. "Social Change, Discipline, and the Common School in Early Nineteenth-Century America." *Journal of Interdisciplinary History* 9, no. 1 (summer 1978), pp. 1–17.

Kaestle, Carl F. and Maris A. Vinovskis. "From Apron Strings to ABCs: Parents, Children, and Schooling in Nineteenth-Century Massachusetts," in *Turning Points: Historical and Sociological Essays on the Family*. Chicago: University of Chicago Press, 1978.

Kendrick, A. C. *The Life and Letters of Mrs. Emily C. Judson*. New York: Sheldon and Co., 1860.

Keniston, Kenneth. *All Our Children: The American Family Under Pressure*. New York: Harcourt Brace Jovanovich, 1977.

Kennedy, David M. *Over Here: The First World War and American Society*. New York: Oxford University Press, 1980.

Kett, Joseph F. *Rites of Passage: Adolescence in America, 1790 to the Present*. New York: Basic Books, 1977.

King, Wilma. *Stolen Childhood.* Bloomington: Indiana University Press, 1995.

Kiple, Kenneth F. and Virginia H. Kiple. "Slave Child Mortality: Some Nutritional Answers to a Perennial Puzzle." *Journal of Social History,* 10, no. 3 (March 1977), pp. 284–309.

Kirk, Robert William. *Earning Their Stripes: The Mobilization of American Children in the Second World War.* New York: Peter Lang, 1994.

Kliebard, Herbert M. "Psychology . . . The Teacher's Blackstone: G. Stanley Hall and the Effort to Build a Developmental Curriculum for Youth." *Journal of Early Adolescence* 5, no. 4 (winter 1985), pp. 467–478.

Kopkind, Andrew. "Coming of Age in Aquarius," in *"Takin' It to the Streets": A Sixties Reader,* edited by Alexander Bloom and Wini Breines. New York: Oxford University Press, 1995.

Kusmer, Kenneth L. *A Ghetto Takes Shape: Black Cleveland, 1870–1930.* Urbana: University of Illinois Press, 1976.

La Guardia, Fiorello H. *The Making of an Insurgent.* Philadelphia, Pa.: J. B. Lippincott, 1948.

Lancaster, Joseph. *Improvements in Education, as It Respects the Industrious Classes of the Community.* London: Darton and Harvey, 1805.

Larcom, Lucy. "Among the Lowell Mill-Girls: A Reminiscence." *Atlantic Monthly* 48, no. 289 (November 1881), pp. 593–612.

———. *A New England Girlhood.* Boston: Houghton Mifflin, 1889.

Larrabee, J. A. "The Schoolroom a Factor in the Production of Disease." *Journal of the American Medical Association* 11, no. 18 (November 3, 1888), pp. 613–617.

Lee, Joseph. *Play in Education.* New York: Macmillan, 1915.

Lenroot, Katharine F. "Children of the Depression: A Study of 259 Families in Selected Areas of Five Cities." *Social Service Review* 9, no. 2 (June 1935), pp. 212–242.

Letchworth, William P. *Homes of Homeless Children.* N.p.: 1903.

Levine, Ellen. *Freedom's Children: Young Civil Rights Activists Tell Their Own Stories.* New York: G. P. Putnam's Sons, 1993.

Lilienthal, Meta. *Dear Remembered World: Childhood Memories of an Old New Yorker.* New York: Richard R. Smith, 1947.

Lindsey, Ben B. and Wainwright Evans. *The Revolt of Modern Youth.* New York: Boni and Liveright, 1925.

Ling, Ping. "Moral Training of Children in War Time." *Pedagogical Seminary* 25, no. 3 (September 1918), pp. 276–301.

———. "The Public Schools and Food Conservation." *Pedagogical Seminary* 25, no. 2 (June 1918), pp. 191–210.

———. "School Children and Food Production." *Pedagogical Seminary* 25, no. 2 (June 1918), pp. 163–190.

Lingeman, Richard R. *Don't You Know There's a War On? The American Home Front, 1941–1945.* New York: G. P. Putnam's Sons, 1970.

Litoff, Judy Barrett and David C. Smith: "'Will He Get My Letter?' Popular Portrayals of Mail and Morale During World War II." *Journal of Popular Culture* 23, no. 4 (spring 1990), pp. 21–40.

Litwack, Leon F. *Been in the Storm So Long: The Aftermath of Slavery.* New York: Alfred A. Knopf, 1979.

Lockley, Fred. *Across the Plains by Prairie Schooner: Personal Narrative of B. F. Bonney of His Trip to Sutter's Fort, California, in 1846, and of His Pioneer Experiences in Oregon During the Days of Oregon's Provisional Government.* N.p.: N.d.

Loiry, William S. *The Impact of Youth: A History of Children and Youth with Recommendations for the Future.* Sarasota, Fla.: Loiry Publishing House, 1984.

Low, Juliette. *Girl Scouts as an Educational Force.* Washington, D.C.: Government Printing Office, 1919.

Macdonald, Mary. "How Kids Cope: Traumatic Images Showing Up in Drawings, Games, Writings After the Assault." *Atlanta Constitution* (September 21, 2001), p. C1

Macleod, David I. *Building Character in the American Boy: The Boy Scouts, YMCA, and Their Forerunners.* Madison: University of Wisconsin Press, 1983.

Magee, J. H. *The Night of Affliction and Morning of Recovery.* Cincinnati: Published by the Author, 1873.

Magill, Edward Hicks. *Sixty-Five Years in the Life of a Teacher, 1841–1906.* Boston: Houghton, Mifflin and Co., 1907.

Malcolm X with Alex Haley. *The Autobiography of Malcolm X.* N.p.: Castle Books, 1965.

Markham, Edwin. "The Child at the Loom." *Cosmopolitan* 41, no. 5 (September 1906), pp. 480–487.

———. "Child-Wrecking in the Glass Factories." *Cosmopolitan* 41, no. 6 (October 1906), pp. 567–574.

Marks, Carole. *Farewell—We're Good and Gone: The Great Black Migration.* Bloomington: Indiana University Press, 1989.

Marrs, Elijah P. *Life and History of the Rev. Elijah P. Marrs.* Louisville, Ky.: Bradley and Gilbert Co., 1885.

Marten, James. *The Children's Civil War.* Chapel Hill: University of North Carolina Press, 1998.

———. "'What Is to Become of the Negro?' White Reaction to Emancipation in Texas." *Mid-America* 73, no. 2 (April–July 1991), pp. 115–133.

Martin, Robert Hugh. *A Boy of Old Shenandoah.* Parsons, W.Va.: McClain Printing Co., 1977.

Martineau, Harriet. *Society in America.* Gloucester, Mass.: Peter Smith, 1968.

Mason, Isaac. *Life of Isaac Mason as a Slave.* Miami, Fla.: Mnemosyne Publishing Co., 1969.

"Maternal Instruction." *American Journal of Education* 4, no. 1 (January and February 1829), pp. 53–38.

Matthews, Ellen Nathalie. "Unemployed Youth of New York City." *Monthly Labor Review* 44, no. 2 (February 1937), pp. 267–284.

May, Dean and Maris A. Vinovskis. "A Ray of Millennial Light: Early Education and School Reform in the Infant School Movement in Massachusetts, 1826–1840," in *Family and Kin in Urban Communities,* edited by Tamara Hareven. New York: New Viewpoints, 1977.

May, Elaine Tyler. *Homeward Bound: American Families in the Cold War Era.* New York: Basic Books, 1988.

May, Henry F. *Coming to Terms: A Study in Memory and History.* Berkeley: University of California Press, 1987.

Mayer, Lawrence A. "It's a Bear Market for Babies, Too." *Fortune* 90, no. 6 (December 1974), pp. 134–212.

Maynard, Joyce. "An Eighteen-Year-Old Looks Back on Life: *New York Times* 1972 Reprint." URL: *http://www.joycemaynard.com.articles/times.html.* February 18, 2001.

———. Looking *Back: A Chronicle of Growing Up Old in the Sixties.* London: Michael Joseph, 1973.

McAdoo, Harriette Pipes and John Lewis McAdoo, eds. *Black Children: Social, Educational, and Parental Environments.* Beverly Hills, Calif.: Sage Publications, 1985.

McCausland, Clare L. *Children of Circumstance: A History of the First 125 Years (1849–1974) of Chicago Child Care Society.* Chicago: R. R. Donnelly and Sons, 1976.

McClintock, Inez and Marshall McClintock. *Toys in America.* Washington, D.C.: Public Affairs Press, 1961.

McCracken, Elizabeth. "Going to School." *Outlook* 102, no. 8 (October 26, 1912), pp. 425–433.

McElvaine, Robert S. *The Great Depression: America, 1929–1941.* New York: Times Books, 1984.

McElvaine, Robert S., ed. *Down and Out in the Great Depression: Letters from the "Forgotten Man."* Chapel Hill: University of North Carolina Press, 1983.

McGhee, Zach. "A Study in the Play Life of Some South Carolina Children." *Pedagogical Seminary* 7, no. 4 (December 1900), pp. 457–478.

McWilliams, John. *Recollections of John McWilliams.* Princeton, N.J.: Princeton University Press, 1921.

Mechling, Jay. "Oral Evidence and the History of American Children's Lives." *Journal of American History* 74, no. 2 (September 1987), pp. 579–586.

Medrich, Elliott A., Judith Roizen, Victor Rubin, and Stuart Buckley. *The Serious Business of Growing Up: A Study of Children's Lives Outside School.* Berkeley: University of California Press, 1982.

Mellon, James, ed. *Bullwhip Days: The Slaves Remember.* New York: Weidenfeld and Nicolson, 1988.

Mencken, H. L. *Happy Days, 1880–1892.* New York: Alfred A. Knopf, 1973.

Merrill, Perry H. *Roosevelt's Forest Army: A History of the Civilian Conservation Corps, 1933–1942.* Montpelier, Vt.: Perry H. Merrill, 1981.

Meyer, Agnes E. *Journey through Chaos.* New York: Harcourt, Brace and Co., 1944.

Miller, Ann with Norma Browning. *Miller's High Life.* Garden City, N.Y.: Doubleday and Co., 1972.

Miller, Arthur. *Timebends.* New York: Grove Press, 1987.

Mirel, Jeffrey and David Angus. "Youth, Work, and Schooling in the Great Depression." *Journal of Early Adolescence* 5, no. 4 (winter 1985), pp. 489–504.

Momaday, N. Scott. *The Names.* New York: Harper and Row, 1976.

Monroe, Paul. *Founding of the American Public School System: A History of Education in the United States.* Vol. 1. New York: Hafner Publishing, 1971.

Montagu, Ashley. *The American Way of Life.* New York: G. P. Putnam's Sons, 1967.

Moore, John Hammond. *Southern Homefront, 1861–1865.* Columbia, S.C.: Summerhouse Press, 1998.

Morris, Willie. *North Toward Home.* Boston: Houghton Mifflin, 1967.

Morton, Marian J. "Homes for Poverty's Children: Cleveland's Orphanages, 1851–1933." *Ohio History* 98 (winter–spring 1989), pp. 5–22.

Moses, Anna Mary Robertson. *Grandma Moses: My Life's Story.* New York: Harper and Brothers, 1948.

Mowry, William A. *Recollections of a New England Educator.* New York: Silver Burdett, 1908.

Moynihan, Ruth Barnes. "Children and Young People on the Oregon Trail." *Western History Quarterly* 6, no. 3 (July 1975), pp. 279–294.

Mundy, Liza. "Sex and Sensibility." *Washington Post Magazine* (July 16, 2000), pp. 16–34.

Munkres, Robert L. "Wives, Mothers, Daughters: Women's Life on the Road West." *Annals of Wyoming* 42, no. 2 (October 1970), pp. 191–224.

Murphy, Lois Barclay. "The Young Child's Experience in War Time." *American Journal of Orthopsychiatry* 13, no. 3 (July 1943), pp. 497–501.

Nasaw, David. *Schooled to Order: A Social History of Public Schooling in the United States.* New York: Oxford University Press, 1979.

The Negro Problem. New York: James Pott and Co., 1903.

Newton, Huey P., with J. Herman Blake. *Revolutionary Suicide.* New York: Harcourt Brace Jovanovich, 1973.

Notestein, Frank W. "The Facts of Life." *Atlantic Monthly* 177, no. 6 (June 1946), pp. 75–83.

"Observations on Infant Schools." *American Journal of Education* 4, no. 1 (January and February 1829), pp. 8–23.

Obst, Lynda Rosen, ed. *The Sixties: The Decade Remembered Now, by the People Who Lived It Then.* New York: Rolling Stone Press, 1977.

Oliver, A. C., Jr., and Harold M. Dudley. *This New America: The Story of the C. C. C.* London: Longmans, Green and Co., 1937.

Orcutt, Hiram. *Reminiscences of School Life.* Cambridge: Mass.: University Press, 1898.

Outland, George E. "Should Transient Boys Be Sent Home?" *Social Service Review* 9, no. 3 (September 1935), pp. 511–519.

Owens, Leslie Howard. *This Species of Property: Slave Life and Culture in the Old South.* New York: Oxford University Press, 1976.

Packard, Joseph. *Recollections of a Long Life.* Washington, D.C.: Byron S. Adams, 1902.

Parks, Gordon. *A Choice of Weapons.* New York: Harper and Row, 1966.

Parr, Joy. *Labouring Children: British Immigrant Apprentices to Canada, 1869–1924.* Toronto: University of Toronto Press, 1994.

Patri, Angelo. *Your Children in Wartime.* Garden City, N.Y.: Doubleday, Doran, 1943.

Patrick, Michael D. and Evelyn Goodrich Trickel. *Orphan Trains to Missouri.* Columbia: University of Missouri Press, 1997.

Paul, James Laughey. *Pennsylvania's Soldier's Orphan Schools.* Philadelphia: Claxton, Remsen and Haffelfinger, 1876.

Peirce, Bradford Kinney. *A Half Century with Juvenile Delinquents: The New York House of Refuge and Its Times.* New York: D. Appleton and Co., 1869.

Pennington, James W. C. *The Fugitive Blacksmith; or, Events in the History of James W. C. Pennington.* London: Charles Gilpin, 1850.

Perkins, Eugene. *Home Is a Dirty Street: The Social Oppression of Black Children.* Chicago: Third World Press, 1975.

Personal Justice Denied: Report of the Commission on Wartime Relocation and Internment Camps. Washington, D.C.: U.S. Government Printing Office, 1982.

Peters, De Witt C. "The Evils of Youthful Enlistments—and Nostalgia." *American Journal of Insanity* 19, no. 4 (April 1863), pp. 476–479.

Petersen, William. "The New American Family." *Commentary* 21, no. 1 (January 1956), pp. 1–6.

Phillips, John Aristotle and David Michaelis. *Mushroom: The Story of the A-Bomb Kid.* New York: William Morrow and Co., 1978.

Pollock, Linda A. *Forgotten Children: Parent-Child Relations from 1500–1900.* Cambridge, U.K.: Cambridge University Press, 1983.

Potter, Ray. *Memoirs of the Life and Religious Experience of Ray Potter.* Providence, R.I.: H. H. Brown, 1829.

Preston, Richard. "A Yearning for Great Teachers." *Washington Post* (May 27, 1979), pp. C1–C3.

"Proceedings of the Annual Meeting of the National Child Labor Committee." *Annals of the American Academy of Political and Social Science* 25, no. 3 (May 1905), pp. 150–171.

Progress and Peril: Black Children in America. Washington, D.C.: Children's Defense Fund, 1993.

Public Agenda Online. *Kids These Days '99: What Americans Really Think About the Next Generation.* URL: *http://www.publicagenda.org/specials/kids/kids.htm.* April 9, 2001.

Puffer, J. Adams. "Boy Gangs and Boy Leaders." *McClure's Magazine* 37, no. 6 (October 1911), pp. 678–689.

Pumpelly, Raphael. *My Reminiscences.* Vol. 1. New York. Henry Holt and Company, 1918.

Quinn, Camilla A. "Soldiers on Our Streets: The Effects of a Civil War Military Camp on the Springfield Community." *Illinois Historical Journal* 86, no. 4 (winter 1993), pp. 245–256.

Raichle, Donald R. "The Abolition of Corporal Punishment in New Jersey Schools." *History of Childhood Quarterly* 2, no. 1 (summer 1974), pp. 53–78.

Rasheed, Haroon. "A Test in Tolerance." *Washington Post Magazine* (November 11, 2001), pp. 20–43.

Read, Georgia Willis. "Diseases, Drugs, and Doctors on the Oregon-California Trail in the Gold-Rush Years." *Missouri Historical Review* 38, no. 3 (April 1944), pp. 260–276.

Reich, Charles A. *The Greening of America: How the Youth Revolution Is Trying to Make America Livable.* New York: Random House, 1970.

Reiman, Richard A. *The New Deal and American Youth: Ideas and Ideals in a Depression Decade.* Athens: University of Georgia Press, 1992.

Reinier, Jacqueline. *From Virtue to Character: American Childhood, 1775–1850.* New York: Twayne Publishers, 1996.

Reissman, Frank. *The Culturally Deprived Child.* New York: Harper and Brothers, 1962.

Restad, Penne L. *Christmas in America: A History.* New York: Oxford University Press, 1995.

Richardson, Martin D. and Le Roy M. Washington. "A Picture of Florida's Schools." *Crisis* 44, no. 9 (September 1937), pp. 270–271.

Rickover, H. G. *Education and Freedom*. New York: E. P. Dutton and Co., 1959.

Riis, Jacob. *The Children of the Poor*. New York: Charles Scribner's Sons, 1892.

Riley, Glenda. "The Specter of a Savage: Rumors and Alarmism on the Overland Trail." *Western Historical Quarterly* 15, no. 4 (October 1984), pp. 427–444.

Robinson, Harriet. *Loom and Spindle or Life Among the Early Mill Girls*. New York: Thomas Y. Crowell, 1898.

Rochelle, Belinda. *Witnesses to Freedom: Young People Who Fought for Civil Rights*. New York: Lodestar Books, 1993.

Rosengarten, Theodore. *All God's Dangers: The Life of Nate Shaw*. New York: Alfred A. Knopf, 1974.

Ross, Jennie E. "A Child's Experience in '49." Part 2. *Overland Monthly* 63, no. 4 (April 1914), pp. 402–408.

Rothman, David J. *Conscience and Convenience: The Asylum and Its Alternatives in Progressive America*. Boston: Little, Brown and Co., 1980.

Russakoff, Dale. "On Campus, It's the Children's Hour." *Washington Post*, November 13, 1998, pp. A1, A12–A13.

Russell, David H. "The Elementary School Child and the War." *California Journal of Education* 11, nos. 3 and 4 (February and May 1943), pp. 144–153.

Ryerson, Ellen. *The Best-Laid Plans: America's Juvenile Court Experiment*. New York: Hill and Wang, 1978.

Sabin, Henry. "Is Your Child in This School?" *Child-Study Monthly* 3, no. 2 (June–July 1897), pp. 95–96.

Satterfield, Archie. *The Home Front: An Oral History of the War Years in America, 1941–45*. N.p.: Playboy Press, 1981.

Schlissel, Lillian. "Mothers and Daughters on the Western Frontier." *Frontier* 3, no. 2 (summer 1978), pp. 29–33.

"The School Garden Army and the State Councils of Defense." *School and Society* 8, no. 199 (October 19, 1918), pp. 464–465.

Schramm, Wilbur, Jack Lyle, and Edwin P. Barker. *Television in the Lives of Our Children*. Stanford, Calif.: Stanford University Press, 1961.

Schubert, Herman J. P. *Twenty Thousand Transients: A One Year's Sample of Those Who Apply for Aid in a Northern City.* Buffalo, N.Y.: Emergency Relief Bureau, 1935.

Schultz, Stanley E. *The Culture Factory: Boston Public Schools, 1789–1860.* New York: Oxford University Press, 1973.

Scott, Donald M. and Bernard Wishy, eds. *America's Families: A Documentary History.* New York: Harper and Row, 1982.

Scott, Emmett J. "Additional Letters of Negro Migrants of 1916–1918." *Journal of Negro History* 4, no. 3 (October 1919), pp. 412–465.

Scott, Rebecca. "The Battle Over the Child: Child Apprenticeship and the Freedmen's Bureau in North Carolina." *Prologue* 10, no. 2 (summer 1978), pp. 100–113.

Scrimsher, Lila Gravatt, ed. "The Diary of Anna Webber: Early Day Teacher of Mitchell County." *Kansas Historical Quarterly* 38, no. 3 (autumn 1972), pp. 320–337.

Seeley, John R., R. Alexander Sim, and Elizabeth W. Loosley. *Crestwood Heights: A Study of the Culture of Suburban Life.* New York: Basic Books, 1956.

Sepmeier, Emma Jane McKee. "Reminiscences of Life in Sheffield, Alabama, 1931–1934." *Journal of Muscle Shoals History* 5 (1977), pp. 112–119.

Seth, Joseph B. and Mary W. Seth. *Recollections of a Long Life on the Eastern Shore.* Easton, Md.: Press of the Star-Democrat, 1926.

Seton, Ernest Thompson. "The Boy Scouts in America." *Outlook* 95, no. 12 (July 23, 1910), pp. 630–635.

Sharlitt, Michael. *As I Remember: The Home in My Heart.* Privately published, 1959.

Shaw, Anna Howard with Elizabeth Jordan. *The Story of a Pioneer.* New York: Harper and Brothers, 1929.

Shepherd, Robert E., Jr. "The Juvenile Court at 100 Years: A Look Back." *Juvenile Justice* 6, no. 2 (December 1999). URL: *http://www.ncjrs.org/html/ojjdp/jjjournal1299/2.html.* October 15, 2000.

Sherman, Edgar Jay. *Some Recollections of a Long Life.* Boston: Privately printed, 1908.

Shinn, Milicent Washburn. *The Biography of a Baby.* Cambridge, Mass.: Riverside Press, 1900.

Sidel, Ruth. *On Her Own.* New York: Viking, 1990.

Silverman, Elaine. "In Their Own Words: Mothers and Daughters on the Alberta Frontier, 1890–1929." *Frontiers* 2, no. 2 (summer 1977), pp. 37–44.

Simpson, Bobby. *Dear Bobby Simpson*. New York: Dell Publishing Co., 1984.

Slater, Peter Gregg. *Children in the New England Mind*. Hamden, Conn.: Archon Books, 1977.

"The Small Arabs of New York." *Atlantic Monthly* 23, no. 137 (March 1869), pp. 279–286.

Sneller, Anne Gertrude. *A Vanished World*. Syracuse, N.Y.: Syracuse University Press, 1964.

Spear, Allan H. *Black Chicago: The Making of a Negro Ghetto, 1890–1920*. Chicago: University of Chicago Press, 1967.

Spock, Benjamin. *Baby and Child Care*. New York: Pocket Books, 1976.

Stampp, Kenneth M. *The Peculiar Institution: Slavery in the Ante-Bellum South*. New York: Vintage Books, 1984.

Stearns, Peter N. and Timothy Haggerty. "The Role of Fear: Transitions in American Emotional Standards for Children, 1850–1950." *American Historical Review* 96, no. 1 (February 1991), pp. 63–94.

Steffens, Lincoln. *The Autobiography of Lincoln Steffens*. Vol. 1. New York: Harcourt, Brace and World, 1958.

Steinbeck, John. *East of Eden*. New York: Penguin Books, 1980.

———. *The Harvest Gypsies*. Berkeley, Calif.: Heyday Books, 1988.

Steinfels, Margaret O'Brien. *Who's Minding the Children? The History and Politics of Day Care in America*. New York: Simon and Schuster, 1973.

Sterkx, Henry Eugene and Brooks Thompson, eds. "Letters of a Teenage Confederate." *Florida Historical Quarterly* 38, no. 4 (April 1960), pp. 339–346.

Stern, Edith M. "Jim Crow Goes to School in New York." *Crisis* 44, no. 7 (July 1937), pp. 201–202.

Sternsher, Bernard, ed. *Hitting Home: The Great Depression in Town and Country*. Chicago: Ivan R. Dee, 1989.

———. *Hope Restored: How the New Deal Worked in Town and Country*. Chicago: Ivan R. Dee, 1999.

Steward, Austin. *Twenty-Two Years a Slave, and Forty Years a Freeman*. Rochester, N.Y.: William Alling, 1856.

Stone, Lawrence, ed. *Schooling and Society: Studies in the History of Education.* Baltimore, M.D.: Johns Hopkins University Press, 1976.

Stone, Richard Cecil. *Life Incidents of Home, School and Church.* St. Louis, Mo.: Southwestern Book and Publishing Co., 1874.

Strong, Josiah. *Our Country: Its Possible Future and Its Present Crisis.* New York: Baker and Taylor Co., 1891.

Stutsman, Rachel. *What of Youth Today?* Detroit, Mich.: Merrill-Palmer School, 1934.

Tarbell, Ida M. *All in the Day's Work.* Boston: G. K. Hall and Co., 1985.

Tashjian, Dickran and Ann Tashjian. *Memorials for Children of Change: The Art of Early New England Stonecarving.* Middletown, Conn.: Wesleyan University Press, 1974.

Tateishi, John. *And Justice for All: An Oral History of the Japanese American Detention Camps.* Seattle: University of Washington Press, 1984.

Terkel, Studs. *Hard Times: An Oral History of the Great Depression.* New York: Pantheon Books, 1986.

Timrod, Henry. *Memorial Edition: Poems of Henry Timrod.* Richmond, Va.: B. F. Johnson Publishing Co., 1901.

Todd, Lewis Paul. *Wartime Relations of the Federal Government and the Public Schools, 1917–1918.* New York: Bureau of Publications, Teachers College, Columbia University, 1945.

Trafford, Abigail. "A New Kind of Normal." *Washington Post* (October 9, 2001), p. F1.

Troen, Selwyn K. "Technological Development and Adolescence: The Early Twentieth Century." *Journal of Early Adolescence* 5, no. 4 (winter 1985), pp. 429–439.

Trowbridge, John Townsend. *My Own Story with Recollections of Noted Persons.* Boston: Houghton, Mifflin, 1903.

Tuttle, William M., Jr. *"Daddy's Gone to War": The Second World War in the Lives of American Children.* New York: Oxford University Press, 1993.

Tyack, David, Robert Lowe, and Elisabeth Hansot. *Public Schools in Hard Times: The Great Depression and Recent Years.* Cambridge, Mass.: Harvard University Press, 1984.

Tyack, David B. "Growing Up Black: Perspectives on the History of Education in Northern Ghettoes." *History of Education Quarterly* 9, no. 3 (fall 1969), pp. 287–297.

U.S. Sanitary Commission Statistical Bureau. *Ages of U.S. Volunteer Soldiery.* Cambridge, Mass.: University Press: Welch, Bigelow and Co., 1866.

Unwritten History of Slavery: Autobiographical Accounts of Negro Ex-Slaves. Nashville, Tenn.: Social Science Institute, Fisk University, 1945.

Uys, Errol Lincoln. *Riding the Rails: Teenagers on the Move During the Great Depression.* New York: TV Books, 2000.

Velie, Lester. "The Shocking Truth About Our Children's Health Care." *Reader's Digest* 104, no. 625 (May 1974), pp. 170–181.

"Ventilation of Public Schools." *Boston Medical and Surgical Journal* 121, no. 6 (October 17, 1889), pp. 394–395.

Vinovskis, Maris A. "An 'Epidemic' of Adolescent Pregnancy? Some Historical Considerations." *Journal of Family History* 6, no. 2 (summer 1981), 205–230.

Violas, Paul C. *The Training of the Urban Working Class: A History of Twentieth-Century American Education.* Chicago: Rand McNally College Publishing Co., 1978.

W., L. B. "The United States Boys' Working Reserve: Boy Soldiers of the Soil." *Michigan History* 4, no. 1 (January 1920), pp. 279–286.

Wald, Lillian D. *Windows on Henry Street.* Boston: Little, Brown and Co., 1934.

Wallace, Anthony F. C. "Childhood, Work, and Family Life in a 19th-Century Cotton Mill Town," in *Family Life in America, 1620–2000.* Edited by Mel Arbin and Dominick Cavallo. St. James, N.Y.: Revisionary Press, 1981.

Wallerstein, Judith, Julia Lewis, and Sandra Blakeslee. *The Unexpected Legacy of Divorce: A 25 Year Landmark Study.* New York: Hyperion, 2000.

Washington, Booker T. *Up from Slavery.* New York: W. W. Norton and Co., 1996.

Washington, E. Davidson, ed. *Selected Speeches of Booker T. Washington.* Garden City, N.Y.: Doubleday, Doran and Co., 1932.

Waters, Lydia Milner. "Account of a Trip Across the Plains in 1855." *Quarterly of the Society of California Pioneers* 6, no. 2 (June 1929), pp. 59–79.

Watson, John B. *Psychological Care of Infant and Child.* New York: W. W. Norton and Co., 1928.

Webber, Thomas L. *Deep Like the Rivers: Education in the Slave Quarter Community, 1831–1865.* New York: W. W. Norton and Co., 1978.

Webster, Noah. "On the Education of Youth in America," in *Essays on Education in the Early Republic,* edited by Frederick Rudolph. Cambridge, Mass.: Belknap Press, 1965.

Wells, Charles Wesley. *Frontier Life.* Cincinnati, Ohio: Press of Jennings and Pye, 1971.

Werner, Emmy E. *Reluctant Witnesses: Children's Voices from the Civil War.* Boulder, Colo.: Westview Press, 1998.

———. *Through the Eyes of Innocents: Children Witness World War II.* Boulder, Colo.: Westview Press, 2000.

West, Elliott. *Growing Up with the Country: Children on the Far Western Frontier.* Albuquerque: University of New Mexico Press, 1989.

West, Elliott and Paula Petrick, eds. *Small Worlds: Children and Adolescents in America, 1850–1950.* Lawrence: University Press of Kansas, 1992.

Wheeler, Homer W. *Buffalo Days: Forty Years in the Old West.* Indianapolis, Ind.: Bobbs-Merrill Co., 1925.

Whitaker, Charles. "A Generation in Peril." *Ebony* 43, no. 10 (August 1988), pp. 34–36.

White, Frank Marshall. "The Epoch of the Child." *Outlook* 95, no. 4 (May 28, 1910), pp. 214–225.

White, Owen P. *A Frontier Mother.* New York: Minton, Balch and Co., 1929.

White, Richard. *"It's Your Misfortune and None of My Own": A New History of the American West.* Norman: University of Oklahoma Press, 1991.

White, William Allen. *The Autobiography of William Allen White.* Edited by Sally Foreman Griffith. Lawrence: University Press of Kansas, 1990.

White House Conference on Child Health and Protection. *Dependent and Neglected Children.* New York: D. Appleton-Century Co., 1933.

Whitman, Walt. *The Whitman Reader.* Edited by Maxwell Geismar. New York: Pocket Books, 1955.

"Why I Joined the Boy Scouts of America." *Scouting* 5, no. 6 (July 15, 1917), p. 4.

Whyte, William M., Jr. "How the New Suburbia Socializes." *Fortune* 48, no. 2 (August 1953), pp. 120–190.

Wiggins, David K. "The Play of Slave Children in the Plantation Communities of the Old South, 1820–1860." *Journal of Sport History* 7, no. 2 (summer 1980), pp. 21–39.

Wiley, Bell Irvin. *The Life of Billy Yank: The Common Soldier of the Union.* Baton Rouge: Louisiana State University Press, 1971.

———. *The Life of Johnny Reb: The Common Soldier of the Confederacy.* Baton Rouge: Louisiana State University Press, 1978.

Wilkerson, Doxey A. *Special Problems of Negro Education.* Washington, D.C.: U.S. Government Printing Office, 1939.

Wiltz, Teresa. "Terror Doesn't Spare Young: Children Witness Horrors Usually Seen Only in Their Nightmares." *Washington Post* (September 15, 2001), p. A10.

Winslow, W. Thatcher. *Youth: A World Problem.* Washington, D.C.: U.S. Government Printing Office, 1937.

Wishy, Bernard. *The Child and the Republic.* Philadelphia: University of Pennsylvania Press, 1986.

Wolf, Anna W. M. *Our Children Face War.* Boston: Houghton Mifflin, 1942.

Wooster, Ralph A. *Texas and Texans in the Civil War.* Austin, Tex.: Eakin Press, 1995.

Wright, Richard. *Black Boy: A Record of Childhood and Youth.* New York: Harper and Brothers, 1945.

Wyden, Peter. *Suburbia's Coddled Kids.* Garden City, N.Y.: Doubleday and Co., 1962.

INDEX

Page locators in **boldface** indicate main entries.
Page locators in *italic* indicate illustrations. Page locators followed by an *m* indicate maps.

FINKELSTEIN
MEMORIAL LIBRARY
SPRING VALLEY, N.Y.
Phone: 845-352-5700
http://www.finkelsteinlibrary.org